'This very fine and readab[...] Churchill family tradition[...] restores Randolph Churc[...] past ... This superb book will help him emerge [...] shadows, a place he has occupied in death though never in life' Andrew Roberts, *Mail on Sunday*

'A narrative of remarkable filial candour'
Anthony Howard, *Sunday Times*

'Winston has done the historical record a service in a thoroughly worthwhile book'
Edward Pearce, *New Statesman and Society*

'Fair and frank, filial yet objective ... This biography sparkles and fizzes with stories and letters and reminiscences' Sir Robin Day, *Daily Express*

'A compelling and engaging narrative ... The quality of Randolph's political journalism in the 1950s and early 1960s is vividly detailed' Roy Jenkins, *Literary Review*

'*His Father's Son* is full of excitement, just as Randolph's life was ... This readable, entertaining and often moving biography (a fine filial tribute) shows just what was lost when Randolph departed this world'
Sir Martin Gilbert, *Observer*

Winston S. Churchill, grandson of his forebear and name-sake, has been a journalist and war correspondent, as well as a roving foreign correspondent for *The Times*. He was Conservative Member of Parliament for the Manchester constituencies of Stretford 1970–1983 and Davyhulme 1983–1997. He is the author of *First Journey*, *The Six-Day War* (with Randolph Churchill), *Defending the West* and *Memories and Adventures*.

HIS FATHER'S SON

THE LIFE OF
RANDOLPH CHURCHILL

Winston S. Churchill

A PHOENIX GIANT PAPERBACK

First published in Great Britain
by Weidenfeld & Nicolson in 1996
This paperback edition published in 1997
by Phoenix, a division of Orion Books Ltd,
Orion House, 5 Upper St Martin's Lane,
London WC2H 9EA

A CIP catalogue record for this book is available
from the British Library.

ISBN: 1 85799 969 X

Printed and bound in Great Britain by
Butler & Tanner Ltd, Frome and London

To the Memory of My Father

CONTENTS

List of Illustrations ix
Acknowledgements xi

Preface 1
I   'The Chum Bolly' 3
II   'Randolph Will Carry on the Lamp' 14
III   Life at Chartwell 32
IV   'More Blessed to Teach than to Learn' 54
V   Telling America 71
VI   A Meeting with Hitler 86
VII   The Father and Son Road Show 101
VIII   Randolph, Hope and Glory 118
IX   Partners in the Wilderness 135
X   'Munich!' 150
XI   Member for Preston 169
XII   North Africa 186
XIII   The Benghazi Raid 205
XIV   A Soldier with the Desert Army 216
XV   Mission to Yugoslavia 232
XVI   Attack on Drvar 242
XVII   Return to Topusko 250
XVIII Victory and Defeat 266
XIX   Life with Father 274
XX   Dreaming of Plymouth Hoe 291
XXI   Across the Naktong 302
XXII   'Culture is for Gentler Creatures' 310
XXIII *What I Said about the Press* 317
XXIV   Action For Libel 323
XXV   Crisis over Suez 330
XXVI   Macmillan it is! 356

XXVII   African Safaris   379
XXVIII The Literary Factory   390
XXIX   *Private Eye*: An Apology   413
XXX   'In Love with the Kennedys'   429
XXXI   The Fight – Continued   435
XXXII   Operation 'Hope Not'   455
XXXIII 'Bumpkin Pasha'   462
XXXIV   Some 'Burnt-Out Case'!   469
XXXV   'Project K'   478

Bibliography   501
Index   503

ILLUSTRATIONS

between pages 212 – 213

Randolph on his father's shoulders, 1912
As page at his Aunt Nellie's wedding, 1915 *Hulton Deutsch Collection*
Playing tennis at Frinton, 1922 *Hulton Deutsch Collection*
With his mother at Eton, 1926 *Hulton Deutsch Collection*
Wild-boar-hunting with his father in France, 1928 *Churchill College, Cambridge*
Visiting America with his father, and Uncle Jack, 1929 *Churchill College, Cambridge*
At Chartwell with his parents, and Charlie Chaplin, 1931 *Hulton Deutsch Collection*
At the Motor Cycle Show, Olympia, 1931
Canvassing in West Toxteth, Liverpool, 1935 *Hulton Deutsch Collection*
At the Ross and Cromarty by-election, 1936 *Hulton Deutsch Collection*
Randolph's wedding to the Hon. Pamela Digby, 1939 *Associated Press Ltd*
With his parents, 1939 *Hulton Deutsch Collection*
In the Western Desert, North Africa, 1941 *Imperial War Museum*
Leading British and American troops onto the island of Lissa in the Adriatic, 1944 *Churchill College, Cambridge*
Making his first parachute jump in the Western Desert, 1944 *Hulton Deutsch Collection*
With Captain Earl Jellicoe and paratroop comrades in the Western Desert, 1944 *Hulton Deutsch Collection*
With Anthony Eden at The Hague, 1948 *Hulton Deutsch Collection*
Randolph's wedding to June Osborne at Caxton Hall, London, 1948 *Hulton Deutsch Collection*
Arabella's christening, 1949 *Hulton Deutsch Collection*
Campaigning against Michael Foot at Devonport, Plymouth, 1950 *Hulton Deutsch Collection*
Three generations of Churchills campaigning in Devonport, 1950 *Western Morning News*

With Winston and Arabella at Chartwell, 1951 *Churchill College, Cambridge*

The Churchill family at Chartwell, 1951 *Churchill College, Cambridge*

At the White House receiving US Honorary Citizenship on his father's behalf, 1963 *Churchill College, Cambridge*

Best man at the wedding of his son, Winston, 1964 *Keystone Press Agency*

Arabella's eighteenth birthday party, 1967 *Churchill College, Cambridge*

Correcting proofs of *The Six-Day War* with Winston, 1967 *Churchill College, Cambridge/Daily Telegraph*

With Natalie Bevan and pugs at Stour, 1967 © *Anthea Sieveking*

Acknowledgements

First and foremost I must express my indebtedness to my father, Randolph Churchill, and to my grandfather, Sir Winston Churchill, for safeguarding for posterity the magnificent exchanges of correspondence between them, as well as for the right, as their heir, to reproduce their letters. Traditionally, the richest seam of gold sought by biographers has been the correspondence of relations, close friends or lovers, parted by duty or travel, who share with each other their private observations and most intimate thoughts. Tragically for the biographers of the future, the practice and art of letter-writing has effectively been killed off by that ephemeral instrument, the telephone.

I must record my appreciation to my aunt, Lady Soames, not only for her permission to reproduce letters from her mother, Lady Churchill, but also for reading and commenting on these pages. I am further indebted to the late Sir John Colville, Private Secretary to my grandfather during his wartime and peacetime premierships, as well as to Anthony Montague Browne, who was his Private Secretary from 1952 until his death, for their comments and criticism.

I am particularly grateful to my grandfather's biographer, Professor Sir Martin Gilbert, who for many years worked alongside my father on the 'Great Biography' of Churchill which he carried forward with such resounding success, not only for his invaluable guidance and advice but also for providing me over the years with a treasure trove of letters – or 'lovely grub', as my father would have called it – with which this work is embellished, many of which are published here for the first time.

I should like to place on record my gratitude to Minnie Churchill, the mother of my four children, who knew and was deeply fond of my father, not only for typing the first half of this book in its original draft, as she has done with each of my books over the past three decades but, above all, for encouraging me to embark upon this work.

I am especially indebted to my father's life-long friend Kay Halle for her presence of mind and devotion in persuading more than two dozen of my father's friends, following his death, to contribute their memories of him in a book she compiled entitled *Randolph Churchill: The Young*

Pretender, as well as for her permission to quote from it. I am also grateful to my late cousin, Anita Leslie, for permission to quote from her book *Cousin Randolph*.

I wish further to express my thanks to Edward Nalbantian, Simon Bird and Simon Moore for their help at various times in collating and marshalling the vast amount of material contained in my late father's archive, as well as to my secretaries, Barbara Ryan and Caroline Rodaway, for their diligence and good humour in typing and re-typing these pages. My thanks are also due to Rebecca Wilson of Weidenfeld & Nicolson and Jane Birkett for their skilful editing of the text and especially to my father's friend, Lord Weidenfeld, for his enthusiasm to publish the work.

Finally, my special thanks are due to Luce Danielson for her encouragement in seeing this work through to completion over the course of the past year.

WSC

Preface

Who was Randolph Churchill? What was it like to be brought up in the home of Winston Churchill, the greatest and most controversial British politician of his age or, as some would say, of all time? And what was Churchill himself like as a father? Was he in his private, family life the same fierce, ogre-like figure that sculptors have delighted to portray defying the Nazi 'Beast', or was there a softer, gentler side to his character? These are just some of the questions I shall endeavour to answer in the pages that follow.

Our subject's lifespan, though barely a decade longer than that of his famous grandfather and namesake Lord Randolph Churchill, who died at the age of forty-six, covers a period unparalleled in world history for its dramatic events and, above all, for the collective and individual sufferings of two generations confronted by the horror of world war. It is against this stark background that I seek to trace the life of my father.

Randolph was born in 1911 when Europe, which for two thousand years had led the world in cultural and technological development and had come to dominate it with economic and military might, was preparing to tear itself apart in the first of two civil wars – conflagrations which were to destroy its pre-eminence and cost the lives of more than 60 million people. From his earliest years these cataclysmic events impinged more directly on the life of Randolph than on that of any of his contemporaries. For, though his father was out of office for the crucial decade of the 1930s, his power and personality – with its growing worldwide influence – dominated the British political scene for almost half a century.

Randolph was brought up in a political powerhouse in which his father was the nuclear reactor. Breakfast, lunch, tea and dinner he was suckled on a diet of politics and passionately argued causes – an upbringing which was to direct and eventually mould his own life. It is perhaps natural for a son – more especially an only son – in the absence of any deep-seated antipathy in their relationship, to follow his father into the family business. This holds good as much for miners and for monarchs as it does for politicians.

Many a son would have been overawed and repressed as a result of being brought up under the influence of so potent a human being and so dominant a personality. Psychoanalysts would no doubt be happy to explain that such a child would inevitably grow up timid, introverted and suffering from an extreme inferiority complex. Many accusations have been levelled at my father, but having an inferiority complex was never one of them. On the contrary, he was to grow up to be the antithesis of what might have been expected. Few who knew him – and those who loved him were at least as numerous as those who could not abide him – would deny that, in power of personality, he was his father's son. Neville Chamberlain once wrote of Winston Churchill, his Cabinet colleague in the Baldwin administration of the mid-1920s: 'Winston ... has *les défauts de ses qualités.*' This was to be even more true of the son.

But, you may ask, can a son write an objective biography of his father? Well do I remember how often this question was put to my father during the many years of preparation and research for his biography of his own father, on which he embarked with such enthusiasm and distinction in the closing years of his life.

'I am going to write a Life of my father which is both filial and objective', Randolph would boldly declare. Invariably the interviewer would remonstrate: 'Surely the two are incompatible?' 'Of course they are not', Randolph would riposte. 'If I were to write a Life of my father that was not objective, it would be laughed out of court ... It would do him no service and would therefore not be filial.' He would then invoke the words of Cromwell, quoted by Winston himself as a 23-year-old cavalry subaltern in a letter to his mother, Lady Randolph, from the North-West Frontier of India:

31 March [1898]

... As to the Biographer – who may investigate another human wretch's life – I would say as Oliver Cromwell did to Sir Peter Lely – 'Paint me as I am' and thereupon was painted wart and all ...

I know that it is in this vein that my father would wish me to embark on his own Life.

Winston S. Churchill
House of Commons
20 March 1996

CHAPTER I

The 'Chum Bolly'

Clementine Churchill was convinced that she was going to give birth to a boy. The Churchills' first child Diana, born two years earlier had been nicknamed the 'P.K.' or Puppy-Kitten, after their own private names for each other: in his letters Winston signed himself, 'Your devoted Pug' and she, 'Your loving Clemmy Kat'. Even before Randolph's birth the new arrival was dubbed the 'Chum Bolly' although when, in 1976, I asked my grandmother why, she could recall no particular reason. I have pondered whether it could be that he was conceived on a fine vintage of Chambolle Musigny. However, Sir Martin Gilbert, my grandfather's biographer, offers two more plausible explanations. He reports that the 'Chumbolly' is a beautiful flower that grows in north-west India, where Winston had served with the Malakand Field Force nearly fifteen years earlier, while in the Persian language, *Farsi*, which also reaches to the North-West Frontier, it means a healthy, chubby new-born baby.

The 'Chum Bolly' puts in his first appearance in a letter written by Clemmie to her husband from Penrhôs in Wales on 18 April 1911: 'I am counting the days till 15 May when the Chum Bolly is due. I hope he will not have inherited the Pug's unpunctual habits!' Regrettably he had: unlike his father who was born seven weeks prematurely, Randolph arrived a fortnight late and, thereafter, a regard for punctuality was never conspicuous among his attributes. Indeed I well recall Randolph in later life lecturing his mother, who invariably arrived for engagements well ahead of time, that 'Punctuality does not rest in being early'. It was on this basis that, after furious and potentially lethal chases to the local railway station, we waved goodbye to many a train which Randolph insisted should be given a 'sporting chance' to get away.

Randolph Churchill was born on 28 May 1911 at 33 Eccleston Square, a terraced house which had been his parents' home since their marriage in 1908 and was just a stone's throw from Victoria Station. Born within the sound of Bow bells, Randolph was fond in later life of claiming to be a 'Cockney'.

His father, Member of Parliament for Dundee, though only thirty-six years old, already held one of the great offices of state, being in his second year as Home Secretary in Asquith's Liberal Government. As President of the Board of Trade, 1908–10, he had been responsible for placing on the statute-book several far-reaching measures of social reform which have survived to this day, including a scheme of National Insurance to provide every citizen with a state retirement pension and the establishment of Labour Exchanges nationwide to assist the unemployed to find jobs. As possibly the only holder of his office to have been in prison – Winston was captured during the Boer War and held captive in Pretoria until his celebrated escape, brilliantly described in his book *My Early Life* – he well understood what it was to be deprived of one's liberty. He was particularly shocked by the large numbers of young people being committed to prison and by the fact that two-thirds of the prison population had been jailed for offences no graver than drunkenness or the failure to pay a fine. The reforms which he instituted led to a reduction in these categories of prisoners from over 170,000 to fewer than 12,000 during the next ten years.

Although Churchill's reforms have benefited millions of his fellow countrymen down the decades, his tenure at the Home Office is more frequently associated with the violent and turbulent events taking place at the time: the Siege of Sidney Street and the Tonypandy riots. In the case of Sidney Street, in the East End of London, the Home Secretary was criticised in Parliament for having visited the scene of action and taken personal charge of operations in the danger zone after a gang of anarchists had killed three policemen and wounded two others. Far graver, however, were the charges levelled against him over his handling of the riots in the Welsh mining valleys of the Rhondda. It is deeply ingrained in the mythology of Socialism in Britain that Churchill sent troops to Tonypandy to 'shoot down the miners' in the autumn of 1910. The charge could not have been further from the truth: it was actually Churchill who, on learning that the War Office had dispatched soldiers, had them detrained at Didcot and substituted mounted police instead. But this has done nothing to prevent the currency of the lie which was regularly thrown from the hustings at the subject of this biography and even, despite the passage of time, at its author.

Among the first to salute Randolph's arrival was Austen Chamberlain, a former Chancellor of the Exchequer in Balfour's Conservative Government of 1902–5 who, despite the passions aroused by Winston's defection to the Liberal Party in 1904, wrote to him from across the floor of the House:

29 May 1911

Hearty congratulations. I hope all goes well with Mother and boy –
It is a pity you cannot yet draw the Maternity Benefit [of 30s per week –
nearly £90 in today's money – proposed by Lloyd George in the House
of Commons three weeks before as part of the National Insurance Bill]
but I understand that you are making it up through Government postage.

Chamberlain was seeking mischievously to suggest that Winston might
be using free House of Commons postage, introduced earlier that year,
to acknowledge the many messages of congratulation.

Winston, who was encamped with the Oxfordshire Hussars in the
grounds of Blenheim Palace doing his military reserve duty, wrote to his
wife at Eccleston Square five days after the birth of his son:

2 June 1911

My sweet & beloved Clemmie,
The weather is gorgeous, and the whole Park in gala glories. I have
been out drilling all the morning & my poor face is already a sufferer from
the sun. The air however is deliciously cool. We have 3 regiments here,
two just outside the ornamental gardens, & the 3rd over by Bladon [where
Winston would be buried].
I have 104 men in the squadron & a vy nice new young officer –
Valentine Fleming's younger brother – 'the lesser flamingo'. F. E. [F. E.
Smith, later 1st Earl of Birkenhead] is here and everything promises to be
vy pleasant. Many congratulations are offered me upon the son. With that
lack of jealousy wh ennobles my nature, I lay them all at your feet.
My precious pussy cat, I do trust & hope that you are being good, &
not sitting up or fussing yourself. Just get well & strong & enjoy the
richness wh this new event will I know have brought into your life. The
Chumbolly must do his duty and help you with your milk, you are to tell
him so from me. At his age greediness & even swinishness at table are
virtues ...

Always my darling your own loving
Winston

The Tories threaten to move a vote of censure on me after Whitsuntide.
I hope they will. They are really too idiotic.

There are scores of precedents for the language I use about the Courts, including Mr Gladstone & many of the great Parliamentarians.

Two thousand kisses my sweet birdling.

Your own for ever.

This goes to you by the King's messenger who is taking the box.

He wrote again three days later:

5 June 1911

Secret
Lock up or destroy

My dearest,
   Both your letters have now arrived. You should address them Q.O.O.H. [Queen's Own Oxfordshire Hussars], Blenheim Camp, not Palace, (wh latter produces delay).
   I am so glad that you are both progressing so well. Ten ounces since last Tuesday is indeed good. I hope he is helping you as well as himself! . . .
   . . . We all marched past this morning – walk, trot & gallop. Jack [Winston's younger brother] & I took our squadrons at the real pace & excited the spontaneous plaudits of the crowd. The Berkshires who followed cd not keep up and grumbled. After the march I made the General form the whole Brigade into Brigade Mass & gallopped 1200 strong the whole length of the park in one solid square of men & horses. It went awfully well. He was delighted. No news about the night march yet.
   . . . & now my sweet little darling with my fondest love I sign myself your devoted friend & husband

W

Much of the month of June was taken up with the preparations for the Coronation of King George V which caused intense excitement throughout the land. This took place on 22 June and Clemmie, as a nursing mother, was granted the special favour of seeing it from the King's box. Indeed this had been arranged even before the birth of Randolph, when Winston received a letter from the King's Private Secretary Lord Knollys:

29 April 1911   *Buckingham Palace*

My dear Churchill,
   I spoke to the King today about his giving Mrs Churchill a ticket for his box in Westminster Abbey on the occasion of the Coronation. He said

he should have much pleasure in giving her one, and you may like to know that he was very nice about it.

Yours sincerely,
Knollys

Three days after the Coronation Winston wrote from Hartsbourne Manor in Hertfordshire where, together with his mother Lady Randolph Churchill, formerly Jennie Jerome of Brooklyn, New York, he was at a house party given by the famous American hostess Maxine Elliott:

25 June 1911

My darling Clemmie,
    It rained all the morning so I stayed in bed & ruminated amid my boxes . . .
    Maxine sends you her best love. She & I spent a long time last night singing your praises. Did the Cat's ear burn!
    The general turn-out on Friday [when Churchill and his wife rode in the coronation procession] made a great impression. Everyone admired the Cat, the carriage, the horses & the tiger – separately, but in combination they fairly lifted the sultana. It really was great fun, & I am sure you will long look back to our drive & will like to tell the PK and the Chumbolly all about it – so it will become a tradition in the family & they will hand it on to others whom we shall not see. Dear me, I have thought of you with tender love to-day. May all blessings be yours & all good fortune . . .
    With fondest love,
    Your own ever loving Husband
    W

Do ask Grey [the Foreign Secretary] to be godfather – I am sure it is a vy good idea, & will give him great pleasure. I am always hearing nice things he has said about me. He likes & wistfully admires our little circle. What do you think?

Clemmie, who had taken her two small children to Seaford on the Sussex coast where they were staying in a boarding-house, replied a few days later approving the suggestion of Sir Edward Grey as a godfather and proposing Lady Ridley, Winston's first cousin, as a 'Fairy Godmother' for the Chum Bolly. Accordingly, on 26 October in the crypt of the House of Commons, he was christened Randolph Frederick Edward Spencer Churchill – Randolph after his grandfather, Lord Randolph Churchill, who had died sixteen years earlier; Frederick after his godfather and his father's greatest friend, F. E. Smith, also a godfather; Edward after Sir Edward Grey; and Spencer, a family name which had ceased to be hyphenated with Churchill because Lord Randolph objected to double-barrelled names.

In late September Churchill had been invited to stay in Scotland with H. H. Asquith, the Prime Minister of the day. According to his own subsequent account, as he was returning from a round of golf – a game at which Winston never excelled – Asquith asked him 'quite abruptly' if he would like to be First Lord of the Admiralty, to which he eagerly replied: 'Indeed I would!'

Due to the prohibitive cost of the extra servants they would need, it was not until well into 1912 that the Churchills, together with the Chum Bolly, moved from Eccleston Square to the more splendid apartments of Admiralty House, Whitehall, overlooking Horse Guards Parade where numerous military exercises took place, including the annual ceremony of the Trooping of the Colour. This was to be their home for nearly four years until, with all the unpredictability attendant upon political life, the turn of events in Europe rendered them homeless overnight.

Following the Agadir incident of 1911, in which Germany sent a gunboat to a Moroccan port to which France laid claim, Churchill, while still Home Secretary, had begun for the first time to foresee the possibility of a European war. In such an eventuality he had no doubt that Britain's duty and self-interest demanded that she actively take the side of France. Thus, over the next three years as First Lord, he laboured unceasingly to strengthen and modernise the Royal Navy, to reinforce the *entente cordiale* with France and to forge a powerful alliance in the hope of deterring Germany from embarking on the path of war.

To Winston this was no drudgery: he was in his element and enjoyed every minute. As recorded in *Irrepressible Churchill* by Kay Halle, he looked back on his time at the Admiralty as 'the four most memorable years of my life' because he could now 'lay eggs, instead of scratching around in the dust and clucking. It is a far more satisfactory occupation. I am at present in process of laying a great number of eggs – "good eggs", every one of them and there will be many more clutches to follow ... New appointments to be made. Admirals to be "poached", "scrambled" and "buttered".'

All the while, Winston paid close attention to his young family. In a letter written from Portland in Dorset on 24 March 1912 he described to Clemmie his visit to the naval base, his discussion about war plans and his intention to go to sea the following day to supervise target practice. The letter concludes: 'I hope Diana is dutiful & that Randolph perseveres in growth & teeth cutting. Unless some crisis occurs I shall not return until Wednesday. I hope you will be well enough to come down to Portsmouth on Friday – we will lie in the Solent & it will do you a lot of good. Good night my darling & sweetest Kat always your loving husband – W.'

A few weeks later, during his wife's absence from home, he reported from the Admiralty:

18 April 1912

I have just returned here after a flying surprise visit to see the P.K. put to bed at 6.30. Both the chicks are well and truculent. Diana & I went through one Peter Rabbit picture book together & Randolph gurgled. You must have his tongue cut when you come home. It hampers his speech. He looks vy strong & prosperous ...

The *Titanic* disaster [the liner on her maiden voyage to New York had struck an iceberg and sunk four days earlier with the loss of two-thirds of her 2,200 passengers] is the prevailing theme here. The story is a good one. The strict observance of the great traditions of the sea towards women & children reflects nothing but honour upon our civilisation. Even I hope it may mollify some of the young unmarried lady teachers who are so bitter in their sex antagonism, and think men so base & vile. They are rather snuffy about Bruce Ismay – Chairman of the line – who it is thought on the facts available should have gone down with the ship & her crew. I cannot help feeling proud of our race & its traditions as proved by this event. Boat loads of women & children tossing on the sea safe & sound – & the rest – silence. Honour to their memory ...

In this letter Winston betrays something of his animosity towards the 'women's libbers' of the day whom he regarded as the worst advertisement for their sex. To the suffragettes the First Lord was something of a *bête noire* and they showed the strength of their feelings by an attempted kidnapping of his children. Randolph recalled the incident in *Twenty-One Years*, the autobiography of his early years which was published in 1965:

Diana and I used to be taken for a daily morning airing in the Green Park in a double pram. This must have been just before the war. There were people called suffragettes who wanted to get votes for women which, I later discovered, was a proposal to which my father and Mr Asquith were strongly opposed; so the suffragettes tried to kidnap me in the park. I have a fugitive memory of being pulled out of the pram and of the nursery maid catching hold of me and pulling me back. More strongly etched in my memory is the detective who thereafter discreetly accompanied us on our morning airings lest this half-hearted attempt should be repeated.

Writing to his wife from the Admiralty yacht HMS *Enchantress* on 23 July 1913, just before going on naval manoeuvres with the Fleet in the North Sea, Winston gave a glimpse of his deep love for his family which was so important a part of his character:

... tender love to you my sweet one & to both those little kittens & especially that radiant Randolph. Diana is a darling too & I repent to have expressed a preference. But somehow he seems a more genial generous nature, while she is mysterious & self conscious. They are vy beautiful & will win us honour some day when everyone is admiring her & grumbling about him.

My dearest you are vy precious to me & I rejoice indeed to have won & kept your loving heart. May it never cool towards me is my prayer, & that I may deserve your love my resolve.

Write daily –
Always your loving husband
W

Of all the matters that commanded the First Lord's attention in the course of his duties, nothing aroused his enthusiasm more than flying, which became his passion in the latter part of 1913 and the first half of 1914. The day before his thirty-ninth birthday he started taking flying lessons under the instruction of Captain Gilbert Lushington of the Royal Marines. Four days later Lushington was killed while coming in to land at Eastchurch while piloting the very same machine in which he had given Winston his first lesson. He had entered a spin from which in those days the means of recovery was unknown. Churchill wrote a moving letter of sympathy to Lushington's fiancée Miss Airlie Hynes, but the incident did nothing to abate his enthusiasm for aviation which was still in its infancy.

In the next seven months he made some 140 flights in different aircraft and with various pilots, several of whom suffered Lushington's fate. At that point Clemmie, who was again pregnant, begged that he cease taking such risks. Winston, albeit reluctantly, agreed in his reply of June 1914:

> It is curious that while I have been lucky, accidents have happened to others who have flown with me out of the natural proportions. This poor Lieutenant, another flying instructor whose loss has disturbed your anxieties again, took me up only last week in this vy machine! You will give me some kisses and forgive me for past distresses – I am sure. Though I had no need & perhaps no right to do it – it was an important part of my life during the last seven months & I am sure my nerve, my spirits & my virtue were all improved by it. But at your expense my poor pussy cat! I am so sorry . . .
>
> I will not fly anymore until at any rate you have recovered from your kitten [Sarah who was to be born four months later]: & by then or perhaps later the risks may have been greatly reduced.
>
> This is a wrench, because I was on the verge of taking my pilot's certificate. It only needed a couple of calm mornings . . . But I must admit that the numerous fatalities of this year wd justify you in complaining if I continued to share the risks as I am proud to do of these good fellows. So I give it up decidedly for many months & perhaps for ever.

In fact he was never to fly solo or to gain his Pilot's Certificate.

That summer Clemmie took the children for a bucket-and-spade holiday on the Norfolk coast. They stayed at Pear Tree Cottage at Overstrand, near Cromer, where many streams run down from low cliffs across the sand to the sea. While still working unrelentingly to bring the Royal Navy up to the highest state of readiness for war, Winston joined them at weekends and would mobilise all the children on the beach to build giant sandcastles and man their defences against the incoming sea.

Meanwhile, unbeknown to the great mass of British holiday-makers enjoying the sunshine of a glorious summer, Europe was sliding remorselessly towards the abyss. The assassination of Archduke Franz Ferdinand of Austria in the faraway Balkan town of Sarajevo on 28 June did not arouse undue attention, although it was this that was to propel Europe into the costliest war of its long and bloody history. On Churchill's instructions the Third Fleet began a test mobilisation on 15 July and two days later King George V reviewed the entire fleet off Spithead. As he recorded in *The World Crisis*, his memoirs of the Great War, the review 'constituted incomparably the greatest assemblage of naval power ever witnessed in the history of the world'.

In the last days of July Winston, abandoning his family by the seaside, hurried back to London to postpone the dispersal of the First and Second Fleets and the demobilisation of the Third. By the end of the month he was able to report to the King:

31 July 1914   *Admiralty*

12.30 a.m.
Secret

Sir,
    Your Majesty is informed of the diplomatic, so I confine myself to the military aspect.
    The First Fleet is now in the open seas. The Second Fleet will assemble tomorrow at Portland. All 'precautionary' measures have (so far) behaved magnificently. The four old battleships will reach the Humber tomorrow. All the flotillas have reached their stations . . .

The following night, acting on his own responsibility, the First Lord issued summonses to all Reservists for the full mobilisation of the Fleet. He wrote to Clemmie at Cromer:

Secret
Not to be left about but locked up or burned

My darling,
    There is still hope although the clouds are blacker & blacker. Germany is realising I think how great are the forces against her & is trying tardily to restrain her idiot ally. We are working to soothe Russia. But everybody is preparing swiftly for war. And at any moment now the stroke may fall. We are ready . . .

Two days later Germany declared war on Russia and on 3 August her forces invaded France and Belgium. Britain's ultimatum to Germany, demanding respect for Belgian neutrality, expired at midnight (German time) the following night. At that instant Churchill flashed the fateful signal to all HM Ships and Naval Establishments:

4 August 1914   *Admiralty*

11 p.m.
COMMENCE HOSTILITIES AGAINST GERMANY

In *Twenty-One Years* Randolph records his memories, as a boy of three,
of the coming of the war:

> We were staying at the seaside ... There was a lot of excitement and my
> father had to go to London. One day we were told that war had come.
> We looked out to sea expecting that German ships would soon come into
> view but nothing happened, except that my father could not come down
> from London. We children were all disappointed – no Germans and no
> Papa.

Writing more than fifty years later, Randolph, in the concluding
passage of the second volume of the 'Great Biography' – the last he was
to complete before his death – reflected on his father at this period in
his life:

> Churchill was a romantic. Tears came easily to his eyes when he talked of
> the long story of Britain's achievement in the world and the many deeds
> of heroism which had adorned it. We have seen how deeply moved he
> had been by the untimely end of his flying instructor Lushington and the
> noble fortitude of his fiancée. Such fortitude in distress warmed and
> comforted his heart in all that he was doing to keep Britain and her Empire
> safe and glorious. If his life had ended in 1914 in his fortieth year we can
> be sure that he would not have been denied a page in history and that his
> epitaph would have been:

When War Came
The Fleet was Ready

CHAPTER 2

'Randolph Will Carry on the Lamp'

One morning looking out of a window at Admiralty House Randolph, aged four, saw a large muster of soldiers in battle kit drawn up on Horse Guards Parade. 'Where are they going?' he asked. 'The Dardanelles,' came back the reply. 'I didn't know where the Dardanelles were or what the war was all about,' Randolph wrote later, 'but the Dardanelles hung like a storm cloud over Admiralty House and I used to end my nightly prayers: "God bless Mummy and Papa. God bless the Dardanelles and make me a good boy. Amen."'

In a matter of weeks the war of barbed wire, mud and rats had begun as trenches were dug across Europe all the way from the Swiss border to the Channel coast. It was not long before the French and British allies began to suffer a terrible toll of life for the sake of gaining a few hundred yards of devastated, bomb-cratered wasteland. Churchill was appalled at the way in which British soldiers were being required, as he put it, to 'chew barbed wire' in Flanders – a toll that was to rise to 20,000 in a single day during the Battle of the Somme. He became convinced that there must be some better way to defeat Germany.

He revolved in his mind two propositions above all. Almost alone among his Cabinet colleagues, he had himself seen action as a soldier and could visualise what it meant to be ordered to charge forward through coils of barbed-wire entanglements only to be shot to pieces by the merciless, withering fire of the machine-gun. He was determined that some mechanical device be contrived that would cross trenches, flatten barbed wire and provide effective protection from the gunfire. Thus he pressed forward with the development of a device codenamed the 'tank'. Before the war was over, General von Ludendorff was to credit the tank with the failure of the German spring offensive of 1918 and the defeat of the Kaiser's armies.

Faced with the difficulties of defeating the Germans in Flanders, Churchill ordered his planning staff to explore the possibility of offensive action on Germany's flanks, either in the north with the seizure of Borkum Island off the Dutch coast from which raids could be mounted against Germany or, alternatively, in the Eastern Mediterranean by knocking Germany's ally, Turkey, out of the war. It was thus that the strategy was conceived of seizing the Dardanelles on Turkey's European coast. Though not Churchill's idea originally, it was one which he was to champion and, though he had charge only of the naval aspects and that for a limited period, he was made the scapegoat for its failure. The Dardanelles campaign shattered Churchill's political career for many years, losing him his job, his home and the esteem of many of his countrymen from whom the true facts were concealed by a government that sought to use the war as an excuse to obscure where the burden of responsibility should be justly apportioned. It was a slur that was hurled at him, at his son and even, fifty years on, at his grandson, at successive elections. I remember leading a team of canvassers down one of the dingy, downtrodden back-streets of Gorton, Manchester, in the by-election of November 1967. All of a sudden, the relative silence of a cold, wet autumn morning was shattered by a cataract of abuse from further up the street. An elderly but none the less powerful man had emerged from one of the terraced houses and could be seen vigorously shaking a Young Conservative canvasser, whom he had taken hold of by the lapels. I hastened to the scene in time to hear the assailant, by now lifting the young man bodily off his feet, yelling: 'Your bloody granddad murdered everyone at Gallipoli!' I hastened to point out that he had his facts wrong and that anyway it was *my* 'bloody granddad'.

To this day the lies and misrepresentations arising from Churchill's part in the affair show scant sign of abating. Yet there are few modern military strategists who doubt that, in concept, the Dardanelles strategy was a stroke of genius which – had the Government pressed it with sufficient drive and resolution – could have brought the war to an end at least two years sooner, with the saving of several millions of lives on the Western Front. Nor is it impossible that the Russian Revolution of 1917 could thereby have been avoided and the world saved from the horrors of Communism which, in Russia and China alone, were to cost over 50 million lives.

The failure of the naval commander on the spot, Admiral Carden, to press home the seaborne attack at a point when the loss of life would have been small; the bungling of Kitchener who, as Secretary of State for War, had overall charge of the military side of the operation; and, above all, the weakness and vacillation of the War Cabinet, meant that the whole enterprise ended in ghastly failure with grave loss of life.

In May 1915, as a result of pressure from the Conservative Party which had joined in a new Coalition Government under Asquith, the First Lord was dismissed from his office and the Churchills, abruptly turned out of Admiralty House, found themselves homeless. The shock and humiliation of the Dardanelles was for evermore to be imprinted in the memory of the four-year-old Randolph. The family was given a temporary home by Winston's younger brother Jack, who – when not himself away on active service in Gallipoli – lived at 41 Cromwell Road in South Kensington with his wife Goonie and their two children, Johnny, aged six, and Peregrine, two. The house was not particularly large and, though the nurseries were amalgamated under one nanny and nursery-maid, the arrival of Winston and Clemmie with their three children made it distinctly overcrowded.

As Randolph recalled:

> The house was almost opposite the Natural History Museum. On wet afternoons Diana, Johnny and I would be taken there. We did not spend much time looking at the exhibits. We preferred to run along its corridors playing hide-and-seek and, since hardly anybody seemed interested in the specimens which had been collected in this fine building, we seldom got into any trouble.

Randolph, though two years younger than his sister Diana and his cousin Johnny, soon became the ringleader in all sorts of pranks and misbehaviour. As Johnny remembered, Randolph used to creep into his Uncle Jack's office, ring up the Foreign Office and announce to the bewildered operator: 'This is Mr Churchill.'

Peregrine still has vivid memories of Randolph's obstreperous behaviour which remained a hallmark of his character. The children's daily outing involved a walk up Queen's Gate to Hyde Park, as Peregrine described to me:

> There would be two perambulators, one each for Sarah and myself. The older children would be hanging on while the two nurses would push us up the long grind to the Albert Hall, where we crossed the road into Kensington Gardens and Hyde Park. There was always a policeman standing at that crossing. Why, I can't think – there wasn't much traffic – but he'd hold up the one and only horse-carriage trotting along and we'd solemnly cross the road. Randolph was an extremely naughty boy and, although barely five, used to make rude remarks and pull faces at the policeman. One day, at the prompting of the nurse, the policeman 'arrested' Randolph who screamed, yelled, and kicked in all directions thinking that he was being taken to the police station.

Randolph's cavalier attitude and instinctive hostility to authority – parental, school, military and political – was something that he never grew out of. If anything, this was a trait that became more pronounced with the passage of time, as more and more powerful people came within range of his abuse.

The mundane routine of nursery life with daily walks in the park, school lessons and early bed, was occasionally shattered by the arrival over London of Zeppelin airships on bombing raids which Randolph described in *Twenty-One Years*:

> These were tremendously exciting since we children would be woken up in the middle of the night, wrapped up in blankets and carried down to the basement where there would be a lot of grown-ups having supper and drinking champagne. We liked Zeppelins very much indeed and thought it a great treat to mix with grown-ups in the middle of the night.

In the summer of 1915 Winston rented Hoe Farm, an idyllic country cottage near Godalming in Surrey, for his family. He visited them at the weekends and it was here, at the age of forty, that he first took up painting. His returns were awaited with great excitement by the children, above all for the chance to play 'Gorilla', described by Randolph as 'The game we used to play in the country. My father would chase us all up the trees and come climbing up after us.'

Deprived of his command of the Admiralty and denied any outlet for his prodigious energies which he wished to devote single-mindedly to winning the war, Winston soon found his new sinecure appointment as Chancellor of the Duchy of Lancaster, with no Department of State to administer, profoundly frustrating. 'Four thousand pounds a year for doing nothing', as he complained. Accordingly, Winston prepared to visit the Dardanelles to make a personal assessment of the situation on the Gallipoli Peninsula where, despite 30,000 killed or wounded, 100,000 British troops were still entrenched. The proposed visit was effectively scotched by his Conservative Cabinet colleagues, but not before he had written a letter which he placed in a sealed envelope marked: 'To be sent to Mrs Churchill in the event of my death'. It is dated 17 July 1915. In it he tells Clemmie that his investments of £2,000 should pay off his debts and bank overdraft and that she will receive £10,000 capital and an income of £300 a year from insurance policies. He concluded:

I am anxious that you shd get hold of all my papers, especially those wh refer to my Admiralty administration. I have appointed you my sole literary executor. Masterton Smith [his Private Secretary at the Admiralty] will help you to secure all that is necessary for a complete record. There is no hurry; but some day I shd like the truth to be known. Randolph will carry on the lamp. Do not grieve for me too much. I am a spirit, confident of my rights. Death is only an incident, & not the most important wh happens to us in this state of being. On the whole, especially since I met you my darling one I have been happy, & you have taught me how noble a woman's heart can be. If there is anywhere else I shall be on the look out for you. Meanwhile look forward, feel free, rejoice in life, cherish the children, guard my memory. God bless you.

Goodbye.

W

In November that year, Churchill resigned from the Cabinet and returned to the army. A week later he left for France. He was relieved to be away from the frustrations of politics and the intrigues of Westminster, referring to himself as the 'escaped scapegoat'.

The commander-in-chief, Field Marshal Sir John French, at his head-quarters at St-Omer in northern France close to the Belgian border, offered Winston the alternatives of a job at General Headquarters or command of a brigade in the line. He at once opted for the latter but, at his own request, first spent a month in the trenches with the 2nd Battalion, Grenadier Guards in which, as he observed to Clemmie in his letter of 21 November, 'once the gt. D of Marlborough served & commanded'.

As for the risks, Winston was prepared to chance his luck with the best of them but, so far as personal discomfort was concerned, he firmly believed in keeping it to a minimum. In his letter a day later he asks:

Will you send now regularly once a week a *small* box of food to supplement the rations. Sardines, chocolates, potted meats and other things wh may strike your fancy. Begin as soon as possible ... Do you realise what a vy important person a Major is? 99 people out of every 100 in this gt army have to touch their hats to me. With this inspiring reflection let me sign myself.

Your loving & devoted husband,

W

Kiss Randolph, Diana & that golden Sarah for me.

On 27 November he wrote to Clemmie at Cromwell Road:

> Hold your head vy high. You always do. Above all don't be worried about me, if my destiny has not already been accomplished I shall be guarded surely. If it has been, there is nothing that Randolph will need to be ashamed of in what I have done for the country.

This sombre reflection was no doubt prompted by the fact that only the day before Winston had narrowly escaped a rendezvous with death. As he was eating lunch in the headquarters dugout of No. 1 Company, he was handed an urgent message: 'The Corps Commander wishes to see Major Churchill at 4 o'clock at Merville. A car will be waiting at the Rouge Croix crossroads at three fifteen.' As he later complained to his wife:

> I thought it rather a strong order to bring me out of the trenches by daylight – a 3 miles walk across sopping fields on wh stray bullets are always falling, along tracks periodically shelled. But I assumed it was something important ... I just missed a whole bunch of shells wh fell on the track a hundred yards behind me; and arrived after an hour's walking muddy, wet & sweating at the rendezvous where I was to meet the motor. No motor! Presently a Staff Colonel turned up saying he had lost the motor wh had been driven off by shells. He added that the general had wanted to have a talk with me but that it was only about things in general & that another day wd do equally well ... another hour across the sopping fields now plunged in darkness. As I walked I cd see our trenches in the distance with great red brilliant shells flaring over them in fours & fives & cd hear the shriek of the projectiles rising like the sound of a storm ... I reached the trenches without mishap & then learned that a quarter of an hour after I had left, the dugout in wh I was living had been struck by a shell which burst a few feet from where I wd have been sitting; smashing the structure & killing the mess orderly who was inside ... When I saw the ruin I was not so angry with the General after all.

Randolph was clearly concerned for his father's safety for, on 23 November, Clemmie wrote to Winston saying that his son wanted to buy him a spade so that if a bomb fell on his trench he could dig himself out sideways. Five weeks later he replied from France: 'Randolph's suggestion is a vy good one & you must tell him it is the vy thing we have all been doing.'

On 30 November Randolph was a page at the marriage of the Prime

Minister's daughter, Violet Asquith, to Maurice Bonham Carter and Clemmie reported the next day to Winston:

> Randolph officiated as one of the pages and looked quite beautiful in a little Russian velvet suit with fur. His looks made quite a sensation & at Downing Street afterwards he was surrounded & kissed & admired by dozens of lovely women.

Winston replied from the trenches in more earnest vein on 3 December:

> The able soldiers here are miserable at the Government's drifting. Some urge me to return and try to break thém up. I reply no – I will not go back unless I am wounded or unless I have effective control.
>
> I am still an optimist about the war. If it were only the Germans we had to beat I should be still more hopeful.
>
> Dearest – continue to write frequently and to tell me all the news & send me heaps of love. I am so glad Randolph had a success at the wedding. Kiss them all for me.
>
> I am in difficulties with my boots . . .

A fortnight later he wrote:

> My darling,
>
> I reopen my letter to say that French has telephoned from London that the P.M. has written to him that I am not to have a Brigade but a battalion. I hope however to secure one that is now going into the line. You will cancel the order for the [Brigadier-General's] tunic!

The offer of the command of the 56th Brigade of the 19th Division had been vetoed at the last minute by the Prime Minister for fear of arousing criticism from Conservative quarters in Parliament. The depth of bitterness of feeling in Conservative ranks towards the man they branded a renegade, and upon whom they sought to lay the blame for the Dardanelles catastrophe, is difficult to gauge across the distance of time, but it is clear that some of his parliamentary colleagues missed no opportunity to spite him and damn his fortunes even as he risked his life in the trenches. Having driven him out of office, they now did their best to damage his prospects in the army. What hurt Churchill most of all was that the Prime Minister, his former colleague, Asquith, was unwilling to incur even the mildest criticism to defend him.

This disappointment had a welcome side-effect for the children at Cromwell Road, however, for it meant that their father was able to take five days' leave and spend Christmas with his family.

On New Year's Day 1916 Churchill was appointed to command the 6th Royal Scots Fusiliers and he spent the next three weeks training with his battalion. The Fusiliers were based in the Belgian village of Ploegsteert, commonly known to the British Tommy as 'Plug Street'. Before going forward with his battalion 'into the line' Winston wrote (in capital letters) his first surviving letter to his son:

[undated]

MY DEAREST RANDOLPH,

I AM LIVING HERE IN A LITTLE FARM. IT IS NOT SO PRETTY AS HOE FARM AND THERE ARE NO NICE FLOWERS AND NO POND OR TREES TO PLAY GORILLA BUT THERE ARE THREE LARGE FAT DIRTY PIGS. LIKE THE ONES WE SAW IN THE WOODS.

THE GERMANS ARE A LONG WAY OFF AND CANNOT SHOOT AT US HERE. IT IS TOO FAR. SO WE ARE QUITE SAFE AS LONG AS WE STAY HERE. BUT WE CAN HEAR THE CANNONS BOOMING IN THE DISTANCE AND AT NIGHT WHEN IT IS ALL DARK WE CAN SEE THEIR FLASHES TWINKLING IN THE SKY. SOON WE ARE GOING TO CLOSE UP TO THE GERMANS AND THEN WE SHALL SHOOT BACK AT THEM AND TRY TO KILL THEM. THIS IS BECAUSE THEY HAVE DONE WRONG AND CAUSED ALL THIS WAR AND SORROW.

GIVE MY VERY BEST LOVE TO DIANA AND KISS SARAH FOR ME. WRITE ME A LETTER YOURSELF SOON AND I WILL SEND YOU AN ANSWER BACK.

YOUR EVER LOVING FATHER
WINSTON S.C.

For the next few months Winston commanded the Royal Scots Fusiliers in the field. In moments of respite from the shelling and the sniping – and even on occasion while it was still in progress – he would set up his easel in the muddy courtyard of his shell-shattered forward headquarters, which he called Lawrence Farm, and embark on painting some of his very first pictures. I am proud to have one which hangs in my home. Another two are on view at Chartwell.

It is clear from the many letters which Clemmie wrote to Winston in the trenches that no man could have had stronger or more loving support than he enjoyed during this difficult and dangerous period of his life. More than that, she kept him fully briefed on the different shifts in the political scene at home, while at the same time affording him loyal and wise counsel regarding his own political position. She too had bitter feelings about the mediocrities who had cast her husband aside, and who still found time to indulge in their spiteful intrigues and to take their grouse-moor holidays while the young men of Britain were so unselfishly laying down their lives by the hundred thousand in the trenches. She wrote on 12 January: 'When it is all over, we shall be proud that you were a soldier & not a politician for the greater part of the war – soldiers & soldier's wives seem to me now the only real people . . .'

Though engrossed in his military duties as a front-line soldier, Churchill could not help brooding over the political situation at home. He sensed a lack of drive in Arthur Balfour, his successor at the Admiralty, and suspected that the massive naval building programme that he and Admiral Fisher had set in train before the outbreak of war, which included fourteen battleships with the new 15-inch guns, as well as the dozen prototype tanks he had ordered, was no longer being driven ahead with urgency and resolve. On hearing a rumour that Balfour was to abolish the Royal Naval Division which Churchill had himself founded and which had served with such distinction at the Dardanelles – despite terrible casualties which included the loss of forty officers and six hundred men in three days alone in June 1915 – he commented acidly on the new First Lord, whom he described as 'the old grey tabby':

> How easy to destroy. How hard to build. How easy to evacuate, how hard to capture. How easy to do nothing. How hard to achieve anything. War is action, energy & hazard. These sheep only want to browse among the daisies.

On his return from the trenches in May, Churchill re-entered the political fray, but his fortunes were still low. He was despondent at the half-hearted way in which the war was being prosecuted by those wielding political power and, inevitably, by his own exclusion from any part in its direction. On 15 July 1916 he wrote from Blenheim to his younger brother Jack who, after nine months at the Dardanelles, was serving with the army in France:

> . . . Is it not damnable that I should be denied all real scope to serve this country, in this tremendous hour? I cannot tell how things political will

turn out: but great instability prevails and at any moment a situation favourable to me might come. Meanwhile Asquith reigns supine, sodden and supreme. LG made a half-hearted fight about Munitions. He is very much alone and none too well qualified for the particular job he has claimed. But very friendly according to the accounts I get from various trustworthy sources.

The Govt. have decided to repudiate their pledge to publish the D'Iles paper. My dossier was more than they could face. There will be a row, but there are many good arguments in the public interest against publishing: and many more good arguments in the Government interest!

I am here at Blenheim for the Sunday – painting. Goonie is here with Johnny: and Clemmie and Randolph. Peregrine develops much character: and like a violet hides his rare merit under abundant foliage. Randolph promises much. He has a noble air, and shows spirit and originality.

Don't be worried about anything my dear and always remember you have me to fall back upon *en tout cas*. I am ashamed of myself for not having been a better correspondent: (you're not up to much). Tho' my life is full of comfort, pleasure and prosperity I writhe hourly not to be able to get my teeth effectively into the *Boche*. But to plunge as a battalion commander unless ordered – into this mistaken welter – when a turn of the wheel may enable me to do 10,000 times as much – would not be the path of patriotism or of sense. There will be time enough for such courses. Jack, my dear, I am learning to hate.

With the formidable Papa now home from the war, life at Cromwell Road became distinctly more lively. According to Peregrine:

All sorts of odd visitors would turn up – people like Lloyd George, Asquith and so on. The house was always full of people going in and out. Cromwell Road had a very large hall with a double staircase leading up from it. Winston had come back from the front and had bought himself an enormous box of meccano. He and all us children thereupon set about building a model of the Forth bridge across the stairs.

My brother Johnny, who was pretty naughty too, and Randolph used to take off the various guests. One day Randolph was standing on a chair in the dining room making a speech in imitation of Lloyd George to the applause of the other children when – horror upon horror – the door opened and in came Winston.

In the spring of 1917, to move the children away from the bombing raids on London, Winston bought a house in Sussex called Lullenden.

After being cooped up in London, the country afforded a wonderful new freedom. Peregrine recounts:

> We literally lived in an old barn. The barn was turned into a glorious nursery for all us children. Randolph was about five then and he, Diana and Johnny used to go to school every day by pony-trap.
> What we liked about Randolph was that if there was trouble for which we the children were inevitably to be blamed – it didn't seem to matter what it was – Randolph would always own up and take the blame. On one occasion when something got broken the nurse demanded to know who had broken it. Nobody owned up, so the nurse said that she would give the person who owned up a chocolate. Randolph couldn't resist this and said he had done it. He didn't get the chocolate, he just got his ears boxed. Years later when we were all together, before Diana's death we were talking about this incident and Johnny said: 'I wonder who did break that object?' Diana owned up and said that she had – after fifty years she confessed!

Randolph's principal recollection of Lullenden is of playing 'Bear', a variant of 'Gorilla':

> Papa was the Bear. We had to turn our backs and close our eyes and he would climb a tree. All us children – six or seven perhaps – had then to go and look for the Bear. We were very much afraid but would advance courageously on a tree and say: 'Bear! Bear! Bear!' And then run away. Suddenly he would drop from a tree and we would scatter in various directions. He would pursue us and the one he caught would be the loser.
> One day we were playing 'Bear' and were chasing Papa through a wood when he disturbed a nest of bees or perhaps wasps. He passed through unscathed, however all of us children in hot pursuit were badly stung!

It was about this time while at his first school – a day school at Dormansland – that Randolph discovered, as he put it 'in a rather macabre way', that his father was different from other fathers:

> I was about five years old at the time and I said to a little boy at school (it makes me blush to recall the episode): 'Will you be my chum?' He said, 'No.' I said, 'Why not?' He said, 'Your father murdered my father.' I said, 'What do you mean?' He said, 'At the Dardanelles.' So when I got home I told this to my mother, who was naturally distressed at what had happened and explained to me about the Dardanelles. I am sorry to say it made me

feel immensely proud, for I realised my father was a boss man who could order other fathers about.

... Often my mother and father were not at Lullenden for many weeks. He was making munitions [in July 1917 Lloyd George had invited him to join his new Administration as Minister of Munitions] and she was running a lot of canteens for munitions workers . . .

Under my father's encouragement I learnt by heart 'Ye Mariners of England who guard our native shores . . .' When my father and mother and their important friends came down for the weekends, I was invited to stand up on a stool and recite this poem. I particularly enjoyed the last verse: 'The meteor flag of England shall yet terrific burn, till danger's troubled night be passed and the star of Peace return'. I remember this quite vividly and I always thought that I had enjoyed these recitations. But it seems that I bore some resentment against my father in the matter. For my mother has since told me that I used to refer to my father as the 'meteor beast'.

Shortly after this, in the autumn of 1918, Winston told them all: 'The war will be over very soon.' A few days later, Randolph and the other children came back in the pony-trap from school to find the gardener up a ladder nailing up a flagpole and a Union Jack on one of the chimneys of the house. The Armistice had been declared.

That year the Churchills were invited by their Marlborough cousins to spend Christmas at Blenheim Palace where Winston had been born in 1874, since his father, Lord Randolph, was the younger son of the then Duke of Marlborough. Randolph and all the children, together with the grown-ups, took part in a paperchase on horseback throughout the grounds of the palace, a whole ox was roasted, and at night there was a gigantic bonfire on top of which was placed an effigy of the Kaiser.

Lloyd George chose this moment, prior to the opening of the Peace Conference at Versailles, to seek a renewed mandate from the British electorate for his Liberal Coalition Government which enjoyed Conservative support. Churchill hastily repaired to his Dundee constituency and the hustings. The heckling was intense and in a letter to Clemmie on 27 November he reported: 'The meeting last night was the roughest I have ever seen in Dundee ... I had to scrap entirely my speech and trust in the main to interruptions and rejoinders, a good many of which came off. We had a great struggle to get into the hall in a very hostile mob.'

When the election results were announced the Lloyd George coalition had been returned with an overwhelming majority, Churchill himself having a majority of more than 15,000. Lloyd George offered him the posts of Secretary for War and Air and he plunged himself immediately into the task of demobilising the nearly three-and-a-half million British soldiers under arms in France and the Middle East who were threatening to mutiny if they were not allowed home.

At about this time Randolph attended a birthday party for the daughter of Lady Curzon, who recorded in her *Reminiscences*:

I have a happy memory of Marcella's party on her eighth birthday. We had the usual amusements for children's parties – a conjuror, and a small orchestra. Jennie Churchill brought her young grandson, Randolph – I can see him now, a very pretty little boy of about Marcella's age. The conjuror's performance was evidently not to the liking of little Randolph and, in the middle of it, he suddenly jumped up on his chair and exclaimed: 'Man, stop! Band, play!' How delightfully Churchillian! And the man did stop, and the band played.

On 18 July 1919 Winston narrowly escaped death in a plane crash. After finishing his day's work at the War Office he had driven down to Croydon Aerodrome for a flight with his Private Secretary at the Air Ministry, Colonel Alan Scott, who had been a fighter-pilot ace in the war. The small biplane with Winston at the controls made a normal take-off. However, while making a climbing turn at a speed of 60 m.p.h. at seventy or eighty feet, the aircraft stalled and spun into the ground with great force. Colonel Scott, whose presence of mind in switching off the magnetos and fuel had almost certainly saved their lives, was unconscious and bleeding. Fortunately the machine did not catch fire. In spite of this, two hours later Winston, with his forehead scratched and legs badly bruised, presided at a House of Commons dinner in honour of the US general, John Pershing.

Following the end of the war the Churchills sold Lullenden and bought a house in London at 2 Sussex Square, Bayswater; at the same time Randolph was packed off to boarding school at Sandroyd, near Cobham in Surrey. On 31 March 1920 Clemmie reported to Winston who was painting and chasing wild boar at Mimizan in France: 'This week has been occupied in taking Randolph to have his school clothes fitted. He looks such a thin shrimp in trousers and an Eton collar!' The school uniform, made to measure from Billings & Edmonds, consisted of two suits, one with knickerbockers and another with long trousers. Randolph was inordinately excited at having his first pair of long trousers and this mitigated the misery of leaving home for the first time.

Before going to Sandroyd, Randolph's father briefed him to look out for a boy called Max Aitken, the son of his great friend Lord Beaverbrook. Beaverbrook in turn instructed young Max to keep an eye on Winston's boy. However, as Randolph reported to his father a week later: 'You will be sorry to hear that the boy I hate most in the whole school is Max Aitken.' Although their parents' efforts to encourage their children to be friends proved vain, in later life they did indeed become firm friends.

In December 1920, at the end of his second term, the headmaster W. M. Hornby wrote of Randolph in his school report: 'A quick boy – at times too quick. He is apt to answer before he thinks.' And a year later: 'He likes to dash ahead too fast. He must learn to digest things more slowly and to be tidier.' And in December 1922, at the end of his third year: 'His clumsy pen does not keep pace with his quick brain and makes for slipshod work.'

Writing to Clemmie in the South of France on 6 February 1921 from Chequers where he and Marigold, the Churchills' fourth child, now aged two, were the guests of Lloyd George, Winston, newly appointed Colonial Secretary, reported: 'The so-called Duckadilly [Marigold] marched into my room this morning, apparently in blooming health. It was a formal visit & she had no special communication to make. But the feeling was good.' He adds without comment that he has had no news from Randolph.

On 13 February 1921 Winston visited his son at Sandroyd and reported to Clemmie:

I went to see Randolph yesterday at Sandroyd and found him very sprightly. The Headmaster described him as very combative and said that on any pretext or excuse he mixes himself up in fights and quarrels; but they seem quite pleased with him all the same.

He was much excited about our inheritance [on the death of a cousin, Winston had inherited an estate in Northern Ireland] and wanted to know all about the house and the lands, etc. I did not gratify his curiosity except in very general terms. He was also anxious to know whether my move to the Colonial Office was promotion or otherwise.

He declared himself perfectly happy and said he did not want anything. Most of the boys have got colds, and he is a happy exception.

The Broadstairs party [presumably Diana and Sarah at the seaside in Kent] are going on all right and I think they had better come back at the end of their third week. Marigold has a little cough again to-day, but otherwise she seems alright. She pays me a visit every morning and takes great interest in everything that is said to her or shown her...

Tonight I give up the War Office seals & take those of the Colonies...

A fortnight later he wrote:

The Broadstairs detachment arrived home yesterday. They were in the pink. I brought them home two days earlier in order to catch a glimpse of them before I left. The Duckadilly received them with joy & is quite free from cold. Indeed she is to go out today. Alas, however, I am the peccant one. I have a horrid cold. I do trust I have not given it to them. It is really impossible to avoid risk at one point or another.

We are going down to see Randolph today. I gave the children the choice of Randolph or the Zoo. They screamed for Randolph in most loyal and gallant fashion. So we arranged for the Zoo too ... Unless I have put things wrong with my cold – I shall leave a vy good state of affairs behind me. The expense of these two mites for 4 weeks is over £60. However it has done them good...

On 29 May that year Randolph's grandmother, Jennie, broke her ankle falling downstairs while staying with friends in Somerset. Soon gangrene set in and, within a fortnight, her left leg had to be amputated. She appeared to be making a good recovery when, on 29 June, she suffered a sudden haemorrhage and died soon afterwards. She was laid to rest in the country churchyard at Bladon where Lord Randolph had been buried a quarter of a century before and where her son and grandson would eventually join her.

Not long after this blow, Marigold's health began to give cause for concern. There had been difficulty with her birth and she had never been a strong child. Randolph, now aged ten, was on holiday at the seaside with the other children and reported to his mother:

August 2nd 1921   *Overblow,*
                                                                          Broadstairs

Dear Mummie,

I hope that you are quite well. My legs are suffering from the sun, it has made them go all red. The other day Falkner lent us his big shrimping net, so we went out and caught lots of shrimps for tea. On Sunday we went out in a little rowing boat, which was great fun! Marigold has been

rather ill, but is ever so much better today. We are all quite well here
except for our legs.

· With much love
Randolph
X X X X X X X X X X X

Nearly three weeks later he wrote from Scotland:

August 20th 1921   *Lochmore,*
                                                        Lairg, N.B.

Dear Mummie,
    We received your letter last night. I am so unhappy to hear about poor
Marigold. Yesterday we went to an island called Handa, and had tea there
... On Wednesday we went crab fishing, and I caught nine but we threw
them all back again into the sea.
    We ride generally in the afternoon on a pony called Flora.

Much love from
Randolph

Four days afterwards, just before her third birthday, Marigold died.
Winston, Clemmie and all the children were utterly distraught. On 3
September Winston wrote to Lord Crewe:

> We have suffered a vy heavy & painful loss. It all seems so pitiful that this
> little life sh'd have been extinguished just when it was so beautiful & so
> happy – just when it was beginning.

Clemmie in particular had been grief-stricken by the loss of Marigold
and her health suffered badly. On Boxing Day 1921 Winston left for the
South of France on a painting holiday. The next day Clemmie wrote
that in the '32 hours since you quitted this house Randolph, Diana and
Sarah had all been stricken with influenza' and she had found herself
running 'a miniature hospital' single-handed. In turn, suffering from
'nervous exhaustion', she too was ordered to bed by the doctor. She
reported a few days later that there had been many deaths in the
neighbourhood, mostly from influenza, 'poor people who did not go to
bed in time & were not properly nursed'. Influenza was to claim 250,000
victims in England, more than half a million in the United States and no
fewer than 16 million in India between 1919 and 1922. Fortunately the

children all recovered, though Clemmie herself remained very weak for some time.

Throughout this period, in addition to all his domestic worries, Churchill was heavily engaged in his work at the Colonial Office, to which he had been appointed in March 1921. Following the collapse of the Turkish Empire he had become responsible for the settlement of the Middle East and chaired a conference in Cairo at which he used T. E. Lawrence – better known as Lawrence of Arabia – as a senior adviser. The upshot was that Churchill placed the Hashemite ruler, Emir Feisal, on the throne of Iraq and created the kingdom of Transjordan for Feisal's brother Emir Abdullah.

One day in late June 1922 Randolph and Diana returned from roller-skating at the rink in Holland Park to find the house in Sussex Square surrounded by policemen. Earlier that afternoon Field Marshal Sir Henry Wilson had been assassinated by an Irish gunman on the steps of his home at Eaton Place. As Churchill had been another of the five British signatories of the Irish Treaty, it was feared that he too might be the target for an assassination attempt. For the rest of his life, except for the period 1932–9, he was guarded by armed Scotland Yard detectives and, initially, by as many as three.

This had its advantages, as Randolph points out in *Twenty-One Years*:

> That summer my father and mother took a house for the summer holidays at Frinton. My father always enjoyed making lakes and damming streams and the three detectives came in very handy on the beaches of Frinton. My father mobilised everybody on the beach and, when the tide ran out, dammed the sunken pools left behind and then dug immensely complicated channels to release the stored up water. Sometimes, instead, we would build an enormous sand castle and seek to resist, like latter-day Canutes, the incoming tide . . .

Clemmie, pregnant once again, wrote on 8 August to Winston, who was holidaying with Max Beaverbrook in Deauville:

> I feel quite excited at the approach of a new kitten. Only five weeks now & a new being – perhaps a genius – anyhow very precious to us – will make its appearance & demand our attention. Darling I hope it will be like you. Three days from now on August 11th [the previous year] our Marigold began to fade. She died on the 23rd.

On 15 September Clemmie gave birth to a baby girl. A fortnight later Randolph wrote from school:

Sunday October 1st 1922   Sandroyd School
                                                      Cobham
                                                      Surrey

Dear Mummie,
  What is the baby going to be christened, I do hope that it will be Mary. I was second this week. I am in the second form for French, English, and Maths . . .
  I hope that you are getting well. I am reading *King Solomon's Mines* which Papa has sent me. [As a boy, Winston had written to tell the author, Rider Haggard, that it was one of his favourite books.] It is very exciting. I am longing to see you and the baby. Please give my love to Papa. I am in the second game this term.

                                                 Much love from
                                                    Randolph

Shortly after Mary's arrival a general election was announced. The result was a disaster for the Liberal Coalition Government and a bitter personal defeat for Churchill who was soundly beaten at Dundee, having been unable to take part in the campaign until the very last days due to appendicitis. As he himself remarked philosophically a few years later, looking back at this moment: 'In the twinkling of an eye, I found myself without an Office, without a seat, without a party *and* without an appendix!'

CHAPTER 3

Life at Chartwell

On 15 September 1922, the day that Mary was born, Winston made an offer of £4,800 for the manor house of Chartwell, near Westerham in Kent – an offer that was initially turned down by the agents Knight, Frank & Rutley on behalf of the owners. However, a week or so later he took his children to visit it and I well recall being regaled by my father with his account of the trip:

> We children – Diana, Sarah and I, aged eleven at the time – all bundled into the motor-car which was driven by Papa. We motored down to Chartwell. The house had been unlived in for years and it was covered in a tangle of creepers. The garden was wild and overgrown but to us children, having lived so much of our lives in London, it was the most beautiful house that we had ever seen. It stood in an upland valley surrounded on three sides by banks of tall beeches, commanding a spectacular view over thirty miles or more of the Weald of Kent.
>
> As we were driving back to London my father asked us if we liked the house. 'Oh, Papa! do buy it! please let's buy it!' – 'My children!' he beamed triumphantly, 'it is already ours – I purchased it this morning.'

For the first time since 1900 Churchill was out of the House of Commons and, after six strenuous years of Cabinet office in which he was successively Minister of Munitions, Secretary of State for War and Air and, most recently, Colonial Secretary, he seized the opportunity of completing the first two volumes of his war memoirs, *The World Crisis*. When Volume I was published in the spring of the following year, Arthur Balfour hailed it as: 'Winston's brilliant autobiography, disguised as a history of the universe'.

Meanwhile he set in hand an ambitious programme which, with many additions and grandiose improvements, involved the virtual rebuilding of Chartwell. In order the better to supervise the work, he rented a house nearby called Hosey Rigge which had once been occupied by Lewis Carroll while writing *Alice in Wonderland*. Winston instantly dubbed it the 'Cosy Pig'.

In a letter from there of 17 August 1923 to Clemmie, who was holidaying with the children at Cromer on the Norfolk coast, he tells of his plans for the children:

I am going to amuse them on Saturday and Sunday by making them an aerial house in the lime tree. You may be sure I will take the greatest precautions to guard against them tumbling down. The undergrowth of the tree is so thick that it will be perfectly safe, and I will not let them go up except under my personal charge.

A year after losing his seat at Dundee, Winston once again threw his hat into the political arena and, in November 1923, was adopted as the National Liberal candidate in the forthcoming West Leicester by-election. For much of the campaign he was laid low in London with a severe bout of influenza and Clemmie carried on electioneering without him. Four days before polling day Randolph wrote to his father from Sandroyd:

Sunday Dec 2nd 1923

Dear Papa,
    I do hope that you will get in for Leicester. Mummie is sending me the Leicester Mercury. I do wish I was in Leicester with you. Yesterday I played in goal for the 2nd XI. We won 2 goals to 1. Will you please send me the books which you promised me? There has been a small fall of snow here, but it has all gone now. We break up on Thursday the 20th.

Much love From
Randolph

His father failed in his bid to return to Parliament, losing to the Labour candidate F. W. Pethick-Lawrence. However, less than six months later, in March 1924, undaunted by this further defeat, Winston contested the Abbey Division of Westminster in another by-election. This time he stood as a Constitutionalist (or Independent Conservative), having broken with the Liberal Party after it had, in January that year, pulled down Stanley Baldwin's new Conservative Government in order to install in office Ramsay MacDonald and the Labour Party. Though standing against an official Tory candidate, Otho Nicholson, he had the support of more than sixty Conservative MPs in what was to prove one of the most exciting by-elections of all time. Randolph, who was on holiday from school, assisted his father by manning the telephone at

Sussex Square. The newspapers reported that it was used 'as never before in the history of the instrument', something that was to remain the case throughout Randolph's adult life.

Polling took place on 19 March and, as the count was entering its final stages, the rumour suddenly spread that Churchill was in by a small majority. A cheer went up from his supporters. As he later recorded: 'The sound was caught by the crowds waiting outside and the news was telegraphed all over the world.' But the report was false: the final tally was a majority, after a recount, of 43 for Nicholson.

This was Churchill's third electoral defeat in a row. Randolph was clearly very upset at the reverses suffered by his father, whom he hero-worshipped, and he hastened to write from school the next day:

20 March 1924

I have just had a telephone message from Diana, to say that you were beaten by 43 votes. I am so sorry that you did not get in. You and Mummie must be very tired after the Election.

We are having lovely weather here. We are not having any work this afternoon as a boy called Williamson got an Exhibition at Harrow. An exhibition is not quite as good as a scholarship. We break up on Tuesday April 8th.

The rebuilding and landscaping of Chartwell, together with his prolific writing, employed Winston's full energies now that he was out of Parliament and unable to play any part in the conduct of affairs of state. In his letter of 17 April – his first from Chartwell – he reported to Clemmie, who was visiting her mother in Dieppe:

The children have worked like blacks & Sergeant Thompson [of Scotland Yard's Special Branch] Aley, Waterhouse, one gardener & six men have formed a powerful labour corps. The weather has been delicious & we are out all day toiling in dirty clothes & only bathing before dinner. I have just had my bath in your de luxe bathroom. I hope you have no *amour propre* about it! . . .

I drink champagne at all meals & buckets of claret & soda in between . . .

On 7 May, with Clemmie at his side, he addressed an audience of over five thousand in Liverpool – the first Conservative Party meeting at which he had spoken for twenty years. Liberals and Conservatives, he declared, now found themselves with many things in common. There was no longer any place for an independent Liberal Party – only the Conservative Party provided an effective means 'for the successful defeat of socialism'.

Eager to know if his father intended contesting Westminster again, Randolph wrote a few days later:

18 May 1924

We are having lovely weather here, but the heat has made lots of boys sick. I was rather ill last night, but now I feel perfectly alright. Yesterday the Queen of Roumania came down here to see her two nephews Alonzo and Atalfo. She kissed two of the boys because she said they had Roumanian eyes. She asked Mr Hornby that we might have a half-holiday . . .

Winston spent much of the month of August at Chartwell with the children and one day took Randolph, now aged thirteen, to lunch with Lord Rosebery, the former Liberal Prime Minister. Their conversation turned to his ancestor, the great Duke of Marlborough, and the attacks on his reputation in Macaulay's *History of England*. This talk, he told Clemmie the next day, 'has turned my mind very seriously to the great literary project which so many people are inclined to saddle me with – a full scale biography of "Duke John" '.

At about this period Bernard Baruch, the distinguished American financier and lifelong friend of Winston's, visited Chartwell. Randolph had obtained advance intelligence of the visit and, as Bernie and Winston were just about to enter the dining-room, Randolph switched on the gramophone which was just inside the door. As his cousin Johnny Churchill recalled the incident: 'The record was a popular item of nonsense of the day. "Barney Google with the Googly Googly Eyes". My uncle was so angry at this cheeky allusion to his honoured guest's name that he snatched the record from the turntable and dashed it to the floor. We were severely reprimanded.'

At the end of 1923 Mr Hornby, the headmaster of Sandroyd, had written of Randolph: 'I should like to see him less the servant of his mood of the moment . . . His thoughts appear to fly from one thing to another with an uncontrolled rapidity that spoils his chances of achieving his best.' And, on his leaving Sandroyd in July 1924, the headmaster percipiently observed the lines on which Randolph's character was set to develop:

He is no willing accepter of drudgery. Indeed he is too anxious to take short-cuts to success. At the same time when he has made up his mind to accomplish a thing he has undoubted power of concentration and persistence. I am heartily sorry to part with a boy so full of the cheerfulness and gaiety of life and one who, though full of mischief, followed by ingenious self defence, is straight as he could be.

My father more than once told me with great approbation how, when he was twelve, his father had given him the option of going to either Eton or Harrow – a choice denied to me. In *Twenty-One Years* he recalled:

> My father had not been happy at Harrow. I doubt if he would have been much happier at Eton, but I was greatly complimented that he gave me the choice. I went down and inspected both institutions. It seemed that there were fewer rules and much less discipline at Eton than at Harrow; accordingly I opted for Eton and joined Colonel Sheepshanks' House in October 1924. This was where I was to board for the next four years.
>
> Before I took the Common Entrance Examination my father said he would give me a pony if I took Middle Fourth. I told one of the masters about it and he said, 'Does your father mean twenty-five pounds or an animal?' I had not then heard of this distinction. In the event I took Upper Fourth and my father gave me one of his polo ponies, called Ostrich.

That October Churchill was at last returned to Parliament as Member for Epping, which he won as a Constitutionalist and Anti-Socialist candidate with a majority of just under ten thousand. A few days later Stanley Baldwin formed his new Conservative administration and, as Churchill later put it: 'I was astonished and the Conservative Party dumbfounded when he invited me to be Chancellor of the Exchequer, the Office which my father had once held.'

On his return to Chartwell he had great difficulty convincing Clemmie that he was not teasing her and, writing to Randolph's new housemaster, Colonel Sheepshanks, on 19 November, he remarked: 'Many thanks for your congratulations. No one was more surprised than I.' This is understandable in view of what he had said of the new Prime Minister less than a year before, at the time of the Leicester by-election: 'Who is Mr Baldwin to acclaim himself such a singularly honest man? He is a man whom we only know in the last few months through the eulogies of the newspapers. He has no achievements to his record. He is an unknown man.'

Shortly after 3.30 p.m. on 28 April 1925 Churchill rose to the Dispatch Box to introduce his first Budget. It was a poignant moment for him – one of which his father had robbed himself when he had resigned as Chancellor nearly forty years before – and Clemmie, together with Randolph and Diana, was in the Gallery to hear him. After announcing the Government's decision to return to the gold standard, the Chancellor went on to deploy his ambitious new insurance scheme which would affect 15 million wage-earners and as many again of their dependents. This involved providing all widows with a pension of 10s 0d a week for life – £14.90 in today's money – plus an extra 5s 0d for an eldest child and 3s 0d for all other children until the age of fourteen and a half. The qualifying age for the retirement pension was reduced from seventy to sixty-five and the means test was abolished. In conclusion Churchill announced a reduction in the standard rate of income tax from 4s 6d to 4s 0d (or 20p) in the pound, with further very substantial reductions for income-tax payers at the lowest end of the scale.

Months of hard work, argument and fierce bargaining had gone into the preparation of his Budget. It had involved pruning the expenditure of all government departments, but most especially cutting back the ambitious naval building programme for which Admiral Beatty fought tenaciously but in vain. This enabled him to achieve the two centrepieces of his programme: a major and overdue piece of social reform and a boost to industry, calculated to reduce the high level of unemployment. When, after more than two and a half hours, the Chancellor resumed his seat he was greeted with prolonged and enthusiastic applause.

Much of the summer of 1925 Winston spent at Chartwell completing his dams and supervising the landscaping of the garden, as well as in painting and brick-laying. Among the regular visitors was the Oxford scientist Professor Lindemann, 'the Prof', who later became Churchill's scientific adviser and whose calculations using a pocket slide-rule and scientific theories, Randolph found fascinating.

Randolph's early school reports from Eton tend to confirm his own self-assessment in *Twenty-One Years*: 'I did not enjoy Eton very much. I was lazy and unsuccessful both at work and at games. I did not conform to the general pattern and was an unpopular boy.'

At the end of the summer half of 1925 his mathematics tutor, A. G. Hudson, observed: 'He is hideously ingenious for a boy of his years. I hope this bodes well for the Country. I must say he is extremely good fun. One does not talk much when he wants to.' His Classics tutor J. D. Harford commented:

His chief fault at present is to strain to breaking-point a natural adroitness of mind by indulging in constant interruptions in the form of queries and quibbles. He shows at present no sign of realising that one of the best forms of discrimination & criticism to develop is self-criticism, a faculty which would enable him to see that his remarks, wasteful of time & fraying to everyone's patience, are very largely cheap, pointless & irrelevant.

And, later in the year, H. G. Babington Smith, another mathematics master, recorded: 'Obstinacy appears to be one of his more prominent characteristics. He has shown himself to be possessed of natural capacity in many directions, but he does not take kindly to being taught.'

The Chancellor of the Exchequer was also taking a close interest in his son's education, as may be judged by his letter of 11 December commenting on Randolph's essay for the Rosebery History Prize for Lower Boys:

I have read the paper and your answers to it. I do not think you have done badly, but it would have been very easy to do better.

Take for instance the question about 'Why Rome won?' [the Punic Wars]. What you say is all right so far as it goes, but surely you ought to have mentioned Sea Power. Quite one of the most astonishing things in history is the way in which Rome, a nation of soldiers and agriculturists, beat the Carthaginians on sea in the first Punic War, and thereafter had the command of the sea. Without this Rome and her Legionaries might indeed have defended themselves in Italy, but they never could have conquered Carthage, still less the world...

I wonder you did not choose to answer the question about whether Hannibal was over-cautious after [the Battle of] Cannae. This is a most interesting topic, and I should like to see what you would have put down about it.

You are quite good at taking a decision as to what your opinion is on these different points, but I am sure to win a prize like this it is necessary to be fuller in your answers...

When will it be known what is to be the subject for next year? You ought certainly to go in for it next time, and if we can get the books early we can read it up together.

That Christmas and New Year the family spent at Chartwell. On 4 January 1926 the Prof came to stay for a week before taking Randolph back with him to spend a few days at Oxford. On his return to Eton, Randolph wrote to his mother, who was holidaying on the Riviera:

Monday January 25th 1926   *A. C. Sheepshanks, Esq.*
                                                       Eton College,
                                                       Windsor.

My darling Mummie,

   I arrived here safely and am now quite settled down to life as an Upper.
It is much more fun, since I can now do most of my work in my own
time.
   I enjoyed my stay at Oxford enormously. The night I arrived we went
to a play called 'The Skin Game' which was very amusing. The next day
the 'Prof' took me down to his laboratory which was very interesting. He
let me blow some glass. In the evening we dined in Hall. I thought the
dons were very nice. The next day we skated in the afternoon which was
great fun . . .

                                               Much Love from
                                               Your loving son,
                                               Randolph

A fortnight later he wrote to his father:

Sunday Feb: 7th 1926.

My dear Papa,

   I am enjoying life here as an Upper very much indeed. I have much
more time for reading. I have read *Ovington's Bank* which I thought was
very good. I have also read *Count Hannibal* by Stanley Weyman. Do you
think you could send me some books, as I have finished all the ones I
have? . . .

                                               Your loving son,
                                               Randolph

Winston replied on 10 February:

I am vy glad to hear from you & that you like the amenities of an Upper
boy's life. Your mother returns on the 18th, so there will be plenty of time
to arrange for a Chartwell week end at yr Long Leave. You will find we
have made a good deal of progress. The orchard will be planted & the
lawns in good order. But one thing leads to another, & '*Le mieux est
l'ennemi du bien.*'
   Have you read *The Long Roll, Cease Firing* & *Dracula* by Bram Stoker?

They interested me vy much when I read them. There is a vy good book of a different character called *The Caravanners* by the author of *Elizabeth & her German Garden* – wh perhaps might amuse you. Let me know . . .

Unfortunately Colonel Sheepshanks did not share Randolph's high opinion of his assiduity with his books, writing to his father at the end of the Lent term that the two zeros for 'Extra Books' or set reading 'show that he cannot be relied on to do any work by himself at his own time . . . I am afraid he has definitely made up his mind that Greek is too hard for him . . . I suppose that he still has a sort of feeling that it is up to him to work at anything he is interested in and to let the remainder of his tasks look after themselves.'

On 27 April 1926, with Randolph again in the crowded Gallery, Churchill introduced his second Budget. He did so against a background of widespread strife in the coal industry, arising from the inability of the coal-owners to maintain the existing level of wages in the pits without a continuing government subsidy. The crisis came to a head on 1 May when the miners rejected outright the owners' insistence on an immediate reduction in wages and the entire workforce of the mines was faced with a lock-out. The same day the TUC Executive called a General Strike in support of the miners, to begin at midnight on 3 May.

The Chancellor was determined that all the forces of the State should be mobilised to ensure the maintenance of law and order, together with the unloading and distribution of essential supplies to the population. Further, he was convinced that the free flow of information, indeed propaganda, would play an essential part in maintaining public confidence and breaking the strike. When all of Fleet Street was closed down, he took over the *Morning Post* on behalf of the Government and, with a skeleton staff drawn from many Fleet Street offices, produced a special government newssheet which he called the *British Gazette*, the circulation of which rose to over 2,000,000 copies on its eighth and last day, after the strike had ended.

Later, in the House of Commons, Churchill was assailed by Labour Members for what they regarded as his partiality in the dispute, which included the requisition by Government of the newsprint stocks of the Socialist *Daily Herald*, thereby effectively putting a stop to the TUC's own rival publication.

Churchill riposted: 'The State cannot be impartial as between itself and that section of its subjects with whom it is contending . . . I decline utterly to be impartial as between the Fire Brigade and the fire.' Finally, winding up the debate for the Government, as tension and fury on the

Opposition benches was rising to fever pitch, he fired his broadside. 'I warn you [*jeers*], I warn you,' he threatened menacingly, as Mr Speaker vainly attempted to maintain order, 'if there is another General Strike, we will let loose on you another – British Gazette!' The bathos was complete and the whole House dissolved into laughter.

From Eton, where he was following the unfolding political drama with intense excitement, Randolph wrote to his mother:

21 May 1926

Have you received a letter from the 'Sheep' [the irreverent nickname by which Randolph referred to his housemaster] inviting you down to lunch on the 4th June? Will Diana be able to come? I do hope so. Perhaps as it is her games afternoon she would be able to come down here in the afternoon, and stay and see the fire-works.

At the beginning of the Strike I asked the 'Sheep' if I could install a wireless set, in order to hear the news bulletins. However he would not let me. So I have fitted up a secret one in the bottom of my arm-chair. It works extraordinarily well and I can hear London quite easily...

I am so glad the *British Gazette* was such a success. I found it impossible to secure a copy down here.

I do hope the Coal Strike will be settled soon. I have just heard on the wireless that Mr Baldwin has gone to Chequers, the owners to their homes and the Miners delegates to their respective districts, and that there will be no further negotiations, which is not very encouraging.

In *Twenty-One Years* Randolph gave a fuller account of how, with the assistance of a school friend, he had installed the contraband radio in his room:

The aerial was put round the top of the picture rail, came down behind a curtain, and went into the bottom of a basket chair. Underneath we installed a piece of three-ply wood on which the set could rest, and in the seat of the chair, cut a small trap door (concealed by a cushion) through which one could manipulate a cat's whisker of this early crystal set, and where one could also conceal the headphones. The set worked beautifully and I had far more fun listening to the BBC in these circumstances than I have ever had since. In 1926 when I was about fifteen I heard on my earphones the news of the end of the General Strike. I have always enjoyed imparting news. Having replaced the receiver of my headphones and disconnected the cat's whisker, I rushed out of my room, but hardly had

I passed the threshold than I realised how dangerous it would be to do so.

I hurried down town and on my return a few moments later communicated my intelligence to one and all, pretending that I had garnered it from some shopkeeper in the town.

Though the General Strike had collapsed after only eight days, the coal strike itself continued unresolved and Churchill was later charged by the Prime Minister, Mr Baldwin, with negotiating a settlement. On 25 August, the eve of a meeting between the Cabinet Committee and the miners' leaders, Churchill invited Thomas Jones, Deputy Secretary to the Cabinet and an avowed Labour supporter, to dine and sleep at Chartwell. In his diary Jones gave an account of the dinner:

Winston plunged into the coal business at once, and I tried in vain to postpone the subject until after dinner when I could have talked in private with my host, but he is the most unsubtle and expansive person. He talked with the greatest freedom and frankness before Lindemann and the rest, making several little speeches in the course of dinner, one especially in defence of a change of opinion which Mrs Churchill alleged against him. The two elder children were with us, Diana about 17, and Randolph about 15. Nothing could be more charming than Winston's handling of the children throughout my short visit.

Lindemann, I quickly discovered, regarded all miners, if not all the working classes, as a species of sub-humans. This drove me to the Extreme Left with Winston at the Right Centre. The ladies left at about 10 p.m. and we carried on till past midnight. Randolph being allowed to stay to the end as a special privilege, and his father frequently deferring to him for his opinion on some phase or other of the coal crisis: the boy was extremely intelligent, and obviously under the influence of the Prof (as he was called).

I was out and about the next morning before 9.00 a.m. and found the Chancellor attired in dungarees and high Wellington boots superintending the building of a dam by a dozen navvies. This is the third lake, and the children are wondering what their father will do next year, as there is room for no more lakes.

As I was going away, he told me 'I am very glad you expounded the democratic faith last night, as the small boy does not often hear it, and it will be very good for him.' I agreed, and said that in view of what was likely to happen in the next twenty years it was desirable he should not be unduly Lindemannised. The father agreed and said he was eager that the boy should get a scientific outlook.

It was at about this time that Randolph fell in love with his cousin, Diana Mitford. Diana, who was a year older, was already a great beauty with her blonde hair and blue eyes. They had first met in early childhood as Randolph's maternal grandmother, Lady Blanche Hozier, and Diana's maternal grandmother, Lady Clementine Mitford (Redesdale), were sisters – the daughters of the 10th Earl of Airlie. Lady Blanche had caused a scandal by separating from her husband, Sir Henry Hozier. Some years later she went to live in Dieppe, on the Normandy coast of France, where she remained until her death in 1925. She was an avid gambler and, according to Diana, the attraction of Dieppe rested in the fact that it had a casino. It was not until after the war and the purchase of Chartwell that Randolph, already a teenager, re-met Diana and her older brother, Tom, who was to become Randolph's best friend at Eton. Most friendships made at school are with direct contemporaries and the fact that Randolph was seeing a great deal of Tom Mitford, who was two years his senior and from another house, aroused the suspicions of Colonel Sheepshanks, who proceeded to question Randolph about it. Hinting darkly that they might be having a homosexual relationship, the housemaster received the monumental put-down from Randolph: 'I happen to be in love with his sister!' By Randolph's account, Sheepshanks was left speechless.

According to my cousin, Anita Leslie, Randolph would have seen a striking resemblance to his own mother, Clementine, in his first love. This is acknowledged by Diana, now Lady Diana Mosley whose second husband, Sir Oswald Mosley, was the leader of the British Union of Fascists. For all her eighty-five years, she remains an exceptionally fine-looking woman, despite spending several years at her husband's side when he was imprisoned under Regulation 18B during the Second World War. When, recently, I sought her out at her home near Orsay, just outside Paris, I asked her about the supposed resemblance between her and my grandmother. She replied:

Well, I think that was Anita's theory and, you see, a lot of people have seen a resemblance between me and Clementine … My Mitford grandfather [Lord Redesdale] had the most extraordinarily brilliant blue eyes. We all had blue eyes, but not particularly those brilliant ones. Now Randolph had brilliant ones and another one who had was Mary, when she was a child, Mary Soames. Another one is my son, Desmond, and my sister, Pam. It crops up and they are tremendously different from ordinary blue eyes, much brighter and my grandfather was rather famous for them. I often thought, 'Well, where *did* Randolph get them? …'

She then added with great warmth and a flash of her still beautiful eyes: 'I loved all the family. I loved your grandfather and grandmother. When people say Clementine was so cold, well, she was extremely kind to us as children and, to me particularly, wonderful.'

Once the coal strike was over, Winston threw himself into two months of sustained work to finish the third volume of *The World Crisis*. And that autumn, having started work on his next year's Budget, he accepted the invitation of his friend Admiral Sir Roger Keyes, who had commanded the Eastern Mediterranean Squadron at the time of the Gallipoli landings and was now Commander-in-Chief Mediterranean, to take a week's cruise on board a destroyer early in the New Year. Winston decided to take his son:

13 *Dec.* 1926   *House of Commons*

My dear Randolph,

I send you herewith £2 [equivalent to £60 today] to wind up the term, but please keep account of the money you have to give in tips & explain it to me later.

We are spending Christmas at Chartwell; & I am going to take you to Malta on Jan. 4. It was vy disappointing to me while arranging this vy interesting expedition for you to learn how little you are using yr abilities & opportunities at Eton.

You will certainly not go to Oxford unless you show some aptitude & love for learning.

Many thanks for yr letter on my birthday & for the cigar cutter. It wd give me much more pleasure to hear something creditable about you from yr masters.

Your loving father,
Winston S. Churchill

The cause of the paternal wrath had been contained in a letter of 10 November from Randolph's housemaster, from which it is evident that he had been flogged:

Just a line to say that Randolph has been 'complained of', i.e. reported by me to the Headmaster for unsatisfactory work and behaviour up to his various division masters. He is 'up to' [i.e. has lessons from] five different men, and all of them independently have complained to me that R. is either being idle or being a bore with his chatter. He is much subdued at the present moment and I hope he will continue to be so. I find it difficult to make him understand that his little wagging tongue makes him, in the opinion of some, a very unpleasant child, whereas by keeping it under control he can be a most delightful member of society. I do not tell him the latter part!

I think this complaint will do good – I hope so. But you will understand that it is nothing very serious, but a cumulation of little complaints –

This had come on top of several less than satisfactory reports Randolph had received earlier in the year. In the view of his science master, C. R. White-Thomas: 'He has plenty of ability but he prefers to be thoroughly idle ... His chief aim in school is to promote discussions which shall be as far removed as possible from the work in hand.'

His mathematics tutor, Mr Kerry, concurred:

The reason for this humble result [14th out of 14] is not entirely that he is the worst Mathematician in the Division – though I think it probable that he is – but he is further handicapped by his obsession for the sound of his own voice. At first, I ventured to answer him back (in fear & trembling) but, finding I was not completely withered, I persevered & have managed to keep his effusiveness slightly in check. It has been good fun (but poor Mathematics).

Similar complaints were to be made of Randolph in later life, not always without justification. Anthony Howard, editor of the *New Statesman*, once wrote of him: 'There was Randolph buoyed up by the reassuring burble of his own voice ...'

Despite these adverse reports Randolph, then aged fifteen and a half, was allowed to set forth for Paris on 4 January 1927 with his father and Uncle Jack. That night, they took the 'Train Bleu' for the South of France, then boarded a steamship for Naples where, as Randolph records: 'We drove off to see the ruins of Pompeii. I was not allowed to accompany my father and Uncle into the newly discovered ruins of Herculaneum with the indecent pictures on the wall. I had to remain above ground, kicking my heels.'

That night Winston reported to Clemmie:

The Rabbit [Randolph] is a very good travelling companion. He curls up in the cabin most silently and tidily. We have played a great deal of chess in which I give him either a Queen or two castles, or even castle, bishop and knight – and still wallop him.

I am shocked to see him wear nothing under his little linen shirts, and to go about without a coat on every occasion. He is hardy, but surely a vest is a necessity to white people. I am going to buy him some.

Next morning in the Straits of Messina they joined a Royal Navy destroyer sent by Roger Keyes and reached Malta four hours later. Here, at the age of fifty-two, Winston played his last game of polo. Two days later, as recalled by Randolph in *Twenty-One Years*:

We sailed in HMS *Warspite* with the whole Mediterranean Fleet and had three days and nights of wonderfully exciting naval exercises. We then arrived and anchored in the Piraeus. We disembarked at once and drove to the Parthenon, where we all had a picnic luncheon while my father painted a picture. That night we embarked in another destroyer, sailed through the Corinth Canal and arrived the following afternoon at Brindisi where we caught the night train for Rome.

Here we had four very exciting days. We saw the Colosseum, the Forum, St Peter's, the Pope, and Mussolini, the latter at a reception at the British Embassy where we were staying. During the next few years there were three separate attempts to murder Mussolini. I remember that my father was beginning to exhaust his stock of congratulatory telegrams on the Duce's preservation; soon, however, the attempts ceased. Of course, we did not then know how tiresome this Socialist dictator was subsequently to prove.

Randolph preserved a lively memory of his meeting with the Pope:

A lot of careful protocol went into the private audience which my father and I had with Pope Pius. As an important minister serving under a Protestant sovereign my father felt that he ought not to kneel, but every-thing was arranged very easily. We were told that we should treat His Holiness merely as a temporal sovereign and bow to him three times: once at the door, once halfway and once when we arrived at his desk. All this passed off very well. The early part of the conversation was a little sticky. Then my father and the Pope got on to the subject of the Bolsheviks and had a jolly half-hour saying what they thought of them.

I had stuffed my pockets with a lot of statuettes of the Madonna and Child which I thought would make acceptable gifts for my Catholic friends if they would be blessed by the Pope. My father detected them on the way to the Vatican and said that I must on no account reveal them. However, when we were taking our leave my father suggested that His Holiness should bless me, though he asked no such benediction for himself. The Pope rose from his seat for the occasion, placing his right hand on my head and a few seconds later his left hand on my father's. Recognising my father's Protestant scruples, he said, 'This is just the blessing of an old man and you can both take it in any spirit that you choose.' He then said a few words in Latin which I fear neither my father nor myself were able to understand. It was very moving and I felt that my statuettes had also been blessed, though I had not revealed them to His Holiness. I was also presented with a silver medal, which I have since seen it falsely stated I sold on my return to Eton. It seems to have disappeared but I am quite sure that I did not 'pop' it.

When, on 11 April, Churchill introduced his third Budget in the House of Commons, Randolph was once again in the Gallery to hear his father, as were Clemmie and the Prince of Wales. The Prime Minister Stanley Baldwin reported to the King:

> The scene was quite sufficient to show that Mr Churchill as a star turn has a power of attraction which nobody in the House of Commons can excel ... His enemies will say that this year's Budget is a mischievous piece of manipulation and juggling with the country's finances, but his friends will say that it is a masterpiece of ingenuity.

Despite an attempt by Leopold Amery, then Colonial Secretary and a right-winger in the Conservative Party strongly opposed to Churchill's free trade policies, to have him removed from the Treasury, the Prime Minister continued to place his full confidence in the Chancellor and personally approved his Budget proposals at every stage. It had been over this very issue that Winston had left the Tory Party in 1905.

Winston spent the summer of 1927 almost exclusively at Chartwell constructing new dams, ponds and waterworks. He started building the lengthy, tall wall around the kitchen garden (today the Golden Rose Garden) and began to write *My Early Life*, an autobiographical account of his first twenty-six years up to his entry into Parliament in 1900.

Meanwhile, in June, Clemmie had been knocked over by a bus while shopping in the Brompton Road and, although she had been able to return to 11 Downing Street by taxi, the effects of the accident were more severe than at first realised. She went to the South of France to recuperate, where Randolph wrote to her from Eton:

> I do so hope you are having a real rest at Eze and are really recuperating
> your lost strength.
> Did the 'Sheep' write you a very rude letter about us going to the play?
> Do let me know what happened. He is absolutely in the wrong but is so
> obstinate that he does not realise it.
> I am so pleased about the enormous [Budget] surplus. The press however
> do their best to belittle the achievement with such headings as 'Surplus
> for first time in three years.' 'Chancellor obtains his first surplus.' However
> I suppose this is only to be expected...

On 9 January 1928 Randolph was again invited to accompany his
father on holiday abroad. This time they took the ferry from Newhaven
to Dieppe to spend a couple of days hunting wild boar with the Duke
of Westminster in the Forêt d'Eu and the Forêt d'Arques. Back at school
Randolph wrote to his father of his hopes of going to Oxford the
following year and of his enthusiasm for history, inspired by his tutor
C. R. N. Routh, an historian of distinction:

> As a result of my stay with the Prof: We have found out that I have to take
> the Scholarship in December of this year. This is rather short notice, and
> should I fail to qualify, I can then come up for Matriculation in March.
> The period of History for the Scholarship is from 1494 to about 1870. At
> the moment we are studying 1640–1660.
> I find it much more interesting specialising in History than doing the
> general curriculum as formerly. I am up to a man called Routh who is
> very intelligent and at the same time amiable...

Randolph's letter was sent back by return of post, marked in red ink
by his father who was less than pleased with his son's calligraphy:

> It is always nice to get a letter from you: & I am vy glad that you enjoyed
> the hunting. I hope things may so unfold that yr undoubted taste for
> riding & love of the chase may be indulged.
> I wish you wd look at yr letter again & see the various 'caligraphic
> elucidations' [sic] wh I have ventured to make upon it. In the early years
> of manhood a really venomous & misleading handwriting will be a serious
> handicap to you. Yr hand-writing is perverse. One can guess what you
> mean as a rule, but proper names remain undecipherable. It cd so easily
> be cured by a little care now. You certainly have been widely taught: but

there is still time to recover. Do try. Send me yr letter back. There ought
not to be doubt about any word. That is the test...
    I was shocked to learn of Lord Haig's sudden death. Yet it is the best of
exits.

Randolph, never one to miss a trick in defending himself or counter-
attacking in an argument – a facility that was the key to his successful
conduct of numerous libel actions in later years – replied on 3 February,
not omitting to draw attention to his father's own spelling mistake:

Many thanks for your letter and for the corrected copy of my letter. I will
try in future to make every letter clearly distinguishable from its neighbours. I had a letter from Eddie [Marsh, Winston's Private Secretary] this
morning assuming entire responsibility for your mistake in 'calligraphic' –
an error which I must confess escaped me.
    I find my studies as a History Specialist more arduous than I had first
anticipated but none the less interesting. I think I shall get on very well
with my new tutor Mr Birley. He is a man of immense height 6ft $5\frac{1}{2}$"!
    Besides Trevelyan's 'England under the Stuarts' I am reading Harold
Acton's 'Lectures on Modern History'. I read these two officially. In my
spare time I am reading Ludwig's Napoleon...
    I do hope that the Budget in general and your rating scheme in particular
are progressing favourably.

Randolph had already been taken into his father's confidence about
his scheme for the de-rating (or relieving from local taxation) of industry
and agriculture in his forthcoming Budget – a measure conceived by
the Chancellor to encourage industry and thereby boost employment,
particularly in the depressed areas where unemployment was high. He
wrote to Randolph two days later warning him against disclosing what
he had told him:

5 February 1928

Many thanks for your letter which is certainly much better written, and
very well expressed. ... I fully approve of your having a thrust at the
Scholarship in December. You of course have to ride hard and fast at a
fence of this kind. One must do one's best to see the hunt and no one can
do more. If you will let me know all the books you are reading I will try
to read them too. The 'Prof' said you had to read John Stuart Mill on
Economics. Which of his various works is it? I could perhaps be of some

help in talking to you about this subject, especially if you could show me a specimen paper on Political Economy. Though quite uneducated on the subject, I have had to argue about it all my life . . .

I am trying a new wireless set with 8 valves and the man was nearly three hours showing me how to work it last night. Afterwards I made it go myself. One can get 15 or 20 foreign stations . . . I do not know whether I shall be able to afford to buy the set but I have got it for a few weeks on approval.

Please do not write any references to my plans as any mention of such topics on paper is dangerous. You will however see from what I said at Birmingham that difficulties are being gradually cleared out of the way and that design is taking the place of chaos. You should also read the King's Speech which will be published on Tuesday with an observant eye.

PS We have bought a fine new carthorse her name is 'Blossom' she can pull a ton & a half!

Since the early autumn of the previous year Churchill had been fighting a running battle with the big spending departments of Government, especially the military, to contain public expenditure so that he could finance his rating scheme, as well as the cost of the General Strike, without any increase in income tax. He fired off a 3,000-word memorandum to Cabinet on the naval building programme, pointing out that even if no new British cruisers were laid down at all in 1928 Britain, by 1930, would none the less have sixty-two cruisers to Japan's twenty-eight and the United States' fifteen.

In early February of 1928 Clemmie was taken ill. Winston wrote to Randolph at Eton:

13 February 1928

We had a vy tiring day yesterday. Two separate operations at 2.30 & midnight! Yr mother astonished the hardened Doctors by her wonderful courage. If you shd turn out as I do not doubt – to be a fearless man, you will know where you got it from.

Today the Doctors declare themselves entirely satisfied, & I hope & believe the corner is turned. She still however has a good deal of pain & is a little disappointed at its not stopping as she had been encouraged to expect. The Doctors say that anyhow, the cavity is open now, & whatever matter forms can drain harmlessly away. Naturally I have cross-questioned them searchingly. And as a result I do not feel particularly anxious at the moment.

If in a day or two you feel you wd like to come up to see her, you shd let me know the most convenient occasion from yr Eton point of view, & I will ask Dr Alington to let you come. Write on receipt of this accordingly.

Randolph replied promptly:

I was so delighted to receive yr letter and to hear that Mummie is all right. I should love to come up to see her. Thursday or Saturday would be the best days – though Thursday being the nearer would be the more welcome.
    Please give her my love and tell her how impressed I am at yr account of her courage. I am so looking forward to seeing you both.

On 8 April, a fortnight before introducing his fourth Budget, Winston wrote to Clemmie: 'Pray God these plans bring back a little more prosperity to Poor Old England.' But much of his letter was devoted to news about Randolph and the development of his forceful character:

There is no doubt he is developing fast, and in those directions wh will enable him to make his way in the world – by writing & speaking – in politics, at the bar, or in journalism. There are some vy strange & even formidable traits in his character. His mind is free & growing more powerful every day. It is quite startling to hear him argue. His present phase is rabid Agnosticism, & last night in argument with Grigg [P. J. Grigg, Churchill's Parliamentary Private Secretary, later Secretary of State for War in the Wartime Coalition] he more than defended his dismal position. The logical strength of his mind, the courage of his thought, & the brutal & sometimes repulsive character of his rejoinders impressed me vy forcibly. He is far more advanced than I was at his age, & quite out of the common – for good or ill . . .

Following the Budget debate a public row broke out within the Conservative Party between Churchill and the Protectionist lobby led by Lord Derby which he dubbed 'the Amery/Page Croft gang' and of which he opined: 'I hate the whole lot of them. They ruined our party once and they will ruin it again if they have their way.' In a letter to his father on 28 July Randolph wrote from Eton: 'I am so glad to see in the Evening papers that the PM has come down on your side re Free-Trade.'

That summer Chartwell was, as always, a hive of activity. In a letter to the Prime Minister, Churchill declared: 'I have had a delightful month building a cottage and dictating a book: 200 bricks and 2,000 words a day.' He was building a cottage and a small brick summerhouse for Mary, who was then six, as well as writing a mammoth biography of his ancestor Marlborough. On 10 October Clemmie reported to Randolph at Eton:

> ... We are still having lovely weather & the trees in the belt [of giant beeches that surrounded the Chartwell valley in a horseshoe, brought down by the hurricane of October 1987] are gradually turning into lovely shades of rose and gold...
> ... On Sunday Papa and the Prof beat Bob Boothby & me. Papa is getting quite fond of the game of golf which is rather nice as it makes a change from the endless work on the estate! The cottage has now got nearly all its roof rafters on, the garden wall is in places 7 ft high & in length extends from Mary's house to the pig-sties. Papa is now trying to buy a second hand motor-lorry, after which we will do all our own carting of bricks coke etc etc. Arnold has built a very nice wooden house for the Emden Geese to sleep in. It appears that these robust not to say coarse looking birds have more delicate constitutions than the graceful swans & cannot stand the winter nights. The house seems to me large enough for 12 geese so I hope our pair may prove fertile.
>
> Tender love my darling
from your Mummie

That year, his last at Eton, Randolph's history tutor, C. R. N. Routh, wrote in his school report:

> He seems to me to be a boy whose ideas and ambitions have outrun his years and capacities ... He brings to his history what very few other boys bring – ardent enthusiasm. He is overflowing with ideas, he has passionate likes and hates, he is as courageous as they make them in defending his theories, and he has a dialectical skill which is often needed if he is going to get out of some of the holes into which he gets himself. But he does get out of them!

Routh concluded by drawing attention to a deeply ingrained facet of Randolph's character which was to lose him many friends and hamper his progress in life:

> Is it unkind – it is not meant to be – to suggest that he is too quarrelsome, that he likes being in a minority, and enjoys, not rubbing people up the

wrong way, but the result of having rubbed them the wrong way?

But it was Robert Birley, headmaster of Eton a quarter of a century later when I was there as a boy, who, in his valedictory report, delivered a judgment on Randolph that was to prove as true of his later life as it was of his schooldays:

Let it be said at once that his work was not always satisfactory . . . His real trouble is his facility. He finds it a great deal too easy to do moderately well, and he is developing too early the journalist's ability to 'work up' a little information or a solitary idea . . . He has a first-rate brain but he must be prepared to do some hard thinking for himself and not to take an easy course. His easy course will not be a dull one, in fact it will be an amusing and interesting one. But it will be second-rate for all that . . .

He is quite one of the most interesting pupils I have had, and he is a very pleasant one. His mind is very vigorous and his interests are wide. At the moment he is going through a mental crisis. I consider it almost inevitable that a boy with a mind as logical as his should experience very real religious difficulties. It is almost a sign of mental honesty. But while it is good that he should be honest in this, and that he should be ambitious, I hope that he will not become too self-centred. There *is* a danger of this.

These were criticisms and warnings that, to his cost, Randolph failed to take to heart. Early in the New Year of 1929 he received a telephone call from the Prof at Oxford to say that a place had unexpectedly become available at 'The House' – as Christ Church is known – for the January term. In great excitement Randolph consulted his father, who was delighted. The very next day, Randolph drove over to Eton with his sister Diana to collect all his belongings, including his 'colours' for football which he had gained only ten days before. Thus, at seventeen and a half years of age, he turned his back on school and launched himself with enthusiasm into the wider world of Oxford.

CHAPTER 4

'More Blessed to Teach than to Learn'

Randolph went up to Oxford a year younger than his contemporaries and without having to take the entrance examination, arriving halfway through the academic year in January
of 1929. He had been glad to leave Eton where he had found the bullying
and restraints on personal liberty increasingly oppressive. He breathed
with relish the fresh air of freedom and adult life afforded by Oxford and
indulged it to the full. In his first letter to his father from Christ Church
Randolph reported:

28 January 1929

Dear Papa,

I am so enjoying being here, and I cannot tell you how glad I am that
I did not have to return to Eton, there are so many interesting and
enjoyable things to be done each day that the time passes very rapidly.

My tutor is a very brilliant man called [Keith] Feiling. He wrote the
History of the Tory Party, which I believe you have read . . .

I am so looking forward to seeing you and telling you all about Oxford.
I shall be in London on Wednesday for Diana [Mitford's] wedding.

Your very loving son,
Randolph

On 15 April Churchill introduced his fifth consecutive Budget. As
Martin Gilbert records, this was 'a count reached previously only by
Walpole, Pitt, Peel and Gladstone each of whom were, or were to
become, Prime Minister'. In his speech he mocked Lloyd George's
proposals for dealing with unemployment as 'paying the unemployed
to make racing-tracks for well-to-do motorists to make the ordinary
pedestrians skip'. The Budget contained one important tax concession –
the abolition of the duty on tea, reducing its price by four pence per
pound. No doubt this step was taken in the interests of national finance
and was in no way connected with the fact that there was to be a general
election the following month for which it might be thought to be a

timely sweetener or, at least, a stimulant. Indeed it was Churchill who, nearly two decades earlier, had enshrined the hallowed British 'tea break' in legislation.

It was in this election campaign that Randolph, not yet eighteen, had his baptism of political campaigning on the hustings. Speaking in Edinburgh, he addressed a large audience following a speech by his father:

I stand before you this evening as a member of a generation which took no active part in the Great War. Those of us who are growing up today were mercifully spared the horrors and the fierceness of that epoch-making struggle ... We rejoice as much as many of the older generation at the amazing fact that our civilisation and our constitution survived, and whatever the older generation may think, the youth of England are today determined that that for which so much blood and treasure was outpoured and which was only preserved with such suffering and with such heroism shall not be idly or wilfully thrown away.

Today we have in our midst a disease, a veritable cancer, which is vitally and fundamentally opposed to our present civilisation and constitution. The Socialist Party base themselves, and rely for their chief support, upon the dissemination of the most poisonous class-hatred, a class-hatred which was unknown in the comprehensive comradeship of the Great War, and which threatens to be destructive to life as we know it in this country ... Do we wish to run the risk of falling into the position of a second-class Power with our Empire disintegrated and our Constitution and our Parliamentary institutions brushed aside? Or do we wish to move forward along the broad, progressive paths of Democratic Government as we have done in the past?

... Let us, in the words of Sir Austen Chamberlain, 'Choose between Conservatism and Confusion'. If we do not desire the latter, let the people of England at this Election return the Conservative Party with a clear majority and thus give the country a further spell of stable government.

The next day, 9 May, Winston was back in London where he lunched with Philip Sassoon, the Conservative MP and dispenser of lavish hospitality. Also present was Thomas Jones, Deputy Secretary to the Cabinet, who recorded in his diary: 'Winston had travelled through the night from two meetings in Scotland, and was very proud to have heard his son address an audience of about two thousand for 20 minutes without a note, just over 17 years of age. So we all stood up and drank the health of Randolph II ...' Later in the campaign Randolph also addressed a women's meeting at Wanstead in his father's constituency of Epping, where Winston had had two large tents erected which could hold five times as many people as the largest available hall.

Although Churchill held Epping, the election of May 1929 went against the Conservative Party. The Liberals, with 59 seats, held the balance between Conservatives and Labour. Baldwin resigned and his place was taken by Ramsay MacDonald at the head of the second minority Labour Government.

As soon as he had returned his Seal of Office as Chancellor to the King at Windsor, Winston returned to Chartwell to resume his biography of the Great Duke of Marlborough. In June he set plans afoot for a three-month visit to Canada and the United States, writing to William Randolph Hearst, the multimillionaire newspaper proprietor: 'We must discuss the future of the world even if we cannot decide it.' He informed Hearst that he would be bringing Randolph and his nephew Johnny, adding: 'I thought it would be a great thing for these two young boys, who are undergraduates at Oxford, to see these mighty lands at a period in their lives when the proportions of things are established in the mind.'

On 5 August Randolph, with his father, Uncle Jack and his cousin Johnny, boarded the Canadian Pacific liner *Empress of Australia* bound for Quebec. This was one of the few periods of his life when Randolph kept a diary:

Tuesday August 6
... It must mournfully be admitted that the vast majority of one's fellow-men and women are dull, graceless, unattractive, gauche and boorish, and yet if one knew them probably very charming. Anyway to themselves they are supremely important and no doubt serve some useful function. But the sight of them makes me sigh for the company of my friends ...

Wednesday August 7
... Papa called the company at dinner several times to bear record that soon there would be grave trouble in Egypt. He seemed very upset about this, but some 1865 brandy cheered him up.

Quebec, Friday August 9
Just 12 p.m. and within less than a week of starting from Westerham, the birthplace of Wolfe, I am in bed 13 storeys above the scene where he met his death. This hotel is situated upon the very summit of the Heights of Abraham. Below us is the St Lawrence bright with the lights of a hundred vessels.

Sunday August 11
From our window we can see at night the Rothermere paper mills all lit up. Papa said à propos of them, 'Fancy cutting down those beautiful trees we saw this afternoon to make pulp for those bloody newspapers, and calling it civilisation.'

Monday August 12
We are certainly being entertained in this country in a most princely fashion. At 11:30 we drove to the station where we found drawn up a most palatial private [rail] car – the Mount Royal – some 90 feet in length. It is to be our headquarters for the next three weeks, and it certainly possesses every convenience and comfort. It comprises a dining room, a sitting room, 3 bedrooms, two bathrooms, 4 lavatories & kitchen and observation platform at the back. We have our own cook and waiter who both live on the car. There are three or four fans in each room, a powerful wireless set which plays in the sitting room and the dining room by the mere pressing a button. One could not travel in more luxurious fashion. The car belongs to Mr Hall, the Vice-President of the Canadian Pacific Railway, and we can just hook it on to any train that happens to be passing, and then stop wherever we like.

We arrived at Montreal at 6:30 having travelled about 180 miles from Quebec. We attended a dinner at the Mount Royal Club . . . Papa made an extremely effective speech of about 35 minutes which was well received. He spoke without notes and without preparation and proved what I have always believed, that the effect on the actual audience is far greater if the delivery is absolutely spontaneous . . . I think Papa is gradually coming round to my point of view and is relying less and less upon notes. John Morley once said, 'Three things matter in a speech – who says it, how he says it, and what he says, and of the three the last matters the least.' How true.

In a lengthy letter to Clemmie of 15 August, Winston reported with paternal pride:

Randolph has conducted himself in a most dutiful manner and is an admirable companion. I think he has made a good impression on everybody. He is taking a most intelligent interest in everything, and is a remarkable critic and appreciator of the speeches I make and the people we meet.

Resuming his diary, Randolph recorded:

'Prince of Wales' Ranch, Alberta
Saturday August 24
I happened to say (after seeing the Calgary oilfields) that it was a depressing
thing to see all these oil magnates pigging up a beautiful valley to make
fortunes and then being quite incapable of spending their money, and
went on to criticise their lack of culture. Instantly Papa flared up, 'Cultured
people are merely the glittering scum which floats upon the deep river of
production!' Damn good.

Banff, Tuesday August 27
At 3 we reached the Emerald Lake, a small lake of an exquisite shade of
turquoise. On the side of it is a little bungalow encampment in which we
are sleeping. In the afternoon Papa painted quite a good picture. I went
in a little boat upon the lake and sunbathed. Later we rode. Uncle Jack
setting out ahead of me met a bear six foot high, which fled.

The same night in a letter to his mother, Randolph described a little
local difficulty:

The only trouble we experienced on our journey is that alcohol may not
be consumed in public. Consequently we have to bring ours in in tea
cups. Tonight we hit on a new device. The ginger ale they sell here is
exactly the same colour as champagne. So we now fill these empty ginger
ale bottles with the proper mixture. And innocently pour it out.
    Papa has bought a gigantic hat such as cowboys wear to protect his face
from the sun. It is called a ten gallon hat. I should think it would hold
about 20 . . .

Winston expressed in a letter to Clemmie his admiration for Randolph's oratorical skill which had impressed him: 'He speaks so well, so
dexterous, cool & finished.' He also remarked on Randolph's sleeping
habits – 'ten or even twelve hours a day – I suppose it is his mind &
body growing at the same time. I love him vy much.'
    Randolph's diary continues:

Thursday September 5
. . . We are now on the ship bound to Seattle, American soil and Prohibition. But we are well-equipped. My big flask is full of whisky and the
little one contains brandy. I have reserves of both in medicine bottles. It is
almost certain that we shall have no trouble. Still if we do, Papa pays the
fine, and I get the publicity . . .

Enroute to San Francisco, Sunday September 8
We got away from Grant's Pass about 8, and at 11.30 we reached Eureka. From time to time on the way we passed great groves of Redwood trees. These are about 10 foot in diameter, about 250–300 feet high and anything between 1,500 and 5,000 years old...
We motored another 20 miles before lunch, making 120 in all. After lunch we bathed, 'au naturel', in a deliciously warm stream, and then inspected the largest tree in California – 380 feet high. We met several naval officers at the tree, and we all joined hands and pressing ourselves against the tree and, stretching ourselves as far as we could, made a circle round the tree. We then numbered smartly from the left, and found it took 14 of us! It must have been more than 20 feet thick.

The same day his mother wrote Randolph a sad, rather nostalgic letter:

Since you left us to go on your travels Diana & I in our miniature way have been almost ceaselessly travelling about England. First of all there was Portsmouth which we both enjoyed tho' we did not see much of Cowes. Do you remember the old *Enchantress* in which we had so many pleasant cruises when your Father was at the Admiralty. No of course you can't because I think you were born in 1911 the very year that Papa was transferred from the Home Office to the Admiralty.
Well there she was tied up by the nose with only a caretaker on board. I remembered my old cabin. The chintzes were new, but some rather pretty cream coloured matting I chose all those years ago was still on the floor – very dirty & worn by now.
Then Sir Roger [Keyes], the Commander-in-Chief, took me over the *Centurion* which is (or rather was) a great battleship I launched in 1909 or 1910 before Papa was First Lord. She now presents a lamentable spectacle being used as a Target in Battle Practice. It gives one a shock to realise that these huge engines of War costing more than 2 million a piece go out of fashion almost like a last year's hat: I had not seen her since I cut the steel cord & she went gliding down to the water & now she is old & bent & rusty & full of holes each neatly patched with a square piece of steel fastened with rivets. However, in some ways she is the most important ship in the Navy. Because when she is to be fired at & all her crew leave her, her engines are left running & she can still steer in every direction. This is done by wireless from another ship. She can also signal back answers to questions such as 'How much oil have you in your tanks?' etc.
We think we are the only Navy who have the secret...

I forgot to tell you that after Lympne I went alone to Dieppe to visit Aunt Nellie [Clemmie's sister] who had been in rather low spirits. I am glad I went tho' to me Dieppe is a sad old town full of the ghosts of my poor brother Bill, my sister Kitty & of Granny Blanche [Clemmie's mother]. Sometimes walking thro' the old streets, passing first the little hotel where Granny Blanche died – then a little further on suddenly I realise I am near the Mortuary where Bill lay in his coffin before they buried him. Presently I walk ... [the rest of the letter does not survive].

Randolph's diary resumes:

San Simeon, Friday September 13
A motley crowd of 25 guests are here. Mostly very inferior. Mrs Hearst who is quite too charming is here and consequently Marion Davies [William Randolph Hearst's mistress] is not.

San Simeon, Saturday September 14
The most deliciously warm weather I have ever known greeted me on arising about ten. I have only had time to examine one-twentieth of the extraordinary products of William Randolph Hearst's fantasies and whims. The outside of the house is of white stone, and towers up to two Moorish turrets. The effect is like the façade of a great cathedral ... The ranch – for so it is termed in false modesty – comprises 300 square miles, stretching along 35 miles of sea. The house is absolutely chock full of works of art obtained from Europe. They are insured for 16 million dollars – i.e. the figure of 3 million sterling. Hearst is reputed to possess an income of 20 million dollars!

Johnny Churchill later recorded his own impressions of the visit in his book, *A Crowded Canvas*:

Butterflies abounded at San Simeon. When two or three large brown striped ones, known I believe as Milk-weeds, settled on my arm my uncle wanted me to collect all the species in sight, but I refused. Randolph and I were already butterfly chasing in the sense that we were paying court to several of the charming women guests. My uncle observed our progress in this direction with great good humour ... His benevolent attitude changed however when Randolph and I decided to make an expedition in the night. Hearst accommodated his guests in two-bedroom villas in the grounds. Randolph forced his way into one of them but made an awful error. It was his father's bedroom. Uncle Winston woke up at once and was exceedingly annoyed. Blasted by a withering reprimand we both retired feeling very sheepish and fed up.

Randolph's diary takes up the tale:

Wednesday September 18
At 12.30 we attended a lunch given at Hollywood in the Metro-Goldwyn-Mayer studios, by Mr Mayer and Hearst ... There were about 200 people at the lunch – mostly film stars and producers. We met Marion Davies – Colleen Moore – Anita Page – Joan Crawford – Douglas Fairbanks Jr. – Ramon Navarro, and many others of whom I had not heard. I thought Marion Davies was the most attractive. After lunch during which an orchestra of about 20 played continuously, various stars appeared on a stage at the far end of the room and performed. It really was astounding...
Then general speeches were made. Hearst very good and helpful, and much more friendly to England than expected ... Throughout lunch we were photographed by hordes of men and after lunch Papa, Hearst and Mayer had a talking film made of them...
One thing particularly amused me in Hearst's speech. He said that Papa had been anxious that there should not be too much speaking, 'like the man who did not take his wife abroad as he was going for pleasure'. Considering that he had just left Mrs Hearst and was in Los Angeles with his mistress – Marion Davies – it seemed to me rather good value!

Hollywood, Saturday September 21
After lunch [with the novelist P. G. Wodehouse] we visited various studios and then went out to Marion's house to bathe ... It is a magnificent place looking on the sea, with a wonderful marble swimming bath of great length and very well heated – all provided by William Randolph. Marion had collected a dinner party of 60 for us. Jim and David Smith were there. The stars included Pola Negri, Charlie Chaplin, Harold Lloyd, Billie Dove & Diana Ellis. I failed to recognise either Charlie or Harold, since moustache and horn-rimmed spectacles were missing.
After dinner we danced and then Marion stimulated Charlie into doing some impersonations. She did Sarah Bernhardt & Lillian Gish, and then he did Napoleon, Uriah Heep, Henry Irving, John Barrymore as Hamlet and many others. He is absolutely superb and enchanted everyone. He also did terribly complicated patter dancing as also did Marion...
Papa & Charlie sat up until about 3. Papa wants him to act the young Napoleon and has promised to write the Scenario.

Wednesday October 2
At 10.30 this morning we arrived at Chicago – reputed the most cosmopolitan town in the world. Its population of 3 millions includes more Poles than there are in Warsaw, more Jews than there are in Jerusalem, and it is also the third largest German city in the world.

We were met by 'Bernie' Baruch, the greatest speculator there has ever been. Mr Baruch was an old friend of my father's since the two of them had been in 1917 and 1918, respectively Chairman of the War Industries Board and Minister of Munitions. He escorted us in another private [rail] car to New York where we stayed with him at the fine house he then occupied on Fifth Avenue. On the way from Chicago he told us the fascinating story of how he had made his first fortune ($700,000 in a single day!) at the age of twenty-six.

New York, Tuesday 8 October
We went down to Baruch's office near Wall Street and visited the Stock Exchange. 'Wall Street is a narrow crooked road with a river at one end and a grave-yard at the other,' someone once said, and it is true.

While this journey for Randolph and Johnny was pure holiday, Winston, though also enjoying it to the full, would relentlessly drive himself to achieve, as is clear from the following reminiscence of Randolph's recorded by Martin Gilbert:

I remember how on a very hot train journey in California, or perhaps further north, he shut himself up in his own small compartment and wrote the article [for *Strand Magazine* which was overdue]. He had for at least the last thirty years had the habit of dictating everything, but he had no secretary with him. In two or three hours he wrote, in his own hand, an article of two or three thousand words, which he read to us at dinner.

He did not do this so much because he needed the money; he had a sense of guilt which he felt he must expiate.

I remember complimenting him on the article when he read it to us. 'You know I hate to go to bed at night feeling I have done nothing useful in the day. It is the same feeling as if you had gone to bed without brushing your teeth.'

The next day Randolph and Johnny sailed on the *Berengaria* for England, arriving back in Oxford two days after the start of term. Also on the ship was Randolph's godfather, the Conservative politician and legal eagle F. E. Smith, with whom they dined and played bridge each evening and of whom Randolph commented: 'F. E. is in terrific form. I know no man who is more amusing company.'

Winston stayed on for a while in America to make a tour of Civil War battlefields for a series of articles he was planning to write. His return to New York just over a fortnight later, on 24 October, coincided with the dramatic collapse of the New York stock market on 'Black Thursday', which marked the start of the Great Crash.

The following morning he was to see at first hand something of the panic that swept New York. 'Under my window,' he recorded, 'a gentleman cast himself down fifteen storeys and was dashed to pieces, causing a wild commotion and the arrival of the fire brigade.' Winston himself lost the greater part of the investments he had laboriously built up from his writing and lecturing over thirty years.

At Oxford, as at school, Randolph made his friends among the older undergraduates: Freddie Furneaux (F. E.'s son, later to be Lord Birkenhead), Seymour Berry (later Lord Camrose) and Basil Dufferin whom Randolph described as: '. . . the most lovable man I met at Oxford. His liquid spaniel eyes and his beautiful charming manner commanded affection. He was the most brilliant of all my contemporaries at Oxford . . . He perished tragically and unnecessarily in Burma in the last week of the [Second World] war.'

Basil Dufferin introduced Randolph to Evelyn Waugh who, after the great success of his first novel *Decline and Fall*, was writing *Vile Bodies* in a Cotswold village not far from Oxford. Although they were all two or three years his senior, Randolph soon found himself part of this 'smart bunch', as Freddie self-mockingly called their small circle.

As Randolph later admitted in *Twenty-One Years*:

I paid little attention to my books at Oxford. I don't think I ever attended a lecture . . . In those days there was still a lot of social intercourse between undergraduates and dons. Some of the cleverest and wittiest of the dons and professors delighted in picking out those whom they thought were the most promising undergraduates and inviting them to luncheon parties. We undergraduates used to give reciprocal luncheon parties in our rooms. So I would give four or five luncheons each term and was invited at least three or four times a week to similar festivities and potations by dons and by my fellow undergraduates.

The dons and professors who had patronised me and entertained me and whom I entertained in return and whom I met at other luncheons were, of course, Prof Lindemann, my father's old friend, who lived in Meadow Buildings in the House [Christ Church], Maurice Bowra, not then knighted and only Dean of Wadham, Lord David Cecil, 'Sligger' Urquhart of Balliol, Roy Harrod of the House and I think John Sparrow, already a Fellow of All Souls. We were all rather cliquey on the undergraduate side; our luncheons were usually given by Freddie, Basil, Seymour and myself.

The luncheons followed a similar pattern. We would assemble at 1 o'clock and drink sherry. We sat down at 1.15; the first course was nearly always lobster Newburg, thereafter some meat dish, vegetables and some over-ornamented confection as a pudding. All of this came from the college kitchens and was really extremely inexpensive. We usually drank a hock with the meal and lots of port afterwards. The luncheons rarely broke up before 4 or even 4.30. It was always stimulating and exhilarating and an education in itself. It was far less laborious than getting up early in the morning and going to lectures. At the luncheons one met the cleverer, witty dons on level terms and learnt a great deal which was later to prove serviceable in the battle of life.

Weekends were spent mostly at Charlton, F. E.'s home some twenty miles from Oxford, as Randolph recalled:

Thither we were all apt to repair on Saturdays and Sundays: tennis, golf, riding, swimming were the order of the day and in the evening anything up to sixteen people, mostly undergraduates, would be crammed into the small, panelled dining room. It was F. E.'s habit to prompt us all to make after-dinner speeches upon which he would make caustic comments. The atmosphere was gay and witty, and I seemed to be moving into an enchanted world...

Into this 'enchanted world', however, there soon intruded a paternal bombshell:

29 Dec. 1929   *Chartwell Manor,*
                                                              Westerham,
                                                                   Kent.

My dear Randolph,
    Before a spark can cause an explosion an atmosphere has to be created.
    Your idle & lazy life is vy offensive to me. You appear to be leading a perfectly useless existence. You do not value or profit by the opportunities

wh Oxford offers to those who care for learning. You are not acquiring any habits of industry or concentration. Even in idleness you find it trying to pass the day.

To these causes of dissatisfaction you add an insolence towards men & things wh is rapidly affecting yr position outside Oxford; & is certainly not sustained by effort or achievement.

You do not try to please me in any of the ways you know so well. Your personal appearance has already deteriorated under the untidy slothful & self-indulgent conditions in wh you choose to live. You do no work: you play no games: you take no exercise. You gossip & chatter & argue unceasingly.

I have tried – perhaps prematurely – to add to our natural ties those of companionship & comradeship. But you do not do your part. You give nothing in return for the many privileges & favours you have hitherto received. I must therefore adopt a different attitude towards you for yr own good.

You must not suppose that merely passing yr overdue examination next term will remove the causes of my disappointment & dissatisfaction. I must be assured that at Oxford you are sedulously devoting yourself to work: I must feel that a much more modest & disciplined spirit animates you – & I hope that these essentials may be combined with a smarter & more athletic appearance.

Unless I am convinced that Oxford is doing you good & that you will be a credit to us there, you will leave after this term. Meanwhile I will consider what form of training is likely to be most helpful to you. Of this however you may be sure that it will require constant exertion on yr part, & will keep you a sufficient distance from London.

The New Year may perhaps furnish you with the resolution to amend not only yr ways but yr outlook. No one hopes so more than

Your loving father,
Winston S. Churchill

There are distinct echoes in this letter of the formidable rebuke that Winston himself had received some thirty-five years earlier from his father after informing him, with modest satisfaction, that he had just scraped into Sandhurst, albeit not into the Infantry (which required a higher standard) but into the Cavalry which would cost his father an extra £200 a year. It is ironic that Winston was exactly the same age as Randolph – eighteen and a half – when Lord Randolph had written to him on 9 August 1893:

... I am certain that if you cannot prevent yourself from leading the idle, useless and unprofitable life you have had during your schooldays & later months, you will become a mere social wastrel, one of the hundreds of the public school failures, and you will degenerate into a shabby unhappy & futile existence ...

In Winston's case the rebuke had been unmerited, but in Randolph's it was undoubtedly well deserved. Sadly, it fell on deaf ears. Nor can Winston be wholly absolved from a measure of responsibility for Randolph's boorish, idle and generally objectionable behaviour. So determined was he not to be to Randolph the cold, distant, irascible father that Lord Randolph had been to him, that he spoiled him at every turn. From an early age, certainly by his early teens, Randolph had been invited not only to join 'men only' dinners, attended by the most brilliant political figures of the day, but his father encouraged him to participate fully in the conversation. This bred in Randolph an unbridled arrogance and, in the political field, a contempt for anyone not of the calibre of F. E. Smith, Lloyd George or Arthur Balfour. Speaking of this period of his life, my father once told me:

I share my birthday [28 May] with Pitt the Younger who entered the House of Commons at the age of twenty-one and became Prime Minister at twenty-four. If anyone suggested that I would not match that record, I should not have been angry, I would just have laughed in their face!

Clemmie had seen the problem developing and tried to act as a brake on Randolph's extravagant ideas of his own importance. This, his sister Mary suspects, was a major cause of the unnatural coolness between mother and son, which was noticeable from an early stage and continued throughout their lives. Winston, on the other hand, was indulgent and, even when exasperated by Randolph's slothful behaviour, he rarely carried through his threats to make Randolph's life less agreeable when the latter failed to mend his ways.

Although, from the distance of a century or more, it is difficult to understand, let alone forgive, the lack of parental love that Winston received in his formative years, it certainly did no detectable harm to his character. The same, alas, cannot be said of the affection and adulation which Winston lavished upon the young Randolph.

Early in the New Year Roy Harrod, who was then Senior Censor of Christ Church and responsible for the administration of 'The House', also entered a plea for Randolph to address himself to his studies:

29 January 1930

I enjoyed your party immensely last night. It was so nice of you to ask me.
I hope that you will soon arise from your slumbers and take the final
schools seriously. I think that you would get solid satisfaction from having
done well at them. You can write – an important and rare asset – you have
energy and will . . . I don't know if you have really put that brain of yours
to the test. There might be magnificent results!

You are quite wrong in supposing that a strong desire to seek society at
10 a.m. is a sort of sign from heaven that you aren't intended for academic
studies. It was always – so long as I was an undergraduate – a tremendous
wrench not to go off in the mornings, to leave work or cut lectures. It
was for me and is for many a case of making a tremendously resolute
effort, yet the day can only contain a limited quantity of pleasure, and
there can always be enough time to spare in which to cull that amount,
so the effort is worthwhile!

There is no evidence that Randolph ever mended his ways: indeed,
the contrary appears to be the case. He did, however, follow through his
father's suggestion that he should take some physical exercise, at least to
the extent of making inquiries of an American friend, a noted sportsman
called Stuart Scheftel. Known to his friends as 'Boy', he was to become
a reporter for the *New York Times* and a businessman. Some fifty years
on from their Oxford days and nearly fifteen years after my father's
death, Scheftel recalled: 'I shared with him a total disinterest in the
academic life of the university and this made a bond between us. One
day he asked me: "Why am I not as popular with my colleagues as I
might be?" – I told him: "Some resent you going across the Quad in
your dressing-gown at 2.00 p.m.!" ' (Peckwater Quadrangle, the 'Quad',
was where the smartest 'sets' of rooms at Christ Church were to be
found and had to be crossed to reach the only bathroom, even in the
author's day.) Scheftel suggested he might take up some sport:

After listing the obvious ones and getting a negative response I was about
to search down other avenues when suddenly he said, 'Of course you
know I ride very well?' I didn't know, but I agreed that that should do the
trick, and as I happened to know that Oxford was having a point-to-point
race the following Saturday, I suggested that Randolph take part. Randolph
now said that he had no horse and no money to rent one, but as I had had
a success on the turf that day I offered to provide the funds and the matter
was arranged.

Unfortunately I could not be present on that historic occasion as I was playing an 'away' match for the University golf team. On my return I sought out Randolph in his rooms where, had it not been that I knew the rooms I was in to be his, I might not have recognised him, so heavily were his head and face bandaged. Naturally I was eager to learn how my friend had been transformed from an English undergraduate into an Egyptian mummy.

Beyond growling that he was 'bloody but unbowed', Randolph seemed far more interested in finding an aperture in his bandages into which he might introduce his cigar than in describing what clearly had been a narrow escape from death. So I had to wait until later to hear what had happened; when I also found out that not only was Randolph's experience with horses extremely limited but he had never before ridden in a race of any kind, much less a steeplechase. Despite this handicap he had made such an excellent showing for himself that he had held the lead all the way to the stands. He had come a cropper at the water jump, receiving a bad roughing up from those following behind.

This for me was the first demonstration of the absolute fearlessness and courage for which Randolph was later so justly admired by those who were with him during the war . . .

'Boy' Scheftel went on to tell me how, while they were at Oxford, Evelyn Waugh, an ardent Roman Catholic, had asked Father D'Arcy, who instructed him, if he thought Randolph would be a good target for conversion to the Roman Catholic faith, to which the prelate perceptively replied: 'No! He'd be like a rogue elephant trumpeting in the sanctuary!' When, in the early 1950s, Randolph had an audience with Pope Pius XII, shortly after it had been announced that his friend Mrs Clare Booth Luce had been appointed United States Ambassador to Italy, he had inquired of His Holiness: 'Do you know my friend Clare Booth Luce?' 'No', replied the Pope. 'But she's a Catholic too!' protested Randolph. According to Scheftel, shortly after the war Randolph had had the presumption to proposition his wife, Geraldine, with the blunt request: 'Will you come to bed with me?' To which she had replied: 'Certainly not and, what's more, I'll tell Boy what you said.' To this put-down a disconsolate Randolph had riposted: 'That would be truly middle class!'

Randolph's days at Oxford were numbered when a seductive offer arrived by post from a top American lecture agency. As Randolph relates:

I was lying in bed about 10.30 in the morning when my great American friend Boy Scheftel passed by my rooms in Canterbury Quad., suitably gowned on his way to a lecture. He said, 'You haven't opened your mail.'

'No,' I said. He said, 'There's one here from America, shall I open it for you?' I said, 'Please do.' He opened it and exclaimed, 'Good God. It's an invitation to make a lecture tour in the United States.'

I was still feeling somewhat lethargic from the evening's exertions and did not betray much interest save to say, 'Do they offer to pay?' 'Yes,' he said. 'Quite a lot of money.' I sat up and read this letter from a respected firm of lecture agents, William B. Feakins, Inc.

At the time I subsisted on an allowance given by my father of £400 a year. This was about the average that undergraduates had at that time. This probably did not apply to the whole University but to undergraduates at the House who were, on the whole, better off than most. I was in debt to the extent of £600 or £700 and was by no means living within my means. The idea of going off to America and teaching, rather than learning, appealed to me strongly and I resolved to go.

The invitation, it seems, resulted from the press reports of Randolph's speech in the Oxford Union debate of 20 February 1930 which had been picked up by the *New York Times* as well as by the *Manchester Guardian* which reported:

... The question for debate was 'That this House disapproves of the proposed Treaty with Egypt', which was moved by Mr Randolph Churchill. He spoke with the utmost confidence and in an easy style. His speech lasted nearly twenty minutes, and with the exception of when turning the pages of his notes his hands were rarely out of his pockets. But he found no difficulty in driving home his points without gesture ...

'I think I can say that our interests in Egypt coincide with Egyptian interests. Under British guidance Egyptians have been able to conduct their affairs better than at any time during the past 3,000 years, but our guidance was only accepted because of the presence of our troops in Cairo, troops which they now propose to remove. The ultimate aim in Egypt is self-government, but to suppose they are ready for self-government is as ridiculous as to say that India is fit to govern itself or that Lord Beaverbrook is fit to rule the British Empire ...'

The motion was lost by one vote, the figures being 101 for and 102 against.

Roy Harrod did not favour the proposed diversion from his studies, as he made clear in his contribution to *The Young Unpretender*, Kay Halle's collection of 'portraits' of Randolph by his friends and colleagues:

About half-way through his prescribed time at Oxford, he came to me

and said that he wanted leave of absence to give lectures in America . . .
and had contracts amounting to more than £2,000 [equivalent to some
£65,000 today]. Rather good for a young man aged about nineteen or
twenty! It is to be remembered that the Churchills were by no means rich.
I remember Winston once saying to me, 'I believe that, if I did not have
to spend so much time earning money by writing, I could one day become
Prime Minister.' Doubtless Randolph was helped in securing his contracts
by his father's name, but this did not boom as loud in the USA in 1930
as it did in 1945. Anyhow, he must have shown some enterprise. So I
congratulated him, but urged him not to go. I said, 'Randolph, you will
not come back to us.' He assured me that he would. I had my own
conviction that he had not struck deep roots in Christ Church, or in
Oxford, such as would pull him back.

Although Randolph subsequently claimed that his American lecture
tour had his father's blessing and encouragement, Roy Harrod recalls
spending a weekend at Chartwell that summer in a joint endeavour with
Winston to dissuade Randolph from the tour:

> . . . it was Winston who did most of the talking. After dinner on the Saturday
> . . . he stood up with his back to the chimneypiece and delivered a great
> oration. He discoursed on the nature of a university and on the merits of a
> university education. He spoke of the ripe judgement and the mellow
> wisdom of the university teachers. They had devoted their lives to reading,
> studying and reflection. They were unique in this respect. Through their
> teaching one could learn to be a wiser man. Then he talked about his own
> experience, in a modest and charming way, about how his lack of university
> education had handicapped him in his political career, about how, in the cut
> and thrust of debate with someone like Arthur Balfour, he had felt himself
> at a disadvantage for lack of the weapons that a university education could
> have given him. It was the most splendid eulogy of the university function
> . . . I was watching Randolph during Winston's discourse. It was all flowing
> over him, so it seemed to me, like water off a duck's back.

Randolph was firmly resolved to go to America, heedless of the
weight of wisdom or good sense deployed by his father. Never short of
self-justifying arguments, on this occasion he excelled himself by calling
in aid the Almighty. As he later put it to me: 'I decided that the time
had come to follow the injunction of Our Lord that "It is more blessed
to teach than to learn"!' After just four terms he thereupon turned his
back on Oxford, preferring to rely upon the university of life, based
upon the unique grounding he had received at his father's table.

CHAPTER 5

Telling America

Randolph set out his preparations for the American lecture tour in *Twenty-One Years*:

Some weeks before I left, my father enquired whether I had yet composed my lectures. I said no, I would do that during the three weeks which I was planning to spend in Venice. He chuckled. When I came back from Venice, on the eve of my departure for the United States, my father enquired what progress I had made. I said, 'I'm afraid not much, I'm going to do it on the ship.' 'Ah,' he said. 'The first day you are on the ship you won't be feeling very well, the second day you will be feeling better, the third day you will meet a pretty girl and then you will be nearly there.'

Thus it turned out, but I consoled myself by thinking there was a whole week after I got to America before I would have to deliver my first lecture.

'*Not so!*' as Randolph's friend (and my godfather), the late Lord Beaverbrook, was fond of exclaiming. Randolph walked down the gangway of the *Majestic* on 7 October 1930 to be greeted by his lecture agent, William B. Feakins, with the news that he had just managed to arrange an extra engagement: Princeton University, that very evening! Worse still, the appearance at the quayside, on the personal instructions of William Randolph Hearst, of his top gossip columnist Maury Paul of the Cholly Knickerbocker column, syndicated coast to coast, robbed Randolph of any opportunity of collecting his thoughts in the train. During the journey Mr Feakins stressed the importance of the Princeton lecture. There would be a lot of press people present and the reports of the event would affect the success (or otherwise) of the three-month tour. Randolph recalled the ordeal:

I tried to look unconcerned but I am bound to say that I felt distinctly queasy . . . My recollection of the lecture is somewhat of a blur. I had three alternative subjects:

1. Why I Am Not a Socialist.

2. Can Youth be Conservative?
3. The British Empire and World Progress.

It seemed to me the same lecture, with adaptations, could be made on any one of these three subjects but I did not even have the material for one.

The lecture took place before a distinguished audience which included André Maurois who, fifteen years earlier, had been the interpreter to Winston's battalion in France. After saying everything he could think of that appeared to be relevant, Randolph looked at his watch and discovered to his consternation that he had only been going twenty minutes:

I was supposed to speak for a full hour; so I took a deep breath and produced a lot of stuff wholly irrelevant to the subject that I was supposed to be speaking on and looked at my watch and found that I had still only been speaking for thirty minutes. I took another big breath and did what in retrospect must have been a brilliant recapitulation in other words, of what I had already said . . . I looked at my watch and it said forty minutes. I had no more to say. I sat down convinced that my lecture tour would have to be abandoned amidst the derision of the press.

A little later I discovered that my watch had stopped in the middle of the lecture and that I had regaled my audience for no less than one hour and a quarter with my unconsidered oratory . . .

The newspaper reports were flattering – even gushing – and I strode on through the Middle West from triumph to triumph.

Randolph was a born orator to whom public speaking came far easier than to his father, who had to overcome both a lisp (which he was later to turn to his advantage) and an instinctive fear of public speaking. Whereas Randolph could jump up on a table and speak brilliantly without a note for an hour or more, Winston, with rare exceptions, would be equipped with a full text or commit to memory his speeches which he prepared with painstaking effort devoting, in the case of his famous wartime orations, approximately one hour of preparation to each minute of delivery. Randolph, on the other hand, because of the very facility with which he could speak extemporaneously, failed to make the effort required to bring him true success.

Immediately after the Princeton engagement and the many press interviews that went with it, Randolph wrote to his father to urge him to ignore any press scribblings that might have reached England: 'I am getting a good deal of publicity. Of course, they publish the most silly remarks which one either makes thoughtlessly or which they have invented. I trust that any reports that reach England will be discounted.' The lecture tour proved a considerable success and was soon extended from the original three months to seven, in the course of which Randolph spoke in no fewer than seventy cities. Having myself done no better than forty-seven cities in fifty-six days, I can confirm that this was a considerable feat of physical, if not mental, endurance. From a town in the Midwest Randolph reported home on 20 October:

... I caught the train to a small village called Mexico in Missouri. I arrived there at six o'clock in the morning and, having had a bath and breakfast at the local inn, I was met by Mr Wood, President of Stephen's College, who was to drive me to Columbia. On the way over, I discovered for the first time that Stephen's College was a seminary for young ladies between the ages of 16 and 20. This came as a great surprise and shock to me, but there was no drawing back.

On arrival in Columbia, I was marched straight into a large hall which contained six hundred girls of varying attractions – some giggling, some smirking and some pensive – and I was forthwith invited to deliver myself on my stock topic 'The British Empire and World Progress'. However, I soon mastered my embarrassment and acquitted myself with credit, considering the trying nature of the circumstances ...

Later the same week his mother wrote with disquieting news from home:

Friday, October 24th 1930

My Darling Boy,

It is now just over three weeks that you sailed away in that gigantic hulk, but to me it feels much longer. I see by looking at your list that by today you will already have given seven lectures. I do hope you are well & not getting over-tired ...

The Book [*The World Crisis*, volume 3] is having a great success here, but your father's pleasure in this is spoilt by the sinister turn which for him politics have suddenly taken. You will of course see that Mr Baldwin has made a complete & abject surrender to Lord Beaverbrook. (The latter by the way is at present not accepting the surrender.) Your Father now feels that he cannot agree to this further step which constitutes a complete contradiction of Mr Baldwin's declarations last spring that he would in no

circumstances come before the electorate with food taxes in his pro-
gramme. He has already told Mr Baldwin & his other colleagues this
privately, & next week he intends to state his position to his constituents.
The first Meeting of the Epping Autumn Campaign is on Monday.
After that the fat is in the fire . . .
Chartwell is very quiet, inhabited only by your Father, me, Mary, the
Pug and the Cat! . . . Colonel Lawrence [of Arabia] came here for a
Sunday & that was really delightful. He is very silent & difficult, but he
likes Papa & enjoyed Chartwell . . .
Then your Father is up to his eyes in work. There is Marlborough, the
Eastern Front & pot boiling newspaper articles waiting to be written. But
of course this sickening political situation is distracting his attention . . .
Good bye my Darling Boy take great care of yourself. I hope someone
darns your socks & irons your clothes so that you always look neat.

Your loving
Mummie

Accounts of Randolph's lecture tour had begun filtering back to
England. Under a headline spanning seven columns: 'Young Randolph
Tells USA How World Should be Governed', the *News Chronicle* of
21 November 1930 carried a report by its New York correspondent:

I have heard 19-year-old Mr Randolph Churchill explain what he would
do if he were Prime Minister of England.
It was his first meeting in New York, following a short tour of the
country and an adoring crowd of 2,000 mostly middle-aged women of
wealth, hung on every word of the romantic-looking boy orator.
One or two elderly men walked out in apparent disgust as Mr Churchill
chanted the praises of Imperialism and denounced the 'sloppy-minded
and mealy-mouthed set of sob-stuff politicians who are at present dragging
England down to the position of a second-rate Power', but his feminine
admirers cheered him rapturously.
'Are there any more at home like you?' asked the venerable chairman
of the meeting, looking at Mr Churchill with wondering eyes when he
sat down after an hour's speech in which he took the modern world to
pieces and put it together again according to his heart's desire . . .
'Who do you think should be leader of the Conservative Party?'
demanded an elderly woman in an ermine wrap.
'It would not be tactful for me to say,' said Mr Churchill with a subtle
smile. 'Of course, I have the greatest admiration for Mr Stanley Baldwin.

He shares all the qualities of a suet pudding, is steady, solid, substantial, but as a leader – NO, SIR!'

... As the large audience streamed away one of the middle-aged women in sables said, 'What a handsome face! What a splendid forehead!' 'And what a cheek!' muttered one of the old gentlemen.

Shortly before Christmas, Clemmie wrote excitedly proposing a visit to Randolph in New York:

21 December 1930

... I have had an inspiration. Papa very kindly has offered me a tiny car as a combined Christmas & Birthday present. But I thought if you liked it I would spend the money on paying you & New York a flying visit?

Shall I hop on to a boat one day at the end of January or beginning of February & come to New York for a week? (I don't think my funds would last longer!) You could take a bedroom (small but comfortable) at the Savoy-Plaza. I should enjoy it so much.

We could go to a play or two together. Perhaps however you won't be in New York about that time? I should love to come to hear you lecture. I feel very nervous & excited about the idea. Papa is amused & rather outraged at the idea of me going to America without him! But I think I should prefer to go alone & not as the appendage of a distinguished man! ...

Early in the New Year Winston reported:

8 January 1931

Secret ...

The political situation is increasingly unsatisfactory and my relations with B. [Baldwin] are chilly and detached. On the other hand R. [Rother-mere] and I have come to a definite understanding about India and his papers are all giving me full support. I am going to fight this Indian business *à outrance* ...

On January 30th I am going to speak at Manchester on the same subject. The Indian Empire Society, who feed out of my hand, have at my suggestion taken the Free Trade Hall, and the *Daily Mail* is going to exploit the meeting to the full. We shall see what support we get ...

I am making good headway with Marlborough but now have to switch off for a couple of months on to the Eastern Front. I have got a good crop of articles for 1931 and indeed am quite weighed down with work. But that is much better than being unemployed.

Very best love my dear Randolph. I pray you may realise all that I hope for you.

Randolph, thrilled at his mother's suggested visit; replied:

11 January 1931

Just over a month from the day I am writing, you will be arriving here on the *Europa*. I really cannot describe to you how excited I am at the prospect...

Meanwhile tonight at midnight I leave for Pittsburgh where I speak tomorrow and on successive days at Dayton (where they make the cash registers), Chicago and Milwaukee. From Chicago I go on to San Francisco, then down to Los Angeles and Pasadena where I shall be for about a week; then up to Portland (Oregon) before rushing back to meet you...

I am dying to see you. I hope you will have a calm crossing and will arrive keyed up for the excitement of New York!

Winston wrote again on 7 February, shortly after his formal breach with Baldwin and the Conservative 'Shadow Cabinet' and twelve days after opening his attack on Indian reform in Parliament:

Your mother is the bearer of this. She is looking forward tremendously to her visit and adventure. She has bought some lovely dresses and is looking her very best...

Now, do please tell her everything and all about the finance of your tour etc. and let me have a full account of your future plans...

You seem to have had a very prolonged lecture tour at Pasadena, nearly a month in fact, and I note that it is not so far away from Hollywood.

I shall be very lonely here now with everybody gone except Maria [Mary]. I shall try and get on with my new series of six articles for the *Strand Magazine* and with the 'Eastern Front' which I am going to call the 'Unknown War'.

Politics have opened out a great deal for me. I had a famous week of action, two most important speeches in the House of Commons and in the two greatest Lancashire halls – The Free Trade Hall and The Philharmonic hall which you know. Baldwin's repudiation of me was couched in terms which went far beyond anything the party will agree to, about India. There is to be a great gathering of Members in the House on

Monday to put him on the mat, or even perhaps on the spot. He will of course wriggle back into a more martial position, but I think he has certainly failed to interpret both the wish of the party and the need of the country. Max [Beaverbrook] is running amok in all directions, but is quite sound on India. He and I are independent but, as I cabled you, converging. Rothermere writes or telegraphs every other day avowing undying fidelity. We are planning a big Albert Hall meeting about the middle of March. At a stroke I have become quite popular in the party and in great demand upon the platform . . .

It is clear that his father was growing concerned about Randolph's decision to prolong the lecture tour to a total of seven months. He was anxious not only about the time being spent 'lecturing' in Hollywood but the fact that Randolph, despite his very substantial earnings, was living beyond his income. In fact, although his lectures earned him $12,000 − £2,500 at the prevailing rate of exchange, equal to £83,800 in today's money − he left the United States owing $2,000 borrowed from his father's friend 'Bernie' Baruch − a debt he did not repay until thirty years later.

But there was another matter nagging at his parents at the time. They appear to have got wind of the fact that Randolph was contemplating marriage.

In the course of his lecture tour he had met and fallen in love with a very attractive young woman a few years his senior − Kay Halle of Cleveland, Ohio. His parents felt very strongly that Randolph, still only nineteen, was too young to marry and this, indeed, was the true reason for Clemmie's descent on New York. In 1976, some years after my father's death, I asked my grandmother about her American visit of which she still retained a vivid recollection:

Randolph met me off the liner and drove me to his hotel where he had taken a very grand suite of rooms. It really was most extravagant of him for, as you know, we were not a wealthy family. He informed me that the next day he had arranged for us to have luncheon on Long Island and that a very nice young lady would be joining us. The next morning Miss Halle arrived at our hotel and we were introduced. It was quite evident that Randolph knew her rather well for the first thing he did was to scold her for not having been to the hairdresser before meeting his Mama.

Clemmie, not content with her efforts at dissuading Randolph, decided to take the bull by the horns and travelled to Cleveland, Ohio, to meet the young lady's father: 'I said to him, "Of course you will understand that there can be no question of our children marrying – Randolph is far too young." To which he replied, "Quite so, Mrs Churchill, I fully agree with you that it would be entirely inappropriate." '

To make doubly sure, Winston, following Clemmie's return to England aboard the SS *Majestic*, bluntly explained to Randolph the facts of life:

6 April 1931

Yr mother has given me a vy full & sympathetic account of yr affairs, & of yr joint adventures. I am sorry that all the fruits of yr lectures have been consumed in expensive living & that there is now no chance of yr being home in time for the Oxford term. You will go out into life practically without any learning or culture, having rejected the opportunities that were offered. This will hamper you as long as you live. On the other hand yr spirit and address are evidently exceptional, & yr natural gifts are such as to enable you to make yr own way to high success, provided you do not hamstring yrself by debts or by inveterate frivolous habits.

You are, as you suggest, the one who will suffer if you make grave mistakes at the outset of yr career. There could be few greater mistakes than for a youth of nineteen to marry on nothing but his wits & expensive tastes. Once married, you are saddled for the rest of yr life with burdens & responsibilities wh absorb the strength of most men. At 21 or 22 you might well have a family. Your effort will be to feed & house them. Good bye to Parliament & early political distinction. Your freedom will be gone. Yr friends male & female will no longer take the same interest in you. Yr own duties & inclinations will keep you at home. And out of doors there will be the struggle for life. Fancy committing yrself to such a round, before you have even tasted the pleasant years of youth & liberty! However as you claim it is to be yr own affair, I say no more, except that it will be an intense grief to me to see the hopes & interests I had founded upon you, my only son, jeopardized, if not indeed extinguished; & to feel that we shall not be able to work together in the political arena, wh is once again becoming filled with lions & gladiators...

Turning to more prosaic matters, I saw Mr Christy of the London Lecture Agency (for whom I lectured 30 years ago). He tells me he could arrange a considerable series of lectures for you in this country in the autumn. You could earn £20 or £25 for each & this wd only mean short journeys. It wd help to carry you along. He wd like to see you when you come back...

I send you my fondest love my darling Randolph, & long to see you safely home again.

PS Yr Mother has taught me backgammon. It is an amusing game. I will take you on when you return.

There is no evidence of any reply to this letter but in due course, having delivered the lectures to which he was committed, an unattached Randolph, for once bowing to parental injunctions, returned to England, where the political scene had taken a turn distinctly unfavourable to his father.

Following Winston's break with Baldwin and the official Conservative Party over India, Brendan Bracken, elected two years earlier as Conservative MP for North Paddington, had made himself indispensable to Winston. On 13 February Bracken reported to Randolph:

> You ask about your parent's activities with regard to India. Well, I am of the opinion that they have been altogether splendid. He has untied himself from Baldwin's apron, rallied all the fighters in the Tory Party, re-established himself as a potential leader & put heart into a great multitude here & in India. By a series of brilliant speeches in the House he has shown the Tories the quality of his genius and the incredible drabness & futility of S.B. The 'boneless wonder' speech [WSC's reference to the Prime Minister, Ramsay MacDonald] is immortal...
> Politics are in an inextricable but deeply interesting tangle. One thing is certain – if this Parliament lasts until the winter Baldwin will depart ignominiously. And your father has more than a good chance of succession.

But Bracken was off-beam in his predictions. The Great Crash in the United States and the Depression which ensued had widespread repercussions on the other side of the Atlantic. The worsening economic situation in Britain caused King George V to favour the idea of a Coalition Government to take the tough and unpleasant actions, including a reduction of unemployment benefit at a time of high employment, necessary to secure an American loan and prevent the collapse of sterling. The King's overtures were successful in winning Conservative and Liberal support as well as the backing of Ramsay MacDonald. In October the latter took his National Government to the country, having abandoned the gold standard on 21 September.

The 1931 election proved a landslide for the Conservatives who won 470 of the 615 seats. MacDonald remained titular head of the National Government, though the old Labour Party had been reduced to 52 seats and two-thirds of the Cabinet posts were held by Conservatives. Baldwin, in fact though not in name, had triumphed and Churchill found himself more politically isolated than ever before, though at his Epping constituency he had been returned with his majority doubled to 10,000.

Randolph, too young to throw his hat into the political arena, embarked in mid-October on a six-month lecture tour of the United Kingdom. He chose as his theme 'Young England Looks at America', making plentiful allusions to the power of the American female, the farce of prohibition and the American way of life in general. But the more serious message underlying his lectures was of the need for closer co-operation between Britain and the United States as the only sure guarantee against another world war – a far-sighted view in 1931 when Hitler had not yet come to power in Germany and the Weimar Republic was not bellicose. He warned against German rearmament and the folly of continuing disarmament by the victorious Allies of the Great War. He dismissed the League of Nations as 'a grand tea-party', incapable of either preventing aggression or of guaranteeing peace.

While far removed from the British political scene in America, Randolph had placed some large and, as it turned out, excessively foolish bets on the outcome of the October election. Whether he acted on his father's forecast in a letter dated 18 October, that 'The Conservatives and National Government supporters will have 430 members in the next House' and his advice to take steps to cut his losses by laying off his bets, is not known. But when the election results came in, Randolph's betting debts amounted to no less than £600 (equivalent to over £20,000 today) – a sum he was unable to meet.

As if this folly were not enough, Randolph proceeded to charter a Bentley motor car complete with chauffeur, which he had seen advertised in the personal column of *The Times*. He compounded this *folie de grandeur* by being so injudicious as to use it for a visit to Chartwell. This incensed his father, who boasted no more than a small, ageing Wolseley, provoking a formidable remonstrance:

3 November 1931

I am ready to pay £600 on account of yr gambling losses on election majorities. But, as I told you, I will only do this if it is necessary for yr well-being. If you feel yrself able to keep a magnificent motor car &

chauffeur at a rate of what must be £700 or £800 a year, you are surely able to pay yr debts of honour yrself.

Unless & until you give proof of your need by ridding yrself of this shameless extravagance, you have no right to look for aid from me: nor I to bestow it. I have many to look after who you should not trench upon.

I grieve more than is worth setting down to see you with so many gifts & so much good treatment from the world, leading the life of a selfish & reckless exploiter, borrowing & spending every shilling you can lay yr hands upon & ever increasing the lavish folly of yr way.

But words are useless.

Four days later Winston wrote again:

7 November 1931

I was vy glad to get yr nice letter, & to learn that you will dispense with yr motor car. I will tell Uncle Jack to credit your account with him with £600. This still leaves you about £80 odd to pay.

I quite understand that you could not have expected such a violent solution of the Election speculation, & many small people have been cruelly nipped. But if you will add up all yr losses through gambling in various ways, you will see what a frightful burden they have been upon yr earning power. One must suffer when one loses: otherwise there is no balance to conduct. But quite apart from this, the motor car & chauffeur would have been a monstrous drag upon you, & all yr best friends would have thought it absurd & unsuitable. Now that you have enjoyed the sensation, you can put it away till some better time.

No one so much as I cares for yr success & reputation. No one I expect cherishes higher hopes of both. But you must give yourself a fair chance in the race of life. The possession of a small store of money alone gives independence, & the power to choose superior tasks.

There were to be further such exchanges between father and son over the next quarter of a century. Winston, as ever, was as generous as he could be within his own limited financial resources which owed everything to his industry as an author and journalist, as well as on the US lecture circuit. Cheques would be forthcoming on receipt of suitable undertakings on Randolph's part to end his profligacy – undertakings that, for the most part, went unfulfilled. The tragic consequence of indulging and spoiling his only son in the formative years of his youth was to poison relations between them in later life.

With his own political and financial fortunes in a precarious condition, Winston set sail for New York aboard the German liner *Europa*, arriving on 11 December to begin a series of forty lectures for which he was guaranteed a sum of £10,000 (equivalent to nearly £350,000 today). But on the day after his arrival in New York he was knocked down by a motor car on Fifth Avenue, having looked the wrong way while crossing the road on his way to the house of his friend 'Bernie' Baruch. The vehicle was travelling at 30–35 mph at the time of impact and he was lucky not to be killed. As it was, he got away with lacerations to the head and a few broken bones. He was already fifty-seven years old and the effect of his injuries was aggravated by the onset of pleurisy. He was forced to remain in hospital for nearly ten days and thereafter to spend two weeks in bed. Fortunately Clemmie was there to look after him. The flow of telegrams to Randolph, starting less than 12 hours after the event, gives some idea of the gravity of the accident:

NEW YORK 5:02 AM 15 DEC 1931
TEMPERATURE 100.6 PULSE NORMAL
HEAD SCALP WOUND SEVERE TWO CRACKED RIBS SIMPLE SLIGHT
PLEURAL IRRITATION OF RIGHT SIDE GENERALLY MUCH BRUISED
PROGRESS SATISFACTORY MUCH LOVE FROM PAPA AND MUMMIE

NEW YORK 5:46 PM 15 DEC 1931
PAPA DOING SPLENDIDLY LOVE = MUMMIE

NEW YORK 2:37 AM 16 DEC 1931
AM MUCH TOUCHED BY YOUR INQUIRIES
DEAR RANDOLPH EXPECT QUITE WELL IN MONTH PRETTY CLOSE
= FATHER

As soon as he was well enough to be moved, Winston sailed to Nassau to convalesce and reported to Randolph:

5 January 1932

I got here on the 2nd intending to return by the *Olympic* on the 10th but I felt the after effects of my accident required a longer convalescence before beginning lectures, so I cabled the long-suffering Alber [his lecture agent] and it is now arranged that I open in New York on January 28th.

You will have read my accounts of the accident in the *Daily Mail*. I rather plume myself upon having had the force to conceive, write and market this article so soon after the crash. I received a great price for it

[£600 – in fact, the exact amount he had paid two months earlier to acquit Randolph's election gambling debts], but find it very dearly bought. I hope and trust I shall be strong enough from the 28th onwards. I have told Alber I will stay until March 15th assuming I do not break down . . . Here I lead the life as nearly as possible of a vegetable . . .

In spite of all the accidents, and pain I have had, I am very glad to be away from this administration and look forward greatly to being back in my corner seat in the House of Commons . . .

Your mother is in love with this Island and nurses the project of buying a house and garden here. The local people said there were no butterflies worth speaking of but I have counted seven varieties in this small garden this morning . . . I wish you were with us. As I told you on the telephone I will settle with Feakins for you as soon as I begin to earn money again.

A week later Clemmie sent Randolph a progress report:

12 January 1932

Papa is progressing but very very slowly. I am sure he will be again as well as before, but he is terribly depressed at the slowness of his recovery & when he is in low spirits murmurs 'I wish it hadn't happened.' He has horrible pains in his arms & shoulders. The doctors call it neuritis but they don't seem to know what to do about it. I think the sunshine & the bathing are doing him good, but of course what is really needed is 3 or 4 months complete relaxation.

Papa is worried about the lectures & thinks he will never be able to stay the course. I hope however that they may actually help his recovery, especially if he starts off with a big success in New York. As for 'staying the course' after he has done say 6 or 10, if he is feeling the strain, I shall persuade him to cancel the rest & I shall bring him home.

Last night he was very sad & said that he had now in the last 2 years had 3 very heavy blows. First the loss of all that money in the Crash, then the loss of his political position in the Conservative Party & now this terrible physical injury. He said he did not think he would ever recover completely from the three events.

You can imagine how anxious I am & I often wish you were here to help & advise me . . .

Ten days later Clemmie wrote in more encouraging terms from the liner bound for New York:

23 January 1931

Papa is now really better. During the 20 days we have spent there the progress, at first imperceptible, became gradually more noticeable & at the end of the time rapid. So that if only we could have stayed another month I believe the cure would have been complete.

Now we must see what effect lecturing has upon him. It may help him to forget the details of the accident which are photographed upon his brain & which sometimes prey upon his mind.

I trust it may be so. Writing that article about the accident made him think about it more & more so that sometimes it is an obsession.

That was a gallant effort. He was still very ill; but he said: 'I must do something to pay the expenses of this illness' – & weak as he was he dictated it & almost collapsed afterwards.

I kept hoping while we were at Nassau that the lovely colours would tempt him to bring out his paint box; at the end of our stay he talked about it once or twice but had not the energy or strength.

I think if we could have stayed on, that in about another week he would have tried – & then I don't think we could have torn him away . . .

A week later, Randolph wrote with home news:

1 February 1932

My lecture went off exceptionally well in Belfast, though my remarks about prohibition stirred up a hornet's nest among the temperance crowd which, though small, is very vocal. Most of the old-fashioned Tories were delighted however, at them being given a prod.

A fortnight ago I went down to stay with Beaverbrook at Cherkley for the weekend. He was most agreeable and I got on very well with him. On the Sunday Brendan and I motored over to Churt for lunch. Lloyd George was in splendid form. I have never seen a man of his age (it was his 69th birthday) who seemed in better health. He was full of vitality and his face had assumed a wonderful tan. He spoke with great affection of you and seemed very worried about your accident. He thinks that neither you nor himself should be in too much of a hurry to speak this session, as he thinks it is only a question of time before the Government becomes extremely unpopular. He is now a convinced food taxer, but I don't know whether he will come out with this publicly or not . . .

I have not been to the Constituency since you left, but am speaking at South Woodford next Thursday and on March 14th at Waltham Abbey. I hear from Hawkey [James Hawkey, Winston's loyal constituency chairman] that they are all in very good shape and are much worried about your illness.

Later in the month Randolph, who had been propositioned to write a Life of his father, telegraphed Winston, still on his American lecture tour:

HAVE BEEN OFFERED 450 POUNDS ADVANCE ON SUBSTANTIAL ROYALTIES FOR BIOGRAPHY OF YOU HAVE YOU ANY OBJECTION TO MY ACCEPTING IF I DO IT IT WILL NATURALLY BE UNAUTHORISED UNOFFICIAL AND UNDOCUMENTED MY AIM WOULD BE PRESENT POLITICAL HISTORY LAST THIRTY YEARS IN LIGHT UNORTHODOX FASHION BELIEVE COULD PRODUCE AMUSING WORK WITHOUT EMBARRASSING YOU MUMMY LOOKING VERY WELL ALL COUNTING DAYS TO YOUR RETURN LOVE R.

His father replied from the Midwest:

STRONGLY DEPRECATE PREMATURE ATTEMPT HOPE SOME DAY YOU WILL MAKE THOUSANDS INSTEAD OF HUNDREDS OUT OF MY ARCHIVES MOST IMPROVIDENT ANTICIPATE NOW STOP LECTURE PILGRIMAGE DRAWING WEARILY FINAL STAGE MUCH LOVE MAMA = FATHER

So it turned out, except his father might have increased the sum a hundredfold. Randolph was prudent enough for once to bow to his father's judgment and, as a result, when he was eventually entrusted with the writing of his father's official biography, in the last ten years of his life, he became solvent for the first time ever.

On Winston's return to England aboard the *Majestic*, which docked at Southampton on 17 March, he was met at the quayside by his friends with a new Daimler motor car which, at Brendan Bracken's suggestion, they – including Randolph – had clubbed together to buy him. He telegraphed Randolph a few days later:

I CANNOT TELL YOU WHAT PLEASURE THE GIFT OF THIS LOVELY MOTOR CAR HAS BEEN TO ME MOST OF ALL FOR THE FRIENDSHIP WHICH INSPIRED IT I WISH I COULD WRITE TO EVERYONE SEPARATELY BUT PLEASE ACCEPT IN THIS FORM MY HEARTFELT THANKS = FATHER

CHAPTER 6

A Meeting with Hitler

On 28 May 1932 Randolph celebrated his twenty-first birthday. Despite a taste for extravagant living, it was already clear that he had inherited many remarkable qualities from his father, principal among them clarity of thought, command of the English language and a fearless courage. He was a fine speaker, and in many ways more assured on the public platform than his father, being able to speak extemporaneously on a wide range of themes. Already he was brimming over with self-confidence and bursting with ambition.

Indeed in the very first of a series of weekly articles for the *Daily Dispatch*, under the headline 'How I Mean to Win Success', he wrote:

> The sky should be the limit of youth's ambition. As one grows older one will probably realise that one cannot win all that youthful ardour desired. But, by that time, one ought to be sensible enough or, perhaps, sufficiently disillusioned, to be satisfied with what one has got...
>
> I am not afraid, however, to reveal to those who have borne with me so far my two main ambitions. I wish to make an immense fortune and to be Prime Minister.

He added, somewhat wistfully:

> In twenty years' time, however, when I shall probably have fought four or five unsuccessful elections and have been bankrupted more than once, I do not see why I should then regret my youthful ambition, however laughable this will appear to my more experienced eye.
>
> Enjoy success to the full and disregard failure – only thus can life be tolerable.

But Winston foresaw at least one major obstacle in the path of Randolph's ambition. Towards the end of his life, my father told me how, when he was just twenty years old his father took him for a stroll on the lawn at Chartwell: 'He was talking about the battle of life and, as we walked, he put his arm around me and said, "My father died when

I was exactly your age. This left the political arena clear for me. I do not know how I should have fared in politics had he lived on."' Winston was certainly right in his view that there was only room for one Churchill in politics at a time. As it turned out, he dominated the political scene like a Colossus for a further generation, not finally resigning as Prime Minister until 1955 by which time he was eighty years old and Randolph forty-four. But Randolph laboured under an additional self-inflicted handicap: his brashness, arrogance and contempt for authority, including especially the leadership of the Conservative Party, made it impossible for him to secure nomination for any seat that was winnable.

To mark Randolph's coming of age and, no doubt, to repair his own political isolation, Winston gave a great dinner at Claridge's on 16 June with the theme 'Fathers and Sons'. As Randolph acknowledged with an unaccustomed modesty: 'It was a splendid occasion and far more than I deserved. The occasion was more suited to my pretensions than to my achievements or abilities.' Among the fathers and sons present were: Viscount Rothermere and the Hon. Esmond Harmsworth; Lord Camrose and the Hon. Seymour Berry; Lord Beaverbrook and the Hon. Max Aitken; Viscount Hailsham and the Hon. Quintin Hogg; Earl Beatty and Viscount Borodale; the Marquess of Salisbury and Viscount Cranborne; the Marquess of Reading and Viscount Erleigh; as well as Viscount Wimborne and the Hon. Ivor Guest. Others among the sixty guests included the Duke of Marlborough, the Earl of Birkenhead (Freddie who, two years earlier, had succeeded his more famous father), Lord Hugh Cecil, Sir Oswald Mosley (not yet the pariah of British politics), Sir Austen Chamberlain, General Sir Ian Hamilton, Admiral Sir Roger Keyes and Sir John Lavery.

The next day the *Evening Standard* carried a report of the dinner, of which Randolph remarked: 'I was only twenty-one but I knew enough of the world and of Fleet Street and of Beaverbrook to detect the hand of the Lord.'

'Great' Men and Their Sons

Mr Churchill gave a dinner to his son last night. The company consisted of many men who are called great and their sons. These 'great' men are convinced, needless to say, that their sons are also 'great'. The sons, or most of them, admire their parents' judgement in this respect. Missing from the list was Mr Baldwin and Mr Baldwin's son Oliver.

Everybody was filled with curiosity about the 'boys'. Yet Mr Churchill put up some of the old codgers to make speeches, and he made a very good one himself...

But what of the younger generation? Lord Birkenhead (aged 24) made a grand speech, carefully prepared, word perfect, witty, with phraseology reminiscent of his father . . .

Randolph Churchill (aged 21) was best described by his own father, who, in speaking of his fluency, said he was a fine machine-gun, and it was to be hoped that he would accumulate a big dump of ammunition and learn to hit the target.

Not a word of Randolph Churchill's speech was prepared, but there was ample evidence of fine natural abilities. To him an old codger may say, 'Work, my boy, work: The way is wide open to you in politics if you do.'

The Hon. Quintin Hogg (aged 24): A very fine speech, with not too much evidence of preparation; an easy passing from gay to grave; finished in form; a shade too nervous in delivery . . .

The last of the quartet who were allowed to provide interludes in the oratory of their elders was to me one of the most interesting. He was the Hon. Seymour Berry (aged 22). His speaking had neither the finished form of the others nor their conscious assurance in addressing an audience. Yet it would not surprise me if he went as far as any of them . . .

Seymour Berry, later Lord Camrose, was for many years editor-in-chief of the *Daily Telegraph* and for much of his life, a close friend of Randolph's.

Winston, delighted at the reception accorded his son's speech, wrote the next day to the Earl of Crawford and Balcarres: 'Naturally I have high hopes of Randolph. He has a gift and a power of presentation which I have not seen equalled at his age. Whether he will be noble and diligent has yet to be proved.' The same day Winston's private secretary, Eddie Marsh, wrote to Clemmie: 'I've never enjoyed a dinner more, & such good speeches. Randolph was delightful & Freddie and Quintin distinguished themselves. What a splendid send off for R!'

Shortly before his twenty-first birthday, Randolph had concluded an agreement with Lord Rothermere for a series of articles for the *Sunday Graphic*, followed by a regular weekly column for the *Daily Dispatch*. As his first foreign assignment, Randolph decided to go to Germany to cover the general election taking place there at the end of July 1932. In the presidential election of March that year, under a system of proportional representation, Hitler and his National Socialist Party had received nearly 13.5 million votes or 40 per cent of the total cast. The lion's share – 18 million votes – had eventually gone to Paul von Hindenburg, who needed a second election in April to be re-elected President. The July Reichstag elections made the Nazis the largest political party in Germany, although they won only 37.1 per cent of the vote. This heralded the accession to power of Hitler as Chancellor of Germany less than six months later, in January 1933.

On arrival in Germany Randolph met Ernst Hanfstaengl, a Harvard graduate and personal friend of Hitler who had appointed him his press secretary. 'Putzi' Hanfstaengl, as he was familiarly known, arranged for Randolph to accompany Hitler in his campaign aircraft. Randolph's first report from Germany was remarkable, not only for his coup in travelling with the 'Führer' in his private Tri-motor Ford aeroplane from rally to rally but in the way he demonstrated a power of prescience equal to his father's. In categorical terms – before even Winston had done so – he predicted that the rise to power of Hitler meant the inevitability of another war between Germany and Britain.

On 31 July 1932, the day of the election, the *Sunday Graphic* carried the following report:

HITLERITES' NEW WAR THREATS
Ex-Soldiers 'Burning for Revenge'
ELECTION CRISIS
Germany Determined to have an Army Again
by RANDOLPH CHURCHILL

Berlin, Saturday: ... All Wednesday afternoon I spent flying round with Hitler from one meeting to another. First of all we lunched at the aerodrome just outside Berlin. Hitler is a teetotaller, a non-smoker and a vegetarian. On this occasion he ate his favourite scrambled eggs and salad. His lieutenants and I fortify ourselves with a more substantial meal. We all climb aboard Hitler's three-motor ten-seater aeroplane. Nazi guards click their heels and raise their hand in the passive salute and we are off.

In twenty minutes we have landed in a field of clover. A special bodyguard – twelve magnificent-looking men in black uniform, all carrying concealed firearms – salute their leader. We drive 12 kilometres to the meeting.

At every corner of the road, at every cottage door, there is a group of people. All the young boys and girls raise their hand to Hitler. A few older people, with a sour look upon their faces, but they are in the minority.

We arrive at the stadium. For 300 yards the road is lined with brown-uniformed Nazis, standing rigidly at attention, and holding hands to keep the crowds off the roads. Hitler mounts the platform; 15,000 arms are raised, 15,000 voices yell 'Heil, Hitler'.

The chairman shouts 'Achtung', and a pin-drop silence ensues. Hitler speaks – quietly at first, but as he proceeds his voice becomes charged with emotion and enthusiasm and rises to a challenging note.

'We are going to end France's European hegemony. A united Germany, morally and economically free, need not fear Moscow nor be subservient to the League of Nations. England does not allow the League to rule her. Why should we?' This is the gist of his message.

We drive off as the crowd sings with impressive fervour 'Deutschland Uber Alles'. Soon we are flying over Berlin again. It is 6.30, and we pass over the enormous stadium where Hitler is to speak in three hours' time. We come down to 300 ft.

At least 100,000 people are already waiting, but it is no use worrying about them. We are over the aerodrome. Five monoplanes circle around us and land simultaneously with us, almost causing an accident. We all jump into the waiting motor-cars, 60 kilometres to Brandenburg, another meeting – the same discipline and enthusiasm.

Hitler is clearly tired, but there is no time to rest. We must start immediately for the last and biggest meeting. By the time we arrive, there are certainly no fewer than 120,000 people crammed into the stadium. Fifteen thousand storm troops are drawn up in the centre.

It is dark, and most of them hold flaming torches. Massed bands play the marching song of the Nazis as Hitler drives slowly round the stadium in an open car. For ten minutes the crowd shout 'Heil, Hitler', until they are almost chanting the refrain.

I can only describe the meeting as a mixture between an American football game and a boy-scouts' jamboree, animated with the spirit of a revivalist meeting and conducted with the discipline of the Brigade of Guards.

Randolph concluded his vivid account with a warning of the threat to world peace posed by the Nazis:

Nothing is more foolish than to underestimate the intensely vital spirit that animates the Nazi movement. Hitler has no detailed policy. He has promised all things to all men. Many Germans say that he no longer wants power – that he is frightened of all the forces he has called into being. They say he does not want a majority and merely wishes to be part of a Coalition. I do not believe this to be true.

He is surrounded by a group of resolute, tough and vehement men who would never tolerate any backsliding from their leader. Nothing can long delay their arrival in power. Hitler will not betray them. But let us make no mistake about it.

The success of the Nazi party sooner or later means war. Nearly all of Hitler's principal lieutenants fought in the last war. Most of them have two or three medals on their breasts. They burn for revenge. They are determined once more to have an army. I am sure that once they have achieved it they will not hesitate to use it.

For the moment, however, the danger is postponed. It is virtually impossible for Hitler to win this election. He will have to continue his support of the present Government.

In the last 12 months there have been four elections, which have cost Germany over £6,000,000. They cannot afford another one yet, but all the time the Nazis will attain strength and impetus, and within three years at the most Europe will be confronted with a deadly situation.

Nothing except a radical revision of the Treaty of Versailles can quench the fire that burns in German hearts. The removal of the sense of injustice which the German nation feels is the most vital task that confronts European statesmanship to-day.

Churchill's biographer, Martin Gilbert, in a letter to me dated 8 April 1976, wrote of this report: 'I must say your father was almost the very first person to see what Hitler and Nazism would lead to. Indeed, I know of no-one else who, as early as July 1932 stated so emphatically: "The success of the Nazi party sooner or later means war."'

More than thirty years on, in an interview with John Summers of the *Sunday Telegraph*, Randolph recalled this time:

I had been going back and forth to Germany and realised the Nazis around Hitler considered that, as Churchill's son, I was a person to be impressed with the rightness of Hitler's purposes ... so I could go home with some 'good' impressions and report to my father.

'They tell me over there the only thing the young Nazis are after is freedom', Summers had asked somewhat naïvely.

'Freedom? What those young men wearing the uniform and singing and marching round Germany are really after is not freedom – it's arms! Arms! And when they have arms – they will want War!'

Outside a Berlin Nazi gathering I asked a leading Nazi – one of the first so-called gentlemen-Nazis: 'What's Hitler really like?' The answer I got was: 'Well, he's really just like your father!' No, I didn't go back and tell my father that. It wouldn't have amused him ...

I have already acknowledged some of Randolph's more glaring faults. But it must also be said that on his very first assignment, at the age of twenty-one, he demonstrated that he was already the foremost political journalist of his generation with a remarkable ability to assess a situation and place it with power and clarity before the public.

Winston, who was at this time heavily engaged in writing his Life of Marlborough, decided to visit the scene of his great ancestor's victories. On 27 August, in the company of Professor Lindemann, he took the car ferry from Dover to Calais for a tour of the battlefields of Flanders and the Low Countries. From there they followed by car the route of Marlborough's brilliant, lightning march to the Danube. After a brief stay in Munich, Winston went on to study the battlefield of Blenheim. On 19 September he wrote to the historian Keith Feiling, who was assisting him with the research on his book: 'The battlefields were wonderful . . . and I was able to re-people them with ghostly but glittering armies . . . I was deeply moved by all these scenes and feel sure I can interpret them for the *first time*.'

While in Munich, Winston and Lindemann had been joined by Clemmie, Randolph and Sarah, and it was here that Churchill came within feet of meeting Hitler. It appears that Randolph, in the course of his recent journalistic foray to Germany, had informed Hanfstaengl of his father's impending visit and had contacted him to arrange a meeting between Hitler and his father. Hanfstaengl recorded the occasion in his memoirs, *Hitler: The Missing Years*:

> I caught up with Hitler at the Brown House and burst into his room . . .
> 'Herr Hitler,' I said, 'Mr Churchill is in Munich and wants to meet you. This is a tremendous opportunity. They want me to bring you along to dinner at the Hotel Continental tonight.'
> I could almost see the asbestos curtain drop down. '*Um Gotteswillen*, Hanfstaengl, don't they realise how busy I am? What on earth would I talk to him about?' – 'But, Herr Hitler,' I protested, 'this is the easiest man to talk to in the world, art, politics, architecture, anything you choose. This is one of the most influential men in England, you must meet him.' But my heart sank. Hitler produced a thousand excuses, as he always did when he was afraid of meeting someone. With a figure whom he knew to be his equal in political ability, the uncertain bourgeois re-emerged again, the man who would not go to a dancing class for fear of making a fool of himself, the man who only acquired confidence in his manipulation of a yelling audience. I tried one last gambit. 'Herr Hitler, I will go to dinner and you arrive afterwards as if you were calling for me and stay to

coffee.' No, he would see, we had to leave the next day early – which was the first I had heard of it as I thought we had two or three days free: 'In any case they say your Mr Churchill is a rabid Francophile.'

I rang Randolph back and tried to hide my disappointment, pointed out that he had caught us at the worst possible time, but suggested, against my better knowledge, that Hitler might join us for coffee. I turned up myself at the appointed hour. There was Mrs Churchill, serene, intelligent and enchanting, Lord Camrose, Professor Lindemann, one of the Churchill daughters and one or two other young people whose names I forget. We sat down about ten to dinner, with myself on Mrs Churchill's right and my host on the other side. We talked about this and that, and then Mr Churchill taxed me about Hitler's anti-Semitic views. I tried to give as mild an account of the subject as I could, saying that the real problem was the influx of eastern European Jews and the excessive representation of their co-religionaries in the professions, to which Churchill listened very carefully, commenting: 'Tell your boss from me that anti-Semitism may be a good starter, but it is a bad stayer.' I had to get this bit of slang explained, which made the rest of the party laugh.

Over coffee, brandy and cigars, my host and I pushed our chairs back and he became confidential in his tone. I can remember the scene to this day. With his left hand, the one next to me, he held a brandy glass almost touching his lips, so that his words reached my ears alone, and in the other a fat cigar. 'Tell me,' he asked, 'how does your chief feel about an alliance between your country, France and England?'

I was transfixed. I could feel my toes growing through my shoes into the carpet. Damn Hitler, I thought, here is the one thing which would give him prestige and keep him within bounds and he does not even have the social guts to be here to talk about it ... I must get hold of Hitler, I thought, and turning to Mrs Churchill made a flimsy excuse about having forgotten to telephone my home to say how late I would be and would she please excuse me while I rang up. 'But of course, ask your wife to join us,' she said.

I got to the Brown House. Hitler had left. I rang his apartment. Frau Winter had not seen him. Then I telephoned my wife to say I did not know what time she would see me. She was tired and preferred not to wait up or come out. I lurched out of the call box into the hall and whom did I see nine or ten steps up the staircase – Hitler in his dirty white overcoat and green hat, just saying good-bye to a Dutchman, whom I knew was a friend of Goering's and had, I think, channelled money to the party in his time. I was beside myself.

'Herr Hitler, what are you doing here? Don't you realise the Churchills are sitting in the restaurant? They may well have seen you come in and out. They will certainly learn from the hotel servants that you have been here. They are expecting you for coffee and will think this a deliberate insult.' No, he was still unshaven, which was true. 'Then for heaven's sake go home and shave and come back,' I said. 'I will play the piano for them or something until you get back.' – 'I have too much to do, Hanfstaengl. I have to get up early in the morning' and he evaded me and walked out. I put the best face on it I could and went back to the party. Who knows, I thought, perhaps after all he will turn up ... So I played my football marches, and 'Annie Laurie', and 'The Londonderry Air' and the party was in high fettle. All except me.

Hitler never turned up. He had funked it. While it remains one of the interesting 'If's' of History, it is idle to imagine that, had such a meeting taken place, the course of history might have been changed. Hitler would never have considered an alliance with the French, nor Churchill an alliance without them and, at the time, he was without influence in the House of Commons.

Following this, his second visit to Germany in two months, Randolph not only warned of the dangers of a second world war but argued strongly against the proposed disarmament of France. On 19 September 1932 he reported in the *Daily Dispatch*:

> ... Mussolini's recent support of Germany's claim to re-arm and have equality of status is an indication of what the French fear. With thirty-five million French menaced from the South by forty-five million Italians, and from the East by sixty millions of Germans, the French are unlikely to acquiesce in any change in the present situation until some guarantees at least as effective as their two million bayonets can be provided.
>
> In this matter Britain has a difficult part to play. Sooner or later the resurgence of Germany has got to be faced, the peace of Europe cannot be indefinitely maintained on its present basis.
>
> There is a dynamic force in Germany to-day which will grow stronger the more it is repressed. The clash between the French desire for security and the German refusal to accept the status of a second-class Power – *there* is the peril of the next war.
>
> European statesmanship must concern itself with this topic above all others if we are to avoid universal annihilation. As a result of the Locarno Pact Britain is definitely involved in all these stresses. We are virtually

committed to take one side or the other in the next war between France
and Germany . . .

Both Randolph and his father were, at this point, 'appeasers' in
the best sense of the word. They strongly opposed the continuing
disarmament of France and Britain, neither of which had any interest in
waging war. At the same time, both father and son wished to see
Germany's legitimate grievances redressed – Randolph favouring a
revision of the Versailles Treaty and Winston going a step further, hinting
at the possibility of an alliance between Germany, France and England.
This vision remained unrealised until a further 20 million lives had been
lost in a second world war, after which these three warring countries
became allies in NATO and partners in the European Union.

Apart from chiding MPs and ministers with articles under such
provocative headings as 'Ministers Must Work Harder', 'Are Our MPs
Too Lazy?' and 'Hundreds of Second-Rate MPs Without a Single New
Idea', a clear and consistent theme of Randolph's articles in the *Daily* and
Sunday Dispatch was the danger of a rearmed and unrequited Germany,
together with the folly of disarmament by her former allies. On 3
October he wrote:

> The world is tired of war. Despite this general and, I believe, increasing
> abhorrence of war there is a wide realisation to-day that if the world
> continues along anything like its present economic and political path war
> will be inevitable sooner or later . . .
>
> Armaments to-day are the defence of civilisation. That is a terrible but
> incontrovertible fact. Despite this, however, we are constantly told that it
> is countries such as Britain and the United States who should lead the
> world in disarmament and set an example to the others. I pray that we
> shall not be deluded by these absurdities. The nations who should give us
> a lead are those who might gain something by war – those who want
> something, not those who have everything they need.
>
> Italy, Russia, Japan, when these start disarming it will be time for us to
> think about it. Until that time, the great Peace-loving nations of the world,
> the British Empire and the United States, should stand together with a
> determined policy against disarmament.

In a debate in the House of Commons on 10 November on the subject
of European disarmament, Mr Baldwin, having warned the young about
the horrors of aerial bombardment, complacently declared: 'When the
next war comes and European civilization is wiped out . . . then do not let

them lay the blame upon the old men. Let them remember that they [the younger generation] ... are responsible for the terrors that have fallen upon the earth.' Randolph riposted in his column a few days later:

> What have Mr Baldwin and the other old men done since the last war to make the next one more remote? What chance have the men under 40 been given to make any contribution in this respect?
>
> Apparently Mr Baldwin's idea is that he shall cling on to office, as long as he can, and go on doing nothing, or, at any rate, as little as possible, and then when the next war arrives, as the result of his generation's inertia, turn round and lay the blame upon the young men whom he has excluded with such success from all power...
>
> Whatever we may think of this point of view, the younger generation can at least find some satisfaction in the fact that they now know where they are; ... no power now; ... when the time comes, not only the burden and the sacrifice, but also the blame.

On 30 January 1933 Hitler became Chancellor of Germany. The Nazi Party had come to power. Ten days later the Oxford Union, to its undying discredit, approved by 275 votes to 153 the motion 'That this House refuses in any circumstances to fight for King and Country'. Within a decade, many of those who so fecklessly supported this shameful motion were to expiate their youthful folly by laying down their lives for 'King and Country'.

In a debate on 2 March, Randolph, though no longer an undergraduate, attempted to reverse the motion and have it expunged from the record. The meeting was packed and passions ran high. Randolph was defeated in his bid by a massive 750 votes to 138. Shortly afterwards Winston wrote to his friend Lord Hugh Cecil of Randolph's defeat: 'He stood a hard test at the Oxford Union. Nothing is so piercing as the hostility of a thousand of your own contemporaries and he was by no means crushed under it.'

Within two days of Hitler coming to power, Hermann Goering declared that the new Cabinet, at its very first meeting, had taken the decision to build up a German air force and, a week later, the first of the anti-Jewish decrees was promulgated. Despite this, in the Air Estimates debate in March, the Government announced a *reduction* of £1,000,000 in resources for the Royal Air Force compared with two years before, because of the 'need for economy'. That same week the Prime Minister, Ramsay MacDonald, presented Britain's proposals – effectively halving the French army and doubling that of Germany – to the Disarmament

Conference at Geneva. In the Commons debate that followed, Churchill – to howls of fury from Labour and Conservative Members alike – fiercely attacked the Prime Minister's conduct of British foreign policy during the past four years which, he declared, 'have brought us nearer to war and have made us weaker, poorer and more defenceless'.

These were Churchill's 'wilderness years', a time when his friends in Parliament could be counted on the fingers of two hands and when bitter criticism, even hatred of him, was widespread. Though he and Randolph were not always close, especially once the office of Prime Minister intruded upon their relationship, during this period they were like brothers and comrades-in-arms. Throughout the next five years, while his father remained politically isolated, Randolph was utterly loyal to him and made himself his lieutenant in all his political battles. Principal of these was their crusade to awaken the British people to the dangers of the Nazi menace and to strengthen Britain's defences in the hope of preventing the war they both so clearly saw coming.

In the spring of 1933 Randolph decided that the time had come for yet another visit to Germany and he telegraphed Hitler's press secretary, Hanfstaengl, on 27 March:

PLANNING COME BERLIN SUNDAY MOST ANXIOUS HAVE OPPOR-
TUNITY EXPOSE ANTIHITLER PROPAGANDA APPEARING ENGLISH
NEWSPAPERS WILL YOU BE BERLIN = RANDOLPH CHURCHILL

Hitler did not fall for this rather obvious stratagem and Randolph never obtained a personal interview with the Führer. Indeed, he added to the 'anti-Hitler propaganda' with an article in the *Daily Dispatch* of 18 April 133 in which he categorically renewed his earlier warning:

The resurgence of the German nation under Hitler sooner or later means war. Nazis with whom I have talked expressed amazement that since they were stamping out Communism they did not receive moral support from Britain. If it had not been for Hitler, they said, Germany would have gone Communisitic...

But the Nazis do not merely intend to stamp out Communism. They will not be satisfied with an economic pogrom against the Jews. They will not be satisfied with equality of status. They would not even be satisfied with the return of the Polish Corridor. Sooner or later, as their appetite is whetted, they will want Alsace-Lorraine...

Throughout the summer of 1933 a flow of disturbing reports from Germany was reaching England. The Nazi Party had established itself firmly in power by declaring all other parties illegal. In the streets a reign of terror was conducted against the Jews. Tens of thousands of Germans were arrested; those imprisoned included not only Jews but political opponents of the Nazi regime as well as trade union leaders, Socialists and Communists. By the end of the year more than 100,000 people had been placed in concentration camps and a further 50,000 had fled abroad. On 27 June Group Captain Herring, the British Air Attaché in Berlin, reported in a secret memorandum to the Foreign Office that Germany had begun to build military aircraft in violation of the Treaty of Versailles and that 'a process of mobilisation' was in progress.

In September Randolph joined the staff of Rothermere's *Daily Mail* for which he was to act as a roving reporter on a wide variety of subjects. At the same time he kept up his weekly feature articles for the *Sunday Dispatch*. On 24 September, under the headline 'Britain Needs Stronger Navy and Air Force', he wrote:

> Germany does not want equality of armaments for its own sake. She demands them in order that they may then be utilised for a war of revenge upon France and for the recovery of her lost Dominions.
>
> The Nazis are not looking for equality of status. They are looking for, and making, GUNS.
>
> It is nothing short of a scandal that, though we emerged from the war with the largest air force in the world, to-day we rank only fifth among the great Powers. Our Naval strength in the narrow seas is by no means as strong as it should be...

A week later, under the headline 'Better to Go to War To-day than in 1937', he wrote:

> Hitlerism spells WAR ... It would be much better to go to war to-day than in four years' time. If joint action could be taken by the Great Powers, Germany could be disarmed to her treaty limitations within a few months. Indeed, no serious resistance could be offered. It is vital, however, to avoid delay.
>
> At the present moment Europe is drifting towards war with far greater certainty than in the year 1913. Britain's position is immeasurably less secure than it was in 1914...

In March 1934, with German rearmament gathering momentum and street violence threatening democracy in Austria and France, Churchill warned the House of Commons: 'Germany is arming fast and no one is going to stop her ... I dread the day when the means of threatening the heart of the British Empire should pass into the hands of the present rulers of Germany.'

In November, at the opening of the new session of Parliament, Churchill attacked the Government for its complacency and warned of the growing air power of Germany:

> It is never quite worth while to underrate the military qualities of this most remarkable and gifted people, nor to underrate the dangers that may be brought against us ...
>
> It sounds absurd to talk about 10,000 aeroplanes and so on, but, after all, the reserves of mass production are very great, and I remember when the War came to an end the organisation over which I presided at the Ministry of Munitions was actually making aeroplanes at the rate of 24,000 a year and planning a very much larger programme for 1919 ... Let the house do its duty. Let the Government give the lead, and the nation will not fail in the hour of need.

Baldwin admitted that the situation gave ground for 'very grave anxiety', but dismissed Churchill's figures which showed that the German air force was rapidly approaching parity with Britain. In fact he asserted that the Luftwaffe was 'not 50 per cent' of British air strength and that Churchill's figures were 'considerably exaggerated'.

But Churchill had made it his business to become the best-informed British politician on the subject. He followed closely the build-up of German power and a key source of information was his near neighbour at Chartwell, Desmond Morton, who was at the time Director of the Industrial Intelligence section of the Committee of Imperial Defence. On 29 November Morton wrote to Churchill:

> Your magnificent exposition of the situation last night has undoubtedly gone far to achieve the object in view. At any rate we have a declaration from SB [Stanley Baldwin] that this Government is pledged not to allow the strength of the British Air Force to fall below that of Germany ... SB was evidently confused when saying the figures given him varied between 600 and 1,000. They did not. The figures given him were as above, i.e. 600 Military planes & something under 400 dual purpose aircraft. = Total: something under 1,000 aircraft capable of immediate use as service aircraft

... How on earth 950 (German) aircraft can be expressed as less than 50% of 1,247 (British) beats me!

In June the same year Randolph went to Doorn in Holland to interview ex-Kaiser Wilhelm of Germany. The Kaiser, who had met Randolph's father on two or three occasions before the Great War, agreed to receive him and, though not in the habit of giving press interviews, invited him to lunch. It was evidently Randolph's intention to draw out his host's views on Hitler, but this the Kaiser adroitly side-stepped. In her biography, *The Kaiser*, Virginia Cowles quotes from a letter written later that month by the Kaiser's wife, Empress Hermine, to an American friend Poultenay Bigelow about Randolph's visit to Doorn:

> Churchill hoped to interview the Kaiser on Hitler, but the Emperor switched the conversation to the Chinese–Japanese war, reverting to the well-worn theme of the 'Yellow peril'. His twenty-three-year-old visitor, however, did not allow His Majesty's reticence to prevent him from stating his own views on Germany's leader; and the Empress Hermine told Bigelow that 'young Churchill knew nothing of the new Germany' which she admired so much and she was shocked when he referred to Hitler as 'A danger and an enemy'.

It was to be another year before the Empress revised the high opinion she held of Hitler.

CHAPTER 7

The Father and Son Road Show

In addition to the danger from Germany, the future of India was a consistent theme of the Churchill *père et fils* team. India was at the forefront of British politics at the time and was the cause of the strongest dissension in Parliament. The Labour Party and a large element of the Conservative Party favoured an early advance to self-government and dominion status for India. Baldwin and the Tories in the National Government sided with Ramsay MacDonald and the Socialists on the issue; Churchill, however, disagreed. Early in 1933 he launched a public crusade against the Government's policy on India, joining the India Defence League of which he became the linchpin.

Both Churchills strongly believed that India was not yet ready for self-government and that any premature step in this direction would negate Britain's efforts of one hundred and fifty years to bring unity, peace and progress to the sub-continent. Furthermore they believed that it would lead to the collapse of any central administration and give rise to blood-shed on a colossal scale – as was indeed to prove the case. More than two million lives were lost in bitter sectarian fighting between Moslems and Hindus within months of India gaining independence in 1947 and the separate state of Pakistan coming into being.

Believing that such a policy was in the interests neither of Britain nor of India, father and son determined to fight it every inch of the way – Winston leading the parliamentary battle and Randolph spearheading a press campaign.

The change of policy towards India by the British Government had led to the imposition of a tariff of 25 per cent on Lancashire cotton goods imported into India – a measure that resulted in the loss of one hundred thousand jobs in Lancashire alone. The industrial situation in the North-West had become critical, with hundreds of mills being driven out of business and an ever-mounting tide of unemployment. For months the Churchills campaigned for the Government to provide safeguards for the Lancashire cotton trade. When their efforts failed they determined to launch a campaign throughout Lancashire.

On 26 June 1934 Churchill addressed a packed meeting at the Free

Trade Hall in Manchester which was attended by more than 3,000 representatives of all sections of the cotton industry. The meeting, by a majority of 3,000 to 15, carried the following resolution:

> This meeting records its thanks to Mr Churchill for his advice and warning, and is of the opinion that a full and true statement of the Lancashire case should be brought by the Manchester Chamber of Commerce before the joint Select Committee and Parliament; that effective guarantees for the maintenance of the mutually advantageous trade between Great Britain and India should be inserted in the proposed new India Constitution; and that all Members of Parliament for the constituencies concerned should be requested to assist Lancashire in this time of distress and peril.

Randolph reported the meeting for the *Daily Mail* whose proprietor Lord Rothermere, a strong supporter of Churchill, offered his full assistance in mounting a campaign in all the Lancashire cotton towns. On 29 June Randolph telegraphed Lord Rothermere at Dornoch in Scotland:

> IT WAS AGREED SUBJECT TO YOUR APPROVAL THAT CAMPAIGN SHOULD BE STARTED MONDAY WITH TWO LOUDSPEAKER VANS, ONE MANNED BY ROBINSON [Secretary of the Manchester Branch of the India Defence League] AND MYSELF, AND OTHER BY [Councillor] WATTS AND BARNES, AN OLDHAM MILL OPERATIVE STOP CONSIDER THIS NUCLEUS OF EFFECTIVE TEAM WHICH LATER MIGHT BE EXPANDED STOP PROVISIONAL ESTIMATE FOR VANS FORTY POUNDS WEEKLY STOP CERTAIN INCIDENTALS SUCH AS PRINTING, HANDBILLS AND CARS FOR SPEAKERS WILL BE NECESSARY BUT DO NOT ANTICIPATE THAT COSTS OF REALLY EFFECTIVE CAMPAIGN WILL BE HEAVY STOP IF YOU APPROVE PLAN PLEASE AUTHORISE ME OPEN JOINT ACCOUNT AT ONCE SO THAT WE CAN START MONDAY STOP CERTAIN GREAT RESULTS CAN BE OBTAINED BY STOUTHEARTED ACTION. BEST WISHES = RANDOLPH CHURCHILL

On Monday 2 July, as planned, Randolph embarked on his Lancashire speaking tour with a meeting at the Imperial Mill in Burnley where he addressed four hundred workers. In the course of the next three weeks he spoke at more than fifty meetings and wrote twenty-eight articles for the *Daily Mail* either under his own byline or thinly disguised as 'Our Special Correspondent'. Typical was the report of 12 July:

HOLIDAY-MAKERS HEAR COTTON'S CALL
INDIA PLAN PERILS
From our Special Correspondent
PRESTON, Wednesday Night.

Bracing Blackpool and proud Preston – the holiday land and the administrative capital of Lancashire have to-day added their quota to the swelling wave of protest against the India White Paper perils.

Speakers in the 'Save Lancashire' Campaign have to-day addressed several thousand people and have obtained many more signatures to the petition they are organising.

Beginning with a dinner-hour meeting at the Leigh Mill, Preston, this morning where they spoke to nearly 500 operatives, Mr Randolph Churchill and Mr Henry Robinson travelled on to Blackpool. There an afternoon meeting was held with Mr Jim Barnes added to the list of speakers.

Thousands of mill operatives from Burnley, Brierfield, Macclesfield, and other towns on holiday this week heard the case for safeguarding trade with India.

Bathers lying on the hot sands, family parties, people sitting in Promenade shelters, on deck chairs, or leaning on the railings – all listened intently to the unanswerable arguments put forward...

On 23 July the Conservative MP for Bournemouth, Sir Henry Page-Croft, wrote to Winston: 'I think there is no doubt that a considerable section of people in Lancashire have been very much stirred at last by this India issue. I heard of Randolph's activities which must have done quite a lot to shake up all the big towns radiating from Manchester.'

Despite all his hard work in defence of the Lancashire cotton trade, Randolph managed to find time to lose money with his proclivity for making foolish bets and frequenting the gaming tables of French casinos. I recall him telling me of an exchange he had about this time with Monsieur Blanc, proprietor of one of the grander casinos. To Randolph's inquiry as to whether there was an effective system of winning at the roulette table, Blanc replied with a disarming frankness which should have been a warning to him: 'Bien sur, Monsieur Churchill, qu'il y a une système: Rouge gagne par fois, Noir gagne par fois ... mais Blanc gagne toujours!' ('Of course, Mr Churchill, there is a system: sometimes Red wins, sometimes Black wins ... but Blanc always wins!')

In May 1933 his father had set up a trust fund in his favour of just under £10,000 derived from his literary earnings. By the autumn of the following year Randolph had had to ask his trustees – his father and Uncle Jack – to advance him £6,100 to meet his debts, including £1,950 in favour of the Palm Beach Casino in Cannes. Before agreeing to make this advance, however, the trustees required him to give a written undertaking that in future he would neither play at any public gaming table nor gamble for sums beyond his present means.

Nevertheless, within a year, Randolph and his father were to be found together at the gaming tables of the French Riviera, despite Clemmie's strenuous disapproval. Many years later Randolph told Martin Gilbert:

> In 1935, while staying at the Château de L'Horizon in the South of France, I went one night with my father to the Casino in Cannes. By five in the morning I had won £200 and my father £500. [Their combined winnings amounting to almost £20,000 in today's money.] We left the casino, but could not find a taxi. 'Let's walk back along the beach, it's only four or five miles,' my father said and off we went, reaching the Château at half past six. My mother, who had never approved of my father's gambling, was still asleep. Father went into her bedroom, woke her up, and showered her bed with one thousand franc notes.

But it was not only Randolph's reckless gambling – a trait perhaps inherited from his maternal grandmother, Blanche Hozier – that ate into his earnings: his extravagance and his generosity were also to blame. On 29 November 1934 Randolph gave a dinner dance at the Ritz Hotel to celebrate his father's sixtieth birthday the following day.

In mid-January 1935, Randolph travelled to Liverpool to report the by-election in the Conservative stronghold of Wavertree. The local Conservative Association had selected James Platt as the official National Conservative candidate, in support of Ramsay MacDonald's National Government. On the night of Friday 18 January Randolph attended one of Mr Platt's public meetings, bringing with him some of his Manchester friends from the India Defence League to liven things up. Between them they subjected the unfortunate candidate to a barrage of hostile questions on India. Following the meeting Randolph and his 'Indian' friends retreated to the Adelphi Hotel where, at about 2 a.m., he resolved to contest the election himself, standing as an Independent Conservative.

The next day, Randolph's decision was reported in the *Sunday Dispatch*:

He [Randolph] made this decision alone. 'I did not want my father to have the responsibility of advising me, as it is quite likely to be a losing fight,' he told the *Sunday Dispatch* afterwards.

'At 4 o'clock yesterday morning after making my decision, I decided to rush back to London to ask the *Sunday Dispatch* and the *Daily Mail* – my employers – if they would support me. Two chauffeurs took turns at the wheel of the car so that not a moment should be lost on the way.'

Rothermere agreed to give him his backing. His father, however, taken unawares by Randolph's decision, was not as pleased as his employers. In a letter to Clemmie, who was on a Far East cruise aboard Lord Moyne's yacht, Winston wrote:

20 January 1935

This is a most rash and unconsidered plunge. At the moment Randolph and his three or four Manchester friends, including Mr Watts who has subscribed £200 to the expenses, are sitting in the Adelphi Hotel at Liverpool without one single supporter in the constituency whom they know of – high or low.

Randolph is to hold his first meeting tomorrow. Of course with the powerful support of the local *Daily Mail* and the *Sunday Dispatch* and with the cause, which is a good one, and with his personality and political flair he will undoubtedly make a stir. But in all probability all that he will do is to take enough votes from the Conservatives to let the Socialist in.

Altogether I am vexed and worried about it. It is nothing like the Westminster Election where we had the local Tories split from top to bottom and where we developed quite rapidly a brilliant organization. Randolph has no experience of electioneering and does not seem to want advice, and the whole thing is amateurish in the last degree. To have a hurroosh in the streets and publicity in the newspapers for three weeks and then to have a miserable vote and lose the election to the Socialist will do no end of harm . . .

Despite his anger at Randolph's action, he hastened to give his paternal support, issuing a statement to the Press Association within hours of Randolph's candidature being announced:

My son has taken this step upon his own responsibility and without consulting me. He is of age; he is eligible; he is deeply interested in Lancashire affairs and in Imperial politics. He has strong convictions of

Tory democracy. He believes it is his duty, at whatever cost to himself, to rouse Lancashire to the dangers of the India Constitution Bill. This is still a free country and he is fully entitled to plead his cause, which is a worthy and vital cause, not only for the wage earners of Lancashire, but for the life of Britain. I know nothing of the conditions in the Wavertree division and cannot form any opinion at this moment upon the prospects of Mr Randolph Churchill's candidature; but I should be less than human if in all the circumstances of these critical times I did not wish him success.

The original draft of the statement contained, at the end, the words 'from the bottom of my heart', subsequently deleted.

The Times greeted the 23-year-old campaigner with somewhat more reserve:

Mr Randolph Churchill's week-end announcement that he intends to join in the contest at Wavertree as a Conservative candidate has quickened interest in the election. That interest was already steadily mounting before his plans were known, and his intervention will certainly increase the pace.

In Conservative circles there is more amusement than resentment over his decision. One prominent member of the party in Liverpool said that, while he regarded the development as a bit of bluff, he was sure that if Mr Churchill did enter the fray the electors of Wavertree would know how to deal with him. This expresses the prevalent feeling in Conservative circles that if Mr Churchill goes to the poll the number of votes he will take from Mr Platt will be negligible ...

The same day, Winston informed Clemmie that Randolph was launching his campaign in Wavertree that night and, although he had 'no friends or supporters' in the constituency itself, Lord Rothermere was giving him 'tremendous support' through his newspapers. Further, the Duke of Westminster had contributed £500 and John Watts a further £200 to his campaign. His letter continued:

I am producing £200. I do not doubt Rothermere will provide the rest. The total expenditure is limited to £1,200, so that is all right. Much depends on whether this meeting goes well tonight and the impression Randolph makes. Of course in action of this kind he has a commanding and dominating personality, and there is a great feeling that Lancashire needs someone of vigour and quality.

Already the election has become a national fight. I shall know at ten o'clock tonight how he gets on. Incidentally before he decided to plunge into the election he wrote a very provocative series of paragraphs about 'a deal in municipal honours' in Liverpool in his weekly letter in the *Sunday Dispatch*. This coupled with the election excitement has led Sir Thomas White, the Liverpool [Conservative Party] 'boss' who was reflected on in these paragraphs, to issue a writ for libel against the *Sunday Dispatch*, and I believe Randolph personally. The contest will therefore not be lacking in bitterness.

At the same time Winston telegraphed Clemmie:

SARAH AND DIANA BOTH GONE LIVERPOOL HELP RANDOLPH THUS HE HAS ALREADY TWO SUPPORTERS . . .

That night, Wavertree Town Hall was packed half an hour before the start of the meeting and arrangements had to be improvised for an overflow meeting. According to press reports the next day, by the time the meeting started all standing room in both halls was fully occupied and hundreds of people were waiting outside. Randolph, entirely alone on the platform, launched a fierce attack on the National Government and the sixty MPs of all parties representing Lancashire. The *Daily Mail* devoted more than ninety column-inches to the meeting:

MR RANDOLPH CHURCHILL'S GREAT START
TWO CROWDED MEETINGS
Scenes of Tremendous Enthusiasm
RUSH OF SUPPORTERS
'Virile India Policy Demanded'

Wonderful enthusiasm marked the start last night of Mr Randolph Churchill's great campaign in the Wavertree by-election, where he is gallantly fighting for no surrender in India and the finest Air Force in the world . . .
   'Our present party leaders were put in their present position by chance. They sit there like toads on the nostrils of the British lion. (*Cheers*). Mr MacDonald is a most grisly and awful liability to the Conservative Party. Lancashire, as far as the Government is concerned, is a forgotten county. But if you return me we shall take the power away from the party caucus and the party bosses.'
   At the overflow meeting at St Mary's Institute, Mr Churchill referred to the question of defence. 'We are,' he said, 'the highest taxed people in the world, and we have a right to say that we should be the best defended and the safest. That need comes before everything else. If we are to be safe we must have the finest Air Force in the world.' (*Loud cheers*).

Following the meeting Winston telegraphed Clemmie:

RANDOLPH MAKING PROGRESS. GREAT LOCAL ENTHUSIASM. INDIA DEFENCE LEAGUE DECIDED GIVE FULL SUPPORT, THEREFORE MANY GOOD SPEAKERS. I GO EVE POLL.

Later he wrote her a full account:

... This is the first time we have definitely opposed a Government candidate at a by-election and it may be we shall lose some of our members for the decision. They even seemed to think that perhaps the Government would refuse the Whip to all members of the League. I do not believe they dare do that. Anyhow all were resolved to go forth, so Randolph will have all our circus at his disposal including Lloyd, Wolmer, Roger Keyes, the D of W! and last but not least Papa. I have promised him to wind up his campaign in the Sun Hall on February 5.

Needless to say this election will cause much heat and bitterness. On the other hand it arouses enthusiasm and will be a national fight. Good judges in the constituency tell me that Randolph will certainly beat the official Tory and that the fight lies between him and the Socialist, who will probably win. In this case the National Government candidate will be at the bottom of the poll. A nasty jar for Ramsay and Baldwin and general anger . . .

Well there it lies tonight, and it must run its course. You will see that I am much more easy in mind about it than I was at first sight. Randolph of course is in the seventh heaven. This is exactly the kind of thing he revels in and for which his gifts are particularly suited. He is reported to be rather tired and no wonder considering his excitement and exertions. I am counselling him bed at eleven and great attention to his vocal cords.

The official Conservative Party, far from treating Randolph's candidature as a joke in bad taste, as *The Times* had hinted, was seething with indignation and deeply apprehensive as to the outcome. Particular resentment focused on Randolph's use of the word 'toad', which Duff Cooper MP, Financial Secretary to the Treasury, claimed in a speech had been used in relation to the leader of the Conservative Party, Stanley Baldwin. This was reported by *The Times* the next day, whereupon Winston entered the fray with a telegram to Duff Cooper:

RANDOLPH DID NOT APPLY WORD 'TOAD' TO BALDWIN BUT TO PARTY BOSSES.

Duff Cooper replied:

I AM VERY SORRY IF I MISREPRESENTED RANDOLPH. I HAD CLEARLY
UNDERSTOOD FROM MORE THAN ONE REPORT THAT RAMSAY AND
S.B. WERE THE TWO TOADS ON THE LION'S NOSTRILS.

Randolph also entered a protest to Duff Cooper from Wavertree:

I NEVER REFERRED TO MR BALDWIN IN SUCH TERMS THE PHRASE
ABOUT TOADS WAS USED IN RELATION TO THE CAUCUS BOSSES
STOP HAVE CHECKED THIS NOT ONLY FROM MY MEMORY BUT
FROM SHORTHAND NOTES OF P.A. [Press Association] REPORTER
WHO IS WITH ME NOW.

This prompted a rejoinder from Duff Cooper:

MUCH REGRET HAVING MISREPRESENTED YOU OWING TO
RELIANCE ON DAILY MAIL REPORT. WILL WRITE TO TIMES WITH-
DRAWING AND APOLOGISING IF YOU WISH IT. DO NOT MYSELF
KNOW WHO CAUCUS BOSSES ARE. PRESUME LEADER OF PARTY
MUST BE ONE OF THEM MUST THEREFORE POINT OUT THAT YOU
COMPARED MR. B TO A PART OF A TOAD. TO WHAT PART I
KNOW NOT = DUFF

Amid all this brouhaha it was announced that Winston would address
Randolph's eve-of-poll rally in Wavertree. Meanwhile he did what he
could to rally support for his son, wiring Lord Carson, the former leader
of the Ulster Unionists and more capable than most of directing the
large Liverpool Orange vote. Carson responded by sending a public
message of support the same day.

On 31 January Winston told Clemmie of his intention to speak for
Randolph at two meetings on the eve of poll for which more than 7,000
tickets had already been issued:

The demand is extraordinary and there is no doubt both these 'Father and
Son' meetings will be crowded out.

All the underlings of the Government have been up, but last night the
Attorney General Inskip had his second meeting only half filled. But they
have crowded in agents from every part of the North country.

It is the machine against popular enthusiasm, and you know what the
machine is. However, as I have said, anything may happen especially as

quite a number of Liberals have come over to us. Long before you get this letter you will have heard the news. If Randolph polls eight or nine thousand, we shall not have suffered a rebuff. If he beats Platt, it is a victory. If he is elected, it is a portent.

Ramsay sinks lower and lower in the mud, and I do not think the poor devil can last much longer. Buchanan, the Clydesider in the House of Commons, called him a 'cur', a 'swine' and 'one who should be horsewhipped'. These brutal insults were allowed to be cast by the Chair and no single member of this great majority – no Minister on the Treasury Bench, no Whip rose to claim a breach of order. Buchanan got off without withdrawing. If I had been there I would certainly have risen to protect this wretched man from such a Parliamentary outrage. What utterly demoralised worms his colleagues and their hangers-on must be to allow their Prime Minister to be insulted in this way in breach of every Parliamentary rule without one daring to stir on his behalf . . .

The same day Sir Samuel Hoare, Secretary of State for India, wrote privately to Lord Willingdon, Viceroy of India:

It is greatly to be hoped that Randolph does really badly and that the effect of his failure will depress Winston before the Committee stage [of the India Bill] comes on.

According to the gossip, Randolph is not doing well. Sightseers crowd to his meetings as they would to a new film, but most of them come from outside the constituency, and as far as one can judge, there has been no serious movement of real Conservatives to him . . .

Winston urged Randolph to stick to the India issue and not widen his attack on the National Government as a whole. He also warned him that any general denunciation of Conservatives co-operating in the National Government would cause serious embarrassment within the parliamentary party. However, within three days Winston was to change his mind and support his son's attack on the Conservative–Socialist alliance, whereby the Prime Minister, MacDonald, and the Conservative leader, Baldwin, were working together.

The same day Winston telegraphed Clemmie in great excitement:

THREE OPPONENTS NATIONAL SOCIALIST LIBERAL RANDOLPH CONSERVATIVE CANDIDATE TREMENDOUS ENTHUSIASM MAG-NIFICENT FIGHT AGAINST GOVERNMENT AND MACHINE CHANCES LIKE ABBEY ELECTION POLLING SIXTH RADIO RAN-DOLPH ENCOURAGEMENT TENDER LOVE = WINSTON

As the campaign reached its crescendo, Platt, the official National Conservative, received a message of support from the Prime Minister, while Randolph received the public support of twenty-three Conservative MPs in defiance of the Party Chairman, Lord Stonehaven, who had threatened that 'disciplinary action' might be taken against these 'rebels' by the Government Chief Whip.

By the eve of poll, 5 February, the odds had shortened from 50 to 1 against Randolph just a fortnight before to make him 6 to 4 favourite. That night, with Winston's arrival in Wavertree, the Churchill political circus was in full swing. The *Daily Mail* report the next day enthused:

WAVERTREE'S MOMENTOUS VOTE TO-DAY
DRAMATIC SCENES ON EVE OF POLL
Randolph Churchill's Confidence
10,000 HEAR FATHER'S HISTORIC SPEECH
Liverpool, Tuesday

... There never has been an election in the last 20 years at which so much popular feeling has been aroused and so much personal enthusiasm created for a candidate ...

The most important part of Mr Winston Churchill's speech was his terrific attack on the continuance of the Coalition Government and the leadership of Mr Ramsay MacDonald ...

Mr Winston Churchill brought all this to a decisive issue. In the presence of the Duke of Westminster, as his Chairman, and nearly 30 Conservative MPs on the platform, he attacked Mr Baldwin with unprecedented vigour.

What, he asked, does Mr Baldwin mean by saying that this is no time for a political dog-fight? What fool's paradise does he live in if he does not realise what is going on to-day? Two dogs are biting us, and our dog is not biting back because he is obliged to wear a Socialist muzzle.

It would be incredible, if it were not true, to see to-day the subservience of the great Conservative Party to Socialist doctrine. We are told we have a National Government. How can it be called that when it is led by an International Socialist and is opposed by two out of the three great political parties in this country ...

Mr Winston Churchill made many moving references to his son's campaign. 'My son Randolph,' he called him, and there were times when tears seemed to be in his eyes as he spoke, with pride but hesitation, of the young man's part in this great campaign ...

'Mr Platt has said that Randolph has no soul. It is a terrible thing to say of any fellow mortal in the precarious and fleeting existence through which we are passing ... I think he has lent his soul to England and his spirit to Lancashire, to the Wavertree electors, who will return it to him in abundant measure tomorrow.'

The cheers that roared back to this peroration lifted our hearts and sent everyone to the last day's campaign tomorrow with a surging hope of victory.

Polling took place at Wavertree on 6 February and the result was announced the same evening. Randolph had secured more than 10,000 votes, 24 per cent of the votes cast, and, by splitting the Conservative vote, had let in the Socialist candidate who romped home with 15,611 votes, pushing the unfortunate Mr Platt into second place with 13,771.

The next day Winston cabled Clemmie, who had reached Australia on her Far East cruise:

RANDOLPH BEATEN AFTER MAGNIFICENT BATTLE NO HARM DONE HAVE YOU SEEN FIGURES SEND HIM A MESSAGE TENDER LOVE FROM ALL = WOW

Clemmie replied with enthusiasm:

HOW TRULY THRILLING ABOUT RANDOLPH DID FUR FLY WHAT REACTION ON INDIAN CAMPAIGN WILL FOLLOW FROM LOSING SEAT TO LABOUR LAST MESSAGE JANUARY 31ST VERY CORRUPT ABOUT DIANA TENDER LOVE = MIAOW

Winston hastened to reassure her:

DIANA ENTIRELY SATISFACTORY RANDOLPH REACTION IMPORTANT EIGHTY FOUR CONSERVATIVES VOTED AGAINST [India] BILL LOVE = WINSTON

The fury in the Tory camp was predictably fierce. The day after the result was announced, Hoare wrote to Willingdon: 'That little brute Randolph has done a lot of mischief ... The fact that he kept our man out will undoubtedly do both Winston and him a good deal of harm in the party. The fact, however, that he got more votes than we expected is disquieting. It shows that there is a great deal of inflammable material about and it makes me nervous of future explosions ...'

But this view was by no means unanimous. Gerald Balfour, brother of the former premier and a former President of the Board of Trade who had served in the Commons with Randolph's grandfather and namesake, hastened to send his congratulations, though misdating his letter by a year:

Feb 7th 1934 [sic]   House of Commons

Dear Randolph,
    Congratulations on the great blow you have struck for the preservation of the soul of the Conservative Party.
    May you go from strength to strength & do much work in the future to reinforce your great achievement.
    I convey this message by favour of your Father who is so justly proud of your victory.

                                                    Yours sincerely,
                                                    G. W. Balfour

On 8 February *The Times* in its leading article roundly denounced both Churchills for their part in securing a Labour victory under the headline 'The Success of Suicide':

Certainly father and son scored a considerable personal success in terms of the number of votes cast for the younger MR CHURCHILL. But what is any single great thing which they have actually done? They have succeeded in returning a Socialist for Wavertree . . .
    India played no real part whatever in the election. It is significant that MR RANDOLPH CHURCHILL, especially during the latter stages of his campaign, widened the front of his assault to attack the whole policy and system of National Government . . .
    The Wavertree election shows nothing more clearly than the fact that those who, in obedience to short-sighted or personal views, seek to destroy the system of National Government, may indeed achieve success, but only the success of suicide.

The Economist, analysing the result in its issue of 9 February, declared:

The chief explanation is, of course, the intrusion of Mr Randolph Chur-chill as an official Conservative candidate running with the backing of the Rothermere Press on a programme of 'No Surrender in India' and 'A Big Air Force'. Mr Churchill junior has secured a personal triumph in polling no less than 10,500 votes against the full might of the Conservative Machine in an area where that machine is reputed to be among the best in the country. Mr Churchill has many personal attractions and has worked extremely hard and ably in his lightning campaign; but even with the help of his distinguished father, a rebel Tory candidate could not have reached a five-figure poll unless the schism in the Tory ranks had gone very deep. The election is a portent . . .

Randolph had succeeded in stirring things up magnificently – something he relished doing and indeed made his prime purpose in life. He had put the national spotlight on India and the plight of the Lancashire cotton industry. Above all, he had rocked the National Government in a dramatic way and had fired a heavy broadside across the bows of a Conservative Party that was supporting a Socialist Prime Minister in office, helping to implement a quasi-Socialist policy and neglecting the nation's defences. By an act that the party machine was never to forgive, he had at the same time jeopardised his own political prospects.

On 19 February the India Bill started its Committee stage on the floor of the House and for the next thirty days Churchill and his colleagues of the India Defence League fought the Bill clause by clause. As he reported two days later to Clemmie in New Zealand:

We do very well in the debate but the Government have mobilised two hundred and fifty of their followers who do not trouble to listen to the debates but march in solemnly and vote us down, by large majorities, usually swelled by the Socialists and always by the Liberals. It is going to be a long, wearing business . . .

At the height of the Committee stage – less than a week after the Wavertree result – Randolph announced his intention to put forward a candidate at the by-election in the south London seat of Norwood, with a view to challenging the National Government's India policy yet again. His father was furious, complaining to Clemmie in a letter dated 23 February:

He has acted entirely against my wishes and left my table three days ago in violent anger . . . He is quite beyond reason or even parley; and I am leaving him alone.

The cost of Randolph's non-stop electioneering was considerable. Fortunately for him he had found a political fairy godmother in Lady Houston, a patriotic but eccentric millionairess who was the widow of a shipping tycoon. Some two years earlier she had written to him out of the blue to deliver a stern admonition over views expressed in his *Sunday Dispatch* column:

> Two weeks ago you were practising Conservatism, last Sunday you were lauding Liberalism. Now my dear boy – take an old woman's advice and make up your mind which Party you stand for and fight for it – tooth and nail – and never have a word to say in praise of your opponent.
>
> By doing this England gained the name of John Bull but – alas – there are none of the John Bull breeds now-a-days. Be one and I would not mind betting you Lombard Street to a china orange that you will be a million times more successful than if you dilly dally – blow hot – blow cold – and one day write one thing and one day another as you now seem to do.

On learning of Randolph's decision to fight Wavertree as an Independent Conservative Lucy Houston had weighed in with further blunt advice: 'Don't call yourself Independent – it is so banal. Isn't *real* better?' However, her letter also brought more tangible assistance to the young campaigner in the form of a cheque towards his election expenses.

Brushing aside his father's objection, Randolph pressed ahead with his plans to defeat the official Conservative candidate at Norwood, Duncan Sandys, who in the event was to win a double victory: he not only vanquished Randolph's candidate but, after falling in love with his sister Diana – who had come to campaign against him – proceeded to win her hand in marriage! On 2 March Winston gave Clemmie a fuller account of Randolph's headstrong action:

> The Norwood by-election, of which I wrote you in my last letter, has absorbed all the children except Mary. Randolph seems to have got a considerable fund through Lady Houston and appears disposed to form an organisation to run candidates not only at by-elections, but against Government supporters at the general election. His programme seems to be to put Socialists in everywhere he can in order to smash up MacDonald and Baldwin . . .
>
> . . . He has for his candidate at Norwood nothing of the powerful support I was able to bring him at Wavertree. Not a single Member of Parliament will, I expect, appear on his platform. The India Defence League will leave him severely alone, and now the *Evening News* whose aid Rothermere had promised him, has made it clear that they will go no further . . .
>
> Now that the Rothermere Press has deserted him, it seems to me that

he is in for a thoroughly bad flop which will strip him of any prestige he gained at Wavertree. This will probably do him a lot of good, and reduce his pretensions to some kind of reason. In every other direction, especially in mine, it will do harm . . .

Though deeply involved in the India issue in the House of Commons where he was leading the fight against the Government, Churchill was day by day growing more alarmed by the situation in Germany. Writing to Clemmie on 8 March he expressed his anxiety at the possibility that Randolph might split the Conservative vote at Norwood, as he had done at Wavertree the previous month, thereby securing the election of 'the Socialist woman candidate [who] is fighting the election on pacifist lines' at a time when the Government 'tardily, timidly and inadequately have at last woken up to the rapidly increasing German peril'. He continued:

The German situation is increasingly sombre. Owing to the Government having said that their increase of ten million [pounds] in armaments is due to Germany rearming, Hitler flew into a violent rage and refused to receive [Sir John] Simon who was about to visit him in Berlin. He alleged he had a cold but this was an obvious pretext. This gesture of spurning the British Foreign Secretary from the gates of Berlin is a significant measure of the conviction which Hitler has of the strength of the German Air Force and Army . . . All the frightened nations are at last beginning to huddle together. We are sending Anthony Eden to Moscow and I cannot disapprove. The Russians, like the French and ourselves, want to be let alone and the nations who want to be let alone to live in peace must join together for mutual security. There is safety in numbers. There is only safety in numbers.

If the Great War were resumed – for that is what it would mean – in two or three years' time or even earlier, it will be the end of the world. How I hope and pray we may be spared such senseless horrors.

Polling at Norwood took place on 14 March. Duncan Sandys was elected with a majority of 3,348 over the Labour candidate – a drop in the Conservative majority of over 20,000 compared to the 1931 election. Randolph's candidate, Richard Findlay, came bottom of the poll with 2,698 votes. Winston wrote immediately to inform Clemmie of the result:

Randolph's candidate thus forfeited his deposit. I do not think the 2,700 votes was so bad considering that no one gave him the slightest support, and Randolph virtually had to fight alone, carrying everything on his shoulders, managing the organisation, making the speeches, answering the questions, writing the election address, interviewing the press etc.

He has now been electioneering for two months continuously but does not seem to be nearly so tired as he was during the Wavertree contest. This result is of course a set back to him and should teach him prudence, and to work with others, without at the same time daunting him. He is now off to Wavertree to form his own small independent Conservative Association there . . . I do not think the result has done me any harm. The fact that the India Defence League stood out of it of course acquits us formally.

It appears that Lady Houston had agreed to underwrite the entire cost of the Norwood campaign for, on 30 March, Randolph wrote to inform her that his and Findlay's expenses amounted to no less than £1,523 19s 0d (over £50,000 in today's money), confessing:

I am afraid that apart from your support we only collected £65.5/-. Still it must be admitted that this is much better than is achieved at most elections, particularly in view of the fact that so few prominent people came forward to support us . . . I should be most grateful if you could let us have this fairly soon as all the accounts have to be settled by the end of next week.

Lady Houston's generosity had been prompted by her desire to smash up the National Government and to force the Conservative Party, which had won no fewer than 470 seats at the previous election, to cease supporting in office Ramsay MacDonald, a forlorn International Socialist, whose party had only thirteen seats.

Randolph, in his early political campaigning, was not the only beneficiary of Lady Houston's impulsive generosity. Significantly, she gave her backing to the British aircraft industry at the most crucial point in its history. By offering £100,000 for the 1931 Schneider Air Trophy contest she provided the key finance – which the Government conspicuously failed to do – for the development of the Supermarine Rolls-Royce S-6 seaplane. This aircraft was the direct predecessor of the Spitfire, which was to play such a decisive role in the Battle of Britain. A year later, acutely conscious of the danger of war and the vulnerability of Britain's cities to air attack, Lucy Houston offered a contribution of £200,000 towards equipment for the air defence of London – the equivalent of more than £6 million today – an offer disdainfully spurned by the Government of the day on the ground that Parliament was the sole judge of what was required for the nation's defences. As events were to prove, the eccentric old millionairess's judgment was the sounder.

CHAPTER 8

Randolph, Hope and Glory

In the Defence debate of 11 March 1935, Churchill warned the House of Commons that disarmament had failed and that 'Germany is arming with furious energy'. Within the week Hitler announced that, in defiance of the treaty limitations upon Germany which restricted her army to 300,000, he already had 500,000 men under arms and was reintroducing conscription. Later the same month – just four months after Baldwin had told the House that Germany's air strength was only 50 per cent that of Britain's – Hitler informed Sir John Simon and Anthony Eden when they met him in Berlin that, in air power, Germany had already 'reached parity with Great Britain'. On 5 April Winston informed Clemmie:

The political sensation of course is the statement by Hitler that his air force is already as strong as ours. This completely stultifies everything that Baldwin has said and incidentally vindicates all the assertions that I have made. I expect in fact he is really much stronger than we are. Certainly they will soon be at least ten times greater than we are so that Baldwin's term that we should not be less than any other country is going to be falsified.

On 13 April, Winston wrote to Clemmie at Marseilles, where she was due to land on her return from the Far East, to inform her that Randolph had been taken ill with a severe attack of jaundice but was now 'decisively better', adding: 'He is in great good spirits and is visited by youth and beauty.' However, he went on to complain:

He has grown a beard which makes him look to me perfectly revolting. He declares he looks like Christ. Certainly on the contrary he looks very like my father in the last phase of his illness. The shape of the head with the beard is almost identical ... All the talk here is about reconstruction [of the Government] as soon as the India Bill is through. Whether that process will lead to my receiving an invitation I cannot tell, and I say most truthfully I do not care.

Meanwhile, Baldwin remains with all his cards in his hands, a power-miser I am going to call him. With the utmost skill and industry, and self-repression, he gathers together all the power counters without the slightest wish to use them or the slightest knowledge how! Ramsay continues to decompose in public...

At sixty I am altering my method of speaking, largely under Randolph's tuition, and now talk to the House of Commons with garrulous unpremeditated flow. They seem delighted. But what a mystery the art of public speaking is! It all consists in my (mature) judgement of assembling three or four absolutely sound arguments and putting these in the most conversational manner possible. There is apparently nothing in the literary effect I have sought for forty years!

The Government was at last forced to concede that Britain's front-line air strength was no more than 453 aircraft compared to a German strength of 880 – precisely the figure that Baldwin had deceitfully claimed for Britain in a Commons debate less than six months before.

Randolph, having decided to give electioneering a rest, much to his father's relief, sailed on 18 May aboard the Royal Mail liner *Arlanza* for Buenos Aires to cover the Chaco War between Paraguay and Bolivia. Five days later, following a Commons defence debate in which Baldwin admitted that he had been 'completely wrong' in the figures concerning the relative air strength of Britain and Germany which he had given the House the previous November, Winston signalled Randolph at sea:

SPEECH SUCCESSFUL BUT GOVERNMENT ESCAPED AS USUAL
MUCH LOVE = FATHER

In the first week of June Ramsay MacDonald resigned, being succeeded by Baldwin who became Prime Minister for the third time. But Winston, passionate to assist in Britain's rearmament, realised there would be no place for him in the new Cabinet. On arrival in Buenos Aires Randolph received an urgent telegram from his father:

IMPERATIVE RETURN FORTHWITH FACE LIBEL ACTION OTHER-
WISE CONSEQUENCES GRAVELY INJURE YOUR REPUTATION
ESPECIALLY WAVERTREE STOP BALDWIN PRIME [MINISTER]
RAMSAY DEFENCE HOARE FOREIGN IRWIN WAR ELECTION
OCTOBER [LLOYD] GEORGE HOSTILE ALL LOVE = FATHER

Immediately prior to the announcement of his decision to stand as a candidate in the Wavertree by-election, Randolph had written an article published in the *Sunday Dispatch* of 20 January 1935 in which he had made a vehement attack on Liverpool's Conservative Party boss, Sir Thomas White. In the article, which appeared under the headline: 'A Deal in Municipal Honours' he disclosed how White had done a deal with the Socialists, who formed the minority group on Liverpool Council, so as to obtain the Freedom of the City for himself. The price paid to obtain this preferment (which required a two-thirds majority of the Council) was the conferring of the Freedom on a Socialist and a Liberal and, more importantly, the election of the first Socialist Lord Mayor of Liverpool. Randolph had concluded his piece:

> Thus, by a happy piece of municipal back-scratching among the ins and outs, a deal was done and both sides obtained the civic preferment they sought.

Two days later Sir Thomas White instructed his solicitor, a brilliant young lawyer with political ambitions, Hartley Shawcross, to issue a writ for libel against Randolph, the editor of the *Sunday Dispatch* and Associated Newspapers Ltd.

In Randolph's absence upon the high seas a date had been set for the hearing of the case before a Manchester jury on 15 July. This, and a timely armistice in the Latin American war, forced Randolph to abandon his plans to report the Chaco War and return to England immediately. Evidently he was considering some swifter means of travel for, before the *Arlanza* reached Rio de Janeiro, he received a cable from his newspaper:

NO NECESSITY TAKE ZEPPELIN STOP ENJOY YOUR REST STOP SHIP WILL BRING YOU HOME IN MORE THAN AMPLE TIME

In the course of the previous six months the two litigants had carried on an unseemly quarrel in public, Sir Thomas calling Randolph variously a 'Lothario' and 'Casanova', while Randolph labelled White 'a pocket Napoleon' and proposed that he should be consigned to 'St Helena, from whence there is no return'. In the event, Randolph felt compelled to submit to out-of-court negotiations and agreed to pay Sir Thomas White £1,000.

Lord Derby, living nearby at Knowsley, had been concerned to bring this damaging dispute to an end and, above all, to dissuade Randolph from his intention of standing once again in opposition to the Conservative Party at the forthcoming general election. He therefore proposed that Randolph should stand down as an Independent in Wavertree and instead become the official Conservative candidate in nearby West Toxteth, a seat held by Labour in a recent by-election with a majority of 5,343 votes. The scheme – initially opposed both by White, who reckoned he owed Randolph no favours, and by Randolph who wished to stand by his supporters to whom he had pledged himself in Wavertree – was eventually agreed to in late October in time for the general election on 14 November. The *Liverpool Star*, reporting his adoption, commented:

> Mr Randolph Churchill's Labour opponent should find the speeches made by Mr Churchill in the Wavertree by-election very useful. If the Opposition has chastised the National Government with whips, he chastised them with scorpions.

One of the quips from the Wavertree campaign that Randolph was not allowed to forget was his declaration that: 'Nearly all the safest Tory seats in England today are represented by old duds.'

The campaign in West Toxteth was predictably lively. Randolph was supported not only by his father and by his mother, who made her first political speech for thirteen years, but by his magnanimous new brother-in-law Duncan Sandys, the victor of Norwood, whom only six months before he had described as 'a political centipede with a foot on every fence'. The public meetings were rowdy and Clemmie had a battle to deliver her speech above the hubbub punctuated with the loud reports of fireworks being discharged, before effectively silencing her hecklers. William Barklay, reporting the meeting for the *Daily Express*, recorded:

> After sitting for safety on top of a school-room blackboard in Liverpool, while a crowd seethed beneath me around Randolph, Hope and Glory, I muttered: 'They say this is a dull election!' Mrs Winston Churchill went in there, stuck her thumbs in her neat waistband and talked them into silence and finally into applause. Afterwards she said to me: 'When I used to go round with Winston twenty years ago there was always blood, and once three men had their thighs broken.'

As the campaign developed momentum, there were indeed scenes of violence. At public meetings chairs were hurled, stewards injured and Randolph's sister Diana had her hat torn off. At a meeting in Birkenhead, Randolph rounded on his hecklers, declaring: 'Free speech is one of the most precious things we have in this country and we are not going to have it stamped out by Hitlerism, Mussolini-ism, Mosleyism, or hooliganism.'

On the eve of poll the *Daily Telegraph* reported from Toxteth:

> Cowardly hooliganism reached its climax here tonight ... Mr Churchill and his son, after addressing five thousand people in the Sun Hall, and St George's Hall, were travelling in an open car ... A stone, about 3 in. long and 2 in. in diameter, struck Mr Winston Churchill's hat and hit another occupant of the car on the arm. Mr Churchill took no notice and made his open-air speech ... Mr Randolph Churchill said afterwards: 'With great difficulty we have established the right of free speech. It now appears that we have left the Socialists bereft of all arguments and they have descended to stone-throwing.'

Randolph, who had opened his campaign by declaring that he did not 'want to go into Parliament to represent a lot of stuffy old ladies in Bournemouth', but wanted to fight for the really hard-pressed people of Liverpool – a statement which was not forgotten when, some twenty years later, he presented himself before a Bournemouth selection committee – fought his campaign on a demand for government assistance for Merseyside and rearmament in the face of the Nazi menace. In the event he was unsuccessful in winning the seat from the Socialists though he slashed their majority by more than 3,500 votes to 2,004. In a brief three-week campaign, Randolph had succeeded in nearly doubling the Conservative vote, which was increased by 7,000. Among the telegrams of congratulation he received was one from Stanley Baldwin – a generous gesture considering that Randolph, barely nine months earlier, had described him and Ramsay MacDonald sitting 'like toads on the nostrils of the British lion'.

Baldwin and the Conservative Party, commanding a majority of 257 over the Labour and Liberal Parties in the new Parliament, felt strong enough to do without Churchill in the Cabinet. He thereupon retreated to the Mediterranean for a two-month holiday. In his absence there was political uproar over the terms proposed by the British and French Foreign Ministers, Samuel Hoare and Pierre Laval, for the future of Ethiopia which, on 4 October, had been invaded by Mussolini's forces. While public opinion strongly favoured backing the League of Nations in imposing sanctions against Italy, the Hoare–Laval plan on the contrary advocated Ethiopia's surrender to Italy of nearly a quarter of Ethiopian territory. Randolph reported to his father in Majorca:

11 December 1935

Baldwin seems to have put his foot into it properly over the Laval/Hoare peace plan. His use of the word 'leakage' gave everyone to understand that the terms printed in the papers are accurate . . .
    I dined last night with Max [Beaverbrook]. Grandi [the Italian Ambassador in London] and Brendan [Bracken] were there. The isolation camp is naturally cock-a-hoop and regard it as a betrayal of the League of Nations. Grandi was just as delighted. Max says that whatever else may happen, no more sanctions can be applied now that Italy has accepted and is prepared to discuss peace proposals.
    I ragged Max about his deal with Hitler. He did not take it at all well and indignantly denied that he had done a deal, but there is no doubt he did. He was very reticent about his conversation, but someone who had a first-hand account of it from him tells me that Hitler expressed himself as most alarmed at the idea of your being in the Cabinet. Hitler's information apparently was that this was a foregone conclusion. He was very angry and said it would be most unfriendly. Max, of course, reassured him and told him there was no possible chance of it . . .

Five days later Randolph cabled his father in Barcelona urging him not to return for the vote on the peace proposals:

GOVERNMENT STANDING FIRM ON PEACE PROPOSALS . . . AND BOUND OBTAIN REASONABLE MAJORITY THURSDAY STOP PRESUME YOU DO NOT WISH SUPPORT SHAMEFUL SURRENDER MUSSOLINI AND OPPOSITION BOUND TO BE MISINTERPRETED . . . FONDEST LOVE = RANDOLPH

In a letter to his father the following day, Randolph welcomed his decision not to return:

From what I hear Baldwin, Hoare and Vansittart [Permanent Under-Secretary at the Foreign Office] who planned this shameful surrender, are extraordinarily confident of the outcome. They are going to raise the cry that they have saved the country from war, and to make it worse from our point of view they are going to suggest that it would have been a war which we might have lost . . .
    Poor Brendan is torn between his desire to see sanctions terminated and Baldwin exterminated . . .

In the event the hue and cry was too great and Baldwin was forced to abandon his proposed agreement. Hoare resigned and the Government obtained a large majority by avowing its support of the League of Nations policy. This stand, though morally high-principled, had the effect of encouraging Italy to join what came to be known as the Axis Alliance with Germany.

Writing to Clemmie from Rabat in Morocco on 26 December, on his way to find a few weeks' sunshine in Marrakech, Winston observed: 'I too thought B.'s speech most damaging to his position and repute. Eden's appointment [as Foreign Secretary] does not inspire me with confidence. I expect the greatness of his office will find him out. Austen wd have been far better.'

In spite of this he was stern in his letter to Randolph the same day:

> It would in my belief be vy injurious to me at this juncture if you published articles attacking the motives & character of Ministers especially Baldwin & Eden. I hope therefore you will make sure this does not happen. If not, I shall not be able to feel confidence in yr loyalty & affection for me.

It is not known what exercise in character assassination Randolph had in mind to prompt this paternal reproof, but events were in train in the far northern fastnesses of Ross-shire in Scotland that were to make for much greater political embarrassment for his father than a bit of journalistic jousting. Both the ex-Prime Minister Ramsay MacDonald, recently appointed Secretary of State for Defence, and his son Malcolm, also in the Cabinet as Secretary of State for Dominion Affairs, had lost their seats standing as National Labour candidates opposite Socialist candidates in the recent general election.

Baldwin, as Prime Minister and leader of the Conservative Party, was most anxious to secure the return to Parliament of the two 'ragamuffin' MacDonalds, as Winston described them in a letter to Clemmie, so that he could prolong the fiction that he was indeed the leader of a 'National' Government. While the Scottish Universities' seat, made vacant by the death of the recently elected Member, was to be the vehicle for returning Ramsay to the Cabinet, Baldwin selected Ross and Cromarty for Malcolm by elevating the sitting member, Sir Ian Macpherson, to the House of Lords.

However, there was immediate resentment among Ross and Cromarty Tories at being treated in so cavalier a fashion by their party leader and a mutiny resulted. On 28 December William Barklay reported in the *Daily Express* from Glasgow: 'The MacDonalds are going native. Beaten out of England at the General Election, Ramsay Mac. and Malcolm, father and son, are heading due North in their efforts to reach Westminster.' However, many local Conservative farmers were refusing to accept MacDonald as a Conservative candidate and were 'reported to be scouring the Mediterranean for Mr Randolph Churchill to ask him whether he will stand. Mr Randolph Churchill sees so red at the mention of a MacDonald that some people think he must be a Campbell in disguise ... It is quite likely, if even one Tory farmer asks him, he will feel disposed to hop all the way from Marrakech in Morocco to Dingwall in the Aurora Borealis without stopping once at Norwood, West Toxteth or Wavertree.'

Although instructed by Baldwin and Conservative Central Office to give their support to Malcolm MacDonald, the local Conservative Association Executive were adamant. They rejected MacDonald at three successive meetings and decided unanimously – with the exception of the Chairman who tendered his resignation – to cable an invitation to ·Randolph inviting him to stand as the official Conservative candidate.

Writing on New Year's Eve from the Mamounia Hotel, Marrakech, where he and Randolph were staying together with Lloyd George, Winston told Clemmie:

> I have been idle today. No Marl [the Life of his ancestor Marlborough], only a little daub & a little bezique. Randolph is of course wanting to fight Malcolm M. but he won't be able to – because it would put a spoke in my wheel and do nothing good for him. I do not think he would really when it came to the point.

Barely a week later, Winston had to admit defeat, informing Clemmie that Randolph had left Casablanca by air that very morning in order to stand against the former Prime Minister's son at the Ross and Cromarty by-election. Winston, who had still not abandoned all hope of being included in the Government, complained to Clemmie:

8 January 1936

> The stubborn and spontaneous character of this invitation, and the refusal even to hear Malcolm MacDonald are remarkable facts. You will see how unfortunate and inconvenient such a fight is to me. 'Churchill v MacDonald'. If they get in, it would seem very difficult for Baldwin to invite me to take the Admiralty or the co-ordinating job [as Defence supremo] and sit cheek by jowl with these wretched people. I therefore

would greatly have preferred Randolph to damp it all down. Instead of this he has had his agent up there feeling around . . .

Rothermere is sending Oliver Baldwin [the Prime Minister's elder son and a former Labour MP] to write up Randolph, which he is apparently ready to do, and to write down Malcolm, which of course is what all other Socialists revel in. So we shall have Ramsay's son, Baldwin's son and my son – all mauling each other in this remote constituency . . .

When the contest gets a little further developed, I propose to utter the following 'piece'. 'I wish Mr Baldwin would tell me the secret by which he keeps his son Oliver in such good order.' However for the present I am keeping completely mum.

Winston was fearful that Baldwin might regard it as a 'definite declaration of war'. But he added with fatherly understanding: 'With Rothermere, Beaverbrook and Lloyd George all goading him on, I cannot really blame him . . . I was reading what Marlborough wrote in 1708 – "As I think most things are settled by destiny, when one has done one's best, the only thing is to await the result with patience."'

William Barklay reported in the *Daily Express* on 8 January that Randolph was due to arrive 'at Toulouse in the afternoon. Early Thursday morning he leaves Paris. He arrives at Croydon at 11.45 on Thursday forenoon and leaves immediately for Dingwall. This must surely be a record feat of endurance in travel for a young candidate flying across a quarter of the globe to uphold a great cause in the North of Scotland.'

The *Scottish Daily Record and Mail* went even further overboard and greeted his prospective arrival with some rapturously heroic stanzas:

> He is coming! The whisper thrills
>   From the Moslem mosques afar
> On the lonely Ross-shire hills
>   Men watch for a moving star,
> For a glitter and a gleam of wings,
>   For a throb on the morning clear,
> And their eyes speak wonderful things,
>   And their hearts say, 'Hush! He is near!'
>
> He is coming! On every croft
>   From Dingwall to Achnasheen
> They are raising their eyes aloft,

They are scanning the blue serene,
Forgetting the oar and the crook,
Forgetting the hoe and the plough,
Forgetting the pot on the hook,
And the rock wi'the wee pickle tow.

He is coming! The Northern gloom
Rolls back for an end of dule,
There is laughter along Loch Broom,
There is singing in Ullapool;
And the jubilant voices swell
Like a roll of exultant drums,
'All's well with the North! All's well!
For Randolph MacChurchill comes!'

When, on landing at Croydon, Randolph was asked by a *Daily Mail* reporter if his intervention in the by-election would mean standing against Malcolm MacDonald, the National Government candidate, he replied blandly: 'I don't know what a National Government candidate is. I must go to Ross to see one.' Although MacDonald enjoyed the backing of Baldwin and the National Government in London, he was finding it difficult to obtain the support of any local political association in Ross-shire. As the *Daily Express* had earlier reported:

He may stand as a Conservative. He may stand as a Socialist. He may stand as a National. He may stand on his head. But we shall not know until tomorrow ... Mr Malcolm MacDonald is not the only pebble on this beach. Another MacDonald arrives tomorrow. But he is the agent for Mr Randolph Churchill ...

Malcolm MacDonald was eventually adopted by the local Liberal Party but not without much dissension and an Independent Liberal candidate being put up to stand against him, while Randolph's candidature was endorsed by a meeting of the Ross and Cromarty Unionist Association by 160 votes to 47.

Randolph had much ground to cover, politically and physically. Ross and Cromarty, which boasted more sheep than voters, had been represented uninterruptedly by Liberals for eighty-nine years and Randolph was the first Unionist candidate to contest the seat for a quarter-century. It had become local practice for the Unionists to give their support to the Liberal candidate so as to exclude the Socialists. Now that the local Liberal Association had announced its intention of supporting the candidature of former Socialist Malcolm MacDonald, the local Conservatives made clear that they could not agree to return him unopposed. They no doubt judged that the strongest riposte they could make to Mr Baldwin was to adopt the *bête noire* of Conservative Central Office. The following day Randolph told a reporter of the *Glasgow News* in mock disbelief:

> I am surprised to see that it has been suggested that my candidature will not receive the approval and support of the Conservative Central Office and Mr Baldwin. I cannot but think that if Mr Baldwin has formed the mistaken view that my candidature was in any sense a hostile act to himself or to this Government, he would, before this late stage, have informed me of his views...

Randolph was swiftly disabused of this idea for the very next morning Mr Baldwin sent a telegram of 'whole-hearted' support to Malcolm MacDonald.

Randolph issued his reply in a press statement the same day:

> Mr Baldwin's telegram of support to Mr Malcolm MacDonald has come as a surprise to me. If the Leader of the Conservative Party finds himself unable, owing to the political entanglement in which he has involved himself, to give his support to the official Unionist candidate I should think that he would have at least refrained from any discrimination. I will not, however, allow myself to be discouraged by this strange political development, but I set myself with redoubled efforts, albeit without my leader's aid, to the task of rallying to the National Government, the forces of Unionism in Ross and Cromarty.

Meanwhile Winston wrote to Clemmie from Meknes in Morocco:

> Today he [Randolph] telegraphs that an unimportant Scottish paper alleges I am wholeheartedly supporting his candidature. I am reluctant to disavow him and have let things drift. Rothermere however is arranging for Oliver Baldwin to write an article examining the relations of fathers and sons in politics and pointing out that sons must take their own line and their fathers cannot be held responsible.
>
> I shall not make up my mind upon the matter further until I get home, but I should think that any question of my joining the Government was closed by the hostility which Randolph's campaign must excite. Kismet!

In a note to Lord Rothermere, who was also in North Africa, Winston pondered further the situation in which his son had landed him:

Modern ideas contemplate freedom of action on their own responsibility for grown sons. It follows that parents have no responsibility for action taken by sons . . . Political divergences between fathers and sons no bar to affection and sympathy.

On his return to Marrakech on 17 January, Winston informed Clemmie that it was not his intention to hurry home; indeed, he felt it would be 'convenient' for him to stay abroad as long as possible: 'without any positive declaration, it would emphasize that I am taking no part in Randolph's campaign'. Besides, a decidedly gloomy telegram was awaiting him at the Mamounia Hotel on the progress of the campaign in the snow-covered Highlands:

RANDOLPH'S PROSPECTS VERY DOUBTFUL STOP SOCIALIST WIN
PROBABLE STOP MORE STAGS THAN TORIES IN CROMARTY =
BRENDAN

On 27 January Winston was cheered to receive a first-hand account of his son's activities on the campaign trail:

The constituency stretches from the Atlantic to the North Sea and covers a million and a half acres. With an electorate of 27,000 odd this makes only one elector to every $55\frac{1}{2}$ acres. In effect, however, it is not as bad as it sounds as more than 70% of the electorate are on the East Coast in fairly populous districts. We can comfortably reach 20,000 of the electorate from our five Committee rooms at Tain, Invergordon, Dingwall, Strathpepper and Fortrose. Between this strip on the East Coast and a much more sparsely populated strip on the West Coast there is no one at all, only vast forests and mountains.

I have not attempted to organise the West Coast, but am concentrating all my efforts on the 20,000 voters in the East. The electorate, as a whole, are by no means as dour as I had anticipated. The Highlander is a very different cup of tea from the Lowlander.

The distress in the farming community is quite appalling . . . Whereas no one up here has heard of Baldwin, you and Lloyd George are extremely popular, with you definitely in the lead. This is one of the most patriotic parts of the country I have ever struck. There are many retired people and the fisher folk all have a great opinion of your services to the Navy. I was not invited to come here because of my reputation as a specialist in wrecking (as you suggested) but solely on account of you. They are all mystified and puzzled as to why you are not in the Government, and think it an abuse and a scandal. Of course I am besieged with requests that you should come and speak. I tell them all that if they make me their Member you will doubtless come . . .

The *Scotsman* and the *Glasgow Herald* which regarded our chances as derisory when we started, have started to become much more respectful since our meeting at Dingwall a week ago last Saturday. We had more than a thousand people in the Town Hall and I made the best speech I have ever made.

You will be shocked, or gratified, to hear that I have taken to using notes. This is not owing to any failing in fluency, but because there are only two telephone lines between Dingwall and Inverness. If, therefore, one is to get a good show in the press it is necessary to hand out the speech at about 4 o'clock. I do not find them nearly so much of an impediment as I used to, and there is no doubt they improve the cohesion of the argument.

Thus, just as Winston, learning from Randolph's example, was abandoning his full notes in favour of 'garrulous unpremeditated flow', Randolph was actually having to marshall his thoughts on paper. Though Winston took no part in the campaign, there were insinuations in the press of paternal involvement and Winston was prompted to reply privately to at least one of these:

I was surprised to read in the leading article of Saturday's *Times* on the Ross and Cromarty By Election, an insinuation that I had prompted my Son's candidature. As a matter of fact, I strongly advised him to have nothing to do with it. Naturally as a Father, I cannot watch his fight, now that it has begun, without sympathy; but I am taking no part in it, though much pressed to do so by the local people. In these circumstances the innuendo of your leading article is neither true nor fair.

Meanwhile, in the far north, heavy snowfalls and gale force winds played havoc with the candidates' electioneering. The Labour candidate, Hector MacNeil, was involved in a road crash, narrowly avoiding a 100-foot precipice, and Malcolm MacDonald, who according to the *Glasgow Evening News* had taken to touring the constituency clutching a hot-water bottle for warmth, had his glasses smashed and received an eye injury when he was struck in the face by a snowball, causing him to spend two days in hospital. Randolph himself had to battle his way through a blizzard in the hills of Wester Ross, as the *Daily Mail* reported:

> He had been 6½ hours covering 50 miles from Dingwall. First his car came upon a lorry which had been ditched by the roadside. It pulled the lorry out. A blinding blizzard came on, but the party pressed forward. A little farther on it found Mr Churchill's loudspeaker van also in a ditch. It pulled that out. Some miles farther on Mr Churchill's own car ran into a ditch.
>
> Whoever goes to Westminster for Ross and Cromarty will represent not only an electorate which wrests from the earth one of the sternest livings known to man, but some of the most savage grandeur in the world...

More than two hours' work with jacks and spades and heroic exertions by the whole party were necessary to extricate the vehicle, when it was found that the engine was frozen and the car disabled. Randolph was forced to continue his journey in the loudspeaker van.

Nor were the difficulties encountered by Randolph confined only to the weather, as the *News Chronicle* of 30 January made clear:

RANDOLPH 'BULL'
THOUGHT HEIFER WAS A MALE
AND SAID SO TO FARMERS

> Mr Randolph Churchill's worst enemy in the Ross and Cromarty by-election last night proved to be – Mr Randolph Churchill. In a flight of rhetoric he referred to a heifer as a 'little brother'. His audience of farmers in Dingwall market place [where he was standing in for the auctioneer at a cattle market] rocked with laughter. It was not until it was explained to Mr Churchill that the heifer could only be a 'little sister' that he appreciated the 'joke'.

It was no doubt this embarrassing episode which prompted Randolph later in the campaign, when some farmers thought they might have fun at his expense, to make so fierce a riposte that it was still remembered thirty-five years later. In 1970, on the first day I took my seat in Parliament, another newly elected Tory MP, Hamish Gray, representing the Ross and Cromarty seat, greeted me warmly in the Members' Lobby and told me with a broad smile: 'You know, Winston, they still haven't forgotten your father in Ross and Cromarty! At one point in the campaign Randolph, due to snow-drifts, arrived more than two hours late for a meeting in a tiny village hall packed with crofters in their heavy coats and boots. After listening respectfully to his speech the audience was invited to ask questions. After a brief silence a dour character from the back of the hall challenged the speaker: "And could Mr Churchill be telling us – How many toes has a pig?" To which your father, stumped for the answer, replied in a flash: "Take off your bloody boots and count!" '

Magnificent repartee! But scarcely the way to win elections, as became evident on polling day. When the ballot boxes were opened Malcolm MacDonald had won by a clear majority, though nearly five thousand votes fewer than that of the National Government candidate in the general election only three months before. The full result was as follows:

M. MacDonald	(National)	8,949
Hector MacNeil	(Socialist)	5,967
Randolph Churchill	(Unionist)	2,427
Dr. W. S. Russell Thomas	(Liberal)	738
Nat. Govt. majority		2,982

The Liberal candidate lost his deposit and Randolph only saved his by 167 votes. Robert Boothby, who had been Winston's Parliamentary Private Secretary during his most recent term of office, commented in a letter to him two days later: 'I am sorry about Randolph although I feel a little chastening at this particular juncture will not necessarily be to his ultimate disadvantage ... There is more sympathy and friendly feeling for him than he suspects. But, my God, you don't challenge that machine with impunity.'

In a leading article on 13 February the *Edinburgh Evening News* offered a damning verdict on the result:

By emphasizing the unpopularity of the Churchillian's attitude, the decisive defeat of Mr Randolph Churchill in Ross and Cromarty seems to be regarded as another nail in the political coffin of Mr Winston Churchill, either as a candidate for the Admiralty or Cabinet Minister charged with the co-ordination of Defence Services.

This was an unduly harsh verdict on both father and son, in view of the fact that the seat had not been contested by a Unionist candidate for a quarter of a century and that Winston had actively sought to dissuade his son from entering the fray. None the less, in the shorter term, Randolph's action did nothing to advance Churchill's ministerial prospects. But even if it did blight his father's chances of early return to office, in the longer view this was perhaps a blessing in disguise, for it meant that he was not tainted by association with a government firmly committed to the path of appeasement.

On 21 February Winston wrote to Clemmie:

> There is no change in the uncertainty about my affairs. Evidently B. desires above all things to avoid bringing me in. This I must now recognise. But his own position is much shaken, & the storm clouds gather.

Two days later Sir Samuel Hoare, who was given the Admiralty post that Winston coveted and for which his talents and experience made him a natural choice, wrote to Neville Chamberlain:

> On no account would he [Baldwin] contemplate the possibility of Winston in the Cabinet for several obvious reasons, but chiefly for the risk that would be involved by having him in the Cabinet when the question of his [Baldwin's] successor became imminent.

The fact that in the space of twelve months Randolph had unsuccessfully fought no less than three elections personally, as well as a fourth vicariously, prompted Noël Coward to pronounce with his great charm but acid wit: 'I am so very fond of Randolph: he is so unspoiled by failure!' This was unfair on Randolph who, though not yet twenty-five years old, had already established himself as a brilliant public speaker and a courageous, if unsuccessful, campaigner. In all three contests he had had no chance of preparing the ground before the actual start of the three-week campaign, although this was extended at Ross and Cromarty because of the death of King George V. In all but one by-election he was challenging the massed resources of the Conservative Party machine. He did so less in the hope of securing a seat in Parliament than to gain publicity for the causes of India and rearmament which he and his father had espoused. It cannot be denied that, in terms of attracting public attention, he had been dramatically successful; nevertheless the two Churchills failed to convert received opinion, either within the Conservative Party or more widely in the country. It is true that they were slowly arousing the sleeping nation by their repeated warnings of the menace of the Nazi war machine and the threat to peace, but the pace of that awakening was being far outstripped by the escalation of German armaments and by events on the Continent.

In an unpublished memorandum a year later Randolph recorded:

March 7th 1936: Hitler reoccupies the Rhineland. Two days later it was estimated that the total number of troops in the demilitarized zone was not more than 25,000 and these were spread over an area stretching from the lower Rhine and the Rhineland proper to south-west Germany and the upper Rhine Valley adjoining the Black Forest. The four principal towns occupied were Cologne, Mainz, Coblenz and Frankfurt. From the first Hitler said that the re-occupation was purely 'symbolic'...

Hitler's re-occupation of the Rhineland was indeed symbolic at the outset, but as soon as he discovered that no one was prepared to turn him out he set to work on a great line of fortifications. Today his occupation is anything but symbolic...

An emergency debate took place in the House of Commons and, on 11 March 1936, Randolph wrote to Lloyd George:

I feel I must write to congratulate you on your really splendid speech. Although I didn't entirely agree with the conclusions about Germany I thought it the best speech I have ever heard in Parliament. May I also thank you for the generous support you gave my father? I thought it really noble of you and cannot express my admiration for the subtle way you handled that part of your speech. It was a great day for both of you and proved to the whole House what I have always believed that all, save you two, are pygmies.

The former premier replied two days later:

Thank you so much for your warm-hearted letter. It had been in my mind to write you for some days. Having regard to all the conditions in Ross and Cromarty, I thought the result you achieved was very remarkable. I have no doubt that you secured two-thirds, if not four-fifths, of the Conservative votes in the constituency. I doubt, if there had been a straight fight between Conservatives, Liberals and Labour in that constituency, whether the Conservative candidate would have scored many more votes than you did.

What a mess we are getting into over this Rhineland business. However, thank God we have got a strong Government at the helm – firm, resolute, inflexible! I sincerely hope they will have the wisdom to choose your father for Defence Minister. It would be a very popular appointment in the House of Commons. But of course he has to deal with Baldwin's dislike of association with a stronger man than himself and Neville [Chamberlain]'s natural jealousy as to the future.

CHAPTER 9

Partners in the Wilderness

Abandoning the hustings, much to the relief of his harassed father, Randolph plunged back into journalism, writing several articles a week for the *Daily Mail*. However, in the summer of 1936 a family drama blew up involving Randolph's sister Sarah, a spirited redhead of twenty-one, who had decided to make her career on the stage. Without informing her parents, Sarah suddenly eloped to New York aboard the liner *Bremen*, announcing to the press at the Southampton quayside that she was going to marry a vaudeville comedian of Austrian origin by the name of Victor Samek, better known by his stage name of Vic Oliver. An added complication was that Oliver was a married man whose marriage had not yet been legally dissolved in Austria. Much consternation was aroused in the Churchill household at the prospect of Sarah marrying a show-business personality nearly twice her age – possibly a bigamist to boot! Randolph was dispatched in hot pursuit with instructions to pour as much cold water as possible on the romance. He decided at the same time to take advantage of the opportunity to report for the *Daily Mail* the imminent US presidential election, in which the Republican, Governor Landon, was challenging President Roosevelt's bid for a second term.

Randolph arrived in New York on 21 September on board the *Queen Mary* just twenty-four hours behind Sarah, to find himself the centre of a blaze of publicity in which the New York press, in its inimitable way, dubbed him: 'The man who wants to trip Cupid'.

Three weeks later Randolph wrote to his father that while he had not been successful in calling off the marriage, he had persuaded the lovers to await the ratification of Oliver's divorce by the Superior Court in Vienna. He added:

We have thus gained two months in which there is a chance that one of them may change their mind. I raised no objections to Sarah joining his vaudeville act as I am sure the only hope of a change lies in them seeing as much as possible of each other without any restraints.

Sarah played in Boston for a week and was paid $300. This week she is in New York at $750. Her name is up in large lights on Broadway, and she is drawing big crowds. She does a little ballroom dance with quite a good young dancer as her partner. I went to see it yesterday. She looks lovely . . . I am afraid they are both very much in love and I am not very hopeful of any change.

Randolph's prediction proved well-founded. Sarah and Vic Oliver married on 25 December 1936 but their marriage, as so many others, did not survive the war and was dissolved in 1945. Randolph's letter continued:

Tomorrow I leave for Toledo where I meet Landon and then go with him to Detroit . . . There is no difficulty getting access to anyone. I had a little trouble with Roosevelt as Bernie [Baruch] did not want to ask any favours! But he undertook to arrange it if all else failed. However I arranged it through R's daughter. R. was very tired and I didn't think I saw him at his best. He does not approach L.G. [Lloyd George] for charm and magnetism. He spoke very appreciatively of you and your books – particularly Marlborough – and, as I wired you, sent you his love. I am still very anti-Roosevelt! But it looks at the moment as if he would win . . .

I am very well and having an absorbing time. As you know I can't resist elections. I wish I were standing myself.

President Roosevelt, together with his mother Mrs James Roosevelt and his wife Eleanor, had received Randolph at his country home at Hyde Park, NY, where they entertained him to tea in the library. Randolph described the scene in a dispatch for the *Daily Mail*:

As he entered, his features broke into a smile which embraced the whole company, and with a wave of the hand which seemed to dismiss his official cares and duties he was among us, more like a country gentleman in the midst of his family, than as a President about to embark on a strenuous campaign in which he will have to resist the bitter onslaught of the most powerful and influential combination which has ever assailed an American President.

I sat beside the President at tea, and for more than half an hour he conversed with me most freely on a variety of topics ranging from social legislation in Great Britain to the influence of broadcasting on politics and the technique of campaigning . . .

Nearly all the men round him are a liability and if he is re-elected, as most people think he will be, it will be by his own unaided force and personality, and in spite of the many measures for which he has been responsible and of nearly all the men who have been his colleagues in the administration.

His stature dominates the political landscape and dwarfs his opponent Governor Landon as much as it does his own Cabinet.

In between his vain efforts to 'trip Cupid' and the hurly-burly of a presidential election campaign, Randolph also did his best to arouse American public opinion to the gravity of the situation developing in Europe. In an Associated Press interview which he gave on arrival in New York and which was syndicated in newspapers throughout the United States, Randolph said of Hitler:

> We are all mugs if we let him make a world issue of Communism and Fascism – an unreal issue as both are dictatorships . . .
> Hitler is out to play Bismarck's game by crushing his opponents one by one. If England stays out now she will just get it in the neck if Hitler smashes Russia and France. A Franco–British alliance is not enough – there must be an alliance of all the peaceful nations.

He also predicted that Britain would come to the aid of the United States in the event of an attack by Japan – an eventuality foreseen by few at that stage – by implication suggesting to his readers that the United States had a similar moral obligation and self-interest to come to the aid of Britain in the event of war with Germany.

Randolph had been in the United States barely a week when he was presented with the remarkable opportunity of making a radio address to the people of America via the Columbia Broadcasting System – two whole years before his father was to do so. He was not one to pass up such an opportunity lightly and in his broadcast can be detected much of the power and prescience of his father:

> Will there be a war in Europe? When will it come? What will be the line-up? These are the questions which millions are asking today and which will soon be answered by an increasingly rapid succession of events . . .
> Many will tell you that the German people do not want war, and many will tell you that Herr Hitler is a sincere lover of peace. But it is surely significant that Germany is the only country in Europe which is not afraid of war . . . Respecting neither God nor Man the Hitler régime has persecuted and suppressed religious sects with the same pride and exaltation with which it has repudiated treaties.

TELLING THE WORLD

He then proceeded to outline the malignant ambitions of Nazi Germany:

The whole brain and manpower of this gifted and scientific race have been ceaselessly employed during the last four years in the most gigantic armament production the world has ever seen. Last year the United States spent $800 million upon national defence. Great Britain spent about $600 million. $4,000 million was the amount expended by the German government. I wish I could accept the suave reassurances of those who visiting Germany for the Olympic games and noticing trivial facts such as the absence of litter in the streets of Berlin, return to praise the demeanour and intentions of the Nazi Government. What is the use of trying to blind oneself to the real facts? . . .

Herr Hitler has called into being passions, forces and instrumentalities which he will be unable to hold in check even if he should so desire. It is impossible to look coldly and dispassionately upon the European scene without an ever growing conviction that sooner or later Germany will fall upon one or the other of her neighbours. Will it be sooner or will it be later? I am afraid it will be sooner. Germany has practically completed her armaments programme while we in England have only just started to equip and repair our national defences, and it has been well said that

England's hours of weakness is Europe's hour of danger . . .

After expanding on the role of the democracies of Europe, Randolph appealed directly to his American listeners:

Whatever part you may decide to play, and it is not for me to say that detachment may not be the part of wisdom, I am reluctant to believe that the United States could watch unmoved and certainly not without ultimate peril to herself, the final collapse in Europe of democratic government and the replacement all over the world of the ballot box by the machine-gun.

We live in dangerous times. For the last three or four years democracy has been on the run and the military dictatorships have been gaining everywhere at its expense. Germany, in defiance of treaty obligations, has re-armed and is fortifying the Rhineland. Italy has conquered Abyssinia. Japan is increasing her grip on China to the detriment of American and British interests. Where will this process end? If the few remaining democracies in the world are unable to show a little more commonsense and resolution in the face of impending disaster, they will assuredly be assailed from without or engulfed from within, one after the other, by the hydra-headed Communist, Fascist or Nazi dictatorships which man has contrived for his own degradation and enslavement.

The broadcast was a remarkable *tour de force*, combining a clarity of vision and power of expression which few 25-year-olds then, or now, could match. It cannot be denied that brash, arrogant and cocksure though he might be, Randolph had a formidable array of weapons in his political armoury.

Even before Roosevelt's landslide victory, Randolph was correctly pre-dicting that Roosevelt would eventually run for a third term. Following the election he headed out to the West Coast to survey the Hollywood scene for the readers of the *Daily Mail*. While there he lunched with eight-year-old Shirley Temple whom he described as 'the biggest single box-office attraction' at the Twentieth Century-Fox Studios. He also played the part of a member of the House of Commons as an extra in the MGM film *Parnell*. 'My fee for the day's work was 30 shillings,' he proclaimed with delight: 'A real MP gets just over a guinea!' He even managed to scoop all the Hollywood gossip columnists by announcing that Charlie Chaplin, to whose dinner party he had been invited, had, more than two years before, secretly married Miss Paulette Goddard at a ceremony aboard Charlie's yacht the *Panacea*, at which the skipper had officiated. In a story immediately snapped up by Hearst's *Los Angeles Examiner* Randolph confided to his readers: 'I am not at liberty to quote Mr Chaplin directly. But I can definitely say they are married.'

In addition he found time to enliven and outrage large sections of Hollywood's film colony. Writing some three years later Oscar Levant, the American pianist and composer, recalled Randolph's visit in *A Smattering of Ignorance*:

> Regardless of whether a visitor to the Coast was a Cabinet member, a banker or the dean of a university, he rarely appeared in Hollywood without a letter of introduction to Harpo. In due course he would make his way to the Marx dinner table where Harpo presided over his cluster of disciples like a mute Socrates.
>
> Only on one occasion did we encounter someone who could euphemistically be described as our match. This was the youthful Randolph Churchill, son of England's First Lord of the Admiralty, Winston Churchill. He came with the reputation of being even more than a London equivalent of me – the most bumptious, loud mouthed, impertinent person that English society has produced in our generation. At dinner he succeeded in insulting everybody at the table before the main course had arrived. It was at the time when Landon was contesting Roosevelt's right to a second term in the White House, and Churchill argued vehemently for the merits of the Republican, as if the election had not already been decided two days before. Since one of Harpo's most treasured possessions was an inscribed photograph of the President, it may be understood how popular this made Churchill with his host.
>
> After dinner we attempted to exact retribution by taking Churchill to a ping-pong parlour and imposing on him the labour of retrieving the balls, which, mysteriously, were being batted consistently to the most inaccessible corners of the room. This did not faze him, however, nor did it diminish his capacity for the querulous ...

When Randolph finally sailed for home in mid-December Heywood Broun, the American columnist, treated him to a valedictory accolade in the *New York World Telegram*:

> Randolph Churchill, England's Ambassador of ill-will, has gone home breathing maledictions upon our native press. I have known Randy, cub and boy for 15 years, and as he approaches maturity he grows more

annoying with every birthday. It is an art with him, and since I recognise it as such he cannot get my goat any more.

When first we met, young Churchill was about 16 [in fact nineteen]. He was engaged on a lecture tour and went about the country telling women's clubs what was wrong with American politics, customs and cookery. He was even then a journalistic delight because if any news reporter asked him what he thought of our skyline or the American woman, Randy would tell him in no uncertain terms. I rather gather the young Churchill thought the American woman looked best in a heavy fog. But, of course, it was seldom if ever necessary to ask Randy. He was the first to volunteer. The Immature Churchill.

At the age of 16 I observed him in drawing rooms interrupting his elders and telling them where they got off. But it came to be so magnificent that you could hardly call it bad manners. It was Promethean, and you could almost hear the flapping of the vultures on their way home to peck at little Mr Churchill's liver.

The reference to Randolph's liver had a distinct echo in a letter from Lord Rothermere who, early in 1937, commissioned him to report the Civil War in Spain which had been raging, with massive bloodshed, for more than six months:

My dear Randolph,

I am consenting to your going to Spain on the very strict understanding that you will under no circumstances expose yourself to any risk.

You will be under the tutelage of Cardozo who has similar instructions from me.

I suggest you stay in Spain for six weeks. You ought to collect quite a lot of material for a good book.

Regarding my bet with you, you have my full permission to drink the wine of the country and beer but no spirits or foreign wines. When you return you will of course go out to win your bet in regard to a strict teetotal regime.

Affectionately yours,
Rothermere

PS Never forget you are an only son.

Lord Rothermere's bets with the Churchills, *père et fils*, to encourage them both to abandon or severely reduce their intake of liquor had become a not unimportant source of income and, for Randolph, they formed an aid to good health. At the end of the previous year and after losing a similar wager Rothermere had written: 'Here is the £500 [over £17,000 in today's money]. I hope the wager has done you a lot of physical good. Everyone seems to think so ...' Sadly, neither the bets nor Randolph's liver were to stand the test of time.

Learning of Randolph's plans Clemmie, on a skiing holiday in Switzerland with her daughter Mary, wrote immediately, displaying all the worries of a mother whose only son is going off to war:

> Do please be very careful and do not get in the way of any bullets or bombs, & take plenty of warm jerseys as I believe Spain can be colder than the North Pole. And what about being inoculated? It will be frightfully interesting, but try not to get ill. I wish I was going to see you before you go? But I send this in case you are starting at once. I'm so much interested about your flat & about Sarah & her husband having the one immediately below you. We are all congregated in a nice little bunch in Westminster...

Winston, too, was apprehensive. As Randolph recalled in the first volume of his biography of his father, Winston, some forty years after his own baptism of fire in the Cuban Revolutionary War in 1896, sought to restrain Randolph from going to Spain:

> He pointed out how difficult it would be to write objectively about a war (quite apart from the difficulties of censorship) when you were on one side of the lines. He further told his son that he must on no account later go to the other side; in that case he would be suspected by both sides of being a spy. This latter advice was heeded. In retrospect – though it was frustrating at the time – it was a good thing that General Franco's public relations officer only allowed the author once to come under fire about two miles outside Madrid.

When, thirty years on, my father sought to give me similar advice, I rejected it. On the contrary I made a habit, when reporting conflicts in the Middle East or Africa, of visiting both sides. Indeed, many were the occasions when I walked with my suitcase across the Allenby Bridge that spans the River Jordan between Jordan and Israel.

Randolph's first report from General Franco's headquarters in Salamanca, published in the *Daily Mail* on 1 March 1937, left the reader in no doubt as to which side he supported:

> 'A humane and equitable clemency is a policy which can ensure a rec-

onciled and united Spain.' This was the keynote of a statement made to me today by General Franco at his headquarters. 'Here in Salamanca,' General Franco declared, 'we Nationalists are prosecuting the war with all possible rigour, but do not forget that from Burgos we are already administering more than half Spain. Soon we shall be ruling all Spain – from Madrid . . .'

General Franco wisely tolerates no politics in the Army, and you do not have to be in Spain more than a few days to realise the power behind him is a straightforward Nationalist and Patriotic movement. The issues at stake today in Spain transcend all party lines. A united Spain which guarantees the rights of property, the sanctity of religion, and the integrity of the courts of justice is the vital need which has brought together all that is best among the Spanish people to overthrow the degrading and tyrannical concepts of the Madrid Communists.

It is impossible to witness at close quarters the struggle that is being fought out here without being convinced that General Franco's victory is essential if Spain is once more to take her place as a great historic and civilised member of the European family.

Two days later Randolph received a telegram of approbation from his parents:

YOUR MOTHER AND I THINK YOUR REPORT EXCELLENT MUCH
LOVE = PAPA

Meanwhile Randolph set about devising a means of beating all his journalistic rivals covering the Franco side in the event of any major developments on the Nationalist side. He confided to his father:

Avila, Saturday, March 13th
3.30 a.m.

For the last three days I have been going daily to Salamanca (about 100 kilometres from here) trying to arrange a scheme whereby the *Daily Mail* news service can be expedited. At last we have triumphed . . . The point at issue was this – Press telegrams even at triple rate are taking upwards of 16 hours to reach London and this all too often means news going stale while the correspondents in Madrid can telegraph direct to London. With infinite difficulty we have at last persuaded the authorities to grant Hartin [Randolph's colleague] a permanent *laisser-passer* across the frontier. We shall telegraph from Talavera to San Sebastian and he will motor across the

frontier and telephone from Hendaye direct to London. This should enable
us to cover the taking of Madrid and beat everybody else by a clear day . . .
    The conditions under which we work are childish in the extreme. We
are never allowed to go near to a front where there is any fighting and are
almost wholly dependent upon the official communiqués. The present
attack upon Guadalajara from the North is not going as fast as we hoped,
but if it succeeds we ought to be in Madrid within 18 or 20 days. If it fails
there may be great delay. From the little I have seen, Franco's victory is,
however, inevitable . . .

Randolph, having had his first experience of shell-fire on the outskirts
of Madrid, described to his father how he was seeking to overcome the
perennial privations confronting a journalist in a war zone:

Tuesday, March 22, 1937   *Hotel Ingles,*
                                                                      Avila

My dear Papa,
    The hotel here boasts every discomfort. Two baths for 70 people and
the water is always cold. The food is typical of the peninsula. Masses of it,
eight courses at every meal, one more unpalatable than the other. We have
bought a leg of mutton and with M. Botto of *Havas* I am just about to
sally forth to a bistro and supervise its preparation . . .
    Both Cardozo and Hartin have been exceedingly kind to me and we
all get on extraordinarily well. Once the fighting starts there will be plenty
of stories for all of us . . . From the little I have so far seen I should judge
that there is no reason for you to alter your basic views upon the general
character of the fighting.
    I have just heard the result of the Oxford by-election. I am indeed sorry
that the Prof [Lindemann] did not get in. However I'm still 2 up on him
in that respect . . . Please don't worry about me. I could not get into
trouble even if I wanted to!

                                                        Your loving son,
                                                        Randolph

After spending Easter in Seville, where his father had urged him to
see the Dance of the Acolytes before the High Altar which he described
as 'unique in the Christian world', Randolph reported that Franco had
assumed supreme power. He wound up his reporting of the Civil War
with an exclusive interview with the Generalissimo published in the
Daily Mail of 23 April:

Salamanca, Wednesday
'Victory will come to us with the close of hostilities. We cannot coun-
tenance any negotiations or compromise.' So declared General Franco to
me today in the first interview he has given since the Guadelajara engagement . . . General Franco at 44 is the world's youngest dictator.

He allowed me to question him freely on a wide variety of topics and,
bearing in mind the wartime need for secrecy on many subjects, his
answers were extraordinarily frank. I asked him about the future relations
of his Government with Great Britain. 'Friendly relations with your
country are traditional in Spain,' he said. 'We would have preferred that
these relations should never have been interrupted and Great Britain has
proof of this. British interests in the Mediterranean are perfectly compatible
with those of a strong national Spain.'

Earlier in the month, in a Commons foreign affairs debate on 14
April, Winston had intervened to press for Britain's continued neutrality
towards Spain:

I refuse to become the partisan of either side. I will not pretend that, if I
had to choose between Communism and Nazi-ism, I would choose
Communism. I hope not to be called upon to survive in the world under
a government of either of these dispensations. I cannot feel any enthusiasm
for these rival creeds. I feel unbounded sorrow and sympathy for the
victims.

Winston culminated his speech with a powerful appeal to the nations
of Europe to abandon the arms race and call a halt to the drift towards
'some hideous catastrophe'. Even one of his strongest critics (Henry)
'Chips' Channon, Conservative MP for Southend, was moved to note
in his diary:

Winston Churchill made a terrific speech, brilliant, convincing, unanswerable and his 'stock' has soared, and today people are buying 'Churchills',
and saying once more that he ought to be in the government, and that it
is too bad to keep so brilliant a man out of office; but were he to be given
office, what would it mean? an explosion of foolishness after a short time?
war with Germany? a seat for Randolph?

Towards the end of the previous year, in the course of Randolph's
absence in the United States, a major constitutional crisis had arisen over

the publicly declared determination of the new King, Edward VIII, to marry an American divorcee, Mrs Wallis Simpson.

Randolph recalled these events twenty years later, in an article for the *American Weekly*:

> ... I arrived in New York on the *Queen Mary* on September 21 and, after a tour of the Middle West, I happened to be back in New York around November 20. I received a telephone call from my friend Lord Beaverbrook asking me to visit him at the Waldorf-Astoria. He told me that he had arrived that morning on the *Bremen* and was returning to England the following day on the same ship. I expressed surprise that his visit should be so brief but he very properly did not disclose to me the reason. Later, back in London, he told me the whole story and in particular of how in mid-ocean, between Southampton and New York, he had received the King's secret summons to return and advise him on the crisis which was about to break on his head and engulf his throne.
>
> It was not until the early days of December that the news broke from London and that the world realised that the King intended to marry Mrs Simpson ... The papers were full of the wildest and most contradictory reports and naturally all my American friends sought me out to know what was the truth. I was no better informed than they were and as a devoted monarchist, surrounded by so many republicans, I experienced many unhappy moments. It was a time when any Englishman acutely felt the need to be at home and I decided to sail on the next ship, which happened to be the *Normandie*. I well remember the mixed but deep emotions with which I heard the King make his abdication speech while the *Normandie* was heading towards Europe. I remember too the civilised comprehension of the French people on board.

Stanley Baldwin, the Prime Minister of the day, had confronted the King with an ultimatum that neither his government nor the Labour or Liberal parties would agree to serve in an administration in the event that the King went ahead with his decision to marry Mrs Simpson, while remaining on the throne. Under this extreme pressure the King took the decision to abdicate but not before Churchill, who was fiercely loyal to the monarchy and deeply sentimental about the plight of the King, had incurred the massive odium of his parliamentary colleagues by demanding that the King should be granted more time to decide his future. In adopting this position he found himself with even less support in the House of Commons than he had had in his fight against the India Bill.

Randolph went on to recount his father's last meeting with Edward as King:

When Sir Winston Churchill had luncheon with the King at Fort Belvedere on the day of the Abdication, the King presented him with a photograph which he signed 'Edward, R.I.' [Rex Imperator]. It was the last time that he was able thus to sign himself. After they had discussed the speech which, as Duke of Windsor, he was going to make that night from Windsor Castle before going into exile, Sir Winston left. The King saw him to his car and Sir Winston, before entering it, deeply moved by the occasion and stirred with emotion, recited the famous lines of Andrew Marvell about the demeanour of King Charles I at his execution:

'He nothing common did or mean
Upon that memorable scene.'

With this Sir Winston took leave of his old friend who, during the luncheon, had ceased to be King.

In May 1937 Randolph went to France to cover the wedding of the Duke of Windsor, as the King had become following his abdication. In the course of the three weeks or so that he was reporting from the Château de Cande, near Tours, Randolph made firm friends with an American, Ken Downs, Paris bureau chief for United Press International, who later had a distinguished wartime career as a commander in the US Office of Strategic Services. As Downs recalled in Kay Halle's book, *Randolph Churchill: The Young Unpretender*:

Those three weeks, some of the most delightful I ever knew, were worth more than a year at any university for me. I was a graduate of the old Front Page school of journalism and rated as a star reporter at home. But I was new to the European scene, and my ignorance was vast. It was great good luck for me to meet this brilliant mind, generous spirit and a mine of information at that time. Randolph loved arguments. He was a verbal brawler by nature . . .
Randolph's love, adoration and respect for his father knew no bounds. His affection was fully reciprocated by Winston, and the relationship between this gifted pair was a thing of beauty in those days. Randolph telephoned him almost every evening to report on the gossip from Cande and Tours, and to receive the news from London. He also made frequent calls to Lord Beaverbrook, the proprietor of the rival *Daily Express* who had an insatiable appetite for gossip.

Randolph was not drinking in those days. He had no need for drink. He was exuberantly gay, vigorous and interested in everything. He required no artificial stimulation. But that was not the reason he was on the wagon. The reason was a bet of £1,000 apiece which he had made with Rothermere and Beaverbrook, the Press lords and Churchill family friends, that he would not take a drink throughout 1937. £2,000 [equivalent to over £65,000 today] in those days was worth $10,000 and constituted a very respectable sum.

Later in that month of May, he was put to a test on the wager when Stanley Baldwin resigned as Prime Minister in London. Baldwin was anathema to the Churchills. Randolph was wildly exultant at news of the resignation. He immediately called his father. After an exchange of felicitations Randolph said, 'Sir, I think this calls for a very special celebration, do you think it would be improper for me to ask Max and Lord Rothermere for a one-day dispensation in my wager?'

Winston chuckled in appreciation and said he did not think such a request would be out of order. Randolph then called Beaverbrook and Rothermere. Both were amused at this request and graciously granted the one-day dispensation...

Apart from Randolph's total honesty, high spirits and sense of fun, Ken Downs saw another side of his character before the vigil outside the gates of the Château de Cande was over:

He had one formidable problem in journalism – the publishers. He would brook no tampering with his copy, and whenever one of his stories was refused, especially if the reason was timidity, he went wild with anger.

I saw the first example of this during the Windsor wedding story. Randolph did not bother with day-to-day reporting, which was handled by other reporters for the *Daily Mail*. Apart from covering the wedding itself, he planned only one big story, a friendly exposition of the position of the Duke of Windsor, based on his private conversations at the Château.

He composed this paper with great care and it was a good one. He read it over the phone to Winston, who suggested a change here and there, including a reduction in the number of mentions of 'the woman he loves'.

'That phrase is getting a little shop worn over here,' Winston said. 'You know, when the plumber is late these days, it is because of the woman he loves.'

But the conservative *Daily Mail* developed cold feet about using a story so friendly to Windsor and decided not to publish. Randolph raged at one editor after another, and appealed all the way to Rothermere. When he failed there, he telephoned Lord Beaverbrook of the rival *Daily Express*, read him the story and asked if he cared to use it. The canny Beaver expressed surprise that the *Daily Mail* would not use such a fine story . . .

Randolph was not prepared to see a major story of his spiked by a weak-kneed proprietor at home. Accordingly, he sent a letter of resignation to Lord Rothermere who accepted it without demur, wishing him well in his future career. The story – a world scoop – was published anonymously in the *Daily Express* of 2 June 1937 under the headline 'The Duke As He Is Today'. Meanwhile, Randolph sold his services to the Londoner's Diary column of the *Evening Standard* for the modest fee of £30 per week which, as he soon complained, only covered his out-of-pocket expenses. Nevertheless his association with the *Standard* was to last, off and on, for the thirty remaining years of his life.

Randolph was one of the very few to be invited to the Windsors' wedding. The Duchess explained why in her memoirs, *The Heart Has Its Reasons*:

Our one desire was to be married in peace and as quietly as possible. To invite all our friends was out of the question. David had asked his old equerry, Fruity Metcalfe to be his best man. And there were other old friends whose hearts and loyalty had remained steadfast in his time of trouble – Hugh Lloyd Thomas, Walter Monckton, George Allen, Lady Selby, Randolph Churchill and, of course, Lady Alexandra Metcalfe, and Eugene and Kitty de Rothschild.

CHAPTER 10

'Munich!'

While England and the world were diverted by royal events the scene was darkening in Europe. In addition to his almost daily contribution of gossip, background and comment to the *Evening Standard* Londoner's Diary Randolph spent much time reporting developments in Germany. On 24 September 1937 he went to Munich to report Mussolini's meeting with Hitler:

> Mussolini comes here tomorrow. The Leader of Fascism will meet the Leader of National Socialism with high ceremony...
>
> Under the photographs of the two great men appears what we must hope will not prove an ironic touch: 'The guarantors of European Peace.'
>
> The most solemn moment of Mussolini's eight-hours' stay in Munich will be when he lays a wreath on the tombs of those who fell in the 'Putsch' of 1923. For it was in Munich that National Socialism, almost unheeded, began. On February 24, 1920, an obscure agitator bearing the unknown name of Adolf Hitler addressed a small meeting of his followers in the Hofbräuhaus and laid down the Twenty-five points of his programme.
>
> In any other town in Germany such a movement would have been treated seriously from the outset, and so perhaps would have come to nothing; but in Munich (where Lenin had once passed a winter without causing any excitement) a man with revolutionary ideas could gain a foothold with little comment or opposition. Soon the foothold became a stronghold, and Hitler had Bavaria at his back while still almost without a following in the North. Now that Hitler is supreme and all the other parties have been liquidated by the triumph of National Socialism, Munich has become the political Mecca of the Nazi party. Here amid the scenes of their earliest struggles are almost sacred shrines of the movement...
>
> Munich enjoys another distinction. It is Hitler's home town. In Munich he has an unpretentious flat in the Prinz Regenstrasse. In Berlin he calls himself a politician. In Munich he regards himself as a Burger or private citizen. He hardly ever wears a uniform and moves about the town almost unguarded. He lunches in public restaurants. In the afternoon he may even be seen drinking his chocolate or camomile tea with a few friends in a café.

A fortnight later Randolph was in Berlin again for the Duke and Duchess of Windsor's visit as the personal guests of the Führer, when the Duke was so ill advised as to offer the Nazi salute. In February 1938 he returned there to report Hitler's latest purge in which thirteen senior army and air force generals and a large number of other officers were dismissed.

Throughout this period Randolph seems to have taken particular delight in 'rotting' (a favourite phrase of his) his cousin, Unity Mitford, one of the six daughters of Lord Redesdale and sister of Tom Mitford, his best friend at Eton, for her overtly pro-Nazi activities. On 7 September 1937 he reported:

> The Mitford family have, as usual, sent a powerful delegation to the Nazi congress in Nuremberg. Three of Lord Redesdale's children are attending this year, as the personal guests of the Führer – Miss Unity Mitford, who spends a large part of the year in Munich and who is a personal friend of Herr Hitler, Mrs Bryan Guinness and Mr T. D. Mitford...
>
> Not all the members of the Mitford family are as well disposed to the Nazi regime as the contingent who are now in Nuremberg. Another of Lord Redesdale's daughters, Jessica, is married to her Communist cousin, Mr Esmond Romilly. She shares her husband's political faith, and accompanied him recently on a political mission to Bilbao shortly before the Basque capital fell into the hands of General Franco.

At this time relations between Randolph and his father were temporarily soured by a foolish and deliberately provocative dinner-table remark of Randolph's in which he suggested that his father had sent Leslie Hore-Belisha, who was Secretary of State for War and had recently paid two visits to Chartwell, a gift with a view to currying political favour with him. Winston, not surprisingly, was outraged and refused to speak to Randolph for the rest of dinner.

This prompted Randolph to write his father a letter, not of apology, but of remonstrance:

14 February 1938

My dear Papa,

I am sorry that you took my jocular remark so seriously. You yourself are apt in conversation to permit yourself many extravagant images and phrases, but I notice that if ever I say anything that is intended ironically you insist on taking it literally.

I quite agree that this particular remark was clumsily worded, but its very crudity would have been enough, I should have thought, to have obviated any chance of your thinking that I meant it seriously.

Yet you proceeded to 'cut' me for the rest of dinner. If there had not been a stranger present I should certainly have left rather than submit to such extraordinary treatment from my host and my father ...

An expression of surprise at my clumsiness would have been quite enough to have bought from me an apology for my stupidity.

When two people know each other as well as we do, it ought to be possible to solve misunderstandings other than by relapsing into moody silence.

Your loving son,
Randolph

His father was not mollified, replying the same day:

14 February 1938

My dear Randolph,

I thought yr remark singularly unkind, offensive & untrue; & I am sure no son shd have made it to his father. Your letter in no way removes the pain it caused me, not only on my own account but on yours & also on account of our relationship. I was about to write to you to ask you to excuse me from coming to luncheon with you on Thursday, as I really cannot run the risk of such insults being offered to me; and do not feel I want to see you at the present time.

Your loving father,
Winston S. Churchill

The next day, Randolph renewed his grudging apology:

15 February 1938

My dear Papa,

Thank you for your letter. I am most upset by your attitude. You described my remark as untrue. I agree. It was so absurdly untrue that I cannot conceive how you ever supposed that it was other than ironic.

But since you chose, I know not why, to take it seriously I took the earliest opportunity of writing to you to explain that it was only an inept gesture and to apologize for it.

I don't see what more I can do ...

If, infected by the violence of your own language, and in the heat of an argument, I used words unbecoming for a Son, I should have thought you might have excused such conduct, particularly when assured that it was accidental.

Your unforgiving and ungenerous attitude can only be explained by supposing that you reject my assurance that I had no intention of insulting you ...

I am sorry you will not lunch with me on Thursday.

Your loving son,
Randolph

But his father was not to be so easily appeased:

16 February 1938

My dear Randolph,

I do not understand how what you said could be looked upon as 'jocular' or ironic. It was grossly rude, & as such wounded me deeply. It is not enough when you have insulted someone to say it was a joke & to reproach them with attaching importance to small things. If, as you protest, you did not mean to be offensive, surely when you saw that I was hurt, you cd have said 'I am sorry. I ought not to have said such a thing.' Instead you complain in yr first letter that I did not continue to converse with you as if nothing had happened. I really did not & do not want such a thing to happen again. I do not see why at my age I shd be subjected to such taunts from a son I have tried to do my best for.

It was a vy base thing for you to suggest that the small gift I gave was given to curry favour presumably in the hopes of gaining political or personal advantage. It was given out of kindness of heart, & of some pity wh I felt, for a man I do not much like, but who had appealed to me for advice & spoken much of his loneliness etc. I wonder you are not even now ashamed that such a thought shd have sprung so readily to yr mind and yr lips. I have not deserved it of you.

There is no question of my 'owing you a grudge'. I shall always do my best to help you, and I have no doubt the extremely unpleasant impression wh I sustained will wear out and pass away in a little while. Meantime you are welcome to yr own self-justification wh appear to be in your eyes complete.

Your loving father,
Winston S. Churchill

Winston evidently felt that this was a rather harsh rejoinder and sent Randolph a further note later the same day:

16 February 1938

My dear Randolph,
  On yr letter I don't see why you did not, as soon as you saw I was offended, say you were sorry. But all the same I forgive you.

Your loving father,
Winston S. Churchill

Nevertheless Randolph's accusation rankled with his father and the dispute rumbled on in a further letter from Randolph who could never accept having the penultimate say in any dispute:

1 March 1938

My dear Papa,
  I'm afraid I was rather *de trop* at your party tonight. I put off a dinner engagement in order to dine with you. Subsequently you told me that you were going to make a speech and suggested that we should have supper afterwards. I was delighted at the opportunity of hearing you speak and was in the House from 8.30 onwards.
  When I asked for you after the debate I found that you had gone without leaving any message for me.
  After a good deal of telephoning I discovered where you were and came along.
  Your reception of me was not very cordial and I felt that I was butting in. In the course of the evening you twice went out of your way to warn me against repeating what you said without making any such admonition to the rest of the company.
  As I wrote to you before, I do not think I have ever betrayed anything you have told me, and I find it intolerable that you should publicly treat me with less confidence than you show towards others whose love and devotion for you is scarcely likely to equal mine.
  I should have thought that a sensitive man like yourself could easily envisage the deep humiliation I feel when my discretion is repeatedly called in question by you in front of hacks like David Margesson [the Government Chief Whip] and Victor Warrender [formerly a Whip, then Financial Secretary at the War Office] and that amiable flibbertigibbet Brendan . . .
  When I was thirteen and fourteen years old you did me the compliment

of treating me almost as if I were a grown up. Now that I am about 27 you treat me as a wayward and untrustworthy child...
Please forgive this lengthy outburst. I hope you will not think it bitter. I know that you are fond of me, and I think you know the love & respect and admiration I have for you. But I cannot comprehend why you should crucify all these feelings by treating me with such obvious contempt before such men of straw.

> Your loving son,
> Randolph

These rows between Randolph and his father were, more than anything, a consequence of the similarities in their characters. In addition to being brilliant, witty and fluent, both were egocentric and opinionated. Each relished verbal duels and rhetorical jousting matches. Randolph, however, carried his enjoyment of what he called 'a jolly row' somewhat further than his father and, all too often, to the point of excess. He just could not resist 'stirring things up' and – without a trace of malice – coming out with the most outrageously provocative statements. He would do this either to discomfit someone whom he thought was behaving badly – especially those in high places who were 'falling below the level of events', to use the judgmental yardstick that he would frequently apply to others – or, as often as not, merely to ensure that the conversation was never in danger of relapsing into tedium. Encouraged by his own natural sense of mischief and high spirits and – when not seeking to win Lord Rothermere's bets – fortified with Scotch whisky, his loquacity and verbal pugnacity knew no bounds. He could never understand that others might not enjoy it all quite as much as he did.

But though his relationship with his father was punctuated by a series of rows – which at times in later life became so blazing that his mother was to ban him from their house – Randolph was always utterly loyal and devoted to him and, except when they were alone together, his fiercest defender and staunchest ally.

These were difficult and trying times for Winston. Out of office and already well in to his sixties, believing he was 'in the last decade of my life', he found himself confronted not only by massive political problems, but financial ones as well. In spite of his very substantial earnings from his vast literary output – *Marlborough*, *Great Contemporaries* and his *History of the English-Speaking Peoples*, in addition to a constant flood of articles for the press – he was faced with the prospects of having to sell his beloved Chartwell. He even considered abandoning his political career to make some money in the City. Underlying these personal worries and frustrations was his deep and gnawing anxiety about the intentions of Nazi Germany which, he saw, were leading Europe remorselessly towards another world war. With equal clarity he saw how the freedom and peace of Europe might be saved but, by a cruel fate, found himself powerless to influence the course of events that continued to spiral downwards towards catastrophe with ever greater rapidity.

By the beginning of 1938 the situation in Europe had become critical. Germany was rearmed and had placed her industry on a war footing. She had already torn up the Treaties and garrisoned the Rhineland. Now, through the powerful local Nazi organisations and relentless propaganda, pressure was brought to bear on Austria. Meanwhile in Britain the Chamberlain Government, which had rejected all of Churchill's calls to launch an all-out rearmament programme – by December 1937 Germany was producing military aircraft at the rate of 600 per month compared to just 200 per month in Britain – found itself powerless to shape the outcome of events in Central Europe. On 18 February Anthony Eden resigned as Foreign Secretary, following Chamberlain's insistence on negotiating, behind his back and against his advice, with Hitler and Mussolini. Barely three weeks later, on 14 March 1938, German forces crossed the border into Austria and Hitler made his way in triumph to Vienna. Austria was at once incorporated into the Nazi Reich.

That same day Randolph, in his report of these events for the *Evening Standard*, could not resist returning his focus to the Mitford sisters:

When Herr Hitler arrives in Vienna this evening his most ardent English admirer will be there to greet him. Miss Unity Mitford, Lord Redesdale's Nordic-looking daughter, had a special pass valid for two persons, given to her yesterday by the wish of the Führer and she and Mrs Victor Cochran Baillie left for Vienna last night . . .

Miss Mitford and her sister, Mrs Bryan Guinness, were in Cologne when Herr Hitler arrived there after the German Army re-entered the Rhineland in March, 1936. Herr Hitler recognised them at once in the Hotel lobby, invited them to join him for lunch and placed them in Field-Marshal von Blomberg's car when he drove in triumph through the streets of Cologne that afternoon.

Field-Marshal Goering admires the Mitford sisters as much as the Führer does. Some time ago they both attended a banquet over which he presided in Berlin. In the middle of the meal the Field Marshal banged the table and, rising to his feet with a cry of '*Ruhe! Ruhe!*' (Quiet, Quiet), proclaimed: 'I want to say that I consider Frau Goering, Lady Guinness and Miss Mitford to be the most perfect Aryan women I have ever seen.' After this brief pronouncement the great man resumed his seat.

A month later, Randolph returned to the saga of Miss Mitford, who had since returned to England:

Miss Unity Mitford, who was attacked by a crowd in Hyde Park yesterday, is returning to Germany immediately after Easter. She hopes that Herr Hitler will give her another Nazi party badge to replace the one she lost in yesterday's scrimmage. Foreigners are not allowed to wear the swastika badge in Germany. The Führer gave Miss Mitford an autographed one he had specially made for her so that she could wear the party emblem without fear of being molested by the secret police . . .

In his column of 25 April, however, Randolph was at pains to pour cold water on any suggestion that Miss Mitford might marry the Führer:

Lord Redesdale's denial of rumours that his daughter, Miss Unity Mitford, is to marry Herr Hitler will carry conviction to all who know the Führer. He is not the marrying type . . .

Randolph's cousin Lord Redesdale – evidently at the end of his tether – felt impelled to write a letter of protest to Randolph: 'Nearly every day now you use some members of my family for two purposes: 1. To make money for yourself. 2. For your anti-Nazi propaganda . . .' Redesdale even had the nerve to offer to pay him to lay off the subject. To this Randolph rejoined:

It surprises me very much to discover that the publicity that some of your relations have achieved is distasteful to them. I had always understood that those of them who suffer from such inordinate admiration for the tyrannous and barbarous methods of the Nazis were extremely proud of their views and did not have the least desire to hide them under a bushel . . .

Undeterred, Randolph reported later in the year:

The wildest rumours continue to circulate about Sir Oswald Mosley's marriage to the former Mrs Bryan Guinness. The facts are as follows: The marriage took place in the private house of Dr Goebbels in Berlin in

October 1936. There is no truth in the story that Herr Hitler was best man. Both he and Dr Goebbels were present, but only as guests . . .

Meanwhile the focus of events began to move sharply East towards Czechoslovakia and, as early as 20 April, Randolph warned readers of the *Evening Standard*:

> I hear that the German general staff have advised Herr Hitler that if he wishes to incorporate the Sudeten Deutsch population of Czechoslovakia in the Reich without bloodshed he must entrust the enterprise exclusively to the army.
>
> The General Staff have pointed out that if the Nazi Party took a hand as they took in Austria by stirring up trouble in advance, the Czech army would be on the alert and resistance would be inevitable.
>
> Apart from the local bloodshed which this would involve, and which Herr Hitler is most anxious to avoid, a determined resistance on the part of the Czechs might provoke a major European war . . .

With developments in Central Europe propelling the continent to war, Randolph decided that the time had come to find a place for himself in the Armed Forces. Three years earlier, in conversation with his father, he had expressed an interest in securing a place in his old regiment, the 4th Queen's Own Hussars. Then, in the summer of 1937, he had explored with Philip Sassoon, of 601 Squadron at Hendon, the possibility of joining an auxiliary squadron of the Royal Air Force. Indeed Vere Harvey, who had recently taken over command of 615 Squadron based at Kenley in Surrey, had written on 1 October 1937 inviting him to join. However Randolph, doubtless wisely, recognised that his talents did not extent to the field of military aviation and decided instead to join his father's regiment. His father was delighted and promptly wrote to the commanding officer of the 4th Hussars, Major General Sir R. W. W. R. Barnes:

6 July 1938

I wonder if, as Colonel of the regiment, you could give me any information on a personal matter? My son Randolph who is twenty-seven years of age and who, as you know, has pushed about a bit in politics, is extremely anxious to join the supplementary reserve of a regular regiment. Although his work as one of the chief contributors to 'The Londoner's Diary' in the *Evening Standard* makes considerable demands upon him, he would be able to go through the necessary courses and to attend such other drills and training as is required. He thinks it his duty to acquire military training and to have a space marked out for himself should trouble come.

I do not know whether cavalry regiments have a supplementary reserve, but if so I thought perhaps you might be able to help me in getting him such a commission in the 4th Hussars. Although we have such a small army it seems frightfully difficult for anyone to get into it.

Randolph was accepted into his father's old regiment and agreed to do the three months' training required to become a reserve officer starting on 1 September. Meanwhile, following a brief holiday in Greece, he wrote on 15 August to a Greek friend:

The news from Germany seems very menacing and it is hard to tell whether they are merely trying to get their way in Czechoslovakia by bluff or whether they really mean business. Most well-informed people here take a grave view, and I think there can be no doubt that if Germany actually does march both England and France will be involved within a week. If only the Germans were sure of us I, personally, believe they would not move...

By late summer Randolph's predictions were on the point of being fulfilled. With Nazi pressure on Czechoslovakia increasing fiercely, Chamberlain decided to fly to Germany on 15 September to negotiate directly with Hitler at Berchtesgaden. The news of Chamberlain's visit was telephoned to Beaverbrook, whose *Daily Express* had long been preaching its soothing 'There will be no war' gospel, that night while Randolph was dining with him at Stornoway House, his London home. As Alan Wood records in *The True History of Lord Beaverbrook*:

Beaverbrook, rather taken aback, decided after a moment's thought that this was splendid, and told the *Daily Express* to be delighted about it. Randolph went to phone the news to his father: Churchill, a political exile at the time, was alone that night at Chartwell where he was finishing his *Life of Marlborough*. At first Churchill thought his son was trying to play a joke on him: as soon as Randolph convinced him that Chamberlain was really going, Churchill saw in a second that the news meant surrender for the moment and war before long. Randolph heard him break down and weep with anger and misery. Back in the drawing room at Stornoway

House they were drinking champagne to celebrate Chamberlain's mission. They asked Randolph: 'Well, what did old Winston say?' Randolph answered: 'He cried.' There was a pause for a time in the synthetic gaiety at Stornoway.

That same night Randolph wrote to his father:

I'm just off to Aldershot – to learn the goosestep. I'm afraid the fun & zest has gone out of my military career.

Please in future emulate my deep-seated distrust of Chamberlain & all his works & colleagues. There is no infamy of which they are not capable. When they are with you they are careful to talk in honourable terms; if I have read them more truly it is because their underlings are less discreet with me.

Three days ago we were insulted; now we have the submission you have so often predicted. Bless you & please in future steer your own course uncontaminated by contact with these disreputable men.

A fortnight later Chamberlain again flew to Germany and, in the early hours of 30 September, signed the infamous Munich agreement in which he, on behalf of the British Government together with Daladier, Prime Minister of France, surrendered to Hitler the liberties and independence of the peoples of Czechoslovakia. The next day Winston was visited at Chartwell by a young BBC producer, Guy Burgess, who, by the end of the year, had joined the British Secret Service and was to defect to the Soviet Union twenty years later. According to Burgess's biographer, the Labour MP Tom Driberg, Churchill greeted Burgess with a builder's trowel in his hand and the news that he had just received a message from Beneš, President of the Czechoslovak Republic (whose name, according to Burgess, he pronounced 'Herr Beans'), asking for his 'advice and assistance'. 'What answer shall I give? What assistance can I proffer?' demanded Churchill. Burgess could think of nothing beyond the assist-ance of his eloquence. According to his account: 'Churchill went on: "You are silent, Mr Burgess. You are rightly silent. What else can I offer Herr Beans? Only one thing: my only son Randolph. And Randolph who is already" – he growled – "I trust, a gentleman, is training to be an officer." '

'Munich!' How vividly I recall the day when, as a schoolboy of fourteen or fifteen, having heard it referred to so many times in the sternest of tones in my father's home, I finally summoned up the courage to ask: 'Father, what was Munich?' Had I known the explosion of wrath that my question would provoke, I would have kept my ignorance to myself: 'Munich? You ask what was Munich?' demanded my father in disbelief, growing redder by the second. 'To think that I spend a fortune on school fees at Eton to have gifted professors instruct you and you ask me: "What was *Munich*?."' Beside himself with rage, he soon lapsed into incoherence.

I never did get the explanation I sought, but had to read it up for myself in the history books. Suffice it to say that, for my father, Munich was the litmus test he applied to all of his political generation. Woe betide those who failed it and were so injudicious as to come within range of the flail of his tongue. He would never forgive those whom he regarded as responsible for leading Britain into what both he and his father were to call 'the unnecessary war' in which so many millions of lives would be lost and which, certainly up to 1936, could have been prevented without bloodshed by decisive, concerted action by the democracies of Europe. Randolph, quite bluntly, regarded them as traitors. As he admitted to Clive Irving in a lengthy interview published in the *Sunday Times* in 1964:

I insulted everybody who was taking what I conceived to be a defeatist view. I dare say this was rather embarrassing for my father because, though he fought these issues very stoutly, he was always very careful to maintain urbane relations with people of all views. But I rather charged out in every way, and was apt to attack people on any favourable occasion.

Churchill's biographer Martin Gilbert recalled one such occasion in the early 1960s in Kay Halle's *Randolph Churchill: The Young Unpretender*:

The Men of Munich were his foes. No attack on them could be too severe ... Some of the great dramas at Stour [Randolph's country home in later life] centred on appeasement. On one occasion the editor of a national newspaper [Donald McLachlan of the *Sunday Telegraph*] arrived with his wife for dinner. Before we had been five minutes at the table the editor revealed that he had served on the editorial staff of *The Times* during the appeasement period and, to the horror of the research assistants present, expressed his opinion that Geoffrey Dawson [the editor] had been right to shorten the dispatches of his Berlin correspondent. 'Surely you could not have approved of that?' Randolph asked in amazement, 'that was censorship of the worst sort, Dawson was a traitor to his country ...' and so on for nearly five minutes, with increasing fury. When the tirade was over the editor, quite unabashed, replied calmly that he had not only approved of the cuts, but actually advised them. With a shaking and trembling of his whole mass, Randolph rose from the table, brandished his [carving] knife at the editor, and bellowed more savagely than any of us had heard before: 'Men like you should have been shot by my father in 1940.' Then, turning from the table, the knife still held high, he left the room. The editor and his wife had both turned white. On the following morning they breakfasted alone and left the house . . .

In the midst of the grave developments in Europe and while still undergoing his officer training with the Hussars, Randolph received the following light-hearted letter from Harpo Marx whom he had befriended the year before in Hollywood and to whom he had written introducing a friend, Robert Byron:

November 22, 1938   *Metro-Goldwyn-Mayer Pictures*
                                                                          Culver City
                                                                          California

Dear Randolph,

Regardless of how quickly I can chase a blonde, it's quite impossible for me to meet Robert Byron. He left town on the 21st and I received your letter on the 22nd!

How about a get-together at the Brown Derby instead of at the Savoy – you, and Marxowish? Stop all that nonsense over there and come over here where the climate is hot and the women cold.

Fondest regards,
Harpo

In the wake of the Munich agreement and the Commons debate which followed it, Winston found himself faced with a revolt in his Epping constituency. In that debate, like the lightning bolt that spells the end of a sultry summer's day, he shattered the euphoria engendered by Chamberlain's 'Peace with honour, peace in our time' claim when he brutally declared:

We have sustained a total and unmitigated defeat . . . all is over. Silent, mournful, abandoned, broken, Czechoslovakia recedes into the darkness. She has suffered in every respect by her association with the Western democracies . . .

I do not grudge our loyal, brave people, who were ready to do their duty no matter what the cost, who never flinched under the strain of last week – I do not grudge them the natural, spontaneous outburst of joy and relief when they learned that the hard ordeal would no longer be required of them at the moment; but they should know the truth.

They should know that there has been gross neglect and deficiency in our defences; they should know that we have sustained a defeat without war, the consequences of which will travel far with us along our road; they should know that we have passed an awful milestone in our history, when the whole equilibrium of Europe has been deranged, and that the terrible words have been pronounced against the Western democracies: 'Thou art weighed in the balance and found wanting.'

And do not suppose that this is the end. This is only the beginning of the reckoning, this is only the first sip, the first foretaste of a bitter cup which will be proffered to us year by year unless by a supreme recovery of moral health and martial vigour, we arise again and take our stand for freedom as in the olden time.

In the Division that followed only thirty Conservative MPs out of 385 abstained – thirteen, including Churchill, ostentatiously remained seated throughout the vote. With a few honourable exceptions the press dismissed Churchill's speech as 'alarmist'. In parts of his own constituency local party members were reported as being 'up in arms' about his criticisms of Chamberlain. The reaction of one of his former leading supporters, Colin Thornton-Kemsley, was not untypical: 'We wanted him to support the Conservative administration, not to discredit them.' Only the steadfastness and loyalty of Churchill's chairman, Sir James Hawkey, headed off attempts to sack him from his Epping constituency for 'disloyalty to Chamberlain'. On 19 October Randolph wrote to Sir James:

My father was telling me last night how splendid you have been over the 'Epping Revolt'. Please forgive this letter dictated in such a hurry on my way back to Aldershot, but I would like you to know how much your loyalty and encouragement have meant to him in these tragic days. I have seen at close quarters how terribly smitten he has been by all the disasters that are coming upon us, and I know how much he has been fortified by your courage and devotion.

Hawkey replied two days later:

... What a tragedy it is that the warnings of your father over the last five years were not heeded by the government. Of one thing I am convinced – that history will justify Winston Churchill and not Neville Chamberlain ...

This was the period of Winston's greatest isolation. Repudiated and reviled in Parliament, only a handful of the doughty band that had fought so fiercely at his side against the India Bill had been prepared to march with him on his urgent, and repeated calls for rearmament and, over the Abdication, he had been alone. Even the small number of supporters who grouped themselves around Anthony Eden and later, following his resignation over Munich, around Duff Cooper – all of whom shared his anxieties about the Nazi threat – were reluctant to be seen to identify themselves too closely with the unpopular and discredited Winston Churchill. Duff Cooper, a close and valued friend, felt obliged to disassociate himself publicly from Winston in the debate of 17 November 1938 on an amendment calling for the immediate establishment of a Ministry of Supply to speed Britain's rearmament. On that occasion only two Conservatives – Brendan Bracken and Harold Macmillan – followed Winston into the Lobby. He felt hurt and rebuffed.

Towards the end of the year Lord Craigavon, Prime Minister of Northern Ireland from 1921 until his death in 1940, presented Winston with a silver goblet of an ancient Gaelic design inscribed with quotations about Ulster by his father Lord Randolph, himself and his son. In writing to express his thanks, Winston confessed: 'Coming as it does at this time of trouble and misunderstanding in which I feel so much alone, tho' constant, it is grateful to me beyond words.' To Clemmie he remarked: 'All round are quotations from my father, from me and one from Randolph, about Ulster. I wish some of these dirty Tory hacks, who would like to drive me out of the Party could see this trophy.'

Through his bitter but glorious 'wilderness years', Winston's one constant ally, who never failed him, was Randolph. In the summer of 1938 Winston published *Arms and the Covenant*, a volume of speeches on defence and foreign affairs covering the previous ten years, compiled and edited by Randolph. In his preface to the volume Randolph declared his boundless admiration of his father:

Observant readers will note the many cases where Mr Churchill's prescience has already been proved beyond dispute, and some will detect occasions when he was alone in giving advice which might have advanced the national cause if it had not been disregarded or accepted only too late ...

In compiling this volume I have read most of the speeches made by the leading spokesmen of all parties, as well as those of Mr Churchill, and I have reached certain conclusions which I trust it will not be thought unseemly, invidious, or unfilial for me to record. As a politician, Mr Churchill suffers from the disadvantage of being strangely free from the prejudices and ideologies which constitute such a large part the mental equipment of our more successful public men. He always finds it difficult to subordinate his views on public affairs to the current exigencies of party position. Such independence of thought and speech is a handicap in the days when party machines are steadily increasing their power. One of the distinctions between a statesman and a politician is that the former indulges in the luxury of subordinating party interests to those of the State . . .

Utterly disenchanted with the Conservative Party, Randolph and his brother-in-law Duncan Sandys set about forming their own party. Winston reported to Clemmie on 29 December:

Duncan and Randolph are forming a new party to bust up all the old ones. The plan is to have a hundred thousand members, who pay a pound a head a year, but after the first hundred thousand are enlisted they are ready to go on even to a million, or more if necessary. No one may belong who is not doing war preparation work of some kind or who has not fought in the last war. Anyone who disagrees with Randolph or Duncan is to be immediately dismissed, and at any meeting only those are to be allowed to stay who are wholeheartedly in favour of the programme. The programme has not yet been settled. I have promised to accept the Presidency when the first hundred thousand is reached. Meanwhile Mary has joined, and has volunteered for any work.

On 3 January 1939 the *Evening Standard* carried a report on the group's proposed inaugural meeting under a banner headline:

'HUNDRED THOUSAND AGAINST THE PREMIER' IS NEW GROUP'S AIM
By Frank Owen

A new attempt is being made to organise a 'front' against the National Government, and especially against Mr Neville Chamberlain's leadership. It is intended to launch the movement at a private meeting at the Caxton Hall tomorrow evening. The conveners of the meeting are described as a New Political Group. They have announced that their objects are:

(i) To strengthen the present Defence programme.
(ii) To supply a firmer foreign policy.

Politicians of all parties and people of no political attachment have been invited to attend tomorrow's meeting ... to register a protest against further 'concessions to the dictators'.

Writing from the South of France on 18 January, Winston reported to Clemmie:

The Duncan–Randolph movement, the Hundred Thousand, has already over-passed its first hundred. Violet [Bonham Carter, later Baroness Asquith] made herself very awkward. Just as she upset Eden's Queen's Hall meeting by her violence against the Government, so now she broke up Duncan's little effort by bolting in alarm. I need scarcely say I did all in my power to dissuade them from it. And no doubt it does me a certain amount of harm. I do not care at all.

The next day, from Barbados aboard Lord Moyne's yacht, SS *Rosaura*, Clemmie wrote anxiously but perceptively: 'O Winston, are we drifting into war? Without the wit to avoid it or the will to prepare for it?'

'The Hundred Thousand' was a fiasco. Almost as soon as it was formed it foundered on personality differences and its inability to agree on any constructive programme. Within three weeks Duncan Sandys had resigned from the chairmanship and the new political party, launched with such gusto, had fizzled out.

Randolph enjoyed a greater success when, on 27 April, at the Oxford Union, he proposed the motion moved by a young undergraduate, Julian Amery, who was to become a lifelong friend, 'That in view of this country's new commitments and the gravity of the general situation in Europe this House welcomes conscription'. As the *Daily Mail* reported the next day:

OXFORD UNION GIVE DECISIVE VOTE FOR CONSCRIPTION

The Oxford Union, who startled the world six years ago by voting that they would not fight for King and Country, reversed that decision last night. By 423 votes to 326, they adopted a motion welcoming conscription. Attendance was a record. Every available space was occupied in the gallery, on the floor, the window sills, and even the President's rostrum. Many had to be turned away. Chief supporters of the motion were Mr Randolph

Churchill, who received a great ovation, and Commander Stephen King-Hall; the opposition was led by Capt. B. H. Liddell Hart...

To carry, by a margin of nearly one hundred, a motion in favour of conscription was a signal triumph and was symbolic of the new generation's determination, albeit late in the day, to resist the forward march across Europe of the dictators. Encouraged by this, Randolph carried the debate on conscription to Gray's Inn, the Manchester Left Book Club and the Stepney Peace Council in the East End of London, where he debated against John Gollan, later for many years Secretary-General of the British Communist Party.

Following the final collapse of the Munich agreement with the occupation of Prague in the spring of 1939, Hitler was ready to make his next move. Through the activities of the Nazi Party in Danzig and a major military build-up on Poland's western borders, pressure was increased during the summer against the Polish Government, as events in Europe moved towards a crescendo. At the beginning of July a major press campaign was launched demanding Churchill's inclusion in the Government, to speed the pace of rearmament and to present a united national front to resist any further demands from Hitler. Even such papers as the *Manchester Guardian*, which had long been hostile to him, now came out in his support. Chamberlain saw in all this a sinister plot but one which, he was confident, had failed. Writing to his sister on 8 July he reported:

This has been a relatively quiet week only enlivened by the drive to put Winston in the government. It has been a regular conspiracy in which Mr Maisky [the Soviet Ambassador in London] has been involved as he keeps in very close touch with Randolph and no doubt Randolph was responsible for the positive statements in the *Mail* that it was all settled as well as the less definite paragraphs in the *Express*. I don't mind them, but I am vexed that Camrose [proprietor of the *Daily Telegraph*] who used to be such a firm supporter should now have committed himself. As soon as I saw the leader in the *Telegraph* I sent for him and explained just why I was not prepared to invite Winston. I did not convince him...

Virginia Cowles, the American newspaper reporter whom Randolph had met while covering the Spanish Civil War, recorded a vignette of life at Chartwell that summer in her book, *Looking for Trouble*:

Randolph took me down to Chartwell for tea, it was beautiful there, with the wind blowing through the grass and the sun streaming down on the flowers – and this time the pond actually had some goldfish in it. Once again I found Mr Churchill with his torn coat and battered hat peering into the water fascinated. After tea, he took me upstairs and showed me the high oak-beam library where he did all his writing. He was working on a three-volume History of the English-Speaking People and over half of it was already completed. 'But I'll never be able to finish it before the war begins,' he remarked gloomily. When it came, he said he was going to close the big house and move into the cottage.

'You won't be living there,' said Randolph indignantly. 'You'll be at No. 10 Downing Street.'

'I'm afraid I haven't got the same fanciful ideas as you have. Things will have to get pretty bad before that happens.' They did. The next time I saw him he was the First Lord of the Admiralty.

The supine leadership of Ramsay MacDonald, Baldwin and Chamberlain and their principal Cabinet colleagues, both by their failure to create an effective system of international collective security and by their refusal to rearm at a pace even remotely reflecting developments in Germany, had brought Britain – indeed all Europe – to the point of war. When, in the last week of August, Churchill returned from a visit to the French Army and an inspection of the Maginot Line defences, he was greeted with the disturbing announcement of a non-aggression pact between Nazi Germany and the Soviet Union.

For more than a year, both privately and publicly, he had been pressing the Government to establish close relations with the Soviet Union and a Triple Alliance between Britain, France and Russia. As a result of the indecision and abject weakness in the conduct of British foreign policy, Soviet Russia was lost as a potential ally, through whose assistance alone Hitler's advance into Eastern Europe could be impeded. Worse, she now felt impelled to seek safety in a direct alliance with Hitler under the terms of the infamous Nazi–Soviet Pact, which contained provisions for the partition of Poland between the Nazi and Communist dictatorships.

On 1 September 1939 Hitler invaded Poland. Two days later, following the expiry of a British ultimatum, Britain, though unable to save her, honoured her commitment to Poland by declaring war on Nazi Germany. That same day Churchill was invited to return to the Cabinet as First Lord of the Admiralty and the signal was flashed to the Fleet, already at its battle stations: 'WINSTON IS BACK.' Within a fortnight Soviet forces crossed Poland's eastern frontier and proceeded to join with the Nazis in dismembering that tragic land and enslaving its heroic people.

CHAPTER 11

Member for Preston

The outbreak of war found Randolph with his regiment. As he recalled in an unpublished memorandum dated 12 June 1954:

When the Second War started, I was serving as a 2nd Lieutenant with the 4th Queen's Own Hussars at Tidworth. I was a Supplementary Reserve officer and when Hitler marched into Poland I was doing my three weeks annual training. We were a cavalry regiment but had been officially mechanised about 18 months before. This meant that our horses had been taken away from us but that no tanks had been supplied in their place. So we did not have very much to do.

About ten days after war was declared, the First Lord of the Admiralty telephoned to me and asked whether I could get three or four days' leave so that I could act as his representative on a mission. This was easily arranged...

Randolph received precise instructions from his father about his secret mission:

My dearest Randolph,

Please be at the house of the Captain-in-Charge at Portland at a quarter to nine on Tuesday morning. He will be expecting you, and I am told his house is well-known. You should wear uniform and look your best. You will have to travel over in the day and sleep on board on the way back. I believe you will land at the other place I mentioned.

I enclose you a letter which you should hand to our friend saying that you have been sent to represent me. You may tell the Colonel, but the whole matter must be regarded as very secret.

I hope you will enjoy your *mission spécial*.

Your loving father,
Winston S. Churchill

Randolph's account continued:

Pursuant to the instructions which I received from the First Lord, I went on board HMS *Kelly* at Portsmouth and reported to the ship's Commanding Officer, Captain Lord Louis Mountbatten. The First Lord had instructed me to wear boots and breeches and my sword. I knew that military officers should not wear spurs on board His Majesty's ships; but I thought they might be needed in the course of my mission and I had therefore brought them with me in my suitcase.

The 'object of the exercise', it transpired, was to proceed to Cherbourg and to bring back to England the Duke and Duchess of Windsor. The Duchess had not been in England since she left a week before the abdication. Both Lord Louis and myself were friends of the Windsors and it seemed to both of us in this phoniest part of the 'phoney war', a very agreeable and jolly expedition.

We arrived at Cherbourg in the morning. I had put on my spurs before going on shore, otherwise I would have been 'improperly dressed'. We were conducted to a large salon on the first floor of the naval headquarters where we were received by what seemed to be at least seven or eight French Admirals. The whole affair was conducted most ceremoniously. After a quarter of an hour, the Duke and Duchess arrived by train from Paris. A *vin d'honneur* was served and toasts were drunk to everyone and everything that seemed appropriate in September 1939. We then sat down, eleven or twelve of us, in large over-stuffed armchairs in a large circle. I was almost immediately opposite the Duke of Windsor and perhaps at a distance of some eight or nine yards. Suddenly, with eagle eye and an accent of triumph, he interrupted the general buzz of stilted conversation: 'Randolph, you have got your spurs on upside down.' Bending my portly figure uneasily and uncomfortably over my Sam Browne belt, and knocking over with my sword a half-filled glass of champagne which I had put by my side on the floor, I found that the Duke was correct in his diagnosis of my military turnout. I made abject and ineffective gestures of apology and exculpation: but it was no good. When royalty can discover a medal put on in the wrong order or any error in dress, it makes their day and they are not to be denied. This occasion was a gala day.

He strode across the floor and said: 'Let me put them right, Randolph.' Scarlet, expostulating and miserable I rose and sought to deter him. 'Sit down, sit down,' he said, 'let me do it.' Obedience is said to be the highest form of politeness and down I sat, and there in the presence of all the French Admirals, scandalised and uncomprehending, the Duke of Windsor knelt down and spent three or four of the happiest moments of his life fussing and fiddling about with the straps by which my spurs were attached to my boots. I kept trying ineffectively to relieve him of his task; all to no avail.

After what I suppose was only three or four minutes but seemed like several aeons of time, the spurs were adjusted to the satisfaction of His Royal Highness. Fortunately the tide proclaimed and compelled our departure and we went aboard HMS *Kelly*. I at once removed the offending spurs in the forlorn hope that I should be twitted no more. It was not to be. The cup was not allowed to pass and all the way through luncheon the Duke continued to tease me about my extraordinary solecism. I bore it with such good nature as I could muster, but eventually as he is a kind man he saw that I had received sufficient punishment. He turned upon Captain Lord Louis Mountbatten and said: 'Dickie, I know you are only a simple sailor man, but you have played a lot of polo in your time. You must have noticed that Randolph's spurs were on upside down. Why didn't you tell him?' 'Well, sir,' replied Lord Louis with that disingenuous charm which has served him so well in his various careers, 'of course I noticed it, but I didn't want to spoil your fun.'

We got back to Portsmouth all right. Eighteen months later HMS *Kelly* was torpedoed. Lord Louis had to swim for it and survived to have two other destroyers sunk under him and to do a number of other things which are a matter of history.

Very soon after his return from his secret mission of 12 September, Randolph telephoned the London flat of his friends Philip and Mary Dunne, only to discover that Philip had already left to join his regiment. The telephone was answered instead by Pamela Digby, the nineteen-year-old daughter of Lord and Lady Digby of Minterne in Dorset. Pamela, a striking redhead, had recently started a £6-a-week job at the Foreign Office doing translations from German and French. Having nowhere to live in London she arranged to rent the Dunnes' flat for £2 10s od a week. Today she lives in somewhat greater comfort, in a former Rothschild residence on the Rue du Faubourg St Honoré in Paris, as United States Ambassador to France and widow of the American states-man, Averell Harriman. In addition to which, she happens to be my mother. She recalls the occasion vividly:

> Philip had gone and Mary was showing me round the flat when the telephone rang. She was by the drinks cupboard so I answered the phone. A voice proclaimed: 'This is Randolph Churchill.'
> 'Do you want to speak to Mary?' I asked.

'No,' he replied firmly, 'I want to speak to you.'

'But you don't know me,' I protested.

At that moment Mary came over from the far side the room, nodding her head vigorously in the affirmative. Meanwhile he continued: 'As a matter of fact I was wondering if you would come and have dinner with me tonight.' Mary was interjecting: 'Please do! Please do!' So I said, 'All right, come and pick me up at seven o'clock,' put down the phone and demanded, 'Mary, what's all this about?' 'Oh, he's an old friend of mine,' she replied. 'He's great fun, he is a bit too fat, but he's very amusing. I told him that you were taking our flat and that I couldn't dine with him but I would try and persuade you to dine with him. Please do – you'll have a very good time!'

I agreed because at that point the war had already started and it was so depressing. Anytime I went to the Four Hundred, whoever you were with would end the evening by presenting the whisky bottle to the head waiter, saying: 'Keep this, I won't be coming here again – I'm going out to get killed.' I was getting so terribly upset by seeing all my friends going off, as they dramatically thought, to be killed, and I thought how marvellous it was to be going out with somebody about whom I didn't give a damn . . .'

These were the days of whirlwind courtships and instant marriages as a whole new generation prepared to go off to war which, it was imagined, would involve slaughter on a scale at least comparable to the one that had decimated their father's generation. Within less than ten days of their first meeting Randolph and Pamela were engaged and a week later they married. Many friends sought to dissuade Pamela from the enterprise. Even one of Randolph's closest friends, Lord Stanley of Alderley, tried to put her off. As Pamela remembers:

Ed Stanley called me up and said: 'You stood me up for dinner last night and I find you dining at a restaurant with Randolph Churchill. He's a very very bad man and you shouldn't go out with people like that.'

'But he's one of your best friends,' I protested.

'Yes, he *is* one of my best friends but he shouldn't be one of *your* best friends.'

That [as Pamela later confessed] rather egged me on though there were moments, every time Randolph disappeared, when I became anxious and said to myself: 'This is absolutely idiotic – I don't know him, he doesn't know me and there's a war on.' The only thing was, everyone else was so scared and so uncertain of what was to happen to them and to the world, while Randolph was totally confident that, though the war was going to be absolutely bloody, we were going to win it, we were going to get through it. It gave one great confidence.

Opposition to the match was not confined to Edward Stanley. According to Pamela:

Everybody was against us getting married except Winston. Clemmie and my mother and father all said it was ridiculous. – 'She's too young!' 'You don't have any money!' 'They don't even know each other!' 'The whole thing is absolutely idiotic – they mustn't be allowed to do it!' But old Winston was splendid. He brushed all those arguments aside and declared: 'Nonsense! All you need to be married is champagne, a double bed and a box of cigars!' He was thoroughly on our side. He was splendid. He even went on to tell us that he had nearly married a 'Pamela' himself [Pamela Plowden], which Clemmie confirmed.

The wedding took place on 4 October 1939 at the beautiful Wren church of St John's, Smith Square, which, later in the war, was to be gutted in a bombing raid. The next day the *Daily Mirror* devoted a whole page to the wedding:

CROWD CHEERS WINSTON AT SON'S WEDDING

Mr Winston Churchill, First Lord of the Admiralty, was cheered again and again yesterday when he arrived at St John's Church, Smith Square, Westminster, with his wife for the wedding of their only son, Mr Randolph Churchill. Large crowds had gathered outside the church ...

It was a real war wedding, with the bridegroom, who is a subaltern in a cavalry corps, wearing uniform ... All the guests carried gas masks and Canon F. R. Barry, Rector of St John's, who performed the ceremony, arrived at the church with his slung over his shoulder in a scarlet satchel.

After the ceremony the couple left the church passing under an arch of drawn swords held high above their heads by two rows of Randolph's brother officers from his regiment before going on to a small reception at Admiralty House.

They spent a brief honeymoon at Belton, near Grantham, as the guests of Lord Brownlow, formerly Equerry to the Duke of Windsor. Randolph and he had become friends at the time of the abdication crisis. However, the marriage got off to a faltering start when Randolph tried to further his teenage bride's education by reading her Gibbon's *Decline and Fall of the Roman Empire* in bed at night. Pamela, many decades later, was still filled with disbelief: 'Fancy trying to read me *Decline and Fall*! Even worse, he would stop and say: "Are you listening?" When I said "Yes I am", he would demand: "Well what was that last sentence?" Can you imagine! Hilaire Belloc was fine, but Gibbon was too much!'

Soon afterwards they spent a weekend with Pamela's parents, the Digbys, at Minterne, near Cerne Abbas in Dorset. By a strange coincidence, Minterne in the seventeenth century had been the home of the first Sir Winston Churchill, a Royalist soldier of West Country stock, who had brought up his children there. His elder son, John, later became the 1st Duke of Marlborough. His younger son, Charles, commanded the British infantry at the Battle of Blenheim, under his older brother's overall command. His daughter, Arabella, became the mistress of King James II, bearing him a royal bastard, the Duke of Berwick, who himself became a military commander second only in repute to his illustrious uncle. Thus it came about that I was to spend much of my childhood, in the post-war years, in the very same magical valley with its woods, streams and rolling hills where my ancestor Duke John had played with his brother and sister three hundred years before.

On 30 November Winston celebrated his sixty-fifth birthday and qualified to draw the old-age pension. Fortunately for the world, retirement could not have been further from his mind. Randolph and Pamela presented him with a gold pen with which he was to sign all his wartime documents.

The winter of 1939–40 was especially harsh. 'Randolph', according to Pamela, 'was really a very unlikely soldier. He was very unfit and it was awful for him because they did all these terrible exercises on Salisbury Plain and he really wasn't cut out for it.' From Tidworth Randolph's regiment moved up to near Hull in Yorkshire, where they lived in a small semi-detached house. As Pamela recalls:

There was snow and more snow. It was cold, there was ice everywhere – it really was ghastly. It was a terribly frustrating time for Randolph. Other regiments were being sent abroad, but not his – he was stuck in Hull. All the sergeants' wives were saying: 'Of course we are all quite safe as long as Mr Churchill's son is in the regiment – none of our husbands will be sent abroad.' One thing that Randolph never lacked was courage. He was desperate to go abroad, yet every regiment except the Fourth Hussars seemed to be sent.

Many criticism could be levelled at Randolph but none that impugned his courage. From the very outset of war he had been pressing his father to use his influence to get him to the Front. But his father made clear in a letter of 15 September that he would pull no strings on Randolph's behalf:

I am sure yr best & indeed *only* course is to obey with good grace, & do whatever duty is assigned to you. In this way you will win the confidence of those in whose power you lie.

I will write to General Barnes about yr grief at being detached from yr regiment for training duties; & of yr desire to accompany them to the front. Such feelings are in no way discreditable; but a good officer wd take care not to show them, while hoping for a better turn of events.

I am always on the look out for any compliment or pleasure I can give you, as you know; but so far as the service is concerned you must make yr own way. I am always thinking about yr interests & yr fortunes.

On top of these frustrations Randolph and Pamela soon found themselves burdened with gambling debts. Randolph not only gambled for high stakes with conspicuous lack of success, but he was what Pamela describes as a 'bill-grabber': 'Rather like old Winston he had a lot of very rich friends and, whenever they went to a restaurant, Randolph would insist on grabbing the bill. This was ridiculous because they could afford it, while he couldn't. It did not help matters that, on joining his regiment, he lost his £30 a week expenses allowed him by the *Evening Standard*.'

However Beaverbrook, with his customary generosity, told Randolph in his letter of 7 November: 'Sooner or later it will be necessary to curtail salaries of men in service and in the office too. However you will not go down until the last man walks the plank.'

Randolph had joined the 4th Hussars to please his father. Had he enlisted in a territorial regiment with friends like Seymour Berry (later Lord Camrose) and Basil Dufferin (Marques of Dufferin and Ava), tragically killed in Burma at the very end of the war, they would all have been junior officers of roughly the same age. As it was, by joining a regiment of the Regular Army Randolph, already twenty-eight years old, found himself with a group of lieutenants who were all nearly ten years his junior and far fitter.

While at Hull, these young officers taunted Randolph about his lack of physical fitness, to which he riposted with predictable Randolphian bravura: 'Rubbish – I am tougher than any of you!' Whereupon they challenged him to prove it, betting him £50 that he could not walk the 104 miles to York and back in twenty-four hours. For three weeks Randolph trained, taking long walks at a brisk pace every afternoon when he got home from his army duties. Pamela vividly recalls the time:

He went on to special foods and took to rubbing his feet with methylated spirits to toughen them up. He took it all terribly seriously and kept on saying how useful the £50 was going to be, how it would pay off so many bills – in fact it wouldn't have paid off a tenth of them.

In between times, Randolph was on to White's Club and Evelyn Waugh and his other friends, all anxious to give him advice. Obviously Evelyn's was of the worst type: 'You know you mustn't start in the middle of the night!', 'You mustn't march in the mid-day sun!' etc. There never was any mid-day sun in Hull anyway. Finally the great day arrived and Randolph set off at a brisk pace for York where we had taken a room at the Station Hotel so he could grab three hours' rest.

It was the return journey that was most painful. We set off at two or three in the morning. I had to follow him with the car headlights on and toot if ever he dropped below 4 mph or was doing more than 6 mph. After many, many hours of walking, Randolph was in such agony from blisters and sores that he finally took off his boots and walked in his socks – two pairs. Then, his socks hurt and we had to stop and pad the socks with cotton-wool. Then that got wet. It was a desperate struggle. I think we made it into the camp just twenty-two minutes under the time-limit. The young officers greeted him with hoots of derisive laughter. They were furious he had succeeded and determined not to pay up. Randolph always thought they would – but they never paid a single penny. The Army then put him on fatigue duties for his trouble . . .

In April 1940, Hitler launched a massive attack against Norway. In spite of naval support and seaborne landings, Britain was unable to prevent Norway falling under the Nazi jackboot. This failure provoked a political crisis at home. By the conclusion of the Commons debate on Norway on 8 May it had become clear that Chamberlain, though he had survived a vote of censure, no longer commanded the support of the House of Commons or even his own party. He thereupon held consultations with the leaders of the Labour and Liberal parties to see if they would join in the formation of a National Government under his leadership. Clement Attlee, the Labour leader, had already pointed out that it might be difficult to get his party to serve under Chamberlain when, on the morning of 10 May, the momentous news broke that Hitler had invaded Belgium and Holland. Chamberlain informed King George VI that he could no longer carry on as Prime Minister and, at 6 p.m., the King summoned Churchill to Buckingham Palace and invited him to form a government. Later that evening, a National Government was formed with the full support of both Labour and Liberal parties. Churchill later recalled in his *Second World War* memoirs:

> Thus then, on the night of the tenth of May, at the outset of this mighty battle, I acquired the chief power in the State, which henceforth I wielded in ever-growing measure for five years and three months of world war . . .
>
> . . . as I went to bed at about 3 a.m., I was conscious of a profound sense of relief. At last I had the authority to give directions over the whole scene. I felt as if I were walking with destiny, and all my past life had been but a preparation for this hour and for this trial.

Later that month Randolph wrote to congratulate Brendan Bracken on his appointment as Parliamentary Private Secretary to the Prime Minister. Bracken replied with a sharp, though friendly, reproof:

12 June 1940

Bless you for your congratulatory epistle.

Please do not regard the rest of this letter as a pompous lecture. But you must give me leave to tell you that I believe you are even more indiscreet than I was at your age!

After you last saw your friend Mrs Luce [Mrs Clare Booth Luce, wife of the proprietor of *Time* magazine, Henry Robinson Luce], she went to the American Ambassador and told him that you had declared that your father 'hated Kennedy' [Joseph P. Kennedy, US Ambassador to the Court of St James, 1937–41].

Kennedy is a very sensitive man, and believing what Clare said to be true, he has turned very sour.

This is a most unfortunate development. Whatever you may think about Kennedy, he has influence with the Government of the United States, and believing as he does that your father is hostile to him, he is not likely to go out of his way to be over helpful in presenting any suggestions made by your father to the Government of the United States.

I have not, of course, had a word with your father about this matter. My job is to minimize his difficulties. But I do beg of you to be a good boy, and above all, to be discreet.

[PS] Looking at this letter it does seem rather pedantic. But you & I love W. – I don't think you will resent faithful tho' reluctant advice.

Randolph was becoming more and more frustrated at seeing no action and at the failure of the 4th Hussars to be posted overseas when, out of the blue, he received an invitation to stand as MP for Preston. It was at this very time that the fate, not only of Britain, but of the world, hung in the balance, as the immortal 'Few' of the Royal Air Force engaged the massed squadrons of the Luftwaffe in the skies above southern England in what came to be known as the Battle of Britain.

Addressing the Preston Conservative Association on 12 September, Randolph bluntly warned of the danger of invasion, as reported in the *Lancashire Daily Post*:

ENEMY WILL BE THROWN BACK INTO SEA

At an enthusiastic special meeting of the Preston Conservative Association in the Guild Hall last night, Mr Randolph Spencer Churchill, the Prime Minister's only son, was unanimously adopted Conservative candidate at the forthcoming Preston Parliamentary by-election...

In a vigorous, realistic speech, confident of the successful issue of the war while not ignoring the stern realities of the present situation, Mr Churchill made a great impression...

Mr Churchill explained that if he was adopted and returned, so long as the war lasted, the Army naturally would have first call upon his time. (*Applause*). He might not, therefore, be able to come to Preston as often as he would wish. He had spent that morning walking round the streets of London, in the City and in the East End, surveying the havoc that had been wrought by the German air bombardment...

'I am sure from what I saw this morning,' observed Mr Churchill, 'that every Londoner would rather see the entire City razed to the ground in a rubble heap than be under the heel of Hitler.' (*Loud applause*). These feelings he believed were shared by all the people of the country ... Fear was the quality that brought ruin to a nation. No nation was ever ruined by courage, sacrifice or suffering. A great nation placed sacrifice and heroism above destruction and death, and if that was their spirit today there could not be the slightest doubt about their ultimate triumph...

This led Mr Churchill to speak of the probability of an attempted German invasion at any moment. It might be tomorrow or the day after, or not for a week, but it was almost certain that their formidable and terrible enemy was going to launch his legions on our shores and there was going to be a fierce and bloody struggle ...

'When we think we fight for all that is most dear and precious to us, our families, our homes, our past, our future, our freedom, our Empire, what a little thing does life seem, weighed in the balance against them! I have said I believe the enemy will come, but I also believe he will be flung back into the sea, and it will not be so easy, once he has tasted defeat, to launch his forces upon us again.'

Since midsummer Pamela, heavily pregnant, had been living with Winston and Clemmie at 10 Downing Street, to be near her doctor. At weekends, and when the bombing of London became intense, she moved down to Chequers, the Prime Minister's country residence. In a letter to Randolph, who had returned to his military duties in the North, she wrote:

My darling,
   I am writing this in the garden at Chequers. It is boiling hot & it would be perfect if only you were here too. Darling I miss you so terribly & just feel I can't wait till next week-end. Where shall we go? Let's have one day all to ourselves. I am so selfish about you – angel – but you're just all I want ...
   ... When is the election? Papa [Winston] says he will introduce you in the House. Do write your Col. a nice letter, as I think his telegram was charming. There was another all-night warning in London last night. I dread going back there, & having to sleep in a shelter every night. There is not room in a very narrow bedstead for Baby Dumpling [the author] & me really, & therefore I get somewhat cramped ...
   I have quite a lot to tell you of our Air Force, but I think perhaps I better not put it on paper ... Max [Beaverbrook, newly created Minister for Aircraft Production] has not been down this week-end, which is sad, but, though the bombs have done quite a bit of harm to aerodromes – Biggin Hill wiped out nearly – I gather they have not hit Max's factories.
                                 All my love to you my darling,
                                               Pamela

Pamela still retains vivid memories of those nights in the air-raid shelter at Number Ten:

The bedrooms at Downing Street were on the top floor and when the raids got bad we went down to the basement. The first air raid shelter they made in the wine cellar. At the far end of the wine cellar, there was a little room where they put two bunks, one above the other. At the other end, there was a room with a single bed. So Clemmie had the single bed and Winston and I – and the 'Baby Dumpling' – shared the double-decker. We used to have dinner at 8 p.m. because most evenings the sirens would go at 9 p.m. As soon as the sirens started I was immediately sent below.

I used to fall sound asleep until 1 or 1.30 in the morning when Papa would come down. He would climb up the ladder into the top bunk. That was the end of my sleep because within two minutes of arriving in his bunk, he started to snore. He snored most of the night and the 'Baby Dumpling' kicked for the rest of it. So between the two of them, the only sleep I got was before Winston arrived and after about 6 a.m. when he would get up and go back to his own bed because the raids were over by then . . .

I remember, at about this time, Winston one evening warning all the family that we might be invaded at any moment and he told us: 'I am counting on each one of you to take at least one dead German with you.' I protested: 'But I haven't got a gun and would not know how to fire it anyway.' To which Winston replied brandishing a table-knife: 'But, my dear, you can use a carving-knife!'

On 8 October 1940 Randolph took his seat in the House of Commons, as reported by John Carvel in the *Star*:

Yesterday was a big Churchill occasion at Westminster. In addition to his review of the war in which he dealt with home and foreign affairs, he [the Prime Minister] introduced his son to Parliament. Mr Randolph Churchill took his seat for Preston. It was a rare spectacle to see a Prime Minister act as one of the sponsors for his son; the other was the Chief Whip. In fact, the last occasion on which a Prime Minister stood sponsor to a new Member was in 1919, when Mr Lloyd George and Lord Balfour escorted Lady Astor – the first woman to take her seat – to the table.

Yesterday's cheers left no doubt about the esteem in which the Prime Minister is held in every part of the House. Here came the third generation of Churchills to a Chamber which has been successively dominated by his grandfather and father. Lord Randolph arrived in 1847, the Prime Minister in 1900. With two short intervals the family have had one prominent member at least for more than sixty years . . .

Randolph's old friend Quintin Hogg – against whom he had campaigned at the time of Munich with the slogan 'A Vote for Hogg, is a vote for Hitler' – greeted his arrival at Westminster with the accolade: 'Well, Randolph, it took a major war to get *you* into the House of Commons!'

It was an irony that Randolph, who was forever looking for a fight and who, though not yet thirty, had contested no fewer than three very lively by-elections, should finally be returned to the House of Commons without a contest. After the drama of Wavertree, the hurly-burly of West Toxteth and tramping through the snows of Ross and Cromarty, it must have been an anticlimax to arrive in Parliament without enduring any of the excitement of campaigning at the hustings.

Two days later, on 10 October 1940, Pamela gave birth to a son at Chequers. He was christened Winston at the nearby parish church of Ellesborough on 1 December 1940, the day after his grandfather had celebrated his 66th birthday. Virginia Cowles, who stood godmother to the child, recalled the occasion in her book *Winston Churchill: The Era and the Man*:

> I had always heard that the P.M.'s emotions were easily stirred and that at times he could be as sentimental as a woman. On this occasion I had proof of it, for he sat throughout the ceremony with tears streaming down his cheeks. 'Poor infant,' he murmured, 'to be born into such a world as this.'

Shortly before I was born, my mother, desperate for a home of her own, had managed to find a small Queen Anne rectory, Ickleford House, near Hitchin in Hertfordshire, for a rent of £52 a year. In late October she wrote to Randolph from Chequers:

> Oh! My darling, how lovely to get into our own house. Too much officialness is getting me beat!
> The news the German Press Agency have put out about Vichy France ... couldn't be blacker. Papa is very upset & says it will lengthen the war considerably – all the fleet, bases, colonies, all to be used against us. Alsace-Lorraine & Savoy all to become German – it's unbelievable isn't it. 'For the French a blush, for France a tear', I only hope it frightens the Americans to action ...
> We had a bomb near here last night – a terrific noise, it even woke Baby Winston up ... Papa came and saw Winston this afternoon & was

very sweet with him. He has so much character now, & I'm getting to know him quite well. Oh! Randy everything would be so nice, if only you were here with us all the time ... Soon, so soon now, I shall be settled in a home of my own, our home – yours & mine & baby Winston's – Oh my darling isn't it rather thrilling – our own family life – no more living in other people's houses.

When, on 26 November, Randolph made his maiden speech in Parliament his father was on the Treasury bench to hear him, and his mother and Pamela were in the Gallery. He began his speech – one of only three which he was to make in the House of Commons during his brief parliamentary career – with a reference to his grandfather and namesake, Lord Randolph Churchill:

> Forty years ago, a young Member, concluding his maiden speech in this House, thanked the House for the kindness and patience with which it had listened to him, not on his account but because of a 'certain splendid memory' which many Members still preserved. I hope that this House will pardon me for striking this personal note, but I today have the personal privilege and satisfaction of having my father here. Therefore, I would like to ask an extra measure of indulgence, on account of the added embarrassment occasioned by the paternal propinquity ...

It is a tradition of the House that maiden speeches should be uncontroversial. However, Randolph was unable to restrain his passion against those whose actions, and above all, inaction, had led Britain into war. In particular he addressed his remarks to those who, having failed to rearm Britain, now complained at the lack of military success. In so doing Randolph was attacking the majority of his parliamentary colleagues. He told the House:

> ... despite the repressive activities of the Patronage Secretary [the Government Chief Whip] some Members have been indulging in a great deal of criticism of His Majesty's Government, and I hope that it will not be thought too inappropriate if I say one or two words in answer to it ... Some hon. Members and some publicists, and some who are both Members and publicists, frequently inquire, 'Why do we not seize the initiative and carry the war into the enemy's country, and why do we not knock Italy out of the war with a few well-directed bombs on St Peter's?' I think that this offensive spirit – I use the word in a military sense – prevails just as much in the Army, but that perhaps there is rather more apprehension in the

Armed Forces of the Crown as to how slender have been our resources in the past and an understanding of the folly of going off at half-cock.

Looking around this House – I say this with all deference – one can see a number of hon. and right hon. Gentlemen, who in a greater or lesser degree, bear some measure of responsibility for the state of our Forces and any shortage of equipment which might perhaps handicap those who plan our strategy. I have no wish to recriminate about the past. We have often been advised from different quarters against this evil tendency, but what about all this recriminating about the present from people whose conduct in the past has largely led up to the not altogether satisfactory position in which we find ourselves today . . .

For good measure Randolph then proceeded to open an offensive against those whom he dubbed the 'war-aim mongers':

In the camps and barracks of the Army you do not hear much argument about war aims. It is not because the Army do not care. They know for what they are fighting – their homes, their lives, their freedom, their right to determine their own future. These are not purely selfish aims; they comprise the future hopes of millions of people outside this country. All Europe knows that our victory will bring to all peace and a new chance of liberty. Of these things liberty is the greatest. Neither Herr Hitler nor Signor Mussolini dares to offer this priceless blessing. It is England's greatest and most historic offering to a Europe enslaved . . .

We make a great mistake in thinking that the world will automatically be a better place after this war. In one way I myself think that this is already a better world, in a spiritual sense, than two years ago. Then we were giving in to evil, and today we are resisting it . . .

Randolph knew all about 'the very great patience which the Army has been able to show under such trying and difficult conditions', to which he referred in his speech. However his own patience was fast running out. After more than a year of war he had yet to hear a shot fired in anger and there was not even a hint of the 4th Hussars being sent overseas. When, therefore, he learned that his friend Lt.-Col. Robert Laycock was forming a Commando unit to be trained for special operations and that many of his friends – in fact most of the White's Club brigade, Peter Beatty, Dermot Daly, Philip Dunne, Peter Milton, Harry Stavordale, Robin Campbell and Evelyn Waugh, were joining – Randolph could not restrain himself. He put in to be transferred to No.

8 Commando which was then undergoing training at Largs on the Ayrshire coast south-west of Glasgow.

No. 8 Commando consisted of ten troops of fifty men, each commanded by a captain and two subaltern section leaders. The men were drawn from the Household Cavalry, Grenadiers, Coldstream, Scots Greys, Irish and Welsh Guards as well as from the Royal Engineers, Royal Artillery and Royal Marines. On top of this tough, rough bunch of soldiers was superimposed the command structure of White's Club, whose members installed themselves in conditions of no great discomfort in the Marine Hotel, Largs, where a country house-party atmosphere prevailed. As Pamela, who went up to Largs with some of the other wives, remembers:

> Bob Laycock's biggest problem was to find functions for this White's Club group because they were absolutely unemployable, while the men under them were excellent. They were all the best, toughest, hardiest soldiers and they had all volunteered for the Commandos. They were being commanded by this crowd who knew nothing but the inside of White's Club.

Evelyn Waugh, who had been seconded to No. 8 Commando from the Royal Marines, recorded in his diary:

13 November–December 1940
The smart set drink a very great deal, play cards for high figures, dine nightly in Glasgow, and telephone to their [race-horse] trainers endlessly ... The standard of efficiency and devotion to duty, particularly among the officers is very much lower than in the Marines. There is no administration or discipline ...

The indolence and ignorance of the officers seemed remarkable, and I have since realised they were slightly above normal army standards. Great freedom was allowed in costume; no-one even pretended to work outside working hours ... Two night operations in which I acted as umpire showed great incapacity in the simplest tactical ideas. One troop leader was unable to read a compass. The troops, however, had a smarter appearance on inspection parades, arms drill was good, the officers were clearly greatly liked and respected. The men had no guard duties. After parade they were free from all restraint and were often disorderly. There was already a slight undercurrent of impatience that they had not yet been put into action ...

No. 8 Command were training for an operation code-named WORK-SHOP: the proposed seizure of the Mediterranean island of Pantellaria near the heel of Italy. This involved several assault landing exercises and especially night operations. Pamela recalls:

They used to go out on these night raids at about three in the morning. At 0500 hours Troop A were supposed to land on the beaches in their landing craft and make their assault. Troop B were to try and catch them at it. Peter Beatty – he was impossible at anything, even worse than Evelyn – was given a stop-watch and was put in charge of the landing group. '0500 hours will be the moment your troops will land,' Bob Laycock had ordered. Well 5 a.m. went by and 5.30 but nothing had happened. So Bob calls down on the phone to Peter Beatty to ask what's happened. Peter explains: 'But it's dark I can't see my watch.' That was the sort of thing they were up against. So then they would give up the water expeditions and start up the mountains. When they got to the other side of the mountains they of course didn't know what they were supposed to do next – how these poor soldiers stood for it! . . .

Then, as Pamela relates:

The worst happened. Almost as soon as Randolph joined the Commandos, the 4th Hussars were sent overseas. All the wives said it was because Randolph Churchill had been taken away so now they knew that their husbands would all be sent to their death. Randolph was most upset at this and was on the point of trying to get transferred back to his old regiment when it was learned that the Commandos were to be sent to the Middle East. As it turned out, because the 4th Hussars were sent to Crete, which proved a disaster, practically all of them were wiped out.

Shortly before Christmas Pamela wrote to Randolph describing a weekend cinema show at Chequers: 'I saw *The Great Dictator* with Charlie Chaplin as Hitler. Papa adored it and thought it frightfully funny when Mussolini & Hitler began throwing food in each other's faces! He is so delightfully naive about films isn't he.' That Christmas Randolph, Pamela and baby Winston, together with Sarah and Vic Oliver, Diana and Duncan Sandys and Mary joined Winston and Clemmie at Chequers. It was the last Christmas the family would spend together for four years.

CHAPTER 12

North Africa

In the New Year of 1941 No. 8 Commando was ordered to Egypt in the face of the arrival in North Africa of Rommel who took command of the Italian–German army which threatened the British position in Alexandria, Cairo and even the Suez Canal. Because the Mediterranean was unsafe for troopships, the only way of getting there was round Africa and the Cape of Good Hope. In early February, they set sail from England in three troopships with the White's Club contingent mostly aboard the *Glenroy*. Evelyn Waugh records in his wartime diary:

July 1940–July 1941
The conditions of overcrowding were worse than ever. No. 11 Commando were very young and quiet, over disciplined, unlike ourselves in every way but quite companionable. They trained indefatigably all the voyage. We did very little except PT and one or two written exercises for the officers. Bob took me for Force HQ as Adjutant, to be promoted to Brigade Major if we became a brigade. There was very high gambling, poker, roulette, chemin-de-fer, every night. Randolph lost £850 in two evenings [equivalent to over £20,000 today]. We stopped at Cape Town where people treated all ranks with the most notable hospitality. Harry [Stavordale] ill-treated the ostriches in the zoo. Randolph lunched with Smuts [the South African Prime Minister]. Dermot [Daly] got very drunk.

On March 8th we reached Suez and proceeded up the Canal, which was reported to be mined, to Kabrit in the Bitter Lakes. ... At Kabrit General Evetts came on board and spoke to the officers. He said we were to serve with his Division (6th) and promised us a bellyful of fighting.

When Randolph sailed for the Middle East Pamela, to economise, had invited his sister, Diana, together with her children, to share the house at Ickleford. At the time she had £12 per week to keep herself and baby Winston and was helping to run a communal kitchen which provided meals for 200–300 people a day, mostly factory workers from the nearby town of Hitchin. As Pamela relates:

Randolph told me, 'It's going to be terrible, being parted like this. But with you living very economically and I living off my Army pay we will at least be able to pay off some of the bills and that will be glorious.' The house was very cold. We didn't have much heat and so I used to go to bed at 6.30 so as to turn off the gas-fire. By day I settled down to life at my communal kitchen.

However, within three weeks of Randolph's departure, Pamela received from Cape Town a bombshell of a telegram which was to shatter their marriage. In it Randolph confessed that he had lost a fortune gambling with his rich friends on the troopship. He asked her on no account to tell his father but to arrange payment 'in the best way possible', suggesting 'payments on the instalments plan of perhaps £10 per month to each of the following...'

Until her marriage, Pamela had never been even a penny in debt but, since then, worries about bills, debts and people threatening to sue for payment had been endless. To Pamela, not yet twenty-one, Randolph's letter was the last straw. In tears she went to see their close friend Max Beaverbrook who was Minister of Aircraft Production and godfather to baby Winston. But Beaverbrook, who was generously continuing to pay Randolph's £1,500 a year salary, was adamant. He would give her a cheque as a present to pay off Randolph's shipboard debt, but he would not advance one penny of his salary. Pamela thereupon decided to rent out the house at Ickleford and park baby Winston with a nanny at Beaverbrook's country home, Cherkeley, so that Winston and Clemmie would not know what had happened, while she took a £12-a-week job at the Ministry of Supply.

Pamela paid off the debts, but things were never to be the same between her and Randolph again. As she told me: 'I sold all my wedding presents, including some diamond earrings and a couple of nice bracelets I had been given. We eventually got it all paid, but it was a lesson. I suddenly realised that if there was to be any security for Baby Winston and me, it was going to be on our own...'

On arrival in Egypt, No. 8 Commando was renamed 'B' Battalion of 'Layforce', as Bob Laycock's brigade became known. But the 'bellyful' of fighting promised by General Evetts was slow in coming. Randolph, in a footnote to his later biography of Sir Anthony Eden, recalled spending several hours at the British Embassy in Cairo with Eden who had, once again, been appointed Foreign Secretary: 'Eden concluded a telegram to the Prime Minister with the words, "Have seen Randolph who has just arrived. He sends his love. He is looking fit and well and has the light of battle in his eyes." It has been said (the author has not been able to verify the tale) that, either owing to a corruption in transmission or to a lively sense of mischief on the part of a Foreign Office official, this telegram was delivered in London with the "a" in "battle" replaced by an "o".'

By mid-May, after two months in the area of Alexandria where, according to Evelyn Waugh, 'the morale of B Battalion began to deteriorate very rapidly', they moved their headquarters to Mersah Matruh in the desert, maintaining advance parties at Tobruk. Here, according to Evelyn's diary, they 'exhausted every means of getting into action ... The feelings of the battalion were well summed up by an inscription found on the troop decks of *Glengyle*: "Never in the history of human endeavour have so few been so buggered about by so many." It was also suggested that the battalion's name should be changed to "Belayforce".'

Writing to Pamela on 24 May Randolph reported:

> ... Our present camp is at a lovely spot in the desert between a blue lagoon & green figgery. We are very near the sea & have the most perfect bathing rather like Antibes. Unfortunately today we have had a sandstorm & life has not been so enjoyable as usual. However, it makes the sea more attractive than ever.
>
> We are miles from civilization. No restaurants, no bars, no baths & hardly any news. But I am enjoying it very much & feeling extremely well. I am getting really sunburnt. If I forgot to tell you earlier the moustache [evidently grown on the voyage round Africa] was shaved off long ago, in fact the day we arrived...

Elsewhere in his letter, Randolph registered a protest about his father's inquiries which had been causing him difficulties with the military: 'I cabled you 2 days ago asking you to stop Papa making inquiries about me through Wavell etc. It really has been v. embarrassing. A cable to me at B. Layforce, is not only more simple, it is nearly always much quicker. He ought to know that in war "no news is good news". He would be sure to hear very soon if anything went wrong...'

Though cut off in the desert and only in the rank of lieutenant, Randolph decided that the command structure of the British Army in the Middle East needed shaking up. On 7 June, in a cable to his father, sent with the knowledge and encouragement of the British Ambassador in Cairo, Sir Miles Lampson, Randolph proposed that the commander-in-chief be relieved of some of his responsibilities:

DO NOT SEE HOW WE CAN START WINNING WAR HERE UNTIL
WE HAVE COMPETENT CIVILIAN ON SPOT TO PROVIDE DAY TO
DAY POLITICAL AND STRATEGIC DIRECTION. WHY NOT SEND
MEMBER OF WAR CABINET HERE TO PRESIDE OVER WHOLE WAR
EFFORT. APART FROM SMALL PERSONAL STAFF HE WOULD NEED
TWO OUTSTANDING MEN TO COORDINATE SUPPLY AND DIRECT
CENSORSHIP   INTELLIGENCE   AND   PROPAGANDA.   MOST
THOUGHTFUL PEOPLE HERE REALIZE NEED FOR RADICAL REFORM
ALONG THESE LINES. NO MERE SHUNTING OF PERSONNEL WILL
SUFFICE AND PRESENT TIME SEEMS PARTICULARLY RIPE AND
FAVOURABLE FOR CHANGE OF SYSTEM. SUPPOSE CHIEF DIFFI-
CULTY WOULD BE WHO TO SEND. THREE POSSIBLE CHOICES
SEEM EDEN SMUTS AMERY. PLEASE FORGIVE ME TROUBLING YOU
BUT CONSIDER PRESENT SITUATION DEPLORABLE AND URGENT
ACTION VITAL TO ANY PROSPECTS OF SUCCESS ENDS

Winston recorded in his *Second World War* memoirs: 'It is the fact that
this clinched matters in my mind ... And thereupon I took action...'

On 24 June Winston replied through Miles Lampson, making clear
that Randolph's suggestion had been well received:

I HAVE BEEN THINKING A GOOD DEAL FOR SOMETIME ON LINES
OF YOUR HELPFUL AND WELL CONCEIVED TELEGRAM STOP LOVE
FROM US ALL

Meanwhile, on 8 June, Winston had written to inform Randolph that
Averell Harriman, President Roosevelt's personal representative who
had visited him on frequent occasions at Chequers and Downing Street
since his arrival in March, would shortly be arriving in Egypt on a fact-
finding mission to report to the President on the progress of the campaign
in the Middle East and on the needs of the hard-pressed British forces:

A gigantic 4,000 pound bomb fell just outside the building of your flat in
Westminster Gardens [No. 70, which Randolph had rented before the
outbreak of war], obliterating the fountain and cracking the whole structure on one side. Unluckily it is the wrong side for you. The CIGS [Chief
of the Imperial General Staff] who was sleeping quite close, in fact about
twenty yards away, seems to have had a marvellous escape and is greatly
exhilarated by the explosion. I am trying to get a similar stimulus applied
in other quarters, but it is difficult to arrange.

The Annexe [the ground-floor rooms of the Cabinet Office Secretariat facing St James's Park which served as the Churchills' wartime home after No. 10 became unsafe] is now becoming a very strong place, but we have only once been below the armour [the Cabinet War Rooms] during a raid. Your Mother is now insisting upon becoming a fire-watcher on the roof, so it will look very odd if I take advantage of the securities provided. However, I suppose everybody must do their duty.

I sent you out an inquiry about the 60 men [commandos who had surrendered two weeks earlier at Castelorizzo, one of the Dodecanese Islands mid-way between Cyprus and Rhodes] because I heard a great deal of criticism here about these special troops surrendering in droves, and so on, and whatever other people may think, I am quite clear that these men ought to have fought till at least thirty per cent. were killed or wounded. Large, general capitulations are of a different character, but small parties are expected to put up a fight and not walk out of a cave with their hands up like a lot of ridiculous loons . . .

The Air attack has greatly lessened, and the Air Force are very disappointed that this moon-phase should have been spoiled by clouds, as they were hoping to make an impression upon the raiders. On the whole, I think the attack will not be so successful as it has been in the past, and at the moment we are having very little of it. Anyhow, I think the Baby is quite safe where he is . . .

Our old House of Commons has been blown to smithereens [by a German bomb on the night of 10 May 1941]. You never saw such a sight. Not one scrap was left of the Chamber except a few of the outer walls. The Huns obligingly chose a time when none of us were there. Oddly enough, on the last day but one before it happened I had a most successful Debate and wound up amid a great demonstration. They all got up and cheered as I left. I shall always remember this last scene. Having lived so much of my forty [parliamentary] years in this building, it seems very sad that its familiar aspect will not for a good many years be before me. Luckily we have the other place [the House of Lords] in good working order, so that Parliamentary institutions can function 'undaunted amid the storms'. We are now going to try the experiment of using the House of Lords. The Peers have very kindly moved on into the big Robing Room, and handed over their Debating Chamber to us. In about a fortnight I expect we shall be there. I never thought to make speeches from those red benches, but I daresay I shall take to it all right . . .

By the time you get this, all sorts of things will have happened which I cannot refer to on paper. At the present time I am hopeful that we shall retrieve and restore the position. Meanwhile, in the larger sphere, not only are we gaining mastery over the Air attack, but making good progress in the Battle of the Atlantic. The United States are giving us more help every day, and longing for an opportunity to take the plunge. Whether they will do so or not remains an inscrutable mystery of American politics. The longer they wait, the longer and the more costly the job will be which they will have to do . . .

Everything is very solid here, and I feel more sure than ever that we shall beat the life out of Hitler and his Nazi gang. We are waiting with much interest to know what fortunes have attended our entry into Syria. No one can tell which way the Vichy French cat will jump, and how far the consequences of this action will extend. It looks to me [from the Ultra decrypts provided by the code-breakers of Bletchley from intercepts of the German High Command's radio traffic] more and more likely that Hitler will go for Stalin [within a fortnight, on 21 June 1941, German forces invaded Russia in defiance of the Nazi–Soviet Pact]. I cannot help it. All my sympathies are already fully engaged.

I am having this letter left for you at the Embassy, Cairo, and am asking them to tell you that it has arrived. I do not want it to go up the line, and after you have received it, you should not take it there. Leave it at the Embassy, or burn it. Do not show it to strangers . . .

PS I send you a cheque for £100 which I expect you can get cashed in Cairo. I am telling Lloyds to notify some Bank or other there in case they have not a Branch, and will send you full advice about it.

Churchill had ordered that Harriman be shown everything and Randolph was detailed to look after him for part of his visit. Randolph reported back to his father a month later:

5 July 1941

It was indeed kind of you to suggest that I should be attached to the Harriman Mission. I have thereby not only obtained all the latest news of you and Pamela, and all my friends in London, but have also had a wonderful opportunity of learning about things out here. I have been tremendously impressed by Harriman, and can well understand the regard which you have for him. In 10 very full and active days he has definitely become my favourite American. He seems to me to possess a quite extraordinary maturity of judgment that is almost on a par with F. E.'s. He got down to work out here with amazing ease and sure footedness, and has won the confidence of everyone he met. I have become very intimate with him and he has admitted me to all the business he has transacted. I am sure you would do well to back his opinions on the situation out here to the limit . . .

Randolph was delighted by the replacement of Wavell by Auchinleck as Commander-in-Chief Middle East and made clear his approval of the appointment:

I have taken a great liking to your Intendant General. He has struck me as incomparably the ablest General I have ever met. Even judged by normal standards, he would be remarkable. It is immensely refreshing to find one man with red tabs whom one can talk to on level terms as an ordinary human being. It is also refreshing to find a General who has a private secretary. It makes it quite a pleasure to do business with him. One of the handicaps that Military people suffer from is that the first 20 years of their life they are never in a position to learn how to run an office or even to dictate a letter. By the time that such amenities are in their power, they are too set in their ways to change; as a result of which you can see Generals wandering round GHQ looking for bits of string and sealing wax. My solution for 'Muddle East', as it is widely known, is to sack half of the people in the office and provide half the remainder with competent shorthand typists. It would treble the efficiency of the Army...

What pleased Randolph most of all was that his father had so promptly taken his advice and appointed a member of the War Cabinet, Oliver Lyttelton (later Viscount Chandos), to be Middle East supremo to give political direction to the war effort in North Africa:

... I think it is the best choice you could have made, but what pleases me most is the change in system. With a good organization, even quite second rate people can do useful work. With a bad system even the best people are paralysed and stultified. The general revolution out here has, I feel, given new hope to all. My only fear is that Oliver's powers may not be quite wide enough. If the Service people are sensible they will make him their friend and advocate, and make the fullest possible use of his services. But I feel that he should have the power and indeed the obligation of presiding over all their meetings, as you do over the Chiefs of Staff. This is the only point on which I have differed with Harriman...

It has been most cheering to hear from Harriman how well and vigorous you are. I am sure you know what a tremendous admiration he has for you. He clearly regards himself more as your servant than R's [Roosevelt's]. I do hope you will keep him at your side, as I think he is the most objective and shrewd of all those who are around you. I hope too you will take his advice about American public opinion. I am convinced his view is right...

I had a talk with de Gaulle two days ago; he had just come back from

Syria, and was very unhappy about the situation there. Though he talked extremely sensibly, he seemed to me very overwrought and highly strung. I think Louis Spiers is a great handicap to him; for though you like him, no one else does.

Finally, Randolph made clear his displeasure at the threatened disbandment of the Commandos:

Our Brigade Commander, Bob Laycock, ought to arrive back in London in a few days. I do hope that you will see him, as he will be able to give you news of my military life, of which I cannot write. He will also tell you of the incredible military boobydom by which your design of having Special Service units has been frustrated out here. Apart from the absurdity of having no DCO [Director of Combined Operations] and only an inactive joint planning Committee which the three service members preside over in turn, our main difficulty has been the CGS, General Smith, who has been our declared and open enemy from the start. He actually told me the other day that the reason for our disbandment was that combined operations were 'too difficult'. Paraphrasing a celebrated retort of yours, I told him that it was a 'very difficult war'. If you still have hopes of engaging in such activities out here, I would recommend Bob Laycock as a perfect DCO. He has spent 12 months on this job, and has a better knowledge than anyone out here of the difficulties involved. He also has the spirit, youth and capacity to overcome them . . .

Thrilled as he was to be involved with Harriman's mission to the Middle East, Randolph's frustrations were mounting. The war had been going two years and still he had seen no action. The anticipated engagement of the enemy, to which he had referred in his letter to his father, never materialised. 'B' Battalion remained firmly stuck in the desert at Mersah Matruh, where Randolph worked ardently with the air force trying to organise a combined operation for a parachute attack against Gazala aerodrome, but the air force refused to co-operate. However, following Oliver Lyttelton's arrival as Resident Minister in Cairo, the major shakeup which Randolph had advocated was at last under way. But, in his letter to Pamela of 29 September, Randolph complained:

We have just heard that Wedgwood Benn [later 1st Viscount Stansgate] has refused job of director of Propaganda out here. So I suppose we will have further interminable delays. I thought of applying for the job myself, but it seems that youth, energy, journalistic experience & a fervent desire to propagand are considered definite disabilities for the appointment! London seems obsessed with the desire to find an octogenarian with no press experience . . .

But Randolph was wrong and, for once, a job suited to his talents came his way. Oliver Lyttelton decided to appoint him to the post despite having no illusions about Randolph, of whom he was to write in his memoirs: 'To say that Randolph is no respecter of persons would be a flaccid understatement: he is by nature critical of authority and vociferous in denouncing its mistakes.'

The decision to turn poacher into gamekeeper by putting Randolph in charge of propaganda and censorship was warmly welcomed by his colleagues in the Cairo-based press. Allan Michie, a Scots-born war-correspondent, recorded in his book *Retreat to Victory*:

During my assignment in the area only one major improvement took place. That was when Auchinleck and Oliver Lyttelton, the Minister of State, who was sent out by the War Cabinet to bring order into the political chaos of the Middle East, picked young Randolph Churchill, son of the Prime Minister, to take over the Army's Bureau of Information and Propaganda.

Randolph, explosive, tireless, imaginative, worked for a time on Lord Beaverbrook's London *Evening Standard* and was smart enough to realise that a co-operative press could be one of Britain's most effective weapons. He had his father's ability to slash through red tape. Like the Prime Minister, however, he creates many enemies by his bull-charging methods. Before he had been on the job for a week fellow army officers, afraid of losing their own soft positions, had begun sabotaging him.

Randolph went ahead with his changes. He fired the Chief Middle East Military Censor and his Assistant and required the new censors to sleep in their offices to give us a 24-hour service. This was a step in the right direction but it was completely nullified when the political and Anglo-Egyptian censors refused to work after 8 in the evening.

'Blind' military censorship was done away with, although both the political and Anglo-Egyptian continued to be done in secret. Doubtful military dispatches were submitted to Churchill or to his assistant, young Captain Robin Campbell, and they invariably applied a common sense rule-of-thumb to our stories.

The chief military censor in the Middle East until Churchill dismissed him was a supercilious young captain whose newspaper experience was limited to a copy of the London *Times* at the breakfast table. He is one of the few British Army Officers who can speak Japanese fluently, but the War Office in Whitehall with its peculiar knack of putting round pegs into square holes, had made him head censor in Cairo . . .

Nor was it only the British press corps that welcomed Randolph's appointment. The Americans were equally enthusiastic, as his friend Ken Downs of United Press International recalled: 'With almost ferocious energy and great skill, he began to transform the inept information section into the most efficient operation of its sort that I saw throughout the war. His experience in journalism and his personal acquaintance with the correspondents, particularly the Americans, paid off handsomely.'

Not only did Randolph at last have a job singularly suited to his talents but, for good measure, it entailed promotion. His friend Evelyn Waugh who had returned home, having taken part in the disastrous battle of Crete, hastened to congratulate him:

26 September [1941]

I hear you have been made a Major & congratulate you with all my stuffy heart. Your father, too, has had a leg up and is Warden of the Cinque Ports [one of the greatest marks of trust the Sovereign can bestow]. On looking the list up I find it vy much more considerable than that of Prime Minister. Always glad to see Churchills doing well.

I have seen Pamela – her kitten eyes full of innocent fun. She is showing exemplary patience with the Americans who now have the place in England which the Germans had in Italy in 1939. They are ubiquitous & boisterous and everyone hides their impatience splendidly . . .

I finished the book [*Put Out More Falgs*], dedicated to you & it is quite funny but paper is so short that it will not appear until it has lost all point.

England is very uncomfortable & everything is being done by the bureaucrats to aggravate the discomfort. There is a splendid new idea called 'Equality of sacrifice' which means that life is reduced to the level of a pre-war unemployed miner – in every sense for extreme idleness is combined with privation.

The only place where one feels at peace is Marine barracks – I spent a delightful two days at Plymouth – band playing, drill sergeants strutting around the parade ground, old Colonels saying rightly, that the Fonseca '22 does not compare with the Campbell '12 which the temporary officers intemperately consumed . . .

When *Put Out More Flags* was published the following year, Evelyn inscribed an early copy (which remains in the author's possession):

> For Randolph
> A minor work for a *Major* friend
> Evelyn 1942

Writing to Pamela from General Headquarters on 21 September, Randolph had told her of his new life in Cairo and that, although he and his assistant, Robin Campbell, had so far been unsuccessful in finding a flat:

> I'm enjoying it very much & think I am beginning to make some headway; but the forces of obstruction are very strong...
>
> So we still hang on at Shepheard's. This is not so inconvenient as it sounds; I leave the hotel at about 8.30 in the morning & seldom get back there 'til 8.30 at night for a bath and then out to dinner – usually at the Mohammed Ali Club which I have joined & is a very swagger affair to which all the rich Pashas belong. For the first time in my life I really have plenty of interesting work to do and am busy from morning to night...
>
> I am sending you some parcels of foodstuffs which with luck should arrive about Xmas. One v. large tin of honey which an Egyptian gave me for little Winston and three smaller parcels each containing sugar, jam, sweets and marmalade. I hope they will be a help. It seems frightful living in this land of plenty while you are all so tightly rationed at home.
>
> Darling, the picture you sent of Baby W. was divine! He certainly doesn't seem to be starving...
>
> Papa tells me in his letter that *Into Battle* [the volume of Winston's immediately pre-war and early wartime speeches which Randolph had compiled and for which he had written the Foreword] has gone so well in America that he is giving me extra. I do think it is generous of him. Mind you use it to pay the most pressing bills and to make a little reserve for emergencies.

He concluded his letter: 'Darling I am so glad that you are hearing good accounts of my work. I do terribly want to do something of which you can be proud...'

In addition to his general duties Randolph launched and edited a weekly newssheet which he called *The Desert News*, later to be known as *Eighth*

Army News, to combat the dearth of information among the troops in North Africa.

In August 1941 Churchill and Roosevelt had met aboard HMS *Prince of Wales* in Placentia Bay, off the coast of Newfoundland, to cement their relationship and to sign the Atlantic Charter. On the return journey, as the ship made its way across the Atlantic at high speed and on a zigzag course to avoid German U-boats, Winston wrote Randolph a long handwritten letter (which no longer survives) telling of the meeting. Ken Downs recalls meeting Randolph for lunch at Shepheard's one day in late September:

> He suggested going to my room before lunch as he had an interesting letter to read to me privately ... Most of the letter was personal, written in high good humour and full of little 'in' jokes about incidents on the voyage to the meeting and observations about various VIPs. But there was a serious paragraph at the end which burned itself into my memory. I cannot quote it verbatim, but it went essentially as follows:
>
> 'I feel that this is the beginning of a great and lasting friendship. The President is a great man, without any doubt. But there is something about him that troubles me deeply. It is his concern about public opinion. He tends to follow public opinion rather than to form it and lead it. I must say that our greatest single preoccupation today is with how the United States is to be brought boldly and honourably into the war.'

Randolph, though based at General Headquarters, never became part of the effete bureaucratic military establishment of Cairo referred to so appositely by the Commandos as 'The Gaberdene Swine', of whom the verse was penned:

> *We fought the war in Shepheard's*
> *And the Continental Bar,*
> *We reserved our punch for the Turf Club lunch*
> *And they gave us the Africa Star.*

Instead he used his new appointment as a roving commission to get out where the action was. Long after the war, Ken Downs had a vivid recollection of one such occasion:

> In November I went out to the Western Desert to cover the grand offensive designed to crush Rommel but which turned into one of his greatest triumphs over the Eighth Army. Early in the battle, I ran across Randolph

and joined him in his desert-equipped Ford station waggon. It was one of the wildest days I have ever known. With our 'soft' vehicle, we were in the midst of a series of swirling tank engagements from about 11 a.m. until dusk. Tanks were hit and burst into flames within fifty yards of us. Once a stick of bombs (from the RAF of course) missed us so narrowly we couldn't hear for a couple of hours. There was nothing quite so exciting as this war of movement in the desert, and I never encountered anyone who enjoyed it more than Churchill. He was like a Packer fan at a game with the Bears. A Packer fan, that is, who could quote poetry, history or classical literature to fit any situation.

Towards the end of 1941 the Commandos mounted a major raid, far behind enemy lines, against Rommel's headquarters near Sidi Rafa in Libya. Their objective was to capture or kill the 'Desert Fox'. The raid failed only because Rommel happened to be absent from his quarters that night attending a birthday party. Many of the Commandos who had been put ashore by submarine were killed in the action. Randolph's assistant, Robin Campbell, was badly shot up, losing a leg and spending the rest of the war in a POW camp. Lt.-Col. Geoffrey Keyes who commanded the raid was killed in the shootout in Rommel's house and was posthumously awarded the Victoria Cross. Randolph's former commanding officer, Lt.-Col. Bob Laycock, survived the raid and, after forty-one days wandering through the desert, managed to get back behind British lines, ragged and emaciated, to tell the tale.

The day after Laycock returned to Cairo, Ken Downs was due to return to the United States to join the army and the Office of Strategic Services (OSS). Writing of the episode many years later, he recalled:

I had to catch that plane in the morning. But I asked Randolph if he would write the story of the raid for me and file it to U. P., when it could be cleared. He said he would. The flight back home took days, down and across Africa and the South Atlantic, with stops in Brazil and the Caribbean, and we finally reached New York the first of the year. When I arrived at the United Press offices on 42nd Street to pick up my pay, I was at once congratulated on my great story. 'Which one?' I asked modestly. 'The Rommel raid of course. What a beaut. We made page 1 of the *New York Times*.' So I knew Randolph had come through again, above and beyond the call of friendship. The story he wrote for me was one of the cleanest scoops and one of the best written ever sent out over my signature.

On the evening of Sunday 7 December 1941, as Winston, Averell

Harriman and US Ambassador John Winant sat at dinner listening to the nine o'clock news on the small black wireless set at Chequers, the dramatic news broke that Japan had attacked the US Fleet at Pearl Harbor. As Roosevelt was to declare to Churchill on the telephone a couple of minutes later: 'We are all in the same boat now.' Within hours, Hitler declared war on the United States and Britain declared war on Japan. As Churchill had so long hoped, the United States at last came into the war at Britain's side. A vital turning-point had been reached. The defeat of Hitler and the ultimate liberation of Europe was at last assured.

Churchill spent that Christmas with the President at the White House planning the next stages of the war. The conflict had now entered a new and momentous phase, in which all the manpower and resources of the United States were to be committed to the struggle. Randolph, briefly back in England, hastened to congratulate his father on his speech to the United States Congress:

6 January 1942

I travelled back with [Poland's General] Sikorski with whom I have made great friends. I expect to be here about a fortnight. I do hope that you will be back before then.

I thought your Washington speech the best you have ever done – particularly the delivery which was wonderfully confident & clear. I only heard the first 10 minutes of the Ottawa speech as I had to leave to catch the flying boat in Cairo; but everyone said it was fully up to the level of the Washington one.

Pamela & Mama are both looking well & lovely. It is a great joy to see them again. Please give my love to Averell & Harry Hopkins.

The New Year of 1942 opened with the war going badly for Britain. Winston returned from Washington to find that Rommel had launched a major counter-offensive in the Western Desert, forcing the Eighth Army to retreat from Cyrenaica. Meanwhile Singapore, defended by 100,000 British and Imperial troops, was on the point of surrendering to the Japanese. At home, where increasing criticism was being voiced, the Prime Minister's conduct of the war was to be challenged in the House of Commons on a motion of 'No Confidence'. Randolph, who had been granted two months' home leave, was in his place for the debate on 28 January, intervening with a powerful and pugnacious speech in which he rounded on his father's critics:

> ... They thought that he had too much power, and that that was very bad and that the power should be removed from him. I should like to ask whether they think that the Prime Minister enjoys as much personal and political power as Hitler, Stalin, or Chiang Kai-shek, or even President Roosevelt? Under the Constitution of the United States, the President has incomparably greater power than any Prime Minister of this country could have under our Constitution...
>
> But what does all this criticism boil down to? It boils down on every hand, to the fact that people say, 'This is a very bad Government.' I was particularly amused by those members of the Conservative Party who were upset at its being such a bad Government and were rather speculating whether they could strain their consciences far enough to support a Government with so many inferior people in it. When one remembers not only the willingness but the pleasure with which they supported administrations composed of incomparably inferior ministers, it really staggers one that there should be this sudden desire among them for perfection. Perhaps, as so many Members say, this is not a very good Government, but ought we not to ask ourselves, is it a very good House of Commons? ... It is the Parliament of Munich, it is the Parliament which failed to rearm the country in time...

Randolph's provocative speech had succeeded in taunting and exposing the shallowness of his father's assailants. Tempers flared. Harold Nicolson recorded in his diary:

> Yesterday, during Randolph's rather unfortunate speech, Southby [Commander Sir Archibald Southby, Conservative MP for Epsom 1928–47] had interrupted and hinted that Randolph was not a fighting soldier ('The Hon and Gallant Member – I call him that because of the uniform he wears'). The Speaker shut him up, and in the corridor afterwards he went up to Winston and said that had he been allowed to finish, he would have congratulated Randolph on his rapid promotion. Winston shook his fist in his face. 'Do not speak to me,' he shouted. 'You called my son a coward. You are my enemy. Do not speak to me.' As I pass the tapes I find it ticking imperturbably. It tells us that the Germans claim to have entered Benghazi, and that the Japs claim to be only eighteen miles from Singapore. Grave disasters indeed...

At the end of the day the Government won its vote of confidence by 464 to 1, with the three Independent Labour Party Members, two of whom acted as tellers in the Division, voting against it.

Six months earlier, following his involvement with the Harriman mission to the Middle East, Randolph, in a letter from Cairo of 5 July 1941, had confided to Pamela:

> This letter will be brought to you by Averell Harriman who will be able to tell you all my news direct. And I am sending back by him a long dictated letter to Papa which you might get him to show you. So I won't give you a long account of our travels. I found him absolutely charming & it was lovely to be able to hear so much news of you & all my friends. He spoke delightfully about you & I fear that I have a serious rival!

Little did Randolph realise the truth of his words. Unfortunately for him, the tall, dashing presidential envoy, with his dark good looks, had also become Pamela's 'favourite American'. Averell, whose wife Marie chose not to accompany her husband to England, had quickly become enchanted by the Prime Minister's daughter-in-law, just twenty-one and abandoned by her husband due to the exigencies of war. Despite the nearly thirty years that separated them, a wartime romance blossomed between the two. Indeed, a further thirty years on, three years after Randolph's death and shortly after the deaths of their respective spouses, Averell and Pamela were to marry. Pamela later described him as 'the most beautiful man I had ever set eyes on'. Meanwhile, she had formed a close friendship with Averell's daughter Kathleen and the two proceeded to share a small house together, where Averell was a frequent visitor. John Colville, one of the Prime Minister's wartime Private Secretaries, noted in his diary how early one morning, following an air raid on Whitehall, he had gone out to see the devastation and had found Pamela and Averell together, examining the debris on Horse Guards Parade.

It was not until early 1942, when Randolph was home on leave, that he got wind of what had been going on in his absence overseas. Efforts to patch up the floundering marriage proved vain. Anita Leslie recorded in her book *Cousin Randolph* that, 'Pamela had developed other interests', adding:

> This situation was not improved by a weekend they spent together with the Roseberys at Dalmeny. Unfortunately Randolph found in the bedroom a copy of his father's Life of Lord Randolph Churchill. He discovered it was

superbly written, and he kept the light on whilst indulging his favourite pastime of reading aloud. At breakfast Pamela complained to Lady Rosebery that she hadn't had a wink of sleep all night because Randolph had kept her awake by loud declarations of what he'd discovered to be marvellous passages. He could not understand that his voice might not prove endearing to a wife for hours on end.

Then, back in London, throughout a trying evening with Pamela and his father-in-law Lord Digby, Randolph tried to be jolly but his exuberance fell flat. Evelyn Waugh, who was as usual a malicious onlooker, wrote that Pamela hated Randolph so much she could not bear to sit in the same room as him. Waugh had previously described her 'kitten eyes full of innocent fun', but on this occasion the fun did not sparkle.

During the year he had spent in North Africa, much had happened at home. Pamela had forsaken country life at the remote Ickleford Rectory in favour of the excitement of wartime London, where she had found a job. With baby Winston parked at Lord Beaverbrook's country home of Cherkley, she had begun to assert a new independence in her life. This was to be given full rein when, at the prompting of Brendan Bracken, she established a social club – known as the Churchill Club – to enable professional men and women from the US and Canadian armed forces, while off duty in London, to meet their British counterparts for a meal and a drink or to attend concerts and lectures. The club, for which Pamela found premises at Ashburton House in the precincts of Westminster School, adjacent to Westminster Abbey, was soon enjoying a huge success.

While, in later life, Randolph was able to look back upon this period philosophically, at the time he was bitterly hurt and humiliated, not least by the fact that his wife's affair with Harriman was common knowledge in social circles. At a time when all important decisions were taken at the top and many Members were away at war, the House of Commons held little appeal for Randolph. He could not wait to get back to active service in the desert where Major David Stirling's newly formed Special Air Service (SAS) had blown up over 250 enemy planes on the ground.

Not only did these events destroy my parents' marriage, but they had a devastating impact on Randolph's relationship with his father. Randolph found it impossible ever to forgive his parents for, as he saw it, condoning what had happened and, worse still, seeming to take Pamela's side by telling Randolph to be kinder to his young wife, of whom they were both so deeply fond. When Randolph levelled this accusation against his father, a battle royal erupted at Downing Street, following which his mother – fearful that Winston might have a seizure – banned Randolph from their home for the rest of the war. His youngest sister Mary, aged just twenty and serving with the Auxiliary Territorial Service (ATS) in a heavy anti-aircraft battery on the outskirts of London, was outraged that her father should be abused in this way. Though loyal to Randolph and, like her sisters, scandalised at what had befallen him, Mary proceeded to write Randolph a furious letter (which does not survive) in which she told him that the best thing he could do was to rejoin his unit and go to the Front. Mary poignantly records in her wartime diary: 'I think the greatest misfortune in R's life is that he is Papa's son – Papa has spoilt and indulged him & is very responsible . . .'

The distraught Randolph turned to an old flame from pre-war years, Laura Charteris who, at the age of eighteen, had married Viscount Long, a 21-year-old officer in the Coldstream Guards, from whom she had already separated. According to Anita Leslie:

Laura's eyes were brown not blue but she was very attractive, very vibrant and magnetic. In his lonely state he naturally became infatuated with her and she enjoyed going around with him in London.

The twenty or more love letters which he wrote her over the next two years all begin 'My darling Laura' or 'My beloved Laura' and all end 'Your devoted – Randolph'.

Randolph, still desperate to see action and smarting from the taunts levelled at him by his father's enemies in the House of Commons, contacted Lord Louis Mountbatten, then Chief of Combined Operations, to inquire if he could find room for him back in the Commandos. Mountbatten wrote on 19 March agreeing to do so. However, almost immediately, Randolph received instructions to return forthwith to Cairo. Here he learned of a malicious rumour that had been put around against him in his absence, which prompted him to write to the Commander-in-Chief Middle East:

Dear General Auchinleck,
Since my return to Cairo I have been told that during my absence a story was circulating to the effect that I had made a speech in the House of Commons criticising the Middle East Command. There is of course no word of truth in this malicious allegation. But since I learned that it has been retailed to you, I think it right to assure you myself of its falsity, more

especially in view of the personal kindness you have shown me since I have been in your command.

Yours sincerely,
Randolph S. Churchill

The commander-in-chief replied:

16 April 1942

My dear Randolph,

Thank you very much for your note. I do not think I heard the story to which you refer. If I did hear a vague rumour to that effect, I certainly paid no attention to it and have forgotten all about it. It would not have rung true in any event as I know it is not the sort of thing you would do. So please do not worry about it. I want to thank you very much for your work here during the past months. You have done a very great deal and the results are lasting. I hope I shall see you soon.

Yours sincerely,
C. Auchinleck

PS I have no similar work to offer you at present but if you have ideas as to what you would like to do in this Command, please let me have them.

Randolph had meanwhile found his own employment of which, evidently, his father had got wind, cabling him on 12 April:

PLEASE LET ME KNOW WHAT YOUR EMPLOYMENT IS AS NATURALLY I LIKE TO FOLLOW YOUR FORTUNES STOP ACKNOWLEDGE

Three days later Randolph replied:

AM JOINING DETACHMENT OF SPECIAL AIR SERVICE UNDER MAJOR DAVID STIRLING STOP I THINK I WILL FIND THE WORK INTERESTING AND AGREEABLE AS I WILL BE WITH A NUMBER OF FRIENDS IN NO 8 COMMANDO PRIOR TO ITS DISBANDMENT

CHAPTER 13

The Benghazi Raid

On learning that his friend David Stirling's SAS regiment had been formed with the objective of carrying out sabotage operations far behind enemy lines, Randolph pressed to be included. He had had enough of his staff job in Cairo and was eager for action. Fitzroy Maclean (Member of Parliament and later brigadier commanding the British Military Mission to Marshal Tito in Yugoslavia) recorded in his book, *Eastern Approaches*:

> Randolph had too good a nose for news not to find out in a very short time that we were going on an operation. And, as soon as he discovered this, he wanted to come too. David objected that he had not done his training and that in any case there was only room for six in the car.

But Randolph was not to be easily put off. According to Virginia Cowles in *The Phantom Major*, Randolph 'had a persuasive tongue and argued that although he had not been through the training course, he had at least done a parachute jump which, he felt, entitled him to accompany the group as far as the rendezvous, if nothing more. David could not deny the jump. Indeed, he had jumped with Randolph to show him how easy it was.'

Ken Downs, with whom Randolph had made friends at the time of the Windsor wedding, had been on hand to record Randolph's impressions of his first parachute jump, which he recounted in Kay Halle's *The Young Unpretender*:

> I asked him if he had been nervous before his first jump. 'Not at all,' he said. 'I have no imagination, so action doesn't bother me in advance. But when I was in the plane, the horrible thought occurred to me, what if I should freeze when I look down the hole? So, I slipped five quid to the sergeant who was next in line behind me and told him to give me a shove if I showed the slightest hesitation.' It wasn't necessary. When the time came, old Randolph hopped right out.

Randolph's parachute billowed open a few seconds behind David Stirling's but, whether due to a faulty parachute or his excessive weight, Randolph came down much faster. He hit the ground hard and was considerably bruised, though not seriously hurt. Perhaps by way of making amends, Stirling agreed to let Randolph come, at least part of the way, on the raid.

Before setting off on the operation, Randolph received a letter from his father which gave him an overview of the war:

2 May 1942

I send this letter by DMI [Director of Military Intelligence], hoping it will make a swift passage. The papers say that you have rejoined the Commandos. Of course I do not wish to hamper you in any way, but I am told that parachuting becomes much more dangerous with heavy people. This no doubt will be considered. I notice that David Stirling has been recalled home, but I hope that you will have found other friends and that the life will be to your liking.

I was very glad to hear from Stafford Cripps that he had met you dining at the Embassy, so I suppose all is put right there.

Things are better here for the time being. I made a speech of an hour and fifty minutes in Secret Session, which opened the eyes of the House so much to the vast panorama of the war and its many grievous dangers, that the debate utterly collapsed and we are not to have one on the war till just before Whitsuntide.

People here are greatly heartened by our Air offensive over Germany. Lübeck and Rostock were practically destroyed, and one German city after another will get during this summer the worst punishment that has yet been inflicted in this war. There are many signs that the Germans will be gravely affected by the prolonged, severe Air bombardment coming upon their homes at the same time that they will be bleeding on the 2,000-miles Russian front. As the summer progresses the weakness of all the Axis powers in the Air will become increasingly apparent, and it is in our interest to force the Air fighting at every point. Our improved methods of dealing with the very puny retaliatory attacks which they have been forced to make on this country, reached their climax last night when we shot down 11 out of less than 50. We have a lot of other things going forward which will become noticeable in due course.

The depression following Singapore has been replaced by an undue optimism, which I am of course keeping in proper bounds . . .

Averell has been quite seriously ill, it seems with a kind of typhoid, but he is definitely better these last few days. Pamela will no doubt tell you more about this, as she and Kathleen are watching over him, assisted by the best doctors and nurses. I earnestly hope he will be better soon, for he is a true friend of our country, and I have taken a great personal liking to him.

Mary has become a Sergeant, and is much counted on in her battery. She tells me that she has written to you. Your Mother has been suffering from tiredness as a result of her Russian Fund and other activities. She has had a sore throat, which is now better.

I went to Chartwell last week, and found Spring there, in all its beauty. The goose I called the naval aide-de-camp and the male black swan have both fallen victims to the fox. The Yellow Cat however made me sensible of his continuing friendship, although I had not been there for eight months.

Pamela seems very well, and is a great treasure and blessing to us all. Winston was in the pink when I saw him last. He has not so far grown old enough to commit the various forms of indiscretion which he would be expected to inherit from his forebears. Sarah and Diana are both well and lively, and send their love . . .

On 16 May a raiding party, consisting of six SAS men, plus Randolph, set out for Alexandria where they were to receive a final intelligence briefing before crossing deep behind enemy lines to Benghazi, which was held by Italian and German forces under the command of Field Marshal Rommel. Writing from his hospital bed some five weeks later, Randolph sent his father a detailed account of the raid:

Secret and Personal   *24 June 1942*

Our object was to sink two enemy ships in Benghazi in such a way as to block the channel to the harbour. The plans had been made and rehearsed before I joined the unit, and I only accompanied the party to study the technique of the Long Range Desert Group whose job it was to take us about 25 miles short of Benghazi. The party which was to undertake the operation consisted of six, and I was only a 'spare file'. But David promised me if anything happened to any of the six, I should be allowed to go the whole way.

Our own car was a Ford utility car stripped down to look like a German staff car. We first drove under our own steam to Siwa; there we joined forces with the LRDG patrol consisting of five trucks. From here we drove about 400 miles, taking four days over the trip. We halted under good cover some 50 miles from Benghazi, and it was here that one of the corporals, while preparing explosives, had an accident with a detonator which injured his hand.

As Fitzroy Maclean recalled in *Eastern Approaches*:

The crack of the detonator had hardly died away when Randolph appeared, jubilant. His exclusion from our expedition had been a sore point, but this it seemed to him, made everything easy. Already he was oiling his tommy-gun and polishing his pistol in preparation for the night's work.

Randolph had secured his seat in the Ford. He continued his account to his father:

As soon as it was dark, we set off with two trucks from the LRDG to guide us. About 11 that night they landed us on the road about 25 miles east of Benghazi. We hit the road within half a mile of where we wanted, which was a very creditable bit of navigation on the part of the LRDG after a journey of 400 miles.

All went well until we reached the fine concrete road about 10 miles outside the town. A screeching noise like a car cornering at a very high speed then began, and persisted however slowly we drove. We stopped to try to put it right, but our efforts were unavailing, and we eventually discovered that, during our long approach march, our front wheels had come out of alignment and in addition our front axle had got bent. So there was nothing for it but to go on, though the noise was frightful and could be heard half a mile away. But the main harm it did was, I think, to our own nerves, as we already had somewhat guilty consciences about what we planned to do and we did not like the idea of attracting so much attention.

We knew our first obstacle would be a road block three miles outside the town; and we hoped to get through this profiting by the linguistic ability of Fitzroy Maclean. He was sitting in the front of the car. David Stirling was driving, and between them was Gordon Alston who knew Benghazi well as he was there for three weeks during the last occupation. I sat in the middle at the back, with Sergeant Rose on one hand and Corporal Cooper on the other, whose duty it was to get out and silently clock the sentries if they failed to yield to Fitzroy's blandishments. We were not going to fire if it could possibly be avoided, but all of us in the back had Tommy guns and several handfuls of grenades.

The guard was alert and well placed. The sentry who challenged us remained about five yards beyond us to the right, while his colleague was about 25 yards to the left. Both of them pointed fixed bayonets at us while another three of their colleagues stayed in the background. It looked as if it would be impossible to dispose of them silently. Fortunately, however, when Fitzroy summoned the right-hand sentry to the car and answered his challenge with the single word '*Militari*', he merely reproved us for showing too much light and stood aside as we drove on with a distinct feeling of elation coupled with relief.

We could not dim our lights any further so we turned them out – luckily there was still another half-hour of moon left so we could see all right.

We saw no one until we came to the centre of the town, when a car came towards us and after it had gone about 100 yards turned round and with another car came after us. They seemed to be gaining on us, and although David accelerated they still seemed to be gaining. Having no lights and making this frightful screeching noise, we already thought we were detected, when suddenly off went a siren. We knew that the RAF were not going to bomb Benghazi that night, though they had been over the three previous nights, so it looked as if we had walked straight into a trap. We crammed on our full speed, getting up to 80 m.p.h. and, relying on Gordon Alston's local knowledge, David by superb driving suddenly crammed on the brakes and shot round a corner into a narrow street and drove on about 500 yards into the native part of the town, where we stopped and awaited developments. Police whistles sounded all over the town, and soon cars were roaring about at top speed. It was clear we could not hope to get out in our car which, in gangster parlance, was 'hot'. So David gave an order for a half-hour time pencil to be put in the car which, as it was chock-full of thermite and plastic, would go off with a pretty detonation.

It seemed our only chance was to get out on foot so, the fuse being set, we legged it through the Arab town, which has been badly knocked about by bombing and which is deserted by night as the Arabs all sleep outside the town. We found a ruined house and there we waited. After about ten minutes we decided we did not want the car to go off while we were still in the neighbourhood, so we changed the half-hour pencil for a two-hour one. Unfortunately the corporal forgot to deal satisfactorily with the discarded detonator which, ten minutes later, went off with what seemed to us an enormous bang.

After about a quarter of an hour another siren went off and quiet began to descend on the town, so Fitzroy and David went back to make a reconaissance [and the decision was taken not to blow up the car after all].

On passing through a breach in a wall, they found themselves suddenly in a narrow side street face to face with an Italian *carabiniere*.

'What,' demanded Fitzroy in faultless Italian, 'is all this noise about?'

'Oh, just another of those damned English air-raids,' replied the Italian gloomily.

'Might it be,' Fitzroy inquired anxiously, 'that enemy ground-forces are invading the town and they are the cause of the alert?' The Italian roared with laughter.

'No,' he replied, 'there is no need to be nervous about that, not with the British almost back on the Egyptian frontier.' Fitzroy thanked him and wished him good night. Although they had been standing under a street light, the Italian never noticed that he and David were both wearing British uniform. In fact, the air-raid sirens proved to be no more than a false alarm. Randolph reflected:

In retrospect, we were perhaps foolish to assume we were the cause of it, but so many circumstances taken together – having no lights, the screeching of our tyres, the sirens and whistles, the supposed pursuit by two cars all conspired to mislead us, and in combination certainly gave me the most exciting half-hour of my life.

We then decided to get on and do the job, but what with the false alarm and the halt on the road trying to mend the car, we had lost about one-and-a-half hours of valuable time, and whereas we had intended to inflate two rubber boats we now decided there was only time for one.

I was left on guard over the car, which Sergeant Rose had another shot at repairing. He got down underneath it with a torch while I kept watch. Five or six times people passed on their way to and from the docks, and we had to suspend work and lie doggo. Meanwhile, the other four carried the boat and explosives down to the dock, which was about 500 yards away.

On reaching the dock, the raiders managed to find a place where they could crawl through the wire fencing, dragging the boat and explosives behind them. From there the small party made its way, in between the cranes and railway trucks, down to the water's edge. No sooner had they unpacked the rubber boat and set about pumping the bellows than they were challenged by a sentry from one of the ships. Fitzroy told him in his best Italian to shut up and mind his own business, and resumed pumping away with his bellows, but to no effect – a loud hissing noise announced that the boat was punctured. Fitzroy thereupon returned to the car to collect the second boat which he lugged down to the dock.

This time it was David's turn to do the pumping. But his efforts proved no more successful. As Randolph related:

Now the challenges from the ships in the harbour had begun to be renewed. It was quite clear that although they might be allowed to blow up the boat on the quayside, they would hardly be allowed to launch it and row out into the harbour and fix their limpets to the side of the ships.

By this time 20 or 30 people were watching, so Fitzroy angrily said to the sentry: 'Who is in charge of this guard?' The sentry, pointing to a tent, said a corporal in it was in charge. Whereupon Fitzroy instructed him to turn out his guard, and proceeded to give them all a terrific dressing-down.

He said (in Italian), 'We are German officers and we have come here to test your security arrangements. They are appalling. We have been past this sentry four or five times. He has not asked us once for our identity cards. For all he knows, we might be English saboteurs. We have brought great bags into the dock. How is he to know they are not full of explosives? It is a very bad show indeed. We have brought all this stuff in here, and now we are going to take it out again.'

This they then proceeded to do, and they were smartly saluted by the corporal as they went.

David meanwhile had told me that he was pretty sure he would not be able to do any good that night, and that I must find a place where we could hide the car and lie up until the following night.

I found a private garage which had been knocked about by bombing. Unfortunately the street was so very narrow the driver had to drive the car back and forwards about 25 times (making the most frightful noise) before it was discovered the entrance was a quarter of an inch too small. Eventually we discovered another similar place, and after a good deal of shunting got the car in.

All this took a great deal of time and was rather alarming, as I did not know how I would fare if anyone came along and asked me what I was doing.

Now it was light, and we all ascended to the house on top of the garage and went to sleep. We woke about 7 o'clock in very high spirits and feeling there was nothing we could not get away with inside Benghazi. Suddenly, however, the whole town became alive. We did not realise that though the Arabs sleep outside the town they all return to their houses during the day. The staircase of our house was in a patio which shared a common wall with the house next door, which had a similar patio to our own. Into this soon came an aged Arab couple who pattered about preparing their breakfast.

This compelled us to keep extremely quiet and talk in nothing but whispers. (I found this extremely difficult.) It also exposed us to the fear that the owner of the house might return, though its incredible state of filth made us feel it had been evacuated. So it proved, but the day was long and very trying. We only had about two books between us – I luckily had F. S. Oliver's *Alexander Hamilton*.

We took it in turns to keep watch, and had decided if anyone should come in our best chance was to have Fitzroy engage him in conversation, then seize him and tie him up.

The hours passed. Then, as Fitzroy recalled:

Suddenly, as we lay dozing, we heard the sound that we had been half expecting all day: heavy footsteps ascending the stairs. Randolph, who was keeping watch, was outside first. There was an exclamation and a stampede. Snatching our tommy-guns, we reached the door to see a frightened-looking Italian sailor disappearing into the street, whilst Randolph, his beard bristling, stood majestically at the top of the stairs.

It had been a nasty fright. Randolph's account to his father continues:

This threw us into a considerable state of alarm, but on thinking it over it seemed most unlikely the sailor had come there looking for us, or that his fleeting glimpse of me would make him guess that in the house there were six fully armed British soldiers together with a car. It seemed most likely he had come there looting, and finding the house occupied had cleared out in a panic. Whatever the explanation, we lay there unmolested, but from now on every sound in the street filled us with apprehension.

We knew the RAF were going to bomb the town that night, so it was decided to have another shot at the ships under cover of the air-raid. About 10.30 the harbour party sallied out to make a reconnaissance, and on reaching the harbour found that there was a ship of about 3,000 tons on fire, which lit up the whole harbour area. No bombs had been dropped, and we still do not know what caused the fire. The light it gave out was a tremendous handicap to our operation and, as an additional disappointment, the all-clear sounded almost immediately.

We subsequently discovered that the RAF, seeing the fire, thought we had caused it and decided they had better not interfere, so went off to drop their bombs on neighbouring aerodromes.

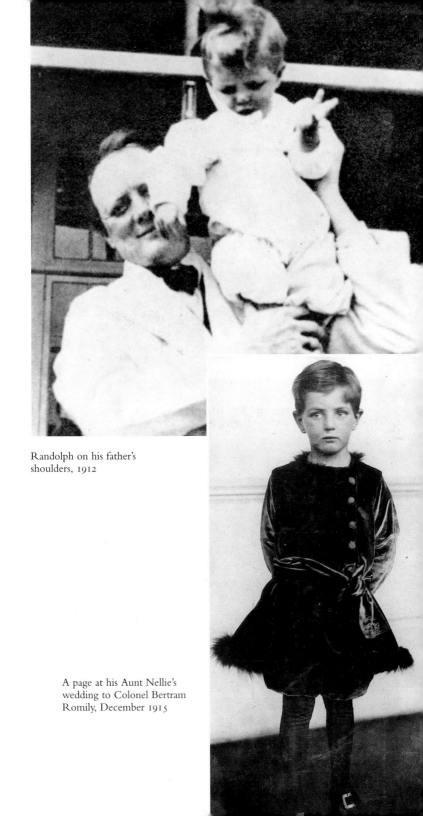

Randolph on his father's
shoulders, 1912

A page at his Aunt Nellie's
wedding to Colonel Bertram
Romily, December 1915

Randolph playing tennis at
Frinton, 16 August 1922

With his mother at Eton, 4 June 1926

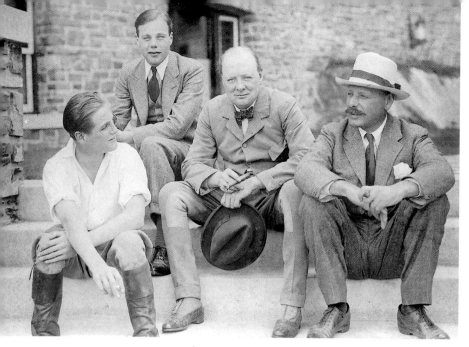

On a visit to America with his cousin Johnnie, Winston, and Uncle Jack, 1929

Wild boar-hunting in France on the Duke of Westminster's estate with Winston and 'Coco' Chanel, Saint Saëns, April 1928

Left to right: Tom Mitford (only brother
of the Mitford sisters), Freddie Birkenhead
(son of Winston's great friend F.E. Smith),
Winston, Clementine, Diana, Randolph,
Charlie Chaplin, at Chartwell, July 1931

With Sir Harold Bowden riding pillion
at the Motor Cycle Show, Olympia,
30 November 1931

Canvassing in West Toxteth,
Liverpool, 11 November 1935

At the Ross and Cromarty
by-election, 10 February 1936

(*above*) Randolph's wedding to the Hon. Pamela Digby at St John's Church, Smith Square, London, 4 October 1939 (*below*) Randolph with his parents, 1939

In the Western Desert,
North Africa, 1941

Leading British and American troops onto the island of Lissa, off the Dalmatian coast in the Adriatic, 1944

Randolph making his first parachute jump in the Western Desert, April 1944

Randolph (second from right standing) and Captain Earl Jellicoe (extreme right standing) pictured with paratroop comrades in the Western Desert, April 1944

With Anthony Eden at the Ridderzaal, The Hague, 1948

Randolph's wedding to June
Osborne at Caxton Hall,
London, 2 November 1948

Arabella's christening, 8 December 1949 –
from left to right: Randolph, Clementine,
Winston, June and Arabella, Colonel and
Mrs Rex Osborne

Randolph campaigning against Michael Foot at Devonport, Plymouth, 20 February 1950

Three generations of Churchills campaigning in Devonport

With Winston and Arabella at Chartwell, 1951

From left to right: Duncan and Diana Sandys, their son Julian, Emma Soames on Winston Churchill's knee, Nicholas Soames (sitting on a cushion), Winston, Clementine, Arabella and Randolph, Chartwell, 1951

At the Whitehouse with Winston receiving, on his father's behalf, Honorary Citizenship of the United States from President Kennedy, 9 April 1963

Correcting proofs of *The Six-Day War* on the terrace at Stour with Winston, 1967

Best man at the wedding of Winston, 15 July 1964

Arabella's eighteenth birthday party – from left to right: Minnie Churchill, Arabella, Randolph, Winston, Sarah, Mary Soames, October 1967

With Natalie Bevan and pugs at Stour, 1967

It was clearly impossible to launch a boat, as there were squads of people standing around to watch the fire and everything was clearly illuminated. David considered the desirability of putting delayed action charges in three MTBs which were right alongside the quay, but eventually decided it was not worthwhile giving away the fact we had been inside Benghazi for so small a prize, as we now felt that we could easily return later and make a proper job of the ships. So he decided instead we would go off and attack our second objective, which was Benina aerodrome.

The men had been working all day on the car, and we hoped now it would make less noise. Unfortunately as soon as we got to the main road the noise was as bad as ever; so we stopped this time in one of the main streets of Benghazi – and had another shot at putting it right.

We went to work for about one and a half hours, and during this time many people passed us, but of course nothing arouses less sensation than people working on a car, and nobody challenged us, no doubt for fear of being asked to give a hand! In fact no one said a word to us, and we worked on as hard as we could.

All, however, to no avail. The car still made as much noise as ever. It was now about 3 o'clock, and we had to get going. There was still time to have beaten up Benina, but the noise our car made might have made escape impossible and would have revealed the fact that we had been inside Benghazi, for our screechings inside Benghazi and at Benina would plainly have been associated once we did anything to provoke inquiry. So there was nothing for it but to go back to breakfast with the LRDG.

We had to negotiate the road block once more. This time they were a little more inquisitive, and upon Fitzroy shouting '*Militari*' they inquired 'What sort of *militari*?', to which Fitzroy responded 'German Staff Officers', and the sentry replied '*Molto bene*'.

The raiding party made its way safely back across the desert to Alexandria. Though bitterly disappointed at having failed to achieve their objectives, they were filled with confidence at their ability to mount future operations of a similar nature. But, on the very last lap, disaster struck as they drove by night from Alexandria to Cairo. According to Randolph:

We had gone about 30 miles, and were passing a long convoy of trucks coming towards us, when suddenly the last one pulled out right in front of us. David swerved sharply off the road but it just touched our near rear wheel and swung us broadside across the road. Our car turned over a couple of times. All of us fortunately were thrown clear, excepting Arthur

Merton, the *Daily Telegraph* war correspondent, whom we had met in Alexandria and to whom we were giving a lift. He was pinned in the car. He had a number of fractures in the head, and unfortunately died before he got to hospital. We were all picked up quite quickly and taken back to Alexandria.

Gordon Alston, Fitzroy, Sergeant Rose and myself all had fairly serious injuries but David, as always, had the luck of the devil, and was wholly unscathed. He left us next morning to go off on another similar enterprise. He is now a few days overdue, but I feel sure he will turn up quite all right . . .

Randolph, who suffered a seriously crushed vertebra, was forced to spend several weeks in a military hospital in Cairo, before being invalided back to England. In a postscript to his account of the Benghazi raid he had better news to report of Stirling's most recent exploit:

David has just got back safe and sound. He burnt down 3 hangers at Benina Aerodrome, destroying about 14 aero-engines, 4 aircraft, and all the aero-engine workshops.

He waited till the first delayed-action charge went up and then opened the door of the guard-house. Inside, facing him, was a German officer seated at a table with about 15 German soldiers drawn up in front of him. David opened his hand and showed the Hun officer a hand-grenade. The Hun wailed '*Nein! Nein! Nein!*' '*Ya! Ya! Ya!*' replied David, lobbing it in and closing the door. There was a fine bang, and as he made off into the darkness a few low moans was all that could be heard from the guard-house.

David then hid up for three days, before returning and shooting up a lot of enemy transport about 4 miles outside Benghazi. He had twin mounted Vickers K. guns on a big truck and destroyed about 15 large lorries, killing about another 10 Huns. He then drove off and made good his escape up the escarpment . . .

Hundreds of miles behind enemy lines with his friends, David Stirling and Fitzroy Maclean, Randolph had felt in his element, relishing the challenge and the excitement. To his frustration, his injuries ruled him out of participating in any of the immediately ensuing raids. By the time he was again fit for active duty, the changing tide of war had shifted the emphasis away from the daring, behind-the-lines raiding parties by the SAS and LRDG to large-scale attacks with massed armour and mechanised infantry.

A bizarre footnote to the Benghazi raid came my way many years later when, in 1992, I travelled to Egypt for the commemoration of the 50th anniversary of the Battle of El Alamein. In the course of a visit to the Cairo Museum with the Prime Minister, John Major, in whose party I was travelling, I was fascinated to hear the curator explain that all those involved, with the 5th Earl of Carnarvon, in the opening of King Tutankhamun's tomb in 1922, had met violent deaths – the last of these being Arthur Merton who, at the time, was on the staff of *The Times* and had been the only journalist present. Merton's death twenty years later completed the supposed curse placed upon those who desecrated the young Pharaoh's tomb.

CHAPTER 14

A Soldier with the Desert Army

Britain's fortunes in North Africa had reached their lowest ebb. Rommel's Panzer divisions, which had swept the British from Cyrenaica, inflicted a further crushing defeat at Tobruk when, on 21 June 1942, they captured 33,000 British and Commonwealth soldiers, together with a vast quantity of stores. Following this latest German advance, Britain's ability to hold Egypt and the vital Suez Canal was in question. Randolph, having been invalided out of Egypt, returned home by air via El Fashr, Kano, Lagos, Accra, Bathurst, Natal, Trinidad, Puerto Rico, Miami, Washington, Montreal and Prestwick – a flight of 17,000 miles by B-24 Liberator bomber.

On his return to England, Randolph prepared a secret memorandum on the conduct of the war in North Africa for his father. Randolph stressed the need for changes in command and for the commander of the Eighth Army to have tank experience:

> Tank warfare is a highly specialised art. It is no use saying that any General worth his salt should be able to handle tanks. No doubt if they had received the right training they could; but they have not, so they can't. It is not merely a question of the technical knowledge involved, it is rather the attitude of mind. Twenty years of peace-time soldiering is itself a bad education for war, and infantry training is the worst possible background for Commanders. I would go so far as to say that the GOC 8th Army ought to be a tank man...

Two nights later Churchill took off by Liberator for Cairo to see the situation at first hand, en route for a first meeting with Marshal Stalin in Moscow. He examined the positions at El Alamein where Allied forces were digging in to resist Rommel's threatened further advance. In the course of this visit, and after consultation with Field Marshal Smuts, he took the decision to appoint General Alexander commander-in-chief in place of Auchinleck. Shortly afterwards, following the death of the newly appointed General Gott whose plane was shot down flying into Cairo on the route taken by the Prime Minister in an unescorted aircraft two days earlier, Churchill gave General Montgomery command of the Eighth Army. Montgomery's selection was popular with the troops, especially as he had a knowledge of tank and desert warfare. This changeover in command marked a turning-point in the desert war. By late October of that year, Tobruk had been avenged by the victory of El Alamein, in which Montgomery's forces routed Rommel's famed Afrika Korps, inflicting massive casualties on the enemy who lost 59,000 men in twelve days' fighting.

Randolph, debarred by his injury from resuming active service for the time being, plunged with almost as much relish, and certainly with equal vigour, into political controversy at home. In a speech to his constituents in Preston on 2 September, he was fiercely critical of all three main political parties, not least the Conservative Party, whose leader happened to be his father. He warned his audience that unless the Conservative party shook off many of its 'retrograde and selfish associations' there was a possibility that a Centre party would emerge, based on the best elements of all existing parties. He went on bravely to declare: 'Though the Conservative Party still retained many of its traditions and principles, those who controlled and dominated the Party increasingly tended in pre-war years to serve the interests of a purse-proud, acquisitive and selfish minority who, for the most part, were more alarmed at the spread of Socialism than by the rise of Hitlerism.'

In a speech a few days later in Tunbridge Wells, Randolph described the British as 'one of the most class-conscious and snob-ridden nations in the world' and called for 'real equality of education' with all children, rich and poor, being taught at state schools where they would grow up to understand each other's point of view. He went on to advance the then novel idea that there should be a weekly family allowance of 10s 0d for the third and every subsequent child in a family, with a view to reversing the decline in the birth rate.

Towards the end of the month Randolph returned to the Preston theme in his third – and, as it proved, his last – speech in the House of Commons in which he publicly exposed the unspoken scandal whereby wealthy candidates could buy a safe seat by agreeing to underwrite the expenses of the local Conservative Association. To the embarrassment and outrage of many of his Tory colleagues he told the House:

I should like to see each party recommending the sweeping away of those abuses from which it profits most itself. There are a number of electoral abuses from which the Labour Party profits, but as I am not a member of that party, it would be ungracious of me to deal with them; but I would like to briefly indicate some of the electoral abuses from which the Tory Party profits and which should be prohibited by law before we have another General Election. Of course the greatest scandal is the black marketeering in constituencies, the sale of seats to rich men, that goes on. It is a scandal to the party and to the House of Commons, and it brings representative government into great disrepute. I would like to see the amount of money that a candidate or member can expend on political organizations severely limited. I would like to see election expenses limited . . .

At this point, Randolph was pulled up by the Deputy Speaker who told him his remarks were digressing from the business under discussion, namely the Prolongation of Parliament Bill. But Randolph had made his point and a predictable outcry ensued.

Captain E. C. Cobb, the senior of the two-Member seat of Preston, formally announced that if Randolph remained as MP for Preston, he would quit. At a special meeting of the Preston Conservative Association on 16 October, called at Randolph's request, party members were given the opportunity of expressing their views on the issue. In the course of a lively two-and-a-half-hour meeting, Randolph received an overwhelming vote of confidence of 44 to 8 while the meeting called on Captain Cobb to resign by a margin of 32 votes to 11. Captain Cobb in fact refused to resign and at a meeting the following month the Preston Conservatives rescinded their call for him to do so, while recording his intention not to seek re-election.

At the end of October Randolph was declared fit by a Medical Board and arranged to return forthwith to his unit. However, getting wind of an important new operation – the first Anglo-American operation of the war – he volunteered to join the British First Army that was on the point of sailing from Scotland. He shared his feelings, though not his plans, with Laura Charteris who had become the mainstay of his emotional life. As Anita Leslie relates, Randolph wrote to Laura in October 1942 before sailing from Glasgow: 'My darling Laura, I am using your beautiful writing case for the first time . . . The place I am off to is extremely inaccessible and I gather I will have to leave for the Middle East at any moment . . . so don't expect to hear from me for some time. It will not mean that I have forgotten you. As I told you the other night it pains me deeply that I should not be in a position to say to you the things I would like to say.'

Four days later Randolph wrote to Laura at sea en route for Algiers, 'I must apologise for the deception which I had to practise on you. As you may hear before you get this letter I am not really going to the Middle East. We are on a much more exciting venture of which you will soon be reading in the papers.'

The endeavour to which Randolph was referring was Operation TORCH, the Allied invasion of French North Africa. This involved a three-pronged assault, with American forces landing at Casablanca and Oran while a joint American and British force, comprised of the British First Army to which Randolph had got himself attached, attacked Algiers. At Oran there was some fierce fighting, but at Algiers the Vichy French put up little resistance and, within two days, Admiral Darlan – second-in-command of the Vichy forces, who happened to be visiting Algiers at the time of the landings – ordered all his troops in North Africa to lay down their arms. This important development – the first direct involvement of US ground forces in the war – came hard on the heels of the Eighth Army's victory at Alamein which prompted the Prime Minister to order church bells – previously the signal for invasion and, consequently, long silent – to be rung in celebration.

On 12 November British airborne forces, supported by commandos from the sea, seized Bône on the Algerian coast, close to the Tunisian border. Randolph, who got there the next day, hastened to send his father a report:

15 November [1942]

... The appointment of Darlan has come as a great shock to most people, particularly to those most friendly to us, and most of all to those who ran the greatest risk for our cause. These last have all been left high and dry, and some of them who committed no other offence than to declare openly for the Allies last Sunday, are now in prison. It may be that our immediate military requirements may be best served by the present policy; but many people feel that this is a poor foundation on which to try and revive a real fighting spirit among the French, either here or in France.

We seem to be getting on to a basis of humbug, which will scarcely stand the test of time. Yesterday Pétain repudiates Darlan, and orders the French to continue to resist the Allies in Africa. Darlan's reply is twofold. He puts the enclosed statement in the local Papers, while he continues to govern and publish decrees 'In the name of the marshal – the chief of the French State'. I suppose that if Darlan succeeds in delivering the Fleet [the French Fleet consisting of 73 vessels including 1 battleship, 2 battle cruisers, 7 cruisers, 29 destroyers and torpedo boats and 16 submarines, was in fact scuttled in Toulon harbour on 27 November to prevent it falling into German hands] the price we shall have paid will not have been too heavy. But it all seems a rather squalid affair.

Randolph went on to give his father a detailed account of his conversation with the former French Prime Minister, Pierre Flandin:

... We talked for about an hour and a half, and the general impression I sustained is that he genuinely wishes to see the Germans beaten. I started by asking him about his own political fortunes. His story is that when he came into Office [as Prime Minister] following Laval's dismissal, the Germans protested vigorously, and that he persuaded Pétain to allow him to send a note to the Huns complaining of German interference in the internal Government of France. The note was about to go when Darlan, through Benoit Mechin, persuaded Pétain against this course, and organised an intrigue as a result of which he was ousted ...

According to Flandin, Darlan told Pétain in his presence in Feb. '41 that it would be unwise to resist the Germans in any way as England would certainly be defeated before the end of March '41 ...

He thinks it vital that British or American troops should reach Vienna, Bucharest and Budapest before the Russians ...

Winston, who evidently had not yet received Randolph's report, wrote to him from Lyneham, the base of RAF Ferry Command:

Midnight 19-xi-42

Dearest Randolph,

I have come down here to see F. M. Smuts off, & I take the chance of sending you a line.

All is well here at home & Winston & his mother are completely installed in their flat [the top floor of No. 49 Grosvenor Square]. He is coming to see me next week. From all I hear he flourishes.

Our affairs have gone wonderfully well, I have had most enthusiastic messages from Uncle Joe [Stalin]. Rommel's remnants are in the toils & it may well be a clean mop up for them.

But the key to the future is the Tunis trip that I hope you will be taking a hand in yourself. All good luck attend you. Write to me when you can. One of these fine days you will see me turn up from somewhere. Your mother sends her love.

Ever your loving father
Winston S. Churchill

General Eisenhower's agreement with Darlan, by which the French traitor was placed in charge of the civil government of North Africa, had the effect of limiting the bloodshed but raised a storm of protest among the Free French as well as in Britain. However the situation was speedily resolved when, on 24 December, a young Frenchman assassinated Darlan at the door of his office. The next morning, Christmas Day, the Prime Minister received the following flash signal from Randolph in Algiers:

HOPE YOU WILL NOT CONSIDER IT UNSUITABLE OR UNTIMELY FOR ME TO SUBMIT FOLLOWING OBSERVATIONS.

I. NATURALLY WE CANNOT CONDONE ASSASSINATION BUT IDLE PRETEND TEARS SHED NORTH AFRICA OR FRANCE. INDEED IF THIS EVENT HAD OCCURRED PRIOR TO NOV. 8 IT WOULD HAVE OCCASIONED WIDESPREAD JOY.

2. I KNOW NOTHING OF ASSASSINS ANTECEDENTS OR CONNECTIONS BUT ONLY FRENCH HAVE RIGHT TO JUDGE HIS ACTIONS AND THAT MUST WAIT UNTIL AFTER WAR. MEANWHILE HE SHOULD BE DETAINED IN AMERICAN CUSTODY.

3. SPLENDID OPPORTUNITY NOW TO MAKE POLITICAL ARRANGEMENTS NOT ONLY SERVICEABLE MILITARY SITUATION HERE BUT ALSO MORE IMPORTANT PROCURE UNITY AND FUTURE STRENGTH OF FRANCE. . . . AM CONVINCED THIS IS RIGHT CARD TO PLAY. . . . HAPPY CHRISTMAS LOVE

Randolph followed this up with a further telegram and a letter to his father:

1 January 1943

Bad weather has stopped all flying and I am still stuck here. As a result I think I have been able to do some useful work. I saw Eisenhower yesterday . . . I told him what a bad impression the recent arrests have made and of the need for Giraud [Darlan's replacement] to liberalise (at least in appearance) his regime. To my surprise he expressed whole-hearted agreement and said that he himself had been urging this upon Giraud. I told him of the widespread fear that repression will only lead to further assassinations. Eisenhower was most sympathetic to all my suggestions . . .

PS Just heard that most of the prisoners have been released, and that Eisenhower is grateful for my intervention.

Shortly thereafter Harold Macmillan was appointed Resident Minister at Allied Force Headquarters, Algiers. Meanwhile, early in the new year, Winston replied with home news and a note of warning:

7 January 1943

Your letters and enclosures have been most interesting and very much to the point. I showed them to Anthony [Eden] who was impressed by them. You do not say anything of your own doings, but I expect you have had a most interesting time and there should be plenty more to come.

Everything here is very quiet and peaceful since our victories and, of course, the Russian triumphs [on the Eastern Front] have been beyond all expectations. The danger now of course is of people running to the other extreme expecting a quick end to the war and the rapid building-up of Utopias and Eldorados. The Parl. is still on holiday which I cannot conceal from you is an easement to those concerned in carrying on the war. There is much I could tell you which I cannot commit to writing. On the whole I am well satisfied with the way things are going, especially when one looks back on what we had come to.

We had a very peaceful and pleasant Xmas; only the family, Brendan and the Prof. You will see how the latter has become Paymaster-General and is now a Minister and a Privy Councillor. He is a great help to me. Young Winston [aged 2] is very good at Bagatelle and plays it with an air of masterly concentration.

I suggested to Harold Macmillan that he should get in touch with you when convenient, as I think he would be interested to hear what you have written to me. Of course, the Americans have managed this show and we have accepted that fact both in the political and in the military spheres.

I shd be careful of Flandin who is a thoroughly discredited man after his Munich telegram to Hitler.

On 12 January Churchill returned to North Africa for a fortnight's conference with President Roosevelt at Casablanca in Morocco, recently liberated by Allied forces, from where he signalled to Algiers for Randolph to join him. Roosevelt brought with him his own sons Elliott and Franklin Jr.

At the Casablanca Conference the shape of the war over the coming months was determined. The conference adopted Churchill's strategic plan for the completion of the conquest of North Africa, the invasion of Sicily, the strategic bombing of Germany, the defeat of the U-boat menace and the preparations for the invasion and liberation of Nazi-occupied Europe later in the year. The decision was also taken to demand the unconditional surrender of the enemy and that the defeat of Germany and Italy should have priority over Japan.

Stalin was unable to attend the conference because of the critical military situation outside Stalingrad where intense and bitter fighting was reaching its climax. On 31 January, General von Paulus and the German Sixth Army, who were encircling Stalingrad, surrendered. The Germans has already lost more than 200,000 men; a further 91,000 were taken prisoner. Throughout the winter, the Russians maintained a vigorous counter-offensive, driving the Germans out of all the territory they had gained the previous summer.

As these momentous events were under way in Russia, Randolph accompanied his father to Adana in Turkey for a conference with President Inönü, whom it was hoped to persuade to join the Allies against Germany or at least to allow British bases on Turkish soil to be manned by their own troops. Randolph was concerned at the security arrangements made for his father's safety, which were in marked contrast to the massive overkill provided by the American forces at Casablanca. Gerald Pawle described the scene in *The War and Colonel Warden*:

> The site of the Adana Conference was a railway siding in desolate open country. All around was ploughed land churned to an impassable morass by torrential rain. The Turks had provided two trains which were coupled together. In them the Prime Minister's party and the entire Turkish Government worked and slept. It was known that many Germans were living and working in the neighbourhood. In the circumstances the arrangements for guarding us seemed a little casual, and Randolph suggested that we might do some patrolling ourselves when night fell ... in the end, however, we came to the conclusion that as anyone who could not speak Turkish would almost certainly be shot if he ventured out after dark, it would be more sensible to remain on board the train and place additional sentries inside the PM's coach.

From Turkey, Randolph flew back to resume his duties in North Africa but even from there he was able to cause a rumpus in Parliament. He had long been concerned about the bitterness and recriminations directed against all Frenchmen who had occupied any official position under the Government of Vichy and the suggestion that they must necessarily be either traitors or Fascists. This prompted him to write a letter from Algiers to the editor of the London *Evening Standard*, calling for an end to this campaign of recrimination in the interest of the successful prosecution of the war and, above all, the rebuilding of a strong, free and democratic France once victory was achieved. That same afternoon the Socialist MP Aneurin Bevan telephoned the Prime Minister's office to say that he intended to put down a Private Notice Question to the Prime Minister in his capacity of Minister of Defence. He was immediately told by the Churchill's Private Secretary that such a question ought to be addressed to the Secretary of State for War. However Bevan replied that he wanted the question answered by the Prime Minister himself as it concerned the Prime Minister's son.

On 16 March Bevan asked the Prime Minister: 'Whether he is aware that a letter appeared in the *Evening Standard* of Wednesday, 10th March, written by a serving officer attached to an intelligence unit in North Africa; whether he can inform the House if this letter was passed by a junior officer; and whether he has any comment to make'. The Prime Minister replied that the Honourable Member had addressed the question to him rather than the Secretary of State for War 'no doubt from those motives of delicacy in personal matters which are characteristic of him', while pointing out that this matter did not fall under the restrictions of paragraph 547a of King's Regulations as it concerned not military but political affairs.

A week later Bevan raised the matter again at some length in a debate. This prompted an Independent MP, the motherly but formidable Eleanor Rathbone, to deliver a fierce and stinging rebuke, as reported by *Punch*:

Miss Rathbone, clutching an armful of loose papers, and with a wisp of white hair escaping from her ample hat, rose. Fixing the back of Mr Bevan's reddening neck with a firm gaze, Miss Rathbone remarked that he had a vicious and venomous dislike of the Prime Minister.

Mr Churchill sat up, clearly wondering what was coming. Mr Bevan sat up, clearly wondering what *had* come. Neither had long to wait.

It was execrable bad taste, said Miss Rathbone, for Mr Bevan to do something to embarrass and to give pain to the Prime Minister just after his return from a long illness, and when he had been on a long journey on the business of the nation. Mr Bevan filled her with disgust and loathing. By this time the House was enjoying it. A 'cattish display of feline malice', the hon. lady remarked, almost gently, as she sat down to applause that would have satisfied the most self-centred of leading ladies. Mr Bevan did not join in. He was (for once) silent.

Randolph had no doubt been right in his sentiments, but had caused his father to be burdened with an unnecessary row at a time when he had weightier matters requiring his attention. Winston none the less was proud of the role his son was playing on, and behind, the front lines. In a letter of 28 March to Harold Macmillan in Algiers he wrote: 'I do not propose sending him a reproving telegraph if he is in action with his unit. After the battle is over and Tunis cleared of the enemy, it might well be that he would be more useful in the House.' In a letter to Randolph he made no complaint, offering no more than a mild and comradely reproof:

16 April 1943

... I send you the extracts from Hansard about your letter to the *Evening Standard*. The House was not particularly friendly, and the little Astor pup nipped in with an awkward Supplementary about which I was not informed. However on the second day it reached a satisfactory conclusion, and the finishing outburst by Miss Eleanor Rathbone was one of the best things I have ever heard in the House of Commons for spontaneous invective and dominating passion. You ought to write to her. Aneurin Bevan took to his bed for some days afterwards. So 'all's well that ends well'. All the same, I was put to a lot of trouble, and I know there were some considerable perturbations high up in Algiers. People are always disagreeable about a serving officer at the front taking part in political controversy ...

The tide of victory has flowed so strongly and swiftly since Alamein, that people are pretty solid in their loyalties. Naturally I wait with strained attention the developments which lie ahead of you. We have, however, so great a superiority in numbers and equipment over the enemy, that we have a right to hope for decisive and satisfactory results.

Baby Winston is extremely well. He came to stay at Chequers the week-end before last, and shows proficiency at bagatelle though he has not yet reached your Casablanca standard. He is coming again tomorrow. Naturally, as he gets older he develops more personality, which takes the form of 'naughtiness'. But his Mother takes infinite pains with him, and with extreme patience makes him yield his point of view. He is very handsome with a noble air. He has got the Eighth Army firmly in his mind, but is not yet apparently aware of the feats of the First ...

Your Mother sends her love. Sarah continues her toil in the Photographic Section [of the Royal Air Force]. Mary has been posted to the heavy battery in Hyde Park, and Diana's event is expected in June. I am going to spend Easter at Chartwell, which I have not seen for many months. The valley must be lovely now.

The German–Italian armies under the command of Field Marshal Rommel had by now been swept off the North African littoral by the Eighth Army under General Montgomery pressing westwards from Libya, linking up with the First British Army, the 2nd US Corps and 19th French Corps advancing eastward from Algeria. Colossal casualties had been inflicted on the enemy, with more than 50,000 dead or wounded and nearly 250,000 taken prisoner by the Allies.

At the end of May, following his third wartime visit to Washington to meet President Roosevelt, Churchill flew to North Africa for a conference with General Eisenhower in Algiers, where he was joined by Randolph. With Eisenhower he planned the next phase of the campaigns including the invasion of Sicily and the liberation of the Italian mainland. As Winston recorded in his *Second World War* memoirs:

> The circumstances of our meeting were favourable to the British. We had three times as many troops, four times as many warships, and almost as many aeroplanes available for actual operations as the Americans. We had since Alamein, not to speak of the earlier years, lost in the Mediterranean eight times as many men and three times as many ships as our Allies. But what ensured for these patent facts the fairest and most attentive consideration was that notwithstanding our immense preponderance of strength we had continued to accept General Eisenhower's Supreme Command and to preserve for the whole campaign the character of a United States operation. The American chiefs do not like to be outdone in generosity. No people respond more spontaneously to fair play. If you treat the Americans well they always want to treat you better. Nevertheless I consider that the argument which convinced the Americans was on its merits overwhelming.

In between his meetings with General Eisenhower and General Marshall, Churchill travelled to Tunisia where, accompanied by General Alexander, he addressed the victorious British forces in the Roman amphitheatre at Carthage. As he recalled the occasion:

> The sense of victory was in the air. The whole of North Africa was cleared of the enemy. A quarter of a million prisoners were cooped in our cages.

Everyone was very proud and delighted. There is no doubt that people like winning very much. I addressed many thousand soldiers at Carthage in the ruins of an immense amphitheatre. Certainly the hour and the setting lent themselves to oratory. I have no idea what I said, but the whole audience clapped and cheered as doubtless their predecessors of two thousand years ago had done as they watched gladiatorial combats.

In fact Churchill's words were to be remembered by tens of thousands, for it was here that he said: '... after the war, when a man is asked what he did, it will be quite sufficient for him to say, "I marched and fought with the Desert Army."'

The invasion of Sicily by Allied forces took place on 10 July. Randolph sailed with the invasion force on HMS *Princess Beatrix* and, the day before the landings, sent his father the following report:

Friday 9 July, '43
9.30 a.m.

My dearest Papa,

We sailed last night from Sousse [on the eastern coast of Tunisia] & here we are now bowling along – our convoy of 4 transports & 4 destroyers is a splendid & exhilarating sight. It is impressive to think that with about 20 LCT [Landing-Craft (Tank)] ahead of us, we only comprise about 1% of the force involved.

I have the rather dull & unimportant job of liaising from a small detachment of 2nd SAS to the Argyll & Sutherland Highlanders. However I shall have a front row seat of the enterprise. If all goes according to plan our small [force] will return tomorrow to prepare other ventures of a more specialised character & for which our unit is really intended.

I had been going on a much more exciting & responsible mission (in which I would have been in command of a small party) but late in the day Gen. Alex issued an order that no-one who knew anything of the main plan could go on the preliminary raids. This ruled out George Jellicoe and another officer who had quite needlessly been told by higher authority some weeks before & myself who as you may recall was unlucky enough to hear one word fall from the lips of a distinguished General. It is all most exasperating...

Despite the disappointment of missing my first 'independent command' it is most thrilling to be involved even as little more than a spectator in this tremendous enterprise. Everyone is cockahoop & the enthusiasm is tremendous both among the Navy & the troops.

4.0 p.m.

We are now steaming a few miles S. of Malta. The golden cliffs look very fine in the afternoon sun. The wind & sea have got up a bit & they say that the landing craft must be having a bad time. One LCT foundered this morning. We hope the wind and sea will drop at dusk. If not, it's going to be v. difficult getting ashore.

12.15 midnight

We're now about 7 miles from shore. The wind has dropped & so has the sea. I'm no longer feeling 'queasy' & can now finish this disjointed scrawl. The assault craft are just being lowered & soon the first flight will be taking off. I'm going in about an hour later with the main body in an LCI [Landing-Craft (Infantry)].

The moon is just coming up & conditions seem perfect. We can see a small amount of AA fire on shore – also a few flares. But the huge armada stretching off on either side of us for miles is wholly unmolested.

I can imagine how anxiously you must all be waiting to hear how it goes off. So far it has been like clockwork – I trust that by breakfast time good news will be flooding in on you.

Your loving son
Randolph

The following night, after taking part in the successful landings, Randolph wrote to his father from HMS *Royal Scotsman*:

10 July 1943

Well here we are safely returning from Sicily. The whole enterprise in our sector was too good to be true. Not a U-boat, not a torpedo-bomber, hardly a shot fired on shore. By 6.0 a.m. the CO of the Argylls authorised our small party who had taken the island lighthouse of Corrienti to return home. I do hope it has gone as well with the Americans. So far the wireless is very non-committal ...

I won't try & give you a description of the landing. You will already know more than I do & all I saw was like a rather dull exercise at Inverary.

This is just to send you my love & warmest congratulations.

Following the successful invasion of Sicily, the Allies decided to attack the Italian mainland without delay. The Germans had strong forces deployed to protect the approaches to Naples, and the Allied landings at Salerno on 9 September met with stiff resistance. At the time Winston was returning from the Quebec Conference aboard the battleship HMS *Renown*. Though fully informed of the progress of the battle, Winston did not know until later of his son's involvement in the fighting. As he commented in his *Second World War* memoirs:

> Our six-day voyage would have been less pleasant if I had known what was happening to some of my children. Randolph had been in Malta recruiting volunteers for the 2nd Special Air Service Regiment in the early days of September. Here he met Brigadier Laycock, who was a great friend of his and mine. Laycock, who knew what was going to happen said, 'There is going to be a show for the Commandos. Would you like to come?' So Randolph went with him, and was closely engaged throughout the battle . . .

After taking part in the Salerno landings with the Commandos, Randolph was invited by his father to join him in Persia for the Teheran Conference, where he met Stalin and Roosevelt to discuss the next phase of the war. High on the agenda were the plans for Operation OVERLORD, the code-name for the Normandy landings and the main invasion of Nazi-occupied Europe. While in Teheran Churchill celebrated his sixty-ninth birthday and a dinner was held in his honour at the British Legation. He gave an account of it in his memoirs:

> This was a memorable occasion in my life. On my right sat the President of the United States, on my left the master of Russia. Together we controlled a large preponderance of the naval and three-quarters of all the air forces in the world, and could direct armies of nearly twenty millions of men, engaged in the most terrible war that had yet occurred in human history. I could not help rejoicing at the long way we had come on the road to victory since the summer of 1940, when we had been alone, and, apart from the Navy and the Air, practically unarmed, against the triumphant and unbroken might of Germany and Italy, with almost all Europe and its resources in their grasp.

Among the guests at the dinner were Harry Hopkins, Averell Harriman, General Marshall, Anthony Eden, General Alan Brooke and Molotov. Winston recorded:

> I felt that there was a greater sense of solidarity and good comradeship than we had ever reached before in the Grand Alliance. I had not invited

Randolph and Sarah to the dinner, though they came in while my birthday toast was being proposed, but now Stalin singled them out and greeted them most warmly, and of course the President knew them well.

A few days later the *Daily Mail* reported:

The biggest celebration party that Persia has seen for many an Eastern moon was the one they threw for Mr Churchill's 69th birthday last Tuesday night in Teheran. Forty toasts were drunk or so it was estimated. And when the Prime Minister proposed 'A toast to Stalin the Great' the 39 guests in the Victorian dining-room of the British Legation got up in a body and sang 'For He's a Jolly Good Fellow.'

It was possibly a feeling of remorse at his effusiveness towards Stalin that prompted Churchill to have the following conversation a few days later in Cairo with Harold Macmillan, to whom I am indebted for the story.

Late one night, following his discussions with President Roosevelt at the Mena House, Churchill invited Macmillan back to his villa. It was already the early hours of the morning. Churchill brooded for a long time in silence. Suddenly he looked up and fixed Macmillan with a penetrating gaze: 'Cromwell was a great man, wasn't he?' 'Yes, sir,' said Macmillan, 'a very great man.' 'Ah,' rejoined Churchill, 'but he made one terrible mistake. Obsessed in his youth by fear of the power of Spain, he failed to observe the rise of France.' After a pause he added poignantly, with the rising power of Russia in mind, 'Do you think they will say that of me?'

Churchill had never harboured any illusions about the Russian Revolution. Indeed, to use his own phrase, he had sought to 'strangle Bolshevism in its cradle'. Nor did he entertain any idealised notions about the Soviet Union or even about Stalin himself. But as he himself had admitted, following Hitler's invasion of Russia: 'If Hitler invaded Hell, I would at least make a favourable reference to the Devil in the House of Commons!' Though full of admiration for the heroic exertions of the Russian people and deeply appreciative of the massive defeats which they were inflicting upon the enemy, he was growing anxious as to what might be Stalin's intentions towards the peoples of Occupied Europe who would be liberated by the Red Army.

Harold Macmillan recalled another conversation with Churchill in Cairo at which Randolph was also present. The British Government had recently taken the decision that they could no longer justify holding the British Fascist leader Sir Oswald Mosley in detention without trial under Regulation 18b and that he should be released. A debate in the House of Commons ensued in which a left-wing attack was mounted against the Government. The Prime Minister inquired by telegram from Cairo whether any Ministers had abstained or voted against the Government. According to Macmillan the reply was disappointing. 'I have made it clear,' asserted Churchill, 'that as regards the present Government, all resignations will be gratefully received!' 'Does that mean,' said Randolph, 'that anyone can join who wants to?' 'No,' replied the Prime Minister with a grin, 'but you can join the queue.'

From Cairo Churchill travelled on to Tunis to see General Eisenhower, whom it had been agreed with Roosevelt would be in command of OVERLORD. However on arrival there, on 11 December, the Prime Minister was taken seriously ill and the next day suffered a heart attack. There was extreme concern for his condition and Clemmie flew out by Dakota from England to be at his side. As Field Marshal Alexander recounted in his memoirs:

> For the second time in ten months he was stricken with pneumonia, and his Doctor, Lord Moran, had to send to Cairo for a specialist in the disease, Doctor Bedford, who knew all about the then new drug M & B, from the initials, of course, of the firm that made it. Thanks to the care of Lord Moran and Dr Bedford, and by M & B, Winston was sufficiently cured [by Christmas Day] to attend a small dinner-party that included his wife, his daughter Sarah, his son Randolph, Moran, Bedford and myself.
>
> Then at the end of dinner Randolph rose and proposed this extremely neat toast: 'Ladies and Gentlemen, let us rise and drink to my father's health and his remarkable recovery, which is entirely due (turning first to Lord Moran and then to Dr Bedford) to M & B!'

CHAPTER 15

Mission to Yugoslavia

While in Cairo, Churchill had seen Brigadier Fitzroy Maclean who, on his instructions, parachuted into Yugoslavia to head a British mission to Marshal Tito and his Partisans, reinforcing the work done earlier in the year by Colonel Bill Deakin, the Oxford don who, up to the outbreak of war, had been helping Churchill on his *History of the English-Speaking Peoples*. On the strength of Maclean's and Deakin's reports and all the other information available to him at the time, which indicated that the partisans were largely responsible for holding down a force estimated at 33 Axis divisions, Churchill decided that the time had come to abandon General Draga Mihailovic and Bozidan Puric, the leading champions of the Royalist cause in Yugoslavia, in favour of Marshal Josip Broz Tito, the Communist leader of the Partisans.

The criterion for this change of allegiance was bluntly simple. 'Who is killing most Germans?' the Prime Minister had demanded. The answer had been Tito. Accordingly Churchill instructed Maclean to prepare to return to Yugoslavia forthwith, with a strengthened mission, to inform Tito that British help was now to be channelled solely through his forces. Maclean, whom Randolph had accompanied on the Benghazi raid and who was a fellow Member of Parliament, invited Randolph to join him. As Maclean recalled in *Eastern Approaches*:

Randolph, it occurred to me, would make a useful addition to my Mission. There were some jobs – work, for instance, of a sedentary description at a large Headquarters, full of touchy or sensitive staff officers – for which I would not have chosen him. But for my present purposes he seemed just the man. On operations I knew him to be thoroughly dependable, possessing both endurance and determination. He was also gifted with an acute intelligence and a very considerable background of general politics, neither of which would come amiss in Yugoslavia. I felt, too – rightly as it turned out – that he would get on well with the Yugoslavs, for his enthusiastic and at times explosive approach to life was not unlike their own. Lastly, I knew him to be a stimulating companion, an important consideration in the circumstances under which we lived.

Following his illness in Tunis, Churchill travelled on to Marrakech to convalesce. There he pondered the Balkan situation, which he was convinced must be exploited to the full, now that the defeat of Mussolini's Italy was certain.

From Marrakech, where Fitzroy Maclean and Randolph had gone to receive their final briefing from the Prime Minister, they were flown on 9 January 1944 in Churchill's personal aircraft to Bari on the south-east coast of Italy, facing Yugoslavia. Here Randolph ran into a friend, Jack Churchill (no relation), who was commanding No. 2 Commando and whom he had met at the time of the Salerno landings. Jack Churchill and his brother Tom, who was in charge of the brigade of which No. 2 Commando formed part, invited Randolph and Fitzroy to a New Year's Eve party they were giving in their mess at Malfetta, near Bari. Fitzroy was thrilled, for he was anxious to acquire a contingent of British forces to join with a Partisan brigade in garrisoning the recently liberated Yugoslav island of Vis, where it was intended to build an RAF airfield for fighter operations over Yugoslavia. Tom Churchill was equally anxious to find an operating base from which the skills of his Commandos could be put to full use. The islands of the Dalmatian coast, many of which were still held by the Nazis, promised to be an ideal hunting ground.

The Germans, whose thirty-three divisions of troops in Yugoslavia included eight Bulgarian divisions, had recently launched an offensive against Tito and his Partisans in the mountain fastnesses of Bosnia. In the depths of winter, the weather over this rugged terrain can effectively rule out night parachute operations. Fitzroy was anxious to make contact with Tito as soon as possible and to deliver to him the letter with which he had been entrusted by the Prime Minister, repudiating Mihailovic and announcing that all future British assistance would go exclusively to the Partisans. In the circumstances it was decided to make the drop by day under cover of a fighter escort at a point near Bosanski Petrovac.

On the morning of 20 January, after a hearty breakfast at Bari aerodrome, Randolph and Fitzroy, forming part of a six-man team, took off across the Adriatic in a troop-carrying Dakota with an escort of a dozen Thunderbolt fighters, flying top-cover. According to Fitzroy Maclean's account in *Eastern Approaches*:

> Soon we had crossed the by now familiar Adriatic and were over the Yugoslav mainland, but there were no signs of life from the anti-aircraft batteries, and no enemy fighters ventured to try conclusions with the Thunderbolts. Then came the mountains, and some cloud. By now we were not far from our destination and it was time to adjust our parachutes.

I felt for the Prime Minister's letter. It was there securely buttoned inside my tunic. Then the doors were opened and the dispatcher signed to us to get into position.

I had decided to jump first with the others following in a 'stick', and I now took my place at the open door with Randolph next to me. Looking down, I could see the houses of a village, with, near them, an open expanse of green grass. A number of figures were running about, and, as I watched, the signal fires were lit and smoke billowed up from them. It all looked very close and I could not help wondering whether we were high enough for our parachutes to open before we reached the ground. Then the light turned from red to green; the dispatcher touched me on the shoulder, and I fell forwards and downwards into space.

I was right: we had been dropped from very low indeed; no sooner had my parachute opened, than I hit the ground with considerably more force than was comfortable. Looking up, I saw Randolph coming down almost on top of me. The expression of satisfaction which dawned on his face as he realised that his parachute had opened, rapidly gave way to one of disgust as he glanced down to see the ground rushing up to meet him. Then, narrowly missing a telegraph pole, he came to rest with a sudden bump in a patch of melting snow and mud.

Prior to this operational jump, Randolph had made only one previous descent by parachute. He had refused to do the three regulation practice jumps, the minimum required before undertaking an operational mission. When a senior officer pressed him on this point and warned him of the dangers involved in jumping without proper training, Randolph rounded on him: 'You bloody fool, if I do three practice jumps, I shall be three times more likely to break a leg.' Randolph's decision was probably wise in the light of the experience of a British agent, Rowley St Oswald, who was to be dropped into the Balkans around this time. Having done his practice jumps St Oswald, challenged to demonstrate his parachuting skills at a bibulous farewell dinner the night before his drop, had jumped off the dinner table and broken both legs.

Maclean described the Yugoslav reaction to the Prime Minister's son dropping in on them out of the blue:

From the moment when his parachute deposited him in a sitting position in a puddle of melting snow in the highlands of Bosnia, until the day some twelve months later when he attended Tito's victory celebrations in Liberated Belgrade, Randolph brought to his job as British Liaison Officer with the Partisans an infectious mixture of courage and enthusiasm. It was,

I believe, one of the happiest periods of his life. He liked the excitement of the guerilla war. He was fascinated by the political implications of everything that was happening around him. Altogether wartime Yugoslavia was full of the kind of problems on which he enjoyed sharpening his wits. He also got on well with the Yugoslavs. There was an explosive Balkan side to his nature which endeared him to them and them to him. They recognized in him, too, some of the qualities they had learned to admire in his father – pugnacity, generosity, curiosity, and a sense of style. And then the very fact that Winston Churchill should have let his own son join them was, they felt, a token of the importance that he attached to them and to their fight.

Due to the difficulties of air communications it was not until mid-March that Randolph was able to give his father an account of his experiences:

15 March 1944

The Russian military mission are now installed here complete with caviar, vodka and epaulettes. The only square meal we have had since arriving here seven weeks ago was when we dined with them about ten days ago. They were stuck at Bari for about three weeks before coming in as the landing grounds were covered with snow and none of them had been trained to jump. In the end they insisted on being provided with gliders and made a spectacular arrival near here on Red Army Day. Two nights ago a Russian plane came over and dropped another two tons of vodka and caviar. The head Russian is Lt. General Kornev who captured Bryansk and Orel. He is a most affable old boy and talks a little English. His number 2 is a Major General, aged 33, who has distinguished himself in guerilla fighting behind the lines in Russia. There are some 20 other officers. Their high spirits have been somewhat dampened in the last few days. Perhaps they have heard, as we have, that an NKVD officer is on his way from London to join them!

We are quite comfortably installed here in the village of Drvar. Most of the village was knocked down by Italian planes 18 months ago. We live in a little group of houses on the outskirts. I have a clean little room which I share with an old friend, Gordon Alston, who went with David Stirling, Fitzroy and myself on our trip to Benghazi. We have a good sized room for our mess but neither very varied nor very much food to eat in it. And nothing to drink except water and very occasionally a little 'rakya', the local form of slibowitz. I am losing a lot of weight and feeling very well as a result.

I have met Tito three times at various dinners. He speaks no English or French and I have to speak to him through an interpreter. He is a very fine man in appearance and appears to be growing rapidly into his job. He seems to be extremely well disposed towards us and our relations with him are excellent. There is no doubt that Fitzroy has done a first class job and has made a great impression on him.

Tito remains however an enigma. Is he still at least a Comintern agent taking his orders from Moscow and acutely remembering the fate of his predecessor [Gorkic, who was recalled to Moscow a few years before the war and quietly liquidated]? Or does he see himself as the leader of a truly independent country? It is impossible to be sure. He has certainly taken great pains since the arrival of the Russians to treat both missions with equal consideration. But the fact remains that he is a convinced Communist of twenty years' standing and I personally find that Communists are impossible to understand – until, like the Russians, they abandon Communism.

Nearly all the most active and vigorous people in the partisan movement are also Communist. The young ones especially have a fanatical worship for Stalin and Russia – based more on their Communism than on any racial sympathy. And of course it will be the leaders of the partisans who will count after the war. The ones who have done the fighting and the sabotage, and no-one else, will be masters of the country ...

I was surprised to hear that the rights of serving members have been curtailed in my absence. I could not quite follow it on the wireless but it said that you had given a ruling that serving members may not address meetings outside their constituencies. I am thinking of putting down a question to ask the Secretary of State for War 'Whether he is aware that the hon and gallant member for Lancaster made a public speech in Drvar on February 22 and what disciplinary action is being taken against him?' I cannot understand the point of these successive whittling downs of the rights of MPs in the Forces ...

Fitzroy Maclean, who had arrived in Drvar before Randolph, describes how in one of the houses there 'had been installed a system of double-decked wooden sleeping shelves sufficient to accommodate the whole Mission. The owner of the house, an elderly peasant, announced with considerable pride that the whole contraption was "specially reserved for President Churchill" himself, who was shortly expected on a State visit to Marshal Tito – presumably a garbled reference to Randolph's impending arrival ...

When I visited Drvar in 1973 I found the small wooden house, set with others amid plum orchards which ran down to a little brook. Its owner, a thin bright-eyed peasant lady in her eighties with silver hair and heavily creased face, remembered Randolph well and insisted on presenting me with a pair of thick woollen socks she had knitted and a bottle of home-brewed slivovitz with a corn cob for a cork. Randolph's billet was just half a mile across the valley from the cleft in a rocky cliff-face where, unseen from the rest of the valley, Tito had his headquarters. On 26 March Randolph sent his father a further report:

We have just heard on the wireless that you are to broadcast tomorrow night. It is a very long time since you have done a broadcast. We are all looking forward to it with the highest interest. We had your last speech to Parliament printed in Jug [Yugoslav] at Bari and it is now distributed throughout this country. It has been welcomed by everyone and has done a lot to improve our stock here.

Two nights ago we had a gala performance of *Desert Victory*. It was a tremendous success. Tito and all his principal military and political chiefs attended as well as the Russian Mission. They were tremendously impressed and I am sure it has done a great deal of good. I am trying to get a lot of other films sent in, including Capra's series *Why We fight*. There is no doubt that the film is the best method of propaganda in a country like this.

After the film we had a great supper party. Altogether we had about 70 people. It was very jolly and the Russians were in particularly good form. They have obviously been told to be extremely civil. When I asked one of them how it was possible for the Red Army to advance so rapidly he replied 'First it is because the threat of a second front holds so many German divisions in the West. Secondly the Allied bombing of Germany has greatly weakened their war production. Thirdly we are much more numerous than the Germans.' I found this a very refreshing attitude for a Russian to adopt . . .

We often see the Foggia-based Fortresses and Liberators flying over us on their way to bomb targets in Austria. Sometimes we see as many as 200. They have a most stimulating effect on the Partisans. Quite a number of crews who bale out are rescued by the Partisans, and pass through here on their way out. I took about 20 of them the other day to see Tito. They were thrilled and of course got him to sign their short snorter bills [local banknotes kept as souvenirs].

Tito lives in an erie with a rocky and precipitous approach. His office is all lined with parachute silk and looks more like the *nid d'amour* of a luxurious courtesan than the office of a guerilla leader. Jumbo [General Sir Henry Maitland Wilson] has sent him a jeep which came in the other night by air. He is delighted with this . . .

Winston, always a staunch royalist, had written to Tito some weeks before, seeking to persuade him to work with King Peter and thereby to unite both Communist and royalist elements in making common cause against the German invaders. But, as Randolph makes clear in a postscript to his letter, Tito was having none of it:

When we discussed all this more than three months ago you will remember that everyone agreed that the only chance remaining to the King to put himself in better relations with the partisans was for him to dismiss Mihailovic; and that this might create an atmosphere in which something might be arranged to improve his fortunes. In the months that have elapsed the King has made no move. We on the other hand have publicly broken with Mihailovic and at the same time have given increasing publicity and recognition to Tito. I am sure that from the point of view of the war and of long term British interests this has been most wise. But I fear it has if anything made matters worse for the King . . .

I think that Tito is perfectly sincere in his view that to bring the King back would seriously compromise the fighting strength of his movement. But in addition it must be remembered that he is a convinced Communist and Republican . . . One of the things that Tito is proudest of is that he has brought about a truer unity among the three races of Yugoslavia than ever existed before; and I think one must credit him with a genuine fear of compromising this important work for the future tranquillity of his country by bringing back the King . . .

It is all very unfortunate and I hope you will not be depressed by the outcome after all the hard work and attention which you have devoted to this affair. I cannot help feeling if you had followed your own instinct in the matter and had sent the telegram to King Peter which you showed me at Marrakech the matter might have gone a bit better . . .

Fortunately no harm seems to have been done to our relations with the Partisans and with Tito in particular. In fact I should say that our stock stands higher than ever before. If we can, as the weather improves, increase air supplies our prestige will grow still more.

I enclose an identity card that was recently found on a captured Chetnik soldier. As you will see it has two stamps – one the German eagle and swastika and the other the arms of the unfortunate King. It is not a very good stamp, but you can plainly see the Crown. In face of such barefaced collaboration by Mihailovic with the Germans it seems incredible to everyone here that the King should continue his association with Mihailovic . . .

One of Randolph's greatest privations, while cut off in the mountains of Bosnia, was an almost total lack of home news other than what could be gleaned from the heavily censored and limited BBC reports over the radio. His friend Max Beaverbrook endeavoured to remedy this:

11 April 1944

. . . I expect that British politics seem very far away as you move about in the Balkan Mountains. Certainly they must lack the glamour and sharpness of Yugoslav political activities. But we have our own mild excitement which keep the House of Commons awake when the war is not dramatic enough for their tastes.

The partisan forces of Marshal Hogg operating on the left flanks of the Tory army staged one successful ambush of the Government during the Committee stage of the Education Bill. It was over the question of equal pay for women. But brief was their hour of triumph! An enormous mass of Government armour along with some famous self-propelled guns was brought into the battle. The Tory Titos deserted their women and fled to the Government lobby. But I expect we shall hear more from them in due course. These political panics do not last long.

I am entirely in favour of such outbursts by the young men of the party. It is good for Parliament, good for the Government, and very good for the young Tories. The principle is an excellent one and well-established, that the Conservative party should provide the Government of the country, and also the most effective portion of the opposition!

Perhaps the news has filtered through to your mountain fastnesses that Anthony Eden is going to give up the Foreign Office. The story has been widely spread and almost as widely denied . . .

Among Randolph's responsibilities was that of being in charge of all propaganda matters affecting the British mission in Yugoslavia. The bureaucracy of the Psychological Warfare Executive which had established itself in Bari had different ideas however, insisting that all propaganda be provided by and channelled through them. By early May, Randolph reported in a letter to Beaverbrook that he had been on a 'short Commando raid to Bari where after a brisk engagement I succeeded in reducing to law and order the Chetnik bands of P.W.E. who for the last three months have been menacing my communications'. In a letter to his mother Randolph told her something of the conditions in which he was living:

> Thank you a thousand times for the lovely parcel of books. They were exactly the sort we need here. They will give immense pleasure not only to me, but to all the other officers here. We always seem to be short of reading matter . . .
> We have just heard of the reopening of the battle for Rome and are all greatly excited. I do hope it goes right this time.
> I got back here to find a new born baby in the house in which I live with the pig, the six Bosnian girls and the Intelligence Officer. The latter is fortunately away at present with Fitzroy, so we are no more crowded than usual. I brought some oranges back for the young children. Most of them have never seen one before and hardly knew what to do with them!

The young King of Yugoslavia, Peter II, continued to be under heavy British pressure to dismiss the pro-royalist Chetnik government of Puric and Mihailovic. In a message dated 24 May, Churchill, who still cherished the notion of a royalist/Communist alliance, informed Tito:

> The King has sacked Puric and Co., and I think the Ban of Croatia [Dr Ivan Subosic, the Governor of Croatia and a member of the Peasant Party, who had been asked to form a new administration] will rally a certain force round him. My idea is that this Government should lie quiet for a bit and let events flow on their course. This, I think, was rather in accord with your idea in the first telegrams we exchanged. I am keeping the Russians and Americans informed of all that goes on between us.
> Give my love to Randolph should he come into your sphere. Maclean will be coming back soon. I wish I could come myself, but I am too old and heavy to jump out on a parachute.

Earlier that month the German army launched a series of new Balkan offensives. In Montenegro these soon petered out, leaving the Partisans in control of more territory than ever before. In Eastern Bosnia and Croatia, however, the Germans made determined advances with more powerful forces. In particular they seemed to be taking a closer interest than previously in the Drvar valley, with an increased frequency of minor bombing raids and strafings. One morning a lone German aircraft appeared over the valley and, unlike all the others, proceeded to spend half an hour or more flying slowly up and down at a couple of thousand feet. There was discussion among members of the British mission as to what this might portend.

Major Vivian Street, who had taken over command of the mission during Maclean's absence in England where he was reporting to the Prime Minister at Chequers, concluded that it was a reconnaissance aircraft taking aerial photographs prior to a major German air attack. Street visited Tito in his headquarters to inform him of his fears and to let him know of his decision to move his mission, with their radio sets and Partisan escort, away from the peasant houses among the orchard trees to a position two or three miles up in the hills. This precautionary move was to save the British mission from imminent disaster.

CHAPTER 16

Attack on Drvar

On 25 May at 0630, just as dawn was breaking, Randolph and his colleagues were aroused by the familiar shout of 'Avioni!' ('Planes!') from the Partisan guards outside their hut. But on this occasion the shout was repeated with a greater sense of urgency. The British team, who had prudently moved higher up the mountainside, dashed outside in time to see fifteen German bombers and Stuka dive bombers unleashing a rain of steel and explosives on the little village of Drvar. The bombers circled and dropped their deadly loads and then moved away, only to make room for new waves of bomber aircraft. The blasts of the bombs re-echoed from the mountainsides and columns of smoke reached up to the sky from the valley below. Then a deeper, more ominous note was heard and six great JU-52 transports appeared in formation over the valley.

Suddenly the sky was filled with billowing brown parachutes. They were followed by further waves of Junkers towing troop-carrying gliders. The bombing had merely been the precursor of an airborne assault by six hundred of Germany's crack SS 'Brandenburg' parachute forces, while further German infantry units came in by glider, followed by much heavy equipment. The situation of all non-Yugoslavs including Randolph was particularly precarious for, although wearing uniform, they were liable to be shot out of hand by the Germans. The Prime Minister's only son would have been a special trophy.

Back in England Fitzroy Maclean, who was preparing to return to the Balkans, was alerted by an urgent signal from Vivian Street. As he recalled:

It was very short, only a couple of sentences. It had every possible indication of priority, and it was the kind of communication that took your breath away. It announced that the enemy had made a large scale airborne attack on Partisan Headquarters with glider and parachute troops; that the Partisans had suffered heavy casualties, although Tito himself was believed to be safe; that the mission had so far managed to escape capture, although whether they would do so for much longer was uncertain, for they were in the woods with strong enemy forces closing in on them from all sides.

A journalist, Stoyan Pribichevich, representing the Combined American–British Press recalled in a dispatch three days later:

At 0700 the bulk of a heavily equipped German with a black steel helmet loomed above our shelter, pointed his submachine gun at us and yelled, 'Heraus!' ('Out!'). He marched us off hands up towards a grove in the back of the house. There another German held his submachine gun ready and two officers stood aside.

One of the officers ordered Fowler, the American, to stand up against the wall, his hands up. Fowler walked up to the wall, and I shouted in German, 'But we are American and British officers!' 'Sorry,' said the officer, 'orders are to execute everybody.' The other officer seemed to hesitate, asked us about our ranks, and after an altercation with his fellow officer, we were led to the village graveyard, where the Germans had established their headquarters. There, standing among the German soldiers and officers, I saw a Chetnik, a rifle across his back and the insignia of the Royal Yugoslav Army on his cap. The job assigned to us was to carry the German wounded from the firing-line across a bullet-swept field back to the headquarters...

As the fighting between the Germans and the Partisans intensified, in and around the village, a group of Germans succeeded in gaining a position from which they commanded the mouth of the cave which was Tito's hideout. Tito and his party had no hope of escape by way of the usual exit from the cave. However, with the use of a rope they succeeded in scaling the rock-face to gain higher ground. Then, after pausing briefly to survey the battle raging in the valley below, they made good their escape.

Randolph and the small British group, grabbing their weapons, wireless sets and anything else they could carry, set off to join the Partisans at their Corps Headquarters in the mountains. For more than ten hours they force-marched across the rugged terrain of rocky hillsides and thick forests. I well remember my father, many years later, giving me a vivid first-hand account of that day. In particular, I recall his description of how, on this brilliant early summer's day, with the Germans hard on their heels, they would occasionally stop to draw breath in lush green clearings and refresh themselves with wild strawberries that were just ripening. Towards nightfall they reached a small group of huts buried deep in the forest which Tito had used briefly as his winter headquarters before moving to Drvar.

Tito and his staff had got there before them. Though Tito and the British mission had thus far eluded capture, their situation remained perilous, with large-scale German forces, estimated at four divisions, closing in on all sides.

Drvar, meanwhile, had fallen to the enemy with heavy casualties among the Partisans. Finding that Tito had escaped, the Germans vented their rage on the civilian population, many of whom they massacred for their known Partisan sympathies. The British sent urgent radio signals to Bari calling for air support, in response to which the RAF and US 15th Air Force began pounding enemy positions with Liberators and Flying Fortresses, while Spitfires and P-38s shot up German troop concentrations.

By now the Germans had reached the edge of the forest in which Tito and the members of the British Mission were hiding. Tito decided that the time had come to break out. According to Fitzroy Maclean, who received a first-hand account from Vivian Street:

The break-out took place at night. Fierce fighting was in progress. Flashes could be seen on the ridge above them. The sound of firing came ever closer. From time to time a Verey star shot up into the sky.

Then Vivian saw something that amazed him. There, on a siding in the woods, was drawn up the Partisan Express (Tito's personal train consisting of a small engine and one box-car looking like a wooden hut on wheels with a stove and chimney in the middle and wooden benches round the walls), with steam up and smoke and sparks belching from the funnel. Solemnly Tito, his entourage and the dog Tigger entrained; the whistle blew; and, with much puffing and creaking, they started off down the five miles of track through the woods, with the enemy's bullets whining through the trees all round them.

During the days that followed, Tito and his staff, with the Allied Mission and a force of two hundred Partisans, were almost constantly on the move; dodging through the woods, lying up in the daytime, moving at night. Again and again they had narrow escapes from the enemy. German patrols, aircraft and light tanks seemed to be everywhere. Food and ammunition were getting desperately short, but once they managed to stop long enough to receive a supply-drop from British planes based in Italy. At the same time other British aircraft were giving much needed air support, wherever they could. During the week that followed the attack on Drvar, our planes flew over a thousand sorties in support of the Partisans, thereby doing much to relieve the pressure on them...

Then one day, as they were resting after a long march, Tito sent for them. Vivian found the Marshal looking tired and depressed. He had, he said, reluctantly reached the conclusion that it was impossible for him to direct the operations of his forces throughout Yugoslavia while being chased through the woods and kept constantly on the move.

Tito thereupon requested the British to fly him out of Yugoslavia so that he could later re-establish his headquarters on Yugoslav soil but on one of the islands off the Dalmatian coast which would afford greater security. That night a Dakota managed to land on a flat piece of land held by the Partisans and Tito, together with his staff and dog Tigger, flew off to Bari.

Three days after the attack on Drvar, on Randolph's thirty-third birthday, his father wrote to him:

28 May 1944

[USAF General] Eaker is here and is starting immediately, so this is a chance to send you a line. We are naturally following with some anxiety the news of the attack on Tito's headquarters. But today the report is that the airborne Huns have been liquidated, and there only remain the forces trying to surround you. I cannot do more than wish you good luck, but you are ever in my thoughts, and in those of all (repeat all) here. We have a lovely day at where we live from time to time [Chequers], and all is fair with the first glory of summer. The war is very fierce and terrible, but in these sunlit lawns and buttercup meadows, it is hard to conjure up its horrors.

Baby Winston, as you will no doubt have been told by Pamela, has developed German measles. I am ashamed to say I told him it was the fault of the Germans, but I shall labour to remove this impression quite soon.

That same day Britain's Resident Minister in Algiers, Harold Macmillan, arrived in Bari with General 'Jumbo' Wilson, where he learned of the German attack on Tito's headquarters. He noted in *The Blast of War*: 'It appears that the attempt to capture him [Tito] and Randolph – which would be the greater prize it would be difficult to say – failed by a hair's breadth, the Marshal having escaped to the hills some two hours previously.'

Randolph remained in Yugoslavia organising evacuation flights from a small landing field as the Germans continued to strengthen their grip on the area. By 8 June, the situation at the airfield was becoming critical. Among Randolph's papers, there survives a sheet of ruled paper torn from a notebook with the following pencil-written message sent from the airstrip:

Major Churchill
Very URGENT

At present, the personnel here are 14 men. NO TOOLS, NO COLONELS, NO CAPTAIN in fact nothing. I'm afraid this is getting beyond a joke, unless the promised Battalion of men arrive I will *not* be responsible for any A/c landing here, so you had better either get the men or cancel the pick-up.

G. Bell Shaw

8 June 44

Randolph stayed on for another forty-eight hours, then he received a signal from General Wilson instructing him to return forthwith to Italy. On arrival in Bari he sent his father a cable from which it is clear that he was not happy with this decision:

Arrived Bari this morning from Ticevo by daylight pick-up operation which was evacuating surplus personnel of Anglo-American and Russian Military Missions. For last fortnight had been in charge our sub-mission with 8th [Yugoslav] Corps in Ticevo area and had expected to stay there until last night when I received a message that General Wilson wished me to come to Italy. I plan return to 8th Corps in three or four days. The last fortnight has been extremely interesting and at times exciting, and I have learned more in these few days about the Partisan Movement than I had in the previous four months.

As a result of a fortnight with nothing to drink, very little to eat or smoke and 20 or 30 miles a day over mountainous country I am fitter than ever before. It looks as if Hun offensive is now petering out. He is retreating to his towns and main lines of communication, and Partisans are rapidly re-occupying their former areas. I believe conditions will soon return to normal.

The opening of the second front [the D-Day landings had taken place in Normandy on 6 June] has thrilled the Partisans, and has raised our prestige to an extraordinary extent. I can now do most useful work in consolidating our relations with them. You can imagine how much my thoughts have been with you in these last few days and how thankful I am that all seems to have gone so well ... My fondest love to all.

Relieved to learn that Randolph was safe, Churchill replied promptly with a request that he return to England to report to him personally:

IMMEDIATE
PERSONAL AND TOP SECRET

I do not want to stand in the way of your wishes to go back to the 8th Yugoslav army. Our authorities are rather concerned lest you should be copped by the Huns. You should talk the matter over with Maclean who will, I am sure, decide what is best from all points of view. Fondest love from all.

11.6.44.

On 15 June, the Nazi-controlled Radio Belgrade, monitored by the Allied Psychological Warfare Branch in Bari, informed their listeners of the German view of recent events in Yugoslavia:

RANDOLPH, THE UNFORTUNATE

During the recent few days, a small misfortune happened to Randolph Churchill, Major in His British Highness's army and son of Winston Churchill, the grave digger of the British Empire. He was surprised in the headquarters of the bandit leader, Josip Broz [Tito], and forced to save his lordly skin as quickly as possible. So Randolph hastened by plane to Italy forgetting his passport, which today is exhibited at the war museum ... of the South-East in Vienna.

His friend Tito forgot his Marshal's parade uniform which also can be seen at the same exhibit. It can be seen that it was pretty hot for them when they had to dash off in order to save their bare lives ...

Harold Macmillan, in his diary entry for 16 June, admitted responsibility for pulling Randolph out of Yugoslavia:

Randolph Churchill was now in our party, I having persuaded General Wilson to give orders for him to be taken out of Yugoslavia. He was naturally indignant of this, but I felt sure this was necessary. I did not want him captured and perhaps tortured by the Germans partly for the PM's sake and partly because I felt sure he knew too much. Anyway, he has not

had a bad time since he came out. He has been to Rome, interviewed the
Pope ... and generally enjoyed himself.

Following his papal audience, Randolph reported to his father:

[The Pope] asked me about conditions in Yugoslavia and in particular as
to the strength of the Communist movement. I explained to him that the
whole trend of today is away from Communism and that private property
and religious institutions are guaranteed and respected by the movement
of National Liberation. I took the opportunity of telling His Holiness how
the civil war in Yugoslavia is to a large extent religious in character,
Serbs murdering Moslems and Catholic Ustachis slaughtering Orthodox.
I explained how Tito was the one focus that could bring all discordant
elements together.

He asked many questions about you and spoke in terms of warmest
admiration. I was with him about fifteen [minutes] and as I took my leave
he asked me to send you his warmest greetings and blessings ...

In an attempt to frustrate the efforts of the politico–military hierarchy
to keep him out of harm's way, Randolph then hastened to the island of
Vis to visit his friend and commanding officer, Brigadier Fitzroy Maclean.
From there, evidently having just heard of the Prime Minister's visit to
the Normandy beaches hard on the heels of the D-Day invasion force,
Randolph cabled his father on 15 June, making clear his eagerness to
return to Yugoslavia:

Reference your telegram No. 128 of 11th June, it is kind of your Generals
to be so worried about my welfare. I am grieved that they allow you to
be exposed to much greater dangers in Normandy while we are poodle-
faking in the Balkans.

I visited Fitzroy this afternoon at Vis and will see General Wilson and
Macmillan at Caserta tomorrow. I will then pay short visit to Yugoslavia
and if your York could pick me up night 18th at Bari would be very glad
to visit you for two or three days to report, prior to my return to our sub-
Mission at Headquarters Croatia to which Fitzroy at my suggestion is
sending me ...

If this suggestion is in any way inconvenient please say so, as what I
desire more than anything else is to return as soon as possible to Yugoslavia
which has been quitted by the Russians and where we now can perhaps
really do some good.

Randolph's visit to Vis was not in vain. The following day Brigadier Maclean signalled the Prime Minister:

> Randolph came over to see me yesterday. He will leave for England in few days. On his return I propose to put him in charge of my mission to HQ Croatia, where he has already made many friends and where there is important work to be done.
>
> As regards risk of capture by the enemy, recent operations have shown that Randolph is well able to look after any subordinate under his command as well as allied interests entrusted to his care.

Maclean had formed a high opinion of Randolph's performance in Yugoslavia, recording in Eastern Approaches that, following the German airborne attack on Tito's headquarters, Randolph was awarded the MBE 'for his courageous and resourceful conduct in the ensuing fighting', though 'the recommendation had been for the Military Cross'.

CHAPTER 17

Return to Topusko

On his brief return to England, Randolph sent his father a memorandum on the political situation in Yugoslavia, dated 27 June, which was subsequently circulated as a secret Cabinet paper. 'There are two reasons,' Randolph reported, 'why it is essential to British interests to give support to Marshal Tito and the Movement of National Liberation:– (a) they are the only Yugoslavs who are fighting the Germans. (b) Whether we help Tito or not he will be the master of Yugoslavia after the War.' Randolph expressed doubt whether, in a plebiscite, more than one per cent of Yugoslavs would vote for a restoration of the monarchy. In the circumstances, he recommended that the British Government continued to give its full backing to Tito and his Partisans, while putting pressure on King Peter publicly to denounce Mihailovic and to dismiss the Puric Government. Randolph also proposed a draft speech which King Peter might be asked to make, concluding with the words so popular with the Partisans: 'Smirt Fascismu – Sloboda Narodu' ('Death to Fascism – Freedom to the People').

Once in London Randolph headed for White's Club. Christopher Sykes, author and later television producer whom Randolph had befriended at Oxford, recalled in his biography of Evelyn Waugh:

I was in White's Club one morning when Randolph burst in roaring: 'Where's Evelyn Waugh? I've got to get hold of him! Where the devil is he?'

I knew the answer, as Evelyn was then training in Scotland with my regiment. I knew that my Colonel was in some perplexity as to how to place Evelyn, never the easiest of men for whom to find advantageous military employment. I said to Randolph: 'I know where he is, and he can be with you here tomorrow morning.'

'You mean it?' cried Randolph.

'I think I do,' I said, 'if you let me get to the telephone. Why do you need him?'

'Because,' said Randolph, standing by the bar and in a very loud voice, 'my father has agreed to me taking charge of a Mission to Croatia under

Fitzroy Maclean, and Fitzroy and I have been hunting for Evelyn every-where, because I need him. I can't go to Croatia,' he added, 'unless I have someone to talk to.' Discretion was never one of Randolph's virtues. I found it a reason for liking him. I telephoned to my Colonel and the deal was settled there and then. I was thus instrumental in organising the raw material of Evelyn Waugh's best and last work, the three novels of his war trilogy.

Evelyn Waugh accepted Randolph's invitation with as much enthusi-asm as his own regiment approved the request for his transfer and, on 4 July, they took off for Bari by way of Gibraltar and Algiers. From there they made a three-day visit to Tito's headquarters on the island of Vis, to be briefed on the latest intelligence reports from Croatia and to receive their orders from Fitzroy Maclean. Evelyn Waugh recorded in his diary on 10 July:

A great banquet for Tito at HQ (a modern villa with all conveniences except water), a bagpipe band, much gin and wine and kümmel. Tito and staff an hour and a half late for luncheon. He in brand new cap and uniform of Russian marshal with Jug badge. Hammers, sickles and Com-munist slogans everywhere. Tito startled all by going back on his agreement to meet Jumbo Wilson at Caserta. Randolph very drunk; bathing. All a little affected by wine in the evening. Maclean dour, unprincipled, ambitious, probably very wicked; shaved head and Devil's ears. I read his reports in one of which he quoted Lawrence of Arabia saying it was a victory to make a province suffer for freedom. Too early to give any opinions but I have as yet seen nothing that justifies Randolph's assertion to the Pope that 'the whole trend' was against Communism. Subsequent conversations have increased my scepticism ... Tito like Lesbian. Randolph preposterous and lovable. HQ in beautiful bay – oleanders and vines, red earth, aromatic shrubs; no road to villa; walk through mined vineyards ...

It is evident that Evelyn, who had a wicked and devious sense of humour, had already formed the theory that Tito, whose true name was Josip Broz, was really a woman, proceeding to dub him 'Our Aunt' – a nickname that he and Randolph were to use until their dying day. Unfortunately for Evelyn, this piece of mischief had reached Tito's ears even before their first meeting. As Selina Hastings relates in her biography of Waugh:

On arrival Evelyn and Randolph were taken down to the sea where most of the party had been swimming. Evelyn, smartly turned out in his regimental khakis, was greeted by Brigadier Maclean, who then introduced him to a handsome, powerfully-built man wearing nothing but a pair of close-fitting bathing trunks. 'Ask Captain Waugh,' said Tito shaking him by the hand, 'why he thinks I am a woman.' . . . Never one to let a good joke drop, Evelyn kept this one going for years. A couple of American military personnel, to whom he propounded the theory, denied it vigorously. 'I know that's not true,' said one. 'I was in charge of the marshal's security when he was in Rome, and I know he went and visited a woman's room on two successive nights.' 'Well,' said Evelyn, unruffled, 'we always knew she was a Lesbian.'

Before leaving Vis, Randolph received the following communication from Fitzroy Maclean:

SECRET

14th July 1944

DIRECTIVE

To: *Major R. Churchill, 4th Hussars*
1. You will proceed to HQ CROATIA, where you will assume charge of the British Military Mission.
   Your responsibilities will include the sub-Mission to 4 Corps, but not that to 11 Corps.
   You will address all official communications to my HQ, forwarding them to my rear HQ at BARI.
   You will not leave your post without prior authority from my HQ.
2. Apart from your responsibilities as Cdr. BMM to HQ CROATIA, you will hold the post of Press and Propaganda Officer on the staff of my Main HQ. As such you will be responsible to me for handling the press and propaganda affairs of my Mission in the field. You will deal in these matters with the PR and PWB Officers on the staff of my Rear HQ at BARI, who will be your channel of communication with PRO and PWB.

Fitzroy Maclean
Brigadier, Commanding BMM

On Sunday 16 July Randolph and Evelyn, after a three-day delay at Bari waiting for an aircraft, finally took off for Yugoslavia, as Evelyn recorded in his diary:

Started in low spirits as the result of indigestion. We got into the aeroplane – a large Dakota transport – at nightfall. Randolph, Philip Jordan, I, Air Commodore Carter, some Yugoslav partisans (one girl), and two or three Russians at the last moment which necessitated our offloading much of our stores. Randolph consequently in a rage. We sat about in and on the luggage. The Russians had a large basket of peaches and grapes and oranges which they passed round. As soon as we flew out to sea the lights were put out and we flew in darkness, noisy, uncomfortable, dozing sometimes.

Philip Jordan, war correspondent for the *News Chronicle*, takes up the account of the ill-fated flight:

Nothing that I know is more forlorn than this corrugated country when you fly over it in the dark night. Once the last faint shimmer of the Adriatic waters has gone it is as though the world has gone also, and you are in a void with neither purpose or direction. The stars went out; the new moon had not yet risen. Even our wings were not visible except when summer lightning gave them substance. The only lights were sparks from the exhausts which flew past like tracers. Once we flew over a road convoy, a row of moving lights that went out as we approached.

When the end came it came slowly. Far below us like an inverted constellation seen in an amber mirror, our own strip came suddenly to view. We saw the safety flare, exchanged recognition signals and then we went down in steep and steady spirals. Until we were within 400 ft. all was well. It was dark when we hit the ground, but when those of us who were lucky enough to regain consciousness, perhaps two minutes later, opened our eyes, the aircraft was illuminated by what seemed thousands of little candles, for the flames were burning from one end to the other, flickering in through every split joint in the flanks.

There had been darkness and cold, but now there was infinite light. It was no more reality than the transformation of a scene in a pantomime. It was enchanting until I realised that my own hair was one of the candles and that a fallen jack was across my body, making movement difficult. When we 'put ourselves out' and went to the door, it was buckled and would not open, but they say we squeezed between it and the aircraft's body. Later, when we had forced the door, others walked or were carried out but they could not get them all . . .

Randolph, dazed and injured in both legs, fought his way out of the plane. But seeing no sign of Corporal Sowman, who had been his batman for eighteen months in North Africa and Yugoslavia, he made at least two attempts to enter the blazing fuselage to rescue him. His efforts were in vain. The faithful Sowman had been incinerated. Evelyn Waugh, badly concussed, had come to seated in a cornfield beside the blazing wreck and recorded:

> The next thing I knew was sitting on a stretcher in a hut. Randolph in tears because his servant had been killed. A good deal of confused talk about who had escaped and who had burned. I was in no great pain though burned on hands, head and legs. Randolph lame in both legs, Philip Jordan with cracked ribs, one Jugoslav with bad burns and an arm broken in two places. I kept saying 'Don't let them put margarine on my burns, it is the worst thing'. Randolph shouting for morphia.

At dawn the next day the survivors were moved by ambulance to the nearby village of Topusko where they were accommodated in a single-storey inn built round a farmyard. According to Evelyn Waugh:

> After a few hours Philip Jordan and I tried our legs and went to visit Randolph in a neighbouring house, lying side by side with a badly hurt Communist commissar of asiatic appearance. He was protesting furiously at our having been moved from the airfield. He had signalled for a fighter-conducted day plane ... Later in the day we went by ambulance back to the airfield; visibility not good enough for landing. Dying air commodore snoring and groaning. An American in charge at the airfield. Randolph upbraided him for moving us. 'It is a golden rule, etc.' At last we bedded down in some straw outside and woke next day very stiff, particularly in the neck, no appetite or energy, no pain ... A Scottish doctor turned up on a motorcycle and bandaged me up. Long medical conferences dominated by Randolph as to whether they should try to operate on Air Commodore Carter who was now becoming paralysed, or take him to Foggia. Randolph drinking brandy hard. One German plane over. Randolph shouting orders to all. At length Spitfires and a Dakota transport and returned to Bari before dark. Taken to 98 General Hospital ...

Among the many messages received by Winston and Clemmie was a telegram from President Roosevelt expressing his relief that Randolph had come through and a letter from Douglas Sowman's mother:

22.7.44

Dear Sir and Madam,

I would like to thank you very much for your sympathy at the loss of such a good son, and for your kindness shown to him when he came home, and also to thank your own son very much for all he has done for Douglas, for I know by the way he has spoke of him he has shown kindness itself to him, and from the bottom of my heart I thank him and wish him all the good luck a mother can.

I am, Sir and Madam,
Yours Respectfully,
Mrs L. Sowman

After a week or so in the British Military Hospital at Bari, Randolph was sufficiently recovered to be able to travel to Algiers to recuperate with his friends Diana and Duff Cooper. Duff, who had taken over as British Minister, recorded in his memoirs, *Old Men Forget*:

> Evelyn had been severely burned and Randolph, when he reached us, had water on both knees. He was however, in high spirits and he gave Monsieur Vincent Auriol at luncheon one day a short lecture on French political and constitutional problems which the future President of the Republic seemed to enjoy. Randolph was about to leave when news arrived that his father would be passing through Algiers on the morrow, so he naturally put off his departure.

On 12 August the first meeting took place between Tito and Churchill in General Wilson's villa overlooking the Bay of Naples. A few days later the Prime Minister summoned Randolph to join him at General Alexander's field headquarters on the shores of lake Bolsena some sixty miles north of Rome. General Lyman Lemnitzer, Deputy Chief of Staff to Alexander (later to be Supreme Allied Commander Europe, 1963–9), recalled in his memoirs Randolph's meeting with his father:

> I was interested in what the reaction of the two would be when they met. I did not have very long to wait. As Randolph entered the dining-room, he promptly became furiously engaged in a heated argument with his father over the policies being carried out by the Allies towards the Partisan forces in Yugoslavia...
> Randolph also argued strenuously for greater Allied material support for partisan activity in Yugoslavia from Italy by the 'Balkan Air Force', the

cover name adopted by the Allies for those elements of the Allied Air Force in Italy participating in that activity. Winston Churchill reminded Randolph of other priorities at this time when Yugoslavia was still almost completely held in the iron grip of the Nazis, and every piece of equipment had to be carefully rationed and dropped with extra care lest it should fall into German hands.

Following this meeting I discussed some of the details of the situation with several of the British Officers at Headquarters. They told me they thought that Randolph was playing a most useful role in discussing face-to-face with his father with courageous candour and directness certain sensitive issues that Government officials and members of the Prime Minister's own staff were frequently loath to raise with him.

I do not know what final results emerged from that particular animated and hotted-up policy debate between the Prime Minister and his son Randolph. But I do know that I had been a first hand witness to a very courageous Randolph Churchill playing the role of 'Devil's advocate' with cool-headed daring.

On 16 September, as soon as they were fit enough to resume their military duties, Randolph and Evelyn Waugh returned to Yugoslavia, flying in uneventfully to Topusko by daylight. Here Randolph established his mission, alongside the headquarters of the National Liberation Movement in Croatia to which he was attached. As he later recorded:

My work in Yugoslavia was mainly concerned with the transmission of intelligence obtained from the Partisans, and organising the arrival in Croatia of military equipment, medical supplies and food. In addition, the small mission which I commanded was responsible for organising the evacuation of many hundreds of Yugoslav wounded and nearly a thousand British and American airmen who had been shot down while bombing targets in Austria.

Furthermore Randolph, while in Croatia, was responsible for the evacuation of several hundred Jewish refugees who had escaped from Eastern Europe and for whom he obtained clearance from the Allied authorities for their evacuation via Bari.

In his diary of 16 September, Waugh describes the small town which was to be the focus of his wartime trilogy of novels:

Topusko is a town laid out for leisure and suitable to our habits. The woods are full of ornamental walks, there is one pretty little garden kept fairly tidy, with the arch of a ruined abbey in it and a little shelter, another garden with a weeping willow and overgrown paths near the bath. Many buildings are ruined and the shops are all gutted and put to other uses. No inhabitants except soldiers and Jews awaiting evacuation who give the Communist salute and write illiterate appeals to Randolph. Permission has been granted to take them to Bari. Plane trees down the street, pretty cobbles in centre, plinth without statue (king?). Baths brand new, clean and still working. We go and take them most days, no charge. The evidence of elaborate therapeutic machinery in surrounding buildings. A few callers – local Communists whom Randolph rags in a salutory [sic] way. He is absorbed in electoral possibilities and undeterred by language limitations. Shouts them down.

Note on Jugoslav soldiers: Simple blue eyes, fair hair, cheerful and respectful, always singing and joking. After the sulkiness of British troops it is extraordinary to see the zeal they put into fatigues.

Evelyn then observed perceptively:

Note on Jugoslav policy: they have no interest in fighting the Germans but are engrossed in their civil war. All their vengeful motives are concentrated on the Ustashe [Croatian allies of the Germans] who are reputed bloodthirsty. They make slightly ingenuous attempts to deceive us into thinking their motive in various tiny campaigns is to break German retreat routes. They want Germans out so they can settle down to civil war . . .

Typical Partisan action: Day before yesterday, 5,000 Partisans attacked 500 Ustashe at Cazin (near Bihac) saying their aim was to hold it in order to attack German road communications. Successful liquidation of Ustashe. Yesterday same party made a half-hearted attack on neighbouring Ustashe village but fled before reinforcements. Today they evacuate Cazin . . .

Writing this fifty years later, with Allied forces once again in the toils of a Balkan conflict, it is sad to reflect how little has changed and how accurate was Evelyn Waugh's diagnosis.

On 13 October, to Randolph's great delight, his friend Freddy, now Major, Birkenhead arrived in Topusko to join them. A week later came the news of the fall of Belgrade to the Partisans. Meanwhile Evelyn Waugh's diary for 23 October recorded:

Yesterday we awoke to an air-raid – six or seven slow machines dropping small bombs and machine-gunning the village without opposition. Randolph became greatly overexcited. This, he said, was just how the Drvar parachute attack had begun.

Randolph promptly ordered everyone to take cover in a slit trench. Evelyn, who made sure that he was last out of the house, refused to obey Randolph's instructions and ostentatiously paraded himself beside their slit trench, wearing a newly acquired sheepskin coat, as the German aircraft dropped their bombs and strafed the village. Randolph yelled at him to get into the ditch and, according to his later account:

Waugh not only refused to get into the slit-trench, but felt that honour required that he should stand on a conspicuous hill in a white coat. I felt that this bravado was needless and shouted at him to take the coat off. With an angry gesture he did so and threw it on the ground beside him.

The party returned to their house for breakfast. Evelyn sulked and was at his most stuffy for the rest of the day. That evening Randolph 'weak-mindedly', as he confessed, in an effort to re-establish relations, apologised to Evelyn in the event that he had been rude to him. This prompted Evelyn to reply acidly: 'It was not your rudeness that offended me but your cowardice.'

Randolph later observed:

Waugh possesses both physical and moral courage in a very high degree. He has seen action in this war at Dakar, in Crete, and in Jugoslavia. His courage, coupled with his intellect, might have won him a distinguished military career. But he was usually more interested in driving his immediate superiors mad than in bringing about the defeat of the enemy.

One of his superiors, an officer of high standing, had a nervous break-down after only two months of having Waugh under his command. I had the doubtful privilege of having Waugh serve under me for some months when I was commanding the British Military Mission in Croatia...

According to Christopher Sykes, in his biography of Evelyn Waugh, this incident made it clear to Randolph that he and Evelyn must split up: 'Now Evelyn,' he said, 'you can't expect me to stand for this. We must go different ways.' Evelyn agreed. 'Can't you find me,' he asked, 'some nice little mission in some other part of the country?' However, such postings were few and far between, as much of Yugoslavia remained occupied by the Germans and their Yugoslav collaborators. 'So Evelyn and Randolph,' Sykes recorded, 'remained doomed to propinquity.'

As Evelyn complained to his diary of 23 October:

At luncheon Randolph and Freddy became jocular. They do not make new jests or even repeat their own. Of conversation as I love it – a fantasy growing in the telling – apt repartee, argument based on accepted postulates, spontaneous reminiscences and quotation – they know nothing. All their noise and laughter is in the retelling of memorable sayings of their respective fathers or other public figures; even with this vast repertoire they repeat themselves every day or two – sometimes within an hour. They also recite with great zest the more hackneyed passages of Macaulay, the poems of John Betjeman, Belloc, and other classics . . .

By November, with little or no action to divert them, Randolph, Freddy and Evelyn were getting increasingly on each others' nerves. Evelyn and Freddy became so exasperated with the endless burble of Randolph's conversation, 'jolly jokes' and ceaseless political argument that, to purchase his silence, they each bet him £10 that he could not read the Bible from cover to cover within a fortnight. Far from procuring the respite they hoped for, they found themselves regaled with a non-stop commentary from Randolph each time he discovered new torments or retribution inflicted by the Almighty upon his chosen people. A week later Evelyn recorded that 'Freddy, having doubled his bet, is now anxious to win it, so that instead of purchasing a few hours' silence for my £10 I now have to endure an endless campaign of interruption and banter, both reader and heckler drunk. Light failed for lack of petrol . . .' Twenty years later, in a letter to Evelyn of 2 September 1964, Randolph recalled: 'I finished the Old Testament and embarked on the New; . . . I was not impressed by "the new truths"; rather by the wickedness of God; and because of an incursion of Americans whom I had to entertain (and whom you teased) the bet to read the Old and New Testaments in a week was called off.'

Finally, in the first week of December Evelyn secured the respite he craved when his request for a transfer was approved and he was ordered to report to Dubrovnik. However, it was not long before he had driven his Partisan hosts to distraction and they were insisting on his removal from the country.

Meanwhile, Randolph received a letter from his father with eagerly awaited news from home:

Fitzroy is bringing you this letter, and I am very glad to hear that you and he will probably meet in Belgrade. It is nice for me to think that Freddie is with you, so that you will have good company even if comfort, victuals and liquor are scarce.

You will have seen how things are going here, and how we all seem set for an Election as soon as the Germans are beaten. Unless some change intervenes in the situation, polling day will be about two months from the official collapse of the Germans. I am expecting of course you and Fitzroy to defend your seats with vigour in these two months. All necessary permissions will be given to Members and candidates subject only to battle exigencies.

He then proceeded to report on the clockwork model railway set he had brought me from America as a present for my fourth birthday and which, on his hands and knees, he had helped to set up:

I have only seen Winston once all these months, but he seems very lively and very well, and I am informed that the train is still running. Considering all the railways that have been cut and the general breakdown of communications over large areas, this peculiarly threatened sector seems to have gone well, especially as I am assured there has been a good deal of traffic . . .

I have been much disappointed with Tito, who has not responded to the generous manner in which I have approached and dealt with him. However my relations with Stalin are so good that I cannot think the two great Powers will be drawn into any great quarrel over Yugoslavia. We have agreed to pursue a joint policy, fifty-fifty, towards Yugoslavia of which the foundation is, 'No needless slaughter of anyone but huns!' . . .

Long before any scientific proof existed of the health hazards of smoking, Winston urged Randolph, sadly in vain, to give up cigarettes:

I had a hope that the difficulties of your commissariat would enforce abstention from the endless cigarette. If you can get rid of your husky voice and get back the timbre which your aged father still possesses, it might affect the whole future of your political life. It may be that abandoning cigarettes may not be the remedy, but it is in my bones that it is worth trying. Your sisters told me that it was in the Liverpool election that, with a very sore throat and against the doctor's warnings, you bellowed for a considerable time in the market-place. Weigh these counsels of a friend, even if you are unwilling to receive them from a father.

All your sisters send their love, and I hope some have written by Fitzroy, though they only knew this morning. Mary has been promoted to Junior Commander with 3 pips, equal to Captain. She is back at the Hyde Park Battery commanding 230 women. Not so bad at 21! The Battery is to go to the front almost immediately, and will be under a somewhat stiffer rocket fire than we endure with composure here. Mary is of course very elated at the honour of going to the front, and at the same time bearing up against her responsibilities. So far we are proceeding on the voluntary basis in regard to young women sent into the fight. If we do not get enough that way, they will have to be directed. Many of them have troubles at home with their papas and mamas. When Mary sounded her girls as to whether they wished to go overseas, the almost universal reply was, 'Not 'arf!' I hope the Battery will produce a record in volunteering. The Battery, I must explain, has eight guns of which only four are in Hyde Park, and Mary journeys from one to the other to discharge her manifold duties. We are well back in the Stone Age now, though, as Stalin pointed out to me, we have not yet reached cannibalism.

God protect us all, especially the young who are retrieving the follies of the past and will, I pray, ward off the worst follies that threaten us in the future.

In the course of the months Randolph spent in Topusko, he had frequent dealings with the local Croatian Communist Party boss, Andrije Hebrang, who had his headquarters adjacent to the Partisans' military HQ. Neither Randolph nor the Partisans had any inkling that Hebrang, a close associate of Tito, was in fact a spy working for the Gestapo. Randolph only discovered this during a visit to Tito some time after the war. He subsequently published in the *Daily Telegraph* in May 1952 one of the most remarkable spy stories of the war:

Hebrang was working underground in Zagreb when the Partisan movement began its resistance. One of his jobs was to infiltrate Partisans into the Domobrans (the Slovene Home Guard), then under German orders. The Gestapo soon got on to his tracks and he was thrown into an Ustashi prison. (The Ustashis were an extreme group which stood for Croat separatism, and had engineered the assassination of King Alexander and M. Barthou at Marseilles in 1934.)

The Ustashis, under Gestapo direction, tortured Hebrang. He broke down and revealed the names of the Partisans he had planted in the Domobran Army. At the same time the Gestapo introduced into the prison a Slavonian girl of whom Hebrang became enamoured to the point of marriage. Either through blackmail or for money this woman was already a Gestapo agent.

He was now completely in the power of the Gestapo and they proceeded to devise a plan of extraordinary subtlety to make use of him. They decided to return him to the Partisans; but they felt that he would be useless unless he had a reliable means of communication.

While I was in Croatia during the war I remember M. Leo Mates [who acted as interpreter at my dinner with Tito] telling me how an enterprising sympathiser, the editor of a newspaper in Zagreb, had waited until a brand-new *Hellschreiber* (radio-teleprinter) machine had arrived at his office from Berlin. It was the first ever seen in Yugoslavia. The editor, without taking it out of its packing case, put it into a truck and drove it out to join the Partisans. Hence a fine daily news service from Moscow.

Little did M. Mates or any of us at Army Headquarters realise that the Partisan editor was a Gestapo spy and that built into the bottom of the *Hellschreiber* was a radio transmitter which Hebrang on his arrival was to use to pass back his messages to his German masters.

Communications assured, the next problem of the Gestapo was to return Hebrang to the Partisans. To let him escape would only excite suspicion. The course they decided on was to arrange an exchange of prisoners. But there was a difficulty; at this time the Partisans had very few prisoners and those they had were unimportant. Accordingly four or five Croatians, 'very courageous Ustashis', said Tito, allowed themselves to be captured. Thus was Tito unknowingly supplied with the currency with which he could purchase the release of Hebrang. Five or six weeks after their capture the deal was completed and Hebrang and his newly married wife were released . . .

Hebrang arrived at Partisan Headquarters towards the end of 1943. Though not remarked at the time, it was later noted that when the Communist Headquarters were side by side with Army Headquarters there were never any German air attacks. When the two Headquarters were apart there were often air attacks on the General Staff but never on the Central Committee.

Except for breakdowns Tito had daily wireless communications with Moscow all through the war. On three separate occasions Moscow warned him that they had information that there was a spy in Croatian Head-quarters with a wireless set. Three times all the wireless operators were changed. The Russians continued their warnings, but still no real suspicion attached to Hebrang. And the radio transmitter built into the *Hellschreiber* and hidden in the woods continued to talk in the silence of the night to the Gestapo in Zagreb.

When in 1945, the Russians entered Berlin the files of the Gestapo were at their disposal and Hebrang only escaped from the clutches of the Gestapo to fall into those of Moscow. Having been tortured, seduced and blackmailed by the Germans he now perforce became a Russian agent.

After the war Tito went on a visit to Moscow. Among other things, he told Stalin and Molotov he was dissatisfied with Hebrang's work [as Minister of Industry]. He was lazy and inefficient and had staffed his Ministry with underlings as lazy and inefficient as himself. Stalin made no comment. Tito then added that when the Partisans had entered Zagreb they had found documents which cast a doubt on Hebrang's integrity; there was no proof, but there was suspicion, that he might have been a Gestapo agent. Still neither Stalin nor Molotov made any comment. Both remained impassive.

Outwardly Tito remained impassive too; but he was thinking furiously. Frequently during the war he had reported to Moscow that he had suspicions of this or that person's fidelity. Previously Moscow had always replied: 'Get rid of him – you can't be too careful.' Why this sudden change? In January 1948, the Ministry of Industry was cut in half; Heavy Industry was taken away from Hebrang and he remained Minister of Light Industry. At the same time Tito removed him from the 11-member Politburo; henceforth he was only a member of the Central Committee of the Communist party, numbering 38. The quarrel with Moscow was now coming to the boil. Envenomed telegrams were passing daily between Moscow and Belgrade. Tito noticed with surprise one day that one of these telegrams started 'Following for Tito and Hebrang', a coupling as unusual as if Mr Attlee were to receive a telegram about Labour Party affairs beginning 'Following for Attlee and Bevan.'

I suggested to Tito that it was rather clumsy of the Kremlin to compromise their agent in this way. 'Yes,' replied Tito, 'it was clumsy but there was a reason. This was the method selected by the Kremlin to indicate to the other members of the Central Committee that Hebrang should be my successor. Meanwhile we had found further evidence in Vienna of Hebrang's complicity with the Gestapo; and in Berlin we had found in the Gestapo archives a file marked "Hebrang". It was empty but we could guess where its contents had gone.'

The telegram was decisive: at once all the other evidence seemed to drop into place. However, Tito still held his hand. When the crucial vote on the break with Moscow was taken in the Yugoslav Central Committee, Hebrang neither spoke nor voted. But Tito's police were by now making urgent inquiries. As a result both Hebrang and his wife were arrested three days after the break with Moscow. Mrs Hebrang at once confessed. Hebrang, though confronted with various incriminating documents, protested his innocence.

Tito told me that since then he had received further evidence which left no doubt that the story was true. He spoke without bitterness and indeed with compassion of the man who had been his comrade for so long and who had fallen upon such hard occasions and evil times.

One last thought occurred to me. 'Marshal Tito,' I said, 'this is a terrible story, but it is right that the world should read about it. It would enhance the authenticity of what I write if I might see Hebrang.' Without waiting for the interpreter to translate he shook his head vigorously and said: 'No.' 'I do not mean I want to have a talk with him, Marshal,' I said. 'Could I just see him from 25 yards away?' Again without waiting for the interpreter, Tito said quite sharply, 'No.'

It would seem that like Mihailovic, and in Mihailovic's famous last words, Hebrang has been 'blown away in the gale of the world'.

By the close of 1944 the tide of war had turned, not only in France and the Low Countries but also in the Balkans. With the Germans beaten in Yugoslavia and the Partisans victorious, Randolph's mission in Croatia was drawing to a close. There was little to trouble the dull routine of the winter months in Topusko, though there was a steady stream of refugees and Allied aircrew requiring evacuation. Randolph's letters to his mother show his preoccupation with surviving the rigours of another Balkan winter without excessive discomfort. Thrilled to receive her Christmas present of a hot-water bottle, he wrote back requesting an elementary cookery book as 'the Croatians are not very enterprising in their cooking – their instinct is to fry everything'.

According to Vladimir Dedijer, an author and academic who fought with the Partisans and became Yugoslavia's first delegate to the United Nations, from 1945 to 1952, the Partisans long cherished fond memories of Randolph and this was certainly confirmed by the warmth of the reception I was accorded in the course of my own visits to Yugoslavia over the years. When Dedijer once asked Tito what he thought of Randolph, he replied with these words:

On 12 August 1944, I met Winston Churchill in Naples. He said he was sorry he was so advanced in years that he could not land by parachute, otherwise he would have been fighting in Yugoslavia.

'But you have sent us your son,' I said. At that moment, tears glittered in Churchill's eyes.

In mid-February 1945 Randolph joined his father in Athens on his way back from the Yalta Conference, which sealed the fate of the countless millions of people of Eastern and Central Europe who had the misfortune to be 'liberated' by the Red Army rather than by the Western Allies. Even while the conference was in progress, on 3 February Randolph had written to Eden to express concern, above all, about the fate of the people of Poland, for whose independence Britain had originally declared war on Germany. Eden replied from Yalta on 7 February: 'We are having a pretty tough time here and, of course, the Polish issue is proving most stubborn of all. I cannot tell how it will all work out. Your father is well, though I think pretty tired...'

From embattled Athens, where the Communist ELAS guerrillas were fighting Greek nationalists for control of the country in the wake of the German withdrawal, on 15 February, Randolph flew in his fathers's plane to Alexandria. There they boarded USS *Aurora* for a meeting with Roosevelt, fresh from his conversations with King Farouk of Egypt, Haile Selassie of Ethiopia and King Ibn Saud of Saudi Arabia on board the USS *Quincy* in the Bitter Lakes. Churchill gave an account of that meeting in his *Second World War* memoirs:

> Later that morning the American cruiser steamed into Alexandria harbour, and shortly before noon I went on board for what was to be my last talk with the President. We gathered afterwards in his cabin for an informal family luncheon. I was accompanied by Sarah, and Randolph, and Mr Roosevelt's daughter, Mrs Boettiger, joined us together with Harry Hopkins [FDR's emissary and closest adviser] and Mr Winant [US Ambassador to Britain]. The President seemed placid and frail. I felt that he had a slender contact with life. I was not to see him again. We bade affectionate farewells...

From the Middle East Randolph flew to Rome where Evelyn Waugh was surprised to encounter him, recording in his diary on 28 February: 'Walking past the Grand Hotel with the intention of visiting S. Maria Vittoria, I found a stretcher being carried out heavily laden with Randolph and went with him to a hospital where he was to have his knee operated on for the injury sustained in the airplane accident.' Since the accident Randolph's knee cartilage had been causing him pain and discomfort. In a letter to his mother from the hospital on 3 March he wrote of his plans to return to Croatia, where he had been in his element and felt he was making a worthwhile contribution to the war effort. But this was not to be. By the time his convalescence was complete, Randolph had to proceed forthwith to a new battlefront – in Lancashire – to defend his Preston seat in the general election which was imminent.

CHAPTER 18

Victory and Defeat

L ate one night in the autumn of 1943 Julian Amery – who shortly before the outbreak of war had, together with Randolph, introduced the motion in favour of conscription at the Oxford Union, successfully reversing the notorious 'King and Country' debate – ventured into the Mohammed Ali Club in Cairo. In the bar he saw a familiar, bulky figure in army uniform, sitting at a corner table alone. In his memoirs Amery records:

> It was Randolph. On the table in front of him was a pile of letters. He handed one of them to me. It was from the chairman of the Preston Conservative Association, for Randolph, at this time, was one of the two Members of Parliament for Preston. The letter stated that the other Member (Captain Cobb) disapproved of Randolph so strongly 'on personal and public grounds' that he was not prepared to run again for Preston in harness with Randolph. The chairman went on to explain that the association would accordingly have to select another candidate. They were naturally anxious to avoid further quarrels. Could Randolph think of anyone with whom he could work in harness and in harmony?
>
> 'Would you like to have a go?' Randolph asked. My mind, at the time, was wholly concentrated on the war in the Balkans. The General Election seemed a long way off and I was not very sure where Preston was. Randolph, however, was at his most persuasive – and he could charm birds off trees when he wanted to and so, rather lightheartedly, I agreed.
>
> A few weeks later Randolph left for Yugoslavia with Fitzroy Maclean. Not long afterwards I jumped into Albania. I had heard nothing from Preston and concluded that Randolph had forgotten to write or that the Preston people had chosen someone else.
>
> In September 1944, when I was on the run in Albania, we received a parachute drop of explosives and other supplies from Bari. These included a packet of mail. In this was a letter from the chairman of the Preston Conservative Association inviting me to stand as their candidate along with Randolph. It was nearly ten months old, and had been misdirected

round most of the Mediterranean. It is easy enough to drop mail by parachute but there is no equivalent method of catapulting back replies.

It was a further two months before Amery, briefly back in Italy, was able to reply. 'Many friends had warned me,' he confessed, 'against the perils of trying to work in harness with Randolph. They told me that I would find him quarrelsome, overbearing and selfish. They begged me to stand almost anywhere but Preston. I am very glad I did not believe them.'

On 7 May 1945 Germany surrendered unconditionally to the Allies and more than five years of war in Europe came to an end. The outbreak of peace found Julian Amery at Chungking in China as part of a British Liaison Mission to Generalissimo Chiang Kai-shek after a distinguished, if unconventional, war as a secret agent and guerrilla leader in the Balkans where he had had the unique distinction of being the only British officer to have commanded Russian troops in action. Winston, clearly anxious that Julian might not return to Preston in time for the campaign, on 30 April cabled Randolph in Rome where he was recovering from his knee operation:

PRIVATE AND CONFIDENTIAL
Let me know how you are getting on and about your future plans. I am rather worried about Julian Amery being away at Chungking. Your mother will be passing through Rome in the first ten days of May on her Red Cross work, and I could, I dare say, find a passage for you in her 'plane. General instructions have been given permitting Parliamentary candidates to return as soon as they can disengage themselves from active military duty. Events are moving very fast. Show this to nobody.

Randolph replied two days later:

Many thanks your telegram and parcel which both arrived today. Am making very good progress and hope to be completely mobile in about a week. I had intended to pay a short visit to Belgrade before returning to England. If I did this I should be home not later than 20 May but if you would prefer me to come home sooner please let me know and I will arrange accordingly . . .

Winston felt that Randolph was cutting things fine:

IMMEDIATE
Personal and Secret
Your mother will probably leave Moscow on 9 May or 10 May [after attending the Russian VE-Day celebrations in Red Square as the guest of Marshal Stalin] and fly by Malta which she should reach next day. I will advise you of exact ETA. I can arrange for you to meet her there. I think it much better for you not to go to Belgrade. You really cannot afford to leave the field open in the constituency so late as 20 May. His father and others have telegraphed Julian Amery here pointing out that he should return at once. The date between an election being declared and the poll is agreed between parties to be 38 days. Very hard work will be required to educate constituency. It was very nice Alex [General Alexander] taking a million prisoners in a single day. I am much worried about Jack [Winston's brother], who is recovering slowly from a heart attack. Much love.

By the time Randolph received this telegram he was already in Belgrade, engaging Tito in discussions about the future sovereignty of the port of Trieste at the head of the Adriatic. On 6 May Randolph, who had assessed the situation in a masterly way, cabled Macmillan in Rome:

MOST IMMEDIATE
TOP SECRET
Personal and Confidential
While talks continue and telegrams pass TITO is rapidly infiltrating TRIESTE. His people will not repeat not go underground but will assert an ever growing political tyranny as the price for giving us military facilities.

The only honourable and effective course for us is to use our military power to impose repeat impose Allied Military Government in TRIESTE and on L of C [Line of Communication] to AUSTRIA as we are entitled to do under terms of Italian capitulation. Our case is as overwhelming as the forces at our disposal and there is no legal reason why TRIESTE should be treated differently than MILAN. But if we argue the matter with TITO we are bound to lose in the long run if not sooner. If we act decisively TITO is bound to acquiesce. Force is the only thing which he respects.

Please repeat this telegram to PRIME MINISTER if you think it helpful.

Randolph's recommendation was heeded and Tito was forced to back down over Trieste. From Belgrade Randolph hurried back to England in time to spend the weekend of 12 May – 'VE plus 4', as it is recorded in the Chequers visitors book, with his father. On his return to London Randolph wrote to congratulate the Supreme Allied Commander:

16 May, 1945

Dear General Eisenhower,

Having had the honour of serving for a year under your command in North Africa, I feel I must write to you this brief line of congratulations on your wonderful victory.

Everyone I meet is singing your praises particularly those who really know how invaluable has been your contribution to the victory.

With every good wish,
Yours very sincerely,
Randolph S. Churchill

Eisenhower replied four weeks later:

13 June, 1945

Dear Major,

This is the first opportunity I have had to write and thank you for your kind note of 16 May. The Allied Victory belongs to all, but I sincerely appreciate your personal congratulations.

Sincerely,
Dwight D. Eisenhower

On 23 May, barely a fortnight after the war in Europe was won, Churchill, as agreed with other members of the wartime coalition government, asked the King for a dissolution of Parliament. The National Government, which had seen Great Britain through five years of World War, now faced a fresh challenge: a general election was called for 5 July.

The election campaign got under way almost immediately but it was not until a fortnight later that Julian Amery was able to get back from China to the battlefront in Preston. While fully expecting disagreements with Randolph, nothing could have prepared him for what was to come. As he recorded in his contribution to Kay Halle's *Randolph Churchill: The Young Unpretender*:

In the course of the election we had only one cross word. I had never spoken on a public platform before and my speech at our adoption meeting had been very carefully prepared. I read it out word for word from a typescript, and was relieved when Randolph turned to me, and said to the amusement of the audience – he had forgotten the microphone was still on – 'Well, at least you can speak.' I accordingly prepared my speech for our next meeting in exactly the same way. Just before the meeting Randolph asked if he might look at it. I took the text from my pocket and handed it to him. He tore it up, explaining that platform speeches were far more effective if made without notes. We were in a crowded hotel bar, full of constituents, otherwise I would certainly have struck him. But he was, of course, quite right, and from then on I spoke only from the briefest notes or from none at all.

After the opening volleys had been fired, Randolph, who believed elections should be fun, was concerned lest the campaign became humdrum and dull. According to Julian Amery:

> Randolph decided that there was too much apathy among the voters and that we must do something to raise the temperature. We discussed different ways of doing this, but there were powerful objections to each. Then suddenly he hit on an idea. He and I would parade down the main street on two elephants. Our *howdahs* could be draped with placards or party favours and we could address the passers-by through loud-hailers as the pachyderms ambled along. Someone raised the question of cost. He accepted this as a valid point and at once got on to the Manchester Zoo to find that elephants could be hired for only £20 each a day [equivalent to over £400 today]. He warmed to the idea and duly booked the elephants for three days later. It was, I still think, a good idea but it had an exotic quality which shocked the officers of our association. 'We don't like stunts in Preston,' they said, and went on to argue that we could not afford the money. Randolph as a concession offered to make do with one elephant. He and I would share it. What could be a more reasonable compromise? But, when this too was refused, he became very angry and told the committee that they were narrow-minded, middle-class provincials with no imagination and no guts. They never forgave him.

With his natural facility for giving offence, Randolph regularly managed to upset party workers during elections. After one such confrontation when he had berated a group of voluntary workers, he turned to Julian and said with an endearing smile: 'You know, Julian, I ought never to be allowed out in private.'

Winston, though over seventy years of age, insisted on coming to Preston to speak in Randolph's support. The previous day he had been mobbed by a gigantic crowd in the centre of Manchester. The *Evening Chronicle* reported on 26 June:

100,000 CHEER CHURCHILL

38 MILES OF CHEERS FROM CREWE

The second day of Mr Churchill's 1,000-mile 50-speech General Election tour, which began at Crewe today – where he was nearly mobbed in the densely-packed market square again took on all the aspects of a victory procession ... In Manchester, the Prime Minister found the greatest reception so far of his tour awaiting him – one of the greatest probably of his lifetime. A crowd of 100,000 people had gathered in York Street, Piccadilly, and the neighbourhood. For three miles through the suburbs the roads were lined with people. The crowd thickened until 200 police at Piccadilly were unable to control it. People swarmed over the blitz sites, climbed air-raid shelters and lamp posts. Police with linked arms were unable to hold them back and the crowd surged forward and almost swamped Mr Churchill's car. It was impossible to move. The whole space was one impenetrable mass of humanity...

The premier's reception was equally warm-hearted in Preston where he addressed a crowd of 10,000 from a balcony overlooking the Market Square. In the course of a twenty-minute speech Churchill told a loudly cheering crowd: 'We are the only unbroken nation to stay the course from start to finish, and which early attacked the foul cancer which Hitler started and would probably have spread all over Europe.' Referring to the war against Japan, which was expected to last for another year or more, he told his audience: 'We must persevere and finish the job. We must stand by the Americans to the end, whatever the cost.'

In early July the Preston campaign reached its climax. Julian Amery recorded:

There was real enthusiasm on our side and, as far as we could judge, very little on the other. We took a theatre for the eve of Poll; and when the curtain went up, Randolph and I marched onto the platform through a Moorish arch, to the strains of 'Land of Hope and Glory'. There were nearly 3,000 people present, and the stage effects and lights helped to convince the audience that they had come to enjoy themselves. They cheered our speeches to the echo. Then when the meeting was over we were literally carried off by our supporters, who chaired us – no easy task where Randolph was concerned – from the theatre down the main street to the Conservative Club.

Randolph had, from the start, been keen to have a campaign song and, under the misapprehension that 'Lily of Laguna' was a Lancashire tune, asked a friend to come up with some suitable lyrics:

> Churchill and Amery,
> We're backing Churchill and Amery,
> They're the pair that Preston needs to-day.
> They're the pair we'll vote for on Polling Day.
> Our votes they won't lack,
> We want them both back,
> Good old Winston wants them with him –
> That's what Preston wants to-day!
>
> Winston for Premier,
> We're backing Winston for Premier,
> He's the one to make a Conference go,
> He's the one who's known to Uncle Joe.
> A true friend of Truman.
> D'you want a new man,
> Some Laski crew man?
> No! We want Winston for our Premier
> That's what Preston wants to-day!

Without opinion polls to provide discomfiture or even to sound a warning note, the mood among Tories, locally and nationally, was buoyant. Indeed, Randolph in a letter to his father of 16 July predicted a majority of at least eighty seats. Intriguingly, the other person predicting a Conservative majority of eighty was Stalin! But when, on 26 July, the result was declared, it all too soon became evident that the people of Preston – indeed the nation – wanted something very different. Randolph and Julian Amery were soundly trounced by a margin of 3,760 votes while, nationally, the Socialists swept to power in a landslide, achieving a parliamentary majority of 146 seats.

That evening they toured the Preston Conservative Clubs to thank their supporters for their work. Julian Amery recalls:

> There were half a dozen such meetings and at each, the Chairman made a short speech, mostly in praise of Randolph and myself. But there was one Chairman who hated Randolph and regarded me as an interloper. In his speech he expressed regret at the defeat of our party, and talked of the country's ingratitude to the Prime Minister. But he made no reference at all to Randolph's efforts or my own. Randolph replied for both of us. I did not take a note of his speech, but it was on the following lines: 'I have

been more touched than I can well say, and so I'm sure has Julian, by the glowing tribute which Mr "X" has just paid to our work at this election. What he said about our eloquence was far too generous. What he said about our assiduity in canvassing touched me to the heart. What he said about the punctuality with which we discharged our many obligations was something I can never forget. I know how bitterly he shares our disappointment at our personal defeat, but the memory of his loyalty to me and to Julian is one that will encourage us both through the years ahead.' The poor man flushed crimson. The audience roared their heads off with laughter; and, for a moment, the bitterness of defeat was forgotten in the universal mirth.

For Churchill, who with selfless and single-minded dedication for five long years had led the British people from the brink of defeat to total victory over Nazism and who, more than any single individual, was responsible for the liberation of Europe, it was painful in the extreme to find himself abruptly cast aside in the very hour of triumph. As the news of his shattering defeat came in, Clemmie did her best to put a brave face on things, venturing the suggestion that: 'It may well be a blessing in disguise.' To which Winston replied soulfully: 'At the moment it appears to be very effectively disguised!'

That same evening, Churchill, who had continued as head of a Caretaker administration pending the outcome of the election, tendered his resignation to King George VI at Buckingham Palace and advised His Majesty to send for his wartime deputy in the National Government, Clement Attlee. Though shocked and deeply hurt by what had happened, he was never bitter. In a message to the nation, he informed the British people that, after serving them for five years and three months of war, he was now laying down his responsibilities. He concluded: 'It only remains for me to express to the British people, for whom I have acted in these perilous years, my profound gratitude for the unflinching, unswerving support which they have given me during my task, and for the many expressions of kindness which they have shown to their servant.'

Nearly ten years on, as Parliament marked his eightieth birthday on 30 November 1954 with a presentation by both Houses in Westminster Hall, Churchill declared of the wartime years: 'It was the nation and race dwelling all around the globe that had the lion's heart. I had the luck to be called upon to give the ROAR!'

CHAPTER 19

Life with Father

Following his election defeat, Randolph moved into the house that he and Pamela had rented at Ickleford in Hertfordshire at the beginning of the war, and it is here that I have my very first memories of my father. As a Blitz-baby I, in common with an entire generation in Britain, never knew my father until I was nearly five years old. I do recall, when I was about three years of age, that a parcel arrived from North Africa containing some hard green objects which, apparently, were called bananas. They arrived 'with love' from someone called 'Father'. Though they were unripe, I was required to eat them – something which prejudiced me against bananas for a lifetime and against my father for a considerable period.

Though I must have met him during his brief spells of leave in the wartime years, my first firm memory of my father was at the time of the VJ-Day celebrations following the surrender of Japan on 14 August 1945 in the wake of the dropping of the atom bombs on Hiroshima and Nagasaki. We were joined at Ickleford by a funny little fat man, whom I later learned was Evelyn Waugh, together with his precocious red-headed son, Auberon, who was a year older than me. There were tremendous celebrations in the village and Father built a huge bonfire, in the embers of which we baked potatoes. There was also a firework display, probably of a very rudimentary nature but to a child brought up in the blackout, it was magical. More than four decades later Auberon – with, I suspect, scant regard for the truth – alleges that I pushed him into the bonfire, but his father's diary entry for 16 August exonerates me: 'Another public holiday. Hangover. Winston a boisterous boy with head too big for his body. Randolph made a bonfire and Auberon fell into it. American came to luncheon and signed R. for highly profitable daily column. Some village sports, a damp bonfire and floodlit green.'

The house at Ickleford had a walled garden with a large tree that was ideal for climbing. We played 'Bears', with Father chasing me up the tree while I tried to escape into the branches. Less happy were the hours spent being made to read aloud – at the age of not yet five – the leading article in each day's *Times*. I never did understand why my father attached so much importance to what seemed to me to be mumbo-jumbo especially when, as I learned later, *The Times* was a newspaper of which he had strongly disapproved ever since it had endorsed Chamberlain's surrender at Munich.

At the time I was living with my mother in London at 49 Grosvenor Square where our sixth-floor flat enjoyed a commanding view over London, making it a grand vantage point for viewing the 'doodle-bugs' and V-2 rockets, as well as the blazing buildings that so regularly illuminated London's blacked-out skyline.

Unbeknown to me, a couple of years earlier, my parents had agreed to separate and, with the end of the war, they proceeded to divorce. As my father once observed to me in a matter-of-fact way, but with a touch of sadness: 'It was a marriage made and broken by Hitler.' This was probably a fair judgment. Their marriage – within three weeks of their initial meeting – would never have taken place had it not been for the outbreak of war; and it was their lengthy wartime separation that drove them apart. How easy for a child to rush to judgment on such matters! I prefer not to. After all, who am I, their only child, to complain that they met and married?

Having never seen my parents together, the fact of their divorce meant nothing to me; indeed, I was not even aware that it was taking place. None the less my four grandparents moved decisively into the breach and, since my mother went to live in Paris soon after the war, I was to spend at least half my school holidays either with my Churchill grandparents at Chartwell or with the Digbys in the small Dorset village of Cerne Abbas. It was there that I spent the first Christmas after the war of which Grandma Digby, who like my mother was also called Pamela (though known as 'Pansy'), gave an account in a letter to Grandpa Churchill:

28 December [1945]

I thought it might amuse you to hear little Winston's remarks at lunch on Xmas day. He was talking about his presents & was especially pleased with the soldiers you sent him and suddenly said: 'Aren't I lucky to have two such nice grandfathers & I've got another grandfather too!' Someone said he must be thinking of Mr Attlee again, but he said, 'No. My other grandfather comes first. I can't remember his name, but he is the one what fighted with the soldiers Grandfather Churchill sent me. He is my great-great-grandfather!' So my short explanation about Marlborough had evidently sunk in!

He is being so good & sweet & is getting very keen on riding. Jacquetta [my aunt, later Mrs David James] takes him out on Twinkle every day & he can guide him quite well.

We also should like to tell you how very nice Randolph has been lately – quite charming to me & very nice to Pamela. The divorce is very sad, but I feel it will be so much better for the little boy if they continue to be on friendly terms as they are at present.

While my parents faced up to the divorce philosophically and resolved at least to put on a show of friendship for my benefit whenever they met, my Grandfather Churchill was deeply distressed that the marriage should have foundered – a sorrow which shows through in his poignant reply to my Grandmother Digby:

6 January 1946

I grieve vy much for what has happened wh put an end to so many of my hopes for the future of Randolph & Pamela. The war strode in havoc through the lives of millions. We must make the best of what is left among the ruins. Everything must be centred upon the well-being & happiness of the Boy. Pamela has brought him up splendidly. There must be friendship to shield him from the defects of a broken home.

It is a comfort that the relations between our families remain indestructible.

Having been cooped up in London for much of the war years, I loved the time that I spent with the Churchills at Chartwell in Kent, and with the Digbys at Cerne Abbas in Dorset, a large farm set in the precincts of what had once been a Benedictine abbey, beneath the awesome prehistoric Giant of Cerne – a fertility symbol, carved out of the chalk hillside. My Digby grandparents had a milking herd of some one hundred Guernsey and Jersey cows, which produced the richest milk, cream and butter I have ever seen. I spent much of the day helping in the farmyard, but my greatest excitement was to accompany my grandfather aboard his electric milk-float on his daily delivery round. Starting at 6.00 a.m. each day, we would deliver milk, cream, eggs and vegetables, produced on the farm, all over the village. I would make the deliveries to the doorstep, while my grandfather would take the money, which he would put in an old cartridge-bag slung across his shoulder.

At the age of eight, Grandpa Digby taught me to shoot with a .410 shotgun. Many were the occasions, on a summer's day after tea, when we would set off in the late afternoon sunlight in pursuit of the rabbits which abounded among the ancient mounds which were all that remained of the old abbey. We would return home when our game-bags became too heavy to carry more. In the evenings, even as a small boy, I would sit up with my grandparents until well past midnight playing cards, usually Canasta.

My visits to Chartwell were every bit as enjoyable. At around nine o'clock each morning I would make my way to my grandfather's small bedroom, beyond his high-vaulted study with its magnificent views over the Weald of Kent. Through wreaths of cigar smoke, I would see the venerable Grandpapa tucked up in bed with a mountain of pillows behind him and a bed-table, cut out to accommodate his ample belly, piled high with papers in front of him. He wore a white silk vest – he never slept in pyjamas – and, sometimes, a red silk dressing-gown. Peering at me over his gold-rimmed spectacles, he would remove a soggy cigar from his mouth, dismiss the secretary to whom he was dictating a letter or a speech, and greet me with a broad smile: 'What shall we do today?'

We would make our daily rounds of the property together. These would invariably start with a visit to the golden orfe – the huge golden-red carp – that lurked silently beneath the waters of a series of fishponds which my grandfather had constructed, linked with cascading waterfalls by a stream that made its way down the valley to the two large lakes he had created in the Thirties by damming the stream. He would summon the golden orfe with calls of: 'Hike! Hike! Hike!', then, from a green-painted box beside the water's edge, he would cast a couple of scoops of food on to the placid surface of water which would turn to turmoil with the large fish fighting for the feed.

Next, we would make our way down past the vast swimming pool, which he had also built, to the upper lake where we would pay our respects to the swans with their jet-black plumage and brilliant scarlet bills, a gift from the Australian Government. The swans spoke a different language and would be hailed with cries of: 'Wow! Wow!' They, too, would be fed from a strategically placed food bin. Finally, we would arrive in the farmyard where my grandfather would reach over the wall to scratch the backs of the Landrace pigs with his walking-stick. They would grunt contentedly at him and he would grunt back. One day he remarked to me: 'Winston, always remember, a dog looks up to man, a cat looks down on man, but a pig will look you in the eye and see his equal!' Whenever the weather was fine we would spend a couple of hours together in the afternoon, completing the great wall with which

HIS FATHER'S SON

he surrounded his large kitchen garden, today the Golden Rose Garden. I would pass the bricks for him to lay, while he mixed the sand and cement which he called his 'Pug', periodically stopping to check with his spirit-level and plumb-line that he was 'building true'.

At this time I was oblivious to the fact that one of my grandfathers was Leader of the Opposition and, in between those responsibilities, working until the early hours of the morning on his war memoirs; while the other grandfather was a peer of the realm and one of the foremost experts on livestock and dendrology. Had anyone asked me, when I was six or seven years old, what my respective grandfathers did for a living, I should almost certainly have replied that one was a bricklayer while the other was the local milkman!

By contrast, life with my father was tempestuous. Being with him as a small boy was like walking hand-in-hand with a mobile volcano. One moment all would be calm, serene and happy; the next, there would be an earthquake of seemingly Vesuvian proportions. It was difficult to forecast the next eruption, though dilatoriness, inefficiency or surliness by a waiter, taxi-driver or a member of the staff of British Railways often acted as a trigger.

One day, when I was about six, Father, who had by now given up Ickleford and taken a small house in London at Hobart Place near Victoria Station, invited me to lunch with him at his club. My mother's Scottish housekeeper, Mrs Martin, who was the sheet-anchor of my childhood, delivered me at the appointed hour into the custody of the hall porter of White's Club, which occupies magnificent premises at the top end of St James's. One of the oldest and most renowned of London's gentleman's clubs, White's remains to this day strictly 'men only'. Over the years I came to know its outer hall rather well, as I frequently had to wait there for Father to 'finish his drink' or to complete dictating an article to the *Evening Standard* by telephone. Suddenly he would appear in his beige camel-hair overcoat clutching a perpetual cigarette in his nicotine-stained fingers: 'Let's go to lunch!' he would boom. While most men's clubs have a ladies' annexe, the members of White's have never felt the need for one since, a stone's throw across the street, there is the Ritz Hotel whose Grillroom has always served this function.

The war having ended some eighteen months earlier, London was still littered with gaping bomb-sites, which were not finally cleared up until fifteen or twenty years later. Rationing of food and other necessaries, including sweets – a matter of particular concern to me – was still very much in force. While, therefore, the bill of fare even at the Ritz was somewhat restricted, to a small boy who had never before been to a restaurant or been offered a choice of food, it was truly amazing. My father and I lunched alone, facing each other across a small round table covered in a crisp white tablecloth. He inquired if I would like a steak. Never having had one before in my life, I fear my look must have betrayed my uncertainty, but a steak was ordered all the same. I could see my father eyeing his watch. I suppose thirty minutes must have passed and nothing had arrived. Suddenly, out of the blue, came a tremor: 'Waiter!' As the head waiter approached, the tremor gave way to a full-scale eruption. After delivering himself of a pithy lecture on how the standards of service had fallen since the pre-war years, he bellowed at the wretched man: 'Bring my son some steak!' The high-ceilinged room with its elaborate gilt décor reverberated with the aftershock; even the chandeliers seemed to quiver. On the instant, the heads of everyone at the other tables turned in our direction and an icy silence descended upon the entire establishment. I was mortified. I felt it must be my fault for having ordered something difficult or out of the ordinary but, as I was soon to learn, this was part and parcel of life with Father.

I once heard it said, though I never witnessed it myself, that on one occasion in a restaurant, unable to secure the level of service which he expected, he started with deliberation to smash the wine-glasses one by one on the marble floor. After the second, the head waiter was on hand and, by the time the third struck the ground, even the general manager had come running up.

I found such episodes traumatic in the extreme and would avert my gaze in embarrassment at his abuse of people who were not in a position to answer back. When, later, I discovered that my father was equally capable of heaping abuse on powerful figures, such as press barons, who could indeed answer back and had armies of flunkies to do so on their behalf, I felt that this was at least more excusable. But the thunder-clouds would clear almost as quickly as they had gathered and he would resume his conversation as if nothing had happened, becoming once again an enchanting companion full of fun and stories.

Having lost both the King's 'Shilling', and his seat in Parliament with the end of the war, Randolph launched himself with vigour back into the field of journalism. He obtained a contract to write a column for the New York *World Telegram*, syndicated in dozens of cities throughout the United States. In addition he contributed numerous articles to the *Daily Telegraph*. His journalism provided not only his one source of finance but also the means of travelling widely, from Stockholm to

Belgrade, Moscow to Madrid, and New York to California. Thus he endeavoured to escape the worst hardships of Socialist austerity in post-war Britain, so vividly described by his friend Evelyn Waugh in a letter thanking him for a box of cigars of 8 October 1945:

> This morning a rare and beautiful gift arrived for me. I thank you with all my heart. The cigars would have been a keen pleasure at any time; doubly so now for I am living in conditions of Balkan austerity. We have no servants; Laura broods despondently over the kitchen range and period-ically raises columns of black smoke, announcing that our meat ration has been incinerated, and drives me to dinner at a neighbouring inn. Most of her day is spent in cooking potatoes for the poultry – 27 hens who lay 3 eggs a day between them. The domestic hot water machine has burst and flooded the kitchen quarters. We have had no hot water for a week but hungry and dirty as I am I shall now be content for an hour a day for 25 days thanks to your munificence.

In one of his early columns for the *World Telegram*, Randolph reported the intention of the Communist Party newspaper, the *Daily Worker*, to more than double its daily sales from 110,000 copies to 250,000 and warned his American readers of a potential threat to freedom and democracy in Britain:

REDS IN BRITAIN AIM TO DOMINATE LABOUR

The *Daily Worker*, the organ of the British Communist Party, has recently announced far reaching plans to transform its existing small sheet into 'a paper equal in size, circulation and technique to the leading daily news-papers.' ... All of this is part of the Communist plan to infiltrate into the Labour movement and gradually gain control. But the moderate elements which today control the British Labour movement are fully alive to these Communist tricks. It is true, that at the last Labour Conference, the Communists' application for affiliation with the Labour Party was rejected only by a very narrow margin. The vote was 1,200,000 for and 1,300,000 against ... Now that the Labour Party has won so decisive a victory on its own, it is safe to predict that the Communist Party's next application for affiliation will be overwhelmingly rejected.

In England, too, as in France, the Communist Party members have been much discredited by their record in the war, which proves that they are not a national party but take their orders from Moscow.

When he visited Moscow in November 1945, Randolph found that one of the principal themes of Soviet dissatisfaction with the West was over the atom bomb, technology which America alone possessed:

Russian officials with whom I talked affected to believe that the declared American intention to retain the manufacturing and engineering technique which has been perfected in the United States shows a desire to use the bomb for 'imperialistic purposes'. They further added that such a policy was bound to cause suspicion and hostility in the Soviet Union. I naturally did not allow these criticisms of my Western Allies to pass without comment ... I tried to reassure my Russian friends by pointing out that though the Americans alone possessed the bomb, they had not dropped it on the Russians nor made the slightest use of any diplomatic pressure which might be thought to reside in the new weapon's extraordinary power. I asked them chaffingly whether in fact anyone in the Kremlin had lost a single minute's sleep worrying about whether the Americans were about to drop an atomic bomb on Red Square. They were all too honest to pretend they had ...

In January 1946 Randolph returned to Yugoslavia. While in Belgrade he was entertained to dinner by Marshal Tito, to whom he subsequently wrote a letter of complaint about the openly hostile line being adopted towards Britain and America by the Yugoslav press. On his return to England he published a series of three lengthy articles for the *Daily Telegraph*, in which he confessed that he and others attached to the Partisans during the war had been innocent in imagining that any kind of democratic government might be established once Yugoslavia was liberated:

If political terminology is to be respected there is only one way of accurately describing Tito's regime – a semi-Communist totalitarian police State. I stress semi-Communist by putting it first because Tito's regime has a long way to go before it becomes fully Communist, but there is no doubt now that this is the path on which it is intended to march.

The British and American officers who served with the Yugoslav Partisans during the war hoped that the National Liberation Front was a reality. And that after the war other parties beside the Communists would play an important role. Events have shown that those of us who cherished this hope were over-naïve. Though there were some non-Communists in the regime, all the key posts are firmly held by Communists. Many of them, like Tito, have been carefully educated in Moscow ...

The wholesale arrests, proscriptions and the general atmosphere of a police State might be written off as the inevitable aftermath of a resistance movement and civil war. Optimists might hope that with the passage of time the regime might become less dictatorial and more liberal in its methods. There was a time when I myself shared such hopes, but I have been reluctantly forced to the conclusion by my recent visit that the Communists, who represent a tiny minority of the whole population, are determined to fasten their rule with iron and unbreakable chains on the whole country in perpetuity ...

It was characteristic of Randolph not only bluntly to criticise Tito, where others would fear to give offence, but also to be the first to spring to his defence three years later when the Marshal was denounced by Radio Moscow with a cataract of abuse. Among the epithets used by the Kremlin to describe Tito following his breach with Moscow were: 'Traitor, Bandit, Scoundrel, Greedy Ape, Chattering Parrot, Egoist, Sneak, Deserter, Coward, Comedian, Hypocrite, Hangman, Insolent Dwarf and Thief'. In addition to these lesser offences the Soviets charged Tito with 'squandering public money on his woman friend who changes cars every time she changes frocks' and of 'drinking with Mr Randolph Churchill at Bari'. This prompted Randolph, on 27 October 1949, to write a rejoinder in the *Daily Telegraph*:

... During the war my duty required me on occasions to have drinks with many outlandish characters, including not only Marshal Tito but also Marshal Stalin. With neither of them, however, have I ever had a drink at Bari.

This, however is by the way. What is of more interest is Moscow's description of Marshal Tito as a 'dwarf'. Neither the Soviet nor the Yugoslav Embassies are prepared to state the heights of their respective dictators; but the Yugoslav Embassy very sensibly suggested that I should consult Madame Tussaud's whose archivist informs me that their wax works of Tito and Stalin are respectively 5 feet 7 inches and 5 feet 8 inches tall ...

Having seen both Tito and Stalin, I would have no hesitation in asserting that Stalin is several inches shorter than Tito and is certainly in no position to go around calling him a dwarf. Indeed, only a very prejudiced person would apply this description to either of these potentates ...

Another to whose defence Randolph rallied was Pierre Flandin, one-time premier of France, who, in July 1946, was brought to trial on charges of collaboration with the Nazis, having served as Foreign Minister of the Vichy Government following the fall of France. Randolph, who had known Flandin before the war and later in North Africa, went into the witness-box to give evidence on his behalf. His evidence, together with a letter Randolph had persuaded his father to write, made a crucial contribution to procuring Flandin's acquittal. One of the key charges against Flandin was that he had sent Hitler a telegram congratulating him on the Munich agreement. Winston, while making it clear that he deplored Flandin's action, felt it only fair to point out 'that the Munich Settlement was supported by very large majorities on both sides of the Channel, not only in the Parliaments but in the countries at large. I did not consider that the differences between us at this time in any way altered our personal relations or weakened my confidence in you as a French friend of England.'

Randolph also refused to go along with the conventional wisdom of the day that backed the trials of the Nazi leaders which opened in Nuremberg towards the end of 1945. He took the strongest exception to the fact that, sitting alongside the British and American judges, were Soviet state officials with, as he reported, 'their hands reeking of the blood of their own countrymen' – a reference to the fact that the Soviet Communists were responsible for the deaths of some 35–50 million of their fellow countrymen. He further objected to the fact that the victorious Allies were implementing laws invented retrospectively. Later, on a lecture tour of Australia, Randolph denounced the hanging of Nazi leaders as 'cold-blooded murder'. On 11 September 1947 the *Melbourne Daily Telegraph* reported him as saying: 'Top Nazis were not hanged for starting the war – they were hanged because they lost it. If the principle was that it was wrong to start war, why was not Stalin in the dock? He conspired to wage five wars of aggression against Poland, Finland, Lithuania, Latvia and Estonia. Stalin was not brought to trial because he won his wars.' Randolph was one of the very few men prominent in public life who had the courage to speak out against this one-sided retribution at a time when such sentiments were far from popular.

Evelyn Waugh, in a letter to Randolph of April 1946, admirably captured the flavour of the Nuremberg scene:

> Surrealist spectacle. Two buildings standing – a luxury hotel & a luxury law-court – amid acres of corpse-scented rubble. Kaiser William baroque hall, functional light, functional furniture, a continuous parrot-house chatter of interpreters. Interpretation almost simultaneous. Curious sensation of seeing two big men bullyragging & their voices coming through the head phones in piping female tones with American accents. Obvious

irony of Russian bullet-headed automata sitting on judges bench. Russian delegation all in top boots, epaulets, everyone else in plain clothes. Russians sit immobile listening hard, quite bemused, as strange as renaissance Venetian ambassadors at the court of Persia. Whenever 'Russia' is spoken they all start guiltily & their spokesman leaps up to say 'I protest that that question is anti-democratic, irrelevant, fascist, cannibalistic & contrary to the Atlantic charter.' Then Lord Justice Lawrence (an entirely admirable man) says: 'It is an entirely proper question' and the trial proceeds. The English are top dogs. Our lawyers six times abler than anyone else. French & Yanks openly admiring. Only obvious criminal in the dock is Kaltenbrunner who is a cross between Noel Coward & Fitzroy Maclean (in appearance). Goering has much of Tito's matronly appeal. Ribbentrop was like a seedy schoolmaster being ragged. He knows he doesn't know the lesson & he knows the boys know. He has just worked out the sum wrong on the black-board & is being heckled. He has lost his job but has pathetic hope that if he can hold out to the end of term he may get a 'character' to another worse school. He lies quite instinctively & without motive on quite unimportant points...

In the autumn of 1946 Randolph embarked on a punishing five-month lecture tour of the United States, during the course of which he gave no fewer than seventy-three lectures in forty-three of the forty-eight States of the Union. Despite his hard work and substantial earnings on the lecture circuit, in addition to a continuous flow of newspaper articles, Evelyn Waugh recorded in his diary for 22 April 1947: 'Randolph is home dead broke, selling all of his possessions ... [he] tried to sell me £100 cigar case. Instead I bought a £20 edition of Pope.'

Soon after his return to England aboard the *Queen Elizabeth*, Randolph, on 28 May, celebrated his thirty-sixth birthday with a column for the *Daily Mail* in which he took stock of his career to date:

I am writing this on my 36th birthday. Birthdays are often the occasion for self-analysis and introspection. Reflecting on my age from a family point of view makes me feel rather old and unsuccessful.

At 36 my grandfather, Lord Randolph Churchill, was Leader of the House of Commons, Chancellor of the Exchequer and, next to Lord Salisbury, the most powerful figure in the Government. At the same age my father had already been a Cabinet Minister for four years, had been President of the Board of Trade and Home Secretary, and was shortly, in 1911, to become First Lord of the Admiralty at the age of 37...

Since the First World War no one, except Mr Anthony Eden, has achieved high political office at an early age. When he became Foreign Secretary at the age of 38 he was regarded as an infant prodigy. There may also be some cynical consolation in the reflection that many of those who achieve success at a very early age did not live long to enjoy it. Danton and Robespierre both died under the guillotine at 34. St Just was executed at 26, Shelley died at 30, and Keats at 26.

Perhaps, after all, it is better to be a late-flowering shrub!

Whether or not prompted by seeing this article, his father ventured to make his own rather harsher assessment of Randolph's career. For some time he had been concerned at his son's inability − despite his many talents − to drive his life towards a specific goal. Only a year before he had written to Randolph: 'You have done vy well & have not had much reward from life. The problem of success requires more calculation than you usually give it ...' Now he felt impelled to write again in a similar vein:

29 June 1947

It seems to me that you always get the Dust without the Palm. At Benghazi, at Salerno, in the motor crash, in the airplane crash, in the parachute jump − in how many other toils & adventures − your life has been preserved, and yr reputation for courage proved. But none of these yielded either fame or command.

Now you traipse around the United States making a lot of money wh is as speedily consumed, & working vy hard & for what? Where is the building up? Where is the structure? Where is the reward & status for the future?

I wd like you to think over all these points, and especially whether you shd not put more *tact, calculation, design & purpose* into your conversation & conduct; so that you will reap some return, and get into some position which will grow by itself instead of trying to live from day to day.

The exertions wh you make, the great & growing capacities you display ought to insure some solid achievement. I recognise how little demands you ever make on me, & admire the independence & fortitude with wh you have endured these disappointing years. But surely you must now steer for some harbour. Surely you must land & try to build a castle.

In my old age I am toiling night & day to provide for those I leave behind me; & events have significantly increased my power. I hope by the time you return to be able to double your present allowance on the 7-year

Deed method. But also I propose to leave you in my will the Farmhouse & its gardens & woodlands [below Chartwell] which I have bought from Major Marnham (keeping the farm in my hands for the present).

This will come to you after my death & yr mother's, entailed for Winston. So that you will have a small but comfortable home close to the Chartwell Museum under the National Trust, & so that the family name association will be preserved by living representatives on the spot.

I have other hopes & plans for yr advantage & for that of Winston. Though my span cannot be long, I build for the future.

The previous year Winston, in dire financial straits, had been forced to sell his beloved Chartwell. Fortunately his friend Lord Camrose, shocked at the news, persuaded ten other wealthy well-wishers each to put up £5,000 and, between them, they purchased Chartwell for £55,000 (the equivalent of £1.1 million today), but on the understanding that Winston and Clemmie would have it for their lifetimes and thereafter it would be given to the National Trust for the enjoyment of the public at large.

At this time Randolph, in addition to maintaining a massive journalistic output on both sides of the Atlantic, undertook lecture tours of Australia, New Zealand and, once again, the United States. His writings covered the entire spectrum of current events, domestic and foreign, but his principal themes were the growing menace from the Soviet Union, in the wake of the subjugation of Eastern and Central Europe by the Red Army, and the importance of maintaining the closest links, political and military, between Britain and the United States. In articles and speeches he promoted the cause of a United Europe and was present to hear his father make his famous 'Europe Unite!' speech at The Hague on 7 May 1948. Furthermore, with the situation in Palestine growing increasingly critical as the British Mandate drew to its close, he proclaimed himself a staunch supporter of the Zionist cause, championing the right of the victims of Nazi persecution in Europe to re-establish their shattered lives in the land of Israel.

In all these themes Randolph was in the closest harmony with his father's thinking and, at the latter's request, he compiled and edited two further volumes of Winston's speeches, covering the years 1945–8. In his preface to *The Sinews of Peace* he described the reaction to his father's famous speech at Fulton, Missouri, in May 1946 which provoked hostile demonstrations outside the Waldorf-Astoria Hotel in New York a few days later:

At Fulton he spoke of the Iron Curtain with which the Russians had divided Eastern from Western Europe and urged a fraternal association of the English-speaking peoples to cope with the dangers of Communist expansion. The Fulton speech drew cries of horrified alarm, not only from Communists and their dupes, but from many usually right-minded and sensible politicians and journalists. Re-reading that speech in the light of after-knowledge, many people may wonder what the fuss was all about. They may perhaps conclude that one of the most dangerous and thankless tasks in politics is to tell the truth and to give warning of danger in good time instead of late in the day.

In his introduction to 'Europe Unite!', Randolph pointed out that the years 1947 and 1948 had been a declining period for Britain's prosperity and prestige but that promotion of the cause of European unity offered a way forward:

The same two years have seen, however, the flowering of the idea of a United Europe, to which Mr Churchill gave a new birth at his famous speeches at Metz and Zurich ... and we have witnessed since then, what seemed scarcely possible three years ago, the meeting at Strasbourg of the Council of Europe. As Britain's Empire has shrunk, her economic situation become aggravated and her military power abridged, thoughtful people have come to see that her place in the world can only be regained by the triple policy of Empire unity, fraternal association with the United States, and the assumption by Britain of a leading role in promoting the unity of Europe. Much of the advice which Mr Churchill has pressed upon his fellow-countrymen in these speeches has thus far been disregarded...

Early in the New Year of 1948 Evelyn Waugh, in the course of Randolph's continued absence on the US lecture circuit, believed he had caught wind of a new romantic attachment in his friend's life:

12 February [1948]

Your long absence has caused comment. John [?] (who rarely leaves the leatherette fender of White's except to doze fitfully on the bench in the front hall where country members leave their dogs) has put it about that you are entangled with a woman and once more about to become a father. I have loyally maintained that you are doing time in Sing Sing or El Cantara for some minor homicide & that you have chosen to suffer under a pseudonym rather than bring further disgrace on your name. Anyway curiosity about you was rife when last I went to London and I shall not be able to confirm that you are at liberty and that Mr Hal R. Peat [Randolph's US lecture agent] was the father in the shot-gun wedding . . .

The White's Club rumour mill was not wholly mistaken for in the autumn of that year, at the age of thirty-seven, Randolph decided to remarry. His bride was June Osborne, the beautiful 26-year-old daughter of Colonel Rex Osborne of Malmesbury in Wiltshire. The announcement of their engagement prompted Evelyn to send Randolph a note of congratulation:

14 October 1948

I read with intense interest the announcement of your engagement in this morning's *Times* newspaper. Please accept my cordial congratulations.

I do not know the young lady but she must be possessed of magnificent courage. Does the Colonel, her father (also notably courageous I observe) receive you in his house? If so it would not be a laborious journey to call here & give me the opportunity of doing homage to the heroine . . .

Ten days later, after meeting Randolph's bride-to-be, Evelyn wrote her a letter of confession:

23 October 1948

My dear June,

I lied when I told you that I had sent flowers to you. I meant to order them after luncheon but got delayed in visiting your new spacious & highly convenient house & went straight to the railway station. Please forgive me & please accept my deep good wishes for your happiness with Randolph.

I have known him for a long time; perhaps before you were born, certainly before you could read & write, and have always felt that he had a unique natural capacity for happiness which, one way and another, has never yet been fully developed. I am sure you will be able to do this for him. He is essentially a domestic and homeloving character who has never had a home. My observation has taught me that the best possible guide for choosing a husband is to go for the child of a happy marriage. That has been a huge source of strength to Randolph's father & I am sure it will be so to him.

I am just off to America & can't hope to see you again before Christmas, but please be assured that you will be much in my thoughts and prayers.

Yours ever affectionately,

Evelyn Waugh

Earlier that summer, I acquired my own passport and was taken abroad for the first time. Father took me to the island of Porquerolles, one of the Iles d'Hyères off the coast of southern France. There we were joined by June, a beautiful lady with long blonde hair who, I learned, was to become my stepmother. She was very kind, especially when I was foolish enough to have an argument with a sea urchin while paddling in the sea, spending long hours patiently plucking the painful needles out of my foot.

Randolph and June were married at Caxton Hall on 2 November. In order to finance their brief honeymoon in Brussels, Randolph was obliged to undertake some lectures in Belgium. Winston, with his characteristic generosity, insisted on presenting them with a home of their own in London, 12 Catherine Place near St James's Park, bought with the proceeds of his own writings.

Early in the New Year of 1949, Randolph, accompanied by June, embarked on a three-month lecture tour of the United States. From North Carolina he informed his father that a letter was on its way to him from the White House, inviting him to address the Massachusetts Institute of Technology in Boston on 31 March, in the presence of President Truman. It was in consequence of Churchill's visit to MIT, which impressed him deeply, that fifteen years later Churchill College, Cambridge, was established in his honour. In accordance with his wishes, it was to have a strong scientific and technological bias. Winston replied on 9 February:

I am still waiting for the President's air mail letter, which has already taken five days since its coming was announced...

I have to go to Belgium on 24 February for four days on our United Europe show. Duncan [Sandys] is doing so well with his tireless persistence and high abilities. The Government are rather puzzled how to make sure I do not become a member of the new Parliament of Europe. What sillies they are!

We have fairly good weather here, and I am just going out to supervise the construction of my new reservoir for the chalk pool. This will give me a respectable cascade for about five hours.

In the autumn of that year, on 23 September 1949, President Truman released the following laconic statement: 'We have evidence that within recent weeks an atomic explosion occurred in the USSR.' For more than four years following the ending of the war in the Pacific with the dropping of atom bombs on Hiroshima and Nagasaki, the United States had enjoyed a monopoly of atomic weapons, never once using its dramatic breakthrough to threaten or even put pressure on any other country. Now that the Soviet Union had, in turn, acquired nuclear weapons technology, Randolph was inclined to treat this as a matter of greater gravity than many other observers of the political scene. In his regular political column for the London *Evening News*, he wrote on 29 September:

> When, four years ago, the secrets of nuclear fission were first penetrated, the possibility of the self-destruction of the entire human race was sufficiently stark and terrible. Comfort, however, could be drawn from the fact that a monopoly of this deadly weapon was in the safe hands of the people of the United States.
>
> Indeed, there were some advantages for the human race so long as the American monopoly lasted in that the world balance of power was decisively tipped in favour of the nations who were satisfied with the status quo and had an enduring interest in peace.
>
> Now, however, that another great Power is hard at work manufacturing atom bombs, the situation has assumed a deadly gravity. Unless some effective means can be found of establishing international control over all atomic developments, an atomic war with all its hideous possibilities seems sooner or later to be inevitable . . .

Randolph was proved right about the gravity of this development which very rapidly tilted the balance of world power to the point where, within barely two decades, the Soviet Union was to rival the United States in military might.

CHAPTER 20

Dreaming of Plymouth Hoe

On 22 December 1949, with the prospect of a general election in the offing, Randolph received an invitation to stand as Conservative and Liberal–National Candidate for the Socialist-held seat of Plymouth, Devonport. His opponent, the sitting member for Devonport, was Michael Foot, the brilliant left-wing firebrand and polemicist. On being informed of Randolph's selection, Foot, defending a Labour majority of 2,013, commented bitingly: 'I do not mind if they put up the Aga Khan or Rita Hayworth!'

'I'M NOT SOLICITING OR LOITERING, OFFICER! JUST WAITING FOR A CALL . . .'

Though he had already fought no fewer than four election campaigns, sat for five years as a Conservative Member of Parliament and happened to be the son of the party leader, there was never any question of Randolph being offered a so-called 'plum' constituency, which is the lot of most up-and-coming Tories after getting their 'blooding' fighting an impossible Socialist stronghold. It was certainly not thanks to Conservative Central Office that Randolph was invited to fight the rough, tough, industrial seat of Devonport with its large Naval Dockyard, but, rather, in spite of it. As Michael Foot himself explained:

> He turned up at a famous by-election in Wavertree, Liverpool, as an Independent Conservative. I happened to be present at one of his packed meetings ... Randolph's achievement was truly amazing. He collected 10,000 Independent votes in a few days and handed the seat on a platter to the Labour Party. And the machine never forgot or forgave him, even when his father had helped lead the nation and, more especially the Conservative Party, cowering beneath his shield, through the Valley of the Shadow of Death.

Randolph and Michael Foot had, before the war, been colleagues on the London *Evening Standard*. Both were staunch individualists and instinctive rebels within their own parties. In later life Michael Foot told one of Randolph's research assistants: 'You and I belong to the most exclusive club in London: the Friends of Randolph Churchill' and, in an obituary published in the *Evening Standard* the day after Randolph's death, he vividly recalled their battles on the hustings:

> Randolph Churchill and I would wake up every morning, for several weeks on end, polishing the thunderbolts which each hoped to unloose on the unbowed head of the other before the night was done. I was the Labour candidate for Devonport, dourly defending my home town against a Churchillian carpet-bagger. He bustled in like something not merely from another world but another century, talking as if the place belonged to him, as the Churchills have often done, from the great Marlborough and his Duchess onwards.
>
> The brilliant cascade of abuse poured forth in all directions, sometimes drenching his own supporters. They say that the joists and beams of Conservative Clubs in Devonport still quiver at the name of Randolph ...

The *Western Morning News* reported on 10 January 1950:

> After his first speech in the division last night, Mr Randolph Churchill, who was given an enthusiastic welcome, was unanimously adopted Devonport's Conservative and Liberal-Nationalist candidate for the forthcoming election. It was impossible for all those who wished to hear Mr Churchill to be accommodated in the Devonport Guildhall, and his speech was

relayed to crowds in the street. Mr Churchill, who was accompanied by his wife, said the one great issue which would dominate the election was: Did we want another dose of Socialism?

... Referring to the mass of controls which operated today, Mr Churchill borrowed his father's famous phrase, 'Set the People Free,' and urged that we had to remove controls which strangled trade and industry ...

With polling day set for 23 February, it was announced early in the campaign that Winston would be coming to Plymouth to speak on his son's behalf. On 5 February Randolph wrote to advise his father:

I think the most helpful line for you to take here would be to deal with the issue of unemployment ... The other note I would like you to strike would be about your Liberal past. Both Plymouth and the West Country as a whole still have a strong Liberal tradition ... You could explain how with Ll. G. and Asquith you laid the foundations of what is today called the Welfare State ... I think it would also be very helpful if you could make a re-statement of traditional Liberal philosophy and show how most of the principles for which Gladstone, John Morley and, to some extent Lloyd George stood, have today been incorporated in Conservative thought. Here you could reiterate your excellent point about the impossibility of anyone being a Liberal-Socialist.

When you suggested Thursday to me I did not realise that Bevan was speaking here that night. It is a very happy coincidence. I hope you will utterly ignore him ... Foot was counting on Bevan's visit to be the high point of the campaign. Your visit on the same day will prick this cherished bubble.

On 9 February a crowd of over six thousand – more than half listening through relay-loudspeakers on a bomb-site outside the Forum Cinema – heard Winston, now aged seventy-five, make a vigorous speech in support of Randolph's candidature. Randolph took the chair at the meeting and started the proceedings with this heartfelt tribute to his father:

From my earliest youth I have followed his political fortunes and have long been baffled that anyone could find inconsistencies in a character which is so strongly woven and whose warp and woof have always been, and still are, so easily distinguishable. The warp is the warp of Old England, of Crécy, of Agincourt, of Sir Francis Drake, and John, Duke of Marlborough, and all that is linked with the fortune, glory and romance of England and her Empire. The woof is that of the great Liberal tradition of Gladstone, of John Morley, of Herbert Asquith, and of David Lloyd George.

This warp and woof, so closely woven together, have produced a web of indestructible moral and physical grandeur which, by its truly unique quality, has flowered into a pattern of leadership unrivalled in English history. There is certainly no other man alive of whom it might be said, as it was of George Washington: 'First in war, first in peace, and first in the hearts of his fellow countrymen.'

In his speech Winston attacked the Socialist passion for controlling and regulating every aspect of the nation's life. He questioned how far it was necessary to maintain rationing, especially of petrol and of food. He derided a recent statement of a government minister that: 'As long as a socialist Government remains in office in Britain it can be expected that a rationing system will be maintained.' Commenting acidly upon the arrogance and inefficiencies of Socialism, he declared:

Thus we have not only rationing for rationing's sake, but the Food Ministry for the Food Ministry's sake. And under Socialist administration these sorts of organisations grow in costs with every month that passes. In wartime, rationing is the alternative to famine. In peace it may well become the alternative to abundance. There is now one Food Ministry official for every 250 families in the country. There are more than 42,000 officials in all . . .

You know, Ladies and Gentlemen, our Socialist masters think they know everything. They even try to teach the housewife how to buy her food. Mr Douglas Jay, Under-Secretary of one of these Departments in which they swarm, has said: 'Housewives as a whole cannot be trusted to buy all the right things, where nutrition and health are concerned. This is really no more than an extension of the principle according to which the housewife herself would not trust a child of four to select the week's purchases. For in the case of nutrition and health, just as in the case of education, the gentleman in Whitehall really does know better what is good for people than the people know themselves.'

Churchill concluded with these words:

No one can tell what the future will bring forth, but I believe that if we act wisely and deal faithfully with one another, and set our country, its history, glorious and inspiring, and its future – unlimited except by our own shortcomings – before our eyes, we should come through. Not only can the dangers of the present be overcome and its problems solved, but, having saved the world in war, we should save ourselves in peace.

Towards the end of the campaign *Picture Post* invited the two contenders for the Devonport seat to write their opinion of their opponent's campaign. Michael Foot wrote:

... One day in December, Mr Randolph Churchill stepped on to the Cornish Riviera Express at Paddington Station. He was at that date the truest of true blue Tories. Up till then his most notable political exploit had been an intervention in Liverpool on behalf of his father's now-forgotten campaign for denying to the Indians even the niggardly freedom wrung from the timorous Stanley Baldwin. Liverpool, he said, 'was his political home'. Not for him any desire to represent 'a lot of stuffy old ladies of Bournemouth'. But Liverpool had no use for the political orphan who had planted himself on its doorstep, so the Everton fan has now became an enthusiast for Plymouth Argyll. The Merseyside was banished from his thoughts, and we were asked to believe that young Randolph, like Sir Francis Drake, had been dreaming all the time of Plymouth Hoe. But that change was comparatively easy. The true blue Tory who had boarded the train at Paddington alighted at North Road Station, Plymouth, half a Liberal. The fun had begun ...

Randolph retaliated with his views on Michael Foot's campaign:

The one blot on what might otherwise be considered a dull, impeccable campaign was contained in a speech which he made on 7 February, at the North Prospect School. This is what the *Western Morning News* reported him as saying: 'First the Tory opponents say that the country is almost ruined, that we are going bust, that we must sound the fire alarm or the gale warnings and generally work up a large-scale panic. Then in the very next breath, in the Tory Manifesto, they promise more for everybody, fewer taxes, more food, cheaper tobacco, plenty of beer, and a grand old orgy all round if only the Tories are returned to power.' 'This,' Mr Foot is quoted as saying, 'was a funny way to behave in a gale.'
    So it would be. Unfortunately for Mr Foot's argument, however, the Tory Manifesto, so far from promising 'cheaper tobacco, plenty of beer and a grand old orgy all round', does not even mention the words 'beer' and 'tobacco'. Nor have I myself during the election made any such promise ... One other thing which surprises me in Mr Foot's campaign

is that under all his photographs and postscripts he prints the corny legend:
'The People's Champion.' The contempt shown for the mentality of the
people of Devonport by his persistent refusal to correct his mis-statement
of fact may lead many people to exclaim: 'The People's Champion – my
Foot!'

When the shindig of the hustings had died away and the ballot boxes
were opened, the count declared Michael Foot to have been returned
with an increased majority and Randolph defeated by a margin of 3,483
votes in a record 85.8 per cent poll. However, Randolph had succeeded
in more than doubling the 1945 Conservative vote, raising it 6,477 votes
above its previous record level. Michael Foot recalled:

> When he learned that he had lost, in the agonising seconds which only
> parliamentary candidates can appreciate, the storm subsided and all was
> sweetness and charm. 'I thought you took that marvellously,' I felt com-
> pelled to acknowledge. 'Yes,' he replied, 'I've had plenty of practice.' He
> had indeed. He lost all the parliamentary contests he ever fought. (When
> he actually got in, he was unopposed.)
>
> Considering his boast at the age of 20, that he might emulate William
> Pitt and become Prime Minister at 24, considering the family background
> and the expectations of a doting father, his whole political life might be
> seen as a crushing defeat. He did not bury his talents; rather he scattered
> them in a riot of political profligacy...

Nor had Winston been successful in his efforts to sweep the Socialist
Government from office. However, he had cut their majority down to
size so that they were returned with a margin so slim – only six seats
overall – that an early general election was inevitable. Undismayed, both
Randolph and his father – despite his great age – were determined to
fight on. Barely three weeks after polling day Randolph was unanimously
readopted as candidate for Devonport at the next election. Meanwhile
he set about organising the largest Conservative Party fair ever held. On
3 July 1950 the *Daily Mail* reported:

BUILDING A 'ONE-DAY TOWN' FOR 150,000

A canvas 'town' for 150,000 people, to be put up on the Earl of Morley's
estate at Saltram, outside Plymouth, will have shops, restaurants, a theatre,
cinema, municipal offices, post-office, police station, and a dance floor
and fair ground ... This town of a day – 15 July – is to house Plymouth

fair, the biggest Conservative rally ever planned. The highlight will be a speech by Mr Churchill ... Special trains and fleets of motor-coaches have been booked to convey the thousands of people to Plymouth.

Last night when 60,000 admission tickets had already been sold, Mr Randolph Churchill, chairman of the executive committee, said to me: 'If the weather is fine we expect 150,000 people. The previous biggest Conservative rally was at Luton Hoo, Bedfordshire, two years ago, when my father spoke to 100,000 people.'

It was typical of Randolph's luck that the day of the Great Plymouth Fair was one of the wettest St Swithin's Days ever recorded. Clemmie put a brave face on things, opening the fair with the words: 'We must always remember that the British people are at their best when things are adverse, we are going to have proof of that today ...' In spite of the deluge more than 5,000 people jammed into a tent to hear Winston's speech and, altogether, an attendance of over 30,000 was recorded.

The Battle of Plymouth Hoe was resumed just over a year later when Clement Attlee decided that he could soldier on no longer with his wafer-thin and ever declining majority and called a general election for 25 October. Randolph opened his campaign with an attack on the extremism and disloyalty of a vocal and growing minority within the Labour Party, which included Michael Foot. The *Western Evening Herald* reported on 5 October:

Speaking at Devonport Guildhall last night, when he was adopted Conservative and National Liberal candidate for the Devonport Division, Mr Randolph Churchill said there were two main sorts of socialist candidates – Grade A and Grade B. 'Here in Plymouth,' he said, 'we can see both types in action. In Sutton Division they have a Grade A candidate, an Attlee candidate, and in Devonport a Grade B, the Bevan candidate. You may say the Bevanites are not very numerous. How, then, was it that they practically swept the board at the Scarborough Conference for the Constituency seats on the Executive and were able to bring about the defeat of Mr Shinwell, the Minister of Defence, and so show what they thought of the rearmament programme, as well as several other of Mr Attlee's colleagues?'

Mr Churchill described Mr Michael Foot as Mr Bevan's principal 'hatchet-man', 'he it is who writes the vitriolic attacks upon Mr Gaitskell and the respected trade union leaders.'

Michael Foot retaliated by cheekily inviting his opponent's father to visit Plymouth. The *Western Morning News* recorded on 10 October:

'Mr Michael Foot, the Labour candidate for Devonport, extended at his adoption meeting an invitation on behalf of the Divisional Labour Party to Mr Winston Churchill to visit the city. Mr Randolph Churchill speaking at Ocean Street School commented: 'I might have invited Mr Clement Attlee, but I thought it might be presumptuous. On second thoughts, Mr Attlee would very likely come rather at my invitation than at an invitation from Mr Foot. I might have my differences of opinion with Mr Attlee, but I would not politically stab him in the back which seems to be the case in this so-called happy family.'

Two days before polling day my grandfather and I travelled down from London on the overnight sleeper to lend our support to my father's campaign. Aged eleven, I had been given special leave of absence from prep school at Ludgrove for the occasion. From Plymouth station we made our way through cheering crowds to the local football ground where a huge crowd was assembled. I suddenly found myself seated on the platform between my father and my grandfather amid an ocean of people with placards and hats, some cheering, some jeering. I cannot pretend to have any vivid recollection of the proceedings beyond the fact that it was a bitterly cold and windy autumn day and I was the only one on the platform without an overcoat. The next day Frank Owen of the *Daily Express* reported Churchill's eve-of-poll appeal to the nation:

PEACE – THE LAST PRIZE I SEEK TO WIN

Winston Churchill stood bare-headed with arms outstretched, on a hill-side in war-battered Plymouth yesterday, and declaimed to a deeply moved crowd of more than 10,000: 'This is the last prize I seek to win – to bring nearer that lasting peace settlement which the vast masses of the people of every race and in every land fervently desire. All the day-dreams and ambitions of my youth have not only been satisfied, but have been surpassed. I pray indeed that I may have this final opportunity . . . My faith is still in the high-progressive destiny of man. I do not believe that we are to be flung back into abysmal darkness by those fearful discoveries which human genius has given us. Let us be sure that they are to be our servants and not our masters.' A great wave of cheering, like the sea coming into Plymouth Hoe, rolled over the crowd . . .

Randolph, in the course of his vote of thanks, commented: 'I was glad indeed that my father, in his speech, took great pains to nail the warmonger lie which has been spread about by our opponents. We have had a good deal of it here one way and another from both Socialist candidates, either directly or by implication. My opponent, in his election address says: "The times are too dangerous to put the Tories in charge. They stumbled into the Second World War." He goes on to say that the Tories would lead us into a third world war through ignorance and "through a failure to understand the forces shaping the modern world in which we live". This is pretty hot coming from one of the leading armchair strategists of the last war...'

I well recall being on the balcony overlooking Plymouth Hoe from which, late the following night, the result was declared to the vast crowd waiting impatiently below. Once again Michael Foot was the victor, though Randolph had succeeded in reducing his majority by over 1,000 to 2,390. Michael addressed the crowd to rapturous cheers but when it came to my father's turn to speak, he could not be heard, such were the jeering and catcalls of the crowd until Michael told his supporters to be quiet.

Afterwards, the chief constable advised that, for our safety, my father, stepmother and I should leave by the back door. 'I don't leave by back doors!' exclaimed my father. We thereupon left by the front door, but it was a frightening experience. I have never seen such hatred in a crowd. Despite the efforts of more than a dozen burly policemen, we were kicked about the shins, spat upon and my stepmother's hair was pulled. There was a bitterness and hatred that, I am glad to say, has gone out of politics today. When, sixteen years later, on the occasion of the 1967 by-election in Manchester, Gorton, where I got my 'blooding' as a parliamentary candidate in a Labour stronghold, the chief constable suggested that my wife and I might care to leave Manchester's town hall by a back door, following the declaration of poll, I knew just what to tell him!

Once again the 85.4 per cent turnout in the Devonport poll had been far above the national average – a tribute to the ability of both candidates to arouse the enthusiasm of their supporters, and to stir up the antagonism of their opponents. In spite of the harsh words and insults exchanged on the hustings, Randolph and Michael Foot – each regarded as the 'enfant terrible' of their respective parties – had a genuine respect, even affection for each other, as is borne out by Randolph's profile of Michael Foot written some ten years later:

To millions of TV viewers, Michael Foot seems an angry, bitter, unattractive human being. The few Tories who still watch him on Sunday afternoons are apt to have their luncheons ruined by what seems to them vicious, vitriolic, virulent observations about many things which they have been brought up to believe are sacred or at least undiscussible. Even those who agree with his political outlook, but have not met him face to face, cannot guess how different he is in private from the image which he has chosen to project on television.

Alone with his friends – and I am proud to number myself among them – he reveals a personality of wit and warmth and of an endearing, almost caressing charm. He is a delightful companion, a man of strong loyalties and a true friend. He is a man of courage, integrity and humanity, which qualities in a world largely dominated by poltroons, crooks and cads is, to say the least of it, refreshing.

Indeed, he is one of the few men I know with whom I would care to go tiger-hunting. But such an expedition would be hard to arrange; for we would almost certainly wish to hunt different sorts of tiger.

It is very much in the tradition of English politics that friendships can be maintained 'across the floor of the House' and even across the hustings. It is part of our English heritage and helps to make us, with all our differences, one of the most truly united nations in the world.

That Michael Foot reciprocated these sentiments is evidenced by the generous and warm-hearted tribute he was to pay his adversary on his death:

He was outrageous and endearing, impossible and unforgettable, a Churchill who scarcely ever tasted victory, and what super Churchillian courage that must have called for. Along with his honesty ('Lies are so dull', he would say) and his streaks of kindness, it was his reckless courage which shone most brightly. It could make him magnificent in political controversy, as he had once shown himself on the battlefield.

Friends and enemies would look on, admiring or aghast. Both enjoyed the witticism when someone [in fact Randolph himself] said that he was the kind of person who should not be allowed out in private. But it is the private Randolph I remember now that he is sadly and prematurely dead. He was a friend and an enemy worth having.

Following his defeat at Plymouth, Randolph received an uncharacteristically warm-hearted letter of commiseration from his friend Evelyn Waugh:

28 October 1951

May I repeat with deeper emotion than would have been appropriate in White's, my condolences on your ill-success at Devonport? Parliament is the place for you while there is a parliament. Your failure and the generally wretched outcome of the election makes it more plain than ever that the present system wont & cant work in present conditions.

England, like every country in Europe, is equally divided on irreconcilable basic assumptions.

This is not the moment for a dissertation on politics, but for a friend to tell you how much he grieves at your most undeserved misfortune.

Randolph had lost his sixth and, as it was to prove, his last election contest. Fortunately his father had been more successful and, though nearly seventy-seven years of age, was set to embark on his second premiership, the Conservatives having secured a slim overall majority of seventeen in the new Parliament. On 27 October, shortly after Churchill had been to Buckingham Palace to receive the King's commission to form a new government, the London *Evening Standard* reported:

Mr Churchill came to the window of his house in Hyde Park Gate last night in pyjamas and dressing gown, in answer to the calls of a big crowd. For five hours they had called 'We want Winston' and had sung 'For He's a Jolly Good Fellow'. At last Mr Churchill appeared with a smile, a wave and the victory sign. He held his poodle in one arm. The Churchill family celebrated the election victory at home. Mr Randolph Churchill and Mrs Soames were with their parents.

That December, for the first time for eleven years, the Churchill family assembled to celebrate Christmas at Chequers, together with a full complement of seven grandchildren including Randolph and June's two-year-old daughter Arabella. I vividly recall the happy atmosphere as we gathered in the Great Hall round the towering Christmas tree lit by more than one hundred blazing candles which, periodically, would set fire to the branches and have to be doused with one of my grandfather's bathroom sponges on the end of a long bamboo. The family rejoicing was perhaps tinged with a certain sadness for Randolph who was not to be at his father's side in the House of Commons and who, at the age of forty, must have realised that his youthful hopes of a parliamentary career, which he had so fervently cherished, would not now be fulfilled.

CHAPTER 21

Across the Naktong

In the summer of 1950, at the start of my school holidays, I spent a few days with my mother at her Paris home, 4 Avenue de New York, just across the Seine from the Eiffel Tower. One day we were invited by the American author Ernest Hemingway to join him for a drink in the bar of the Ritz Hotel. The Ritz Bar was a favourite haunt of Hemingway, who claimed to have been the first to liberate it from the Nazis at the end of the war. To reach the bar, which is by the Rue Cambon entrance, from the main part of the hotel on the Place Vendôme, one passes down a long corridor flanked by brilliantly lit showcases containing a dazzling array of exotic and highly priced merchandise. No sooner had we sat down and ordered our drinks than Mr Hemingway – a huge man with sparkling eyes and a grisly grey beard – made some excuse and left. He was gone five minutes, perhaps ten, and my mother was becoming apprehensive as to whether he would return. Suddenly he was back with a look of triumph on his beaming face, brandishing a box which he proceeded to give me. I was not quite ten years old at the time and he must have seen how my eyes had popped out when they fell upon a huge ivory-handled clasp-knife from one of the display cases, for he had gone back to negotiate its purchase. I was thrilled: my mother, appalled.

My Hemingway knife, with its large and lethal-looking blade, was my pride and joy and, on my return to England to spend a few days with my father, I proudly showed him my new trophy. This proved a terrible mistake. He opened up the magnificent weapon and was admiring the sharpness of its flashing steel blade when, all of a sudden, he looked up at me with his penetrating blue eyes and said: 'Winston, I am off in a few days' time to Korea where there is a war going on. One lot of Koreans who are Communist from the North have invaded South Korea which is our ally. I am going to report from the South where the Americans are fighting. Will you lend me your knife so that I can cut off a hunk of Communist?' Somewhat baffled by all this and mortified at the thought of being parted so soon from my new and most treasured possession, I did not see how I could very well refuse.

Randolph's arrival in Korea, in mid-August 1950, came at a crucial juncture in the war, just six weeks after the North Korean invasion of 25 June 1950. The United Nations forces, at that time overwhelmingly American and South Korean – were engaged in a desperate struggle to hold on in the south-east corner of the Korean peninsular around Taegu which, following the fall of Seoul and Pusan, had become the temporary capital. Ansel E. Talbert, Korean War bureau chief of the *New York Herald Tribune* recalled in Kay Halle's *Randolph Churchill: The Young Unpretender*:

> Some 25,000 North Korean troops had just swept Eastward across the Naktong River, which constituted the western flank and a major defensive line of the embattled American and South Korean forces. They had, in fact, cut the main North/South road up the Korean Peninsular only fifteen miles from Taegu.
>
> With other members of the Allied Press Corps Randolph personally witnessed the almost miraculous turn in the tide within a three-day period, which he credited to the heroism of 'the tired US 24th Division ... In action longer than any other unit, fortified by elements of the US Marine Brigade.' With some air support, they saved Taegu and probably the entire UN position on the Korean peninsula.

Randolph had arrived armed with a handwritten letter of introduction from his father to General MacArthur, Commander of the US forces:

28 July 1950

Randolph has a considerable political experience in England and was for five years in the House of Commons. He did not see much of it as he served in the Commandos most of the time, and was an officer in my own regiment, the 4th Hussars (of which he is a reserve member). He has lectured all over the United States, and is fully versed in all forms of public discussion. He was with me at Casablanca and Teheran and heard many very confidential things. I found his discretion impeccable on all these serious matters. His out-look is broadly mine; and I therefore feel I may trespass upon you in these days of growing stress by commending him to you as a comprehending admirer of all the work you have done and are doing.

But Randolph had not been in Korea more than a fortnight – and had only filed a few stories for the *Daily Telegraph* – when he was wounded while taking part in a night patrol behind enemy lines across the Naktong River. The *Telegraph* of 25 August carried his own account of the incident on its front page:

Two newspaper correspondents, Frank Emery of International News Service, and myself, were last night privileged to accompany a crack reconnaissance unit of the First Cavalry Division on routine night patrol across the Naktong River.

The reconnaissance was uneventful and produced no information about the enemy until we were preparing to recross the river.

A mortar bomb fired from about 400 yards away fell among us, about 15 yards to my right. One member of the six-man patrol was gravely injured and despite three separate subsequent attempts by his comrades to rescue him he failed to recross the river. The correspondents were slightly wounded but returned with the rest of the patrol.

It was about 10 p.m. when the patrol silently filed down through an orchard to the river bank a few miles south of Waegwan. A lopsided, bulbous moon had momentarily found a hole in the dark protective clouds. So we waited for six or seven minutes until it was obscured. Thereupon Master-Sgt. Roy Pruitt, from El Paso, Texas, who was in command of the shore party responsible for launching the patrol, gave us the word to go.

Led by Sgt. Earl Johnson of San Rafael, California, we clambered down the 20ft bank into the sandy bed of the river. At this point the bed of the Naktong River is about three-quarters of a mile broad, but at this season the river itself is no more than 600 yards wide ... No sign of enemy observation greeted us as we quietly climbed the gentle sandy slope on the far side and knelt down behind the thick and friendly scrub which lined the river-bank. There for a few moments we conferred. Then two of us moved inland on the right and two of us on the left. The other four were detailed to remain by the edge of the scrub to cover our return.

The main object of our reconnaissance was to determine in which direction the enemy was moving along the road about half a mile from the river.

Between us we had the road under observation for some minutes. But the result of our vigil was nugatory – the road was empty of enemy traffic ... Our orders were to leave the North Korean bank by midnight. Accordingly, shortly after the hour for our withdrawal had come, Sgt. Johnson instructed five of us to move down to the water's edge and to wait there while he collected the two men on our left flank ...

We were still more than 100 yards from the water when, glancing over my right shoulder, I saw a vivid flash about 400 yards behind us. It could have been the explosion of a friendly shell fired to cover our withdrawal.

But it was followed almost immediately by the sharp and unmistakable bark of a mortar bomb being fired. Something like two seconds later it reached the summit of its trajectory and slowly started on its downward path.

The shrill swish of its approach admitted not the smallest doubt – it was hostile and we, not our friends on the farther shore, were the target. I fell flat in the sand. A split second later the bomb burst. I felt a slight pain in my right leg, but did not at first realise that I had been hit. I seem to recall a fleeting impression that I had bruised my shin against a rock.

Should we lie where we were? Or should we stumble onward to the water? I was on the extreme left of the patrol. The smoke was clearing and I could see two or three of my friends moving forward in short sharp rushes.

I staggered forward, crouching down three or four times in the sand, and before it seemed possible I was at the water's edge. Now there was no protection to be found in the shallow stream of the Naktong. Wade for dear life!

It was so quiet that we could hear the pounding of our own hearts. Once more we had dry sand under our feet, and only 50 yards to go.

Urgent American voices guided us to the easiest inclines: we fell exhausted on the summit of the bank, comforting arms supporting us over the rough ground.

While the two wounded in our party had their wounds simply dressed we made our report at the battalion command post.

MR R. CHURCHILL FLOWN TO JAPAN

Tokyo, Thursday

After spending four hours on his despatch to the *Daily Telegraph* Mr Randolph Churchill was flown to Tokyo.

At the battalion aid post where his wound was first treated, surgeons found a hole the size of a florin near his shinbone. Splinters were buried in the wound. – A.P.

According to Ansel Talbert: 'It was characteristic of Randolph that he insisted upon writing his story and arranging for it to be flown back before he would submit even to emergency repairs. As he lay on a litter waiting to be flown to Tokyo a GI enquired of him whether he was Winston Churchill's son. "Well, I'm certainly not one of Clem Attlee's offspring," Randolph growled.'

From the 49th General Hospital in Tokyo one of Randolph's press colleagues reported to the *Daily Telegraph* on 25 August:

CHURCHILL OPERATED TWO PM TOKYO TIME FRIDAY SHRAPNEL
FRAGMENT REMOVED FROM LOWER FRONT LEG SLEEPING
SOUNDLY SNORING LOUDLY DOCTOR UNEXPECT ANY COM-
PLICATION BUT SHOULD REMAIN IN BED LEASTLY WEEK
REGARDS FOLSTER

The editor of the Rengo Press Agency in Tokyo, Togo Sheba, meanwhile wrote to reassure Winston:

4 September 1950

This is just to inform you that your son is recovering rapidly from his leg
wound. I had the opportunity of meeting your son on the fourth floor
room of the Tokyo Army Hospital this morning. He shares his small room
with another soldier.

When I entered he was resting comfortably, his wounded leg above the
covers, and was reading a novel. Rather a brusque man, but kind hearted
when I began talking to him ...

You had a narrow escape in the Boer War. So had your son recently.
God be with you both.

Randolph had been lucky – he had lost nothing more than a small
hunk of flesh to the Communists, not to mention my treasured Hemingway knife. However it had been his unpleasant task, almost as soon as
he had arrived in the Korean theatre, to report the deaths of Christopher
Buckley, chief correspondent of the *Daily Telegraph* and Ian Morrison,
Far East correspondent of *The Times*, who had been blown up by a land-
mine. In the absence of other volunteers, it had also fallen to Randolph
to break the news to Buckley's wife who was in Tokyo. As Ansel
Talbert recorded: 'Even the British Minister and members of the British
Diplomatic Mission ducked the unpleasant task. But Randolph, on
instant impulse, performed the task with such warmth, tact and sincere
sympathy that even his long-time friends who were aware that such
qualities existed beneath his flamboyant and argumentative exterior, were
astonished. Randolph told me later, that he was too.'

Frank Emery – who had so recently accompanied Randolph on the
night patrol across the Naktong and had complained about his non-stop
talking – was killed less than a fortnight later in a plane crash in Japan,
together with two American photographers. Altogether no fewer than
seventeen of Randolph's fellow war correspondents lost their lives covering the Korean War or in air crashes on their way to or from the front.

It is easy to criticise Randolph for being loud, argumentative and too frequently drunk; equally, to use the yardstick he applied to others, it was rare for him ever to 'fall below the level of events'. Indeed, time and again, in his clarity of journalistic expression, his maturity of political judgment or, as here, in his steadiness under fire and his loyalty to his comrades, Randolph would rise to the occasion.

Following his release from hospital, Randolph spent three weeks recuperating in Tokyo, Formosa and Hong Kong. I recall him telling me – it is the sort of thing that sticks in a small boy's mind – how in Hong Kong he had indulged himself by ordering a white sharkskin suit. The first evening he wore it coincided with the day on which the Communists were celebrating the anniversary of the Chinese Revolution and tension was high among the colony's many Communist sympathisers. Over dinner with a fellow journalist at a rooftop restaurant overlooking the harbour, Randolph, as was his wont, had a row with the management who proved surly and unco-operative. But the management had the last laugh. When the meal was over, Randolph and his colleague got up to leave. The manager saw them into the lift which, curiously, was operated from the outside. They had only descended half a floor when the iron-cage lift came to an abrupt halt, with the restaurant floor at eye-level. With profuse, but wholly synthetic, apologies the staff opened the lift doors and proceeded to haul Randolph and his companion out, managing to cover Randolph's new white suit in thick black grease in the process. Quite recently Alan Whicker, presenter of the television programme *Whicker's World*, mentioned to me that he had met my father in Korea where he, too, had been a war correspondent. When I recounted this story he proceeded, to my great surprise, not only to confirm my own childhood recollection of what my father had told me, but to assert that it had indeed been he who had been my father's dinner companion on the occasion!

From Hong Kong, Randolph returned to Korea in time to report the dramatic Inchon landings of United Nations forces under General MacArthur's command – an event which might have persuaded the North Koreans to end hostilities, had the Chinese Communists stayed on their side of the Yalu River. He was also present to witness the recapture of Seoul and the reverse crossing of the 38th parallel before returning to England towards the end of November.

Though Randolph's injury had not been serious, it continued to cause him trouble for several months and, on 6 February 1951, he entered the London Clinic to undergo a further operation on his leg. Soon afterwards an incident occurred which in many ways typifies the kind of verbal scrape in which he regularly became embroiled. On 22 February Randolph took the afternoon train from Marylebone Station to Nottingham where, in the evening, he was due to address the City of Nottingham Conservative Supper Club. In a subsequent legal statement of 2 April, Randolph gave his account of what happened:

> While buying my ticket I sent the porter ahead with my luggage telling him to get me a seat in a first-class smoker. When I arrived on the platform I found him outside the restaurant car which was locked. He told me that there were no seats left in the train and that he was trying to persuade the restaurant car attendant to let me in there.
>
> There were two or three stewards at the window but they refused to open the door because, they said, tea could not be served till 15 minutes after leaving Marylebone. I explained that I did not want tea but merely to get on the train. They persisted in their refusal. As the train was due to leave, I told the porter to put the bags in anywhere he could. At this moment a guard or inspector appeared and pointed out that there was a reserved seat which had not yet been taken up and suggested that I sat there. This I did.
>
> This seat was in a non-smoking compartment, so when we had been going rather more than an hour I went into the corridor to smoke a cigarette. While I was there, one of the restaurant car conductors arrived carrying a suitcase and followed by a lady. They went into the carriage which I had just left, and she produced a ticket which plainly entitled her to the seat. I then continued to stand in the corridor looking out of the window. After the steward had seated the lady he came out into the corridor and the following dialogue ensued:
>
> STEWARD: 'Ha ha! In the soup again.'
>
> RSC: 'Shut up, you bastard. It isn't funny at all.'
>
> STEWARD: (*leering and whimpering*) 'You can't say that to me. I'm illegitimate. I'll have the law on you.'
>
> RSC: 'I'm very sorry I didn't know. But please go away.'
>
> A short time later I found a seat in the neighbouring coach. When the train stopped at Leicester the steward reappeared accompanied by a uniformed constable and a plain-clothes policeman. The plain-clothes man asked me to go into the corridor; he showed me his card, and told me that a complaint had been made against me of using obscene language. This I denied, since I was at that time unaware that the word 'bastard' was

obscene within the meaning of the act. The plain-clothes man said that the steward claimed to have a witness. I then observed another white-coated steward in the background, but am quite sure that he was not in the corridor when the incident occurred. (On the face of it, it seems unlikely that two stewards would have been required to escort one lady to her seat.)

I made no statement to the plain-clothes man beyond denying the charge and stating that I considered in so far as anything had occurred I was the injured party.

I heard no more of the matter until the receipt of Messrs. Pattinson & Brewer's letter of March 29.

In consequence of this incident, my father found himself on the receiving end of an action for slander. It was typical of Randolph's misfortunes that he should have addressed his remarks to one of the (presumably) few British Railways stewards who was illegitimate. The steward's lawyers sought to advance the proposition that, since there was no 'public interest' in this fact being broadcast publicly, Randolph could not claim truth as a defence and indeed that it was one of those rare instances when the dictum 'The greater the truth the greater the libel' (or, in this case, the greater the slander) applied. Though in fact this can be invoked only in cases of criminal libel, it required all the skill of Hartley Shawcross, the leading advocate of the day, finally to persuade the man, after a long-drawn-out legal correspondence extending over eighteen months, to abandon the case.

CHAPTER 22

'Culture is for Gentler Creatures'

It was the tragedy of Randolph's life that during his five years as a Member of Parliament the exigencies of active service precluded him from making more than a token contribution to the parliamentary life for which his gifts, talents and upbringing so richly suited him and that he was never to win a seat again in Parliament. That Randolph had an important contribution to make is evident not only from the causes he espoused but from his powers of expression. At a time when few in the Conservative Party had brought themselves to accept the concept of a wider European unity, Randolph was a crusader for the cause. On 24 January 1952 he delivered a powerful address to members of the European Movement at a conference at the Albert Hall, called to discuss the situation in Central and Eastern Europe:

... A dark Arctic night of Asiatic slavery, torture and death has descended upon eight nations which are historically and geographically part of Europe and which run in a broadening belt from the Baltic to the Black Sea. Latvia, Lithuania, Estonia, Poland, Czechoslovakia, Hungary, Bulgaria and Rumania have by a devilish turn of the screw of Fate fallen victims to a tyranny longer and more agonising than that of Hitler.

It is the alien Soviet Communist absorption and enslavement of the 100,000,000 people who live in these eight countries which has made the negotiation of a peace treaty impossible. And we are gathered here tonight as representatives of all the nations of Europe, East and West, slave and free to proclaim that there can be no true peace in Europe until all Europe is free. So long as those nations remain in bondage there will be no peace and we will not seek to make any peace; for such a peace could not endure, and in any case would be founded upon a wicked abandonment of the rights of others, of the cause of Western civilisation and of the Christendom of Europe ...

Therefore, at this magnificent meeting in this famous hall where the European Movement was launched less than five years ago, we pledge ourselves as good Europeans to be unwearying in the pursuit of our ideal which is the only true bond of peace – a Europe happy, prosperous, united and free ...

... I believe, however, that Europe can never be truly united or truly prosperous without full German participation on equal terms; and I am even more certain that the defence of Europe cannot be secured over the next four or five years without powerful German support for what is now called the European Defence Community...

Winston, returning aboard the *Queen Mary* from his first visit to the United States since once again becoming Prime Minister, evidently received a report of Randolph's Albert Hall speech, for he wired a cable of congratulations from mid-Atlantic.

Following the death two weeks later, on 6 February 1952, of King George VI and the accession to the throne of Queen Elizabeth II, the nation's attention came to focus almost exclusively on the Coronation of the new Sovereign, to take place on 2 June 1953. Randolph, a staunch and sentimental monarchist like his father, determined to produce two books in the intervening period – *The Story of the Coronation*, tracing the history of the monarchy and detailing the ceremonial of the Coronation, and *They Serve The Queen*, an illustrated volume describing the personalities and functions of the Officers of State closest to the Sovereign.

While immersed in research, Randolph was invited to address a Conservative Party rally in Hove. He decided to use the occasion to launch a fierce attack on what he regarded as the republican tendencies of his friend Lord Beaverbrook and on the anti-royalist propaganda appearing in the Beaverbrook press. Beaverbrook's *Daily Express* of 20 November reported Randolph as saying: 'Lord Beaverbrook is always ready to hire Socialists (prominent among them Michael Foot) and crypto-Communists to insult and deride nearly all those institutions which most Englishmen revere...'

Alleging a 'notorious Beaverbrook campaign to wreck the Coronation', Randolph declared in his Hove speech:

Just as Lord Beaverbrook thinks it is good business to praise the leader of the Conservative Party while denouncing his colleagues, so he finds it good business outwardly to praise the Queen while attacking everyone connected with the Court as stupid, reactionary and old-fashioned. But this should not deceive you. In his heart, as I have reason to know, Lord Beaverbrook is a republican, and he is as much opposed to our monarchical institutions as he is opposed to nearly everything else which has made our country glorious and free. You will remember: 'THERE WILL BE NO WAR THIS YEAR OR NEXT YEAR EITHER', screaming banner headlines across the *Daily* and *Sunday Express* in 1939. Always wrong on every public issue...

The *Toronto Globe* concluded its report of Randolph's speech: 'Reached by telephone in Nassau, the Bahamas Islands, Lord Beaverbrook listened attentively to quotations from Churchill's denunciations and requested that they be repeated twice. When he was asked for comment there was a moment's silence and then he said: "Much obliged, I have no comment to make at all."'

That spring Tito visited Britain as the guest of the Foreign Secretary, Sir Anthony Eden, prompting Evelyn Waugh in a letter to Randolph to return to his mischievous suggestion, conceived when they were in Yugoslavia together during the war, that 'Our Aunt' Tito was really a woman:

29 March 1953

It is most kind of you to offer your services on my behalf with *Punch*. I thought the contribution I submitted might set the right tone of farce for Tito's visit, but that has already been abundantly supplied by the politicians. Catcalls behind her back as she leaves would not be worthy of our national weekly (which I confess I never see)...

The politicians must be heartily sorry they imported the wench. I note that her baleful eye brought down another two aircraft yesterday. The army seem to be more cautious.

How the Brooklyn Jeromes must be blushing in Purgatory to see Clarissa [Anthony Eden's wife and Winston's niece] entertaining a woman of Tito's reputation ... Since you were so good as to send me your review of *Tito Speaks* [by Vladimir Dedijer], I enclose an uncorrected of my own.

For Winston, the high point of his second premiership was undoubtedly to be First Minister of the Crown at the time of the Coronation of Britain's young and beautiful new Queen. He gloried in the re-enactment of the ancient ceremonial and in the act of national homage to the Sovereign at Westminster Abbey. Elizabeth Kenward recorded in *The Tatler*: 'The Prime Ministers of the countries of the Commonwealth had taken up their places with our own Prime Minister, Sir Winston Churchill, who was wearing the uniform of Lord Warden of the Cinque Ports under his Garter Mantle, and Lady Churchill. Their son, Mr Randolph Churchill wearing Court dress, was in the Abbey in the role of a Gold-Staff Officer, and their grandson, Winston Churchill, was page to Marshal of the Royal Air Force, Viscount Portal, who carried the Sceptre with Cross.'

Following the Coronation, the Churchill clan gathered for a celebration luncheon at Downing Street, where photographs were taken of the three generations of male Churchills together in our Coronation robes. I was twelve years old at the time and shall always remember it as one of the most exciting days of my life. However, the strain of the Coronation and of the great additional burden of public duties involved in receiving all the Commonwealth Prime Ministers and other Heads of State, as well as running the Government, proved too great for Winston. Three weeks later, Clemmie confided to Randolph that his father had suffered what was evidently a stroke:

25 June 1953

Papa is not well. After the dinner party on Tuesday (for the de Gasperis) he felt overpowered with fatigue & we got him to bed as soon as we could. Lord Moran [Winston's physician] came early the next morning – & later brought Sir Russell Brain. They both think & hope that after 48 hours complete rest the symptoms (slightly slurred speech & slight loss of power in the fingers of the left hand) will subside. I am just taking him to Chartwell & Bermuda is 'on' [for a meeting with President Eisenhower, in the event postponed until December] – if the symptoms subside (they may even disappear). If anyone says to you: I hear your Father is very tired – Please say 'yes he is very tired, & he is resting as much as possible over this week-end so as to be fresh for the voyage.'

I am very sad & anxious & Papa is in very low spirits. But Charles Moran is optimistic so I will be too.

Randolph, deeply distressed, replied on 30 June:

I do want you to know how much I am thinking of you at this sad & difficult time. I thought you were magnificent on Saturday & doing everything possible to maintain Papa's morale. So long as that persists no miracle is impossible...

Once again Winston proved formidably resilient, and not only recovered, but continued for two more years as Prime Minister.

No sooner had Randolph completed his two books on the Coronation than he embarked on the writing of yet another book, entitled *Fifteen Famous English Homes*, an illustrated work about the great houses of England, their history and their occupants. I have a shrewd suspicion that this volume, coming as it did at a time of very considerable financial stringency, was undertaken by my father neither from altruistic motives nor solely for financial reward, but as a means of providing a free holiday, together with some good shooting, for his twelve-year-old son as, together, we toured the country visiting one ancestral home after another. One of the houses at which we hoped to stay was Chatsworth, home of the Duke and Duchess of Devonshire. Unfortunately it was being restored at the time and the Devonshires recommended that we put up at the local Trust House hotel. My father, under the misapprehension that such establishments formed part of the Temperance movement, arrived in a bad temper armed with plentiful supplies of whisky.

In the summer of that year, Randolph and June moved to the country where they installed themselves in a fine Georgian manor house called Oving, which enjoyed a splendid view across the Vale of Aylesbury. It was a lovely house which my father hoped, but could not afford, to buy. Accordingly he rented it for a year and, eventually, it became the home of his friends Michael and Pam Berry, later Lord and Lady Hartwell. Among the many guests at Oving that summer was the Democratic contender for the US presidency, Adlai Stevenson, who unsuccessfully challenged Eisenhower in the 1952 election and again in 1956.

When *Fifteen Famous English Homes* reached an advanced stage, Randolph ventured to send some chapters to 'the Little Captain', as he fondly called his friend Evelyn Waugh:

2 July 1953

In an unguarded moment you very kindly undertook to read and criticise some chapters in my book on English Country Houses. I have now completed five on Blenheim, Wilton, Chatsworth, Althorp and Hatfield. If you can spare the time to correct the orthography and make suggestions for improvement in style, I shall be most grateful. Also if you could suggest some architectural comments, which would embellish the text, I should be your debtor for life.

We are now installed in this agreeable and comfortable house, and we should be delighted if you and Laura could visit us any weekend, or, indeed, for a night or two at any time.

Evelyn Waugh replied, pouring buckets of cold water on the project:

4 July 1953

I do not think that you have chosen a subject well suited to your genius. You have no appreciation of architectural beauty or of the paintings & decorations & treasures which enhance it.

The only family with whose history I have any familiarity is the Herberts and I have supplied a few corrections to your account of them.

I do not know what reader you seek to interest. Certainly not the specialist or the amateur.

Forgive my bluntness. This is not your proper work. You need hot, whisky-laden, contemporary breath, the telephone, the latest gossip, the tang of the New World, to bring out what is lively in you. History & culture are for gentler creatures...

It is most kind of you to invite me to your new home. If my preceding comments have not caused deathless offence, I will come with great pleasure. Would early August be suitable?

Randolph, undaunted, made clear his intention to persevere:

7 July 1953

Thank you for your letter and for your helpful corrections to the chapter on Wilton. When Nancy [Mitford] sent you one of her books you advised her to abandon it and start again. Myself you advise to abandon the attempt altogether. Unfortunately the state of my finances does not permit me to accept this well intentioned advice, and I must, therefore, persevere. But I assure you that your criticisms will act as a spur and indeed as a goad to my endeavours.

I am delighted that you will visit us in early August. Please say when you would like to come. My son will be here then, and if you have a boy of around his age, perhaps you might like to bring him with you. I trust Laura will also come.

Waugh, who was unrelenting, replied on 12 July:

If you have engaged yourself to deliver those articles for publication there is of course no alternative to their completion. I hope your next work will be topical. There lies your proper field.

Laura, alas, will be busy with farm & children all the summer, sends her love & regretfully declines your kind invitation. The boy Auberon Alexander is available for little Winston's entertainment. His chief interest is shooting sitting birds with an airgun & making awful smells with chemicals. He is devoid of culture but cheerful & greedy for highly peppered foods. If not closely watched he smokes & drinks.

Shall I bring him for the first week-end of August? I look forward greatly to seeing you.

When *Fifteen Famous English Homes* was published the following year, it contained the following dedication:

To
EVELYN WAUGH
Sometime Captain RHG
who
when advising the author to abandon the project
urged that
'History and Culture are for gentler creatures'
this book is defiantly dedicated

On being sent a copy Waugh, mollified by the dedication, recanted his earlier over-hasty criticism:

13 April 1954

Very many thanks indeed for your handsome present. It is a fine volume, full of information on a topic near my heart. I congratulate you on the depth of research and the elegance of presentation.

I am full of pride at the dedication both as a token of your continued kind feeling toward me and as an association with so considerable a literary work . . .

It was during a visit to Knowsley in Lancashire, in the course of his researches on the stately homes of England, that Randolph was asked by his friend, John Derby, to write the Life of his grandfather, Edward George Villiers Stanley, 17th Earl of Derby. He responded on 1 May:

I have given a lot of thought to your very flattering suggestion that I should write your grandfather's life, and have come to the conclusion that I would very much like to do so. I discussed the matter today with my literary agents, Curtis Brown, and they were of the opinion that it could be an important and popular book and that it should be published by one of the four or five leading firms of publishers . . . Allowing two years for the research and writing and nine months for the production, it could be published in the autumn of 1956 . . .

Randolph's purpose in undertaking this major and laborious work was to demonstrate his ability to write a serious historical biography, in the hope that one day his father might be persuaded to entrust to him the writing of his own Life, which was Randolph's remaining ambition and to which he was to refer as the 'Great Biography'.

CHAPTER 23

What I Said About the Press

Before settling down to the tranquil task of writing his biography of Lord Derby, Randolph decided to launch a one-man crusade to clean up the Augean stables of Fleet Street – a campaign that was to send shock waves throughout the national and provincial press, and to cause extreme embarrassment to a small number of enormously powerful men who had arrogated to themselves the right to invade the privacy of any of the Queen's subjects – and even of the Queen herself. Randolph took the strongest exception to those press lords in Fleet Street who sought to increase their already vast fortunes by prying into the private lives and misfortunes of others while confidently supposing that they themselves should be immune from any such intrusion or attacks on their behaviour. At the same time Randolph castigated them for peddling pornography to the masses under the pretence of selling newspapers. As he explained in the introduction to his polemic, *What I Said About the Press*:

In September 1953 I took the chair at a Foyle's Luncheon at the Dorchester Hotel. I seized the opportunity to make some observations which had long been on my mind about some sections of the British Press. Subsequently, I made two further speeches on the same topic. I couched what I had to say in the most provocative way I could, since I knew that it was unlikely otherwise that any notice would be taken of what I had to say. In doing this I ran some risks.

Indeed, I was told by my legal advisers that it was possible that I might be sued for libel. With my lawyer's approval I accepted this risk with open eyes. Since very few newspapers were likely to report what I intended to say (because of the tacit and clandestine arrangements of the Newspaper Proprietors' Association), I would have welcomed an opportunity to test these issues in court. One of the most brilliant lawyers practising at the bar [Sir Hartley, later Lord, Shawcross] with whom I discussed these matters and whom I consulted about the second speech I made said 'Are you trailing your coat?'. I replied 'Certainly.'

'Well then,' he replied, 'I'd go ahead.'

In the event, none of the rich, powerful and influential people whom I had attacked saw fit to make any reply, either in writing or in the courts. Instead, one of them, after waiting for many months without defending himself in any way against the serious charges that I brought against him, chose to strike at me with entirely different weapons...

Randolph, as he was fond of putting it, did not believe in making scapegoats out of small fry and he once remarked to me: 'Never blame the man who shins up your drainpipe to poke a lens through your bathroom window – blame the man who sent him!' He rightly held that the rich and powerful proprietor, who profits from a newspaper, cannot disclaim responsibility for the way it is run. Having set the scene at the Foyle's Literary Luncheon, Randolph launched into his attack on Britain's newspaper proprietors with criticism which, sadly, is even more valid today than when he embarked on his campaign more than forty years ago:

A number of public-spirited people and organs have recently been concerned about the vast outpourings of pornography from the presses of Fleet Street. There is no doubt that pornography, even its crudest forms, makes a very wide appeal to a large section of the human race. Despite this, the man who dedicates his life to earning his living by the manufacture and sale of pornography is not generally considered a particularly esteemed member of the community.

He went on to propose the creation of a new office:

... so deep and lush and fast flowing has become the river of pornography and crime which streams today from Fleet Street, that there has recently been some talk behind the scenes that the more important pornographers and criminologists should receive some public recognition of their tireless labour. One suggestion I have heard is that it would have been appropriate in Coronation Year to have appointed a Pornographer Royal and Criminologist Extraordinary. The project even went so far that a short list of suitable candidates for this new appointment was drawn up. I do not wish to appear discourteous to Mr Cudlipp [Hugh Cudlipp, editor of the *Daily Mirror*], and I am sure he can take his medicine like a man, but I am sorry to say that I don't think he even got on to the short list...

He then proceeded to evaluate the claims of the rival candidates:

A Mr Clapp, the editor of the *Daily Sketch*, entering new into the race, has set so fast a pace that old hacks like Mr Eade [editor of the *Sunday Dispatch*] have now seriously to look to their laurels. It was, I understand, the rise of Mr Clapp which robbed his stable companion, Mr Eade, of the coveted and envied position of Pornographer Royal and Criminologist Extraordinary. It was thought to be a dead-heat for Lord Rothermere's two horses ...

Randolph thereupon addressed himself to what he termed the power of the '*sup*-press', as used by newspaper proprietors to protect themselves from all criticism or intrusion:

It is a curious thing that, while these wealthy men who own papers set themselves up to criticise every kind of institution, they themselves are the one institution which is totally immune from criticism. They have the power not only of the press but of the *sup*-press.

Dog Don't Eat Dog. That is one of the reasons why the London press is so very bad. This handful of wealthy men have formed a cartel to immunise themselves from anything said about them, though some of them dish out a cataract of dirt and filth at every institution and individual they feel moved to criticise.

Though we may not approve, everyone can understand the position of an unfortunate man who has no other trade or livelihood save pornography; but it is, I think, a little disquieting when you find a man like Lord Rothermere, who inherited three or four million pounds from his father, romping around in the gutter ...

Finally, Randolph exposed the way in which large sectors of the British press, while affecting to support the Royal Family, never let pass an opportunity of trivialising or denigrating the institution of monarchy and those who represented it – a situation that has become totally out of hand today: '... there are almost no limits to the disgusting impertinence which a large section of the press allow themselves in handling the private lives of a family whom, of course, they always affect to love and revere ...'

Randolph was correct in his surmise that the gravamen of his charge would be suppressed in almost all the press reports. There proved to be only two honourable exceptions. Undaunted, he returned to his theme, in a speech to the Manchester Publicity Association on 7 October, explaining:

Although attempts were made to suppress the speech, they failed. The management ran down the safety curtain, but a little too late. One of Lord Rothermere's shoes was left on the wrong side of the curtain and the public, through the courtesy of the *Manchester Guardian*, caught a glimpse of it. The management then panicked and the curtain was partially raised and a scene of utter confusion became evident, in the course of which Mr Michael Foot turned on all the lights and printed the speech verbatim in the *Tribune*. Lord Rothermere of course was quickly smuggled off the stage and has since offered no defence of his conduct. He desires not only what his father was accused of by the late Lord Baldwin – 'power without responsibility, the prerogative of the harlot throughout the ages' – but the cash that comes from the sale of pornography without the shame attaching to this squalid way of life . . .

He went on to attack the way in which even newspapers of high repute sought to suppress news of which they did not approve:

There is no doubt that a lot of papers, particularly *The Times*, think that if something is not reported in their columns it has not really happened. They believe that they can overlook it and that the public will be too stupid to notice it. On the whole they succeed in this almost unconscious policy. It is candidly my intention to make this policy fail and it is in that sense that I think I can say that my speech in London has achieved some success . . .

Randolph concluded his remarks by mischievously suggesting that he had recently heard it whispered that Lord Kemsley was considering founding the Kemsley School of Journalism which would provide:

. . . a school for Press Lords, where the more backward ones could be taught some of the more elementary rules of honour and human decency with which their preoccupation in making money has so far not brought them into contact. I have heard it said that Lord Rothermere intends, out of his huge profits from the sale of pornography, to endow a chair at Lord Kemsley's school for backward press lords and editors and means to enrol himself as the first student in the school.

Randolph even volunteered his own services:

If this school for press lords materialises I shall be very happy to give a series of lectures there free of charge. I trust that I shall be put in charge of the night class for backward boys. I shall not waste too much time on

old lags like Lord Rothermere, but I shall have a special rod in pickle for
that clever, but in some ways backward new boy, Sir William Haley [the
newly appointed editor of *The Times* whom Randolph accused of arriving
hotfoot from the BBC with 'banks of electronic suppressors'].

These exchanges have weathered the years astonishingly well and
indeed are more pertinent than ever today. Because of its criticism of the
barons of Fleet Street, the book in which they were later published,
What I Said About the Press, was banned by the retail newsagents W. H.
Smith & Son. Randolph retaliated by producing postcards advertising
his book under a headline, 'BANNED BY W. H. SMITH!'. As a boy
at Eton, armed with a fistful of these postcards, I would launch raids
against the W. H. Smith bookshop opposite Windsor Castle, inserting
my father's contraband leaflets as I thumbed through their stock. Meanwhile, my father's friends were doing likewise in other parts of the
country and, in this way, Country Bumpkins Ltd., the company formed
by Randolph to market his banned book, managed to make many
hundreds of sales.

Soon after these withering and unprecedented attacks on a number
of hitherto respected newspaper proprietors, Randolph was invited to
contribute a regular weekly column entitled 'Guide to the Press' for *The
Recorder*. When that ceased publication, he wrote a series of political
feature articles for another weekly called *Truth* under the *nom de plume*
'Tarquin' because, as Randolph explained: 'Like him, I prefer to cut off
the heads of the tall poppies.' One of the few newspaper proprietors to
give Randolph support and encouragement in his crusade against the
seamier sections of the British press was Lord Beaverbrook. Though
brazenly admitting that he had acquired his newspapers solely for propaganda purposes, he was also the only proprietor in Fleet Street to allow
them to print criticisms of himself.

Although he maintained a constant output of articles and comment
for the press, Randolph was now settling down to the more serious
labour of his biography of Lord Derby. This change of direction from
the choppy, sometimes raging waters of polemical journalism, which so
suited his impetuous nature, towards the calmer, deeper waters of political
biography, coincided with a determination to turn his back upon the
noisy, vain and flighty life of London, in favour of the richer, more
enduring rewards of life in the country. Though he was never to abandon
his brash, lucid and lively brand of journalism, nor wholly to forsake the
bar and card-room of White's Club which, more than anywhere, had
been his London home, the change marked a definite turning-point in

his life. At last, as his father had enjoined him to do several years earlier, he was steering for harbour with a determination to land and build his castle.

On 30 November 1954 Winston celebrated his eightieth birthday. In Westminster Hall he was presented with an Address by both Houses of Parliament, together with a portrait of himself by Graham Sutherland, which, tongue-in-cheek, he dubbed 'a remarkable example of modern art!'. Afterwards a family celebration was held at Downing Street. However, his great age, combined with the likelihood of another general election within a year, gave rise to more speculation than ever as to when he would step down as Prime Minister. For fourteen years he had been leader of the Conservative Party and, throughout that time, there had been a general assumption, growing latterly to conviction, that Sir Anthony Eden would be his successor.

On 24 December Randolph, writing in *Truth* under his pseudonym Tarquin, cheekily speculated – some months before Eden was to succeed Churchill – as to who Eden's successor might be, correctly forecasting that the contest would be fought out between Rab Butler and Harold Macmillan. A few days later he published a detailed and informative article under his own name in the *Evening Standard* on the complex and mysterious procedures by which the Conservative Party in those days chose its leader. Although previously his father had frowned on such speculation, Randolph received a letter of congratulation from him early in the New Year:

2 January 1955

I have read your article about 'Who Chooses the Tory Leader?', and was most interested to learn of these facts, of most of which I was unaware. I like the terse and cool method you adopt in your recent writings.

I have also read in the *Evening Standard* of yesterday your article about Yugoslav politics. This also was good and clear, and I am particularly grateful to you for telling me how to pronounce 'Geelas' and 'Ded-ee-ay'. I have not yet read the article about Anthony's successor. It seems to have got mixed up with other papers, or did you take it away?

On 4 April the Queen paid Sir Winston and Lady Churchill the great – indeed, up to that point, unprecedented – compliment of dining with them at Number Ten and, the next day, my grandfather formally tendered his resignation as Prime Minister, recommending as his successor Sir Anthony Eden who, almost immediately, called a general election.

CHAPTER 24

Action for Libel

In the course of the May 1955 general election campaign Randolph, in an article for the *Evening Standard*, accused Mr Cyril Lord, the Lancashire cotton tycoon, of uttering 'loud-mouthed vapourings' when he had claimed that the Conservative Government would lose every marginal seat in Lancashire. The following Sunday *The People* newspaper attacked Randolph in an article headed 'VOTERS BEWARE!' which contained the following paragraph:

... Most of all, beware of the party propagandists – those who haven't seen fit to fight openly for a seat but prefer to be paid hacks to write biased accounts of the campaign. Chief among these – as usual – is Randolph Churchill, that slightly comic son of our greatest statesman ...

Randolph promptly wrote a letter to the editor-in-chief of *The People*, Mr Harry Ainsworth, pointing out the falsehoods and inaccuracies contained in the article. He concluded with the following warning:

I have never been paid by any party or any individual to write articles to order. My opinions, popular or unpopular, are my own. I would have thought that this was notorious. In consequence your statement that I am a party propagandist and paid hack is false and a gross libel on me in my professional character.

I have taken counsel's opinion and I am advised that I have strong grounds for bringing an action for libel against you and your paper. I am, however, disinclined to go to law and will not do so if you will publish this letter textually in your next issue with the same prominence which you gave to your false statements about me and, at the foot of it, publish a full retraction. I do not demand an apology as in my view an apology procured by threat of legal action is worthless. However, if your sense of honour and sense of decency should prompt you to offer me one, I shall be glad to accept.

When *The People* published the letter only in part and without a retraction, Randolph instructed his solicitors, Oswald, Hickson, Collier & Co. – 'the Old Firm' as he was fondly to dub them during the succession of legal actions in which their libel ace, Peter Carter-Ruck, acted for him – to issue a writ for libel the next day against Mr Ainsworth and Odhams Press Ltd., the publishers of the newspaper.

While the generality of the human race allow themselves to be overawed by professional men, especially in the medical and legal fields where ordinary mortals are liable to feel out of their depth, Randolph regarded it as the height of folly to fall into the hands of professional advisers. I remember listening to a radio report with my father when it was announced that President Eisenhower had cancelled his engagements on 'doctor's orders'. My father exploded with fury: 'Presidents don't take orders from damn doctors! How monstrous! How ignominious! Grown-up people consult professional men for their advice, but it must be *they*, not the professionals, who take the decisions.' It is to this wise counsel that I owe the successful outcome of each of the half-dozen actions for libel which I have had to fight over the years.

Randolph always insisted on making crystal clear his views on the matter from the very start, whenever a new professional man entered his life. In the case of a lawyer, most especially if he were a grand leading counsel, Randolph would insist on 'testing the mettle' of the new recruit by declaiming from Swift's *Gulliver's Travels* the appropriately offensive passage about lawyers. Gulliver, having arrived in a faraway land where he is taken prisoner by the Lilliputians, a race of midgets, is brought before the ruler and asked to tell of his native land – England – and its customs. He was at pains to describe the function and character of lawyers to the ruler:

> I said there was a society of men among us, bred up from their youth in the art of proving by words multiplied for the purpose, that white is black, and black is white, according as they are paid. To this society all the rest of the people are slaves. For example, if my neighbor has a mind to my cow, he hires a lawyer to prove that he ought to have my cow from me. I must then hire another to defend my right, it being against all rules of law that any man should be allowed to speak for himself.

Randolph's purpose in doing this was not only because he found it a 'jolly tease'. Above all, it was to make clear to the newcomer that he knew about lawyers and their tricks and that no one was going to pull the wool over his eyes. He also wanted, crucially, to assess by his reaction whether the new recruit was suitable material with whom to go 'tiger-hunting'. If the lawyer flinched or took offence too easily, Randolph would reckon himself better off without him. He demanded of his lawyers not only a first-class legal brain, but that they should be 'on our side' – by which he meant men who would fight the good fight alongside him, neither wilting under the heat of the noonday sun nor flagging in the watches of the night. He would unequivocally accept the advice of his barrister or solicitor on points of law – but on these alone. Everything else was in his domain to decide.

Many were the calls that he made to his legal advisers in the watches of the night. Indeed, on one famous occasion he set up, on the spur of the moment, a legal conference for midnight, requiring all the briefs, statements of claim and legal depositions to be prepared and typed by dawn, in order to obtain a legal injunction, which was delivered before the offending party had even finished breakfast. The secret of Randolph's success as a litigant lay in his precise attention to detail, his own detailed cross-examination of his lawyers in advance of a case to make sure that they were fully apprised of every salient fact, and the fact that he was briefed on the intricacies of the law. Above all, he remained at all times in strategic command of the battle. He would constantly chide his solicitors and leading counsel with the query: 'Have we done our prep?' Occasionally he discovered they had not and disaster was thereby averted.

Randolph's friend, the distinguished barrister and politician Sir John Foster, described Randolph's performance in the witness box during his action for libel against Odhams Press: 'Under cross-examination for the Defence Randolph showed himself extremely quick-witted. One of the most difficult exercises when asked a question is for the witness to retain its exact formulation. The answer is apt to reflect the general impression of the question not its precise wording. Throughout he showed great accuracy in his treatment of words. As always, very articulate and precise, he revealed any ambiguity in the words used.'

Randolph's libel action against Odhams was a classic case and he went on to publish the lively courtroom exchanges in *What I Said About the Press*. Learned counsel, as a matter of course, adopt an overbearing, hectoring manner in an attempt to intimidate and bully the witness. It is a cardinal rule that leading counsel, examining the witness in the box, should retain the initiative and remain intellectually in command of the situation at all times; they like to have their questions answered with unadorned 'yeses' or 'nos'. However, the unfortunate Mr Gilbert Paull, Counsel for the Defendants, conducting his last case at the Bar before retiring to the judge's bench, found it uphill work with Randolph in the witness box:

COUNSEL: Tell me this: in your opinion who first tried to bring the other into contempt, you or Mr Ainsworth?

RSC: I think that Mr Ainsworth brought himself into contempt by the scandalous character of the paper which he edits and I drew attention to the scandal which he was creating for himself. After all, the paper is read by five million people.

COUNSEL: That is a very good answer from your point of view . . .

RSC: I do not think you objected to us putting any of these papers [copies of *The People*] in [as evidence]?

As the exchanges continued, it was clear that Mr Paull had more than met his match. The tension rose in the packed courtroom in the High Court in the Strand as Mr Paull attempted to assert himself:

COUNSEL: You must not ask me questions: let us have a look at a little something which you said in that speech of yours. Let us look at page five, shall we? Did you use this sort of language about Lord Rothermere: 'But it is, I think, a little disquieting when you find a man like Lord Rothermere, who inherited three or four million pounds from his father, romping around in the gutter with those whose cruel economic fetters still deny them an escape into a more honourable and salubrious profession.' Is that the sort of language you thought it useful to use?

RSC: Rather good stuff, I think. If you read it again I think the words are perfectly chosen to do the thing they are meant to do, which was to try and make Lord Rothermere ashamed of making money out of pornography. That was the object of the exercise and I am not ashamed of it at all.

COUNSEL: You are complaining about our language about you –

RSC: Not the language. I am complaining about the lies which are told about me. I do not tell lies about Mr Ainsworth, and Mr Ainsworth should not tell lies about me. That is why I am here now, for that precise thing. I am complaining about the untrue statements made about me . . .

COUNSEL: You think the remark: 'Romping around in the gutter' perfectly justified?

RSC: Perfectly justified. I am quite sure if he thought it untrue he would have brought an action for libel against me long ago, but he has not, because he knows it to be true, and he is ashamed of it. He will not thank you for giving publicity to it in this court, but I do not mind.

COUNSEL: That is awfully clever.

RSC: It happens to be truthful . . .

COUNSEL: When you criticise you have not the slightest hesitation in using language which is really very offensive, have you?

RSC: I often take a great deal of time in my choice of words, and I do not think it would be true to say I have not the slightest hesitation. Sometimes words come to me very hurriedly, and sometimes I search a long time to find the right word.

COUNSEL: So it was quite deliberate, was it, in saying about Mr Attlee that he was a tardy little marionette?

RSC: One does not write by accident. I am not a monkey on a typewriter from whom the words come out by accident. Of course I apply my mind to my work. Sometimes one is rather hurried and has less time than usual, and I had to write that late at night after the meeting. Personally, I am rather proud to be associated with the phrase; I think it is rather good.

COUNSEL: I am not complaining about your criticising, I am suggesting to you that the language shows a complete lack of –

RSC: You would rather I wrote what people like –

At this point the referee stepped into the ring to protect Mr Paull who was on the ropes, but Randolph boxed on regardless:

MR JUSTICE JONES: Let Counsel finish the question.

RSC: You said you were complaining about the language I used, and I said: Would you rather I wrote like they write in *The People*. Is that the sort of thing you prefer me to write?

COUNSEL: That is a very clever remark, but let us pass on . . .

Mr Paull, desperately endeavouring to bring his cross-examination to a climax, tried to show how Randolph himself had used the word 'hack' of others and therefore, he argued, it was unreasonable for him to complain if the word were applied to him:

COUNSEL: Did you think it right and proper to call Mr Eade, the editor of the *Sunday Dispatch*, an old hack?

RSC: I did indeed, and I suppose if he had thought it wrong he would have sued me for libel, but he did not.

COUNSEL: You mean everybody ought to have sued you?

RSC: He might have complained about it; written to me and said: 'This is unfair', and given me an opportunity to apologise; but he never made one point of denial of this allegation . . .

COUNSEL: You spend your life, do you not, saying most dangerous things about everybody?

RSC: Not everybody, only those whom I think are acting contrary to the public interest. Why do you say 'everybody'?

COUNSEL: You thought it right to call the editor of the *Sunday Dispatch* an old hack?

RSC: So he was. Have you read the *Sunday Dispatch*? Perhaps you do not. I do not blame you for not reading it, but it is part of my duty to read it.

Mr Paull, unsettled by a witness who refused to be intimidated by the wig, gown and overbearing manner of leading counsel, and increasingly desperate to deliver his intended *coup de grâce*, became flustered and demanded:

COUNSEL: Is it criminal to call you a hack?

RSC: I am not suggesting it is criminal – this is a *civil* action, Mr Paull!

Mr Paull's discomfiture was complete and, by now, Randolph had the jury rollicking on their bench. When they returned to the court, following their retirement, they awarded Randolph £5,000 damages against *The People* (equivalent to over £65,000 today), together with his legal costs.

John Foster delivered a perceptive judgment of Randolph before the law and in life: 'As a litigant Randolph was courageous, articulate, quick and, unlike his usual nature, completely self-controlled. With his intelligence he understood the principles on which cases were fought . . . when dealing with the law, [he] showed up in his best light because he respected its rules, and the limitations imposed on him by the legal system. If he had recognised the even more important limitations sought to be imposed by society and his fellow human beings he would have been as successful in his life as he was in his contact with the law.'

Later that year Randolph gave an object lesson on how a private citizen might protect himself from the invasion of his own and his family's privacy by the minions of an all-powerful press baron. The *Spectator* Notebook, in its issue of 9 December 1955, revealed to its readers what it described as 'The Great *Sunday Graphic* Mystery':

The week before last the *Graphic* announced that a serial on 'THOSE CHURCHILL GIRLS' would begin on the following Sunday. 'This fascinating story', so the *Graphic* informed us, 'has been compiled from sources close to Chartwell, from friends who have known them individually'. The series was to be, it was claimed, moving, revealing, exciting, touching. After this appetising build-up it must have been a sad disappointment to readers to find in the following Sunday's *Graphic* not a line about those Churchill girls, and not a word of explanation about their non-appearance. (Not even the acres of nonsense about Signorine Sophia Loren and Gina Lollobrigida were adequate compensation.) My own view is that the key to the mystery lies in a telegram sent by Mr Randolph Churchill to Viscount Kemsley at 9.30 p.m. on 27 November. It read:

YOUR SUNDAY GRAPHIC ANNOUNCES SERIES ARTICLES START-
ING NEXT SUNDAY QUOTE THOSE CHURCHILL GIRLS UNQUOTE
STOP WONDER WHETHER I COULD HAVE YOUR COOPERATION
FOR SERIES I AM PLANNING FOR DAILY MIRROR AND GLASGOW
DAILY RECORD ENTITLED QUOTE THOSE BERRY GIRLS UNQUOTE
FEATURING LADY KEMSLEY MARCHIONESS OF HUNTLY MRS
LIONEL BERRY MRS NEVILLE BERRY MRS CUBITT ETC. WARMEST
REGARDS TO YOU AND ALL THE BERRY GIRLS — RANDOLPH

No further word was ever heard of the announced serial on 'Those Churchill Girls'. If there is one thing newspaper proprietors refuse to tolerate, it is any unauthorised intrusion, into their own private lives or that of their families, of the nature that they presume to inflict upon the highest and the lowest in the land.

CHAPTER 25

Crisis over Suez

There were no national newspapers on 6 April 1955 to record the resignation the previous day of Sir Winston Churchill – they were all strike-bound. The *Manchester Guardian*, however, the only newspaper of consequence still publishing, carried the following report:

> ## BRITAIN CHANGING THE GUARD
> ### A Constitutional Delay
> #### by Randolph S. Churchill
>
> Westminster, Tuesday
>
> An hour before Sir Winston Churchill arrived at the Palace to tender his resignation to the Queen, there was a crowd of perhaps a thousand people, but as there were no newspapers to speculate rightly or wrongly about the hour of his arrival, they gradually melted away. When he arrived at 4.30 p.m. not more than three hundred or four hundred people stood at the gates . . .
>
> Everyone expected that Sir Anthony Eden would be sent for within an hour or two of Sir Winston's resignation. As the hours passed, it became apparent that though it is as certain as tomorrow's sunrise that the Queen's choice will fall on Sir Anthony, he will not, in fact, receive his summons to the Palace until tomorrow.
>
> The delay which has bewildered many people is constitutional and not political. It is not generally realised that under the traditions of the British Constitution the Sovereign is under no obligation to consult a retiring Prime Minister about his successor, and it would be unseemly for him to volunteer advice . . .

The months that followed his resignation were ones of sadness and frustration for Winston, deprived of the adrenalin of power which had coursed through his veins for so many years. He found himself stranded, like some beached whale, on the sands of old age, all too aware of the dangers confronting mankind at the height of the Cold War, yet powerless to influence events. Perhaps, too, he shared in some measure the view trumpeted so loudly by Randolph that his successor, Anthony Eden, was not up to the job of Prime Minister but, if so, he kept such doubts strictly to himself.

In consequence of the mischievous and shameful book written in 1966 by his private physician, Lord Moran, many of those who did not know Churchill have accepted the notion that, for long periods in his life, he suffered from a 'Black Dog' of melancholy; some ill-informed historians have even sought to elevate this to a clinical condition. The notion was effectively demolished by Sir Martin Gilbert in his recent book *In Search of Churchill*. There is no doubt that there were short periods of Winston's life when he was depressed, not on his own account but because of his inability to shape events when danger threatened. This was especially true during his 'wilderness years' in the 1930s when his warnings of the mortal danger posed by Hitler fell on deaf ears and, again, during his second premiership when neither Eden nor Eisenhower supported his efforts to seek a reconciliation with the incumbents of the Kremlin following the death of Stalin in 1953.

Undoubtedly, another such low point came when Churchill relinquished power in 1955. Randolph evidently sensed this when, one evening, he dined and stayed the night at Chartwell, as he did from time to time. Before retiring to bed he felt moved to write his father a letter of encouragement in which his devotion to the man he termed 'the author of my being' shines through:

> Power must pass and vanish. Glory, which is achieved through a just exercise of power – which itself is accumulated by genius, toil, courage and self-sacrifice – alone remains. Your glory is enshrined forever on the imperishable plinth of your achievement; and can never be destroyed or tarnished. It will flow with the centuries. Please try to be as happy as you have a right and (if it is not presumptuous for a son to say it) a duty to be. And, by being happy, make those who love you happy too. All on one sheet of paper!
>
> > With devoted love,
> > Randolph

Randolph refused to be reconciled to the new administration. Even before Sir Anthony had kissed the Queen's hands on his appointment as Prime Minister, Randolph had managed to fall out with his first cousin, Clarissa, who was Eden's wife. Randolph had long since made up his mind that Eden would never make a good Prime Minister and, with his talent for brashness, lost no time in communicating his view to the new mistress of 10 Downing Street. He did not even wait for the Edens to move in. With the indelicacy for which he was notorious, he chose the occasion of his father's farewell dinner party at Downing Street on 4 April, attended by the Queen and the Duke of Edinburgh, to charge up to Clarissa and make his declaration of war: 'You ought to know,' he told her bluntly, 'that I am against the new régime.' He further informed her that he had just written an article for the news weekly *Punch*, proclaiming this. Not surprisingly, this prompted a sharp riposte, hand-delivered the next morning, from the fiercely loyal Clarissa:

5 April 1955

As I believe you do not remember our conversation of last night, here is what I said.

I am sad that you should value our friendship below the pleasure you get from your cheap and futile campaign against Anthony in clubs and, no doubt, in print.

I cannot see what advantage it can possibly be to yourself, Winston or the Conservatives. That is has material advantage for you I can well believe, and I am hurt that you should sell our friendship in this way.

Randolph, apparently amazed that his provocative remark should have given offence, replied on the same day:

Your letter grieved me. I realised last night that I had upset you and I telephoned you this morning to see what I could do to put it right. Your secretary asked me to call back ... When I telephoned this evening the Foreign Office operator told me 'Lady Eden says she has written to you' ... Meanwhile an hour before I got your letter ... Jock Colville [Churchill's former Private Secretary] rang me up to say that you had telephoned him and wanted him to stop the publication of the *Punch* article. Although I had not heard from you, I immediately telephoned to *Punch* to find out if this was possible. It was too late, owing to the Easter holidays, and it had already been printed.

I am bound to say, however, that if I had received your letter earlier its tone would have deterred me from such action. If I may speak frankly, your letter is so silly and misguided that it might have been written by Pam Berry ...

It is true that I earn my living by writing for the papers but I have always made a particular point of writing what I want to write and not what the editor would like. If you don't understand this, I fear you understand nothing about me at all.

I have no desire to quarrel with you, but you seem to be insisting on having a quarrel with me ... I have written two other articles about current events, one of which you will be able to read in tomorrow's *Manchester Guardian*. I do not think there is anything in any of these three articles offensive or derogatory either to Anthony or yourself; but if you insist on embarking on your splendid new situation with a chip on your shoulder, you will doubtless find ample cause for complaint, not only in my writings, but in those of many other people. Such hypersensitivity will not be helpful to Anthony.

Clarissa, not surprisingly, remained unmollified:

I cannot find in your letter any reason given as to why you prefer attacking Anthony to our being friends.

Of course I never thought you wrote what your employers wanted – but the idea of lashings of money would have been an excuse for so wantonly destroying our cousinship. You say even this is not the reason . . .

But I think you do not remember that all this began because you came up to me at the party the other night, said 'You ought to know that I am against the new régime' and spoke of your forthcoming article. It was unfortunate that you brought your position to light so forcefully, otherwise we could have gone on amicably living apart.

I am genuinely amused and curious of all that the press write on A. but sustained attacks from *friends* I find impossible to take. You must understand that surely and appreciate my dilemma . . .

Jock (later Sir John) Colville, who was assisting Eden during the change-over period, did his best to defuse the cousinly feud in a letter to Randolph of 6 April:

I have been thinking about your articles on Anthony, quite apart from the *Punch* one. Your Father has written a letter to the Chairman of his constituency, which is being delivered today, and which strongly supports his successor. Moreover, when the election comes he intends to lend his influence to supporting Anthony and the Conservative Party. I am sure that articles by you attacking Anthony, if indeed that is what you intend, will distress him and also embarrass him . . .

I do not want to be officious, but I do think it is important to keep your Father out of this dispute and to save him from having to arbitrate between his son and his successor in matters of this kind.

Randolph took Colville's advice and sent Clarissa a copy of his proposed article which was nothing like as hostile as she had been led to believe.

The seeds of Randolph's vendetta against Eden – though he would have strenuously denied such a characterisation of his conduct – are perhaps to be found in a passage contained in an article published in the *Evening Standard* of 23 May, just three days before the general election. After describing Eden's spectacular early career, which saw him enter Parliament at the age of twenty-six and rise to be Foreign Secretary at thirty-eight, Randolph remarked:

Eden had already caught the public imagination with his good looks, his charming smile, his elegant clothes and his evident attachment to the cause of the League [of Nations] won him golden opinions from the public ... It was clear that a new star had been born in the political firmament and he soon far outshone in public favour the mediocrities from whose ranks he had risen.

However, dealing with the period immediately following Eden's dramatic resignation as Foreign Secretary in 1938, Randolph was sharply critical of his decision to stand apart from Churchill at a crucial juncture:

On leaving the Government Eden did not attach himself to the powerful and growing group of members whom Mr Winston Churchill had gathered round him while preaching the cause of collective security and rearmament.

On the advice of Lord Baldwin (as he had by then become) he joined a small group which was presided over by Captain Sidney Herbert and which included the veteran statesman Mr Leopold Amery. When a few weeks after he had left the Government Hitler marched into Austria, Eden conspicuously failed to add his views to that of Churchill in protesting against this unlawful act of violence. None the less, when Neville Chamberlain invited Winston Churchill to join the Government on the outbreak of war, the latter insisted that Eden should also be included ...

Eden's disaffection with Churchill is confirmed by a letter many years later from Martin Gilbert to Randolph, who was in Marrakech at the time:

6 February 1964

I lunched last week at Haseley Court, the home of Mrs Lancaster – formerly Mrs Ronald Tree. Among those present were Lady Gage (the daughter of Lady Desborough), the Marquesa de Casa Maury and Nancy Astor...

I sat next to Nancy Astor at lunch and persuaded her to talk about your father. She at once launched into a bitter attack upon him, describing him repeatedly as 'half alien and wholly reprehensible'. She insisted that one of his worst faults was that he fell at once under the influence of anyone who was polite to him. 'Indeed,' she said, 'if a nigger flattered him he would have supported *him*.' She then launched, somewhat irrelevantly, into an attack on F. E. Smith whom she described as 'unfit to hold even the lowest public office' ... 'He [Winston] once even flattered me' she said, 'but I saw through his flattery and told him that nothing he would ever say or do would alter my opinion that he was no good, absolutely no good'...

Nancy Lancaster told me the following story. In 1937 her husband, Ronald Tree, had invited a number of anti-Chamberlain politicians to spend the weekend at Ditchley. They were to be addressed by Eden on the need to form an anti-Tory group led, naturally, by Eden himself. Tree had met your father in London and had asked him to come along to the weekend gathering. Nancy Lancaster saw Eden shortly after your father had accepted the invitation and said to him: 'You will be pleased to know, Anthony, that Winston will be coming down to our weekend gathering.' Eden turned towards her with a wry grimace and said testily: 'I don't like that at all. Winston will only try to get on our bandwagon' ... Eden and his supporters were like violets scattered on the grass; your father was an oak which towered above them and sheltered them from the blizzard...

A few years later a profile of Randolph in the *Observer* commented perceptively on his bitter hostility to Eden which manifested itself long before the fiasco of Suez:

Churchill's personality seems fuelled by an apparently endless flow of truculence. He dare not dodge a fight or ignore a challenge just in case it might be remotely thought to seem pusillanimous. The only son of a father who has bubbled over with a natural, unthinking courage from his earliest days, and courted danger like a lover, Randolph Churchill has always known that many an unfriendly eye would be watching for any weakening of the standard, any dilution of the fighting blood. Compulsive pugnacity was the quickest escape route from Sir Winston's giant shadow.

This bottled aggression may explain his bitter vendetta against Sir Anthony Eden which has often embarrassed even some of his most sympathetic partisans. It could be analysed as an unconscious rivalry directed against pretenders to his father's throne.

But it must also be remembered that even in the Thirties Randolph regarded Eden as a vain man kept afloat by a certain anaemic charm. Before, during and after Eden's premiership, he has never spared Eden. His admiration for other Lieutenants of Sir Winston – a Macmillan or a Sandys or even a Soames – is often gushingly effusive.

Randolph's mock-paranoid view of Eden was noted by Leonard Lyons, the American columnist of the *New York Post*: 'On the day Sir Winston resigned as Prime Minister and was succeeded by Anthony Eden, his son Randolph went, as usual, to his London club – White's – in St James's Street. On leaving, he saw an unusual sight – a policeman tagging a ticket on the car parked outside White's. "The Eden terror has begun," said Randolph.'

Following his resignation, Churchill was offered a dukedom – a distinction unprecedented for any politician in modern times – but not before it had been established that the offer would be declined. The Queen wanted to pay her first and favourite Prime Minister the highest compliment she could; the Palace, on the other hand, took the view that 'poor Dukes were bad for business' and, no doubt, the prospect of a future 'Duke Randolph' was more than the Establishment could take. Jock Colville was therefore instructed by the Palace to make discreet inquiries as to Sir Winston's likely reaction to being offered the Dukedom of London.

Colville, having cast a fly over Winston jointly with Clemmie, felt able to report back with confidence that the former Prime Minister would regard the offer as the greatest honour ever paid him, but none the less would feel unable to accept it. Central among his reasons was that, at a time when there was no provision for renouncing a peerage, his acceptance would have presented an insuperable obstacle to either his son or grandson pursuing a career in the House of Commons.

Reassured, the Palace formally conveyed the offer to Sir Winston some weeks later when, to the horror of Clemmie and Jock Colville, Winston began to voice second thoughts. 'It is a remarkable honour,' he mused, 'and I certainly should not wish to give offence to my Sovereign.

Perhaps,' he added mischievously, 'I should accept after all!' To the relief of all concerned, it turned out that my grandfather, well aware of what had been going on behind his back, could not resist having some fun at Clemmie's and Jock's expense.

After a two-year sojourn in Buckinghamshire, Randolph, in the course of the summer, found a new home at East Bergholt in Suffolk. Though not as beautiful as Oving, it commanded an even finer view – over the Stour valley towards Dedham Church, a scene which features in many paintings by the celebrated artist, John Constable, himself a one-time resident of East Bergholt.

Randolph named the house Stour, after the river valley it dominates, and it was to remain his home until his death. Few of his White's Club friends ever imagined that such a confirmed townee as Randolph could survive in the quiet solitude of the countryside. Perhaps they had failed to detect his new mood or underestimated his ability to make up for being cut off from the hot gossip of White's bar by constant use of the telephone. He would think nothing of waking a Cabinet minister friend in the early hours of the morning, when his resistance might be expected to be at its lowest, with a view to either seeking information or imparting advice. In fact, contrary to all expectations, Randolph put down roots that were deep and strong in his beloved East Bergholt, amid the rolling and picturesque landscape of East Anglia. He rapidly became, as he thereafter joyously proclaimed, a confirmed 'country bumpkin'.

That autumn, Randolph and June took time off from organising their new home to visit Israel, where Randolph represented his father at the laying of the foundation stone of the Winston Churchill Auditorium at Technion, Israel's institute of technology in Haifa. Tension was already building in the Middle East with increasing cross-border raids into Israel by Palestinian *fedayeen* and, on occasion, by groups of Egyptian saboteurs. These in turn prompted retaliatory raids by Israel. More seriously, barely six years after the creation of the state of Israel and the 1948 War of Independence, a fierce Middle East arms race was under way.

From Israel Randolph reported that although Egypt had already acquired 200 Sherman tanks against Israel's 100, and 100 Meteor and Vampire jets against Israel's 50, the British Government was planning to sell a further 64 Centurion tanks to Egypt, despite repeatedly rejecting similar applications by Israel. The situation was rendered even more precarious, and the imbalance of military hardware accentuated, by a secret negotiation between Egypt and the Soviet Union, skilfully disguised as a Czech arms deal. The full implications of the deal had yet to be appreciated by Western political leaders who were to become increasingly alarmed as more and more MiG fighters and Stalin tanks were delivered to the Egyptians with each month that passed.

On returning from his Middle East visit, during the course of which he had lengthy talks with the Prime Minister, David Ben-Gurion, and other Israeli leaders, Randolph called upon the British Government to redress this dangerous imbalance of armaments. He went on to propose a six-point plan to safeguard peace in the Middle East, based on international guarantees by Britain, France and the United States to defend any Middle Eastern country that became the victim of unprovoked aggression. The failure of the Western allies to heed this advice and act in concert to maintain the peace, led to the scene being set for a Middle East crisis and a second Arab-Israeli war.

In the wake of the Conservative victory in the May general election, Clement Attlee stepped down as leader of the Labour Party, his place being taken by Hugh Gaitskell for whom Randolph expressed a fulsome admiration in his article for the *Evening Standard* of 17 December 1955:

> Let no one underrate the character and potentialities of the new Leader of the Socialist party, nor the grandeur of his political achievements. In this politically drab age of the bureaucrat and of the managerial revolution, when advancement is almost exclusively reserved for the good boys and time-servers who toil their way patiently up the rungs of the political ladder without ever having an idea or running a risk, Hugh Gaitskell stands out as a first-class politician of patriotism and ambition, who has fought his way to the top with speed, courage and tenacity. And who deserves to be there because of sheer political guts and merit . . .

Randolph's praise of the Labour leader was in sharp contrast to his view of the leader of his own party whose Government, after only six months in office, he described as being in a 'condition of moral and physical paralysis'.

Early in the New Year of 1956 Randolph travelled to Washington to report on Eden's talks with Eisenhower. He commented unfavourably on the lack of any pre-conference planning which might have provided a basis for realising some concrete achievement in the talks themselves; and was especially critical of the way in which the two leaders failed to come to grips with the growing Middle East crisis, fuelled by the decision of the Soviet Union to involve itself directly in the area.

Randolph complained at the way in which the talks concluded with a 'pompous declaration and uninformative communiqué', and added: 'when statesmen and politicians can't think of anything else to say, they always drag in God. Last night's declaration did it twice over, both in the preamble and peroration. It was obvious from the start of the conference, as I indicated last night, that as no planning had been done by either side, no joint plan could be produced'. On returning home, Randolph continued his warnings of a Middle East explosion unless the British and American administrations took some firm initiative in the area and, because of the conspicuous failure of the British Government to sponsor any such initiative, he redoubled his criticism of Eden's leadership to the point of calling for the Prime Minister's replacement in his *Evening Standard* column of 5 March:

> Three months ago I wrote in this column that British foreign policy in the Middle East lay in ruins. I was rebuked by many friends who said that this was an exaggerated and alarmist view. I doubt if these friends would rebuke me today. I also wrote in these pages of the Washington Conference and faithfully reported that no substantial results had come from the meeting between Sir Anthony Eden and President Eisenhower because no joint plan had emerged for coping with the deadly situation in the Middle East.
>
> Again I was told how unkind it was of me say such disagreeable things and that the Prime Minister was doing his best. I do not doubt it, and that is why I am sure there has got to be, and quickly, a change in the occupancy of 10 Downing Street ... If either Mr Macmillan or Mr Butler had the political guts of the late Mr Lloyd George or the late Mr Bonar Law they would push Sir Anthony Eden to one side and in concert kick him upstairs to the House of Lords and lay their own hands upon the supreme instrument of British Government, while time remains.

Not surprisingly Conservatives in the House of Commons were outraged by Randolph's attack on their party leader. Dame Irene Ward, that formidable but delightful battleaxe of the Tory Party, riposted in a letter to the *Evening Standard* under the heading 'I don't like Randolph':

> I read Mr Randolph Churchill's references to the Prime Minister with the greatest contempt. As an old member of the House of Commons I do not know a single Conservative member who would welcome Mr Randolph Churchill as a colleague either for his views or for his personality. This letter may be crude, but it's true.
>
>   Irene Ward, House of Commons

A few days later, in his *Evening Standard* column of 13 March, Randolph sought to rebut the charge that he was carrying on a vendetta against Eden:

> ... Nothing could be sillier. I have known [Eden] and liked him all my adult life, and his beautiful wife is my dearly loved cousin. But it is quite contrary to the tradition of British public life that those taking part in politics should allow themselves to be swayed by personal affection. Indeed, such a process would smack of nepotism.
>
> From the earliest days I never thought that he would make a good Prime Minister. When he reached this office nine months ago I publicly explained in these columns why I did not think so, but added that I might very likely be wrong, since people often grow into a bigger job. I don't think he has. I have said so and given my reasons. This is a free country and politicians and journalists, whose business it is to think about politics, have a duty to say bluntly what they think without regard to personal or party advantage. Only the timorous and unthinking could interpret such action in terms of a vendetta ...

The next day, in his political column for the *Spectator*, Henry Fairlie commented: 'Meanwhile Sir Anthony Eden's position does not improve. The only consolation he has had during the weekend has been a second attack on him by Mr Randolph Churchill in the *Evening Standard* – the kind of support which any Conservative in trouble looks for hopefully ...' However, shortly thereafter Ian Trethowan reported in the *News Chronicle*: 'Sir Anthony Eden has ridden out the storm and during the ten-day Easter recess he will celebrate his first birthday as Premier. Truth to tell, there was never much chance that he would fail. The idea of a mutiny was never more than a gleam in Mr Randolph Churchill's eye. Prime Ministers are almost unsinkable.'

Immediately in the wake of his attacks Randolph was surprised to discover that, miraculously, a new star had been born in the firmament of Fleet Street columnists. The newcomer (of whom none had previously heard) went by the name of 'Richard Strong' and was promptly accorded top billing in the *Evening Standard* for a series of articles purporting to defend the Prime Minister from the scabrous attacks of his fellow columnist, Randolph, under such titles as 'Eden is a Good Prime Minister' and 'Who Are the Enemies of Sir Anthony?' Randolph, writing the day after the appearance of the latter article, evidently felt confident that he had penetrated 'Richard Strong's' disguise:

> Lord Beaverbrook is back in London, which to my mind, is never quite

the same place without him. Wherever he is, he adds to the gaiety of nations. Lord Beaverbrook will be 77 in May, but his sense of fun, appetite for life, and unique powers are wholly unimpaired. Most of his political life has been devoted to attacking and destroying Governments. Now in a mellow old age he has dedicated himself to the task of defending a Government, that of Sir Anthony Eden. Indeed, the Beaverbrook papers today are the only national papers which give consistent support to the Tory Government...

Within a very few days of his return he had given new proof to Fleet Street and Westminster that he is still firmly in the saddle by discovering and establishing an outstanding new political journalist, a Mr Richard Strong. This brilliant young writer, whose talents had so far been over-looked by all the editors in Fleet Street, and whose name cannot be found in any work of reference, was singled out with lightning and unerring intuition by Lord Beaverbrook himself...

Mr Strong is a generous opponent. For while his main concern is to defend Sir Anthony and to attack his critics, he showered a generous measure of praise upon myself. For why? Mr Strong is obviously an objective writer. So objective that while praising the Prime Minister he yet finds room for criticism.

After saying that in view of my failure as a politician humility should subdue my criticism of Sir Anthony's performance in the House of Commons, he adds: 'No one has ever heard the whole of a speech by Sir Anthony. That is perfectly true. He drawls. His delivery is poor. He has to be read, and the clichés removed, to get the significance – if there is any.' As a matter of fact I have never criticised Sir Anthony's Parliamentary performances which, except for his fiasco in the recent Middle East debate, are generally of a high level...

It is difficult to judge which was the more damaging to the Prime Minister – Randolph's attacks or 'Richard Strong's defence. The magazine *Forward*, in its issue of 31 March, went on to aver: '. . . As Beaverbrook is one of Sir Anthony's lifelong enemies and bitterest critics, the PM does not much relish finding him as his only defender. The kiss of death from a malicious octogenarian is not a very exhilarating form of embrace. Nor is the kiss very tender . . .'

At Stour, Randolph had set about establishing one of the most comprehensive libraries of reference books and political biography to be found outside the London Library. Meanwhile June had thrown herself with enthusiasm into the task of decorating their new home. In the tradition of many Suffolk houses, they painted the outside pink, while decorating their drawing-room with an apricot-coloured flock on the walls and beige silk curtains. Between them they transformed the whole house, and a large nursery was created on the top floor for Arabella who, although only six, was already entrancing visitors with her blue eyes and blonde hair.

Randolph, between writing his biography of Lord Derby and frequent journalistic forays, threw himself with relish into the task of bringing some order to the seven-acre garden where the flower-beds were overgrown with weeds and the lawns had become a hayfield. Dead trees were felled, views were opened up, 'young gentlemen' researchers were set to mowing the lawns and I, in my holidays from school, was given the task of taming the woodland with a huge Allen motor scythe, almost as heavy as I. A blue 'river' of polyanthus was planted to bring colour to the woodland, a new rose garden created and a magnificent avenue of pleached limes established under the guidance of Xenia Field, an expert gardener and friend. Large chestnuts, oaks and cedars were strategically pruned, so as to frame the tower of the neighbouring church, the clock of which Randolph arranged to have restored. The kitchen garden was gradually reclaimed and provided a plentiful supply of fresh fruit, flowers and vegetables for the house, which was always filled with glorious blooms.

One day my father collected me from Eton and took me for lunch with his friend, Sir George Bellew, a high functionary in the Royal Household who rejoiced in the title of Garter Principal King-at-Arms, and who had a lovely home in Windsor Great Park. Spying four Corinthian columns awaiting disposal, my father bought them for £100 and had them set up on the terrace at Stour, to create a pergola, covered with clematis, wistaria and honeysuckle. Here, for eight months of the year, whenever the weather was fine, Randolph would entertain his guests to raucous al fresco luncheons as the scudding clouds and sunshine endlessly chased each other across the panorama of broad meadows of the Vale of Dedham where the River Stour meanders lazily through cattle pastures.

Tragically, even such an idyllic setting as this was not enough to persuade June to stay with Randolph. She had a temper too and, between them, their yells and tantrums rocked the house, embarrassing guests and staff alike. Randolph's friend from Oxford days, Christopher Sykes, witnessed one such row at a dinner given at the Queen's Restaurant in Sloane Square by John Sutro, as my cousin, Anita Leslie, recorded in her book *Cousin Randolph*:

Randolph was late because he had arranged to meet June at their home and he had difficulty in getting someone in the house to hear him as he hadn't the key. All of which had put him in a bad humour. The subsequent quarrel did not cease quickly owing to the fact that Randolph had been drinking. As things got worse Randolph turned to abuse his wife, describing her among other things as 'a paltry little middle-class bitch always anxious to please and failing owing to your dismal manners', and other endearments of the same kind. All this was shouted in a loud voice in the restaurant and as Randolph was recognised as the son of our great Prime Minister, it caused a great deal of interest among the customers and Randolph soon had a large appreciative audience.

During this painful scene I had said nothing, nor had Sutro, but as it went on increasing in violence and arousing yet more interest amongst the people in the restaurant, I felt I must intervene, or I would feel a worm for the rest of my life – so when Randolph next paused for breath in his denunciation I said in a conciliatory way, 'Randolph, you really should not talk to your wife in that way ...' For a moment Randolph was silent. Then he roared out, 'What the hell do you mean by butting in to a private conversation?' I could not think of a witty rejoinder so said, 'I am sorry but I thought you were having a public conversation.' John Sutro saved the situation by starting to laugh – with some embarrassment I admit.

Anita Leslie continued:

Randolph had been oblivious to the fact that he was in a restaurant; shouting in front of a riveted audience, he had really imagined he was giving June a dressing-down out of earshot. She, meanwhile, sat blinking back her tears, unable to swallow the dinner ordered. In the following year she left him. Randolph never understood how appalling his behaviour had been, and he had lost two old friends that night, as well as his pretty if unsuitable wife. But who was suitable for Randolph? Arabella, a lovely little girl, disappeared with her mother but later came down to Stour for weekends. No matter how remorseful he might be, Randolph had to face the fact that he had lost June. From now on he had only himself and his garden and his fertile mind ...

That summer, after reporting the Democratic and Republican Party conventions in Chicago and San Francisco, Randolph went on to New York to take part in the *$64,000 Question*, then America's most popular television show with an audience estimated at 13 million. At the time, as I vividly recall, Randolph's finances were in a particularly sorry state. The small traders in the local village of East Bergholt were refusing him credit and it was rare that we could afford to put more than one or two gallons of petrol at a time into my father's ageing and battered station wagon. However, with his sights firmly set on winning that $64,000 – equivalent to £22,500 in 1956 or £300,000 in today's money – Randolph felt that things were looking up.

For ten days without ceasing, he mugged up his Kipling – the subject chosen by the programme organisers. This was an exercise that involved everyone in the household, including secretaries, 'young gentlemen' researchers and myself. Passages were read aloud, vast tracts were memorised and this process, including arduous testing, would go on until three or four each morning. At the end of ten days, Randolph felt sufficiently confident to indulge in the purchase of a splendid and most expensive croquet set for my amusement in the school holidays. Other extravagances were embarked upon and it seemed to me that the whole $64,000 would be spent before he had even set foot in the United States.

This mood of exuberant over-confidence was temporarily shattered by a transatlantic telephone call from the programme's producer who announced: 'Say Mr Churchill, we kinda think that Kipling is too narrow a subject, how would it be if we made it the entire English language?' Though only three days remained before he was due to leave for the United States, Randolph, unwilling as ever to admit that anything was beyond him, accepted the proposal with resignation. More than two weeks' work, involving a staff of at least half a dozen, down the drain! While it is possible to 'mug up' Kipling, where does one start in the case of the entire English language?

After two weeks of the hurly-burly of the Chicago Stockyards and the San Francisco Cow Palace, the outlandish venues of American political conventions, Randolph presented himself on the programme. He skipped with ease over the $64-hurdle which required him to name 'A certain English nobleman who gave his name to the English language by being so absorbed in gambling that he would not leave the table in order to eat'. 'The Earl of Sandwich!' exclaimed Randolph triumphantly. However, he came a cropper at the $128 fence when he was unable to name 'The land agent of the Earl of Earne in County Mayo who was so tyrannical that in 1880 the people banded together and refused to have any dealings with him.'

To console himself after this fiasco Randolph went out and bought a small black pugdog which he named 'Captain Boycott'. In due course the 'Good Captain' acquired a wife who, after due consultation with the

Dictionary of National Biography, was named 'Annie' who, in turn, bore a son named 'Cunningham'. The fame of 'Captain Boycott' spread far and wide and soon his progeny was in demand among Randolph's friends on both sides of the Atlantic. Indeed, I remember crossing the Atlantic with my father and two baby puglets with silky black coats, one for Mrs Janet Auchincloss, mother-in-law of President Kennedy, and the other for Mrs Babe Paley, wife of his friend Bill Paley, President of the Columbia Broadcasting System. Disaster struck, however. Within a few weeks the proud new owners of the two baby 'pugs' remarked that their coats were turning brown, their legs getting rather long and their tails becoming bushy. Suspicion fell on 'Orlando', a gallant and handsome King Charles cavalier spaniel, the gift of the artist Paul Maze.

As he saw the mirage of $64,000, on which he had set his hopes, vanish into thin air, Randolph commented phlegmatically, as recorded in the *Observer*'s Sayings of the Week column: 'At forty-five one cannot become a "Quiz kid".' At this point the Fates repented of their disfavour and, only three weeks later, allowed him to triumph in his libel action against Odhams Press which had dragged on for more than a year. He won not only honour but £5,000 (£65,000 in today's money), tax-free to boot!

Meanwhile, events in the Middle East were heading rapidly towards crisis. On 26 July 1956, Colonel Nasser announced that Egypt intended to nationalise the Suez Canal. This followed hard on the heels of an American decision to withdraw its offer to finance the building of the High Dam at Aswan, in retaliation for Egypt's secret arms deal with the Russians the previous year. The Egyptian action was a calculated challenge to Britain's position in the Middle East and placed in jeopardy British and French oil supplies from the Persian Gulf, all of which passed through the Suez Canal at the time.

Sir Anthony Eden acted with speed and resolution in the face of Nasser's challenge and entered into immediate consultations with the French and American governments. He called an international conference in London of all Suez Canal users for August, while the governments of Britain and France took urgent steps to mount a military operation aimed at toppling the Egyptian dictator. Secret talks were held with Israel which, in the wake of numerous cross-border attacks by raiding parties of Egyptian commandos and Palestinian *fedayeen* as well as the threat posed by Iraq moving forces into Jordan, was persuaded to take decisive military action. Accordingly Israel, on 29 October, made an armoured thrust west across the Egyptian-held Sinai Desert towards the Suez Canal, dropping a battalion of paratroops to seize the Mitla Pass, thereby blocking the retreat of the Egyptian army which found itself ambushed from the rear.

Shortly afterwards Britain and France, acting in close and covert collusion with the Government of Israel, attacked Egypt under the bogus pretext of protecting her from Israeli aggression and safeguarding the Suez Canal. After the RAF had destroyed much of the Egyptian air force on the ground, an Anglo-French airborne assault force seized Port Said and Port Fuad on the Suez Canal, supported by a seaborne invasion force which had taken ten days to arrive from Algiers, Marseilles and Malta, the nearest deep-water ports from which the invasion could be mounted. Randolph recorded in his 1959 biography of Anthony Eden:

> The author arrived in Tel Aviv on the evening of Monday, 5 November, hot-wing from New York and London to find an uproarious party proceeding in the Dan Hotel at which some twenty French pilots were being fêted by all the pretty girls in Tel Aviv for the aid which they had given Israel with their *Mystère* fighters. Everyone seemed highly collusive and why not? It looked like a splendid victory.

But that was before the UN Security Council and, above all, the United States Government had got to work, exerting pressure on Britain and France to accept a cease-fire. Unbelievably, the British Cabinet, which had foolishly failed to square the Americans, capitulated to the pressure. The operation was halted within thirty-six hours of the landing of the main Anglo-French invasion force, though they were within forty-eight hours of achieving all their military objectives, including the seizure of the entire length of the canal.

The essence of failure rested in the weakness of Britain's political leadership, compounded by the serious illness now afflicting the Prime Minister and the ten-day delay between the launching of the operation and the landing of the first seaborne troops in the Canal Zone. Randolph commented:

> This difficulty could only have been surmounted if the planners had been content with a plan of a lighter, speedier, more daring and more flexible character. As one French critic of the ultimate plan remarked to the author: '*Il faut arriver vite à la guerre.*' The failure to adopt such a strategy was more the fault of the generals than of the politicians. Unfortunately, Sir Anthony Eden was misled by Sir Walter Monckton and Mr Antony Head into the

classical error of falling into the hands of his generals, a fate almost as dreadful as being in the hands of lawyers, almost as ghastly as being 'under doctor's orders'. But the politicians must bear part of the blame since, instead of goading the generals into swift and ruthless action, they kept impeding and rattling them with every artful contrivance of indecision. Here the nervous hand of Sir Anthony Eden could often be detected...

No assessment of the rights and wrongs of the Suez story can even be tentatively formed without bearing in mind the fact that Sir Anthony was a sick man throughout the crisis ... Courage, both physical and moral, is something which Sir Anthony has never lacked in peace or war, and even those who feel most strongly that he must bear the main responsibility for the mismanagement of British policy at this time cannot withhold an honourable salute to a man who, in the grip of recurrent pain, worked himself unsparingly to the verge of the grave doing his duty as he saw it with selfless devotion. Sir Anthony's ill health must nevertheless be reckoned as a national, no less than a personal, tragedy.

Prior to the publication of his account of the Suez operation, Randolph sent copies of the typescript to several of the political figures involved, among them Antony Head of whom he was severely critical in his role as Minister of Defence. Head replied with a defence both of the military plan and of his political chief:

20 November 1958

I have returned your draft under separate cover. As far as the bit I am concerned with, it is full of distortion and inaccuracies. The underlying factor in the Suez operation was from the moment it was decided to leave Egypt, both the Cabinet and the Chiefs of Staff were aware, and accepted the fact, that the most eastern deep water port in the Mediterranean was Malta. Owing to vast expense and impracticability, it was never at any time considered feasible to create a deep water port in Cyprus.

This dominated the whole operation. It meant that from the time the button was pushed until a landing could be made was inescapably the steaming time of LSTs [Landing-Ships (Tank)] based on Malta. Every feasible effort was tried to reduce this highly unacceptable interval, but there was no way in which it could be dramatically reduced except if the whole operation was done by an airborne landing, or one accepted a long interval between an airborne landing and the arrival of the seaborne forces. This neither the Chiefs of Staff [misreading the lessons of Arnhem] nor the French were at the time prepared to accept...

Although you state that there should have been more LSTs and transport aircraft, neither the timing nor the successful execution of the operation was affected by this. The airborne drop was completely successful and the assault landing took place exactly as planned, and its success was extremely rapid.

Suez failed because it did not have the three extra days required to reap the advantages of the operation as a whole. When it was stopped prematurely and followed by withdrawal, the wave of frustration which swept this country was to a large extent directed in criticism of the operation. I have yet to hear of any alternative operation which would have been a practicable and reasonably safe method of occupying the Canal Zone.

So far as your remarks about Anthony Eden are concerned, a large part of them are in my opinion extremely unfair and some of them inexcusable. I cannot see that they will do anything but harm your journalistic reputation.

Randolph answered by telegram the following day:

MOST GRATEFUL FOR YOUR LETTER STOP EYE WELCOME CRITI-CISM BUT WOULD BE STILL MORE GRATEFUL IF YOU WOULD INDICATE QUOTE DISTORTIONS AND INACCURACIES UNQUOTE OF WHICH YOU COMPLAIN STOP REFERENCE YOUR LAST SEN-TENCE WHAT EYE AM TRYING TO DO IS TO PRODUCE AYE PIECE OF CONTEMPORARY HISTORY COLON CONSEQUENTLY MY QUOTE JOURNALISTIC REPUTATION UNQUOTE IS NOT INVOLVED — RANDOLPH

There is no record of any reply among Randolph's papers.

A key question at the time was whether or not the governments of Britain, France and Israel had acted in collusion in their attacks on Egypt. The official British line was that the objective of the Anglo-French force was to separate the belligerents, Israel and Egypt, and to safeguard the Canal. It was on this basis, as the Prime Minister explained in the House of Commons on 30 October, that Egypt was asked to agree 'that Anglo-French forces should move temporarily, I repeat temporarily – into key positions at Port Said, Ismailia and Suez'. It was even suggested that the real purpose behind the intervention was to stop the wicked Israelis beating up the unfortunate Egyptians. However, Randolph did not 'buy' this Foreign Office line and realised immediately that there had, indeed, been collusion. When this charge was repeatedly and vigorously denied,

Randolph retorted: 'Well, if there was no collusion – *why* was there no collusion? No wonder it was all a shambles!' It is clear from Randolph's 'Child's Guide to the Tory Party', published in *Punch* on 19 December, that he did not take at face value the Government and Foreign Office denials:

Q. Uncle Randolph, what is all this talk about collusion?

A. You mean the horse belonging to your grandfather [Colonist].

Q. No, of course not. I meant this thing the English, the French and the Israelis are supposed to have done together.

A. Well, when I was in Jerusalem the other day I asked that nice Jewish Uncle, David Ben-Gurion, whether there had been any collusion. He smiled and said 'I didn't think Uncle Anthony had it in him.'

Q. Well, Uncle Randolph, please tell us all about the war and what they fought each other for.

A. Well, dear, a great many different reasons have been given. The one I like best is that given by Uncle Anthony before he went to Jamaica.

Q. What was that?

A. He said that we had invaded Egypt to stop the war, and that was why he had destroyed the Egyptian Air Force.

Q. But why didn't he destroy the Israeli Air Force too? and why didn't he land in Haifa as well as in Port Said?

A. Well, that would have meant destroying a lot of the French Air Force too, because they were helping the Israelis, with their *Mystère* fighters and their fighter pilots in destroying the Egyptian tanks and aeroplanes...

Q. I see it says that the French transport aeroplanes brought jeeps and petrol to the advancing Israelis to help them get to the Suez Canal more quickly.

A. Yes.

Q. Where did the French planes come from?

A. From Cyprus.

Q. Doesn't Cyprus belong to us?

A. I hope so.

Q. Well, if Uncle Anthony wanted to stop the war couldn't he have told the French that they mustn't use Cyprus to send the petrol and the jeeps to the Israeli army?

A. Well don't be tiresome or you will upset Uncle Anthony...

Even two years later, at the time of the serialisation of Randolph's biography, *The Rise and Fall of Sir Anthony Eden*, in the *Daily Express*, the 'collusion' charge remained a political hot potato and his repetition of it provoked renewed and vigorous Foreign Office denials, prompting an Osbert Lancaster cartoon in which one member of White's Club turns to another at the bar and inquires: 'Do tell me, just when did the F.O. take over the publicity for Randolph's new book?' Though these official denials gave the book a massive publicity boost, Randolph was angered that, so long after the event, the same lies should be trotted out by the Macmillan Government. It was these hurt feelings that prompted him to send the following telegram dated 8 December 1958 to Harold Macmillan, who had succeeded Eden as Prime Minister in January 1957:

PLEASE SEE ZECHARIAH CHAPTER THIRTEEN VERSE SIX = RANDOLPH

The reference in the King James Bible reads: 'And one shall say unto him, What are these wounds in thine hands? Then he shall answer, Those with which I was wounded in the house of my friends.'

The same telegram could well have been sent in the opposite direction, for the serialisation of Randolph's book provoked a major parliamentary row which broke the next day over the head of the Prime Minister. It all started innocently enough with the Labour MP for South Ayrshire, Emrys Hughes, asking the premier if he would appoint an official historian of the Suez campaign. However, it was not long before violent accusations of 'guilty men' were being thrown at the Government front bench by Labour MPs scenting blood in the run-up to a general election. Demands were made for a parliamentary inquiry into the charges of collusion and a cover-up. A heated four-hour exchange then ensued in which Opposition big guns such as Aneurin Bevan, Emanuel Shinwell and even the Labour Party leader, Hugh Gaitskell, all joined. Richard Crossman in his political column in the *Daily Mirror* of 12 December recorded:

The scuffle in the Commons last Tuesday about Mr Randolph Churchill's articles on Suez made one thing clear. Suez is still a live political issue which could even tip the balance in the forthcoming General Election.

What Mr Macmillan has to fear was clearly revealed in the last article Mr Randolph Churchill published in the *Daily Express* this week.

'In common with many other people,' he wrote, 'I feel compelled to revise the judgement and opinions which I held in October 1956 ... If we had known with what INEPTITUDE the campaign had been planned, if we had detected the INHERENT FRAUDULENCE of the Anglo-French ultimatum, if we had known of the Government's MISCALCULATIONS about the American reactions ... many of those who, like me, applauded the action on the day might have adopted a very different line. I, for one, am prepared to stand in a white sheet and admit that I was wrong.'

Mr Randolph Churchill – even without full access to the facts – has been driven to accuse his own party leaders, Sir Anthony Eden and Mr Macmillan, of 'ineptitude' and 'inherent fraudulence'. No wonder the Premier is afraid that if the whole of the facts about Suez were revealed, tens of thousands of Tory voters might agree with Mr Randolph Churchill!

The following week, with the Suez row still in full swing, Antony Head intervened in an adjournment debate initiated by the Labour MP, George Wigg. According to the *Times* Parliamentary Correspondent on 17 December:

Mr Head who was Minister of Defence at the time ... reduced the crowded House to fascinated silence with his version of events.

He called Suez an operation in a strait-jacket dictated by geography and he was at pains to explain that those military authorities responsible were not the 'half-witted, infatuated fools' they had been made out to be. He said the expedition was extremely well planned and operated within its limits but the tragedy was that the operation stopped.

Then Mr Head launched into a vigorous attack on Mr Randolph Churchill. He said he did not know what purpose was behind Mr Churchill's writing his 'very peculiar book'. He bore perhaps the most illustrious name in England today and that fact gave a certain authority to his book.

This life of Sir Anthony Eden and particularly the parts of it published were a smear not on Sir Anthony Eden but on Mr Randolph Churchill. History would look on this episode of Mr Churchill's journalism as a disgrace to the proud name he bore ...

Among those who sprang to Eden's defence was the Conservative MP for Kidderminster, Gerald Nabarro, a vain and pompous man with large handlebar moustachios who affected the manner of a jumped-up sergeant-major. In the florid style of speech for which he was noted, Nabarro declared at a public meeting at Halesowen on 6 December 1958: 'This was a pernicious, cowardly, and uncalled-for action in the present circumstances. This should have been a national crusade. Mr Churchill made his attack in the newspapers, knowing full well that Sir Anthony could not reply. That is the action of a coward. I grieve that these things should have been done when Sir Anthony, like other

Ministers of that time, cannot reveal Cabinet secrets in his lifetime, and has remained silent.'

On seeing press reports of this speech Randolph despatched the following telegram to Nabarro:

YOU ARE REPORTED BY THE PRESS ASSOCIATION TO HAVE SAID AT A PUBLIC MEETING IN YOUR CONSTITUENCY THAT MY WRITINGS WERE QUOTE COWARDLY UNQUOTE STOP YOU ARE FURTHER REPORTED TO HAVE CALLED ME A QUOTE COWARD UNQUOTE STOP I CALL UPON YOU TO RETRACT THESE WORDS IMMEDIATELY OR FACE THE CONSEQUENCES OF AN ACTION FOR SLANDER = RANDOLPH CHURCHILL

The next day, no reply having been received, Randolph issued a writ for slander. When, some three months later, Randolph received Nabarro's statement of defence he was amazed to discover that Nabarro was seeking to deny that he had ever uttered the words complained of. Whereupon, on 2 March 1959, Randolph wrote to Nabarro:

It is now more than ten weeks since the Press Association attributed these words to you and since I brought them to your attention. If what you are asserting is true; why did you not say so at the time? It seems to me astonishing that a public man should allow the Press Association to put such reckless, untrue and damaging words into his mouth without issuing any *démenti* . . .

Nabarro ostentatiously refused to reply himself, instructing his solicitors to inform Randolph: 'Our client asks us to say that he does not buy expensive dogs and bark himself.' This was later to provide Randolph with the opportunity of having some fun at the expense of Learned Counsel for the Defence when, eventually, the case came to court. On the second day of the hearing Nabarro's counsel, Geoffrey Lawrence QC, read to the court an article written by Randolph in March 1956:

MR LAWRENCE: Sir Anthony was Prime Minister at the time you wrote that article?
RSC: I think that is stated in the article. I was wondering when the question would come.
MR LAWRENCE: Don't be impatient!
RSC: I am not. I am being marvelliously patient – more patient than I was yesterday.

MR LAWRENCE:	Is it clear from that article that you are saying that Sir Anthony Eden was unfit to be Prime Minister of Great Britain?
RSC:	Yes, and I am grateful to you for having revived my recollections of this article. I am astounded at the knowledge it shows and also the prescience.
MR LAWRENCE:	So this article was a very severe attack on Sir Anthony?
RSC:	No, it was a warning to the nation of the troubles we were likely to get into if the nation went on being governed in that way.
MR LAWRENCE:	Don't fence with words please.
RSC:	Who is fencing? Don't accuse me of fencing with words. I don't go back on a word of it.
MR LAWRENCE:	And you described Sir Anthony Eden as a man of exceptional vanity?
RSC:	I was attacking his public life – which is the only thing I ever do attack.
MR LAWRENCE:	You were saying not only that this man had laid our policy in the Middle East in ruins, but that he is so exceptionally vain that he has tried to evade looking facts in the face?
RSC:	I think I expressed it better than that. Why recast my thoughts in less precise words?
MR LAWRENCE:	Do you agree with my interpretation of what you wrote?
RSC:	No. I agree with what I wrote – every word of it. (*Addressing Mr Justice Gorman*): My Lord, Counsel is trying to put words into my mouth which are not true. I was setting out to write the truth as God has given me to see it, which is not what happens to every lawyer.
MR LAWRENCE:	Was that meant to be offensive to me, Mr Churchill?
RSC:	No. I was thinking of the profession in general. Lawyers are after all 'expensive dogs' as your client describes it, paid to argue a case in which they have no personal stake. That is a perfectly fair comment on a matter of public interest...
MR LAWRENCE:	Would you not accept the proposition that your articles in the *Daily Express* constituted an attack

	on Sir Anthony Eden?
RSC:	I am not paid to accept propositions put by expensive dogs – your client's phrase not mine.
MR LAWRENCE:	You adopted it to be personally offensive to me?
RSC:	No; to be personally offensive to Mr Nabarro who has called me a coward and that is why we are here. I have not said anything about him yet...

On the fifth day of the case, after a two-and-a-half-hour recess, the jurors, three of them women, returned to the courtroom where Mr Justice Gorman required them to answer two questions:

Q: 'Were the words complained of fair comment on a matter of public interest?' – 'No.'

Q: 'If the answer to question one is 'No', what damages should be awarded to Mr Churchill?' – '£1,500.'

In addition to the damages, Randolph had costs awarded in his favour. It was estimated that the case had cost Nabarro in the region of £10,000 (equivalent to £120,000 today), although no one would have guessed as much from his beaming smile over his mutton-chop moustachios as he emerged from the court, evidently feeling that the self-advertisement which he relished was worth every penny.

On his return to his Suffolk home that evening, Randolph found the following amid a shower of congratulatory telegrams on his doormat:

MY BEST CONGRATULATIONS I AM SO GLAD DEAR RANDOLPH =
PAPA

Beneath his grin, however, it is evident that Nabarro was far from amused at the outcome of the case. Ten days later, in the course of a debate on the economy in the House of Commons, he felt impelled to interrupt the Labour MP Fred Lee who was accusing the Government of political cowardice. According to the report in the *Guardian* of 10 November 1960, Nabarro interjected: 'Oh be careful (*laughter*). You must realise that free speech means that you may call a spade a spade but not a coward a coward.'

Randolph, returning from the United States a few days later, saw the report and wrote a letter to the editor of the *Times* which appeared on 15 November:

Sir,

... Unless Mr Nabarro's words have no meaning at all, they were a plain reference to my recent action for slander against him, in which the jury awarded £1,500 for the very word about me which he has chosen to repeat in the House of Commons.

Surely this is an exceptionally gross abuse of the privilege of Parliament? Mr Nabarro knows that statements in Parliament are covered by absolute privilege and are not open to challenge in any Court of Law. For this very fact there is a Parliamentary tradition that decisions of other Courts should not be challenged in Parliament, particularly by interested parties.

I am, Sir, your obedient servant,

RANDOLPH S. CHURCHILL
Stour, East Bergholt, 13 Nov.

The same day the Labour MP for Dundee East, George Thomson, requested the Speaker, Sir Harry Hylton-Foster, to rule on the matter. In his ruling on 16 November, the Speaker implied that the Kidderminster MP's conduct represented an abuse of the privilege of the House of Commons, although he was not prepared to grant time for a debate. Thereupon Nabarro rose to make a personal statement, withdrawing his remarks:

The word 'cowardice' was strangely reminiscent to me, having regard to my activities during the last few weeks. As I have unintentionally – I emphasise 'unintentionally' – been guilty of an abuse of Parliamentary Privilege, as you have just ruled, Mr Speaker – (*Hon. Members*: 'No') – I should like to seek your permission and the permission of the whole House unreservedly to withdraw the words referred to, though I recognise that they cannot now be expunged from the Official Report.

CHAPTER 26

Macmillan It Is!

The failure of the Suez operation created a crisis in British politics which Eden, because of his central responsibility and his failing health, was unable to survive. According to Randolph's account in *The Rise and Fall of Sir Anthony Eden*:

> The British Government had capitulated over Suez on 6 November. It was announced from 10 Downing Street on 22 November that the Prime Minister, on the advice of his doctors, would spend a three-week holiday in Jamaica. He returned from Jamaica on 14 December. On 8 January, he went down to Sandringham and on the following day, tendered his resignation to the Queen, who had travelled up to London in his wake so as to be at Buckingham Palace to receive it.

Who was to succeed Eden as leader of the Conservative Party and as Prime Minister? That was the question on every lip. On 10 January, the day when the Queen was to announce whom she would call upon to form the next administration, political pundits throughout the land and every national daily newspaper were forecasting that her choice would fall upon 'Rab' Butler. In lonely isolation Randolph, in an article for the London *Evening Standard*, took a contrary view, going nap on Macmillan, though the *Evening Standard* headline betrayed all the anxiety of a newspaper with a world scoop on its hands:

IS IT MACMILLAN?
Butler started favourite – then came a change
From Randolph Churchill: East Bergholt (Suffolk), Thursday

> By tea-time today Mr Harold Macmillan, Chancellor of the Exchequer in Sir Anthony Eden's former Government, will have been invited by the Queen to form a new administration. That seems the only reasonable prognosis as seen in the early hours of this morning from East Anglia ... We country bumpkins down here supplement our radio and TV communications with a liberal use of the telephone. Until seven or eight

o'clock last night there were many good judges of political form in London who seemed to think that Elijah's mantle might fall upon the Lord Privy Seal, Mr Butler.

But opinion hardened itself and judgment became more acute in the bars, the clubs, the salons, the flats and private houses where Tory politicians tend to congregate during a crisis – partly to form a cohesive front and partly to keep away from the press.

Consequently, Butler moved back in the betting and Macmillan became a strong favourite ... It became known that the Queen's advisers were aware that not only the Tory Suez group, but also a considerable body of senior and central opinion in the party were opposed to Butler ... There seemed by midnight to be a unanimous acceptance, save for a few fringe and frenetic females, of the idea that Macmillan would have the job ...

Unanimity in public at all costs has long been the recipe, if not the slogan, of the Tory Party. It will prevail today. Butler could not get it unanimously, but Macmillan can ...

By brow-beating, hectoring and cajoling his many friends, former friends and acquaintances with a ferocious use of his telephone until three or four in the morning, Randolph had scooped the field. The proprietor of the *Evening Standard*, Lord Beaverbrook, holidaying in the Bahamas cabled:

CONGRATULATIONS ON TODAYS ARTICLE IT IS BRILLIANT JOURNALISM = MAX

The plaudits flowed in on all sides. Even Socialist Tom Driberg averred: 'So Randolph Churchill's much-talked-of scoop in the *Evening Standard* – he gave Macmillan as the new Prime Minister several hours before the official announcement – really was the result of intelligent guesswork and of frequenting the right clubs, and not, as some supposed, of a 'leak' from his father ...'

Randolph himself commented: 'It's not often in life that something you very much desire coincides with what you think is likely. That is one of the reasons people lose so much money betting. I have always been a Macmillan fan. I saw a lot of him in the Mediterranean during the War and early came to appreciate and respect his qualities of judgment and statesmanship. He is certainly the best educated man among the Tory politicians.' When asked on a television programme whether it was not the case that Macmillan had 'the common touch' Randolph exploded: 'Common touch? To hell with the common touch! He's got the *un*common touch. We want men of distinction and education.'

Some six weeks later Randolph discussed the selection of Macmillan with his father and later recorded their conversation in his diary:

27 February 1957

After lunch at Hyde Park Gate on Thursday I discussed with WSC Macmillan's appointment as Prime Minister. He said that he had not consulted Lord Salisbury as to the advice he was going to tender nor had he received any communication, even indirectly, as to the nature of Salisbury's advice. He had had a talk three or four days before on the telephone with Butler and had indicated to him that his views in these matters were strongly influenced by his belief in seniority and that his being so much younger than Macmillan would be a strong factor in his judgment.

I told WSC how I put this argument to Rab two years ago when he came on board Onassis' yacht in Monte Carlo at the time of the Kelly–Rainier wedding and I was condoling with him about his disappointment.

Though WSC had no knowledge of the advice or even of the temper he must have known when he went to the Palace that the overwhelming majority of the Party were for Macmillan. Sandys and Soames must certainly have let him know this. (I MUST CHECK THIS AS I OMITTED TO ASK HIM ABOUT IT AT THE TIME.)

WSC also told me that he came up from Chartwell to London assuming that Michael Adeane [the Queen's Private Secretary] would know and he took it as a mark of favour when Adeane led him straight in to the Queen.

Randolph then told his father that only one member of the Cabinet, Patrick Buchan-Hepburn, had backed Butler and remarked: 'It's funny that even now Rab can't see what he did.' Randolph recorded: 'WSC glared and spat one word: "Munich!" Personally I don't think that is the whole explanation.'

The way in which a new leader of the Conservative Party 'emerged' without any formal procedures, let alone a democratic election, and the apparently great, if not decisive, influence of the leading grandee of the party, Lord Salisbury, is something that would surprise, even shock, a later generation. Although Iain Macleod was to inveigh against the machinations of the so-called 'Magic Circle' when, a few years later, Lord Home was picked to succeed Macmillan, it is clear that the choice of Macmillan reflected, by and large, the wishes of the party. A much later entry in Randolph's somewhat fitful diary – which was not hand-written but dictated and typed – reads as follows:

MOST SECRET 3 COPIES ONLY
Iain Macleod talked to RSC. Sunday 15 September 1963

Mr Macleod explained what happened just before Sir Anthony Eden resigned in 1956.

During the Suez Crisis at the end of a Cabinet meeting on [date left blank], when it was obvious that Anthony could not continue as Prime Minister, Harold Macmillan, Duncan Sandys, David Eccles, Peter Thorneycroft and Iain Macleod went across to the Treasury.

There was very little discussion; the reality was clear. Two points were instantly settled.

   1. Eden had to go.
   2. It must be Macmillan.

In his spare moments between political punditry, journalistic joustings, berating press barons, pursuing pornographers, fighting libel actions and his biographies of Lord Derby and Anthony Eden, Randolph took an active and increasing interest in the laying out of the garden at Stour, now his home base and the focus of his new life as a 'country bumpkin'.

Two years earlier, the garden had been a hayfield but, as Randolph made clear, he did not see it as his job to get down on his hands and knees or get earth under his fingernails. 'My role,' he would declare loftily, 'is that of the constitutional monarch, as defined by Bagehot, to warn, encourage and advise!' When in the course of a BBC Television interview at his home he was asked by Berkeley Smith about 'the big research teams' that were assisting him with his books he replied:

Well, not big research teams. You saw Mr Molian weeding in the garden in his spare time – he is helping with research on the *Life of Lord Derby*. Then there is Mr Maunthner mowing the lawn – he is very keen on fresh air – he is delving out the life of Sir Anthony Eden ... If you live in the country you've got to have a hobby and we Country Bumpkins have planted trees which you saw in the film. But our hobby, principally, is sort of teasing rich press lords who behave very badly and who really ought to behave better.

When the interviewer inquired why he had chosen to call the company

he had formed to market his book *What I Said About the Press* 'Country
Bumpkins Ltd', Randolph answered:

> Well, it just tickled my fancy. I thought it was a thing that might tickle the
> fancy of the public too and I gather it has. People think of me rather as a
> 'City Slicker'. I was born a cockney within the sound of Bow Bells at 33
> Eccleston Square, which later for many years, strangely enough, was the
> headquarters of the Labour Party. I lived in London for 25 years of my
> adult life, and I had got rather bored with it. I know Dr Johnson said that
> a man who was bored with London was bored with life; but I had seen
> enough of it and I thought I would rather have an opportunity of reading
> more and writing more books, which is quite impossible in London today.
> That's what led me to come and settle down here in the country.

A few days later he received a letter from his friend Lord Beaverbrook
from his home in the South of France:

> *28 April 1957*
>
> My dear Randolph,
>   I have been reading Percy Cudlipp on your appearance on television.
>   It is a wonderful triumph and I am telling my undertaker to engrave on
> my tombstone: 'But it will be a duller world when Lord Beaverbrook is
> no longer among us – Randolph Churchill.'
>
> Yours affectionately,
Max

Following a visit to Stour in the early summer of that year, Madame
Escarra, for many years a close friend of Beaverbrook, sent him this
account of Randolph's new home:

> It is very pretty, an eighteenth-century house, all pink – with old windows
> and white shutters. As soon as you enter the hall you are fascinated by the
> view. You go to the terrace and you see a real Constable landscape (it was
> his country), with magnificent trees under a vast sky, and far away the
> famous tower [Dedham Church] represented in most of his paintings. The
> sun is just shining out on it now, and is coming galloping through
> the fields to reach us. Long shadows are stretching over the lawns, making
> the curves of the slopes even more harmonious. It is the hour when all is
> quiet, peaceful. No noise, only 'melodious birds, singing madrigals'.
>   Close to the house, to be seen from the rooms, is a rose garden, which

Randolph is watering with love. He has discovered in himself a passion for his garden. He is planting and planting again trees and flowering bushes. He is building a new avenue. We can imagine it in a few years – on each side lime trees, making a vault, edged by lavender and farther on, in the middle of the path, a maple tree, a circle where you can sit and see the old church, and dream – and behind, lost in the background, white camellias, gardenias, a symphony of colours – poetry – mystery.

A tremendous carillon suddenly stirs the air. We go towards it. The bells are not in the church, they are enclosed in a wooden house, where four men are moving them like '*Vulcans aux Enfers*'.

A telephone rings. 'My mother is coming here tomorrow. I want to make everything enchanting for her; "beds of roses and a thousand fragrant posies, a cap of flowers and a kirtle embroidered all with leaves of myrtle, a belt of straw and ivy buds . . ." Let us go to the garden and pick all the flowers we can find – rhododendrons and honeysuckle, lilac.' The house is now crowded with flowers. Lady Churchill will be in the panelled room, with pictures of birds covering the walls, as well as the walls of the bathroom and sitting room. Francis Bacon's Essays are placed on her bedside table. There are six other bedrooms and bathrooms, very comfortable, all decorated differently, with great personality. Everywhere engravings and pretty furniture.

Early in 1958, Randolph embarked on a hectic tour of the United States, undertaking more than thirty lectures in the space of six weeks. His theme was 'The Defence of the West' and he was at pains to play down the significance of the launching of Sputnik I, which had placed the Soviet Union firmly ahead in the space race, causing a major sensation, even alarm, in the West. He did not believe that this development would in any way affect the military balance between East and West and he was opposed to engaging in an arms race with the Soviet Union which might bankrupt the West.

Randolph had a conviction that, as he put it, 'Enough is enough': that it would not matter if the USSR built more nuclear weapons than the United States, so long as the latter maintained the unquestioned ability to inflict unacceptable damage on the Soviet Union in the event of any attack on the West. I recall, as a seventeen-year-old schoolboy at Eton, my father telling me of an exchange with General Curtis LeMay, at the headquarters of the United States Strategic Air Command, buried deep underground at Omaha, Nebraska. On asking the commander-in-chief if he had enough nuclear bombs, LeMay drawled: 'Say, Mr Churchill, we've kinda run out of targets!'

Upon his return to England, Randolph received an anxious letter from his mother in the South of France where his father had been taken ill:

21 March 1958

Although 'Papa' has made an excellent recovery from his illness, it has left him very weak. We have had 2 set-backs, minor in themselves but it has delayed things. Now all being well we hope to fly back on Sunday the 30th March. We shall go straight to Chartwell and stay there for Easter. Would you like to visit us there some time? Will you dine & sleep on my birthday, 1 April?

I'm planning a bed-room on the ground floor of Hyde Park Gate as I doubt if your father can climb the stairs. When do Winston's holidays begin? & what are the plans? He sent me such a nice telegram when he heard of 'Papa's' illness.

I have been following your doings with affectionate interest...

In fact a birthday telegram from Randolph to his mother, addressed to Roquebrune, makes clear that Winston was not well enough to return to England as planned.

Immediately following a journalistic sortie to Britain's Mediterranean and Middle East bases – Malta, Cyprus and Aden, in each of which trouble was brewing – Randolph dashed off to Algeria where the French Army, 450,000 strong, had mutinied under its commanders, Generals Salan and Massu, in sympathy with the more than one million French colonists in Algeria who felt they were being betrayed by the French Government. The famous revolt of 13 May was to lead to the overthrow of the French Republic and the installation of General de Gaulle as President. Although commercial air traffic between France and Algeria was suspended, Randolph managed to find a pilot in Switzerland with a five-seater aeroplane, willing to fly him from Zurich to Algiers where he arrived early one morning to find himself surrounded by twenty soldiers toting sub-machine-guns. As he remarked good-humouredly in his *Evening Standard* column: 'Despite the excessive precautions I was amiably received...'

Soon afterwards Stephen Barber of the *Daily Telegraph* (in whose company, some ten years later, I was to be assaulted and beaten over the head by Mayor Daley's Chicago police while reporting the Democratic

'Prenez Garde! Je crois que c'est Randolph!'

National Convention of 1968) arrived on the scene with the rest of the world's press, aboard an Air Algérie plane. Much to Barber's surprise, Randolph was already there. As he recalled:

The big coup every reporter was out to make at that moment was to interview the shadowy M. Soustelle, who was obviously the grey *éminence* behind the whole Gaullist plot – although he was later to fall out with the General. Randolph was then representing the *Evening Standard*. I ran into him on the steps of the Aletti Hotel near the waterfront, where our tardily arriving crowd of journalists from Paris found themselves billeted. It was, by then, too late for me to file anything to my paper, so I proposed dinner. Randolph demurred. Then he gave me a crafty look and said: 'If you'll keep the others off my back, I'll fill you in on what I'm going to find out tonight. I am due to be picked up in a few minutes by a man who is going to take me to see Soustelle himself.' He then vanished.

Early next morning I was awoken by a telephone call to my room. It was Randolph. 'Come round and have breakfast,' he said. 'I need your help.'

A few moments later I was to find him sitting on his balcony overlooking the harbour. He was working on a curious meal of orange juice, fried eggs and Veuve Clicquot and insisted that I join him in his menu. But he was in an awkward bind. He had secured his interview with Soustelle. The great man ... had been most informative. They had talked at length. And there had been a good deal to drink.

The only serious snag, Randolph at length admitted, was that not only had he neglected to take notes, but he could not remember a solitary thing Soustelle had said. What was more, at any moment a telephone call was due to come in from the Paris office of the *Evening Standard*. The editor knew he had achieved the splendid coup – a veritable scoop of an interview with the top mystery man of the whole affair. What was Randolph going to say when he started demanding 'copy'?

We worked hard on the problem. I tried one idea after another to prod some recollection out of the recesses of Randolph's memory. What had he said about de Gaulle? What role were the generals – Massu and Salan – going to play in the future development of the drama? When was de Gaulle going to come to Algiers? – in fact, he came some days later.

It was hopeless.

Then suddenly the telephone rang. It was Paris. Randolph took the receiver and plopped down on the bed with it in his hand. And, all at once, a beatific smile came over his face. 'I've got it,' he chortled. 'Just you listen to this...'

Whether or not anything really came back to him at that juncture I shall never know. All I do remember is that it went rather like this: 'Last night I had the privilege of meeting the grey eminence of the Algiers uprising. He is M. Jacques Soustelle ... We met in the handsome Villa des Oliviers, high in the hills above the city and looking out over the bay of Algiers ... It was at this self-same spot that Sir Winston Churchill conferred during an earlier French crisis with General Charles de Gaulle ...' He paused at this point and then went on: 'I wish I was at liberty to tell you exactly what M. Soustelle told me ... but my lips are sealed. However, I think it fair for me to tell you what I told M. Soustelle ... I told him that I believed that civilians must always be in control of the military ... while the reasons behind the 13 May rebellion could be understood and even approved ... the sooner the supremacy of civil authority was re-established, the better. I think you may take it that M. Soustelle agreed with me ...' There was a good deal more in this vein.

It was so highly thought of by Lord Beaverbrook, the owner of the *Evening Standard*, that he caused the whole article to be reprinted in the paper's morning stablemate, the *Daily Express*, next day – a rare honour indeed.

Frankly, I do not know whether Randolph had a sudden total recall of his conversation with' M. Soustelle of the previous evening. I doubt if it matters. It was undoubtedly off the record anyway. And the story did have Randolph's competitors in a great rage of envy, which is really what the game is all about.

In fact, the published article, as it is to be found in the pages of Randolph's large and weighty press-cutting books that fill several yards of my library shelves, though clearly identifiable, bears little resemblance to the more splendid Barber version. Could it be that Stephen Barber's recollection was somewhat hazy – not to say extravagant – after that unaccustomed Veuve Clicquot breakfast?

Having exhausted the possibilities in Algeria by also gaining scoop interviews with Generals Massu and Salan, who declared that only a de Gaulle government would satisfy them – it was in fact the latter which the *Daily Express* reran from the *Standard* of the night before – Randolph decided to press on to Corsica, the island of Napoleon, to which the mutiny had spread. Barber takes up the story:

After that Randolph developed an alarming enthusiasm for chartering singularly dangerous-looking light aircraft in which to sally forth on further exploits. We flew one anxious dawn in a twin-engined five-seater of indeterminate ancestry across the Mediterranean to Ajaccio in Corsica, I remember, in order to get the story of how that island was seized by the rebels. The rebel chief who carried this out was Pascal Arrighi, a member of the Paris Chamber of Deputies who was, in due course, to fall foul of de Gaulle, like Soustelle, and escape to exile.

We were arrested by paratroops twice in a matter of hours, coming and going, but it never worried Randolph. While military policemen and bureaucrats sought either to impound our plane, arrest us or, finally and in desperation, expel us, my dear old friend never lost sight of the main objective. We had the knack of getting hold of the only telephone around that could be coaxed into reaching London or Paris to enable him to dictate copy.

What made this all the more remarkable was the fact that Randolph's

French was, to say the least, rudimentary. That was my job – dealing with
the natives. Yet somehow, when it came to my turn to have a go at reaching
my paper on the same telephone that had just performed splendidly for
'Church-eel', the line went down abruptly.

That year, Randolph celebrated his forty-seventh birthday bobbing
around the Mediterranean aboard a small cargo vessel, the *Charles Plumier*,
bound from Corsica for southern France. On his return to Stour, he
found the following letter, as always handwritten, from his mother:

28 May 1958

To-day is your Birthday and I am thinking of you and so is Papa & we are
hoping you will have a happy year ahead of you. Papa was so excited 47
years ago when you were born; & he went off for a solitary ride in
Richmond Forest to cogitate & dream about his son . . .

Yesterday we sent you a birthday telegram in French becos we were
told that an English one would not get thro' the censorship! I hope you
are having a thrilling & interesting time – Sarah is in Jerusalem or Haifa
opening the Technion of which you laid the foundation stone a year or
two ago. I would have liked to do it, but did not dare to leave your father
in his precarious state of health. I hope to see you soon my darling Boy.

Back at East Bergholt after further journalistic forays to Nicosia,
Istanbul, Amman and Tel Aviv, Randolph received a letter from the
Prime Minister:

> *10 Downing Street*
> *Whitehall*

1 September 1958

Dear Randolph,

I was very interested to see your article in the *Standard* the other day. It
was very well written and as usual very friendly to me.

If you are to be in London in the next fortnight I hope you will come
and see me. After that I am going to try to get a little holiday but shall be
back towards the end of September.

> Yours ever
> Harold

At the time Randolph was engaged in making preparations for his parents' golden wedding anniversary on 12 September, the centrepiece of which was to be the presentation by Randolph and his sisters of a Golden Rose Avenue to be planted in the Walled Garden at Chartwell. So that Winston and Clemmie could gain some impression of what it would ultimately look like, Randolph was busy arranging for a cross-section of distinguished artists to do individual paintings of varieties of golden rose to be planted. The book containing these, together with a plan of the proposed layout of the avenue, beautifully illuminated in gold-leaf by Randolph's neighbour and expert calligrapher, Denzil Reeve, was intended as a surprise. However, word evidently reached Cap d'Ail, where Winston and Clemmie were staying with Max Beaverbrook, for on 1 September Randolph received the following telegram:

MY DARLING RANDOLPH I AM THRILLED BY YOUR ROMANTIC PLAN FOR OUR ANNIVERSARY THANK YOU SO MUCH FOR ALL YOUR LOVE AND THOUGHT = MAMA

Meanwhile Randolph replied to Harold Macmillan's letter by return of post:

2 September 1958

I was much touched by your kind letter. I should very much like to come and see you as you suggest.

I am flying out to Nice on the afternoon of Thursday, 11 September in order to present a book of paintings on behalf of myself and my three sisters to my Father and Mother on their Golden Wedding. It is a very grand affair and contains portraits of 29 individual roses painted by some of the leading English artists and is meant to serve as a guide to the Golden Avenue of rose trees which we are presenting.

I thought you might like to see the book even more than myself . . .

Following his interview with the Prime Minister, Randolph reported in his *Evening Standard* column of 11 September:

MACMILLAN WILL STAND BY IKE

One thing critics of the Government do not understand is that Mr Harold Macmillan is loyal to his Allies and would be very unlikely to rat on them; for the simple reason that if he were to rat on his Allies, his Allies might rat on him.

Of course, there are people in the British Government today who would like to do another Munich. Fortunately, they are not in the majority.

I was lucky enough to see the Prime Minister last night and am happily in the position to tell the world that Britain will stand by the United States in the Far East. Some people feel that the United States let us down over Suez. We ain't going to let the United States down over Quemoy and Matsu . . .

Randolph's article, which purported to imply that Britain would fight alongside the United States to defend the Nationalist-held offshore islands against invasion by Communist China from the mainland, sparked a major political storm and provoked a *démenti* from Downing Street. The *Standard* reported in its front-page lead the following day:

Randolph Churchill's news commentary in yesterday's *Evening Standard* sparked off political uproar in London. Every newspaper today carries quotations from the article and an official statement was issued from 10 Downing Street last night. This said: 'We have no commitment of any kind with the United States over the Far East situation.

'With regard to Mr Randolph Churchill's article, this represents Mr Churchill's own view and was not authorised by the Prime Minister. The position of Her Majesty's Government remains as stated by the Foreign Office last Friday.' . . .

In his TV speech to the American people last night President Eisenhower himself took up the 'No Munich' theme . . .

Randolph's article had occasioned the Prime Minister extreme embarrassment and brought him under strong attack from the Socialist leader, Hugh Gaitskell, and the left-wing press. Randolph, already in the South of France for the celebration of his parents' golden wedding, cabled a message of apology to Macmillan.

In the Prime Minister's absence on a brief holiday in Scotland his Private Secretary, John Wyndham, acknowledged the cable:

14 September 1958

Thank you for the telegram which you sent me from Monte Carlo. I passed on your message to the Prime Minister. He says that although he is angry, his motto still is 'If you call a dog *Churchill*, I shall love him.'

Winston and Clemmie were thrilled by the Golden Rose Book, as may be judged from the rapturous letter Randolph received a few days later from his mother:

16 September 1958

Your swift visit was a joy; like a meteor flashing across the sky. And it was an inspiration to bring Arabella [Randolph's seven-year-old daughter, who recited to her grandparents 'The Garland of Meleager']. I look at that glorious book every day.

I'm longing to get to Chartwell & watch the planting of the Golden Rose Avenue.

Your Father sends his fond love.

The Golden Rose Book is now on display to the public at Chartwell.

Early in the new year of 1959, it was reported that the Conservatives of Bournemouth were refusing to readopt their sitting Member of Parliament, Nigel Nicolson, due to his failure in 1956 to support the Suez fiasco. It might have been thought that Randolph's ardour to enter Parliament would have cooled after three unsuccessful attempts in the mid-thirties, his defeat as Member for Preston in the 1945 landslide and his failure to beat Michael Foot at Devonport in the 1950 and 1951 elections. But clearly this was not the case for he proceeded to take both his friends and the Bournemouth Tories by surprise with a statement to the press on 16 January, declaring his intention to offer himself as a candidate for this plum Conservative seaside seat.

The following day Randolph wrote to the Prime Minister, boldly seeking to enlist his support, if not for Bournemouth, then at least for the vacancy that had also arisen in Chelsea:

My Bournemouth excursion will I expect persuade the land-ladies to re-adopt Nigel. And of course, I wouldn't think of standing against a duly adopted candidate who was also the sitting member. I assume this is also your view.

What about Chelsea? I don't know at all whether you would like to see me in the H of C or not. I might not be much help to you, but I don't think I would be a hindrance.

If you are not already bespoken and you are not hostile to this venture, a discreet word to Bill Cadogan (who is the Chelsea Chairman) might fix it.

If this letter embarrasses you in any way, please chuck it in the fire.

Macmillan, wisely, was not going to be drawn:

19 January 1959

I have just received your letter. I am very glad to hear what you say about Bournemouth. I am hoping the position will be cleared up.

About Chelsea: I have made enquiries and find that the following is the practice as regards Conservative ex-MPs. They either ask the Chairman of the Party to include their names on the Central Office list which is sent to the Chairman of the vacant constituency – in which case it is included automatically. Alternatively they apply direct. There is no reason why they should not adopt both these courses.

As Leader of the Party I carefully abstain from making any effort to promote or discourage any particular candidature. I have kept to this rigidly – and did so even before I became Leader of the Party. If you consult Maurice he will confirm this. I never made the slightest effort to get him any kind of favour – I am sure you will understand how I am placed.

That weekend Cross-bencher in the *Sunday Express* predicted with confidence:

Mr Nigel Nicolson, Tory MP for Bournemouth East, will hum with joy this morning as he knots his Old Etonian tie . . .

Nothing in Mr Nicolson's opinion, could have helped him more than Mr Churchill's announcement that he would stand as a candidate at Bournemouth, independently if necessary.

For Mr Nicolson will argue that if anyone has done harm to the Tories over Suez it is Mr Churchill by his recent fascinating articles in the *Daily Express*. And that by comparison his own little criticisms of Sir Anthony Eden were as insipid as watered ginger beer.

Furthermore he realises that Mr Churchill's 1 a.m. intervention has caused great annoyance to the Bournemouth Tory leaders. And he is sure they are dreading far more trouble in the future . . .

On the same day, the *Sunday Dispatch* commented: 'It's not so much who will stand for Bournemouth, but who Bournemouth will stand for.'

Interviewed by Robin Day for Southern Independent Television,

Randolph described Nigel Nicolson as 'an able and good MP' and said that he would not be standing against him if Nicolson were still the official candidate. 'Poor dears,' he observed patronisingly of the Bournemouth Tories, 'now they haven't got a candidate at all, this great and famous constituency of Bournemouth, with all its Tory voters. I thought I ought to give them a lead. I don't think they know a great deal about politics, the people who are running this association.'

Asked why he had not been elected to Parliament since the war, Randolph replied: 'I choose constituencies without enough Tories – there are enough Tories for anybody down here. Conservative associations like people to stand in queues. They ask impertinent questions about buying a house and living in the constituency and a lot of rot of that type. I don't care to stand in queues!'

Clearly, in a quarter of a century of campaigning, Randolph had learned little of the art of making friends and influencing Tory selection committees. *Time* magazine of 2 February inconveniently recalled his quip to the electors of Liverpool twenty-five years earlier when he had declared: 'I don't want to go into Parliament to represent a lot of stuffy old ladies in Bournemouth, I want to fight for really hard-pressed people.' The news weekly went on to report:

In London the Tory Party's inner council reacted to the news of Randolph's foray into Bournemouth like a military headquarters that has just learned of an enemy breakthrough. Party Chairman Lord Hailsham galloped off to Bournemouth post haste. At week's end, in a tense, three-hour session with Bournemouth Tory leaders, Hailsham persuaded them to accept the hated Nigel Nicolson again, if a private postal poll shows that he would win a majority of the 7,500 Tory votes [i.e. Association members] in the constituency.

Hailsham's intervention temporarily assuaged the crisis. Meanwhile Clemmie, on holiday with Winston in Marrakech, was observing the scene from a distance and not without a hint of disapproval:

6 February 1959

I have just had a letter from Sylvia [Clemmie's lifelong friend and cousin, Sylvia Henley]. She is so fond of you & through my long life I have liked her & then loved her more & more. She told me a little about Bournemouth & your motives . . .

Papa is very well physically but alas his memory is failing & he is

*'Well, all I can say is if Randolph and Quintin get themselves
photographed bathing together, the Tories have had it!'*
Daily Express, 22 January 1959

becoming more & more deaf. When we leave here we are going for a
short cruise with Mr & Mrs Onassis in the *Christina*...

Randolph, on the point of leaving for Copenhagen and then Moscow
to cover the Prime Minister's meeting with Khrushchev replied on 12
February:

I was so very glad to get your letter and to hear your news. I am off
on Saturday to Copenhagen to address – of all improbables – a Youth
Organisation! I shall spend four or five days there, and then fly on to

Moscow to report on Harold's visit for the *Evening Standard* and the United Press. I expect I shall be gone about a fortnight.

All the lovely bulbs that you and Papa gave me for my Birthday are thrusting up and I expect that some of them will be in bloom by the time I get back. I think they are going to be a great splendour in the garden . . .

I don't quite understand your reference to my 'motives' at Bournemouth. Of course I don't know what Sylvia has told you. My motives are to get elected to Parliament, which as you know, I have been trying with little success to do for the past twenty-five years. I have made friends with one of the Vice Chairman, Miss Mary Dyson. I enclose two directives I have sent her to assist in her political education. I expect you know how politically backward people are in English seaside resorts, like Southend and Bournemouth.

With Randolph Moscow-bound, his friend Osbert Lancaster summed up the situation admirably in his cartoon in the *Daily Express* of 19 February which appeared with the caption: 'Keep your fingers crossed, boys! Peaceful Co-existence is about to face the acid test!'

However, even Osbert Lancaster cannot have known how prophetic these words would be. Within days Randolph was overheard at a British Embassy reception in Moscow, given by Macmillan in honour of his Soviet hosts, out-Khrushchev-ing Khrushchev in rumbustious, explosive and outrageous behaviour.

Noticing Randolph, chain-smoking with whisky-and-soda in hand, surveying the superb panorama of the Kremlin with its magnificent domes and cupolas across the Moskva River from a first-floor Embassy window, a Soviet official at the reception made bold to approach him in an endeavour to make polite conversation. 'Don't you think that is a fine view of the Kremlin?' inquired the Russian. 'Yes, indeed,' rejoined Randolph, 'and, furthermore, I have a brother-in-law called Sandys [Minister of Defence in the Macmillan Government] who could send the whole place to kingdom-come in three hours and twenty minutes!' At this point, the fire hoses were sent for and the Ambassador intervened to prevent an actual outbreak of hostilities. The incident served to liven up what might otherwise have been a formal, rather stuffy, diplomatic occasion.

But for Randolph the party was not yet over. Always with his eye on the main story, he lay in wait for Secretary-General Khrushchev on the Embassy staircase. The *Observer* reported in its Pendennis column of 8 March:

'Keep your fingers crossed, boys! Peaceful Co-existence is about to face the acid test!'
Daily Express, 19 February 1959

He (Randolph) was in many ways too Russian for them – larger-than-life, explosive, extrovert, capacious. In many respects, one might think he might be a good sparring-partner for Khrushchev: but their encounter was not fortunate. Churchill stood at the top of the Embassy stairs waiting for K to pass by on his way out. K. appeared.

CHURCHILL: Sir, may I call on you tomorrow?
K: I am very busy tomorrow.

Though unsuccessful with Khrushchev, Randolph had an unexpected visitor at his suite in the National Hotel, to which he had been moved after complaining volubly about being allotted a shoddy room with no bath at the Hotel Ukraina where the rest of the foreign press had been billeted. According to Randolph's report in the *Evening Standard* on 22 February:

> On Saturday evening I was sitting in my apartment, minding my own business with my secretary and interpreter Miss Lidiya Dubininskaya, when the telephone rings. A chap announces himself as Burgess [Guy Burgess, a British Foreign Office official who, together with Donald Maclean, had defected to Moscow in 1951] and asks whether he can come and call on me. I think that it is probably a practical joke played by some other journalists. But I play it 'deadpan' and say yes, come around as soon as it's convenient.
>
> Well, he does and he's wearing an Old Etonian tie. I know that it is not Mr Macmillan because neither he nor I would perpetrate the social solecism of wearing an old school tie in Moscow.
>
> Well, there we are in the National Hotel – and Burgess, wearing his Old Etonian tie, says to me: 'I am still a Communist and a homosexual.' I replied: 'So I had always supposed.' Burgess claims that he never 'carried a card'. I don't know about this: but I expect that MI5, for whom Burgess claims he worked before the war, would have a view about this.
>
> Burgess further told me that he was thinking of coming back to England to see his aged mother to whom he speaks every week on the telephone. I warned him that the Attorney-General, Sir Reginald Manningham-Buller [dubbed 'Bullying-Manner' by *Private Eye*], might have a word or two to say about that...
>
> After his seven long years in Moscow Burgess is very lonely and avid for news about top people in England. I was naturally guarded in my reply ... I told Burgess that I had long cherished the hope that he was really a double agent and that he was working for our side.
>
> He said: 'If I were doing that I naturally wouldn't tell you or anyone else...'

While in Kiev covering the Macmillan tour, Randolph received a telegram from a close friend and neighbour in Suffolk, Natalie Bevan, giving the result of the postal ballot at Bournemouth:

NICOLSON BEATEN BY 91 VOTES HAS OFFERED IMMEDIATE RES-
IGNATION LOVE = NATALIE

Randolph promptly issued a statement to the press in Kiev reaffirming his intention to stand for the seat, declaring: 'These are serious times and at a period when the First Secretary of the Communist Party of

Russia, Mr Khrushchev, is treating the British Prime Minister in so impudent a fashion we must all rally around Mr Macmillan. In these circumstances I feel it my duty to return from Kiev as soon as possible. I hope to be in Bournemouth on Monday.'

Osbert Lancaster again captured the spirit of the moment in the *Daily Express* of 4 March 1959 with a cartoon showing Randolph arriving at Bournemouth railway station with snow on his boots and a fur hat on his head, being greeted with the words: '*Droshky*, Sir?' by a porter offering to call a taxi.

'*Droshky*, Sir?'
Daily Express, 4 March 1959

Randolph's haste was in vain for, as he put it, while wandering around in the slush of a collective farm he had failed to appreciate that Nicolson's proffered resignation was not to be immediate and there was to be no early by-election. In fact, it was not until May that the Bournemouth Tories announced their choice. Not only was Randolph not among the eight candidates short-listed for the seat; he was not even accorded an interview.

According to a report in the *Daily Express* of 14 May, Randolph received the news without much regret:

> 'I shall now stay at home cultivating my garden unless someone sends for me ... It was a bit of a snub not even being asked for an interview. On the other hand, in a way it's a relief. That's not sour grapes. I wanted the seat but it would have meant a complete dislocation of my life.'
>
> Mr Churchill's life is a full one. His biography of Sir Anthony Eden is due to be published next month and his Life of Lord Derby in the autumn. And now he is working on his autobiography [*Twenty-One Years*].
>
> 'If I had been elected,' he added, 'it would have meant attending the Parliament and going to Bournemouth at least one weekend a fortnight. I like my home. I spend as much time here as I can. Particularly now, in the summer.'
>
> Mr Churchill has a very beautiful garden. It is looking its best just now. The roses are far advanced. I can't blame him for preferring it to the dust and heat and baby-kissing and hand-shaking of Parliamentary politics.

That summer, in the course of a visit to America to see my mother and the Broadway producer Leland Hayward, who was to be her future husband, somebody suggested that I might find it interesting to work as a volunteer at the Washington campaign headquarters of Senator John F. Kennedy, who had put his hat in the ring as one of the Democratic Party candidates for the following year's presidential election. Aged eighteen and midway between Eton and Oxford, I was filled with excitement at this idea and cabled my father forthwith. This provoked the bluntest telegraphic response I have ever received in my life. Randolph was evidently under the misapprehension that Jack Kennedy, himself, had offered me the job:

ASK JACK WHAT HAPPENED TO BRITISH AMBASSADOR SACK-VILLE-WEST 1886. SUGGEST YOU FIND SOMETHING LESS POL-ITICALLY AND CLIMATICALLY HOT THAN WASHINGTON. LET ME KNOW IF I CAN HELP. LOVE = FATHER

It took me a while to discover the fate of Ambassador Sackville-West three-quarters of a century before: he was thrown into the Potomac

River for interfering in American party politics. It was a crushing reply but this advice, which I accepted, was entirely right. As several of my father's friends have told me, his advice to them, about their problems or a course of action, was often both dispassionate and wise.

Unfortunately I had less success, despite repeated efforts, in persuading successive Chairmen of the Conservative Party under Margaret Thatcher in the 1980s of the folly of a British political party taking sides in American party politics. Full of admiration for her friend Ronald Reagan, the Prime Minister was determined to equate the Republicans in America with the Conservatives in Britain, thereby foolishly relegating the Democrats to the same camp as the British Labour Party. When, as was inevitable, the Republicans lost the presidency in 1992, following a campaign in which a handful of Conservative Party members and officials had been actively engaged on the Republican side, it was not surprising that relations between the new President, Bill Clinton, and Margaret Thatcher's successor, John Major, were distinctly frosty and, for a while, the Anglo-American 'special relationship' slumped to an even lower ebb than at the time of Suez.

Heeding my father's advice, I took a three-month job on the news desk of the *Wall Street Journal*, an experience which propelled me towards a journalistic career on leaving Oxford three years later.

That autumn Harold Macmillan and the Conservative Party won a landslide victory, in spite of Randolph's failure to secure a High Court injunction to prevent the Labour Party including, without copyright permission, liberal quotations from his highly critical book on Eden in their election pamphlet 'The Tory Swindle 1951–1959'.

CHAPTER 27

African Safaris

On the evening of 30 November 1959 the Churchill family gathered for dinner at 28 Hyde Park Gate to celebrate Winston's eighty-fifth birthday. Earlier in the day Winston had attended Prime Minister's Questions in the Commons where, as the oldest member and Father of the House, he received a great ovation.

A few days later, Randolph left for Nairobi to accompany, in a journalistic capacity, his friend Iain Macleod who, as Colonel Secretary, was making an official visit to East Africa. Macleod was apprehensive on hearing of Randolph's intentions, commenting: 'The last thing I wanted was to have Randolph's genius for uncovering secrets added to my worries.' On boarding the aircraft at London airport, Macleod was much relieved to see no sign of Randolph. By the time all the passengers had taken their seats and the aircraft was preparing to depart, he was already congratulating himself on having given his prospective 'shadow' the slip. But his relief was short-lived and, as he recalled: 'We waited and waited. Finally after a small commotion Randolph appeared through the pilot's cabin. Brushing aside my papers and my civil servants, Randolph seated himself beside me. "Ho!" he said. "I suppose you thought I'd missed it?" "No" I said, "I just hoped."'

Randolph, having fallen out with the *Evening Standard*, for which he had written regularly since before the war, had recently been appointed roving correspondent for the *News of the World*, which claimed a readership in excess of 15 million. Following a two-week tour of Uganda, Kenya and Tanganyika, Randolph confided to his readers in an article dated 27 December:

I had a particularly personal and filial interest in all I saw in East Africa. For I was following for the most part the trail blazed by the Under-Secretary of State for the Colonies fifty-two years ago. In 1907 Mr Winston Churchill traversed all this area on foot or bicycle ... Mr Churchill was then 33 years old; but he already commanded a journalistic style incomparably more vivid than anything the present writer can aspire to at 48.

Consider the following passage from *My African Journey* . . .: 'We are steaming ten miles an hour across an immense sea of fresh water as big as Scotland, and uplifted higher than the summit of Ben Nevis . . . The air is cool and fresh, the scenery splendid. We might be yachting off the coast of Cornwall in July. We are upon the Equator in the heart of Africa and crossing the Victoria Nyanza, 4,000 ft. above the sea! . . . The Nile springs out of the Victoria Nyanza, a vast body of water nearly as wide as the Thames at Westminster Bridge: and this imposing river rushes down a stairway of rock . . . in smooth, swirling slopes of green water. It would be perfectly possible to harness the whole river and let the Nile begin its long and beneficent journey to the sea by leaping through a turbine. It is possible that nowhere else in the world could so enormous a mass of water be held up by so little masonry.'

Randolph continued: 'The dam was built – 50 years later; it cost £24 million; it produces enough electricity to light half of Birmingham . . .'

Among the political figures that Randolph met during his visit to Kenya was 28-year-old Tom Mboya, whom he described as: 'the most brilliant political personality in the whole African continent'. According to Randolph, Mboya 'made a pronouncement of immense and hopeful significance. Whereas before he had always clung to the claim of "one man, one vote" which would have meant that the European and Asian minorities would have been wholly unrepresented both in the Legislative Assembly and the Government, he has now let it be known that he is prepared to concede, at least for the time being, some reserved seats for the minorities. Mr Macleod, by his personal impact on Mr Mboya, deserves a good deal of credit for what he has accomplished. But he must share the credit with Mr Nyerere, the high-minded and resolute leader of African opinion in Tanganyika . . . He has set an example which Mboya has been brave enough to follow.'

The Kenyan *Sunday Post* reported:

Most colourful of an impressive press corps in Kenya to cover the visit of the Secretary of State for the Colonies, Mr Iain Macleod, is another politician and journalistic *enfant terrible* Randolph Churchill . . . Mr Churchill was of the opinion that Mr Macmillan is determined that there will be no more 'undignified scrambles' out of any more British possessions but that, realising what Mr Churchill described as 'the inevitable', the Prime Minister intends to lead African dependencies into independence, 'but just when and how is certainly not for me to comment,' he said.

In the course of his brief visit to Nairobi Randolph, with a couple of hours to kill before the plane's departure, went for a drive through a nearby game park. On coming across a pride of lions basking placidly in the equatorial sunshine, he instructed the driver to stop and – contrary to all the rules – dismounted from the vehicle. Randolph thereupon strode up to the lions, brandishing a walking-stick and roaring: 'Call yourself lions? You should hear a British lion roar, you sissies!' After an initial indication of surprise the lions, who evidently had killed the night before and consequently had no stomach for Randolph, resumed their slumbers.

As Randolph headed for home, the Prime Minister, Harold Macmillan, was setting out on a six-week tour of African Commonwealth countries, starting in Ghana and ending in Cape Town, where he delivered his famous 'Wind of Change' speech to the South African Parliament. Africa was very much in the spotlight of British politics in 1960, given the large number of British colonies in West, East and Central Africa, in each of which there were powerful forces straining for independence. The problem of transferring power peacefully to responsible successor governments, following the end of colonial rule, presented the British Government with a major challenge, nowhere more so than in Kenya and Rhodesia where large numbers of British citizens had been encouraged to settle.

Over the next few weeks Randolph covered the crushing of an insurrection of the French Army in Algeria by General de Gaulle, reported from Cyprus on the progress of Julian Amery's negotiations with Archbishop Makarios to secure indefinite Sovereign Base rights for Britain on the strategic Eastern Mediterranean island, and declared himself opposed to the Labour Party's proposed boycott of goods from South Africa. He then headed back to the African continent, this time to South Africa, travelling with his friend Stephen Barber, correspondent of the *Daily Telegraph*. In Kay Halle's *Irrepressible Churchill*, Barber recorded:

Randolph tended, most days, to line up on the side of the underdogs of the world. While he was not notably sentimental about Africa's downtrodden blacks, for example, he was none the less contemptuous of those who thought themselves superior by virtue of the colour of their skins. I remember once in the spring of 1960 – early in what became known in Britain as 'Africa Year' because so much happened then in that continent – I found myself on a plane flying with Randolph from Salisbury, capital of what was then the Rhodesian Federation, to Johannesburg.

There had just been an ugly police incident at a Transvaal town named Sharpeville. Afrikaner troopers had lost their heads and shot up a crowd of black Africans. Dr Verwoerd's government had told lies about it. Emergency laws had been proclaimed. It looked for a moment as if a massive native uprising against the Whites was about to begin ... Soon after we took off, the stewardess came round handing out long immigration forms to fill up for the Johannesburg authorities. They asked many more questions than most and Randolph, who never cared much for bureaucratic nonsense of any sort, was soon showing exasperation. He was incensed over a question relating to his 'proposed means of financial support while in the Union of South Africa'. He wrote down: 'This is an impertinence but you may take it that I am most generously treated by my employer.'

Then came the question on race – the burning issue in a country where apartheid is strictly practised. 'Damned cheek!' said Randolph. He then began writing furiously across the form, filling up the small space allotted and spreading himself down the margins of the paper. 'They can try and make something of that!' he muttered. Peering over his shoulder I read the following:

Race: human. But if, as I imagine is the case, the object of this inquiry is to determine whether I have coloured blood in my veins, I am most happy to be able to inform you that I do, indeed, so have. This is derived from one of my most revered ancestors, the Indian Princess Pocohontas, of whom you may not have heard, but who was married to a Jamestown settler named John Rolfe. ...

In reply to a question demanding the object of his visit, Randolph had answered 'Fun'. At the bottom of the form, where he was given the choice of putting his 'Signature or mark', he exercised the latter option by covering his thumb with ink from his ballpoint pen and imprinting it on the form.

Not surprisingly, on arrival at Johannesburg airport, the Afrikaner immigration officials were not amused. The *Rand Daily Mail* of 25 March reported:

Mr Churchill was asked politely by immigration officials to surrender his passport. Then he saw red, white and blue. I could hear him bellowing away – 60 feet down the subterranean immigration hall, his gesticulating arms and corpulent figure silhouetted behind a glass partition ... a policeman asked him if his baggage had been checked. Mr Churchill snorted: 'Probably confiscated.' Finally through the doorway he greeted a friend and bellowed: 'Ah well, let's enter the ... police state.' Walking up to the baggage hall, he added: 'They've told me to collect my passport tomorrow morning. Ha! What a ... hope. They can damn well send it round to me.' I asked Mr Churchill – politician and journalist – whether he had been to the Union before: 'Yes – I was in the Cape in Smuts's time. Things were much different then.'

Randolph, as so often, got his way and was able to report in the *News of the World*:

Next morning the Chief Immigration Officer waited upon me in my hotel. He offered profuse apologies, admitted I was fully entitled under South African law to put my mark instead of my signature, and returned me my passport. Thus this small incident was settled in a manner wholly satisfactory to me – unconditional surrender by the Union authorities.

On the more serious subject of the Sharpeville massacre, he reported:

There has been a large-scale massacre which has attracted world-wide attention ... seventy-one Africans were shot to death by the police at Sharpeville on Monday for not carrying passports: on Thursday the immigration authorities here confiscated my passport, thereby presumably exposing me to the bullets of their colleagues in the police force ...

If you are going to run a Police State you would surely be well advised to have an efficient police force. It must be recorded that Dr Verwoerd has not got such a force at his disposal. Ten London Bobbies could easily have dispersed the 10,000 or 20,000 Africans who demonstrated at Sharpeville ...

Randolph was echoing his father's faith in police rather than troops for it was Winston who in 1911, during the disturbances in the mining valleys of Wales, had replaced troops on their way to Tonypandy with mounted police.

Having filed his story to the *News of the World*, Randolph proclaimed to Stephen Barber: 'Now we will go and interview Dr Verwoerd!' As Barber recorded:

The South African premier was not in a loving mood towards the British at that time. Nor was he anyone's pin-up in England. But he was making a speech at an Afrikaner township some distance across the *veldt* from Johannesburg and it seemed to Randolph both obvious and simple to climb into a taxi and demand to be taken thither. I tagged along, becoming increasingly alarmed at the enormous sum we soon began running up on the meter.

In due course, we got to the place. Verwoerd had made his speech and was riding slowly in stately triumph through dense crowds of tow-headed Afrikaners, surrounded by exceedingly tough-looking jack-booted body-guards at the head of a motorcade. Randolph was dressed rather casually in a sloppy pair of grey flannels and a white shirt. It was hot and he was also sweating. He did not, in short, cut an awesome figure. But that did not prevent him from diving through the mob and reaching the premier's car – an open Ford convertible – to demand an interview.

With Verwoerd's bodyguards gripping the safety-catches of their revolvers, Randolph reached into the open car, proffering a handshake, and inquired: 'Dr Verwoerd, I presume?' before proceeding to demand an interview. According to Stephen Barber:

> Verwoerd looked stunned, as well he might have been. But he quickly realised who Randolph was, which probably saved us both from being locked up, if not actually shot on the spot. Randolph was very pleased by this journalistic enterprise. I must confess, I did not myself see where it had got him. The good doctor never did agree to see him. But it so happened a week later, by which time Randolph had reached Nairobi, the Kenyan capital, on his way back to London, that an eccentric Anglo-South African liberal confronted Verwoerd at a Johannesburg agricultural fair and shot him in the head with a .22 pistol.
>
> Verwoerd survived. But Randolph felt totally vindicated. He was able to write a splendid column for the *News of the World* that weekend, telling his readers how he could have forewarned the South African leader that an assassination attempt was going to be made against him. During his Johannesburg visit, Randolph had heard a number of important people remark that it was high time someone shot Verwoerd. And he had not been impressed by the quality of local security arrangements...

As a parting shot at the heavy-handed officialdom of the apartheid republic, Randolph, before leaving Jan Smuts Airport for Nairobi, took huge delight in ceremonially burning his South African press card, to the obvious amazement of a two-year-old girl who was photographed sitting on the bench beside him eating an ice-cream – a photograph which appeared on the front page of the Johannesburg *Sunday Times*.

During the course of his visit to South Africa, Randolph had made a pilgrimage to the State Model School in Pretoria where his father had been imprisoned during the Boer War and from which, as he put it, he 'escaped from a W.C. to freedom and worldwide acclaim'. Randolph's visit sixty years later prompted correspondence in the columns of the Johannesburg *Star*, including a contribution which suggested that Winston had been mistaken in believing that he had been captured by the Boer leader, General Botha, when in fact his captor had been by one of the soldiers under the general's command. Randolph forwarded the clipping to his father who remained adamant that it was Botha who had captured him.

On his way back through Kenya, Randolph spent a few days with his friends Tom and Diana Delamere in their magnificent home, Soysambu, set in the spectacular Rift Valley where, two years later, they were to receive me most hospitably when, with a companion from Oxford, I piloted a single-engine aeroplane round Africa. Tom Delamere was among the most prominent and distinguished of Kenya's white settlers and almost the only one who, throughout Kenya's 'Mau Mau' emergency, let it be known that he did not carry a weapon for his own protection. Diana, of *White Mischief* fame, was still a lady of great beauty and charm. She had been at the heart of the greatest scandal of Kenya's settler community when her first husband, Sir Jock Delves Broughton, stood trial for the murder of her lover, Josslyn Hay, Earl of Erroll, in January 1941. Delves Broughton, though acquitted, later committed suicide. Breaking his homeward journey in Cairo, at his old wartime haunt of Shepheard's Hotel, Randolph cabled his friends:

YOUR PRINCELY HOSPITALITY CALLS NOT FOR A BREAD AND BUTTER LETTER BUT FOR A CAVIAR AND CHAMPAGNE CABLE LOVE TO YOU BOTH = RANDOLPH

Towards the end of the year, Randolph's American literary agent, Alan Collins, made the mistake of confiding to Randolph his plans to drive by Land-Rover from Benghazi, on the Mediterranean coast, across the Libyan desert to the Tibesti Mountains in Tchad. Jokingly, he suggested that Randolph might care to join the expedition. The very mention of North Africa and the desert conjured up memories for Randolph of Monty and Rommel, as well as his own exploits behind enemy lines with the SAS and the Long Range Desert Group twenty years before. To the surprise of Alan, who was already beginning to regret having mentioned it, Randolph found the suggestion irresistible. He quickly established that a brand-new

Land-Rover could be acquired for an export price of £800 and forthwith placed an order for one to be delivered by sea to Benghazi. The six-week expedition, which involved crossing some of the world's most inhospitable terrain was set to leave in the spring of 1961. To my great delight, my father invited me to join him. 'The trip,' he averred, 'would be highly educative for a budding historian as there are many Roman ruins and historic oases to be visited. It is a rare opportunity to see this little-known part of the world and I should love it if you could come. Please let me know as soon as possible ...' I accepted with enthusiasm and was promptly dispatched to acquire camp-beds, ground-sheets, sleeping-bags, collapsible chairs and table, a camping cooker, cooking pots and utensils. Meanwhile my father acquired a large insulated 'Magic Box' which he proceeded to fill with such rations as he judged necessary for survival in the desert. The list of items which he purchased from Fortnum & Mason survives and includes the following items:

8 tins of Pâté de Foie Gras
2 tins of Coq au Vin
2 tins of Quennelles Nantua d'Écrevisses
6 tins of F & M Real Green Turtle Soup
6 tins of Bisque d'Homard
6 tins of Clam Chowder
1 tin of Bath Oliver [chocolate biscuits]

As soon as I could get away from Oxford for the Easter vacation, we flew out to Benghazi. We arrived to discover that it was the middle of Ramadan, a holy festival guaranteed to bring any strict Muslim country to a grinding halt for an entire month. Despite long hours spent at the port which my father, together with David Stirling and Fitzroy Maclean, had unsuccessfully tried to blow up in 1942 – our efforts to extricate our Land-Rover from the hands of the Libyan Customs officials proved of no avail.

Only when my father produced a large wad of local banknotes did they feel able to overlook their religious susceptibilities, calling to mind the scene in Evelyn Waugh's *Decline and Fall* in which the Llanaba Silver Band is invited to play at a school sports day in Wales. On being instructed to play something more lively than lugubrious religious anthems, the bandmaster declared brazenly: 'No music can we play, whatever, on the Sabbath but Holy music – except you pay us double!'

The expedition was led by Alan Collins's appropriately named brother-in-law, Livingstone ('Liv') Pomeroy, an American working for the US Embassy in Libya which, at the time, was ruled by King Idris, a loyal ally of the West. Nobody had then heard of Gaddafi, and the United States still retained Wheelus airbase near Tripoli while the British had a battalion of troops at Benghazi, together with an RAF detachment at the nearby airbase of El Adem. When Colonel O'Lone of the Royal Scots Greys, stationed in Benghazi, learned of our expedition, he offered to send with us one of his young officers, Lt. Francis Gibb, together with five men from the British Army under the pretext of conducting 'desert trials' on their newly acquired long-wheelbase Land-Rovers.

With the return of Pomeroy from Tripoli, where he had gone to take some examinations connected with his foreign service work, the expedition finally got under way. My father, convinced that 'Liv' was in fact a CIA man, teased him with having taken the exams to secure promotion from 'Spy, Third Class' to 'Spy, Second Class'. With such raucous banter, our convoy, fourteen strong in five Land-Rovers, headed down the flat coastal road towards Agedabia where we made camp for the night.

Each vehicle was loaded with twenty five-gallon metal jerricans of petrol together with five plastic cans of equal size containing water. Since there were no more than three points in the course of the 5,000-mile expedition where we could refuel, we had to carry sufficient petrol for two weeks' motoring. Supplies of drinking water were equally limited and, in spite of the twenty-five gallons carried by each vehicle, a daily ration of one gallon per person was strictly enforced. Each vehicle also carried ten cases of British Army 'Compo' rations, containing such delicacies as steak and kidney pie, treacle pudding and other items more suited to survival in the Arctic. In addition, we had all our personal kit, including camp-beds and sleeping-bags. As if this were not enough, our Land-Rover was allocated the bulky 200-pound generator required to power the expedition's radio, on which my father had prudently insisted.

While another member of the expedition, Professor 'Hank' Setzer of the Smithsonian Institute in Washington, who was conducting a study of small mammals, especially the jerbil or desert rat, went off to set his traps, Liv's English wife, 'Miggs', and Alan Collins's wife, Catherine, prepared dinner. Meanwhile my father, seated by the blazing camp-fire and armed with a stock of Scotch whisky, instructed me to open some of the Fortnum & Mason provisions. Noticing that a pair of Dutchmen from a neighbouring oil rig were paying too much attention to our 'white ladies', Randolph bellowed: 'Leave the women alone! Bugger off!' Then he proceeded to regale the company with tales of the desert war, quotations from Belloc's *Modern Traveller* and other gems from his extensive repertoire. When the time came to go to bed, Randolph demanded boiling water for our hot-water bottles. The incredulous Americans protested that there would not be enough water to drink if the Churchills had hot-water bottles every night: 'Silly-billies!' chided Randolph. 'You boil up the same water each night.' Then, in a loud aside to me: 'That's the trouble with Americans – they don't know the desert!'

Once we had left the coastal strip behind us, there was virtually no humidity in the air and, in consequence, the galaxies, nebulas and planets sparkled with a brilliance not seen in other climes. There is a magic to sleeping beneath the stars, with the whole firmament of heaven revolving above one from horizon to horizon. By dawn the temperature would drop close to freezing and the Churchills' hot-water bottles were the envy of the expedition.

The Americans – a race that cannot exist without ice – had been filled with disbelief when Randolph had asserted that he would find ice in the Sahara to keep his pâté de foie gras cool in his 'Magic Box' and, at least for the first few days, as we made our way through the newly established oilfields of northern Libya, we had no trouble in securing abundant supplies from the oil rigs that we passed. After five days, however, with the delicacies from Fortnum & Mason running low, realising that the desert was much less fun without Monty and Rommel and concluding that the Americans 'had no conversation' – by which he meant they were tiring of his monologue – Randolph decided the time had come to head for home, where his daffodils and tulips would be bursting into bloom. On his last evening we held a farewell dinner to which we invited five oilmen, including a delightful bearded Frenchman called André. Miggs Pomeroy describes the scene in *A Sahara Mouse-Hunt*:

The last of Randolph's pâté is delectable, served with the crisp toast which our guests have brought us. For dinner we have green turtle soup, also from Fortnum & Mason. It is flavoured with sherry and we tell Randolph that he is a great gourmet, with which he readily agrees. We also have tamales, hot chilli beans, beet salad and whisky. André holds a lantern for the women to do the dishes and Randolph complains that American women demand too much attention and that Frenchmen give them too much. An Englishman, now, knows how to treat women! Catherine thinks she has earned the Victoria Cross for not throwing the dish-water at him . . .

Accordingly, we dropped Randolph off, together with Alan Collins who was suffering from the heat, at one of the last oil rigs on our route, where the weekly re-provisioning flight was due the next day. Before leaving, he bequeathed me not only his Land-Rover but the few remaining supplies in his 'Magic Box'.

From there we struck south across the desert into Tchad and the Tibesti Mountains. Ours was the first expedition since the war to trace the route taken by the Free French General Leclerc, when he had marched north into Libya to join forces with the Allies against Rommel's army.

There may have been a more serious reason for Randolph's abandonment of the Sahara expedition. Even before his fiftieth birthday, which he celebrated a month later, his health had been giving grounds for concern. It had been noticeable to everyone on the expedition, that while the rest of us ate our meals, Randolph only drank his. Though he would have a nibble of foie gras or a bowl of soup, for the most part he would play with his food and push it to one side, though this did not prevent him from bellyaching fulsomely if it had not been prepared to his satisfaction. In addition to smoking eighty to a hundred cigarettes a day, he had been in the habit, for the past twenty years or more, of drinking up to two bottles of whisky daily – far in excess of anything consumed by his father. The human constitution, even one as strong as Randolph's, is not designed to take such punishment and it seems likely that, even as he was so proudly embarking upon the Great Biography of his father, he was already suffering from the chronic alcohol poisoning that would kill him seven years later.

CHAPTER 28

The Literary Factory

Bournemouth had finally dispelled any lingering ambition Randolph may have had of re-entering Parliament and making a political comeback in the House of Commons. It was evident from the political campaigns of his youth that his temperament and character were not tailor-made to appeal to Conservative Party selection committees, especially those to be found in the safer seats. As he advanced in years, far from mellowing, he became even less inclined to moderate his views or to compromise his way of life to accommodate the ever greater demands made by constituency associations of their MPs, let alone to curry favour with the local party notables whom he could not resist antagonising. Never again would Randolph threaten a Tory selection committee with the offer of his services. Nor were his hopes that Harold Macmillan might make him a peer in the 1963 resignation honours to be realised: in a fanciful moment he had imagined that the Prime Minister might relish the idea of an independent Tory spirit in the Lords.

He was now more than ever confirmed in his determination to devote himself to a literary life, to which his talents were more suited and which enabled him to carry on his work from the comfort of his Suffolk home, amid the delights of the garden he had created overlooking the broad meadows of the Stour valley. Each year he came to share, in fuller measure, the judgment of his fellow villager of an earlier age, John Constable, which he had engraved on a plaque on his terrace-wall: 'I am come to a determination to make no idle visits, nor devote my time to commonplace people. I shall return to Bergholt – John Constable.'

The spring of 1960 saw the publication of Randolph's *Lord Derby: King of Lancashire*. Six years of effort, assisted by a team of three 'young gentlemen' researchers and two secretaries, had gone into the production of the 300,000-word work that covered 618 pages. The reviews were overwhelmingly favourable, some ecstatic. The *Guardian* praised it as 'the best political biography we have had for many a long year' and Roy Jenkins in the *Spectator* found it 'one of the best accounts yet to be published of the quarrels which rent the Conservative Party between the last days of the Lloyd George Coalition and the formation of the second Baldwin Government'.

His friend and political opponent, Michael Foot, proclaimed in the *Daily Express*:

> ... The safe arrival on the bookstalls of a new book by Mr Randolph Churchill is something of a legal and diplomatic as well as a literary event. Downing Street, I trust, is alerted. Foreign Office public relation officers must be at their action stations. And who can estimate how many lawyers' palms must be itching to get their cut from these prospective royalties?
>
> But wait. This is a less rumbustious Randolph who has turned his hand from polemics to biography. True, an occasional outburst against the Randolphian *bêtes noires* – the Municheers, the Press, and the 'self-made self-seekers' of the Tory party – enrich the proceedings. But, for the rest, the achievement is sober, scholarly, and more elegant than explosive...

Of all the letters that he received following publication of the book, there was none that Randolph valued more than one from Harold Macmillan, the Prime Minister:

22 April 1960

I have just read your Life of Lord Derby. I feel I must write to tell you how admirably you have handled the whole period. Your book constitutes in my opinion an absolutely first-class account of the politics of some thirty or forty years. You have used very skilfully the figure of Lord Derby on which to hang this admirably written and very well documented work. I congratulate you most sincerely.

PS I dined with your father two nights ago and thought him pretty well. I told him my view about your book which pleased him very much.

Randolph, greatly touched, replied:

25 April 1960

Of all who have written in letters or reviews, about my Life of Derby, you are the only critic who has understood what I was trying to do. That you should think that I have succeeded is gratifying to me in the highest degree. I can think of no-one from whom such a tribute would have been so acceptable.

I am complimented that you should have found time to read this long book and also that you should have the kindness to write to me.

However, soon afterwards Randolph received what he regarded as the supreme accolade, from his father:

May 1960

My dear Randolph,
I have reflected carefully on what you said. I think that your biography of Derby is a remarkable work, and I should be happy that you should write my official biography when the time comes. But I must ask you to defer this until after my death. I would not like to release my papers piece-meal, and I think that you should wait for the time being and then get all your material from my own Archives and from the Trust. In any case I do not want anything to be published until at least five years after my death.

Your loving father,
Winston S. Churchill

Randolph's reply betrayed his devotion to his father and his eagerness to embark upon what he regarded as a labour of love:

Your letter has made me proud and happy. Since I first read your life of your father, thirty-five years ago when I was a boy of fourteen at Eton, it has always been my greatest ambition to write your life. And each year that has passed since this ambition first started in my mind, has nurtured it as your heroic career has burgeoned.

When the time comes, you may be sure that I shall lay all else aside and devote my declining years exclusively, to what will be a pious, fascinating and I suppose, a remunerative task.

Thank you again from the bottom of my heart for a decision which, apart from what I have already said, adds a good deal to my self-esteem and will, I trust, enable me to do honour in filial fashion, to your extraordinarily noble and wonderful life. . . .

Randolph had, at last, secured the prize on which his sights had so long been set and for which he had slaved so diligently. It was this that he craved more than anything else, though pride had always prevented him from asking his father for it. In 1947 Winston had urged him to give his life a purpose: 'Surely you must land & try to build a castle.' By turning his back on the shallowness of a life that centred around the bar and gambling tables of White's Club, putting down deep roots in the countryside and producing a serious political biography, he had made his landfall. Aged forty-nine, he now set about building his castle, which was to be a monument to the father he loved so dearly and admired so intensely but with whom he could not resist repeatedly having the most heated of rows. It was a tragedy that these two human beings, so deeply devoted to each other, sharing many characteristics and espousing all the same causes, should have had such an antagonistic relationship.

Few of Randolph's relationships could survive the fiery arrogance of his temperament, especially when fuelled by a liberal intake of whisky. In consequence of this he was, for much of his life a very lonely man – something that led him to drink more than was good for him. The mixture of temper and alcohol made him impossible to live with, as June had discovered after seven years of marriage. A couple of years after her departure, however, Randolph met the last and great love of his life, Natalie Bevan – a friendship that would endure until his death. Natalie lived in the nearby village of Boxted, with her ex-naval officer husband, Bobby, the son of Robert Bevan, a distinguished artist of the Camden Town group. Anita Leslie records their first meeting:

> The Bevan home lay only fifteen minutes' drive away. Natalie had come to Stour for the first time in 1957 to see her friend Lord Kinross who happened to be staying with Randolph. Patrick Kinross opened the front door and Randolph had walked across the hall to greet her. He stopped in his tracks and stood looking at Natalie for a long time in the strangest way. She looked back at him silently. The rapport was instantly established. After a moment of what one might almost call extraordinary recognition, Randolph stepped forward and took her by the hand. 'Come out on the terrace,' he said, 'and smell the roses.' Then without more ado he addressed her almost tearfully, 'I have been waiting for you so long. I love you.' And wildly he began kissing her. Randolph had always been a pouncer but this was not his usual way at all. He felt the love of his life had arrived at last and although it was late in the day he was profoundly grateful.
>
> Natalie was the same age as Randolph – forty-six – and as well as being beautiful she was a most unusual woman. She had first married Lance Sieveking and had two daughters. Then after the war she had married Bobby Bevan and come to live in Essex. In her, Randolph recognised something he had always been searching for. It was a curious liaison but she admitted the strength of it and Randolph was overwhelmed from the start. Natalie accepted the sudden link – and still remembers the scent of the roses that night.

Randolph and Natalie immediately became lovers, a situation which

Bobby accepted with amazing good grace. While continuing to live at Boxted, she would make regular visits to Stour and from time to time accompanied Randolph on trips abroad to the South of France, Marrakech or America. Natalie was warm-hearted as well as beautiful and brought a joy and peace into my father's life such as he had not known before. I became deeply fond of her, as did all at Stour who welcomed her frequent arrival, above all for the miraculously calming effect that she had on Randolph. Martin Gilbert recalls that the early-evening buzz of the battery-powered shaver that Randolph kept in his desk, would herald the arrival of Natalie and a night off for the Young Gentlemen.

Many years after my father's death, I asked Natalie if she had ever had trouble with him: 'Certainly not,' she replied forcefully, 'he knew I would not have stood for it!' I certainly never heard them have a row – in sharp contrast to the temper tantrums that he would inflict upon poor June. Indeed, it is probably true to say that the only friendships of my father that stayed the course of time were with those who made clear from the outset that they were not prepared to be bullied. Sylvia Henley, his mother's cousin and lifelong friend, was one of that breed. But to others he could behave insufferably.

Nancy Hare, wife of the Tory minister John Hare, who was Randolph's friend and neighbour, told Anita Leslie: 'We were discussing falling in love. I made some comment to the effect that after a certain age, people didn't really fall in love. Randolph turned on me and said: 'Age has nothing to do with it,' and added, 'I am more in love now than I have ever been in my life before.' I was then give a long lecture on the subject . . .

Natalie reciprocated Randolph's love and in her diary wrote: '1958–9. The most golden of my years.' After a three-year romance and just as soon as his divorce from June came through, Randolph wanted to make Natalie his wife. Accordingly, he wrote to her proposing that they marry the following year:

4 August 1960

My own darling Natalie,

There is no need to say much after all that has been said in the last three days. I want you to know what I said this morning is true, I want you to be my wife as soon as possible. My love for you can stand many afflictions and will, I know, endure. You have had a lot to put up with from me. But I believe you still love me?

'Come then. Let us act with courage, conviction and good sense. Let us so arrange our lives that we may start a new and permanent life together on your fiftieth birthday or on mine; or, if you should prefer a compromise on any convenient date between 24 May and 28 May 1961. That only leaves 25, 26 and 27 May. I see that my birthday falls next year on a Sunday – which wouldn't do, so please choose 25, 26 or 27 – Thursday, Friday or Saturday.

Whatever you decide I shall love you, now and forever. Please help me to make us both happy.

> Your devoted and unhappy,
> Randolph

Natalie was being forced to choose between the two men in her life. In the end she could not bring herself to leave her husband. Perhaps instinctively she knew that the love and friendship which she and Randolph shared might not survive living permanently under the same roof. It was undoubtedly a wise decision and almost certainly because of it their friendship endured to the end, while Randolph's relations with Bobby remained most cordial. I have warm memories of the many happy lunches that we all enjoyed together at Boxted House, where Bobby was the most genial of hosts.

Armed with his father's commission, Randolph set about further changing his way of life. Apart from American conventions and elections, which he could not resist being on hand to report, his journalistic forays abroad became far fewer as he buckled down to the gargantuan task that lay ahead of him.

A purpose-built strongroom with a massive Chubb safe-door was built at the back of the house to accommodate the more than one million documents of the Churchill Archive, weighing some one-and-a-half tons. The top floor of the house was cleared to provide offices for the enlarged staff of 'young gentlemen' researchers, sometimes amounting to four and even five in number, backed up by a team of four secretaries.

Through his literary agent, Graham Watson of Curtis Brown, Randolph struck a deal to sell the serial rights in the work to the *Sunday Telegraph*, which also acquired the right of 'access to documents' from the Chartwell Trust, established by my grandfather for the benefit of his children and heirs. The *Telegraph* established a company called C&T Publications Ltd., in which was vested the Churchill copyright. Meanwhile the volume rights were acquired by the publishers Heinemann in Britain and Houghton Mifflin in the United States – the 'Heinemen' and the 'Mifflemen', as Randolph dubbed them. Meanwhile, Winston relented over his earlier suggestion of an embargo on publishing anything within five years of his death.

Early in 1961 Randolph appointed Michael Wolff, a lovable bear of a man who had a first-class brain, to head his team as director of research. Following his visit to Stour, Michael took the initiative in writing a letter of confirmation:

25 January 1961

I am writing to confirm our agreement that I should be your principal assistant in the preparation of your life of Winston Churchill at a fee of three thousand pounds per annum, payable by you in equal monthly instalments...

Our agreement is to take effect on 1 February 1961, and to remain in force unless otherwise agreed by mutual consent until 31 July 1962. After that the agreement may be terminated on either side by six months' previous notice.

Randolph took as the theme of his work the words of Lockhart: 'He shall be his own biographer.' Rather than paraphrase the letters and documents of Winston and others, he thought it preferable – as indeed I have done in this work – to let the reader have sight of the actual text, allowing the subject to speak for himself wherever possible. He planned it as a five-volume work, with each volume having several ancillary or companion volumes in which all relevant documents and correspondence were to be published for the benefit of researchers and historians, so as to avoid the main volumes becoming too ponderous and expensive for the general reader.

Randolph's high-powered research team at various times included such distinguished individuals as Martin Gilbert, Alan Brien, Michael Molian, Ivan Yates, Martin Maunther, Frank Gannon, Tom Hartman and Andrew Kerr. On occasion, one or other would give in their notice, exasperated at working for Randolph or offended by one of his tantrums. But most relented before reaching Manningtree railway station or after sleeping on it over a long weekend. Certainly I never met one who regretted their involvement with Randolph or their labours on the Great Biography.

In addition to ploughing through and reducing to coherent order the massive quantity of documents in the strongroom at Stour, they mounted raiding expeditions to the Royal Archives at Windsor, the Public Record

Office in Chancery Lane and the Beaverbrook, Asquith and Lloyd George Archives, as well as those housed in the muniment rooms of stately homes up and down the country or in the Library of Congress and other collections in America.

I have a vivid recollection of one such raiding expedition in which I became engaged with my father and Michael Wolff while still an undergraduate at Oxford. The object of the exercise was to carry away letters from Winston and his parents, Lord Randolph and Jennie, reposing in the muniment room in the basement at Blenheim Palace where, allegedly, they were suffering from damp. Our cousin, Bert Marlborough, the 10th Duke, invited us to dine and stay the night at the magnificent palace set in its stately park beside the village of Woodstock in the rolling Oxfordshire countryside. It had been the gift of Queen Anne to John Churchill, whom she created 1st Duke, on behalf of a grateful nation, for the splendid victory of Blenheim – in stark contrast to the treatment meted out two-and-half centuries later to Marlborough's descendant who, after saving the world from Hitler, was given the order of the boot by the British electorate and forced to sell his beloved Chartwell to stave off bankruptcy.

After being affably received by the duke, we were shown to our rooms, where our bags had already been unpacked. We were only four for dinner, including our host, so we ate off a table set up in the smoking-room, which for many years had been used as a drawing-room. No sooner had we embarked on the first course than Bert instructed his butler, Mr Wadman, a tall, distinguished-looking man in a tailcoat, to move the television closer to the table and turn it on. My father, sensing that this was a deliberate ploy to impede conversation, or at least to put a break on any Randolphian monologue, took umbrage and asked for the television to be switched off. When Bert refused, my father exploded: 'Television is for the lower orders – not for dukes!' Intransigently, Bert proceeded to instruct Wadman to turn up the volume on the television. Thereupon my father asked him if he would have one of his footmen pack our bags. 'Certainly not!' exclaimed the duke. 'You can pack your own bloody bags!'

Thus we beat an unceremonious retreat from Blenheim Palace and headed for Oxford, where we put up for the night in the appropriately named Randolph Hotel. When, a few weeks later, Michael Wolff returned on his own to Blenheim, without Churchillian or even ducal encumbrance, he had no difficulty in completing his assigned task of carrying off all the papers relevant to the Churchill biography.

Randolph would make light of such incidents, joking to his friends that he was 'not fit to be allowed out in private' but, tragically, through his heavy drinking he was not only making impossible the fulfilment of his ambition to complete the Great Biography but also losing many of his friends. He even fell out with his close friend from Oxford days, Pam Berry, the daughter of his godfather F. E. Smith. I have to this day a photograph of the two of them aged twenty, looking lovingly at each other, with the inscription: 'To the Boy Orator from the Child Vamp!' The photograph always stood on the mantelpiece at Stour. But, following a report in the *Evening Standard* of a charity function she had organised, in which Randolph had gratuitously insulted her by reporting that she had 'omitted to shave her upper-lip', Pam considered their friendship at an end. When Randolph later called on her with a Christmas present, no doubt intended as a peace-offering, he found, to his amazement, that the door was shut in his face, for reasons that Pam explained:

3 January 1961

... I understand you think it unreasonable of me not to want to see you. As you know I used to be very fond of you. But the simple fact is that after a sufficient number of wounds and injuries have been inflicted, indeed repeated, with monotonous regularity, over the years scars are produced which cannot be assuaged by a few words at a wedding reception or by a personal visit at Christmas.

I am so made that if someone is my friend I remain in most cases entirely and uncritically devoted to them for all time. But in the event (happily rare) of finding myself the recipient of a series of knife-thrusts from the said friend my affection simply withers on the vine and that's that. In its place there's nothing left but hurt.

In such conditions I am sure you can see it's easier for me to have a no-relationship with you than a semi-relationship? The latter could only be artificial and forced on my part.

Believe me I feel no ill will to you and hope you will prosper in anything you do. On our old days of companionship and fun I look back with regret and sadness. But it wasn't I that put an end to them.

Fortunately for Randolph there were other friends to whom he was devoted, and who remained devoted to him. One of them was John Betjeman, of whose work Randolph was a fervent admirer, knowing many of his poems by heart. Indeed Betjeman credited Randolph's enthusiasm in their undergraduate days for giving him the courage to persevere with his poetry. At luncheon or dinner parties Randolph would encourage the embarrassed young poet to recite his latest offerings. As Betjeman recalled: 'He used to ask for special favourites and then listen with his eyes wide open, and laughter in his face, and lead the applause at the end. It was through him that I gained self-confidence.' It was also thanks to Randolph, who persuaded their wealthy friend Edward James to fund the venture, that Bentjeman's poems were first published. When, later in life, Randolph wrote asking Betjeman to sign a limited edition of his latest work, *Summond by Bells*, he replied enthusiastically:

30 January 1961

Dear Randolph,
    Of course I'll sign it, old top. As my oldest and loyalist poetical supporter I should have made sure that you had one right at the beginning. I'd very much like to see the file you mention. Bung it along here, old boy. I look forward to a return to Country Bumpkin, Ltd. and to see how your landscape garden progresses. I go to Belfast quite soon so it will have to be when the primroses send their shy blossoms through the Suffolk earth.
                                                    Your equally affectionate
                                                                    John B

    Another friend who stayed the course was John Sutro, a contemporary of Evelyn Waugh's at Oxford, who recorded in Kay Halle's *The Young Unpretender*:

    Finally, let me mention an incidence of Randolph's magnanimity. There was a plan to start a magazine on the lines of *Time* magazine [to be called *Topic*], and the suggestion was made that Randolph should become its editor – an admirable idea, for he was a first-rate journalist and had the gift of inspiring others. I was to join the editorial board, and out of the blue on the telephone Mr Onassis offered to put up a substantial sum of money to join the other sponsors in launching the magazine. We spent the weekend planning and had many good ideas – the position would have been the salvation of Randolph and occupied his eager and creative mind. Then, at the last moment, when all seemed settled, some enemy of Randolph, or someone whom he had offended – we never knew who – torpedoed the whole plan and he was excluded. Instead of being angry and vindictive Randolph behaved with dignity in spite of the crushing disappointment, 'I wish them the best of luck,' he said. It only remains to say that after a few months the magazine failed completely and a very large sum of money was lost. Randolph would have made the magazine a success – it was a shame.

In Randolph courage, loyalty, wit and gaiety were mingled with a certain intransigence, sometimes too fiercely expressed. He was, none the less, always honest and sincere, and I am proud to have been his friend.

Randolph had no idea how unpleasant and offensive he could be when he was drunk. By the time that he was sober he had largely forgotten, or become oblivious to, what had passed. When in good form, he could be the best of companions, a brilliant conversationalist, bubbling with wit and panache. A dinner hostess could be assured that, whatever else might happen, the evening would not be dull if Randolph was among her guests and, in a crisis, there was no friend more loyal. That said, there was a limit to what even his friends could accept of the other side of his character.

The mainstays of Randolph's secretarial staff were Eileen Harryman, who was appointed archivist, and Barbara Twigg, a bright young girl just out of secretarial college who joined the team in May 1963 and was to remain with Randolph until his death. Utterly loyal and infinitely adaptable, her remit went far wider than private secretary. Randolph, as might be surmised, had trouble keeping staff, but Barbara Twigg would be there to step into the breach, equally at ease whether cooking a meal, taking dictation at 2.00 a.m., packing Randolph's suitcase or coping with the dogs' indiscretions, and managing to smile through it all.

Unable to retain resident domestic staff, due to the demands that he would place upon them, Randolph came to rely heavily on a stalwart team of dailies from the village: Mrs Sexton, who invariably applied too much rouge but was a passable cook; Mrs Gunn, of gypsy origin who insisted on being known as a 'travelling lady'; and Mrs Hiersum, a small but spirited seventy-year-old. Meanwhile, the jovial Mr Mark, assisted by two under-gardeners and an amiable 'loony' from the local asylum, kept in order the extensive grounds including the large kitchen garden. Randolph took the closest interest in his garden, supervising the layout and forever ordering new varieties of specimen trees and flowering shrubs. Although this enthusiasm did not extend to getting his hands dirty, on one occasion, shortly before the arrival at Stour of Loelia, Duchess of Westminster, he did condescend to dead-head the Duchess Loelia roses – possibly because his greenhorn assistant, Martin Gilbert, had no previous experience of dead-heading roses.

This entire team – the 'young gentlemen' researchers, the secretariat and the domestic and garden staff – Randolph proceeded to claim as tax-deductible in his tax return to the Inland Revenue. This proved too much for the lady tax inspector in Ipswich, who refused to accept that the four gardeners were a legitimate 'business' expense. Randolph decided to contest the matter and went off to do battle with 'the moustachioed bitch of Ipswich', as he unchivalrously dubbed her, before the local Tax Commissioners who, being lay persons, were not instinctively sympathetic to the Revenue. He proceeded to argue that what was sauce for the corporate goose, should also be the perquisite of the individual gander: just as Shell or ICI were allowed to set against their tax liabilities the cost of landscaping and maintaining gardens in front of their offices, so, by the same token, since he was running a literary factory, Randolph asserted, he should be entitled to make comparable deductions. Sensing that the Commissioners were inclining to accept Randolph's arguments on this point, the inspector moved on to query some of his other expense claims, especially in respect of overseas travel, including one or two trips from which no press articles had resulted. Randolph countered this by saying that if a large corporation sent a representative to Latin America, for example, without any specific deal being secured, they would none the less be able to claim the cost of the journey for tax purposes, a point that seemed perfectly fair to the Commissioners.

Exasperated, the inspector produced what she believed to be the clincher, dramatically brandishing a bill from a strip joint that rejoiced in the name of 'Churchill's'. 'Is that not a night-club?' she demanded in a shocked tone. 'Yes, indeed,' countered Randolph, 'and from time to time I entertain foreign guests there, though it is not an establishment in which my family has any financial interest!' By this time, the Commissioners, who were enjoying the proceedings hugely, were thoroughly on Randolph's side and he went on to win his case.

On returning from a brief visit to the United States to report the Democratic and Republican conventions in Los Angeles and Chicago respectively, Randolph found that, in his absence, Harold Macmillan had shuffled the Cabinet. In the *News of the World* on 31 July he recorded both his delight at the promotion of his two brothers-in-law, Duncan Sandys and Christopher Soames, and his displeasure that Lord Home should have been appointed Foreign Secretary:

Well, it's lovely to be back again with my roses and dahlias and to discover that I now have two brothers-in-law in the Cabinet. It would be idle to pretend that I am happy about Lord Home's appointment to the Foreign Office. Like Mr R. A. Butler who fortunately stays where he is [at the Home Office], he was a man of Munich as Parliamentary Private Secretary . . . to the late Neville Chamberlain. As my readers know I am a tremendous Macmillan fan. I could never have supposed he would commit such an act of political indecency . . .

Having made his public declaration of war, Randolph proceeded to write to the new Foreign Secretary stating that his selection was intolerable and that he intended to denounce it in his next column. Despite this, Alec Home invited my father to join him for luncheon at the Ritz Hotel so that, as he elegantly put it, 'Randolph could confirm his impressions and improve his copy.'

The piece that appeared was very different. Randolph had allowed himself to be bowled over by Alec's charm and frankness, helped no doubt by the quality of the wines. Alec told him: 'The lesson I learned from Munich was that one must be in a position to talk to a dictator or would-be aggressor from strength. We shall not surrender to aggression while I am at the Foreign Office.' Randolph, never too proud to admit a mistake, declared: 'I came away from the Foreign Office vastly reassured about the qualities and character of our new Foreign Secretary. He is a brave and honourable man and I have confidence that he will be unrelenting in his care for British interests . . .'

In November Randolph returned to the United States to cover the US election, having already in July interviewed the two successful candidates, Senator John F. Kennedy and Vice-President Richard Nixon. While he had formed a high opinion of both, he had evidently come under the spell of Jack Kennedy's captivating charm, making reference in his subsequent report to Kennedy's 'guts, charm, intelligence and political horse-sense . . .' While most pundits were hedging their bets and declaring that the outcome was too close to call, Randolph, who had had a world scoop with his prediction of Macmillan's victory three years earlier, had no such reservations. Sticking his neck out, he ended his report for the *News of the World* of 6 November:

Usually in the Gallup Poll there are 11 per cent who say they 'Don't know'. Dr Gallup has recently joined this minority and has explained that he has not got a clue himself. I am not sure that I know the answer, but I will be braver than the doctor. I think Kennedy will be the next President of the United States.

Randolph had a personal stake in the Kennedy victory as, some seven weeks before, he had bet Herbert Nelson, a New Yorker whom he had met aboard the *Queen Elizabeth*, $400 against $600 that Kennedy would win the presidential election. In a letter of condolence to Richard Nixon, he wrote: 'I greatly admired the manful and effective way in which you fought. I, on a tiny scale, have had several election defeats. I admired more than I can say the courageous and dignified way in which you accepted yours, and the tears which your wife so heroically held back at 3.30 on Wednesday morning were coursing down my cheeks as I watched on television your necessarily qualified concession of defeat . . .'

Nixon replied:

19 December 1960

Pat and I want you to know how very much we appreciated the letter which you sent us after the election.

A message of congratulations after winning an election is of course always appreciated although not unexpected. But nothing could have meant more to us than to receive such a warm and thoughtful message after losing.

In the years ahead as we look back to 1960, the disappointment of losing the closest election in history will fade into the background. But your act of thoughtfulness will always remain close to our hearts.

Early in the new year of 1961, the editor of the *News of the World*, Stafford Somerfield, refused to publish one of Randolph's articles which the paper's legal adviser judged to be libellous. This provoked a furious telegram from Randolph who could not abide having his articles 'messed about' by editors:

FREEDOM OF THE PRESS DOES NOT MEAN FREEDOM FOR PRO-PRIETORS OR EDITORS TO SUPPRESS THE TRUTH AS WRITTEN FOR THEM BY THEIR GIFTED CORRESPONDENTS PLEASE REFLECT ON THIS REGARDS RANDOLPH

To this ringing declaration of press freedom, Somerfield replied with mock humility:

IT IS NOT GIVEN TO US ALL TO BE GIFTED. SOME OF US WITH WHATEVER JUDGMENT WE MAY POSSESS CAN ONLY ACT AS WE

'The club seems strangely quiet with Randolph sub judice.'
Daily Express, 25 October 1960

THINK BEST. THANK YOU FOR YOUR REGARDS WHICH I VALUE.
AS EVER = STAFFORD

Although Randolph had a close personal knowledge of the law of
defamation and felt that he was the better judge of what was, or was not,
libellous and of how far he could afford to 'trail his coat', his judgment
was by no means infallible. When, on 11 June 1961, the *News of the
World* published an article by Randolph referring to the political editor
of the *Daily Express*, Douglas Clark, as a 'hack' whose opinions were
dictated for him by his employers, Clark sued for libel. Randolph, in his
depositions for the defence, tried to argue that:

All employees of the Beaverbrook Press, with very few exceptions, are hacks. *Vide* Lord Beaverbrook's testimony before the Royal Commission on the Press. Two or three years ago Hugh Gaitskell was entertained at a Lobby luncheon and made an amusing speech in which he divided the various Lobby correspondents into a number of categories. One category he said were the hacks. 'Chief among the hacks,' said Gaitskell, 'was Mr Douglas Clark.'

Despite a spirited defence entered by Randolph the case, which ran on for more than a year, was eventually settled out of court at considerable cost to his employers and to his own pride, but not before he was made to eat humble pie by Somerfield, who insisted on receiving Randolph's request in writing before his costs would be met:

23 October 1962

PERSONAL

Dear Somerfield,

    I would be obliged if the *News of the World* would pay my damages and costs in the matter of Douglas Clark. I am sorry that the article I wrote has caused all this bother particularly as you were so enthusiastic about it at the time.

Yours sincerely,
Randolph S. Churchill

As a teenager I could never understand why what were quaintly termed 'debts of honour' (such as those run up at the gambling table) should take precedence over all others. My father clung to the notion of a bygone era that 'Gentlemen live by credit'. While that may have been in order with tailors, wine merchants or establishments such as Fortnum & Mason, so long as they were prepared to stand the racket, I found it mortifying in the extreme when from time to time, a desultory queue of local shopkeepers from the village formed at my father's door, seeking payment of long overdue accounts. The local publican was never among them. He was smart enough to insist on cash for all purchases of cigarettes and whisky. As a last resort my father would arrange to visit his London bankers, Coutts & Co. in Old Park Lane, where the manager would invariably be formally attired in a black frock-coat. Once, when the circumstances were dire and he urgently needed his overdraft limit to be increased, he too dressed up in his frock-coat so as not to be at a disadvantage. His ultimate threat, as he saw it, was the removal to another establishment of his already large overdraft, on which the bank was raking in interest at an extortionate rate.

Mercifully for Randolph and the retailers of East Bergholt, his days of living from hand to mouth were now behind him. Thanks to the provision made for him by his father through the Chartwell Trust, which had successfully negotiated the sale of the Great Biography to various publishers worldwide, for the first time in his life Randolph had an assured income. On learning from his mother, who was chairman of the Chartwell Trust, of the arrangements that had been made, he hastened to write to her:

3 July 1961

Thank you very much for your letter of 1 July, enclosing the memorandum about the Chartwell Trust. It is the hardest thing in the world to say 'Thank you' in a graceful & acceptable fashion. But I think that both you and Papa know how abidingly grateful I am to you both that I can sit on my lovely terrace at Stour and do my work in such exceptionally attractive surroundings. The memorandum about the Chartwell Trust shows how well you & your fellow trustees have guided & guarded the interests of your children & grand-children. Bless you. Please tell Papa that not a day goes by without my thinking of him as the saviour of our country & the founder of all the family's fortunes.

That summer, my grandfather invited me to spend ten days with him in Monte Carlo where, thanks to the generosity of his friend Aristotle Onassis, he was installed in circumstances of considerable splendour in the penthouse of the Hôtel de Paris. From there I reported to my father:

1 September 1961

I've been having a wonderful time here – water-skiing & diving underwater with an 'aqualung'. Grandpapa is in very good form and insisting on going to the casino – we both lost the other evening. Ari who has been here has now left for London & Greece. Miss Garbo came to dinner the night before last & earlier this week we dined with the Lord [Beaverbrook] and Lady D. [the widow of Sir Philip Dunn, whom Beaverbrook was later to marry] ...

Much looking forward to S. America!

As part of the sales of the foreign rights of the biography, Randolph had been invited to Argentina by his publishers in Buenos Aires, who had recently acquired the Latin American rights and who had sent him two first-class tickets. My father very generously invited me, *faute de mieux*, to join him – an invitation I accepted with alacrity. However, he was insistent that we flew in separate aeroplanes – not an easy matter at a time when there were no more than one or two flights per week to Latin American destinations. Like my grandfather, he was a great dynast. Conscious of the fact that we were both only sons and recalling that none of the great Duke of Marlborough's male heirs had survived to marriageable age, he had long made it a rule that we should never fly together. For some strange reason the logic of his argument did not extend to travel by motor car which, with him at the wheel, was infinitely more hazardous, especially given his inability to drive even the sixty miles from London to East Bergholt without stopping at least once at a pub to 'fill up'.

Accordingly, I flew out ahead of my father to spend three days with friends in Rio de Janeiro, before joining him in Argentina. There, in addition to a few days in Buenos Aires where we visited his publishers, we spent a weekend at a magnificent *estancia* or cattle-ranch called La Concepción. But the high point of the trip was, undoubtedly, our visit to Peru. After being lavishly fêted by our Ambassador in Lima, Sir Berkeley Gage, we flew to Cuzco, the ancient Inca capital in the heart of the Andes – for once breaking our rule of not flying together, as there was no alternative flight available. The flight, in an unpressurised DC-4 aircraft of Fawcett Airlines, left at dawn and, though we flew at 20,000 feet sucking oxygen from individual plastic tubes, the snow-covered peaks of the Andes towered spectacularly above us to 22,000 feet or more.

On landing at Cuzco, which stands nearly 12,000 feet above sea level, we discovered that the departure of the daily train to Machu Picchu, the Lost City of the Incas, was craftily synchronised by the locals to ensure that it left shortly before the once-daily flight from Lima was due to land, requiring visitors to night-stop in Cuzco whether they liked it or not. My father managed to discover that, for a reasonable sum, we could charter our own diesel-propelled railcar. However his lungs, already badly damaged by his immoderate consumption of cigarettes, could not cope with the 12,000-foot altitude so we were forced to delay our departure by two or three hours and to find a hotel room where he could lie down to catch his breath.

From Cuzco, where the ancient Incas had their Sun Temple in which, reputedly, human sacrifices had on occasion been offered, we embarked on the most exciting railway journey either of us had ever made. Our private British-made railcar climbed laboriously for a few miles up the mountainside to a 13,000-foot pass which stands at the Grand Divide of the Andes, at which point every stream and river flowed west to the Pacific, while ahead of us to the east lay the headwaters of the mighty Amazon, which wound its way through 4,000 miles of jungle and rain forest to the Atlantic. On reaching the summit of the pass, the driver switched off the diesel engine and we proceeded to coast downhill at a steady 30–35 m.p.h., in complete silence apart from the rhythmic 'clickety-clack' of the wheels on the rail-joints. At first the country before us was a broad plain of fertile grasslands such as one finds in the Basque country around Pamplona in northern Spain. But soon the single track plunged more steeply, requiring the driver to apply the brake as we entered the narrow valley of the Urubamba River, which had carved its path out of the rock over the centuries. At this point the dry savannah of the plain rapidly gave way to a lusher, greener and ever more tropical scenery as we found ourselves hemmed in on all sides by dark towering mountains.

After a journey of some five or six hours, we reached our destination, a tiny station deep in the valley beside an already wide and swiftly flowing river. High on the hillside above us stood the amazingly well-preserved ruins of Machu Picchu, to which the Incas had retreated in the fifteenth century in the face of the Spanish Conquistadors. These remarkable and extensive ruins, made out of hand-carved stone and fitted together without the use of any mortar, had remained undiscovered until the beginning of the twentieth century, surrounded by the high, forbidding rock-faces of the Andes which, for centuries, had kept sacred the secret hideaway of the Incas.

From Peru I flew on to New York to celebrate my twenty-first birthday with my mother and her new husband, Leland Hayward, before returning to Oxford to resume my final-year studies. My father, meanwhile, travelled on by way of Mexico City to Los Angeles, where he had been invited by the Hollywood movie mogul, Otto Preminger, to visit the movie set at Columbia Studios where the film of Allen Drury's *Advise and Consent* was being produced. There, at a dinner party at Romanoff's restaurant, a favourite watering-hole of the Hollywood set, Randolph disgraced himself by becoming atrociously drunk and abusive. The *Los Angeles Mirror* the next day gave prominence to the story on its front page under the headline, 'Churchill's Son Irks Film Party':

A re-enactment of the Boston Tea Party – with libations stronger than tea – occurred Tuesday night at Romanoff's restaurant in Beverly Hills.

Not a drop of liquid was lost, but Randolph Churchill, garrulous journalistic son of Winston Churchill, was deserted at a party table by a group of Hollywood guests and a napkin was hurled in his face.

Mrs Billy Wilder, wife of the director, admitted today she was the one who threw the linen at Churchill. The guests included the Wilders, Charles Laughton and Elsa Lanchester, director-producer Otto Preminger and I. A. R. Diamond, writer. While Mrs Wilder felt free to discuss the incident this morning, the irate Churchill slammed the door in my face and said, 'I don't want to talk to anyone.'

Mrs Wilder said Churchill, whom she claimed had indulged in some forthright drinking, 'was tossing insults around all evening.' 'It wasn't only what he said but his manner and tone,' she complained. 'He turned to me once and remarked nastily, "Oh, your hyena laughter!" I laughed again, but I was very angry. Billy couldn't hear what Churchill was saying but he knew something was wrong and got up and said, "Let's go." Then I tossed my napkin in his face. The others at the party left with us.

'Young Churchill is a colossal bore and I feel sorry for his father.' Mrs Wilder said Preminger, who had never met Churchill before, 'was a bit stunned by it all . . .'

That same day Preminger left Randolph in no doubt of the offence he had caused:

18 October 1961

Last night your condition and my desire to avoid more scandal prevented me from making the situation clear to you. I hope this morning will find you sober enough to realise that your behaviour was quite unforgivable. You insulted without provocation my very good friend Mrs Wilder and, with your incredible rudeness, spoiled the evening for my wife and our dinner guests.

Naturally I expect you to cancel any further visits to my set.

Please notify my office of your intended departure date so that they can make the necessary arrangements.

Randolph refused to apologise but, a week after the dinner, riposted with an account to United Press International of an earlier meeting with Preminger. The story appeared in *The Stars and Stripes* of 24 October:

'I am a singularly articulate human being,' said Randolph Churchill, son of Sir Winston Churchill. 'You do not spik Eenglish. You spik British,' said Otto Preminger, son of Mark Preminger, an Austrian District Attorney. 'I can express myself better than being misquoted by your rawther worse English,' Churchill retorted. 'Really, my good man, you do not make yourself clear.'

'Vot? You tink I haff an axsent?' Preminger demanded. 'Of course you have an accent,' Churchill replied airily. The men were sitting across from one another in a Hollywood restaurant arguing the merits (and demerits) of Preminger's new movie, *Advise and Consent*. Sitting in on the meeting was Allen Drury, author of the bestseller. 'You have completely ruined a great work of art,' Churchill went on. 'Your script of the book is quite terrible, you know. You have sold your artistic talents to comply with the lowest intelligence.'

'May I please get a vord in now, iff you pleese,' Otto said, forcing a smile. 'I von't be a party to anything that puts President Roosevelt in a bad light. Vot are you now, a movie critic?' 'I'm a critic of politics,' Churchill answered firmly ... 'When you took this splendid book to transform it into a script you should have used a physician's scalpel instead of a meat ax [*sic*].' Preminger, a bombastic soul in his own right, was clearly at a loss. He pounded the palm of his hand against his bald head and explained: 'See vot you haff done. In vun you right off my movie, you criticise this government und you have something unkind to say about my axsent. How could you?' 'I was just offering my advice without your consent,' Churchill said, enjoying his play on words. 'I don't mind takink advice,' Preminger said unhappily, 'but I also don't use it.'

Preminger to Drury – who incidentally is suing Otto over release date of the picture – trying to explain Churchill's presence in Hollywood: 'Ve met 30 years ago in Vienna,' he said, 'I was vorking and he vas visiting. It is the same thing now. He is visiting and I am vorking. He asked to zee my script, zo I gave him vun. Now, bleef me, I am sorry.'

'Speaking of the dreadful script,' Churchill said as Otto winced, 'why do you have the Senator cut his throat instead of shooting himself as he does in the book?' 'I haff my reasons,' Otto replied. 'It is quieter and less messy. It chust fits into the movie better.' 'Rubbish,' said Churchill. 'A knife is quite messy. The only sure way is to jump off a high building.' 'I'll chump right after lunch if I can find a building that high in Hollywood,' Preminger said moodily.

By the time he reached Washington, however, Randolph was on his best behaviour for meetings with the Secretary of State, Dean Rusk, and

Defense Secretary, Robert McNamara, as well as with President Kennedy. He was particularly impressed by the 45-year-old McNamara, previously chief executive of the Ford Motor Company, who confirmed that Polaris – the submarine-launched ballistic-missile system which was to be the mainstay of Britain's nuclear deterrent – was 'invulnerable'. Thereafter, when either my father or I visited Washington, we would invariably call upon McNamara in his vast office at the Pentagon to be assured that, despite advances in underwater acoustics and the launching of orbiting satellites, the deterrent remained 'invulnerable'.

Randolph's visit to Washington coincided with the Berlin crisis, caused by the Kremlin's decision to erect the infamous wall that divided Berlin. The *World Press News & Advertiser's Review* of 3 November reported, under the headline 'Randolph's Scoop':

Last Sunday the *News of the World* justified its claim to seriousness by publishing an important exclusive by Randolph Churchill, who had been strangely tame for months. This – while Russian and American tanks stood threateningly face to face in Berlin! – was a Churchill interview in the Pentagon where Robert McNamara, the American Secretary of Defence, had said: 'Please, Mr Churchill, make no mistake about this. I am preparing to fight a nuclear war. It would be crazy to spend all this money' – he has increased his country's defence expenditure by two billion pounds in eight months! – 'as a bluff. If we are attacked, we shall strike. We have three or four times as much stuff as the Russians have. Even if they make a sneak attack, it would be in our power to destroy Russia. And we shall, if they attack us.'

As he left the Pentagon, Randolph recorded: 'The most pregnant thought which Mr McNamara left in my mind was this: "We have the tackle. Some doubt our will to use it. I don't." Nor do I.' Heedless of these pressures, Kennedy, whose election Randolph had tipped on the eve of poll a year earlier, was in a relaxed mood when he received him in the Oval Office, putting his feet up on his desk while they chatted away about the critical situation in Berlin, America's budding involvement in Vietnam and Anglo-American relations. Despite Randolph's strong antipathy to Kennedy's father – 'Wicked Papa Joe' as he called Joseph Kennedy who had been Ambassador in London at the outbreak of war and had predicted Britain's defeat – he was completely won over by Jack Kennedy's charm and, later, by Bobby's.

On the occasion of Winston's eighty-seventh birthday at the end of the month, it was reported in the press that he was the sole surviving officer of the 21st Lancers' famous charge at the Battle of Omdurman in 1898 – one of the last great cavalry charges of history. In proposing the toast at a family dinner party at 28 Hyde Park Gate to mark the occasion, Randolph declared:

> Of Winston Churchill it may be said, as it was said of Washington and could have been said of only one other Englishman, Chatham: 'First in war, first in peace and first in the hearts of his fellow countrymen.'
>
> But here tonight we are not met around Mama's elegant and sumptuous board to sing the praises of the Winston Churchill who saved the world. This is a family celebration. We who are here are the kith and kin and friends who have lived their lives with my father and mother ... We can testify with gratitude how he has brought honour and security to his own family no less than to the nation and the world. The toast is: 'Papa!'

CHAPTER 29

Private Eye: An Apology

O n 28 May 1962 Randolph celebrated his fifty-first birthday, an
event that provoked a reflective letter to his father:

Immersed as I am in the study of your wonderful and fascinating life, I fell
to speculating this morning while walking round my garden on my fifty-
first birthday of what you had accomplished by the time you had reached
my present age. It is extraordinary to realise that you had been Chancellor
of the Exchequer for about a year; that you had already lived several lives;
that you had served in six wars and campaigns; that you had written nine
successful books and were, on your fifty-first birthday, while Chancellor
of the Exchequer, working on Volume 3 of *The World Crisis*. You had
been Under-Secretary of State for the Colonies, President of the Board of
Trade, Home Secretary, First Lord of the Admiralty, Minister of Munitions,
Secretary of State for War and Air and Secretary of State for the Colonies.

It is a sobering thought for me, but an encouraging one, that on
your fifty-first birthday very much less than half your life's work was
accomplished. For this I 'take heart of grace' (from one of your favourite
operettas, *The Pirates of Penzance*) and derive many encouraging thoughts
for the future of my son Winston who is only twenty-one and who flew
over today from Oxford for my birthday luncheon.

We both salute you, the author of our being.

Work was now well in hand at Stour, with Randolph and his powerful
team of 'young gentlemen' researchers making advances across a broad
front, unravelling the early part of his father's life. The midnight oil
burned until the early hours throughout the house, as the team continued
their labours under Randolph's vigilant eye and with his frequent promp-
tings to 'Box on!' Indeed, according to Michael Wolff, 'Box on!' became
the team's motto.

Randolph had been thrilled beyond measure when his father, as a
mark of favour, gave him the narrow upright desk which had once been
the property of Benjamin Disraeli at his country home of Hughenden

and which had been given to his father, Lord Randolph, in the 1930s by an admirer. He wrote to his parents on 28 August:

> I so much enjoyed lunching with you both last Thursday at Hyde Park Gate. It was exciting to see Papa looking so well after his vexatious time in hospital. [Winston had broken his thigh in a fall two months before.] I drove Papa's and Disraeli's desk safely back to Stour, where it is happily installed in my library. It is very much admired by those friends and neighbours who have visited me in the last few days.
>
> The desk is my greatest treasure; it will inspire me to write an even better life of Papa than I had been planning. Bless you both.

Readings-aloud from the Disraeli desk became a central feature of life at Stour. In the early hours, in the drawing-room where the air was heavy with smoke from Randolph's chain-smoking and from the blazing log fire, the 'young gentlemen' would share with the assembled company of guests the latest fruits of their researches – their 'lovely grub', as Randolph termed it. Any whose eyelids were becoming heavy or who might be minded to slink off to bed, would be encouraged with a fortissimo rendition of one of Randolph's favourite quotations from Longfellow:

> The heights by great men reached and kept,
> Were not attained by sudden flight,
> But they, while their companions slept,
> Were toiling upward in the night!

While alternately encouraging, berating, directing or prodding his gifted team, Randolph himself would be hard at work producing his 'purple passages' for inclusion at appropriate places in the text, drawn from his incomparable knowledge and understanding, gained at his father's knee, of the ancestors, relations, political allies and foes of yore, all of whom were lining up in the wings preparing to play their part in the Great Biography.

Despite the devotion with which he laboured at this task, Randolph remained at heart a political and polemical journalist who was never so happy as when he was reporting from where the action was, be it party conferences, conventions or elections on either side of the Atlantic. He continued to keep up a regular flow of contributions to the press and managed to become involved in various libellous skirmishes.

That year, the Stour research team was strengthened by the arrival of

Martin Gilbert, a bright young history don from Merton College, Oxford. Martin had been recommended to Randolph by Diana Cooper, whose husband Duff had resigned from Neville Chamberlain's Government in October 1938 over Munich and whose papers he had asked to see with a view to a sequel to his first book, *The Appeasers*. Diana had written: 'Darling Randy, Here is Martin Gilbert, an interesting researching historian young man, who loves Duff and hates the Coroner [Neville Chamberlain]. He is full of zeal to set history right. Do see him.' Martin Gilbert, in his book *In Search of Churchill*, recounts:

Randolph sent me a letter inviting me to his home in Suffolk. 'I am nearly always here,' he wrote. But I was extremely reluctant to take up his offer to visit him. I had once seen him at the bar of the Randolph Hotel in Oxford, apparently drunk and certainly loud-mouthed. I had heard stories of his extreme right-wing attitudes, bordering, it was said, on the Fascist. I was busy with my new book, had many other people to see ... Having spent a pleasant afternoon with Arnold Toynbee ... I saw no particular point in having what might prove to be an unpleasant evening with Randolph Churchill. 'He'll just shout and scream at you,' one friend told me. I had no reason to disagree.

The day came when I succumbed to Randolph's third or fourth telegram asking me when I was going to visit him. It was in March 1962. I travelled by train from Oxford to London, crossed London from Paddington to Liverpool Street, and took the train to Manningtree ... It was a journey that I was to make many times, but I shall never forget the first venture into the unknown. I was very nervous and, as the train pulled out of Colchester, the last station before Manningtree, I wondered if I were doing the right thing...

Gilbert recalls his first impressions of Randolph on arrival at Stour:

There was Randolph, in a deep armchair, out of which he rose slowly: a large, rather cumbersome man, with a somewhat pasty, battered-looking face, ill-fitting trousers which he hitched up even as he was rising from his chair, and the look of an elderly patriarch (he was my age as I write these words). The effect of this slightly alarming appearance was quickly dispelled: he was full of charm, had an engaging twinkle in his eye, and expressed his appreciation that I had made the long journey from Oxford: 'It was kind of you to come.'

It was well after 2.00 a.m. before Randolph allowed his guest to retire for the night. The next morning, while Martin was having breakfast before catching his train back to Oxford, Randolph appeared in his dressing-gown:

> He was all smiles and asked me if we could have a talk. He walked out on to the terrace, his dressing-gown blowing open in the wind, his slippers shuffling on the flagstones. As we walked up and down, he explained that six months earlier he had been asked by his father to write a four-volume biography based on his father's private papers. These papers were even then being brought to Stour, and three researchers were working on them. He wanted a fourth person to help. Would I be willing to join his team? I was quite thrown by this, and asked if I could think it over. He agreed, and said he would wait to hear from me . . .
>
> I hesitated. Some of my friends warned me that working for Randolph would be a dead-end. Many new universities beckoned in those years, their history departments calling out for young graduates. To work for Randolph would be to put oneself outside the academic world, to appear to be lacking in seriousness. The very subject of Churchill, let alone Randolph's reputation as a buffoon, would mean an end to all sorts of possibilities. Other friends thought differently. Here was a chance to work on a major archive, to study Churchill's personal and political papers, to get a glimpse of the closed world of a large private collection. I could work there for a year, then return to academic life with enviable knowledge . . .
>
> More telegrams came from Randolph, saying that he hoped I would come to work for him. Suddenly I panicked. Was this an absurd thing to do, to move out of the Oxford cocoon to which I had for so long aspired and in which I was just beginning to flourish? I went to see the Warden of St Anthony's, Bill Deakin, who had been Winston Churchill's literary assistant from 1936 to 1940 and again from 1945 to 1955. Bill knew Randolph well and encouraged me to try. The whole thing could not possibly last more than six months, he said, a year at the most. But it would be an experience . . . I wrote to Randolph, accepting his offer.

Thus began Martin Gilbert's co-operation with my father, which was to prove so fruitful and beneficial to them both.

Soon after his arrival, Martin was despatched on visits to many of the stately homes of England and Scotland where, not infrequently, his hosts, oblivious of the treasures contained in their family archives, would gaily say: 'Take away anything you like!' It was not long before Randolph dubbed Martin his 'Tiger for Research', a billing which, over the decades, he has fully lived up to.

After Martin had been on the team for several years, Randolph, referring to Barbara Twigg, the mainstay of his secretarial staff who arrived at Stour in 1963, as someone who would go on to 'the bitter end', added: 'I hope, dear boy, you will be a "bitter ender?"' None could have served my father better, above all by carrying forward the biography to its triumphant conclusion with zealous research and a faithful regard for the truth which, Randolph once told him, was 'The only thing that interests me.' Nearly thirty-five years after their first meeting, having completed the main work, together with a single-volume version, Martin Gilbert, recently knighted, still labours to conclude the final companion volumes of documents, for which space could not be found in the main work.

In the Autumn of 1962 Randolph, for once, decided not to attend the various party conferences, choosing instead to watch them on television. This prompted the following exchange via the telegraphic service – which in those days was in efficient working order and much used from Stour – between Randolph and the Conservative Party Chairman, Iain Macleod at the seaside resort of Llandudno in North Wales on 10 October:

12 noon
RT HON IAIN MACLEOD
URGENTLY RECOMMEND ALTERATION OF PLATFORM SEATING. BEHIND CHANCELLOR ON ONE SIDE WAS VERY PUZZLED LOOKING WOMAN ON OTHER WISE MAN WITH MARKED RESEM-BLANCE TO DOCTOR GOEBBELS.
WARMEST REGARDS = RANDOLPH

12.15 p.m.
RT HON IAIN MACLEOD
FURTHER – STRAIGHT BEHIND CHANCELLOR REINCARNATION OF HITLER. IN BACK ROW LEFT THERE IS A MAN LOOKING LIKE DUNCAN SANDYS EATING A SANDWICH = RANDOLPH

4.40 p.m.
RT HON IAIN MACLEOD
MUCH BETTER THIS AFTERNOON = RANDOLPH

CHURCHILL EAST BERGHOLT
GRATEFUL FOR GUIDANCE. HAVE WHITEWASHED ALL ON PLAT-FORM. NOW WHITER THAN WHITE. LOVE IAIN

RT HON IAIN MACLEOD
THOUGH BLUE COMES OUT WHITE ON TELLY WOULDNT BLUER
THAN BLUE BE BETTER POLICY. LOVE TO EVE = RANDOLPH

More serious events were meanwhile taking place on the far side of the Atlantic where the Soviet Union was seeking to install nuclear missiles in Cuba, aimed at the soft underbelly of the United States. While many politicians and journalists in Britain and elsewhere in Europe thought that it was the Americans who were being provocative by insisting on a showdown, Randolph gave his full support to President Kennedy in his *News of the World* column of 28 October:

I have not seen anyone make what I believe to be the true and vital point about the Cuban situation or 'crisis' as it is called by windy people. Indeed many commentators have entrenched themselves in utterly false positions by suggesting that President Kennedy has fallen into a Russian trap by getting involved in Cuba when he ought to be keeping his eye on Berlin. Of course it is very much with Berlin in mind that President Kennedy has acted with such courage and sagacity . . .

How could the Russians conceivably believe that America would stand firmly against aggression in Berlin if the President showed that he was not prepared to take necessary action to protect his own front doorstep? One of the points about the deterrent is that it must be credible to those whom it is intended to deter . . .

The Russian bluff has been called; and the President has shown that he is not bluffing. The Russian ships with their missiles have very sensibly turned away and have avoided the necessity of being boarded, taken into American ports and searched . . .

When Britain ruled the world we looked after free men everywhere. This obligation has now devolved upon the Americans who, I doubt not, will discharge it with fidelity.

Randolph proceeded to back up his journalistic support with a telegram to President Kennedy's press secretary, Pierre Salinger:

ITS A GREAT DAY FOR THE IRISH = RANDOLPH

Salinger replied promptly:

31 October 1962

I appreciated both your wire and the copy of the article in *News of the World*. Nowhere have I seen the fundamental relationship between Berlin and Cuba exposed with such clarity as in your article. It struck at the very heart of the point which was uppermost in the President's mind.

I know also how much the President valued your telegram and support during the very difficult week.

The Prime Minister, likewise, lost no time in congratulating Randolph on his piece:

29 October 1962

Dear Randolph,

I read your article in the *News of the World* yesterday with great pleasure. In the end it was the Russians' nerve which broke first. I think this has been due not only to the President's very skilful handling but also to the firmness of the Western Alliance. It has been a fascinating week and has ended in a sort of Munich in reverse. Your article helped.

Yours ever,
Harold Macmillan

Not every commentator had been as 'steady on parade' (another favourite phrase of Randolph's). As Arthur M. Schlesinger Jr. records in *A Thousand Days*:

The British had greeted Kennedy's Monday night speech with surprising scepticism. Some questioned whether nuclear missiles really were in Cuba; maybe the CIA was up to its old tricks again; or maybe this was a pretext to justify American invasion ... A group of intellectuals – A. J. Ayer, A. J. P. Taylor, Richard Titmus and others – attacked the quarantine and advocated British neutrality. *Tribune* wrote, 'It may well be that Kennedy is risking blowing the world to hell in order to sweep a few Democrats into office.' Among the pacifists, Bertrand Russell, who was already on record calling Kennedy 'much more wicked than Hitler', sent messages to Khrushchev:

MAY I HUMBLY APPEAL FOR YOUR FURTHER HELP IN LOWERING THE TEMPERATURE ... YOUR CONTINUED [SIC] FORBEARANCE IS OUR GREAT HOPE.

And to Kennedy:

YOUR   ACTION   DESPERATE   . . .   NO   CONCEIVABLE   JUS-
TIFICATION. WE WILL NOT HAVE MASS MURDER . . . END THIS
MADNESS.

It was just at this time that, having graduated from Oxford, I embarked on
a 20,000-mile flight round Africa with an Oxford friend, Arnold von
Bohlen. To make up for the fact that we had less than 250 flying-hours'
experience between us, that summer while visiting my mother and her
husband Leland Hayward, at their home near Mount Kisco, an hour's
drive north of New York City, I had undertaken an intensive six-week
Commercial Pilot's and Instrument Rating course at La Guardia Airport.

It was not long before my grandfather got wind of my plans and, on
my return from the United States, I was summoned to lunch with him
at 28 Hyde Park Gate. We lunched alone, together with my grandmother.
My grandparents did not conceal their anxiety: 'This is a very hazardous
enterprise,' Winston declared gravely, 'I am not at all sure that I approve.'
I had long since learned from experience that the only way to deal with
cantankerous Churchills – whether my father or my grandfather – was
to stand up to them. They understood and respected no other language.
'How dare you, Grandpapa!' I rejoined. 'When *you* were my age, you
had already come under fire in Cuba, fought on the North-West Frontier
of India and were on the point of charging with the 21st Lancers at
Omdurman!' He paused for a moment's reflection and replied with a
smile: 'I think you have a point,' adding, as I took my leave of him, 'You
have my blessing!'

In early October Arnold and I took off in a single-engine Piper
Comanche which we had rented from Oxford airport for £7.50 per
flying hour. We flew east across the Mediterranean to Beirut, Damascus
and Amman, where we were enthusiastically received by King Hussein,
himself a keen aviator. From there we flew to Cairo and on up the Nile
to Sudan and the battlefield of Omdurman, where I found an unspent
cartridge on Jebel Surghum, the vantage point from which my grandfather nearly sixty-five years before had reported to Kitchener that the
Dervish army, tens of thousands strong, was advancing in order of battle
across the plain stretched out beneath him. To a letter telling my father
of this I added the postscript: 'I have just met a man who is the grandson
of the Khalifa [and] whose maternal great-grandfather was the Mahdi
[the Dervish leader].'

My father had been full of encouragement when I had told him of
my African plans and had persuaded his brother-in-law, Duncan Sandys,

then Secretary of State for Commonwealth Affairs, to write letters of introduction on our behalf to British High Commissioners and Ambassadors throughout the Middle East and Africa. Then, acting as my literary agent – the best in the business – Randolph persuaded Jocelyn Stevens, editor of *Queen* magazine, to commission a series of articles on our adventures and arranged for the sale of any hot news stories through United Press International. This proved invaluable when we flew to Yemen, where I reported on the civil war in which Egyptian forces were engaged at Nasser's behest, and again in the Congo where we arrived in time to witness the final drama of the bid for seccession by the province of Katanga with the capture of Moïse Tshombe by UN forces. On reaching Cape Town an enthusiastic letter from Randolph was waiting for me at the British Embassy:

25 January 1963

I find it difficult to express the pleasure with which I read your second long despatch from Ndola ... This is very high class stuff. Persevere and keep it up ...

All is well here though we have been infested with snow and ice and frost for about a month. However, the house is warm and the roads in our neighbourhood are reasonably negotiable.

It was sad about Gaiters. [The leader of the Labour Party, Hugh Gaitskell, for whose integrity and ability Randolph had the highest admiration, had died on 18 January 1963.]

Do please keep in touch with me ...

While in South Africa we were invited to a barbecue party beside the swimming-pool of a beautiful Cape Dutch house at Stellenbosch in the hills above Cape Town. I soon found myself engaged in a political discussion with one of the other guests – an elderly Boer. In a loud voice he proclaimed: 'It'll be fifty years before these people learn even to pull a lavatory-chain!' When I inquired how long he thought the whites in South Africa could maintain their supremacy, our fellow guest fell into a paroxysm of rage. 'Before we surrender,' he declared, 'we'll kill every bloody nigger in the place, and you bloody liberals [pointing at Arnold and myself] will be the first to be shot.' At this juncture, Arnold and I, standing with our backs to the pool, were unable to restrain a laugh and the next minute we found ourselves sailing backwards through the air into the swimming-pool, though we had the compensation of bringing our fellow guest with us into the water. This incident was swiftly relayed, in somewhat fanciful terms, to Martin Gilbert at Merton College, Oxford, via one of his pupils, a young South African. Martin wasted no time in passing on the story by telegram to my father:

FOLLOWING LETTER RECEIVED BY SOUTH AFRICAN UNDER-GRADUATE DATED JANUARY 31ST FROM CAPETOWN QUOTE DAD DISGRACED HIMSELF BY HURLING YOUNG WINSTON CHURCHILL AND GERMAN FRIEND INTO THE SWIMMING POOL. I DO ADMIT HE WAS PROVOKED BEYOND MEASURE AS THEY TOLD HIM THEY WERE ALL FOR THE NATIVES AND WOULD HELP TRAIN THEM IN SABOTAGE AND OTHER UNPLEASANT THINGS. POOR OLD REACTIONARY WHITE SOUTH AFRICAN DAD COULDN'T STAND THAT AND REALLY BLEW HIS TOP. HE GOT A BIT BRUISED IN THE PROCESS AND VERY WET INDEED. UNQUOTE. SO THE CHURCHILL TRADITION LIVES ON = MARTIN GILBERT

Shortly thereafter my father wrote to me in Lagos in a state of some excitement, suggesting I might fight the Labour-held seat of North Paddington in the next general election. He bombarded me with detailed statistics and historical background on the constituency, which he described as 'largely populated by black men, Irish, railway workers, tarts and building operatives; and much of the property is owned by the Ecclesiastical Commissioners of the Church of England'. He also informed me that my great-grandfather, Lord Randolph Churchill, had represented South Paddington from 1892 until his death in 1895 at the age of forty-six. I turned down the proposition, which I judged to be premature, preferring to stick to my intended career as a journalist and war correspondent.

On 2 March he wrote to me in the Canary Islands on the final leg of our African adventure: 'Snowdrops and yellow aconites are just beginning to show their heads ... I am suing *Private Eye* for libel. It all looks very promising, but of course in these affairs you can never tell...'

From Morocco, our last port of call on the African continent, we set course for home, leaving a cold, fog-bound Tangier at dawn. By late afternoon, ten hours after leaving the shores of Africa, we landed at Oxford where everyone seemed most surprised to see us and astonished that we had brought the Comanche back from its 20,000-mile safari without so much as a scratch. My flying instructor, Jeremy Busby, rubbed his eyes and heaved a sigh of relief. He climbed aboard with us and we immediately took off for a disused airfield near my father's Suffolk home. It was already half an hour after sunset and Randolph was at the end of the runway with his car headlights on to guide us in. As the roar of the engine died and the propeller swung to a halt, he embraced me and greeted us with the words 'I have killed the fatted calf!' For the return of the prodigal son?

Randolph had something else to celebrate: he had secured an interim mandatory injunction against the publishers, directors and members of the editorial board of the satirical magazine *Private Eye* for making a vicious attack on Sir Winston Churchill in a back-page strip cartoon. This suggested that Churchill, who was tastelessly tagged the 'Greatest Dying Englishman', had sent soldiers to Tonypandy in 1911 to shoot striking Welsh miners and had gloried at the scale of loss of British and Allied

'Look, darling! Signs of spring!'

soldiers at Gallipoli and Dieppe. It was further claimed that Randolph, in his '500-volume Official Biography', would gloss over these unpleasant 'facts' and that he employed an army of hacks to write his books for him. Randolph wrote to *Private Eye* on 14 February denouncing 'the lies and libels about my father and myself contained in your issue of February 8' and giving the editor the opportunity of retracting them. When, by 20 February, he had received no reply, he instructed his solicitors to issue writs for libel against the editor and a dozen of his associates. Believing it to be a false economy to go for the second best, Randolph retained a formidable covey of barristers, including two 'silks', Gerald Gardiner (later Lord Chancellor) and Helenus Milmo, together with Colin Duncan as junior counsel and Randolph's nephew, Julian Sandys, to complete the team.

Private Eye, a £100-company which up to that point had never successfully been sued, did their very best through approaches to some of Randolph's researchers, including Martin Gilbert, to secure sufficient ammunition to fight the case, but in vain. It cannot have been entirely by coincidence that Martin Gilbert found himself in the office of *Private Eye* shortly after 5.00 p.m. on the very day that Randolph's writs were being handed to members of the staff. As Martin reported back to Randolph:

CONFIDENTIAL
In the course of selecting back numbers, I was able to take down, on the blotting pad of my cheque book, the following conversation.
    'I've had a letter from the Queen [High Court writs come in the name of the Queen]; so have we all; from old Churchill . . .'
    'This is a case that's worth fighting, in my mind.'
    'I think we can win, too.'
    'I think this is fabulous. I daresay it will be costly, but it will pay off. We must go through with this.'
    'We're going to have a wonderful time. We will have to have a new magazine – *New Private Eye* – and devote an issue to Randolph (query Rudolph) Rednose himself. The fact that he has waited so long to sue us is a good sign.'
    'Oh! I'm looking forward to this.'

Meanwhile *Private Eye* decorated their window with a display dedicated to Randolph, the centrepiece of which depicted him as a pig defecating into a bucket, entitled 'THE GREAT BOAR OF SUFFOLK, together with other abusive material that characterised him, among other things, as 'SELFISH, MEAN and DIABOLICALLY CUNNING' under a huge headline entitled 'THE REDNOSE AFFAIR'.

While Randolph's friend, the satirist and author A. P. Herbert, failed in his efforts to persuade the Director of Public Prosecutions to issue proceedings for criminal libel, *Private Eye* played into his hands by sending one of their staff, Peter Usborne, to see Martin Gilbert at Merton College in a vain attempt to suborn him and secure him as a witness in the pending libel action. As Martin reported to Randolph:

[Usborne] told me that what he wanted to know was:
(a) Did RSC actually write the 'Eden' [book]?
(b) Was the 'Eden' an accurate book?
(c) What were RSC's motives in suing *Private Eye*?
(d) Could the *Private Eye* account of WSC's past stand up to serious historical justification?

He said he had evidence that (a) RSC did *not* write his 'Eden'; but he would not give me the source.

He was convinced that (b) the 'Eden' was inaccurate, and said that he had approached certain historians who were willing to testify to this.

He thought that (c) was explained either by the fact that RSC was an 'evil man'; or that he was temporarily angered, and could be appeased.

He said that *Private Eye* were not yet certain whether to fight the case on justification, but that if they did, (d) would become all-important. He thought that he *could* find historical evidence for all the *Private Eye* assertions.

For my part, I expressed total ignorance of (a); said that (b) was beyond my period of expertise, but warned him against his expressed intention of basing his belief that it was an inaccurate book solely on the reviewers, a list of whom he already possessed.

I said that (c) could surely be answered by a careful scrutiny of the issue of *Private Eye* about which you had taken offence, and that (d) was not an easy matter, since in my opinion every single historical assertion made by *Private Eye* was false.

Mr Usborne pressed me to tell him where he could find similar accusations against WSC in earlier accounts. This I refused to do. He did not seem a very wise young man – though full of enthusiasm for his self-appointed tasks . . .

Mr Usborne was not merely unwise, he was incompetent, leaving behind him his notebook which was then forwarded to Randolph by one who described himself as 'An Anonymous well-wisher' and who reported: 'The notebook, at a cursory glance, seems to indicate the plan adopted by Mr Usborne to build up a defence – even an attack! – against yourself...'

Randolph took much pleasure in returning the notebook to Nicholas Luard of *Private Eye*, not omitting to send a copy to his solicitor, Peter Carter-Ruck. Meanwhile, on 2 March, Randolph had secured a mandatory interim injunction against the magazine, as reported in the *Evening Standard* the following day:

> Yesterday's proceedings in Chambers before Mr Justice Paull [Randolph's sparring partner from *The People* libel action] granting the injunction which Mr Randolph Churchill successfully obtained against *Private Eye* must have been among the most expensive of such litigations. The proceedings only took forty-five seconds.
>
> Mr Gerald Gardiner QC, I understand, never goes into court, even for the shortest appearance, for less than one hundred guineas; and his junior Mr David Hirst (for a silk cannot appear without a junior) would have received a fee of two-thirds of this amount (roughly seventy pounds). I calculate that Mr Gardiner must have been paid rather more than two guineas per second. And that is taking no account of the solicitors' fees on both sides, which will not have been trivial.
>
> But then, as Whistler said in the witness box in his case against Ruskin, he did not charge for a picture for the time he spent on it, but 'for the knowledge of a lifetime'. Who will ultimately have to foot these bills will of course be a matter for the courts.

This injunction, coupled with Randolph's letter returning Usborne's notebook, prompted Luard to make settling noises: 'I think we all feel that the time may have come to discuss the whole problem. Fundamentally I am sure that our enemies are common ones and it seems a pity to find ourselves in the position of opponents. The editors and myself would certainly like to come down and meet you if you feel that a discussion would be of value to both of us...'

A meeting at Stour was duly arranged and, to their mortification, the bright young humorists of *Private Eye* had to swallow the novel form of humble pie that Randolph served up for them. *The Times* of 13 March 1963 reported:

> Mr Randolph Churchill claimed yesterday he had made legal history by the manner in which he had settled his differences with *Private Eye*...
>
> 'Instead of the usual out-of-court settlement I have insisted that they buy a full-page advertisement in the *Evening Standard*, which will appear

in the next few days,' he told *The Times*. 'It will contain a letter I wrote to them, and with my costs and their own, the bill will be about £3,000.'

'I am fed up with lawyers and as I didn't want any money myself I decided to cut them out of the case,' he added. 'I was told I might get damages of £100,000, but I didn't want to close the magazine down.'

The full-page 'advertisement' duly appeared in the *Evening Standard*:

WITHDRAWAL

The following letter from Mr Randolph Churchill was sent to *Private Eye* on 14 February 1963. It is printed here at the expense of *Private Eye*.

The Editor,	Stour,
Private Eye,	East Bergholt,
22, Greek Street,	Suffolk.
London W.1.	

Sir,

I write to call your attention to the lies and libels about my father and myself contained in your issue of February 8.

I   Your allegation that I am planning to write a biography of my father of a tendentious character amounting to a falsification of history is unfounded . . .

II   Your suggestions that I intend to omit or gloss over unpleasant alleged episodes in my father's life are abominable . . . The lies you tell about my father are exceptionally gross and offensive.

III   Your allegation that my father was responsible for 'shooting Welsh miners' is not only a lie, but the reverse of the truth . . .

IV   Your suggestion that my father had a callous disregard for loss of British and Canadian lives in two World Wars, and in particular that he made light of the casualties at Dieppe, is the vilest libel I have ever seen . . .

I shall be glad to have your observations on the foregoing as soon as possible.

Yours faithfully,
Randolph S. Churchill

Beneath, there appeared an unreserved retraction signed by each member of the *Private Eye* staff who had received a writ. Aloysius Pepper, in the *Spectator* of 22 March, reported:

The reason for *Private Eye*'s withdrawal would appear to be a simple one. It seems to be generally agreed that any jury confronted with remarks that in any way impugn the divinity of Sir Winston Churchill would need hear no more argument. And that the total cost of the case to *Private Eye*, if it were fought and lost, thanks to Mr Churchill's care in engaging sufficient legal representation to ensure that his case did not, at least, go by default, could have been in the region of £40,000.

As it is, it cost them a bare £3,000 – and their pride, in having to furnish Lord Beaverbrook with advertising revenue . . .

Not long after my father's death and hard on the heels of my election to Parliament in 1970, *Private Eye*'s bunch of talented wiseacres could not resist trying to level the score by taking a tilt at me, forcing me to issue a writ for libel against them which led to a further climb-down on their part. I devoted the modest damages I had demanded to the creation of an avenue of a hundred Lombardy poplars in Trafford Park, the industrial complex that forms part of my Manchester constituency. Twenty-five years on, my '*Private Eye* Avenue' still flourishes.

CHAPTER 30

'In Love with the Kennedys'

In December 1962, just two months after the Cuban missile crisis, Randolph flew to Nassau to report the conference between Macmillan and Kennedy. At that crucial meeting the elderly Prime Minister, who had an excellent rapport with the youthful President, persuaded him to allow Britain to purchase the Polaris missile for installation in her nuclear submarines. Previously the intention had been to purchase from the US the Skybolt stand-off missile to maintain the effectiveness of Britain's V-bomber force, but the missile had been cancelled. Randolph's reporting of the conference earned him a bouquet from the President, relayed to him by his ex-wife, Pamela, who wrote early in the New Year of 1963 after attending a reception at the White House with her Broadway producer husband, Leland Hayward: 'By the way, over New Year's the President told me that you had done by far the best and fairest reporting job on the Nassau Conference.'

Following my return from Africa in the spring of 1963, my father and I received a most exciting invitation from the White House. Plans set in train by his devoted Washington friend, Kay Halle, had come to fruition with the decision of President Kennedy, backed by Congress, to confer Honorary United States Citizenship upon Sir Winston Churchill. This signal honour had been granted on only one previous occasion, to the Marquis de Lafayette, the French Revolutionary leader who, in the American War of Independence, had befriended George Washington and fought with distinction alongside the American colonists against the British at the Battle of Yorktown.

My grandfather, who had always taken great pride in the fact that he was half-American, was overjoyed and accepted the compliment with enthusiasm. Addressing a Joint Session of Congress on 26 December 1941, shortly after the Japanese attack on Pearl Harbor, he had teased his audience with the observation: 'I cannot help reflecting that if my father had been American and my mother British, instead of the other way round, I might have got here on my own!' Sadly, more than twenty years later and at eighty-eight years of age, he was not well enough to make the journey to Washington himself. He therefore asked my father and

me to represent him. We cabled our acceptance to the President and a
week later flew off to Washington.

Jack Kennedy, unlike his father Joe, was a staunch Anglophile and held
my grandfather in the highest regard. He went to great lengths to make the
occasion a memorable one, arranging a splendid ceremony at the White
House on 9 April 1963. Immediately following the formal signing of the
Act of Congress by the President in the Oval Office, where Father and I
were received by him, we adjourned to the Rose Garden of the White
House, where the President paid this heartfelt tribute to Churchill:

> Whenever and wherever tyranny threatened, he has always championed
> liberty. Facing firmly towards the future, he has never forgotten the past.
> Serving six monarchs of his native Great Britain, he has served all men's
> freedom and dignity. In the dark days and darker nights when Britain
> stood alone – and most men save Englishmen despaired of England's life –
> he mobilized the English language and sent it into battle. The incandescent
> quality of his words illuminated the courage of his countrymen. Indifferent
> himself to danger, he wept over the sorrows of others. A child of the
> House of Commons, he came in time to be its father.

It was a deeply moving moment and it was with pride that I stood
between the President and my father as he read out, in stentorian tones,
my grandfather's letter of acceptance:

> I have received many kindnesses from the United States of America, but
> the honour which you now accord me is without parallel. I accept it with
> deep gratitude and affection . . . I am as you know half American by blood,
> and the story of my association with that mighty and benevolent nation
> goes back nearly ninety years to the day of my father's marriage. In this
> century of storm and tragedy I contemplate with high satisfaction the
> constant factor of the interwoven and upward progress of our peoples.
> Our comradeship and our brotherhood in war were unexampled. We
> stood together, and because of that fact the free world now stands.

Following my father's death, Jackie Kennedy recalled that day most
movingly in the tribute she paid to Randolph in Kay Halle's book:

> I remember Randolph, on a spring day after rain, with the afternoon sun
> streaming into the Green Room.
>   We sat around a table – Randolph and young Winston, Sissie and David
> Harlech, Kay Halle and Jean Campbell, with glasses of warm Champagne –
> and I was so happy for Randolph, I wished that moment to last for ever for
> him.

It was the day Jack had proclaimed Sir Winston Churchill Honorary Citizen of the United States. There had been the ceremony in the Rose Garden, a reception in the White House. Now Jack had gone back to his office, the last guest had wandered out, and we had gone to sit in the Green Room to unwind together.

Jack had cared about this day so much.

We met in his office, Randolph was ashen, his voice a whisper. Someone said he had been up most of the night. 'All that this ceremony means to the two principals,' I thought, 'is the gift they wish it to be to Randolph's father – and they are both so nervous it will be a disaster.'

The French windows opened and they went outside. Jack spoke first but I couldn't listen – every second was ticking closer to Randolph. Then the presentation.

Randolph stepped forward to respond: 'Mr President.' His voice was strong. He spoke on, with almost the voice of Winston Churchill, but Randolph's voice was finer.

He sent his words across the afternoon, that most brilliant, loving son. His head was the head of his son beside him – Randolph and Winston – those two names that would for ever succeed each other as long as Churchills had sons. And Randolph speaking for his father. Always for his father.

But that afternoon, the world stopped and looked at Randolph. And many saw what they had missed.

After – in the Green Room – the happy relief – Randolph surrounded, with his loving friends – we so proud of him and for him – he knowing he had failed no one, and had moved so many.

I will for ever remember that as Randolph's day.

Randolph reported the following Sunday to the readers of the *News of the World* under the headline 'Citizen Winston':

... The [US] Administration have had a difficult time so far in the 88th Congress. There as been much obstruction and it was pointed out to me that the only Bill which so far has been enacted is the one that the President signed in the attractive surroundings of the Rose Garden on Tuesday ...

One of the attractive features of the new Kennedy Administration is the much more free and easy atmosphere which prevails ... As one moves around the capital from house to house one can run into five or six key figures in the course of an afternoon and evening.

One such encounter was with the Bobby Kennedys, at a small dinner at the British Embassy, on the night of the White House ceremony. I had only met the Attorney-General once before and only very briefly. Last week I had a chance of a most amusing and high-spirited conversation with him. He has a wonderful gift of quick repartee, a delightful smile and a most engaging personality. I met him again the following night at a dinner party at Mr Averell Harriman's and the following morning called on him at the Department of Justice . . .

According to Arthur Schlesinger Jr., Robert Kennedy, thanking Randolph for something nice he had written about him, added: 'This does not happen with overwhelming frequency here in the United States so I am having your piece made into leaflets and have instructed the Air Force to take them and drop them all across this country so that people will come to realise that they have a fine fellow as Attorney General. Our U-2 pilots will also drop some in Cuba.'

As one of my father's researchers, a young American called Frank Gannon, rightly observed: 'Randolph was in love with the Kennedys.'

Later that week, Bobby invited us to Hickory Hill, his home in Maryland, just twenty minutes' drive across the Chain Bridge from Washington. It was in the course of this visit that my father and I formed a close friendship with Bobby and his wife, Ethel, who has a bubbling sense of humour and a full measure of the Kennedy *joie de vivre*. Visits to Hickory Hill were always a riot. There was no question of any formality. Children of all ages would spill out of cupboards and rampage through the house which was filled with shrieks of laughter. Visitors were regularly co-opted into lively games of touch-football and both Bobby and Ethel were aces on the tennis court. Indeed, on one occasion I was soundly trounced by my hostess when she was eight months' pregnant! They insisted, should we be over later in the year, that we visit them at Hyannisport, where the Kennedy clan spent their summer vacation.

Accordingly, that summer, while I was staying with friends at that mecca of sailing, Newport, Rhode Island, my father arrived and a plan was made to visit Bobby and Ethel at Hyannis the next day. They invited us to join them for a cruise aboard the family's large cabin cruiser, the *Honey Fitz*, to Martha's Vineyard, a lovely island off the New England coast, where we met up with a large number of their friends for a barbecue and a day on the beach. In fact we were all having such a good time that the decision was taken to stay on for dinner at a local inn. By the time we headed back to Hyannis night had fallen. A stiff breeze and choppy sea had got up, causing the *Honey Fitz* to pitch and wallow in a lively fashion. As I helped the young boatman – he had confided to me that he had never navigated at night before – the weather became rougher still and matters were not made easier by the fact that there were no charts on board. Meanwhile, on the afterdeck Father, who could not sing to save his life, was somewhat implausibly leading Bobby and Ethel in choruses of 'Lloyd George knew my Father . . .' to the tune of 'Onward Christian Soldiers', as the waves crashed over the boat, drenching us all.

It was nearly midnight before we made harbour on the far side of the Sound and secured the *Honey Fitz* for the night. Nearly all the lights were out at the Kennedy compound where the clan lived as on a commune, with each branch of the family having a holiday home of their own. Bobby suddenly remembered that they had the Chief of Naval Operations, who was there as the guest of the President, billeted with them in their only spare room. 'Don't worry, Randolph,' assured Bobby, 'I'll sneak you and Winston into Teddy and Joan's house. They have a spare room. But be sure not to make any noise otherwise you'll wake everyone up!' So saying, in the pitch black of the night, Bobby led us straight into a bed of tall and very prickly roses and started cursing and swearing in a loud voice. He took us into his brother Teddy's house and showed us up to a small twin-bedded room, since our unwitting host and hostess were already asleep. It was not long before Father, exhausted by the exertions of the day and the rigours of the return journey, was fast asleep and snoring so loudly that I was unable to sleep myself. After aiming first one slipper, then the other, in the general direction of the offending noise, in a vain effort to procure a respite, I gave up, took my blanket downstairs and stretched out on the living-room sofa. Determined to be back in my own bed at dawn, before being discovered by my host or hostess, I too fell into a deep sleep.

To my horror I was still there when Joan appeared in a dressing-gown on her way to the kitchen. With considerable embarrassment I introduced myself and endeavoured to offer an explanation for my presence. But my hostess seemed not in the least surprised to find a strange man sleeping in her living-room. Evidently it was all part and parcel of life at Hyannis with the Kennedys, to which she had long since become accustomed. In due course Teddy, by then already a Senator, appeared and, after a hearty breakfast, we all walked across in brilliant sunshine to the main house clad in the white clapper-board characteristic of New England homesteads. As I recorded in an article of tribute I wrote on Jack Kennedy for the *News of the World* following the tragic news of his assassination later that year:

It was shortly after nine on a Monday morning. Two helicopters, each with twin jet engines, had just landed on the lawn in front of his father's house, ready to take the President on his way to Washington. He had instructed the helicopters to land here, rather than at a field nearer his own house, as he knew it would give pleasure to his old and infirm father.

The President arrived, driving himself in an open car. The helicopters were waiting with their engines running, all set to take him to Otis Air Force Base on Cape Cod, where he would board a Boeing jet liner for the 400-mile flight to Andrews Air Force Base near Washington. From there he would fly in yet another helicopter to the lawn of the White House, and by 10.30 he would be at his desk.

The President found time for a friendly word with everyone. Recognising my father and me as we stood by the driveway, he came over to say good morning. Then, as he turned to board the helicopter with his brothers, Bobby and Teddy, he added, 'Be sure and visit Jackie. It will cheer her up.'

Never did I imagine that this would be the last time I would see the young President upon whom so many hopes – by no means only American – were founded. Within three months he was dead, cruelly cut down by an assassin's bullet in the prime of his life.

Randolph was distraught when he heard the news, penning his tribute in the *Evening Standard* of 22 November under the headline 'I Loved Him as a Brother':

The news from Dallas saddened and sickened me. For a few moments I could hardly believe it and my mind was half-paralysed by shock. I had known President Kennedy and several members of his family for a long time, and had had talks with him three times this year . . .

. . . of all the Heads of State that I have met, he was the most rewarding to meet; despite his busy life he enjoyed seeing people from overseas, and above all from England, a country for which he had a deep respect, and a government which he regarded as America's staunchest ally . . .

If it is not presumptuous to say so, I not only admired him as a great statesman, but loved him as a brother. I feel afflicted in my heart, no less than in my mind . . . He was the best emblem of hope and leader of our generation in the free world. He had served gallantly, indeed heroically, in the Second World War; he knew the hell of war. He was the surest guarantee that there would not be another war, and that mankind, somehow, would move forward into a sunlit age.

As Milton wrote:

> For Lycidas is dead,
>   dead ere his prime,
> Young Lycidas and
>   hath not left his peer.

CHAPTER 31

The Fight – Continued

In the spring of 1963, the Profumo crisis burst on the heads of Harold Macmillan and an unsuspecting Conservative Government. The Secretary of State for War, John Profumo, initially denied newspaper reports that he had had an affair with Miss Christine Keeler, whom he had met at Lord Astor's home at Cliveden in Buckinghamshire. It transpired not only that she was a call-girl but, unfortunately for the Defence Secretary, that simultaneously she happened to be enjoying a liaison with the Soviet Naval Attaché in London, Captain Eugene Ivanov. This latter fact gave Fleet Street and the Opposition the spurious excuse they needed to elevate the whole affair into a 'Security' scandal. Profumo, while admitting that he and his wife had met Miss Keeler at Cliveden, denied any impropriety. However, two months later he was forced to admit the untruth of his statement to the House of Commons and resigned.

Though Chancellors of the Exchequer quite regularly 'lie' to Parliament when asked if they have any intention to devalue the currency, the press were in full cry and the Opposition baying for blood. In any other European country, the fact that Profumo had misled the House in a matter regarding his private life would have been regarded as no business of either press or Parliament. Anyone who knew Jack Profumo knew there was never any question of his passing state secrets to Miss Keeler or her Russian lover, nor of his submitting to threats of blackmail, had any been made.

Randolph, writing the following year in his book *The Fight for the Tory Leadership*, quoted in full Profumo's personal statement to the House of Commons, italicising the final sentence: '*There was no impropriety whatsoever in my acquaintanceship with Miss Keeler.*' He went on to comment:

> The words italicised by the author constituted the lie which Profumo told to the House of Commons. They were the cause of his downfall and disgrace.
> It is a question of only academic interest: but what would have happened

if these eleven words had been omitted? Suppose, alternatively, he had told the whole truth to the Prime Minister and to the House of Commons. Would he have been forced to resign merely for having gone to bed with a woman who was not his wife? Probably.

Randolph was especially outraged by a leading article in *The Times*, as was Hugh Trevor-Roper, Regius Professor of History at Oxford, who later wrote: 'I ceased to take that infamous, nauseating rag after the leader "It *is* a moral question" '

Loyalty to his friends – especially to a friend in need or in trouble – was one of Randolph's finest and most endearing qualities. His affection for Profumo probably stemmed from the fact that, as the youngest Member of Parliament, newly elected just two months before the crisis that shook the Government in the spring of 1940, he had been one of the Conservative Members who voted against Neville Chamberlain on 8 May, making possible Churchill's accession to power two days later.

It was typical of his sense of loyalty that, at a moment when all were shunning the Profumos, who were besieged by thirty or forty of the gutter press camped on their doorstep, Randolph staged a public dem-onstration of his enduring friendship. As he tried to make his way through the throng of reporters to the Profumos' front door, they demanded to know the purpose of his visit. Randolph turned on them in scorn, proudly and loudly proclaiming: 'I have come to visit my friends! What the hell are *you* doing here?'

At this point Randolph swung into action with 'Operation Sanctuary', his plan for spiriting the Profumos away from their own home to the safe haven of Stour, East Bergholt. As Martin Gilbert recalls in his book *In Search of Churchill*:

I still have the instructions we were all given, headed with the code name 'Operation Sanctuary' marked 'Secret', and explaining how we were to look after 'OGs' ('Our Guests').

Randolph would leave the country to be with his father aboard Aristotle Onassis's yacht *Christina*. 'Our friends will seek to come here to Stour unobserved.' If they were observed 'admission of Press to the house or garden will be denied.' If interlopers broke into the garden 'they will be requested to leave'. If they refused, the police would be called, 'during which time our guests will retire upstairs. We will not stand any rot.'

The Profumos were to be treated as if they were in their own home. Randolph's staff were instructed not to 'blab' in the village. If the Profumos wished to go abroad 'they should fly from Southend to Dieppe and should charter a car on arrival on the continent and "disappear none knows wither".' In fact there was never any idea in the Profumos' mind that they would go abroad, despite newspaper speculation. Randolph, as usual, was trying to cover all possibilities.

I was impressed by Randolph's gesture, one of real affection and goodness.

Jack Profumo later wrote a letter of warm appreciation:

2 July 1963

I know Valerie is writing but even though I add to your correspondence I *must* send you a few lines to tell you how much operation 'Sanctuary' meant to us & how grateful we are for all the trouble you took to arrange it so happily – in your absence [Randolph's assistant] Andrew [Kerr] was perfection as Host/Cook/Chief of Staff!

... Far more than just for a weekend of refuge I want you to know how deeply I value your ready & robust friendship & help in our almost unbearable plight especially in the face of my lack of frankness when you sought to help me earlier on.

I shall always remember that & what it has meant to Valerie & me. Bless you & again all my thanks.

In a letter of her own Valerie wrote poignantly: 'I want you to know at once and from my heart how deeply grateful both of us are to you for your unfailing help during these last terrible weeks – Nobody could have striven for us or supported our (poor) cause more loyally or lovingly. My dear friend: I can only say from a very broken but still undaunted heart, "Thank you" – My love, Valerie.'

That summer Ari Onassis invited my grandfather, my father and me to join him on a cruise in the Adriatic aboard the *Christina*. We left Piraeus on 8 June on what Anthony Montague Browne, Churchill's last Private Secretary, has described as 'the last and the least fortunate cruise' that Winston was to make on the yacht. In his memoirs, *Long Sunset*, Montague Browne relates: 'The guest list was partly ours and partly our host's. I had suggested Jock and Meg Colville (Sir John Colville was Private Secretary to Churchill during the War) both because WSC enjoyed their company and because Jock had long hoped to be invited.

Young Winston (Churchill's grandson) came, and finally, after a tussle, WSC was persuaded to include Randolph...'

At first all went well and, with Ari's good humour to jolly us along, the three generations of male Churchills seemed to be getting on wonderfully well. Randolph treated his father with respect and affection to the point that Montague Browne was congratulating himself on having pushed for his inclusion. But, as he was forced to acknowledge, his self-congratulations were premature:

Suddenly at dinner he erupted like Stromboli. For no apparent reason his rage was directed at his father, then he began to particularise with violent reproaches relating to his wartime marriage. What he said was unseemly in any circumstances, but in front of comparative strangers it was ghastly. Nonie [Montague Browne's first wife] intervened with great courage, but Randolph, who was fond of her and normally treated her with regard, swept her aside as 'a gabby doll' – the mildest of his remarks that evening. I was equally unsuccessful in trying to divert his abuse from his father. Short of hitting him on the head with a bottle, nothing could have stopped him. Ari did his best, but was ignored. It was one of the most painful scenes I have witnessed. I had previously discounted the tales I had heard of Randolph. Now I believed them all.

WSC made no reply at all, but stared at his son with an expression of brooding rage. Then he went to his cabin. I followed him and found him shaking all over. I feared that he would suffer another stroke, and sat drinking whisky and soda with him until he was calmer. I will not record what he said, but it was plain that means must be found to remove Randolph from the ship.

Onassis was mortified at what had befallen but, a step ahead of Montague Browne, he came up with a masterly stratagem. He knew that Randolph was anxious to interview the King and Queen of Greece prior to their imminent state visit to Britain, particularly in view of the fact that Queen Frederika was a controversial figure in Britain at the time. Without delay and unbeknown to Randolph, Ari telephoned the Royal Chamberlain to the King of Greece and arranged for Randolph to be accorded an exclusive interview at their palace twenty miles outside Athens. The next morning Randolph found on his breakfast-tray a cable inviting him to dine with the King and Queen at the Royal Palace the following evening. Flattered and delighted, he hastened to tell his host his good fortune and to inquire how he might get to Athens in time. As Montague Browne records:

Ari said that we would put into Corfu that evening and an Olympic Airways aircraft would fly Randolph to Athens. After a harmonious but silent dinner Randolph departed, humming 'Get me to the Church on time'. I accompanied him in the launch to the harbour. After a while he fell silent and I saw he was weeping.

'Anthony', he said, 'you didn't think I was taken in by that plan of Ari's and your's, do you? I do so very much love that man (WSC) but something always goes wrong between us.' I could only hope there would be enough time left for Randolph to demonstrate his love, and WSC his...

The *News of the World* duly got its scoop interview with the Greek Royals, but the incident was a desperately sad one and showed that, even more than twenty years later, Randolph could neither forgive nor forget the fact that his father appeared, at least in his eyes, to have condoned Harriman's wartime affair with his wife, prompting him to unleash a torrent of abuse upon the head of his defenceless 88-year-old father.

With the Conservative Government reeling in the wake of the Profumo affair, a 'Macmillan Must Go' campaign had been started within the Tory Party, prompting Randolph to mount a fierce pro-Macmillan defence. As Martin Gilbert attests:

Randolph's efforts to keep Macmillan at Number Ten were intensified by his contempt for Butler, whom he accused of being one of the worst of the pre-war appeasers, a man who would have done anything, however dishonourable, to keep Britain out of the war. By contrast, Macmillan was Randolph's ideal of the patriotic anti-appeaser, the man who had fought throughout the First World War, and who had supported his father's call for rearmament in the 1930s. Hence the zeal to champion Macmillan's cause even when it had almost no other champions.

I was a bystander as Randolph tried to mobilise support for the Prime Minister... I waved him off from the lawn at Stour as he flew by helicopter to Macmillan's house at Birch Grove, then on to Lord Beaverbrook at Cherkley, then on to his father at Chartwell, in an attempt to show the flag.

Meanwhile, closer to home, he and Martin Gilbert drove across country to Rab Butler's constituency at Saffron Walden where Randolph's brother-in-law, Christopher Soames, then Minister of Agriculture, was due to address a public meeting. Martin recalled:

Randolph stood quietly at the back until the local Party Chairman asked for questions. He then called out in his booming voice: 'What I want to know is – Is Mr Butler loyal to the Prime Minister?' There was consternation on the platform. The Chairman tried to have the question ruled out of order. But Rab, recognising his adversary, agreed to answer it and, somewhat nervously, attested to his loyalty.

Randolph, who was keeping a political diary at the time, made a note of a telephone conversation he had with the Prime Minister's daughter in the early hours of 10 July:

12.45 a.m. RSC talked to Catherine Amery

She seemed saddened by the disloyalty of Harold's colleagues, practically none of whom had spoken up for him.

She said Harold was fully aware of the attitude of Tory MPs.

RSC reminded her how some months before she had told RSC how her mother [Lady Dorothy Macmillan] had said to her: 'Isn't it ghastly, darling. Everybody's saying we may win the next General Election.'

Catherine replied: 'She is in a very different mood now. Nothing short of dynamite would get her out of Admiralty House [where the Prime Minister was living while Downing Street was being renovated] at a time like this.'

Three days later Randolph went to see Macmillan and recorded:

Spent 30 minutes at Admiralty House with PM. He was looking younger and better than I had seen him for a long time.

Tho' he only indicated it obliquely, I was satisfied that he means to fight the next general election; and that he thinks he can win it.

What he wants, is to persuade Kennedy to jolly the Russians along and to persuade them that they are a European not an Asiatic Power. He hopes that the next stage might be non-aggression pacts and some form of disarmament. The great thing, he thought, was to keep moving along. If he were convinced (and I believe that he could easily be so convinced) that he could play a hand with Kennedy in wooing Russia to the West, he would certainly fight the next election – possibly in October '63. I stressed the need for grabbing the initiative...

As part of his campaign to rally support for the Prime Minister, Randolph wrote to Alec Home, the Foreign Secretary, urging him to speak out:

14 July 1963

... I tried to get you this evening at Whitwell and received the majestic and ennobling utterance from the butler 'My Lord, I am sorry his Lordship is walking in the garden with Her Majesty.' Accordingly I decided to write to you on a matter which is very near my heart.

I have found it odious to a degree that for several weeks the Prime Minister has been assailed by the fabricated rumours of the gutter press and that so few of his colleagues should have come to his defence. In the last week we have seen two of his closest colleagues, one of them, Maudling, who should be beholden to him, attacking him with sly innuendo and fishing around to get his job.

Surely it is time that some of his colleagues spoke up for him or else got up and openly poleaxed him. What Harold is undergoing is not the death of a thousand cuts but the death of a thousand innuendos.

Since our first meeting, just after you became Foreign Secretary, I have regarded you, together with Quintin [Hailsham] as one of the two most honourable members of the Cabinet. In Quintin's absence in Moscow I appeal to you to stop the rot...

Please forgive this lengthy exhortation — I know how busy you must be — but I am so nauseated by the disloyalty which started in the Cabinet last July, which has suppurated downwards and is now pullulating on the backbenches. Fortunately the rank and file in the country seem still to be very loyal. Can't you please give them early and timely encouragement?

Following a brief visit to Canada where, at the invitation of Lord Beaverbrook, he addressed the University of Fredericton, New Brunswick, Randolph flew on to Washington, where he stayed a few days with Kay Halle. Concerns about the situation at home preoccupied him even there and, two days later, he recorded in his political diary:

SECRET
Tuesday, 8 October 1963:

Telephoned SLO 1938. Eve [Macleod] says that their daughter is v. ill. Telephoned Iain Macleod at Blackpool to ask how conference was going. He refused to say anything on grounds which he said I would understand when I heard the news. He cut short the conversation at the end of one minute. I at once saw that something was up. Tracked Julian [Amery] down at about 5 o'clock (Washington time) at his home. He told me that Harold [Macmillan] was going into hospital for a prostate operation and would have to resign. A few moments later the President's secretary, Mrs

Evelyn Lincoln, rang to say that the President would be delighted to see me at 12.30 the next day. I said: 'Delighted', and asked whether he would spare a moment on the telephone as I had important news. I was put through straight away. He [President Kennedy] sounded very sad to hear about it ...

Never one to let a hot news story get away from him, Randolph hurried home where all the resources of the Stour telephone network were brought to bear as, in relentless late-night telephone calls, he urged Cabinet ministers and other opinion-formers within the Conservative party to support Quintin Hogg for Prime Minister. Meanwhile, he had some blue 'Q' for Quintin lapel button printed which unfortunately arrived with neither pins nor adhesive. Randolph thereupon charged up to Blackpool and tried to pin his 'Q' buttons on to the lapels of some of the leading lights of the Tory Party and even, irreverently, on the ample posterior of the Lord Chancellor, Lord Dilhorne.

Randolph thereupon retreated to East Bergholt, from where the battle for Hogg was carried on with salvoes of telegrams from himself, members of his staff and – somewhat implausibly, given the 'East Bergholt' date-line – from the 'Young Tories from Scunthorpe', all targeted upon the unfortunate Rab Butler at the Imperial Hotel, Blackpool.

The enemies of Quintin were meanwhile putting it about that he was mad – a mischievous rumour which did not take long to reach East Bergholt. As Randolph's political diary of 13 October records:

7.15   Ali Forbes [a political and literary journalist] was called by RSC. He was hostile. He said that Lord Hailsham was mad, RSC was mad and so was Hitler. RSC said that he did not know about the other two but he did not think Hitler was mad. Forbes said that there was madness on both sides of Lord Hailsham's family. RSC said he could easily disprove the Tweedmouth madness as having anything to do with Lord Hailsham. Forbes said 'What about the maternal side who came from Tennessee?' ...

10.00   RSC rang Nancy Hare [wife of the Minister for Labour, John Hare] and told her to stop saying that Lord Hailsham has a mad look in his eye ...

11.30   Lord Hailsham rang. RSC had two pieces of news for him. (1) That people were going round saying that he was mad and that there was madness in his family. Lord Hailsham said that he had a forebear who had built a copy of the Parthenon in Tennessee and that was pretty mad; apart from that he knew of none. (2) That Lord Salisbury was on his side.

11.45 RSC told Iain Macleod that there was a swing to our cause. Mr Macleod said that RSC was doing the cause no good; RSC said that must please him. The conversation was short.

Clive Irving, a friend of Randolph's and managing editor of the *Sunday Times*, had a ringside view of these shenanigans as he happened to be staying at Stour at the time:

He relied on the telephone to keep him in touch, and he elevated its use as a political intelligence system and provocative weapon to that of a fine art: his one acceptance of electronic aids. It cost him a fortune in phone bills – £400 a quarter at 1964 prices. He had two lines at East Bergholt, controlled from a push-button system which he kept by the fireside chair; quite often one Cabinet Minister would be held on one line while another was being interrogated on the other. I wondered how it was that they always talked to him, even if it was only to pass the time of day. Partly it was that all of us are particularly vulnerable to the telephone, the absolute violator of privacy ... Another reason, and probably the decisive one, was that whatever the perils of talking to Randolph, there was often a useful piece of gossip to be picked up. Whatever the reasons, people did answer the phone to Randolph, and at any hour, as I saw in a set-piece demonstration of his technique during the scheming for the leadership of the Conservative Party after Harold Macmillan's fall in 1963.

Randolph had been waging a misguided and foredoomed campaign on behalf of Lord Hailsham, the putative Quintin Hogg [as he would have become after renouncing his peerage]. This, as Mr Hogg must have realised, was the kiss of death. Although Randolph's support was well meant and robust it was, in the current jargon, counter-productive to a disastrous degree ... One night he got word that the pro-Hailsham lobby was close to disintegrating. At about 12.50 a.m. Randolph rang Mr Selwyn Lloyd, who was said to be wavering. The somnolent Mr Lloyd was instructed to remain 'steady on parade'. Next on the list was Mr Iain Macleod, one of the few people who knew how to cope with and dispatch Randolph's calls. His response was short and expletive.

Other leaderless Tories were pursued, and the last name on the list was that of Lord Home. Randolph reached him at about 1.30 a.m. The phone rang, and an understandably distant peer replied. But Randolph was taken aback. It was, he felt, a terrible sign of the attrition of the aristocracy's living standards that Lord Home had himself answered directly. Without bothering to reply at once, he put his hand over the speaker and said: 'Goodness, how sad. They live like bloody coolies, these days.' He then opened the conversation. 'Is that you, Alec? Randolph. Look here, I hope you're advising the monarch that it should be Quintin. It is being said that you might yourself be in the ring. I trust that that is not so ...' Lord Home, three days later to become Prime Minister, was remarkably polite and patient, and utterly enigmatic.

That was one rare occasion when Randolph's political antennae let him down; but since every other commentator was backing the wrong horse it was, perhaps, forgivable...

Despite his disbelief and outrage that Lord Home should have the temerity to put himself forward for the leadership, renouncing his peerage to become Prime Minister, my father and I won a bet on the outcome and I have in my possession a card bearing the legend: '23 Oct 63. Your share of the spoils – Father', to which was attached a cheque for £20. Randolph thereupon managed to secure one of the first interviews with the new Prime Minister, Sir Alec Douglas-Home, as he chose to style himself, but when the *News of the World* gave the story second billing to one on traffic problems Randolph was outraged and promptly withdrew his services. The editor, Stafford Somerfield, commented defiantly: 'Neither Mr Churchill nor any other writer decides where in the paper a story shall go. That is the editor's responsibility.'

It remained a mystery in the minds of the public, and indeed among many well-placed Conservatives, as to how, within a fortnight of behind-the-scenes soundings and manoeuvrings, Lord Home, the no-hoper of the party conference, was transformed into Sir Alec, the victor and incumbent of Number Ten. Randolph was determined to get to the bottom of the plot and there was none better placed to do so. He thereupon set about producing an 'instant' book to throw light on the machinations within the upper echelons of the Tory Party. The book, *The Fight for the Tory Leadership* was published in paperback within two months of the Blackpool conference, giving rise to much excitement. Hugh Trevor-Roper hastened to write on New Year's Eve:

Your book arrived yesterday. I thought I would begin reading it before going to bed last night. I like going to bed fairly early in these rural solitudes. I couldn't. I simply couldn't stop reading, and went to bed at 2.0, having finished the book.

You are incomparably the best political journalist writing in England today ... You write so *well*! The pace is so good, you have Gibbonian touches and you never miss a point. Also your judgement is so good. How I agree with you! ... Especially about *The Times* ...

Few things are so delightful as to find one's dislikes shared. *The Times*, RAB, *The Daily Express*, that snivelling pedant E. Powell ... I am with you all the way. I hope that your book is so violently attacked in *The Times* that everyone will read it ...

Randolph also received a brief note in a shaky hand from the former Prime Minister, still writing on 10 Downing Street notepaper:

What you write about me is much too flattering. But I will not pretend that is has not given me much pleasure.

Yours ever,
Harold

Meanwhile, in his review of *The Fight for the Tory Leadership* for the *Observer*, Anthony Sampson remarked:

It shows signs of being informed from at least two very important sources. It seems clear that Mr Churchill enjoyed the close confidences of Harold Macmillan and Quintin Hogg; and he produces some intimate glimpses of the operations of these two men.

Most important, he gives a detailed and vivid account of the last days of Macmillan's Premiership, when he lay in bed in hospital, defying his doctors, trying to secure a solution to the leadership crisis. This account effectively dispels accusations that Macmillan was 'fixing' his successor ...

Randolph's book, predictably, put the cat among the Tory pigeons, most spectacularly by provoking Iain Macleod, who refused to serve in Alec Home's Government, to break cover, accusing the Government Chief Whip of rigging the ballot, and denouncing the Old Etonian 'magic circle' which he alleged had blocked Rab Butler from securing the leadership: 'The truth is that at all times, from the very first day of his Premiership to the last, Macmillan was determined that Butler, although incomparably the best qualified of the contenders, should not succeed him.'

A glorious row resulted in which Randolph revelled. Questions were tabled in Parliament by Labour frontbencher Douglas Jay, demanding to know 'why permission was given to Mr Randolph Churchill to see a Cabinet paper?' This referred to the magisterial memorandum drawn up by the Prime Minister from his hospital bed, detailing how soundings were to be taken within the party to find a successor. In fact, Randolph had not seen the document although he had a shrewd idea of what it contained. For a while mayhem ruled in the Conservative Party, as different factions waged war on each other.

Soon after this fracas, Randolph started to receive important advance payments for the biography of his father. It was typical of his generous nature that, having some money in the bank for the first time in his life, his top priority was to share his good fortune with his friends. Accordingly, he went off to town to purchase from Asprey's of New Bond Street half a dozen or more hugely expensive black pigskin 'dressing-cases', containing silver hair- and clothes-brushes among other items. These he proceeded to bestow upon his closest and most favoured friends, one of whom was Quintin Hailsham, perhaps as a consolation prize for not winning the leadership of the Conservative Party the previous autumn, or possibly to make amends for the fact that his cause was torpedoed by Randolph's over-enthusiasm. Quintin was overjoyed:

31 January 1964

Sometimes one is quite bowled over by generosity. A dressing case arrived today from Aspreys, my initials on it, to prove that I had made no mistake. I wondered what it was, who had sent it? An anonymous admirer? An American millionaire? A bribe from a tycoon which would have to be returned? I numbered my relations and found them wanting either in cash or kindness. I enumerated enemies and found booby-traps with hidden murder devices unlikely. I rang up Aspreys, and discovered the truth. Randolph, the magnificent. At all events, thank you, and bless you.

Early in the new year of 1964 Randolph, detecting signs of drift at Number Ten, fired off a 'back-stiffening' telegram to Alec Douglas-Home:

UNLESS YOU DECLARE INSTANTLY THAT YOU MEAN TO REMAIN OUR LEADER UNTIL NEXT ELECTION TORY PARTY WILL BE DESTROYED. SEE TODAY'S GUARDIAN. ALL WOULD RALLY IF YOU WOULD LEAD. OTHERWISE DISASTER. BESEECH ACTION. REGARDS = RANDOLPH

Later the same day, after talking to the Prime Minister by telephone, Randolph followed up with a letter:

8 January 1964

I am so glad to hear that you are going to make a powerful speech in a week's time and that meanwhile your determination to lead us all at the next election will be made plain in the *Sunday Times*.

It is a dangerous thing to leave a political vacuum. All sorts of bad types are apt to move in ... This is a time when all good Tories should be attacking Harold Wilson. Most of them, one way or another, seem to be attacking you with varying forms of disloyalty. A firm pronouncement by you will end all this rot.

So far I have only noticed two of your colleagues – Quintin and Ted Heath – who have spoken up for you. The rest seem to be calculating the odds at Ladbroke's...

Please forgive this exordium but I have been most worried. The country is in a terrible mess and you – only you – can provide the alternative government that will save it.

Meanwhile, even as *The Fight for the Tory Leadership* was selling like hot cakes, Randolph found that he had another fight on his hands. His daily consumption of eighty to a hundred cigarettes had caught up with him and, shortly before his fifty-third birthday, he had to undergo an operation at the Brompton Hospital in London for the removal of part of his lung. His friends were concerned. Bobby Kennedy cabled from Washington:

HOPE YOU WILL BE WELL SOON ENGLAND NEEDS YOU BUT WE ALSO NEED YOU BACK HERE TO STRAIGHTEN US OUT REGARDS = BOBBY

Another well-wisher was his old political sparring partner, Michael Foot:

10 March 1964

Jill and I were concerned to read the reports in the papers this morning which might have meant anything. However, we were greatly relieved & gratified when Andrew [Kerr] told us the facts of your vitality & high spirits. This is just a line to wish you the speediest of recoveries. We greatly enjoyed the meeting at Marrekech. It was impossible to think of you really ill ...

Iain Macleod, writing in his *Spectator* column under the pen-name of 'Quoodle', drawn from G. K. Chesterton, declared:

'Randolph is Randolph, is Randolph', wrote Quoodle in his first Note-book. He has all the swashbuckling virtues of the Churchills – eloquence, loyalty, truculence, magnanimity and above all courage. First, last and always, courage. It was an unforgettable sight to see him in hospital earlier this week on the eve of a major operation dictating his column for the *Spectator*, dispensing Pol Roger 1955, and instructing his surgeon on the conduct of the operation.

Some weeks ago Randolph and Quoodle exchanged some reasonably rough words in print on a matter of high political and constitutional policy. Nevertheless, we continued to phone each other almost every day as if nothing had happened, making no reference at all to the argument still raging. Pique is for political adolescents, and Randolph, to use one of his favourite words, is 'grown-up'.

Quoodle

Alan Brien, who had been one of Randolph's assistants in the 1950s and went on to become the diarist of the *Sunday Times* and a columnist for the *New Statesman*, recalled in Kay Halle's book:

Death itself did not frighten him. 'I'd like to go just like that – pop!' he once said to me. 'It can be tomorrow. I've enjoyed myself and I won't complain.' In hospital for the operation on his lung, it was a treat to see him refuse to be reduced to a vegetable, as most people are, ticking off the eminent surgeons for talking about doctor's orders (*'I'm paying. It's my lung. I give the orders. I take advice, but I give the orders'*) and instructing the formidable Matron in how to make a decent cup of tea. He insisted on seeing what had been removed before allowing it to be disposed of. 'It was rather nasty-looking, really,' he told me. 'Like a fat mutton chop you wouldn't even give to the dog. Well rid of that, I'd say.'

Immediately following the operation, Randolph's doctors put out a statement that, in the event, the tissue removed had proved 'non-malignant'. When word reached the bar of White's Club, his erstwhile friend, Evelyn Waugh, was prompted to exclaim: 'Trust those damn fool doctors to cut out of Randolph the only part of him that was not malignant!' This *bon mot* was relayed to Randolph by his friend Ed Stanley, prompting an instant reconciliation between the two old comrades who, because of some offence taken by Evelyn, had scarcely spoken for twelve years.

A few weeks later Randolph, garnering information for an article on tulip trees which he was writing for the *Sunday Times*, had sought to enlist his refound friend's assistance. Evelyn replied mischievously following the *Private Eye* line by referring to Randolph's army of researchers as 'Ghosts', prompting an exchange between the two:

13 May 1964

I hope that your convalescence is rapid.

It is kind of you to offer me one of your father's books. Please choose yourself whichever you think best entitles him to the Companionship of Literature. I shall read it with respect & close attention.

An old man who works about the place tells me I have 8 tulip trees − some decrepit, some mere saplings. I beg you not to let Ghost reveal this. The wood is in demand for veneers and timber poaching is becoming a grave danger. All my neighbours have tulip trees. I think if Ghost flits from Tewkesbury to Exeter he will find one every five miles. Perhaps the Eastern counties have been ravaged by American aeronauts. Ghost will only cause trouble to tree-lovers if he gives publicity to these modest adornments. Timber-merchants are predatory vandals.

RSC to EW

12 June 1964

Ghost received your request that you should not be reported as owning tulip trees. Your request will, of course, be complied with. I merely mentioned to Leonard Russell [features editor of the *Sunday Times*] that I had had a funny letter from you about them. I never suggested that he should send Lord Snowdon, or any of his other photographers, to intrude upon your privacy.

I am sending you today under separate cover the two-volume edition of *Marlborough* which is unabridged. I shall value your views upon it.

EW to RSC

15 June 1964

Very many thanks for *Marlborough* which I shall study with attention.

Thank you also for calling off Lord Snowdon. I can now remove the false beard I have worn since I got Mr Russell's alarming letter.

EW to RSC

19 June 1964

For Ghost's (not Snowdon's) information my tulip trees are now in full flower.

I am enjoying *Marlborough*. The author has no specifically literary talent but a gift of lucid self expression in words – lost when least excited. His military reports are in the same class (though lower) as Belloc & Duggan.

Later in the year when Randolph inquired if he had persisted with his reading of *Marlborough*, Evelyn replied: 'I read *Marlborough* throughout. Were I reviewing the work of a novice I should fall on it furiously but in the case of a man of your father's distinction, I think it would be impertinent. I was everywhere outraged by his partisanship & naive assumption of superior virtue. It is a shifty barrister's case not a work of literature.'

Randolph recorded: 'Miss Nancy Mitford told me that *Marlborough* almost drove him [Evelyn Waugh] to apoplexy, and that as he read it he would exclaim, "God, I hope that when I turn the next page this bloody Grand Alliance will get into trouble."'

That summer, Randolph's friend and my godfather, Lord Beaverbrook, died shortly after celebrating his eighty-fifth birthday. Randolph paid tribute to him in the *Evening Standard*, saluting him as 'a true friend and, above all, a staunch ally in adversity'. He concluded: 'He was a good man and a bad man in exceptional degrees; but only history will decide which characteristics prevail. I do not doubt that whichever way he is going "all the trumpets will be sounding for him on the other side".'

Although Randolph had a deep love for the cantankerous old Canadian with his impish sense of fun, he also saw in him a mischievously wicked side. One of Randolph's favourite stories to illustrate the point occurred in the late 1950s when Beaverbrook was taken ill in the South of France. His doctor, Sir Daniel Davies, was a delightful Welshman who hailed from the valleys of Aberystwyth and was physician to the Queen. He was preoccupied with the hectic last-minute arrangements of a family wedding when a summons came by telephone from Beaverbrook: 'Dan, is that you?' demanded the gruff, instantly recognisable voice with its broad Canadian accent that forty years of living in England had done nothing to tame. 'Yes, Lord Beaverbrook,' replied the doctor in his gentle Welsh lilt. 'Dan, I'm sick and I need you out here right away.' 'Well, Lord Beaverbrook,' protested the doctor, 'I'm afraid that will be difficult as it's my daughter's wedding day.' This excuse served only to produce a roar of protest from the grumpy old Canadian who thundered in peremptory tones not usually expected from those about to expire: 'Dan, I'm a dying man. You can't abandon me just when I need you. Now, listen carefully. There is a Viscount airliner waiting for you at Northolt airport. It will be ready to leave in one hour's time and you're to be on it. A car will be outside your home in fifteen minutes.'

The saintly, mild-mannered doctor succumbed to these hectoring blandishments and dutifully flew to his dying patient's side. However, by the time he reached La Capponcina on Cap d'Ail some four hours later, having abandoned his daughter's wedding, Lord Beaverbrook was sitting up in bed feeling somewhat better. The local English doctor from Monte Carlo, Dr Roberts, had meanwhile dropped by, prescribed some tablets and pronounced that there was nothing seriously wrong with the old man, a diagnosis in which Sir Daniel concurred.

Arriving at La Capponcina a day or so later, Randolph found his friend already out of bed and clearly on the mend. Beaverbrook, the son of a Presbyterian minister, disapproved of my father's partiality for whisky and had, for a while in Randolph's youth, bribed him to stay 'on the wagon'. Whenever they met Beaverbrook invariably and ostentatiously would draw attention to this vice by summoning his butler and, in a loud voice, commanding: 'Albert, bring Mr Churchill some Scotch whisky!' To which the elderly retainer would reply in a mournful tone: 'Yes, Lawd!' After three or four minutes Albert reappeared bearing a silver salver on which was set a bottle of whisky, a soda-water siphon, a tumbler and some ice. Beaverbrook, instantly spotting that the whisky bottle was new, bellowed: 'Albert! That's a new bottle of whisky! What happened to the old bottle?' 'Well, Lawd,' lamented the butler, 'there was not much left in the other bottle and the doctor from London drank it.' 'That goddamn doctor!' growled the crotchety old Beaver, grudging every drop, but clearly well back on form.

In the course of the summer of 1963, soon after returning from my flight round Africa, I had met once more and fallen in love with the beautiful, dark-eyed Minnie d'Erlanger, a childhood friend who had captivated me from the moment we first met, at the age of thirteen, on the ski-slopes of Kitzbühel in Austria. Embarrassed by my father's heavy drinking and unpredictable outbursts of rage, I had avoided inviting friends to my father's various homes during the school holidays. This changed during my university days when, with two or three friends, I would leap into a small plane at Oxford airport and fly cross-country to a disused airfield near Stour. He would invariably greet my friends affably and entertain us all to a jolly lunch under the pergola on the terrace. But until I took Minnie to Stour for the occasional weekend from the autumn of 1963 onwards, I had never asked any of my friends to stay.

To Minnie, who had heard terrible stories of my father's temper, rudeness and drunkenness, he was charm itself. He invariably treated her with the greatest courtesy and respect, always taking much pride in showing her the latest embellishments to his garden. In the spring of 1964, shortly after his lung operation in the Brompton Hospital, he was the first to congratulate us upon our engagement and to encourage the match, though we were both just twenty-three at the time.

When we were married, on 15 July 1964, my father was my best man, looking rather like Stanley Holloway in *My Fair Lady*, all togged up in his frock-coat and top-hat. After a small reception for closest family given by my grandparents at 28 Hyde Park Gate, we went on to a much larger party, given by Minnie's mother, 'Smut' d'Erlanger, at the Hyde Park Hotel, where my father's friend, Natalie Bevan, had done beautiful arrangements of flowers from Stour and from her own garden nearby. My father had the idea of persuading the Duchess of Buccleuch to lend for the day the Sword of Ramillies, with which John, 1st Duke of Marlborough, had led the charge of his troops against the French. The sword came with its own minder, but disaster struck when I sought to drive it into the cake. Being a rapier, not a sabre, it had been designed for running through something softer than the rock-solid icing of one of Madame Floris's wedding-cakes and it buckled under the strain.

That autumn Randolph was, as always, having 'cook problems' at Stour. Few stayed for long and of one he remarked: 'She was good as cooks go – and as cooks go, she went!' These considerations prompted him to record in his political diary:

Sunday 15 November 1964
THE BACKSTAIRS APPROACH TO THE CORRIDORS OF
POWER

Read in the newspapers that Mrs Harold Wilson had sacked the cook who had worked for Alec Douglas-Home for twelve months at Downing Street. One of the papers said that she had previously worked for Lady Rosebery and Lady Pamela Berry. Tried, but failed, to contact Lady Douglas-Home. Tracked down Eva Rosebery at Dalmeny ... She said that she had heard of Mrs Green [the cook] some years ago and had tracked her down in Stevenage New Town.

'I happened to be driving a Bentley,' Eva said. Mrs Green said she would be very glad to come for a week four or five times a year when the Roseberys were at their Newmarket house. So it was agreed that she should come the following week and that Eva Rosebery should send a car for her. She sent over the station wagon. Mrs Green refused to get in it. She said she would travel in nothing else except a Bentley or a Rolls-Royce. She could not find Mrs Green's number listed either under cooks or Green, but said she would send someone down to get her file and would call me back.

This she did . . . Eva said that she was temperamental like all cooks.

'Is she a good cook?' I inquired.

'Adequate,' was the reply.

'I suppose you judge by Rothschild standards of cuisine,' I said.

'Not at all,' Eva said, 'she just provided plain simple wholesome food that Harry likes.'

I have been brought up to believe that one should always check carefully on references, particularly with the most recent employer. So I tracked Mrs Harold Wilson down at Chequers. She was out walking with the Prime Minister but when I called back at 4.15 p.m. through the Downing Street exchange she came to the telephone. She gave Mrs Green a good reference. I told her about Lady Rosebery's experience with the Rolls-Royce and the Bentleys and she said that this had not been a preoccupation of hers in the short time they had been in Downing Street. Whereas Eva had said that Mrs Green was 'adequate', Mrs Wilson said: 'Well, if you want a *Cordon Bleu*, you had better have her.' Time alone will tell!

I said that I was very sorry that I had never met Mrs Wilson. She said she had long wished to meet me. I said I trusted it could be speedily arranged. I then said: 'Is the Prime Minister around? Do you think he would care to have a word with me?'

Mrs Wilson said: 'I think he is. Hold on. – Harold!'

I had eight or nine minutes' chat with him. Like his wife, he behaved in a most grown-up fashion. He did not seem at all windy of talking to me. I thanked him for his nice letter and simultaneously he was reiterating his thanks for my nice telegram [re WSC's illness].

RSC: 'I wonder if I could come and see you some time before you go to America?'

HW: 'On what basis?'

RSC: 'Nothing to do with journalism but I like to get acquainted with the people who govern our country.'

HW: 'Fine. I will try to fit you in.'

RSC: 'Well I would come to London any day to see you: just tell your people to let me know when it is convenient. I am going to New York and Washington just after you, to make sure that you haven't got rid of our bomb.'

HW's answer was muffled and incomprehensible . . .

Randolph's fears were, in fact, unfounded for the new Prime Minister, keeping the majority even of his Cabinet colleagues in the dark, was working to maintain the effectiveness of Britain's nuclear deterrent with a programme code-named CHEVALINE to replace the single nuclear warheads on Britain's Polaris missiles with triple re-entry vehicles – a decision which outraged the majority of his Labour Party colleagues when eventually they learned of it.

CHAPTER 32

Operation 'Hope Not'

On 30 November 1964 the Churchill family gathered at 28 Hyde Park Gate to celebrate my grandfather's ninetieth birthday with a family dinner party. It was a fine and memorable occasion with nearly every member of the family present, including all his children – with the exception of Diana, who had died the previous year – his more grown-up grandchildren and the closest of family friends. Mary Soames, who inherited much of her father's descriptive powers, has given by far the best account of this at once happy, but also sad, occasion:

> Clementine's present to him was a small golden-heart enclosing the engraved figures '90'. It was to hang on his watch-chain, and joined the golden-heart with its central ruby 'drop of blood' which had been her engagement present to him fifty-seven years before. During the afternoon the Prime Minister called to bring Winston good wishes from the Cabinet.
>
> That evening there was the usual hallowed family dinner party: Randolph, Sarah, myself and Christopher, Winston and Minnie, and Arabella, Julian Sandys, Edwina and Piers Dixon, Celia Kennedy (Sandys); and cousin Sylvia. The only guests not members of the family were Jock and Meg Colville, and Anthony and Nonie Montague Browne. Monty [Field Marshal Montgomery] had been invited but was himself ill in hospital.
>
> The house glowed with candlelight and flowers, and we were united yet one more time in drinking first Winston's health and then Clementine's. But his birthday evening had for us all a poignant quality – he was so fragile now, and often so remote. And although he beamed at us as we all gathered round him, and one felt he was glad to have us there – in our hearts we knew the end could not be far off.

The evening concluded with Randolph proposing the toast to Winston as 'the author of our being'.

The end was not long in coming. During the night of 9–10 January 1965, Winston suffered a massive stroke and thereafter never regained consciousness. For so many years he had fought a valiant and long-drawn-out battle against the infirmities of old age which, due to his formidable constitution and, above all, his indomitable spirit, he had managed to keep at bay since his first heart attack more than twenty years before, and through several subsequent strokes and bouts of pneumonia.

The family were alerted to expect the worst but, amazingly and tenaciously, he held on for another fourteen days. For much of that time a member of the family kept vigil at his bedside. Finally, as the moment approached when we knew he would not be with us for much longer, the family assembled around his bed to take leave of him. We knelt in the dimly lit room in silent prayer, each with our own precious memories of this man we loved so deeply and who had meant so much to each one of us, indeed to the whole world. It was not until the morning of 24 January 1965 that he gave up the struggle, having – seemingly by a supreme act of will-power – clung on until the very same day and month of his father's death seventy years earlier.

The Queen had decided that her first and most loved Prime Minister should be accorded the exceptional honour of a state funeral – a distinction reserved for Sovereigns and for the nation's greatest heroes. Granted to a commoner just four times in the nineteenth century – to Pitt (the Younger), Nelson, Wellington and Gladstone – it had never once been bestowed in the twentieth century. Buckingham Palace, in consultation with 10 Downing Street, had charged the Earl Marshal of England, the Duke of Norfolk, with responsibility for the arrangements, which had been drawn up several years before under the code-name of Operation 'Hope Not'. Two weeks before, Anthony Montague Browne, my grandfather's faithful and – after Eddie Marsh – his longest-serving Private Secretary, flashed the cryptic prearranged telegram to Bernard Norfolk who was in Scotland: ' "Hope Not" imminent'. As Montague Browne recalls:

> Bernard's wife Lavinia later told me that he had been out all day and, in the evening, when he asked if there had been any communication, she replied: 'Only a nonsense telegram.' Later he saw it and leapt into action, and all his superb organisation was brought to complete readiness for the State Funeral.

At an early stage in the advance planning both my grandmother and father had been advised and kept informed of the arrangements, which had been drawn up in meticulous detail and involved the marshalling of many thousands of troops, nine military bands, six Sovereigns and fifteen Heads of State, among them the Queen, accompanied by Prince Philip, General de Gaulle and President Eisenhower. When my father had inquired of the Earl Marshal: 'Well, Bernard, at the end of the day, what *is* a state funeral?' 'Why, you bloody fool, Randolph,' the Earl Marshal had replied pithily, 'it's a funeral paid for by the State!'

Prior to the funeral, by order of the Queen, my grandfather's body lay in state in Westminster Hall for three days during which, despite a biting wind, the people of Britain – together with many from overseas – queued for hours round the clock to file silently past the coffin and pay their last respects to the man they revered as their saviour. So great were the numbers that the queue extended more than two miles from Westminster Bridge, along Albert Embankment on the east bank of the Thames, across Lambeth Bridge and along Millbank to Parliament Square and, finally, to Westminster Hall itself, the oldest surviving part of the Palace of Westminster. As I described the scene in my book *Memories and Adventures*:

> In the gaunt hall with its high hammerbeam wooden ceiling, my grand-father's coffin was set on a catafalque. A Union flag draped the coffin on which his insignia as Knight of the Garter rested on a silk cushion. Candles flickered round the funeral bier, which was guarded at each corner by officers of each of the three services in turn, with clasped hands resting on their drawn reversed swords. People filed past in their thousands and tens of thousands to bid farewell. So many were to say: 'But for him . . .'

Saturday, 30 January, the day appointed for his funeral, dawned steely grey with a searingly cold east wind. Despite the cold, the route of the procession was already lined, many deep, with those who had come – some thousands of miles – to pay their last respects. Seven thousand soldiers and eight thousand police had already taken up their positions on either side along the route between Parliament Square and St Paul's.

My father and I, together with my grandmother and other members of our family assembled in New Palace Yard, just beneath Big Ben, shortly before a bearer-party from the Grenadier Guards lifted the heavy lead-lined coffin from its catafalque in Westminster Hall and lowered it on to the naval gun-carriage that was to carry him on his final journey through the streets of London. While my grandmother and the other female members of the family followed in carriages, the men walked. Despite his recent lung operation and continuing poor health, my father insisted, come what may, in marching behind his father's coffin. In morning-coats, top hats and greatcoats, he and I followed immediately behind as, on the stroke of 9.45 a.m. from Big Ben, the great black gun-carriage, drawn by 140 naval ratings, moved off from the Palace of

Westminster to the clatter of horses' hooves on the cobblestones, the muffled beat of drums and the distant boom of the guns of the Royal Horse Artillery in St James's Park, firing a ninety-gun salute – one for each year of his life.

My Aunt Sarah, the actress, captured the scene and the sounds in her poignant memoir of her father, *A Thread in the Tapestry*:

> The Queen's town carriage swayed and creaked gently. The horses' hooves were the most decided noise, after them came the distant guns and the drums beating out the relentless precision of the slow march. One could not hear the music.
>
> The silence in the creaking carriage was audible above all. So it had happened: the inevitable Operation Hope Not was nearly over. The days of almost peaceful coma, the Lying in State, and now the last of all journeys that we would ever take with him was on its way.
>
> The curve of Whitehall lay ahead: the Home Office, the Cenotaph, Downing Street, the Treasury, the balcony on the right from which Charles I had made his farewell, the Admiralty, the little Whitehall Theatre of laughter, and Nelson brooding over Trafalgar Square.
>
> The people lining the streets did not seem to be alive, no-one batted an eyelid. I looked at them, and yet our eyes could not meet, for behind their eyes lay their own visions, their own memories...
>
> As we passed the Cenotaph, one hundred flags borne by men and women of the wartime resistance movements in France, Denmark and Norway were raised in a last salute to the man whom they considered in their darkest hours a chief and a leader...
>
> Now we were nearing St Paul's Cathedral. I remembered seeing it silhouetted in flames from the roof of the Savoy, standing by my father's side ... all those years ago...

As we climbed Ludgate Hill on the final lap to St Paul's, the naval gun-carriage crew strained at their heavy load and the horses pulling the carriages were slipping. I glanced anxiously at my father by my side who, by now, was very out of breath. It was an ordeal for him but, determined as always to be 'steady on parade', he gritted his teeth, stuck out his jaw and soldiered on. At St Paul's the Royal Navy detachment made way for an eight-man bearer-party of Grenadier Guardsmen, who hoisted the heavy coffin to their shoulders and bore it haltingly up the steps of the great cathedral. Again Sarah captured the moment:

> We had been told it was not necessary to curtsey to the Queen and her

family. They were already in their pews. For the first time in English history, the monarch waived her prerogative and waited for her humble servant...

'The Battle Hymn of the Republic' crashed through the great cathedral, as the bombs had crashed around it in 1940 ... Ghosts? They only live in our desire ... it is perhaps our memories that see the mist hover over the lake and fireflies dance where no human could ... He is gone ... a barge did come and carry him on ... the steel cranes bowed their heads ... the gull-grey sky held and the Thames ran softly on ... He is gone. What is mortal of him lies at Bladon...

The service at St Paul's was a great national outpouring of emotion and grief before the representatives of 110 nations. All present sensed that they were witnessing the passing of an era – the severing of the link with the man who had led them through the years of 'blood, toil, tears and sweat' to glorious victory. As the service drew to its close, trumpeters, high above in the gallery, sounded the Last Post which reverberated hauntingly under the great dome. Total silence followed as the echoes died away, before a single trumpeter sounded Reveillé.

The procession re-formed and we marched down Cannon Street to Tower Hill, where the massed pipe bands of the Highland regiments played the lament 'The Flowers of the Forest' as the bearer-party placed the coffin on the deck of the launch, *Havengore*. With my grandfather's flag of Lord Warden of the Cinque Ports, of which he was so proud, fluttering at the bow in a stiff breeze and the Union flag draping the coffin on the quarter-deck, we headed up the Thames. Sixteen Lightning jets of the Royal Air Force flew overhead, while dockers manning the cranes on the south bank of the river spontaneously lowered their giant booms in silent tribute.

At Waterloo Station the coffin was placed aboard a Pullman train, drawn by a steam locomotive of the Battle of Britain class, bearing his name, which was to carry my grandfather to the Oxfordshire village of Bladon, hard by Blenheim Palace where he had been born ninety years before. That journey – the last we would ever make with him – was the most moving of my life. The train took a route through the southern suburbs of London before striking west on the old Great Western line. Outside every home, at the bottom of each garden or crowded at level-crossings, people of every age and walk of life had gathered to see the train pass. Old soldiers, some standing smartly to attention, others in wheelchairs, with rows of medals proudly pinned to their chests, made a final tearful salute to their chief as we passed by. Women and children gathered round, many clutching Union Jacks.

Then, at a brief graveside service, attended only by family and closest friends, we committed him to the earth, surrounded by a mass of wreaths, including one of daffodils from the Queen, bearing the inscription: 'From the nation and from the Commonwealth. In grateful remembrance, Elizabeth R.'

But in the midst of death, there was life. On 22 January, my wife Minnie had given birth to our firstborn, a boy. Out of deference to family tradition which, for four generations, had alternated the Christian names of Randolph and Winston, we christened him Randolph, after both his grandfather and his great-great-grandfather. For thirty-six hours, as my grandfather's life ebbed away, the new generation overlapped with the old, like runners in a relay race, passing the torch from one to the other. By a strange quirk of fate the same issue of *The Times* which devoted its front page to my grandfather's death, recorded on the back page our son Randolph's birth.

Among the many letters of condolence that Randolph received was one from Michael Foot:

25 January 1965

You were no doubt prepared, over many years, for the blow to fall, but it falls none the less heavily for that. Jill and I send you our deepest sympathy and our love. We know, however faintly, how deep was your admiration & affection for your father, & therefore how difficult these times must be. We are sure you will surmount them splendidly & write the biography in the way it should be written & only you can write it.

Don't bother to answer this. But we hope to see you in a few weeks, & meantime will be thinking of you constantly.

No tribute was more poignant than the majestic verse that had been penned by Winston's ally from his days in the political wilderness, Duff Cooper, 1st Viscount Norwich:

> When ears were deaf and tongues were mute,
>   You told of doom to come.
> When others fingered on the flute,
>   You thundered on the drum.

When armies marched and cities burned
    And all you said came true,
Those who had mocked your warnings turned
    Almost too late to you.

Then doubt gave way to firm belief,
    And through five cruel years
You gave us glory in our grief,
    And laughter through our tears.

When final honours are bestowed
    and last accounts are done,
Then shall we know how much was owed
    By all the world to one.

CHAPTER 33

'Bumpkin Pasha'

Immediately following his father's funeral, Randolph, together with his assistant Andrew Kerr, set out for North Africa with his car laden down with tin boxes bursting with files, typescripts and galley proofs. After a journey of some ten days they reached Marrakech, from where Randolph wrote to his mother:

14 February 1965

I have been thinking so much about you, dearest Mama, and am very glad to hear that you are going to Barbados and to Jamaica. I know what a terrible time you have had in the last ten or fifteen years and trust that you have realised my understanding of this. When you have had a good holiday and rest you must try to create a new life for yourself. To begin with you will probably feel a vast void. No doubt you are making plans; I would suggest that you sell 27 and 28 Hyde Park Gate, and move to an attractive commodious flat in Belgravia; and that meanwhile you should do a good deal of travelling...

I trust that you will have a lovely time with Ronnie Tree in Barbados and with Sarah Russell in Jamaica. And I hope that you will continue to follow the sun by spending a week with me in this spacious and commodious villa.

PS Love to Mary. I am very glad to hear that Christopher [Soames] is rising in the political firmament. I think it would be a terrible pity if he forsook politics for commerce. R.

Like his father, Randolph relished escaping from the mists and cold of the English winter to the sunshine of North Africa. He found the crisp desert air with its sparkling clarity exhilarating. He loved Marrakech with its subtle mingling of French and Arab culture and cuisine and, especially, the Mamounia Hotel, where he proceeded to install himself in circumstances of no great discomfort. His suite looked out upon the fine walled garden of the hotel, with its tall palm trees and vibrant colours set against the incomparable backdrop of the snows of the High Atlas.

Here, uninterrupted by the relentless intrusion of the telephone, he found the tranquillity to 'box on' with the monument he was constructing to his father's memory. Working in shirtsleeves on the terrace, under the African sun, despite his now numerous infirmities, he pressed forward with his great work, correcting galley proofs, dictating new chapters and sending back to Stour a flow of instructions to the team of researchers that formed his back-up. Occasionally, at weekends, together with Natalie Bevan, who joined him there, and Andrew Kerr, Randolph would venture across the desert for a picnic beside a cool mountain stream in the Ourika Valley of the Atlas Mountains, a spot where his father had painted some of his most brilliantly coloured canvases.

After six weeks in the African sunshine, Randolph flew home for a luncheon which he and his sisters gave at the Café Royal to mark their mother's eightieth birthday and to attend a service at St George's Chapel, Windsor, for the 'laying up' of their father's Garter banner. This was followed by a luncheon with the Queen at Windsor Castle at which Randolph, entirely in character, had the temerity to raise the sensitive subject of the Windsors. He thereupon promptly cabled the Duchess in Paris:

THE QUEEN TELLS ME YOU WOULD LIKE BLACK PUG COULD EYE
GIVE YOU ONE OF MINE WHAT WOULD YOU PREFER TRUST HRH
IS BETTER REGARDS TO BOTH = RANDOLPH

But the duchess declined:

GREATLY APPRECIATE GENEROUS OFFER OF ONE OF YOUR PUGS
UNFORTUNATELY I BOUGHT ONE BEFORE LEAVING ENGLAND
BRINGING FAMILY UP TO FIVE WHICH IS ALL WE CAN MANAGE
WARM REGARDS FROM US BOTH = DUCHESS OF WINDSOR

During a fleeting visit to his beloved Stour, before flying back to Marrakech to resume his labours, Randolph was thrilled to find a fine pair of monogrammed evening slippers awaiting him, the gift of his friends the Profumos. In writing to thank Valerie, he remarked: 'I wear them nearly every evening and then announce myself as Bumpkin Pasha.'

Later that month his mother wrote with exciting news:

April the 27th 1965

Dearest Randolph,

This morning the Prime Minister offered me a life peerage & I have accepted. I hope you approve. He is seeing The Queen to-night & it will be published on Saturday morning. I am so much looking forward to my visit that day. I do hope my dear boy you will soon be feeling better.

Your loving Mama

The gazetting of this honour prompted Evelyn Waugh to inquire: 'Does your mother's recent ennoblement entitle you to the prefix "Hon"? If so I apologise for omission.' Randolph replied somewhat soulfully: 'I am afraid you were right. I am now an Hon, not a Rebel.'

In the course of his absence, Randolph's essay in autobiography, *Twenty-One Years*, was published. His friend Charles Wintour, editor of the *Evening Standard*, praised it as: 'One of the most charming accounts of a rather belligerent adolescence that I can remember'.

That summer Minnie and I christened our son. The proud Grandpa arrived from Stour laden with magna of champagne. Writing to thank him for the handsome pen-stand which Randolph gave his grandson, I expressed the hope that one day he would wield the pen as sharply and well as his grandfather and great-great-grandfather, his namesakes. *Private Eye* marked the occasion by publishing on their front cover a photograph of me holding baby Randolph high above my head, with a balloon coming out of his mouth proclaiming: 'If you call me Randolph – I'll sue!'

That autumn, accompanied by Minnie, I embarked on my first lecture tour of the United States, speaking in forty-seven cities in fifty-six days and driving 12,000 miles coast-to-coast and back again. On completion of this marathon, I was propositioned by Mike Cowles, proprietor of *Look* magazine, to report the Vietnam War. I hastened to share the good news with my father who was predictably enthusiastic, offering to help organise the logistics. However, on later learning of my plan to visit North Vietnam, as well as South, he wrote to me in Saigon to sound a note of caution:

7 March 1966

I have been greatly impressed by the extracts of your diary which have reached me. You are certainly having a fascinating time and learning a lot. Naturally none of us like you being out there too long...

Minnie rang up last night and told me of your telegram with the idea of going to Hanoi from Hong Kong. I would have thought this was very difficult to achieve though it would be a tremendous scoop. I think you will remember the arguments which I had from my father and which I passed on to you about the danger in war, particularly one which in some senses is a civil war (whatever the Americans may say), of going to both sides. They may both distrust and treat you as a spy. If you can go and so decide, mind you leave all incriminating papers with you in Hong Kong. And don't make any notes except of a most flattering kind while you are in Hanoi. However, I would stick to Hanoi and not go into the areas where the Americans are bombing. It would be too boring to be done in by them. All this, however, you must decide for yourself – you are on the spot. But don't act without good advice . . .

I gather if you get back in time you are going to help Ted Heath [in the forthcoming General Election]. I expect he is alright; so I wouldn't hurry home on his account. I would complete your important journalistic plans. We don't seem to have a hope in hell of winning but I think their majority may not be worse than 40 or 50; others say they may get a landslide. Michael Wolff has been conscripted by Ted Heath to be a back-room boy in the Central Office . . .

I didn't feel very well in Switzerland [where he had spent six weeks working on the Great Biography] so I came back two weeks early and find that I have anaemia and all that sort of rot and have to take a lot of pills. But today I am beginning to feel a lot better. Except for the index and the preface, Vol. I is absolutely locked in a strait-jacket and they have already started printing some parts of it. We managed to do about half of Vol. II in Switzerland but before we get on with that we have got to tidy up the Companion to Vol. I. So I am not going to do anything for the election except two articles a week on how the clowns perform on television for the Evening Standard, who say they are going to call it 'Box on with Randolph'.

Spring seems to have come the last three days and everything is bursting out . . .

From Saigon later the same week, I sent my father an account of my activities:

12 March 1966

I have not sat still for a moment since I arrived 'in-country' a month ago. I have travelled to almost every part of the country: I have seen the Marines, the 1st. Cav., the 1st Division, Special Forces, the Vietnamese Army (ARVN) and the popular forces – all operating in different parts of the country. I have met buddhists & catholics, 'montagnards' and people of the Delta, Wahau & Cao Dai (who incidentally regard grandpapa as a God).

I have flown on two air-strikes, one on an F-100, the other on an F-4C (Phantom); I have also gone on a FAC (Forward Air Control) mission –

in a light, unarmed aircraft which pin-points the objectives to be hit by the fighter-bombers. I spent a day and a night on the carrier *Ranger* which is striking N. Vietnam from 'Yankee' station in the Gulf of Tonkin – this is a fantastic operation: every 90 minutes from twelve noon to twelve midnight a full flight of aircraft – Phantoms, Skyraiders, reconnaissance a/c, tankers, radar a/c – is launched & the previous wave is recovered. Then the operation is taken over by a second carrier to keep up a round-the-clock momentum. Carriers have never operated on such a sustained basis in any previous war . . .

A couple of nights ago I was out in the field with the Australians – it was quite lively: a few enemy mortars landed in the camp and there was plenty of small arms fire and, to make things even more exciting, a whole lot of 'friendly' .50 calibre machine-gun fire – tracer – started flying past a few feet from where I was sleeping. I found myself diving with four 'Aussies' into a two-man fox-hole; it was amazing how we all managed to fit in – you've never seen people move so quick. The following morning everyone was digging like hell . . .

That same day my father cabled me in Hong Kong where I was shortly due to arrive:

DIARY RECEIVED UP TO MARCH 3 FIRST CLASS. GALLUP POLL SHOWS LITTLE DOG TEN POINT FIVE PER CENT AHEAD HURRY HOME TED NEEDS YOU EVEN BEXLEY POTENTIALLY VUL-NERABLE. WE HAD TOM LEHRER DAVID FROST AND CLIVE IRVING TO LUNCHEON FOR PATE EN BRIOCHE FONDEST LOVE = ARA-BELLA FATHER

'Little Dog' was a reference, with scant respect, to the Prime Minister, Harold Wilson. During the post-war Labour administration, Wilson, who was short of stature, was regularly seen trotting along beside Dr Dalton, the enormously tall Chancellor of the Exchequer.

Although, by this stage of his life, Randolph did little more than pick at his food, he none the less required a stately procession of fine dishes to grace his table whenever there were guests to be entertained. The American Frank Gannon, one of Randolph's 'young gentlemen' researchers, recalled Tom Lehrer in his contribution to Kay Halle's book:

One Saturday David Frost brought Tom Lehrer to luncheon. Preparations for a Royal visit could hardly have been more elaborate. A piano was hired and a special menu devised. The meal centred on a Pâté de Foie Gras en

Croute, and an hourly kneading schedule was arranged for the dough. Everyone was called upon and after eighteen hours of virtually continuous kneading, the crust was a deserved triumph.

He had derived a mock-blasphemous enjoyment from the fact that I, as a Roman Catholic, could be amused by Lehrer's song 'The Vatican Rag', and wherever we might go where there was a piano, he would insist that I perform it:

> *You can do the steps you want if*
> *You have cleared them with the Pontiff.*
> *Everybody say his own Kyrie eleison*
> *Doin' the Vatican Rag.*

According to Gannon:

Randolph's sense of humour was a very American one. He would enjoy the most sophisticated joke, but just as frequently he would repeat the apocryphal *Variety* headline about the mad rapist who fled: 'Nut, Screws and Bolts'. He liked the new wave of stand-up comics like Mort Sahl and Shelly Berman, and Bob Newhart's Eisenhower-welcoming-Khrushchev routine was his favourite.

He was a great fan of Tom Lehrer's, and playing at least one side of the latest Lehrer record became part of the nightly after-dinner ritual, along with the ten o'clock news, and the reading aloud, usually from the 'Courtship and Marriage' chapter of Volume Two (with the charming letters between his father and mother) or the section on the 'Naming of the Battleships' (with the King's Secretary's classic line: 'Monosyllables are as a rule a mistake when applied to Battleships ...'). Lehrer's offhand phrase 'or one of that crowd' (as in 'Mozart or one of that crowd') became a standard part of Randolph's speech, like his unvarying reference to the Luce magazines as '*Time, Life,* and mis*Fortune*'.

A week later my father wrote to me in New York:

18 March 1966

I am very glad to think that you are on your last leg and soon returning home. Do try and get back before the Election. Ted Heath [to whom I had been Personal Assistant in the 1964 Election] would like you for the last three or four days and you should certainly try and be back in time to vote. The current odds are ten to one on Labour.

Arkle won the Gold Cup at Cheltenham yesterday by thirty lengths at a hundred to nine on.

I am longing to see you again and hear all your news. I hope you will be very careful before you commit yourself to any too decided opinions on Vietnam. Opinion here is much less wobbly than when you went away. That is because Harold Wilson can't quarrel with LBJ as he owes him such a lot of money. On the other hand, as you will have found in America, a lot of opinion – and well respected opinion – is going soft on the war. Since you have been out there I have read everything I have been able to and I must say I don't see how the Americans can win. It looks as if their own casualties are now getting fairly high while the Vietcong and North Vietnam seem to be able to replace whatever losses they may have. If you get down to Washington, mind you see Scottie Reston of the *New York Times* as well as McNamara. That will give you the two sides of the case. Perhaps the truth lies somewhere in between...

Towards the end of the month Randolph wrote to his old friend Evelyn Waugh:

27 March 1966

I was away in Switzerland when your [*Sword of Honour*] trilogy arrived and it has only just come to light buried under a big pile of my father's books that have come from Chartwell. So please forgive my delay in thanking you.

I have read it all in the individual volumes twice. I certainly mean to read the final version, though I doubt whether I shall show the perception and assiduity of the reviewer in the *Times Literary Supplement*. He must have fed it all into a computer.

Incidentally, why did you scrap your phrase about my father's 'sham Augustan style'?

I heard reports that you had been rather low and were abandoning a book on the crusades. Frankly I think I shall myself prefer the second volume of your autobiography. When does it come out?

Two weeks later Evelyn, his friend since Oxford days and his companion in arms in Yugoslavia, was dead. Randolph commented: 'He was most punctilious in his correspondence and I had been concerned at receiving no answer to my last letter. His death came to me as a grievous loss and shock.'

CHAPTER 34

Some 'Burnt-Out Case'!

In the spring of 1966 Randolph was shocked to learn that his father's personal physician, Lord Moran, in contravention of his Hippocratic oath, was publishing a book about his most famous patient. Entitled *Churchill: The Struggle for Survival 1940–1965*, it was based on the medical diaries that Moran had kept. Randolph joined battle with a letter to the independent medical journal, *The Lancet*, on 23 April 1966:

> Lord Moran's diaries covering the quarter of a century in which he knew Sir Winston Churchill as patient and friend are to be published in the spring...
>
> A doctor, like a lawyer or a priest, does not readily recount his professional dealings with an identifiable person; and the public's trust in the medical profession derives largely from its conviction that what transpires between patient and doctor will not be bandied about. If this confidentiality is owed to the living, it is doubly owed to the dead ... Lord Moran, by writing publicly about the medical condition of an identified patient, is creating a modern precedent. It is a bad precedent which none should follow.

A spirited correspondence ensued in the columns of *The Times*, but it was Randolph who won the day with an article in the *Daily Telegraph* of 15 June. This was as fascinating for its insight into his father's struggle against bouts of ill-health over the final twenty-five years of his life from 1940, as it was damning of Lord Moran:

WAS HE A BURNT-OUT CASE?

A lot of people in many lands are beginning to ask whether Winston Churchill was fit to conduct the war to a successful conclusion after 1943; whether he did as well as he should have done for the Western world at Potsdam; and whether his health justified him in persevering in Opposition in 1945; and then in 1951 resuming the government of Great Britain for three-and-a-half years.

Most of this disquietude, which has shown itself particularly in Britain,

France and the United States, is due to the recent book by Lord Moran, my father's doctor for the last 25 years of his life.

It has led people in Britain to ask whether there should not be a statutory committee of doctors which should at regular intervals inquire into the health of the Prime Minister, as is done in the case of the senior executives of many of the great corporations in the United States. People are getting worried lest some utterly incapable person should be in charge of important affairs at some moment of crisis.

Do these suppositions rightly apply to Sir Winston Churchill?

It is not my purpose here to review Moran's book but merely to cite and refute a few statements which have given rise to these questions. A very few will suffice.

We are told, for instance, by Lord Moran in an interview in the *Sunday Times* of April 3: 'Oh, after the war. He was burnt out. It was the exhaustion of mind and body and the series of strokes that accounted for much that is otherwise inexplicable.' In fact, as Moran reveals himself, Churchill had no stroke until 1949.

Apart from some pneumonic attacks in the war and a 'coronary insufficiency' in Washington in December 1941, he enjoyed, for a man of his age, labours and responsibility, good health – sufficient enough to do the job. And during none of these illnesses did he ever relax his control over the British war effort...

Yet men in charge of great destinies are apt to worry when things go wrong. They don't disclose *all* their worries to their colleagues or the House of Commons; only, alas, do they confide some of the more physical of them to a doctor, who after death turns out to be a sneak guest.

Later Moran tells us: 'The end of the war found Winston spent.'

While Churchill was forming his new Cabinet in 1951 Moran revealed an extraordinary and previously unsuspected political ambition. He wished to serve in the Government of this 'burnt-out case', the man whose forces had eight years before been 'spent' and had now 'crawled back to No. 10 Downing Street', to quote a somewhat inelegant phrase used by Lord Moran about his patient.

My brother-in-law, Christopher Soames, recalls that while the Government was being formed Moran approached the new Prime Minister and asked to be made Minister of Health. This was met with a hilarious and incredulous response. After all there were many doctors in the Ministry of Health – what was needed was an experienced politician in charge.

When the Prime Minister said that the matter could not be considered Moran, according to Soames, flew into a great tantrum and ranted and raved and said that it was most unfair after all he had done for the Prime

Minister that he should not be awarded this office. He withdrew and a week later his wife wrote to apologise for his having behaved so foolishly and rudely . . .

In most professions there are definitely set retiring ages such as 60 or 65. This has never applied to politicians nor has anyone ever suggested that it should. In politics experience, wisdom and judgment may grow with advancing years; achievement and stature may be *all*-important. Gladstone formed his fourth administration at the age of 82, though it is true that the Liberal Cabinet quite soon wanted to get rid of him, as did the Tory Cabinet when Churchill achieved a similar age.

Winston Churchill was 65 when he became Prime Minister in May 1940. He had for five months been qualified to draw the old-age pension. It appears from the general consensus of mankind that he made a valuable, even indispensable, contribution to the war. Indeed, almost anyone else would have tried to have made a negotiated peace and the whole world might then have fallen under the sway of Hitler . . . He was the unanimous choice of all parties in the State as the one man who could unite the nation in its dread hour of danger.

I have been appointed by my father as his official biographer. It will certainly be no part of my tale to pretend that he never made any mistakes, either before, during or after the war. Of whom could that be said? But who else could have done any better?

Well after 1943, when Moran tells us that he was 'spent', he made powerful contributions to the Allied victory. Of course he had his arguments and his ups and downs with Roosevelt, with de Gaulle and with Stalin. What grand alliance has ever prevailed without disagreements?

Moran says of Churchill: 'It was exhaustion of mind and body that accounts for much that is otherwise inexplicable in the last year of the war – for instance the deterioration in his relations with Roosevelt.'

But at Yalta it was not Churchill who was dying. Roosevelt was dead five months later. Churchill lived another 21 years. So much for medical prognosis!

As for Churchill's 'failing powers' at Yalta, one of his closest confidential advisers recently wrote to me:

If Britain's influence declined in 1944, this was primarily due to a shift in relative military strengths. By then the USA had more divisions in the field. This meant, as WSC had long foreseen, that within the Alliance Britain's role became one of counsel rather than command. This change coincided with the decline in FDR's judgment – he *was* dying – and a growing disposition on the part of senior American advisers to believe that they could do a bilateral deal with the Russians.

It was these conditions, and not any lack of grip by WSC, that led to lost opportunities at the Yalta Conference – and, to a lesser extent, at Potsdam.

Throughout these difficult times WSC preserved his judgment and foresight undiminished. He was, after all, the first to appreciate the gravity of Russia's threat to Europe.

When the war ended Churchill was 70. This is the moment at which Moran thinks he was 'burnt out'. Churchill was certainly greatly distressed at the outcome of the election in 1945, as he had been by many things that had happened in the last year of the war . . .

Of course he hoped he would be re-elected and have some share in the framing of a peace. Whether he would have succeeded or not is anybody's guess. He certainly couldn't have done much worse. Those who took over failed to make any peace at all and 21 years later there is no German Peace Treaty.

For three or four months after his electoral defeat he was like a bear with a sore head. He did not show his mortification in public and he gradually regained his equanimity.

Moran says that his defeat in 1945 left 'a permanent scar'. I believe this scar healed easily and without any therapeutic treatment. But I do remember some six or seven weeks after the election walking around the gardens with him at Chartwell. He was very morose and I tried to cheer him up. He stopped and turned on me and said quite angrily: 'It is very silly of the child to mind when his toys are taken away from him. But he *does* mind.'

Of course, by his 'toys' he meant his Red Boxes with all the Foreign Office telegrams. He felt isolated from the great world of power. But quite soon he recovered his equilibrium and decided to continue as leader of the Tory Party and to write his six-volume account of the Second World War, which was widely acclaimed and certainly got a better press than did Moran's book. This work earned him the Nobel Prize for Literature in 1953.

Not bad for a burnt-out case!

At the same time he managed, with able lieutenants, to reform the Tory party so that five years later they were able to come within six seats of defeating the Socialists in 1950 and in 1951 when the Socialists threw in their hand he was able, as Moran says, to 'crawl back' to 10 Downing Street with a majority of 17 . . .

When he became Prime Minister again in 1951 there is no doubt that he dominated his Cabinet colleagues . . . It may be that he had not quite the same strength and resilience as he had in 1940. Indeed, it would be surprising if this had been so; for he was by now a man of 77. But he certainly had enough drive and vigour to provide leadership for this country, at home and also in international affairs, viz. his visits to the United States and Canada and his speeches there.

Even in 1953, after the most severe of the strokes which afflicted him, he did not lose heart. To Moran he may have shown apprehension. To his personal staff and others close to him he showed only determination – to recover and carry on.

When he had the stroke I was ill with influenza. As soon as I recovered I went down to see him at Chartwell. There were three of us for dinner – WSC, Jock Colville and myself. WSC was in a wheelchair. After dinner, in the drawing room, he said that he was going to stand on his feet. Jock and I urged him not to attempt this and, when he insisted, we came up to either side of him so that we could catch him if he fell. He waved us back with a stick, he then lowered his feet to the ground, gripped the arms of his chair, and by a tremendous effort – with sweat pouring down his face – levered himself to his feet and stood upright. Having demonstrated that he could do this, he sat down again.

I shall never forget this demonstration of will-power. It was like 1940 in person – 'you can't do this to me'. He was determined to recover.

He did recover. Though he had what he called 'a kick in his gallop', he could go regularly to the House of Commons and could still dominate it.

In the House of Commons he was perhaps at his best, in these last days, when answering Parliamentary questions. Right up to the end he was adept in dealing with supplementaries – for which he never needed any notes and relied wholly on his power to improvise ...

I regret that on reading the book one might have the impression that my father was a hypochondriac, perpetually concerned about his health. But frequently throughout the 25 years during which Moran was my father's doctor, many months would pass between visits, months of enormous creative activity and sparkling health and vigour which Moran never had the opportunity to observe.

It is quite natural that as a doctor his observations should be chiefly concerned with ill health, but this limitation imposed considerable restrictions on his opportunity for presenting a really complete portrait of my father.

Moran was a gloomy figure, and on one occasion abroad one member of my family said to him: 'You know, Charles, you have been here for five days now, and you have not said a kind word about anyone.' This made him very angry.

Let us take up once more the accusation of the 'burnt-out case'...

Between his 80th birthday on November 30, 1954, and his retirement on April 5, 1955, parliament sat for 13 weeks. During this time he took part in three major debates, answered Questions on 23 days – giving 103 answers to 122 questions and dealing with 183 supplementary questions...

But even after he had resigned in 1955 his capacity for interest in world affairs had not been drained away. He was not – even yet – a burnt-out case.

He joined in debates on German rearmament, the future of the European Defence Community; made at least three notable speeches in the 1955 elections; and a distinguished and noteworthy address at Aachen in May 1956 where he received the Charlemagne Prize...

It may be that his hopes [of organising a 'Summit' meeting with the Americans and Russians] were chimerical. But he persevered; in any case it is quite ludicrous for anyone to pretend that his second administration was in any sense a failure, or a stain on his reputation.

No great miscalculation or disaster marred these years. He did not, like Lloyd George, traffic in honours; nor like Baldwin lie to the country about its defences; nor like Chamberlain dishonour the country by a Munich.

He would never have made the shambles that Sir Anthony Eden created at Suez. Shortly after Suez someone asked whether he would have undertaken this operation. He reflected for quite a time then replied – 'I would not have done it without squaring the Americans – but if I had, I would never have dared to stop.' He was retired and after 80 when he made that sagacious statement.

Randolph's article gave rise to numerous letters of congratulation including one from his father's old friend Violet Bonham Carter who was now Baroness Asquith:

19th June 1966

Dear Randolph,

I must write you a line of fervent congratulation on your 'Burntout Case' article in the D.T.

It was I felt the *coup de grâce* to Moran (though 'grace' is the least thing he deserves!). The revelation of his grotesque demand to be made Minister of Health & subsequent tantrums was especially effective.

I cannot tell you what I feel about his abuse of his (fortuitous) & confidential function & of his lack of elementary loyalty to one whom he had the honour to serve. I knew of the existence of the book as long ago as '62 from a private source. (It was then in *12* volumes!) If ever we meet I can tell you more about this in confidence...

Once more *all* my congratulations – 'Sneak Guest' was a good touch.

Ever yours,
Violet

Another congratulatory missive came from Nigel Lawson, the new editor of the *Spectator* and future Chancellor of the Exchequer:

24 June 1966

I very much enjoyed your piece in the *Telegraph* the other day: the revelation about Moran asking for the Ministry of Health was an absolute block-buster. My only regret is that the article appeared in the *Telegraph* and not in the *Spectator* ... There is nothing I should like better than to see your name in our pages again.

Among those who contacted Randolph following his article was Dr J. Tudor Pembleton from Chelmsford who, in common with the great majority of the medical profession, shared the family's sense of outrage at the betrayal of a patient's confidences by a past President of the Royal College of Physicians and who had lodged a formal complaint about the conduct of Lord Moran. The complaint – that Moran had published 'for his private profit, details of Sir Winston Churchill's life which were gained in his relationship as Sir Winston Churchill's medical practitioner' – was to be heard before a meeting of the Central Ethical Committee of the British Medical Association (BMA). Randolph was invited to submit evidence to the Committee or to appear before it. Primed by Randolph, Clemmie joined the fray:

4 October 1966

Dear Dr Tudor Pembleton,

Thank you for your letter of the 29th of September. I have been in touch with my son and we both feel that it would be wrong to decline your request, knowing that the evidence given before the Central Ethical Committee is strictly confidential.

I am therefore sending you a copy of a letter I wrote to Lord Moran on the 30th of July 1964. I think that it is self explanatory ... I should perhaps explain that at that date, seven months before my husband's death, his health had deteriorated to a point where it would not have been feasible to discuss this matter with him.

I enclose an extract from a letter I addressed to Lord Moran on January the 21st 1966 when he had asked for permission to reproduce the Orpen portrait of my husband in his book.

Yours sincerely,
Clementine S. Churchill

In her letter to Moran Clemmie had made clear her strenuous opposition to his intended breach of confidence:

30 July 1964

Dear Charles,

I am seriously disturbed by our conversation yesterday. I think that you should have told me of your intentions: it was only through the matter having been mentioned in the Press that I found out you intended to write a book about Winston, and I subsequently raised the matter with Jock [Colville].

I had always supposed that the relationship between a doctor and his patient was one of complete confidence.

Had you been writing your own biography, with passing references to Winston, it would have been understandable, though I would have hoped that you would tell us what you intended to say. But I do not see how you can justify your present course. An impartial observer would, I think, consider that your career had been a successful one and had not been damaged by your association with Winston, and I think he has not shown himself ungrateful to you.

Incidentally, I have seen Anthony [Montague Browne]'s letter to you, which Jock informs me you found 'intolerable'. I do not see how this adjective can be applied to a mildly phrased letter which Anthony was bound to write in his capacity as the legal Trustee of the copyright in Sir Winston's and my own papers. I do urge you to reconsider your intentions.

C.S.C.

Randolph, too, gave evidence to the Central Ethical Committee of the BMA, which recommended that the noble doctor be expelled for unethical conduct likely to bring the profession into disrepute. The resolution was to have been considered by the Council of the Association at its meeting on 21 December. However, before it could do so, the wily old doctor issued writs for libel against the BMA for publishing a letter containing the resolution of the Central Ethical Committee, thereby preventing any consideration of the resolution by the Council. Having succeeded in his stratagem, Moran withdrew the writs unconditionally and asked to appear before the BMA at its meeting early in the New Year to speak in mitigation. As Dr Tudor Pembleton reported to Randolph:

> I was invited to attend this meeting of the Council, as an observer. This I did and listened to Lord Moran repeat his contention that he had been given verbal permission by Sir Winston Churchill to write his book. He produced no evidence and made all the remarks that he had made in the various letters to the newspapers in, what seemed to me, a manner of some arrogance. He repeated the inference that he had not been paid but remarked that he had refused remuneration, which did not seem to me to be entirely consistent...

In the event, Moran got away with a severe censure.

The excuse advanced by Moran for publishing his memoirs, namely that he had received no remuneration from his patient, was typical of the disingenuousness which led him to be known within the medical profession as 'Corkscrew' Charlie. The truth was, as my father told me at the time, that because he was one of the most highly paid doctors in the land, paying surtax at 19s 6d in the pound (97.5 per cent), he had particularly asked *not* to be paid. Instead he requested his patient to pay for his sons to attend public school – an arrangement to which Winston had, most willingly, consented.

CHAPTER 35

'Project K'

That summer of 1966 Randolph spent three weeks in the South of France as the guest of his friend and former fighter-pilot ace, Max Aitken, at La Capponcina, the home of Max's late father, Lord Beaverbrook. Though surrounded by family and friends, Randolph was on edge, awaiting the verdict of the reviewers of Volume I of the Great Biography, which was shortly to be published. He suspected, not entirely mistakenly, that some of the reviewers whom he had offended or carved up in his journalistic columns over the years, might use the occasion to retaliate with reviews of Randolph himself, rather than of his *magnum opus*, to which he had devoted the past five years. Frank Gannon recalls:

> The waiting was the worst part. He tried to occupy himself with the beginnings of Volume Two, but the tension was too great. He began to sleep later into the afternoon, and to be more irritable. He would constantly shift the conversation back to what he was thinking about all the time: how would it be received; who would they get to review it in the *Sunday Times*, in the *TLS* . . . Would the countless people to whom he had been rude, whom he had cut, who had mocked his life as frivolous and flamboyant, who had objected that so great a work should have been entrusted to a competent professional historian – would these people now write their reviews of Randolph S. Churchill instead of the book he had laboured five years, laboured in fact all of his life, to produce?

Randolph need not have worried. The reviews were overwhelmingly favourable, apart from a sour note struck, predictably, by *The Times* whose reviewer, hiding under the cloak of anonymity, loftily declared: '. . . had there been open competition, Mr Randolph Churchill might not have come in first. He is his father's biographer by inheritance, rather than on the record of his past work.'

But A. J. P. Taylor in his review for the *Observer* praised Randolph's 'courageous frankness' in drawing attention to his father's 'egocentricity which was to become such a predominant characteristic, and to which must be attributed alike his blunders and his triumphant successes'.

Among the flood of congratulatory letters Randolph received was a most generous one from my mother in America: 'I am so happy & proud of you, on volume I. It is rare in this country to read reviews that are all raves! It must be so very gratifying & I know well deserved. Please know how happy it makes me, for you. It is a truly just reward...'

But just as Randolph was savouring the deserved success of his labours, his health problems were mounting. Though reluctant to discuss such matters, even within the family, he had evidently shared his anxieties with his sister, Mary Soames, who was already embarked upon the Life she was writing of their mother and who had visited him at Stour to discuss their respective literary ventures. On her return home, she hastened to write to him:

3rd October 1966

... It was so interesting (& also helpful to me) to be able to discuss so many family things with you – your views on Mama & your recollections will be of immense value to me, in trying to get a reasonably detached view.

I am so dreadfully sorry about your health, & touched & glad you confided in me to some extent about it. I only wish I could do or say something helpful. It's so easy to *say* it – but please, please try not to get too down & depressed. You *must* finish this wonderful & important book, and I am quite sure mind-over-matter is not a myth – but a very real ingredient (I don't put it higher) in ill-health. Also – you know – I think we are all blessed with something of Papa's marvellous constitution – and we really are tough & resilient – look how often Papa confounded his doctors – & even at the end. Think of all the people who have done marvels in the past despite rotten health. Superb physique & freedom from disease have never been the guarantees of art or literature or political prowess. Think of the Brontës – tho I'm sure you would have thought them gabby girls! Still they were physical wrecks & yet produced these extraordinary books ... I feel so much for you, as of course it's wretched trying to work when you're feeling ill. But *please* box on – because no one can write this book as you can – & it will be not only a splendid memorial of Papa, but also the vindication & apotheosis of all your life's labour & ambitions, and will have a place always in history & literature.

Following his severe pneumonia in 1963 (not aided by his 80–100-cigarette-a-day habit) and his lung operation in the spring of 1964, Randolph, in April 1965, had a mild stroke – an event which he kept from his family. According to his local physician, Dr Marshall, he had for many years been suffering from hypertension and high blood pressure, as well as from cirrhosis of the liver. However, in July 1966, Dr Marshall noticed that his liver had started to shrink. Despite massive doses of iron orally and intramuscularly, he had become severely anaemic and required a transfusion of three pints of blood. Further investigation revealed gross gastritis and two gastric ulcers. It is no wonder that Randolph was virtually unable to eat and, when he tried to do so, was unable to keep it down. Furthermore, since 1963 he had suffered five minor heart attacks which Dr Marshall suspected might be due to failure of the left side of the heart.

Dr Marshall told Randolph bluntly that he had to give up the whisky to which he had long been addicted and all other spirits, placing him on a liquid diet of milk and Complan, a dietary supplement rich in vitamins. Refusing, as ever, to take 'orders' from doctors (or anyone else), Randolph none the less consented to accept the kindly doctor's advice and, thereafter, restricted his drinking habits to the occasional lager and one or two glasses of wine a day. All too late, he had seen the writing on the wall. Though he faced the future with stoicism and without complaint, he realised that, though only fifty-five years old – my exact age as I finish this work – he had a major battle on his hands if he was to survive to complete the great monument that he was labouring to build as a filial tribute to his father, whom he had loved so deeply and who, even beyond the grave, continued to dominate his life.

Putting his health worries behind him, in late November Randolph set sail for New York aboard the *Queen Mary*, en route for Barbados where he planned to spend a working holiday. He sent me a copy of his diary entry at the time:

RMS Queen Mary at sea

Thursday November 24

Noon. Sailing briskly across the Channel. Calm sea. Slight haze, after sunshine in Solent. Last night we rang Mr Vincent of the Verandah Grill who said that he was keeping my 'usual table' for me in the window: he was keeping a large one 'in case I wished to entertain'. A scrutiny of the passenger list reveals no-one suitable for entertainment, save Yehudi Menuhin and Sir Isaac Wolfson, and perhaps Lady Bird [Johnson]...

Life at sea is good for the appetite. For breakfast I had: orange juice, tea, porridge with cream, and brioche with strawberry jam. Andrew [Kerr], who never eats breakfast, was persuaded to eat a brace of kippers.

Just going up to deck to take the temperature. Social temperature: low. Except for ourselves and children no one under 60. Perhaps the *jeunesse d'orée* will board at Cherbourg, which we reach in half an hour, when we shall be lunching in the far-famed Verandah Grill.

Mill-pond crossing. In the crowded bar a fiddler – not Yehudi I apprehend – has been playing for the pre-luncheon guests. In Winston's honour we are singing:

> Hail the *Wehrmacht*
> I mean the *Bundeswehr*
> Hail our glorious ally!

This was one of his favourite Tom Lehrer ditties and I happened to be in Germany at the time, reporting on the rising fortunes of the neo-Nazi party in Germany for the *News of the World*. I had secured an interview with its leader, Herr von Thadden, who turned out not to be an Austrian house-painter about to set the world ablaze, but a dispossessed Pomeranian squire anxious for the return of his lands behind the Iron Curtain.

Randolph's transatlantic diary continues:

Friday November 25

4.00 p.m. No *jeunesse d'orée* at Cherbourg ... Early in the evening, while still tied up at Cherbourg, I dictated the first 500 words of the Irish Chapter. So good that we thought of sending them by Radio Press Collect [to the] *Sunday Times* [for whom Randolph was now contributing the occasional column] for *Sunday Telegraph* and Heinemann; but Andrew found out that even at Press rate it would cost, at 5d per word, about £12. The *Sunday Times* might object if we send the whole chapter Collect. Andrew has saturated himself all morning in Irish affairs. We plan to do another 1,000 words before dinner.

I nearly forgot, last night an aged American couple approached very sweetly and introduced themselves to me. They looked towards Andrew and said: 'And is this Yehudi Menhuin?' I resisted the temptation of saying: 'No, he's Sir Isaac Wolfson.'

Today Wolfson and his wife lunched with us in the Verandah Grill. They wanted to take us down to the dining room as they had already ordered their Kosher luncheon there. I said 'Nonsense, Andrew will arrange for the Kosher luncheon to be served in the Verandah Grill'. So it was, however the Verandah Grill has no Kosher plates and no Kosher knifes and forks, but the Wolfsons said that it didn't matter. Lady Wolfson is a pretty red-headed woman of Russian Jewish extraction. Sir Isaac's father was a Polish Jew who came to Glasgow in the 1890s.

After she had left to see a movie we drew him out. He was even more forthcoming than Roy's the Boy [Roy Thomson, later Lord Thomson of Fleet, proprietor of the *Sunday Times* and later of *The Times*], in fact he only needed about two questions to get him started. He told us in minute detail how he made his money and how he has and is giving it away. Around 1924 he settled about £10,000 of Gussie's [shares in Great Universal Stores] on all his brothers, sisters, nephews and nieces, about twenty all told. He doesn't think that people ought to have too much money and it was all put into Trusts intended to bring them in about £500 a year. Today each of the £10,000, all still in Gussies, is worth £625,000 ... the money given to the Wolfson Foundation is worth £80 million [over £750 million at today's values], they only give away the income – so far £15 million has been dispersed.

He told us a lot of jolly jumble jokes ... [and] that RSVP on invitations meant 'Remember Send Vedding Present' ...

In the final instalment of his transatlantic diary Randolph records:

Monday 28 November 1966 – Midnight

We get in at crack of dawn tomorrow. It has been a very steady journey. The stabilisers really work. There has been no motion at all. We haven't done as much as we would have liked of the Irish Chapter owing to a number of factors, one of which has been getting to know our great new friend, Sir Isaac Wolfson. I have arranged with Denis Hamilton to do a 5,000-word profile on him for the *Sunday Times*. And we have got two hours of him on tape. I did the first hour on how he made his money and Andrew did the second hour on how he is giving it away ...

Wolfson and I exchanged balance sheets. We have shown him ours which records a net profit of £3,000. He showed us his which shows a net profit of £43 million. We picked up a lot of tips from him as to how to run our business in the future ...

We made friends on board with Yehudi Menuhin ... I told him straight away that I knew nothing about music and he agreed it was much better people should say so instead of affecting the interest they do not possess. He talked in the most intelligent way about a wide variety of topics. He has very great charm. He has a striking looking wife who is extremely gabby and noisy with other people but when she's talking to him is very quiet and discreet. They seem an extremely happy couple. They have a son who wants to become a film director...

There have been reports of very bad lethal smog hovering over the Atlantic seaboard, stretching from Massachusetts right down to Washington DC. I wired Bobby Kennedy and said please send two gas masks to meet us at the pier. We haven't had any answer. Perhaps he is offended. We pointed out he had grave responsibilities both in Massachusetts and in New York. If he doesn't send the gas masks, we'll turn Republican and ask Governor Rockefeller to send them instead.

Before leaving for Barbados, where he had rented Queen's Fort, a fine house on the island's west coast, close to Ronnie Tree's magnificent mansion of Heron Bay, Randolph made sure to spend a few days in Washington with his lifelong friend, Kay Halle, in her Georgetown home. It was while there that he received a most exciting proposition which he hastened to share with Natalie Bevan at home in Suffolk:

5 December 1966

I had dinner with Bobby Kennedy at his farm, Hickory Hill in Virginia, twenty-five minutes outside Washington. Now fasten your safety-belt. After dinner I got Bobby alone. We talked for half an hour about the forthcoming Manchester book on the Kennedy assassination. This was rather painful to Bobby and he twice said he did not want to talk about it; but then he reopened the topic himself. Then he started talking about my book. He had not read it – only the reviews. He suddenly said: 'When will you finish your book?' I said: '1970.' He said: 'By then we will have all President Kennedy's papers sorted. Would you like to edit them?' I was staggered, but said quite calmly, 'Yes, of course, and should I write his Life too?' Bobby said, 'Certainly', and said that he would like it done in the same objective manner as my book on my father.

It was like being given three Nobel prizes for Literature piled on top of each other. It is the greatest compliment ever paid me in my life. After all, despite what [Sir William] Haley [editor of *The Times*, in his review of Volume One] wrote, I had a natural right to do my father's Life. This is something so extraordinary that I could hardly believe it. I shall now have to plan to live an extra five years till 1976. You must look after me.

This is Top Secret. Tell no-one except Bobby [Natalie's husband] who I know is a tomb of discretion: and keep this letter under lock and key. When writing to me refer to it as 'Project K'.

As Martin Gilbert recorded in his contribution to Kay Halle's *The Young Unpretender*:

> But of greater encouragement to Randolph than all the reviews was Robert Kennedy's invitation to him to write the biography of John F. Kennedy as soon as the Great Work was complete . . . plans for 'Project K' were discussed around the fire at Stour late into many nights. Randolph envisaged a two-volume work, the first on Kennedy's rise to power, the second on his Presidency. At one stage he hoped to begin 'Project K' in 1969, while nearing the end of the fifth and last volume of *Winston S. Churchill*.

Despite his frenetic schedule, Randolph was able to record:

> Thursday 21 December 1966, the shortest day of the year, was one of great satisfaction to me. I finished Volume II of my Life of my father: Lord Thomson was confirmed in his purchase of *The Times*: Mrs John F. Kennedy succeeded in enforcing her contract and protecting her copyright in *Death of a President* [by William Manchester].
>
> I was only directly concerned in the first of these events, but my mind was actively preoccupied with the second and my heart with the third.

The next day Randolph cabled Jackie Kennedy:

> WARMEST CONGRATULATIONS YOUR VINDICATION OF CON-
> TRACT AND COPYRIGHT LAW AND YOUR VICTORY FOR PER-
> SONAL PRIVACY FONDEST LOVE = RANDOLPH

Despite his high hopes he was not well. With Randolph under the weather, it was inevitable that the Great Biography progressed more slowly. This, in turn, upset and depressed him. In mid-May of 1967, hearing that he was in low spirits, I rented a single-engine plane and flew up to East Bergholt to spend a couple of days with him. As I recorded in *Memories and Adventures*:

> Over dinner the conversation turned to world affairs. All at once my father remarked: 'It seems to me that the situation in the Middle East is warming up. Winston, why don't you go and visit our friends in Israel? – so far you have only seen the situation from the Arab side.' Like many young men of my age – I was twenty-six at the time – I was reluctant to accept parental guidance and ever ready to assert an independent view. Far from accepting my father's suggestion, I disputed it. However . . . by the time he awoke, I had already booked myself to Tel Aviv on an El Al flight leaving London

at 1.00 p.m. that day. I had called *The Times* to ask if they would be interested in having some articles from me on the Middle East, only to learn that they had, that very morning, sent their defence correspondent, Charles Douglas-Home, on an early flight to Israel.

Having drawn a blank at the quality end of the market, I decided to try the mass circulation end instead ... I left a message for Mr Somerfield [the editor of the *News of the World*], who was not yet in the office, to the effect that I presumed they already had a correspondent in the Middle East to cover the situation but, in the event that they did not and he wished me to represent them, he could leave word with El Al at Heathrow before 1.00 p.m. Meanwhile I bade farewell to my slightly amazed father ... and flew back to Redhill, where Minnie met me with a passport and packed suitcase and we raced from there to London Airport. Though we did not arrive until the scheduled departure time, El Al had held the flight and there was a message from Mr Somerfield commissioning me to write a series of three articles for them on the Middle East situation.

Ever eager to give me his full backing for such ventures, my father fired off a salvo of telegrams to journalistic contacts in Tel Aviv and Jerusalem, as well as to the Foreign Minister, Abba Eban, and Israel's former Prime Minister, David Ben-Gurion. Two days later, at dawn on the morning of Monday 22 May, I was in the latter's suite at the King David Hotel in Jerusalem when word came over the radio that Nasser had closed the Straits of Tiran, blockading Israel's access to the Red Sea and Persian gulf oil supplies. As I recalled:

[Ben-Gurion] motioned with his hand for the radio to be turned off. He was visibly shaken, but not surprised, by the news. He shook his head gravely and declared: 'This means war!' Then there followed a lengthy silence before, with deep emotion in his voice, he went on: 'I am very frightened! Not for Israel – she will survive – but for the youth of our country. It is always the finest of their generation who never return.' he went on to expound his unequivocal conviction – as assured as had been my grandfather's in 1940 – that, come what may, Israel would survive. 'For the Arabs, what is military defeat?' he mused, before answering his own rhetorical question: 'It is the loss of an army. In ten years they will have another. But Israel can never afford to be defeated. Defeat for us would be the end – the end of everything, the end of our homes, our families, the end of the Jewish state, the end of the dreams of centuries. That is why we shall never be defeated!'

Taking me by the forearm, the old man led me out on to the balcony where Jerusalem the golden lay before us, and proceeded to give me a lesson in Jewish history which, seen through his mind's eye, stretched out in a seamless panoply of time. 'This,' he declared with a gesture, 'is the city of David – Jewish for 3,000 years. But travel a few miles down that road', pointing the way with his finger as he spoke, 'there you will find Hebron, the city of Abraham – 4,000 years Jewish!' It was a moving and magical moment.

Just over two weeks later, on Monday 5 June, Israel launched her devastating pre-emptive strike against her neighbours, destroying over 300 out of some 340 serviceable Egyptian combat aircraft at nineteen airbases within 170 minutes. Not since Pearl Harbor had there been such a devastating surprise attack. Meanwhile on land, the Israeli Army unleashed its lightning attack across the Sinai Desert, outmanoeuvring the 100,000-strong Egyptian Army and blocking their retreat to the Suez Canal. When, later in the week, Jordan and Syria joined in the conflict, they too were dealt devastating hammer blows, which were to deprive Jordan of the West Bank and East Jerusalem, and Syria of the Golan Heights.

If the Israelis moved fast, so did my father. Appreciating the frustration of writing for a Sunday newspaper under such circumstances, he swiftly fixed me up an assignment with the London *Evening News*, which had five editions in the day, making it the ideal platform for a story that was developing with breathtaking speed. Two days later my father cabled me in Tel Aviv:

SUGGEST WE DO JOINT RUSH BOOK STOP WHAT DO YOU SAY
STOP LOVE = FATHER

I cabled back my instant and enthusiastic agreement. Meanwhile Minnie, despite being six months' pregnant with our third child, Marina, gamely volunteered to fly out to type the book, arriving on the last day of the war. Thereupon my father promptly negotiated a deal for the volume rights with Heinemann and for serialisation in the *Sunday Telegraph*.

While my father concentrated on the historical and global perspective, I was to be responsible for those chapters detailing the political events in the Middle East that built up to the crisis, as well as those giving a blow-by-blow account of how Israel secured her remarkable victory. My father proceeded to install a telex machine in his East Bergholt command bunker, where all available research assistants and several 'new boys' were mobilised to draft material. Martin Gilbert's task, for which he was given forty-eight hours, was to write the history of the Jews from Moses to Nasser in 4,000 words while, by telephone, other leg-men were recruited in Washington, New York and the Middle East, so as to build up a picture that would enable my father to write the story of the international power-play behind the conflict.

The collaboration with my father – never the easiest person to work with – went amazingly well, except for the fact that he could not bring himself to accept that anyone could stay anywhere but at the Dan Hotel in Tel Aviv, where he had lodged at the time of the Suez conflict of 1956 and on subsequent visits to Israel. Consequently each evening a bellboy would be dispatched from the Dan to the Hilton Hotel where we were staying, bearing sheaves of telexes – at least half of them demanding to know why I had not replied to earlier ones!

The day after the war ended I went to see the Israeli military censors – three very able colonels, based at the Public Information Office in Beit Sokolov Street – and gave them a list of all the senior military and political figures I wished to interview. They smiled politely but, as I expected, I heard nothing from them. Accordingly, I made my own arrangements and set about debriefing the top Israeli military commanders and interviewing the key political figures, all of whom were only too anxious to reveal how they had won the war.

After three weeks, just as I was on the point of leaving the country having completed my work, all three censors suddenly asked if they could wait upon me in my hotel suite, to which I readily agreed. Somewhat uncomfortably, they said they understood that I had, even without the benefit of their assistance, seen almost everyone on the list that I had submitted to them. I confirmed that this was indeed the case and that, certainly, it had been no thanks to them. One of them then pointed out that I would of course have to submit everything I had written to Israeli military censorship before it could be allowed out of the country. When I told them that all my chapters were already in England being set up in print, they were stumped. At my father's suggestion I had been sending material back, two or three chapters at a time, by the 'safe hand' of various distinguished members of Britain's Jewish community, such as my father's new-found friend, sir Isaac Wolfson, who were returning home after visits to Israel to savour the heady wine of victory.

Even in the final three weeks when I was working alongside my father and his team at Stour, buttoning up the book and getting the corrected proofs away to the publishers, the harmony between the two of us was remarkable, partly due to the clear-cut division of labour and partly to the extraordinarily tight deadline we had set ourselves. Precisely two months after the end of the Arab–Israeli war, *The Six Day War* hit the bookstalls in paperback and rapidly went into multiple reprints as well as eighteen foreign editions. The *Sunday Telegraph* ran the story in five successive issues and for a whole month our faces peered down from hoardings throughout the land, advertising the serialisation under the slogan 'The Churchills go to War Again'.

Considering the speed of its production, the reviews that we received were amazingly friendly and enthusiastic. The distinguished military historian, Sir Basil Liddell Hart, wrote in his review for the *Daily Telegraph* of 11 August 1967:

> *The Six Day War*, the combined work of Randolph S. Churchill and Winston S. Churchill, is a remarkable achievement, and a much better blend than most books produced under joint authorship. It is very well written on the whole, and in parts brilliantly, with a turn of phrase as superbly apt as that of Sir Winston Churchill himself, while free from any rhetorical note. It is a fine piece of journalism and some of the chapters can rightly be termed fine contributions to historical literature, even though they can be classified as 'instant history' because of the shortness of time since the event.

Another reviewer, General Sir Hugh Stockwell, who had commanded the 6th Airborne Division in Palestine in 1947–8 and was General Officer Commanding Ground Forces during the Suez operation of 1956, also gave the book a warm welcome:

> The brilliant military campaign fought by the Israelis at the beginning of June this year, in which they defeated, in the remarkably short space of 6 days, Egypt, Jordan, and Syria, is excitingly described by Randolph and Winston Churchill in *The Six Day War*.
>
> One can hardly put down the book ... in the search for how their victory was achieved...

Cyrus Sulzberger of the *New York Times* wrote to Randolph from Montevideo to say: 'It is far and away the best "quickie" book I have ever read, and I am really impressed by the thoroughness and speed with which you two accomplished the job. You really have every reason to be proud of yourselves. It will stand up over the years and is a thoroughly fine job.'

At the time, though I knew my father had been unwell, I had no inkling that he had less than a year to live. In retrospect, I was thrilled to have had this chance of working so closely with him and collaborating on such a successful joint venture, which immediately became a best-seller.

Shortly afterwards, Randolph's second volume of his father's Life, *Winston S. Churchill: Young Statesman 1900–1914*, was published, dealing with the period of Winston's early political career, from his maiden speech in the House of Commons in 1900 up to the outbreak of war in 1914 when, as First Lord of the Admiralty, he flashed the momentous signal to the Fleet: 'COMMENCE HOSTILITIES AGAINST GERMANY'. The reviews were mixed but, overwhelmingly, favourable.

But the strain of endeavouring to reduce some one million documents to an accurate, coherent and readable biography, especially with diversions such as *Twenty-One Years* and *The Six Day War*, was taking its toll on Randolph's team and, one suspects, upon Randolph himself. Just ten days into *The Six Day War*, Randolph received a bombshell from Martin Gilbert in Oxford:

June 17 [1967]

Dear Randolph,

I'm afraid that I have bad news. The doctors say that I cannot continue as I am without *serious* danger to my health. They say I am taking on far more than I can manage, both in the amount of work, the time spent travelling, and the psychological dislocation. They urge me immediately to cut down my work load drastically, and, for at least a year, to give up travelling and 'devilling'. I cannot cast my health into jeopardy, or risk leaving Helen and the baby with a weakened or broken breadwinner.

I know you will understand how upset I am to have to bring to an end so unexpectedly and so abruptly my work with you, which has been a source of deep satisfaction to me. You have treated me with greater kindness than any other person has ever done, and I shall never forget how much you have done to make me what I am now . . .

My years with you will never be forgotten or surpassed. You have meant more to me than I could ever say or try to write.

Please don't be angry.
Yours ever,
Martin

This was a devastating blow to Randolph, who, already so seriously ill himself, replied:

20 June 1967

I am more grieved than I can say at getting your letter of Saturday. Of course you must be guided by your doctors in this matter. I have long suspected you were doing too much and doing it too quickly; and you would be mad if, at your age, you were to put your health in jeopardy.

It follows that I must find help elsewhere for Volume III. Do you think I can count on your being available for Volume IV? ... As to our current quickie, I shall expect no more work from you save delivery of the finished maps...

Please give my love to Helen and tell her to worry about nothing except the health of the father and the child. If she does this, as I know she will, she will have no time to worry about herself.

Just a month later Cameron Hazelhurst, who had secured a job as A. J. P. Taylor's deputy at the Beaverbrook Library, cited pressure of work caused by *The Six-Day War* venture, and his wife Janette's physical and emotional problems as reasons why he, too, could not go on working for Randolph.

Despite the abrupt ending of their co-operation on the Great Biography, Randolph and Martin Gilbert remained close friends and the latter continued to supply titbits from the spires of Oxford:

8 October 1967

A piece of 'Oxford intelligence'. At dinner on Friday night Robert Blake spoke *very* highly of volume two, commenting on how well the techniques of volume one worked for a more historical period. A. J. P. Taylor, who was present, did not dissent – he said the gem of the volume was the letter about Asquith's drinking habits – and was generally well-disposed to the great work. Blake certainly gave the impression that he had written a 'rave review'.

Meanwhile I had decided to throw my hat in the political ring and had been selected to fight the staunchly Labour seat of Manchester, Gorton, in a by-election. Aware of the indelicacy with which my father was liable to treat voluntary workers, I resisted his offer to 'PROCEED BATTLEWARDS!' as he was minded to do in the jargon of Fleet Street. None the less he despatched his ever loyal secretary, Barbara Twigg, to assist in the campaign. She reported back: 'The other evening when I was canvassing, I knocked on one door and said: "Would you like to meet your Conservative candidate, Winston Churchill?" "No thank you, dear," she said, "I knew him well when he was MP for Preston in 1935 [*sic*]!" And she continued to expound in your favour...'

On my birthday my father sent me a bullish cable of encouragement:

MANY HAPPY RETURNS OF THE DAY AND TO PARLIAMENT PRESENT AWAITS YOU WESTMINSTER LOVE AND GOOD WISHES FATHER

Though I reduced the Labour majority from 8,308 to 577, following a recount, the Labour candidate, a local schoolmaster called Ken Marks, was elected. It was to be another two-and-a-half years before I secured a seat in the June 1970 general election as Member of Parliament for Stretford and, sadly, my father would never know of it.

That autumn it was reported that the German playwright Rolf Hochhuth had written a play, *Soldiers*, which was shortly to be staged on Broadway, alleging that the crash at Gibraltar of the Liberator transport carrying the Polish leader, General Sikorski, on the night of 4 July 1943, had not been accidental, but had been deliberately contrived by the British Secret Service on Churchill's orders. David Frost decided to devote a television programme to the subject: among the participants were Randolph, together with Kenneth Tynan, who as Director of the National Theatre was eager to bring the production to London, and David Irving, Hochhuth's researcher who, over the years, has made himself an unashamed apologist for Hitler.

When, more than a year later, following my father's death, it transpired that the Liberator's Czech pilot, Ed Prchal, the sole survivor of the crash, was still alive and well, living in Los Altos, near Stanford University, California, I approached David Frost to see if he would do a further programme on the subject – a proposition to which he agreed with alacrity and enthusiasm. 'Let's do a Savundra on them!' he exclaimed with excitement. 'Would that fit the bill?' I told him it certainly would. Up to that point the only authenticated case of assassination by television had been Frost's devastating demolition job on Emil Savundra, a crooked insurance tycoon.

David arranged for Prchal to be flown over from California to do battle at my side against Messrs. Tynan and Irving. I was anxious to persuade Prchal to launch an action for libel against the German playwright who had branded him and my grandfather assassins. Given that there is no law of libel against the dead, he was the only one who could sue. But he beat me to it and, over our first handshake, inquired: 'Mr Churchill, where can I get a good libel lawyer?' I referred him to the 'Old Firm', as my father and I called Peter Carter-Ruck and his team, who handled all my father's libel actions; as well as my own over a span of forty years. Prchal went on to win the case hands down but, sadly, it was a pyrrhic victory. Hochhuth had no assets within the jurisdiction of the court, beyond his future UK earnings.

Hochhuth and his supporters were firmly on the run as we approached the end of the programme but Frost realised that the best was yet to come. The moment we were off air, he turned to the principal protagonists and asked if we would all be available to participate in a further programme the following week. At this point Ken Tynan and David Irving began shifting uncomfortably in their seats, giving various reasons why they would be unable to do so. It looked for a moment as if they were going to get away with it. But David was superb. He was having none of it: 'Hold it everyone!' he told the studio audience and participants alike. Then, though it was nearly midnight, he turned to his team and declared: 'Triple-time to the camera crews, we'll tape another show right away!' By the end of the second programme the Hochhuth camp, having tied themselves in knots, had been utterly discredited. From that moment onwards, this lie – fabricated by Dr Goebbels within twenty-four hours of the Gibraltar crash – has never been given credence in Britain or elsewhere.

In the spring of 1968, I travelled to the United States to report on Harold Wilson's visit to Washington, where I had the strange experience of being introduced to the British Prime Minister by the President of the United States, Lyndon Johnson. Soon after my return, I spent a few days at Stour visiting my father, who was eager as ever to know the latest news from Washington and to have word of his many friends there. Despite his poor health he insisted, as always, on staying up until a late hour.

I told him that I had seen Bob McNamara and that Polaris was still secure. However, when I made mention of the fact that Averell Harriman had invited me to lunch with him at his Georgetown home, he became reflective and seemed far away in his thoughts. Suddenly his eyes came into sharp focus and he abruptly declared: 'You should never boast about your conquests!' I was taken aback and could not think what on earth he could be alluding to. Then I realised that he was being autobiographical and that my mention of Averell had reminded him of their first meeting in Cairo more than a quarter of a century before. He then went on to describe how, while in a foxhole in the desert, he had received a telegram from Winston, stressing the importance of Harriman's forthcoming visit to the Middle East on behalf of President Roosevelt.

In compliance with his father's request to do what he could to make Harriman's visit enjoyable, he had one evening chartered an Arab dhow and given a dinner in his honour as they cruised up the Nile under a moonlit sky. Telling the story against himself, without bitterness or rancour, he confided to me: 'We had had a fine dinner and [speaking no doubt for himself] rather too much to drink, which led me to do the unforgivable. I boasted to Averell of an affair I was having with the American wife of a senior British officer in Cairo.' He then added, somewhat wistfully: 'I had no idea what Averell was getting up to in London.' He would have been as astonished as I to have been told that, within barely three years of our conversation, shortly after my step-father Leland Hayward's death in the spring of 1971, Averell and my mother would be married. Considering that Averell was, at the time, on the point of celebrating his eightieth birthday, he and my mother were fortunate to enjoy fifteen years of happy marriage together.

In the previous weeks, concern had been voiced to me by several of those involved with the production of the Great Biography that all was not well at Stour. Not only was my father in very poor health but, in the absence of both Michael Wolff, who was then at Conservative Central Office, and Martin Gilbert, the ship was becoming rudderless. Andrew Kerr, though a wonderfully loyal amanuensis, who would turn his hand to everything from mowing the lawn and collecting guests from the station to researching the book and accompanying my father on trips abroad, was none the less no substitute for either of the previous directors of research. Accordingly, since no one else dared to do so, I ventured to suggest that my father should take steps to strengthen his team. The result was a furious row in which wild accusations were levelled at me and in which both my statements and my motives were misinterpreted.

On returning home, I received an outraged letter from my father, who had been angrier than I had ever seen him:

4 May 1968

My dear Winston,

I have long suspected that the ability to say you were sorry was alien to your nature; but your conduct last Friday week was so gratuitously outrageous that I had thought that ere now I would have heard from you.

Your silence compels me to write, not that I owe you any explanation but so that you can, in a cold light, reflect upon your unnatural and unfilial attack upon myself, my work and one of my staff.

The gravamen of your case which you yelled at me seven or eight times was that '*everybody* felt bitter resentment towards Andrew and thought him negligent and quite unsuited to his work'. You refused to tell me who these accusers were though I pointed out to you that by the nature of things they could not be very numerous since few people are in a position to form a view on this topic ... I have therefore instituted an inquiry to find out who is 'everybody'. It turns out to be nobody ...

Martin Gilbert, who you said did not leave me because of a nervous breakdown but because he could not abide working under Andrew, has written me a most warm-hearted letter in which he says he is very upset by the allegation ... It has been painful and laborious for me to discover all this and to set it down. I have done so with two objects. The first is to convince you of the monstrous untruths that you have been putting forward in the hope that you will now desist. The second is that you may consider your own general conduct with an eye to the future. If you were to go about treating other people as your presume to treat me it would augur ill for your success in life.

Your loving but affronted father
Randolph S. Churchill

Though bitterly resenting my intrusion, my father evidently took my point to heart for, in the course of the week, he telephoned Martin Gilbert to tell him: 'A lamp is always burning for you here.' Following my return from Paris where I was reporting the progress of the Vietnam Peace Conference for the London *Evening News*, I replied to this blockbuster:

13 May 1968

Dear Father,

I received your letter shortly before leaving for Paris and, now that I am back, hasten to reply. I am sorry that there should have been this disagreement between us and, above all, that you should have imputed that my motives were at the very least unfilial. Perhaps I explained myself maladroitly when I came to see you, but nevertheless my motives were of the best. Not having seen you or having heard of the progress of the book since you came to stay with us over Christmas I was most surprised when four people – all of them either close to you or connected with the book – sought me out independently within two or three weeks of each other to express their anxiety over the way the book was going. Naturally, I was most concerned to hear this and felt it my duty to bring the matter before you and discuss the situation with you.

Though you may feel that the life you are writing of my grandfather is none of my business, nevertheless, my interest in it is twofold:

(1) That the Biography should stand as a worthy memorial to my Grandfather, and that the subsequent tomes are of as high a standard as Volumes I and II;

(2) That the book should be finished by you, under your direction and in your name.

These two considerations – and none other – have prompted me to make the following suggestions to which, whether you are prepared to accept them or not, I trust you will at least give due consideration.

The organisation at Stour of research workers, young gentlemen and secretaries, as you established it when you began your great labour, was conceived at a time when you were in good health and, even so, provided for Michael Wolff and after him Martin Gilbert to be what the American Military would call your Executive Officer or Number One below you in your organisation. For the past few months you have not been enjoying particularly good health, and in the past twelve months (which included the two you most kindly gave up to *The Six Day War*) you have not been able to make the progress you would have wished with the big book. During this period you have not had Martin Gilbert assisting you and only recently has Michael Wolff come back on a part-time basis...

In my view you need, more than ever, Michael, or someone of his calibre, on what would virtually be a full-time basis, so that when you are well you are able to steam ahead and, should you be under the weather, the ship will at least not be rudderless and will be able to maintain a certain momentum.

I am afraid you missed my point about Andrew completely. I did not say, and it would not be true to say, that 'everybody felt bitter resentment towards Andrew'. Andrew has done an enormous amount for you, not only in helping you with the book, but in accompanying you on your journeys abroad and making himself serviceable in every way possible. He has certainly been most loyal and, far from resenting him everyone, myself included, has the greatest admiration for him and likes him enormously. What you quoted of Martin Gilbert's letter confirms this. Nevertheless, this does not alter the fact that he is not the person best suited to have, what to all intents and purposes is the Number One job on the book at a time when your health is not of the best. I feel sure that he too would agree with this . . .

Please do not resent the suggestions I have made. They do not represent an attack on you, on Andrew or on your staff. But I do feel I was not unjustified in putting this before you as, above all, I would like to see this work, which will be the crowning glory of your life and a magnificent memorial to your father, finished, as far as possible, by you and not by some hack Oxford historian. Please believe me when I say that I have no motives other than what I have set out in this letter, and no interest other than to see you finish your great work.

I am sorry if I have angered you by setting forth my views so bluntly – and perhaps ineptly, but not for having brought this to your attention.

Your loving son,
Winston S. Churchill

My father replied by return:

14 May 1968

Dear Winston,

Thank you for your letter of May 13. If you will read my letter again you will see that I nowhere impugned your motives: it was your conduct of which I complained. I note that 'everybody' is now reduced to 'four'. It seems to me that your proper course of action should have been either to inform me who was saying what, or to have told these critics that they should communicate with me direct. What I resented and I still resent was your purveying of anonymous gossip and the violent and offensive manner in which you spoke to me. It is in your power to put both these matters right: the first by giving me the names of the four people; secondly by expressing some regret for the violence of your behaviour.

Your loving father,
Randolph S. Churchill

Death, as the Bible says of the second coming of the Lord, comes 'as a thief in the night'. Sad to say, that was the last letter I received from my father. We did however meet briefly at Harold Macmillan's Sussex home, Birch Grove, just five miles from where I was living at the time. Harold had invited my father to stay and Minnie and I were asked to lunch, together with Young Randolph, who was now three years old and Jennie, aged eighteen months. At least at that, our last meeting, cordial relations were re-established. Randolph placed his grandson and namesake upon his knee, pulled out his father's Bréguet pocket-watch, making it chime the hour and the minutes and declaring: 'I am so very proud of this young man!'

When, two or three days later, I spoke to my father on the telephone he told me how, while at Birch Grove, some time around midnight he had asked Harold if he would be so kind as to have one of his Young Gentlemen look him up a train and book him a taxi for the morning. 'I couldn't believe it,' he told me in horror, 'the old boy got up and went to a bookshelf to get his Bradshaw's [Railway Guide] to look up the train *himself* and then telephoned the station to book me a cab!'

On the evening of Tuesday 4 June, word came of the tragic assassination of Bobby Kennedy, of whom Randolph had been so deeply fond, just five years after that of his brother, the President. The following day I set about writing a tribute to him for the *Evening News*. Preoccupied as I was with the news from America, nothing had prepared me for an even more personal tragedy.

On the morning of 6 June 1968 – the anniversary of D-Day – Andrew Kerr telephoned from Stour to report that my father had died in his sleep. Minnie and I hastened up by car from London. Andrew told us that, late the previous evening, when he had informed my father: 'They've caught the fellow who shot Bobby!', he had replied: 'Good, good, but have they caught the fellow who's done me in?'

Among the many tributes received was one from Marshal Tito addressed to my grandmother:

WE HAVE LEARNED WITH DEEP SORROW THE NEWS OF THE GREAT LOSS WHICH HAS BEFALLEN YOU AND YOUR FAMILY THROUGH THE DEATH OF YOUR SON RANDOLPH STOP WITH RANDOLPH CHURCHILL WE ARE LINKED BY MANY MEMORIES OF THE DIFFICULT DAYS OF THE LAST WAR AS WELL AS OUR LATER FRIENDLY MEETINGS STOP ON BEHALF OF MY WIFE AND IN MY OWN NAME I EXPRESS YOU MY DEEP AND SINCERE CON-DOLENCES = JOSIP BROZ TITO

My father left the following instructions as to the disposal of his mortal remains:

I desire that my corpse shall be disposed of either in the churchyard of East Bergholt or in the gardens of Stour, as speedily as possible and with the least inconvenience to other people or expense to my Estate. Any of my friends who care to attend my sepulture shall be entertained to baked meats and a cold collation at Stour and drink anything that may happen to be in my house. There shall be no memorial services. Bones (not my own) shall be provided for my dogs and bitches: but steps must be taken that the bones shall not be bones of contention nor treated like those of Jezebel [which were eaten by dogs].

Randolph had never been religious. However, according to a friend of Michael Wolff, Mr McGregor-Craig, the subject had come up a couple of years earlier as they sat with Randolph around the swimming-pool of the Mamounia Hotel in Marrakech. When Michael remarked: 'I have often wondered what Winston's views on religion really were', McGregor-Craig ventured to say that he thought they were best summed up in *My Early Life*, to which Randolph had replied: 'Rubbish!' As McGregor-Craig relates:

A copy was produced and I had no difficulty in turning to the appropriate place and proving that it was not 'Rubbish'. I then quoted the following extract:

If you are the recipient of a message which cheers your heart and fortifies your soul, which promises you reunion with those you have loved in a world of larger opportunity and wider sympathies, why should you worry about the shape or colour of the travel-stained envelope; whether it is duly stamped, whether the date on the postmark is right or wrong? These matters may be puzzling, but they are certainly not important. What is important is the message and the benefits to you of receiving it.

'That's news to me,' was his [Randolph's] comment, and then, 'If there is some all wise omniscient Creator up aloft, why doesn't He ring me up on the telephone?'
'Perhaps,' I replied, 'he's been waiting for you to ring Him up.'
'How do I know His telephone number?' he went on, and I answered, 'Perhaps you haven't looked in the right telephone directory.' And then realising I was treading across a minefield I concluded, 'Isn't it just possible, Mr Churchill, that on more than one occasion He tried to ring you up and found the number engaged? Why not try just once more, for His phone is never engaged, and you can always reverse the charges!'

Frank Gannon, recalling his first days at Stour as an impressionable young American, captured so well the memories that are still vivid for all those who knew Randolph and fell under his spell – of long evenings beside the blazing log fire in the library at Stour with Randolph firmly planted in his green velvet chair, reading aloud or quoting from his remarkable repertoire of poetry:

We talked for hours and then he began to read. He read Belloc's 'In Praise of Wine'; then selections from John Betjeman (his favourite was 'The Arrest of Oscar Wilde'); then several of his father's speeches from *Step by Step*. Then, for some reason, he picked up the *Rubaiyat* from the shelf. I had never heard all the poems read aloud. And by the time he reached the end, after many hours of reading, he was whispering hoarsely, breathlessly:

And when Thyself with shining Foot shall pass
Among the Guests Star-scatter'd on the Grass,
And in Thy joyous Errand reach the Spot
Where I made one -- turn down an empty Glass!

He closed the book and then rose, stirring up the dogs with the usual, 'Come on, doggies, out you go for a minute. Annie! Boycott!' and went about getting ready for his customary sleep till noon. When I went up to my room, the dawn mist was already rising over the Vale of Dedham. The chill autumn air had made the covers very cold, but I scarcely noticed. I was still transfixed by his extraordinary reading of those extraordinary poems . . .

I last left him as I first saw him: sitting in the great green chair by the fireplace. But everything was different. November had turned to May, and for all the springtime pressing over the terrace, the room was dark and foreboding. His last words, as we rushed for the train, were the usual ones: 'Do keep in touch Frank. Don't be such a stranger.' I do keep in touch; so frequently a bit of reading or a phrase of conversation will bring him back to mind. And whenever I work or write, I do turn down an empty glass for Randolph. I remember him and I miss him.

Following the funeral service which we held in the church of St Mary's, East Bergholt, I had invited, as instructed, all his family and friends back for a light 'collation' and to finish up what was left in his cellar. After lunch Harold Macmillan, who had spoken movingly of Randolph in his funeral oration, took me aside on the terrace and said with his engaging smile: 'You know, Winston, your father was the last to live in the grand manner!' Remembering the final telephone conversation I had had with my father, I knew exactly what Macmillan had in mind. Though never rich, Randolph invariably aspired, and for the most part succeeded, in living his life 'in the grand manner', with retinues of Young Gentlemen and secretaries on call until the early hours of the morning.

Among Randolph's papers at his death were these two verses written out in his own hand and, apparently, of his own composition:

> Oh foolish one! Why seek to know the truth?
>   Its agate shroud betokens the despair
> That must be yours when all is known;
>   Too soon we pass the threshold of this life
> For us to preen ourselves on knowing all.
>   We nothing know and nothing care.
>
>   Except our love divine, enchanted, rare
> As little tissue cobweb clouds
>   Flecked with the rosy tints of summer skies
> Abiding as the ageless rocks
>   Whipped by the boiling sea.

We buried him in Bladon churchyard, beside his grandfather, and his father, whom he loved and revered so deeply. To this day the memory of him lingers on in the hearts of his friends.

Bibliography

Amery, Julian, *Approach March* (Hutchinson, 1973)
Amory, Mark (ed.), *The Letters of Evelyn Waugh* (Weidenfeld & Nicolson, 1980)
Churchill, John Spencer, *A Crowded Canvas* (Odhams, 1961)
Churchill, Randolph S., *They Serve the Queen* (Hutchinson, 1953)
    Fifteen Famous English Homes (Derek Verschoyle, 1954)
    Churchill: His Life in Photographs (with H. Gernsheim) (Weidenfeld & Nicolson, 1955)
    What I Said About the Press (Weidenfeld & Nicolson, 1957)
    Portraits and Appreciations (privately printed, 1958)
    The Rise and Fall of Sir Anthony Eden (MacGibbon & Kee, 1959)
    Lord Derby: 'King of Lancashire' (Heinemann, 1959)
    The Fight for the Tory Leadership (Heinemann, 1964)
    Twenty-One Years (Weidenfeld & Nicolson, 1965)
    Winston S. Churchill, vol. I, *Youth: 1874–1900* (and Companion volume) (Heinemann, 1966)
    Winston S. Churchill, vol. II, *Young Statesman: 1901–14* (and Companion volume) (Heinmann, 1967)
    (ed.) Sir Winston Churchill, Speeches and Addresses:
        Arms and the Covenant (1938)
        Into Battle (1941)
        The Sinews of Peace (1948)
        Europe Unite (1950)
        Stemming the Tide (1953)
        The Unwritten Alliance (1961)
Churchill, Sarah, *A Thread in the Tapestry* (André Deutsch, 1967)
Churchill, Sir Winston, *My African Journey* (Hodder & Stoughton, 1908)
    The World Crisis 1911–1918 (6 vols) (Thornton Butterworth, 1923–31)
    My Early Life (Odhams, 1930)
    Marlborough: His Life and Times (Harrap, 1933–8)
    The Second World War (6 vols) (Cassell, 1948–54)
Churchill, Winston S., *The Six-Day War* (with Randolph S. Churchill) (Heinemann, 1967)

Memories and Adventures (Weidenfeld & Nicolson, 1989)

Cowles, Virginia, *Looking for Trouble* (Hamish Hamilton, 1941)
   Winston Churchill: The Era and the Man (Hamish Hamilton, 1953)
   The Phantom Major (Collins, 1958)
   The Kaiser (Collins, 1963)

Cooper, Duff, *Old Men Forget* (Rupert Hart-Davis, 1953)

Curzon, Lady, *Reminiscences* (Hutchinson, 1955)

Davie, Michael (ed.), *The Diaries of Evelyn Waugh* (Weidenfeld & Nicolson, 1976)

Gilbert, Martin, *In Search of Churchill* (HarperCollins, 1994)

Halle, Kay, *Randolph S. Churchill: The Young Unpretender* (Heinemann, 1971)
   Irrepressible Churchill: Stories, Sayings and Impressions of Sir Winston Churchill (Robson Books, 1985)

Hanfstaengl, Ernst, *Hitler; The Missing Years* (Eyre & Spottiswoode, 1957)

Hastings, Selina, *Evelyn Waugh: A Biography* (Sinclair-Stevenson, 1994)

Leslie, Anita, *Cousin Randolph* (Hutchinson, 1985)

Levant, Oscar, *A Smattering of Ignorance* (Garden City Publishing Co./Doubleday, New York, 1940)

Lyttelton, Oliver, *Memoirs* (Bodley Head, 1962)

Maclean, Fitzroy, *Eastern Approaches* (Jonathan Cape, 1949)

Macmillan, Harold, *The Blast of War* (Macmillan, 1967)

Michie, Allan, *The Invasion of Europe: The Story Behind D-Day* (Dodd, Mead, New York, 1964)

Montague Browne, Anthony, *Long Sunset* (Cassell, 1995)

Nicolson, Harold, *Diaries* (Collins, 1954)

Pawle, Gerald, *The War and Colonel Warden* (Harrap, 1963)

Pomeroy, Miggs, *The Great Saharan Mouse-hunt* (with Catherine Collins) (Hutchinson, 1962)

Rhodes-James, Robert (ed.), *Chips: The Diaries of Sir Henry Channon* (Weidenfeld & Nicolson, 1967)

Roberts, Brian, *Randolph: A Study of Churchill's Son* (Hamish Hamilton, 1984)

Schlesinger, Arthur M., *A Thousand Days: John F. Kennedy in the White House* (André Deutsch, 1966)

Sykes, Christopher, *Evelyn Waugh* (Collins, 1975)

Windsor, Duchess of, *The Heart Has Its Reasons* (Michael Joseph, 1956)

Wood, Alan, *The True History of Lord Beaverbrook* (Heinemann, 1965)

INDEX

Abdullah, Emir, 30
Adeane, Michael, 358
Admiralty House, 8, 14, 16
Ainsworth, Harry, 323–4, 326
Aitken, Sir Maxwell, 27, 71, 87, 478
Alber (lecture agent), 82–3
Alexander I, King of Yugoslavia, 261
Alexander, General Harold George, 216, 226–7, 255, 268
Allen, George, 149
Alston, Gordon, 208–14, 235
American Weekly, 146
Amery, Catherine, 440
Amery, Julian, 166, 266–7, 268–73, 441
Amery, Leopold, 47, 189, 334
Anne, Queen, 397
Arlanza, 119, 120
Arrighi, Pascal, 365
Asquith, Herbert: WSC's positions in government, 4, 8; women's suffrage issue, 10; wartime government, 15, 23; daughter's wedding, 20; WSC's army career, 20; Liberal tradition, 293, 294; drinking habits, 490
Asquith, Violet, *see* Bonham Carter
Astor, Nancy, Lady, 180, 335
Astor, William Waldorf, 3rd Viscount, 225, 435
Atlantic Charter, 197
Attlee, Clement, 176, 273, 297–8, 338
Auchincloss, Janet, 345
Auchinleck, General Claud, 192, 194, 203–4
Auriol, Vincent, 255
Aurora, USS, 265
Ayer, A.J., 419

Babington Smith, H.G., 38
Bagehot, Walter, 359
Baldwin, Oliver, 87, 126, 128
Baldwin, Stanley: fall of government (1924), 33; forms government (1924), 36; WSC as Chancellor of Exchequer, 36, 47; WSC's opinion of, 36; miners' strike, 41, 42; resignation (1929), 56; WSC's relationship with, 73–5, 76, 79, 87, 122, 133, 134, 148; 1931 election, 80; disarmament debate, 95–6; German air power issue, 99, 118–19; India policy, 101; 1935 election, 108–11, 122; RSC's speech (1935), 108–9; Hoare-Laval plan, 122–4; Ross and Cromarty election issue, 125–6, 128; abdication issue, 146;

resignation, 148; responsibility for WWII, 168; on Rothermere, 320; advice to Eden, 334
Balfour, Arthur James, 4, 22, 66, 70, 180
Balfour, Gerald, 112
Barber, Stephen, 362–5, 381, 383–4
Barklay, William, 121, 124, 126
Barnes, Jim, 102, 103
Barnes, Major General Sir R.W.W.R., 158, 175
Barry, Canon F.R., 173
Barthou, Louis, 261
Baruch, Bernard, 35, 62, 77, 82, 136
Beatty, Admiral of the Fleet David, 1st Earl, 37, 87
Beatty, David Field, 2nd Earl, 87
Beatty, Peter, 183, 185
Beaverbrook, William Maxwell Aitken, 1st Baron: WSC's friendship, 27, 30, 367; son's relationship with RSC, 27; relationship with Baldwin, 73, 126; India policy, 77; 'Fathers and Sons' dinner, 87; Hitler policy, 123, 159; abdication issue, 146; relationship with RSC, 147–9, 175, 187, 239, 311–12, 321, 340–1, 360, 405, 441; RSC's debts, 187; young Winston's childhood, 187, 202; RSC's attack on, 311–12; Eden government policy, 340–1; admiration for RSC's journalism, 357, 365; second marriage, 406; *Private Eye* case, 428; Macmillan premiership policy, 439; death, 450–1
Bedford, Dr, 231
Bellew, Sir George, 342
Belloc, Hilaire, 499
Ben-Gurion, David, 338, 349, 485–6
Beneš, Eduard, 160
Benn, William Wedgwood (*later* 1st Viscount Stansgate), 193
Berengaria, 62
Berry, *see* Camrose, Hartwell
Berwick, James Fitzjames, 1st Duke of, 174
Betjeman, John, 398–9, 499
Bevan, Aneurin, 224–5, 293, 297, 350
Bevan, Bobby, 393–5, 483
Bevan, Natalie, 375, 393–5, 452, 463, 483
Bevan, Robert, 393
Bigelow, Poultenay, 100
Birkenhead, Frederick Edwin Smith, 1st Earl of: friendship with WSC, 5; RSC's godfather, 8; relationship with RSC, 62–3, 64, 66; Nancy Astor's attack on, 335; daughter, 398

Birkenhead, Frederick Winston Furneaux (Freddie), 2nd Earl of, 63–4, 87, 88, 257, 259
Birley, Robert, 49, 53
Blake, Robert, 490
Blenheim Palace, 23, 25, 397
Blomberg, Field Marshal Werner von, 156
Boettiger, Mrs, 265
Bohlen, Arnold von, 420–2
Bonham Carter, Maurice, 20
Bonham Carter, Violet (*later* Baroness Asquith of Yarnbury), 20, 166, 474
Boothby, Robert, 52, 132
Botha, Louis, 385
Botto, M., 144
Bournemouth constituency, 369–71, 373
Bowra, Maurice, 64
Bracken, Brendan: relationship with WSC, 79, 154, 177, 222; political predictions, 79; relationship with RSC, 84, 154, 177; WSC's car, 85; Hoare-Laval plan issue, 123; Ross and Cromarty election, 129; rearmament issue, 164; Churchill Club, 202
Brain, Sir Russell, 313
Bremen, 135, 146
Brien, Alan, 396, 448
British Gazette, 40–1
British Medical Association, 469, 475–7
Brooke, General Alan, 229
Broun, Heywood, 140–1
Brownlow, Peregrine Cust, 6th Baron, 173
Buccleuch, Duchess of, 452
Buchan-Hepburn, Patrick, 358
Buchanan, George, 110
Buckley, Christopher, 306
Burgess, Guy, 160, 375
Busby, Jeremy, 422
Butler, R.A. ('Rab', *later* Baron) 322, 356–8, 402, 439–40, 445
Byron, Robert, 162

C&T Publications Ltd, 395
Cadogan, William, 369
Campbell, Lady Jean, 430
Campbell, Robin, 183, 194, 196, 198
Camrose, Seymour Berry, 2nd Viscount, 63–4, 87, 88, 175
Camrose, William Ewert Berry, 1st Viscount, 87, 93, 286
Carden, Admiral Sir Sackville, 15
Cardozo, 144
Carroll, Lewis, 32
Carson, Edward Henry, Baron, 109
Carter, Air Commodore, 253–4
Carter-Ruck, Peter, 324, 426, 492
Carvel, John, 180
Catherine Place (No. 12), 289
Cecil, Lord David, 64
Cecil, Lord Hugh, 87, 96
Centurion, HMS, 59
Cerne Abbas, Dorset, 275–7
Chaco War, 119, 120

Chamberlain, Sir Austen, 4–5, 55, 87
Chamberlain, Neville: on WSC, 2; Hoare correspondence, 133; relationship with WSC, 134, 167, 334; negotiations with Hitler, 156, 159; Munich agreement, 160, 162, 275; opposition to, 165; responsibility for WWII, 168; resignation, 176–7, 436
Channon, Henry ('Chips'), 145
Chaplin, Charlie, 61, 139–40, 185
Charles Plumier, 366
Charteris, Laura (*later* Lady Long, *then* Mrs Michael Canfield, *eventually* Duchess of Marlborough), 203, 218
Chartwell, Kent: WSC's purchase, 32; WSC's work, 37, 47, 51–2, 277–8; Jones visit, 42; geese and swans, 52, 207, 277; Hore-Belisha's visits, 151; WSC considers sale, 156; life at, 167–8; purchased for nation, 286; Golden Rose Avenue, 367
Chartwell Trust, 395, 406
Chelsea constituency, 369–70
Cherkeley, 187, 202
Chiang Kai-shek, 267
Christ Church, Oxford, 53, 54
Christina, 436, 437–8
Churchill, Arabella (mistress of James II), 174
Churchill, Arabella (daughter of RSC), 301, 342, 343, 369, 455
Churchill, Charles, 174
Churchill, Charles Richard John Spencer, 9th Duke of Marlborough, 87
Churchill, Clementine (mother of RSC, *née* Hozier): birth of son, 3–7; husband's flying experiences, 11; family holidays, 11; support for husband, 21–2, 33, 34; daughter's death, 29, 30; influenza, 29–30; electioneering, 33, 121; Diana Mitford's opinion of, 44; accident, 47–8; illness, 50–1; relationship with son, 66, 203, 264, 366, 371–2; American trip, 75–9; husband's New York accident, 82–4; Munich visit, 92–3; disapproval of gambling, 104; West Toxteth speech, 121; family Christmas (1940), 185; illness, 207; husband's heart attack, 231; Red Cross work, 267; Moscow VE-Day celebrations, 268; general election (1945), 273; Plymouth Fair opening, 297; husband's stroke, 313; husband's dukedom question, 336–7; husband's old age, 362, 366, 371–2; golden wedding, 367–9; Chartwell Trust, 406; husband's ninetieth birthday, 455; husband's funeral, 456–7; life peerage, 463–4; response to Moran memoirs, 475–6
Churchill, Diana (sister of RSC, *later* Mrs John Milner Bailey, *then* Mrs Duncan Sandys): birth, 3; childhood, 7, 9, 16, 24, 29, 32, 37; kidnap attempt, 9–10; political involvement, 42, 121; brother leaves Eton, 53; travels with mother, 59; parental concern for, 112; marriage, 115; wartime life, 185, 186, 207, 225; death, 455

Churchill, Lady Gwendoline (Goonie, aunt of RSC), 16, 23
Churchill, Jack, 233
Churchill, Jack (uncle of RSC), *see* Churchill, John Strange Spencer
Churchill, Jennie, Lady Randolph (grandmother of RSC, *née* Jerome, *afterwards* Mrs George Cornwallis-West), 7, 26, 28, 397
Churchill, Jennie (granddaughter of RSC, *later* Mrs James Repard), 496
Churchill, John, 1st Duke of Marlborough, 35, 52, 56, 92, 126, 174, 397, 452
Churchill, John George Spencer ('Johnny', cousin of RSC), 16, 23–4, 35, 56, 60–2
Churchill, John Strange Spencer ('Jack', uncle of RSC), 6, 16, 22, 45, 56, 58, 81, 104, 268
Churchill, June (RSC's second wife, *née* Osborne), 288–9, 314, 337, 341–3, 394
Churchill, Marigold (sister of RSC, died in infancy), 27–9, 30
Churchill, Marina (granddaughter of RSC), 486
Churchill, Mary (sister of RSC, *later* Lady Soames): birth, 31; childhood, 52, 76, 142; political activity, 165; family Christmas (1940), 185; war service, 203, 207, 225, 260–1; relationship with brother, 203; general election (1951), 301; father's ninetieth birthday, 455; biography of mother, 479
Churchill, Minnie (RSC's daughter-in-law *née* d'Erlanger): engagement and marriage, 451–2; WSC's ninetieth birthday, 455; children, 460, 464, 486, 496; husband's lecture tour, 464; husband's Israel assignment, 485, 486; lunch at Birch Grove, 496
Churchill, Pamela (RSC's first wife, *née* Digby, *later* Mrs Leland Hayward, *then* Mrs Averell Harriman): first meeting with RSC, 171–2; engagement and wedding, 172–3; honeymoon, 173–4; pregnancy, 179–80; birth of son, 181–2; Ickleford House, 181, 186–7; family Christmas (1940), 185; motherhood, 187, 202, 225; wartime life, 186–7, 195, 202, 220; husband's gambling debts, 187; affair with Averell Harriman, 201–2, 207, 439, 493; breakup of marriage, 201–3; divorce, 275–6; Paris home, 302; life in America, 377, 408, 420, 429; marriage to Averell Harriman, 493
Churchill, Peregrine Spencer (cousin of RSC), 16, 23–4
Churchill, Lord Randolph, (grandfather of RSC): name, 8; Blenheim, 25; political career, 37, 180, 182, 284, 422; relationship with son, 65–6; grave, 28; biography, 201–2; letters, 397
Churchill, Randolph Frederick Edward Spencer: LIFE: birth, 3; godparents, 7–8; kidnap attempt, 9–10; family holidays, 11, 28–9; page at Asquith–Bonham Carter wedding, 19–20; Dormansland School, 24; poetry recitation, 25; children's parties, 26;

Sandroyd School, 26–7, 31, 33, 34, 35–6; school reports, 35–6, 37–8, 40, 44–5, 52–3; sister's death, 29; influenza, 29; reading, 31, 39–40, 49, 174; Chartwell, 32; by-election assistance, 33–4; behaviour to father's guests, 35; Eton, 36–45, 48–51; General Strike, 41–2; political education, 42; love for Diana Mitford, 43; trips with father, 44, 45–7, 48, 56–63; audiences with Pope, 46–7, 248; Oxford entrance plans, 48; debating skills, 51; Oxford entry, 53, 54; electioneering (1929), 55–6; public speaking, 55, 58, 72, 119, 130, 133; North American trip (1929), 56–63; at Oxford, 63–70; ambitions, 66, 86; Oxford Union debate, 69; American lecture tour (1930–31), 69–70, 71–9; marriage plans, 77–9; chauffered car, 80–1; twenty-first birthday, 86–8; journalism, 86, 88–92, 95–100, 119, 135; reports from Germany, 88–9; German issues, 91–2, 94–5, 98, 100, 133–4, 137; India issue, 101–3; Lancashire speaking tour, 102–3; Wavertree by-election candidacy, 104–14, 121, 181; Norwood by-election, 114–17; jaundice, 118; White libel action, 119–21; West Toxteth candidacy, 121–2, 181; Ross and Cromarty by-election candidacy, 125–33, 134, 181; sister Sarah's marriage, 135–6; American trip (1936), 135–41; radio address, 137–9; Spanish Civil War reporting, 141–5; Windsor wedding, 147–9; Queen's Own Hussars, 158–9, 162, 169, 174–6, 178, 183; attitude to Munich agreement, 160–2, 275; edits father's speeches, 164, 286–7; new political party plans, 165–6; Oxford Union conscription debate, 166–7; Windsor mission, 169–71; first meeting with Pamela, 171–2; engagement and wedding, 172–3; honeymoon, 173–4; Preston election, 178–81; birth of son, 181; maiden speech, 182–3; No. 8 Commando transfer, 183–5; family Christmas (1940), 185; Middle East wartime experiences, 186–201; breakup of first marriage, 201–3, 439; joins SAS, 204; Benghazi raid, 207–15; back injury, 214, 216, 218; political speeches (1942), 217–18; North African operations, 218–23; accompanies father to wartime conferences, 222, 223, 226, 229; *Evening Standard* letter, 223–5; invasion of Sicily, 227–9; Maclean's opinion of, 232, 249; Yugoslavia mission, 232–49; MBE, 249; Croatia mission, 250–64; knee injury, 265; Roosevelt meeting, 265; general election (1945), 265, 269–73; fatherhood, 274–9; divorce, 275–6; journalism, 279–81, 290, 321–2, 349, 362–5, 379–85, 395, 429; lecture tours (1947), 284–7, 289; view of career, 284–5; second marriage, 288–9; Plymouth (Devonport) election campaigns, 291–301; daughter, 301; Korean war reporting, 302–7; leg wound, 305–6, 307; British Railways slander suit,

Churchill, Randolph Frederick Edward
Spencer – *cont*
308–9; European Movement speech, 310–
11; attack on Beaverbrook, 311–12;
Coronation (1953), 312; father's stroke, 313;
press crusade, 317–21; Odhams Press libel
action, 323–8, 345; stops 'Churchill girls'
story, 328–9; vendetta against Eden, 331–6,
338–40; *Observer* profile, 335–6; Israel visit,
337–8; Middle East concern, 337–9; breakup
of second marriage, 342–3; *$64,000 Question*,
343–5; dogs, 344–5, 463, 498, 499; Suez
crisis, 345–51; Nabarro libel action, 352–5;
Eden succession issue, 356–9; gardening,
359–61, 373, 377; BBC TV interview, 359–
60; lecture tour (1958), 361; Algerian
reporting, 362–6; parents' golden wedding,
367–9; parliamentary selection attempts,
369–73, 375–7; Soviet Union visit, 372–6;
Africa trips, 379–85; Sahara expedition,
385–9; biography of father, 392, 395–401,
478–9; love for Natalie Bevan, 393–5; staff
at Stour, 400–1, 452; Clark libel action, 404–
5; South American travels with son, 407–8;
US trip (1961), 408–11; Romanoff's dinner
disgrace, 408–10; fifty-first birthday, 413;
Private Eye libel case, 422, 423–8; father's
Honorary US Citizenship ceremony, 429–
31; Profumo crisis, 435–7; *Christina* cruise,
437–9; Macmillan resignation and succession
issue, 439–47; lung operation, 447–8, 452,
479; son's wedding, 452; father's ninetieth
birthday, 455; father's death, 456; father's
funeral, 457–60; writing in Marrakech, 462–
3; grandson's christening, 464; Moran book
response, 469–77; stroke (1965), 479–80;
Kennedy biography project, 483–4; *Six Day
War* collaboration with son, 484–8; death,
497; funeral, 497–500; PERSONAL
THEMES: arrogance, 66, 87; attitude to
authority, 16–17, 87, 194; appearance, 20,
26, 118, 415; combativeness, 27, 52–3, 155,
267, 307, 335–6, 398; courage, 249, 300;
drinking, 141–2, 148, 307, 389, 398, 408–9,
451; finances, 69–70, 77, 80–1, 103–4, 175,
187, 284, 344–5, 405, 446; gambling, 103–
4, 175, 186, 187, 392, 405; generosity, 175,
446; handwriting, 48; health, 29, 118, 389,
407, 447, 479–80, 493; kindness, 300, 306;
mimicry, 23; schools' view of character, 35–
6, 52–3; smoking, 260, 389, 407, 447, 479;
taking the blame, 24; temper, 155, 278–9,
342–3, 400, 451; unpunctuality, 3;
RELATIONSHIPS: in love, 43, 77–8, 203,
393–5; with father, 66, 78–9, 81, 97, 105–6,
114, 118–19, 124, 128–30, 147, 151–5, 164–
5, 188–9, 202–3, 331, 379, 392–3, 406, 413–
14, 438–9; with friends, 292, 300, 398–400;
with mother, 66, 75–6, 203, 264, 361, 371–
2, 406, 462, 479; with son, 274–9, 302, 313–
14, 377, 405, 420–3, 451–2, 487–8, 493–6;
with wives, *see* Churchill (June), Churchill

(Pamela); WORKS: *Europe Unite!*, 287;
Fifteen Famous English Homes, 313–16; *The
Fight for the Tory Leadership*, 435–6, 444–5;
Winston S. Churchill Vols I & II ('Great
Biography' of father), 13, 85, 389, 392, 395–
401, 465, 478–9; *Lord Derby*, 316, 342, 359,
377, 390–2; *The Rise and Fall of Sir Anthony
Eden*, 346–7, 349–51, 377, 378; *The Sinews of
Peace*, 286; *The Six Day War*, 486–9; *The
Story of the Coronation*, 311, 313; *They Serve
the Queen*, 311, 313; *Twenty One Years*, 9, 13,
17, 30, 36, 37, 41, 46, 71, 377, 464, 489
Churchill, Randolph (grandson of RSC), 460,
464, 496–7
Churchill, Sarah (sister of RSC, *later* Mrs Vic
Oliver, *then* Mrs Anthony Beauchamp, *then*
Lady Audley): birth, 11; childhood, 16, 29,
32; Munich visit, 92; marriage to Vic Oliver,
135–6; career, 135–6; flat, 142; family
Christmas (1940), 185; wartime life, 207, 225,
230, 265; Technion opening, 366; father's
ninetieth birthday, 455; father's funeral,
458–9
Churchill, Tom, 233
Churchill, Sir Winston (seventeenth century,
father of John, 1st Duke of Marlborough),
174
Churchill, Winston Spencer (father of RSC):
birth of son, 3–7; African experiences, 379,
385; early political career, 3–4, 284; First
Lord of the Admiralty (1911–15), 8–9, 11–
13, 14–16; finances, 8, 17, 63, 70, 80, 81–2,
83, 155; fatherhood, 9–11; Dardanelles
campaign, 14–16, 20; Chancellor of Duchy
of Lancaster, 17–18; war service, 18–23;
Minister of Munitions, 25; Dundee election
(1918), 25; Secretary for War and Air, 26;
Dundee defeat (1921), 31; Colonial
Secretary, 30, 32; by-election defeats, 33–4;
horses, 36, 50; Epping election success, 36;
Chancellor of Exchequer, 36–7, 40–1, 47,
49–51, 54–5; bricklaying, 37, 47, 51–2, 277–
8; General Strike, 40–1; Naval cruise with
son, 44–7; opinion of son, 45–6, 51, 57, 58,
64–5, 70, 78, 88, 115–16, 285–6; general
election (1929), 55–6; North American trip,
56–63; relationship with son, 66, 78–9, 81,
97, 105–6, 114, 118–19, 124, 128–30, 147,
151–5, 164–5, 188–9, 202–3, 285–6, 331,
379, 392–3, 406, 413–14, 438–9; general
election (1931), 80; car, 80, 85; New York
accident, 82–4; Munich visit, 92–4; German
policy, 95–7, 99, 116, 118, 133; wilderness
years, 97, 164; India issue, 101–2, 114, 116,
164; son's by-election candidature, 105–6,
108–14; drinking, 141; Spanish Civil War
stance, 145; abdication issue, 146–7, 164;
response to Chamberlain–Hitler meetings,
159–60; Epping revolt, 162–3; First Lord of
the Admiralty (1939), 168; son's wedding,
173; forms government (1940), 177;
sponsors son, 179, 180; birth of grandson,

Churchill, Winston Spencer – *cont*
181; Middle East war policy, 189; Roosevelt meeting (1941), 197; North Africa visits, 216–17, 226–7; Casablanca Conference, 222–3; Adana Conference, 223; Teheran Conference, 229–30; heart attack, 231; Tito meeting (1944), 255; Yalta Conference, 264–5, 471–2; general election (1945), 273; postwar speeches, 286–7, 295–6, 297, 298; second premiership (1951), 301; Coronation (1953), 312–13; strokes, 313, 473; eightieth birthday, 322; resignation, 322, 330–1; dukedom question, 336–7; Eden succession issue, 358; ill health in old age, 362, 366, 371–2, 455–6; golden wedding, 367–9; eighty-fifth birthday, 379; in Monte Carlo, 406; eighty-seventh birthday, 411–12; grandson's African trip, 420; *Private Eye* article (1963), 423–4; Honorary US Citizenship, 429–31; last *Christina* cruise, 437–9; ninetieth birthday, 455; death, 455–6; funeral, 456–61; Moran's memoirs, 469–77; WORKS: *Arms and the Covenant*, 164; *Great Contemporaries*, 155; *History of the English-Speaking Peoples*, 155, 232; *Marlborough*, 52, 56, 75, 92, 155; *My Early Life*, 4, 47; *The World Crisis*, 12, 32, 44, 73
Churchill, Winston Spencer (son of RSC): birth, 181; infancy, 187, 196, 202; childhood, 220, 222, 225; childhood memories, 160–1, 274–9; German measles, 245; train set, 260; education, 36, 161; Cairo visit, 215; Drvar visit, 237; relationship with father, 274–9, 302, 313–14, 377, 405, 420–3, 451–2, 487–8, 493–6; father's second marriage, 289; father's election campaign (1951), 298–9; Coronation memories, 312–13; Sahara expedition, 385–9; Monte Carlo visit, 406; South American travels with father, 407–8; African trip (1962–63), 420–3; *Private Eye* libel damages, 428; grandfather's Honorary US Citizenship ceremony, 430; Kennedy visit, 432–4; *Christina* cruise, 437–9; journalism, 142, 362–3, 378, 421–2, 433–4, 464–6, 492, 494; political career, 131, 299, 377–8, 422, 428, 467, 490–1; in love, 451; wedding, 452; grandfather's ninetieth birthday, 455; grandfather's death, 456; grandfather's funeral, 456–60; birth of son, 460; lecture tour, 464; Vietnam trip, 464–6; Six Day War, 484–8; last meeting with father, 496–7; father's death, 497
Churchill Archive, 395
Churchill Club, 202
Churchill family, 174
Clark, Douglas, 404–5
Clinton, Bill, 378
Cobb, Captain E.C., 218, 266
Cochran Baillie, Mrs Victor, 156
Collins, Alan, 385–9
Collins, Catherine, 387, 388
Colville, Sir John (Jock): Pamela-Averell Harriman affair, 201; RSC's relationship with Eden,

332, 333–4; WSC dukedom issue, 336–7; *Christina* cruise, 437; WSC's ninetieth birthday, 455; at Chartwell, 473; Moran book, 476
Colville, Margaret, ('Meg'), Lady, 437, 455
Constable, John, 337, 390
Cooper, Corporal, 208
Cooper, Diana, 255, 415
Cooper, Duff, 1st Viscount Norwich, 108–9, 164, 255, 415, 460
Coronation of Elizabeth II, 312–13
Coronation of George V, 6–7
Country Bumpkins Ltd, 321, 360
Coutts & Co., 405
Coward, Noël, 133
Cowles, Mike, 464
Cowles, Virginia (*later* Mrs Aidan Crawley), 100, 167, 205
Craigavon, James Craig, 1st Viscount, 164
Crawford, Joan, 61
Crawford and Balcarres, David Lindsay, 27th Earl of, 88
Crewe, Robert Crewe-Milnes, 1st Marquess, 29
Cripps, Stafford, 206
Cromwell, Oliver, 2
Cromwell Road (No. 41), 16, 23
Crossman, Richard, 350
Cuba crisis, 418–19
Cudlipp, Hugh, 318
Cudlipp, Percy, 360
Curtis Brown, 395
Curzon, Grace Elvina, Lady, 26

Daily Dispatch, 86, 88, 94–5, 97
Daily Express, 124, 126, 127, 147, 149, 159, 298, 311, 349–50, 365, 370, 373, 376, 391, 404, 445
Daily Herald, 40
Daily Mail, 75, 82, 98, 102, 105, 107, 111, 127, 135–6, 139, 142–4, 148, 166, 167, 284, 296
Daily Mirror, 318
Daily Telegraph, 88, 122, 167, 279, 282, 303–4, 305, 469, 488
Daily Worker, 280
Daladier, Édouard, 160
Daley, Richard J., 362
Dalton, Hugh, 466
Daly, Dermot, 183, 186
D'Arcy, Father, 68
Dardanelles campaign, 14–16, 20, 22, 24
Darlan, Admiral Jean Louis Xavier François, 219–21
Davies, Sir Daniel, 450–1
Davies, Marion, 60, 61
Dawson, Geoffrey, 161
Day, Robin, 370
Deakin, Bill, 232, 416
Dedijer, Vladimir, 264, 312
de Gaulle, Charles: Middle East wartime experiences, 192–3; Algeria crisis, 362, 365, 381; WSC's funeral, 456; relationship with WSC, 471

Delamere, Diana, 385
Delamere, Tom, 385
Delves Broughton, Sir Jock, 385
Derby, Edward George Villiers Stanley, 17th Earl,
    51, 120, 316, 317, 321, 390–2
Derby, Edward John Stanley, 18th Earl of, 316
d'Erlanger, Minnie, see Churchill
d'Erlanger, 'Smut', Lady Gerard 452
Desert News, The, 196–7
Diamond, I.A.R., 409
Digby, Edward Kenelm Digby, 11th Baron, 171,
    174, 202, 275–7
Digby, Jacquetta (later Mrs David James), 276
Digby, Pamela ('Pansy'), Lady, 171, 174, 275–7
Digby, Pamela, see Churchill
Dilhorne, Reginald Manningham-Buller, 1st
    Viscount, 375, 442
Disraeli, Benjamin, 413–14
Dixon, Edwina, 455
Dixon, Piers, 455
Dormansland School, 24
Douglas-Home, Sir Alec, see Home
Douglas-Home, Charles, 485
Dove, Billie, 61
Downs, Ken, 147–8, 195, 197–8, 205
Driberg, Tom, 160, 357
Drury, Allen, 408, 410
Drvar, Yugoslavia, 236–7, 240–1, 242–5
Dubininskaya, Lidiya, 375
Dufferin and Ava, Basil, 4th Marquess of, 63–4,
    175
Duncan, Colin, 424
Dunn, Marcia Anastasia, Lady, 406
Dunne, Mary, 171–2
Dunne, Philip, 171, 183
Dyson, Mary, 373

Eade, Charles, 319, 327
Eaker, General Ira, 245
East Bergholt, Suffolk, 337, 405
Eban, Abba, 485
Eccleston Square (No. 33), 3, 5, 8
Economist, The, 113
Eden, Anthony: Moscow mission (1935), 116;
    Hitler meeting (1935), 118; Foreign Secretary,
    124, 285; WSC's opinion, 124; resignation
    (1938), 156, 334; supporters, 164; Queen's
    Hall meeting (1939), 166; RSC's biography,
    187, 378, 425; Foreign Secretary (wartime),
    189, 222, 239; Middle East visit (1941), 189;
    Teheran Conference, 229; Yalta Conference,
    265; Tito's visit (1953), 312; Conservative
    Party leadership, 322; Prime Minister, 330–
    1; RSC's vendetta, 331–6, 338–40;
    Eisenhower talks, 338–9; Suez crisis (1956),
    345–8, 351–4, 356, 474; resignation, 356, 359;
    succession issue, 356–9
Eden, Clarissa (née Churchill, later Lady Avon),
    312, 331–4
Edinburgh Evening News, 132
Edward, Prince of Wales (later Edward VIII, then
    Duke of Windsor), 47, 146–9, 151, 170–1

Eighth Army News, 196–7
Eisenhower, Dwight D.: Darlan agreement, 221;
    Italian campaign, 226; OVERLORD, 231;
    victory in Europe, 269; doctor's orders, 324;
    Soviet policy, 331; Eden Middle East talks,
    338–9; China crisis (1958), 367–8; WSC's
    funeral, 456
Elizabeth II, Queen: Coronation, 311, 312; dines
    at Number Ten, 322, 332; WSC's
    resignation, 330; WSC's successor, 330, 331;
    WSC dukedom question, 336; Eden's
    resignation, 356, 358; Home's premiership,
    447; WSC's funeral, 456–60
Elliott, Maxine, 7
Ellis, Diana, 491
Emery, Frank, 304, 306
Empress of Australia, 56
Enchantress, HMS, 10, 59
Epping constituency, 36, 55–6, 80, 162–3
Erroll, Josslyn Hay, Earl of, 385
Escarra, Madame, 360
Eton, 36–45, 48–51
Europa, 76, 82
Evening Chronicle, 270–1
Evening News, 115, 290, 486, 494, 497
Evening Standard, 149, 150, 156, 158–9, 165, 175,
    223–4, 278, 292, 301, 322, 334, 338–40, 357,
    362, 365, 367–8, 375, 379, 398, 426–7, 434,
    450, 464
Evetts, General Sir John Fullerton, 186, 187

Fairbanks, Douglas, Jr., 61
Fairlie, Henry, 340
Farouk, King of Egypt, 265
Feakins, William B., 69, 71, 83
Feiling, Keith, 54, 92
Feisal, Emir, 30
Field, Xenia, 342
Findlay, Richard, 116–17
Fisher, Admiral John Arbuthnot, 22
Flandin, Pierre, 220, 222, 282–3
Fleming, Valentine, 5
Foot, Jill (née Craigie), 447, 460
Foot, Michael: Plymouth (Devonport) election
    campaigns, 291–301; relationship with
    RSC, 292, 300, 447, 460; anti-monarchist
    articles, 311; Tribune, 320; review of Lord
    Derby, 391
Forbes, Alistair, 442
Forward, 341
Foster, Sir John, 325, 328
Fowler, 243
Franco, General Francisco, 142–3, 144–5
Franz Ferdinand, Archduke, 11
Frederika, Queen of Greece, 438, 439
French, Field Marshal Sir John, 18
Frost, David, 466, 491–2
Furneaux, Freddie, see Birkenhead

Gage, Sir Berkeley, 407
Gaitskell, Hugh, 297, 338, 368, 405, 421
Gannon, Frank, 396, 432, 466–7, 478, 498–9

Garbo, Greta, 406
Gardiner, Gerald (*later* Baron), 424, 426
General Strike, 40–2
George V, King, 6, 11–12, 47, 79, 133
George VI, King, 177, 273, 311
Gibb, Francis, 387
Gilbert, Helen, Lady (*née* Robinson), 489, 490
Gilbert, Sir Martin: on origins of 'Chum Bolly',
    3; on WSC's budgets, 54; on WSC's
    writing, 62; on WSC's perceptions of
    Nazism, 91; on Churchill gambling, 104; on
    Men of Munich, 161; on 'Black Dog', 331;
    on Eden and WSC, 334–5; on RSC–Natalie
    relationship, 394; RSC's research team, 396,
    415–17; gardening experience, 400; South
    African story, 422; *Private Eye* libel case, 424–
    5; on 'Operation Sanctuary', 436–7; on
    Macmillan leadership crisis, 439; on 'Project
    K', 484; *Six Day War*, 487; stops work on
    Great Biography, 489–90, 493–5
Giraud, Henri Honoré, 221
Gladstone, William Ewart, 293, 294, 456
Glasgow Evening News, 130
Glasgow Herald, 130
Glengyle, 188
Glenroy, 186
Goddard, Paulette, 140
Goebbels, Joseph, 157–8, 492
Goering, Hermann, 96, 156, 284
Gollan, John, 167
Gorman, Sir William, 353–4
Gott, General William Henry Ewart, 216
Grandi, Dino, 123
Gray, Hamish, 131
Gray's Inn, 167
Green, Mrs (cook), 452–3
Grey, Sir Edward, 7–8
Grigg, P.J., 51
Guardian, 390, *see also Manchester Guardian*
Guest, Ivor, 87
Guinness, Mrs Bryan, *see* Mosley
Gunn, Mrs (daily at Stour), 400

Haggard, Rider, 31
Haig, Douglas, 1st Earl Haig, 49
Haile Selassie, Emperor of Ethiopia, 265
Hailsham, Douglas Hogg, 1st Viscount, 87
Hailsham, Quintin Hogg, 2nd Viscount: 'Fathers
    and Sons' dinner, 87–8; relationship with
    RSC, 181, 446; Bournemouth constituency
    intervention, 371; Macmillan succession
    issue, 441–7
Haley, Sir William, 321, 483
Halle, Kay: *Irrepressible Churchill*, 8, 381; *The Young
    Unpretender*, 69, 147, 205, 269, 303, 399,
    430–1, 466, 484; question of marriage to
    RSC, 77–8; WSC's Honorary US
    Citizenship, 429; RSC's Washington visits,
    441, 483
Hamilton, Denis, 482
Hamilton, General Sir Ian, 87
Hanfstaengl, Ernst ('Putzi'), 89, 92–4, 97

Hare, John, 394, 442
Hare, Nancy, 394, 442
Harford, J.D., 37
Harlech, David Ormsby-Gore, 5th Baron, 430
Harlech, Sissie, Lady, 430
Harmsworth, Esmond, *see* Rothermere
Harriman, Averell: Roosevelt's representative,
    189, 191–3, 198–9, 493; Middle East
    mission, 189, 191–3, 492–3; affair with
    Pamela, 201–2, 439, 493; illness, 206–7;
    Teheran Conference, 229; Kennedy dinner
    party, 432; marriage to Pamela, 493
Harriman, Kathleen (*later* Mrs Stanley Mortimer),
    201, 207
Harriman, Marie, 201
Harrod, Roy, 64, 66, 69–70
Harryman, Eileen, 400
Hartin, 143, 144
Hartman, Tom, 396
Hartwell, Michael Berry, Baron, 314
Hartwell, Lady Pamela Berry (*née* Smith), 314,
    332, 398, 452
Harvey, Vere, 158
Hastings, Selina, 251
Hawkey, Sir James, 84, 163
Hayward, Leland, 377, 408, 420, 429, 493
Hazelhurst, Cameron, 490
Hazelhurst, Janette, 490
Head, Antony (*later* 1st Viscount), 346–8, 351
Hearst, William Randolph, 56, 60–1, 71, 140
Heath, Edward, 447, 465, 467
Hebrang, Andrije, 261–4
Heinemann, 395, 486
Hemingway, Ernest, 302
Henley, Sylvia, 371, 373, 394, 455
Herbert, A.P., 425
Herbert, Captain Sidney, 334
Hermine, Empress, 100
Herring, Captain, 98
Hiersum, Mrs (daily at Stour), 400
Hindenburg, Paul von, 89
Hirst, David, 426
Hitler, Adolf: 1931 position, 80; rise to power,
    88–9, 96; RSC's reporting, 88–91, 97, 137,
    150–1; nearly meets WSC, 92–4;
    rearmament, 96, 116, 118; Beaverbrook
    relationship, 123; Rhineland occupation,
    134; Mussolini meeting, 150; Windsor
    meeting, 151; occupation of Austria, 156;
    Mitford relations, 156–8; Chamberlain
    meetings, 159–60; Munich agreement, 160,
    167; Polish threat, 167; attack on Norway,
    176; invasion of Low Countries, 177; US
    war, 199; WSC's warnings, 331; sanity
    question, 442
Hoare, Sir Samuel, 110, 112, 119, 122–4, 133
Hochhuth, Rolf, 491–2
Hoe Farm, Surrey, 17, 21
Hogg, Quintin, *see* Hailsham
Home, Alexander Douglas-Home, 14th Earl, 358,
    401–2, 440–7, 452
Home, Elizabeth Hester, Lady, 452

Honey Fitz, 432–3
Hopkins, Harry, 199, 229, 265
Hore-Belisha, Leslie, 151
Hornby, W.M., 27, 35–6
Hosey Rigge, 32
Houghton Mifflin, 395
Houston, Lucy, Lady, 114–15, 117
Howard, Anthony, 45
Hozier, Lady Blanche (grandmother of RSC, *née*
    Airlie), 34, 43, 60, 104
Hozier, Sir Henry, 43
Hozier family, 60
Hudson, A.G., 37
Hughes, Emrys, 350
Hundred Thousand movement, 165–6
Hussein, King of Jordan, 420
Hylton-Foster, Sir Harry, 355
Hynes, Miss Airlie, 10

Ibn Saud, King of Saudi Arabia, 265
Ickleford House, Herts, 181, 186–7, 274
Idris, King of Libya, 387
India Defence League, 101, 104, 108, 114, 115,
    117
Inönü, Ismet, 223
Inskip, Sir Thomas, 109
Irving, Clive, 161, 443, 466
Irving, David, 491–2
Irwin, Edward Frederick Lindley, Baron, 119
Ismay, Bruce, 9
Ivanov, Captain Eugene, 435

James II, King, 174
James, Edward, 399
Jay, Douglas, 294, 445
Jellicoe, George, 227
Jenkins, Roy, 390
Johnson, Sergeant Earl, 304
Johnson, Lady Bird, 480
Johnson, Lyndon B., 468, 492
Jones, Thomas, 42, 55
Jordan, Philip, 253–4

Kaltenbrunner, Ernst, 284
Keeler, Christine, 435
Kelly, HMS, 170–1
Kemsley, James Gomer Berry, 1st Viscount, 320,
    329
Kennedy, Celia (*née* Sandys, *later* Mrs Ken
    Perkins), 455
Kennedy, Edward (Teddy), 433, 434
Kennedy, Ethel, 411, 432–3
Kennedy, Jackie (*later* Mrs Aristotle Onassis), 430,
    434, 484
Kennedy, Joan, 433
Kennedy, John F.: presidential campaign (1960),
    377, 402–3; RSC's reporting, 410–11, 418–
    19, 434; RSC's relationship, 411, 432–4, 442;
    Cuban crisis, 418–19; WSC's US
    citizenship, 429–31; assassination, 434;
    Macmillan's resignation, 442; biography
    project, 483–4

Kennedy, Joseph P., 177, 411, 430
Kennedy, Robert (Bobby): RSC's relationship,
    411, 431–3, 434, 447; RSC Kennedy
    biography proposal, 483–4; assassination, 497
Kenward, Elizabeth, 312
Kerr, Andrew: RSC's research team, 396, 493–6;
    Profumo 'Operation Sanctuary', 437;
    RSC's illness, 447; Marrakech work, 462,
    463; *Queen Mary* voyage, 480–1; RSC's
    death, 497
Keyes, Lt.-Col. Geoffrey, 198
Keyes, Admiral Sir Roger, 44, 46, 59, 87, 108
Khrushchev, Nikita, 372–4, 419
King-Hall, Commander Stephen, 167
Kinross, Patrick, 2nd Baron, 393
Kipling, Rudyard, 344
Kitchener, Field Marshal Sir Horatio Herbert, 15
Knollys, Francis, 1st Viscount, 6–7
Korean War, 302–7
Kornev, General, 235

Lampson, Sir Miles, 188, 189
Lancashire Daily Post, 178
Lancaster, Nancy, 335
Lancaster, Osbert, 350, 373, 376
Lancet, The, 469
Lanchester, Elsa, 409
Landon, Alfred M., 135, 137
Laughton, Charles, 409
Laval, Pierre, 122, 220
Lavery, Sir John, 87
Lawrence, Sir Geoffrey, 284, 352–4
Lawrence, Col. T.E., of Arabia, 30, 74, 251
Lawson, Nigel, 475
Laycock, Lt.-Col. Robert (Bob), 183–4, 185–7,
    193, 198, 229
League of Nations, 122, 124
Leclerc, General Jacques, 389
Lee, Fred, 354
Lehrer, Tom, 466–7, 481
LeMay, General Curtis, 361
Lemnitzer, General Lyman, 255
Lenin, Vladimir Ilyich, 150
Leslie, Anita, 43, 201, 203, 218, 342–3, 393–4
Levant, Oscar, 140
Liddell Hart, Sir Basil, 167, 488
Lincoln, Mrs Evelyn, 442
Lindemann, Frederick Alexander ('the Prof', *later*
    1st Viscount Cherwell): Chartwell visits, 37,
    37, 38, 52; influence on RSC, 37, 39, 42, 48,
    53, 64; European tour with WSC, 92–3;
    Oxford by-election (1937), 144; Christmas
    (1942), 222
Liverpool Star, 121
Lloyd, Harold, 61
Lloyd, Selwyn (*later* Baron Selwyn-Lloyd), 443
Lloyd George, David: relationship with WSC, 23,
    27, 84, 119, 125; general election (1918),
    25–6; WSC's budget (1929), 54; RSC's
    relationship, 66, 84, 119, 125, 134, 136;
    Baldwin relationship, 126; Nancy Astor
    sponsorship, 180; Liberal tradition, 293, 294

Long, Laura, Lady *see* Charteris
Long, Walter Francis David, 2nd Viscount, 203
Longfellow, Henry Wadsworth, 414
Lord, Cyril, 323
Los Angeles Examiner, 140
Los Angeles Mirror, 408
Luard, Nicholas, 426
Luce, Clare Booth, 68, 177
Luce, Henry Robinson, 177
Ludendorff, General Erich von, 14
Lullenden, Sussex, 23–6
Lushington, Captain Gilbert, 10, 13
Lyons, Leonard, 336
Lyttelton, Oliver (*later* Viscount Chandos), 192, 194

MacArthur, General Douglas, 303, 307
MacDonald, Malcolm, 124–5, 127–8, 130, 132
MacDonald, Ramsay: Labour premierships, 33, 56; National Government, 79–80; Disarmament Conference, 96; India policy, 101; RSC's speeches, 107, 108–10, 122; WSC's speeches, 111; resignation (1935), 119; Ross and Cromarty election campaign, 124–5; responsibility for WWII, 168
McGregor-Craig, 498
MacLachlan, Donald, 161–2
Maclean, Donald, 375
Maclean, Fitzroy (*later* Sir Fitzroy: Benghazi raid, 205, 208–14, 386; Yugoslavia mission, 232–3, 236, 240–1, 242, 244, 247–9, 251–2, 259–60
Macleod, Iain, 358–9, 379–80, 417–18, 441–5, 448
Macmillan, Lady Dorothy, 440
Macmillan, Harold: relationship with WSC, 164; Resident Minister in Algiers, 222, 245; Cairo wartime memories, 230–1; relationship with RSC, 247–8, 268, 350–1, 366–8, 370, 391, 439–40, 445, 496–7; Suez issue, 350–1; succeeds Eden, 322, 356–9; Soviet tour, 372–6; general election (1959), 378; Commonwealth tour, 381; Cabinet reshuffle, 401; Cuba crisis, 419; Nassau Conference, 429; resignation and succession, 390, 439–44; RSC's funeral, 499
Macmillan, Maurice, 370
McNamara, Robert, 410–11, 468, 492
MacNeil, Hector, 130
Macpherson, Sir Ian, 124
Maisky, Ivan, 167
Majestic, SS, 71, 78, 85
Major, John, 215, 378
Makarios, Archbishop, 381
Manchester, William, 483, 484
Manchester (Gorton) constituency, 299, 490–1
Manchester Guardian, 69, 167, 320, 330, 333
Manchester Left Book Club, 167
Manningham-Buller, Sir Reginald, *see* Dilhorne
Margesson, David, 154
Mark, Mr (gardener at Stour), 400
Marks, Ken, 491

Marsh, Eddie, 49, 88, 456
Marshall, Dr, 480
Marshall, General George C., 226
Martin, Mrs (housekeeper), 278
Marx, Harpo, 140, 162
Massu, General Jacques, 362, 364, 365
Masterton Smith, Sir James, 18
Mates, Leo, 262
Maudling, Reginald, 441
Maunther, Martin, 359, 396
Mayer, Louis B., 61
Maze, Paul, 345
Mboya, Tom, 380
Mechin, Benoit, 220
Melbourne Daily Telegraph, 283
Menuhin, Yehudi, 480–1, 482–3
Merton, Arthur, 213–14, 215
Metcalfe, Lady Alexandra, 149
Metcalfe, Maj. E.D. ('Fruity'), 149
Michie, Allan, 194
Mihailovic, Draga, 232, 233, 238–9, 250, 264
Milmo, Helenus, 424
Milton, Peter, 183
Minterne, Dorset, 174
Mitford, Lady Clementine, 43
Mitford, Diana, *see* Mosley
Mitford, Jessica, 151
Mitford, Nancy, 315, 450
Mitford, Pamela, 43
Mitford, Tom, 43, 151
Mitford, Unity, 151, 156–7
Molian, Michael, 359, 396
Molotov, Vyacheslav, 229, 262–3
Monckton, Sir Walter, 149, 346
Montague Browne, Anthony, 437–8, 455, 456, 476
Montague Browne, Nonie, 438, 455
Montgomery, General Bernard Law, 217, 226, 455
Moore, Colleen, 61
Moran, Charles Wilson, Baron, 231, 313, 331, 469–77
Morley, John, 57, 293, 294
Morning Post, 40
Morrison, Ian, 306
Morton, Desmond, 99
Mosley, Desmond, 43
Mosley, Lady Diana (*née* Mitford, *then* Mrs Bryan Guinness), 43–4, 54, 151, 156–7
Mosley, Sir Oswald, 43, 87, 157, 231
Mountbatten, Lord Louis, 170–1, 203
Moyne, Walter Edward Guinness, 1st Baron, 166
Munich agreement, 160–1
Mussolini, Benito, 46, 94, 122, 150, 156

Nabarro, Gerald, 351–5
Nassau Conference, 429
Nasser, Gamal Abdel, 345, 421, 485
Navarro, Ramon, 61
Negri, Pola, 61
Nelson, Herbert, 403
Nelson, Horatio, Viscount, 456

New Statesman, 448
New York Herald Tribune, 303
New York Post, 336
New York Times, 67, 69, 198, 468, 488
New York World Telegram, 140
News Chronicle, 74, 131, 253, 340
News of the World, 379, 383–4, 401–5, 411, 418–19, 431, 439, 444, 481, 485
Nicholson, Otho, 33–4
Nicolson, Harold, 200
Nicolson, Nigel, 369–71, 375–6
Nixon, Richard M., 402–3
Norfolk, Bernard Fitzalan-Howard, 16th Duke of, 456–7
Norfolk, Lavinia, Duchess of, 456
Normandie, 146
Norwood constituency, 114–17
Nuremberg trials, 283–4
Nyerere, Julius, 380

Observer, 335, 345, 373, 445, 478
Odhams Press, 324, 325, 345
Oliver, Vic, 135–6, 185
O'Lone, Colonel, 387
Olympic, 82
Onassis, Aristotle, 358, 372, 399, 406, 436, 437–9
Operation TORCH, 219
Osborne, June, *see* Churchill
Osborne, Colonel Rex, 288
Oswald, Hickson, Collier & Co., 324
Oving, 314
Owen, Frank, 165, 298
Oxford Union, 166–7

Page, Anita, 61
Page-Croft, Sir Henry, 103
Paley, Babe, 345
Paley, William S. (Bill), 345
Parnell (film), 139
Paul I, King of Greece, 438, 439
Paul, Maury, 71
Paull, Gilbert, 325–8, 426
Paulus, Friedrich von, 223
Pawle, Gerald, 223
Pear Tree Cottage, Overstrand, 11–13
Pearl Harbor, 199
Peat, Hal R., 288
People, The, 323–8
Pepper, Aloysius, 427
Pershing, General John, 26
Pétain, Marshal Henri Philippe Omer, 219–20
Peter II, King of Yugoslavia, 238–9, 240, 250
Pethick-Lawrence, F.W., 33
Philip, Prince, 456
Picture Post, 295
Pitt, William (the Younger), 66, 296, 456
Pius XI, Pope, 46–7
Pius XII, Pope, 68, 248
Platt, James, 104, 106, 111–12
Plowden, Pamela (*later* Lady Lytton), 173
Plymouth (Devonport) constituency, 291–301
Pomeroy, Livingstone ('Liv'), 386–7

Pomeroy, 'Miggs', 387, 388
Portal, Charles, 1st Viscount, 312
Powell, Enoch, 445
Prchal, Ed, 491–2
Preminger, Otto, 408–10
Preston constituency, 178–9, 180, 217–18, 266, 267, 270–2
Pribichevich, Stoyan, 243
Prince of Wales, HMS, 197
Princess Beatrix, HMS, 227
Private Eye, 422, 423–8, 464
Profumo, John (Jack), 435–7, 463
Profumo, Valerie, 436–7, 463
Pruitt, Master-Sgt. Roy, 304
Punch, 312, 332, 349
Puric, Bozidav, 232, 240, 250

Queen Elizabeth, 284, 403
Queen Mary, 135, 146, 311, 480
Queen's Own Hussars, 158–9, 162, 169, 174–6, 178, 183, 185
Quincy, USS, 265

Radio Belgrade, 247
Rand Daily Mail, 382
Rathbone, Eleanor, 224, 225
Reading, Gerald Isaacs, 2nd Marquess of, 87
Reading, Rufus Isaacs, 1st Marquess of, 87
Reagan, Ronald, 378
Recorder, The, 321
Redesdale, David Freeman-Mitford Mitford, 2nd Baron, 43
Redesdale, Lady Clementine Mitford, Lady, 43
Reeve, Denzil, 367
Renown, HMS, 229
Reston, Scottie, 468
Ribbentrop, Joachim von, 284
Ridley, Lady, 7
Roberts, Dr (from Monte Carlo), 451
Robinson, Henry, 102, 103
Romilly, Esmond, 151
Rommel, Field Marshal Erwin, 186, 197–9, 207, 216–17, 226
Roosevelt, Eleanor, 136
Roosevelt, Elliott, 222
Roosevelt, Franklin D.: presidential elections (1936), 135–7, 140; RSC's visit, 136–7; Harriman's mission, 189, 192, 493; Atlantic Charter, 197; WSC's Washington visits, 199, 226; Casablanca Conference, 222; Teheran Conference, 229–30; telegram to WSC, 254; meeting with WSC (1945), 265; relationship with WSC, 471
Roosevelt, Franklin Jr., 222
Roosevelt, Mrs James, 136
Rosaura, SS, 166
Rose, Sergeant, 208, 210, 214
Rosebery, Albert Edward Primrose, 6th Earl of, 201
Rosebery, Archibald Philip Primrose, 5th Earl of, 35
Rosebery, Eva, Lady, 201–2, 452–3

Ross and Cromarty constituency, 125–33, 181
Rothermere, Esmond Harmsworth, 2nd
     Viscount, 87, 319–21, 326
Rothermere, Harold Sidney Harmsworth, 1st
     Viscount: relationship with WSC, 75, 77;
     India policy, 75, 102; 'Fathers and
     Sons' dinner, 87; RSC's journalism, 88,
     98, 102, 149; RSC's election campaigns,
     106, 115, 128–9; influence on Baldwin,
     126; Churchill drinking bets, 141–2, 148,
     155
Rothschild, Eugene de, 149
Rothschild, Kitty de, 149
Routh, C.R.N., 48, 52
Royal Scotsman, HMS, 228
Rusk, Dean, 410
Russell, Bertrand, 419
Russell, Leonard, 449
Russell, Sarah, 462

Sackville-West, Lionel Sackville, 377
St Oswald, Rowley, 4th Baron, 234
Salan, General Raoul, 362, 364, 365
Salinger, Pierre, 418–19
Salisbury, James Gascoyne-Cecil, 4th Marquess
     of, 87
Salisbury, Robert Gascoyne-Cecil, 5th Marquess
     of, 87, 358, 443
Sampson, Anthony, 445
Sandroyd School, 26–7
Sandys, Duncan (later Baron Duncan-Sandys):
     Norwood election, 115, 116; marriage, 115;
     West Toxteth support for RSC, 121;
     Hundred Thousand movement, 165–6;
     Christmas 1940, 185; political career, 289;
     Macmillan leadership, 358; Minister of
     Defence, 373; Cabinet reshuffle, 401;
     Commonwealth Secretary, 420–1
Sandys, Julian, 424, 455
Sassoon, Philip, 55, 158
Savundra, Emil, 491
Scheftel, Geraldine, 68
Scheftel, Stuart ('Boy'), 67–9
Schlesinger, Arthur M. Jr., 419, 432
Scotsman, 130
Scott, Colonel Alan, 26
Scottish Daily Record and Mail, 126
Selby, Lady, 149
Setzer, Professor 'Hank', 387
Sexton, Mrs (daily at Stour), 400
Sharpeville massacre, 382, 383
Shaw, G. Bell, 246
Shawcross, Hartley (later Baron), 120, 309, 317
Sheba, Togo, 306
Sheepshanks, Colonel, 36, 40, 41, 43
Shinwell, Emmanuel, 297, 350
Siege of Sidney Street, 4
Sieveking, Lance, 393
Sikorski, General Wladyslaw, 199, 491–2
Simon, Sir John, 116, 118
Simpson, Wallis (later Duchess of Windsor), 146
Smith, Berkeley, 359

Smith, David, 61
Smith, F.E., see Birkenhead
Smith, Jim, 61
Smuts, Field Marshal Jan, 186, 189, 216, 220, 383
Snowdon, Antony Armstrong-Jones, 1st Earl of,
     449
Soames, Christopher (later Baron), 358, 401, 439,
     455, 462, 470
Soames, Mary, see Churchill
Somerfield, Stafford, 403–5, 444, 485
Soustelle, Jacques, 363–5
Southby, Sir Archibald, 200
Sowman, Corporal Douglas, 253–5
Spanish Civil War, 141–5
Sparrow, John, 64
Special Air Service (SAS), 202, 204, 205–14
Spectator, 328, 340, 390, 427, 448
Spencer-Churchill, John Albert Edward William
     ('Bert'), 10th Duke of Marlborough, 397
Spiers, General Louis, 193
Stalin, Joseph: WSC Moscow meeting, 216;
     Stalingrad siege, 223; Teheran Conference,
     229–30; WSC relationship, 230, 260–1, 268,
     471; Tito relationship, 262–3, 282; 1945
     election prediction, 272; death, 331
Stanley of Alderley, Edward Stanley, 6th Baron,
     172–3, 448
Star, 180
Star, Johannesburg, 385
Stars and Stripes, The, 409
Stavordale, Harry, Viscount, 183, 186
Stepney Peace Council, 167
Stevens, Jocelyn (later Sir), 421
Stevenson, Adlai, 314
Stirling, Major David, 202, 204, 205–6, 207–14,
     386
Stockwell, General Sir Hugh, 488
Stonehaven, John Lawrence Baird, 1st Viscount,
     111
Stour, Suffolk: RSC's purchase, 337; library, 341;
     decor, 342; garden, 342, 359–61; Natalie
     Bevan, 393–4; Churchill Archive, 395–6;
     staff, 400–1, 452; Great Biography, 414–17,
     493–5
Strand Magazine, 76
Street, Major Vivian, 241, 242, 244–5
Strong, Richard, 340–1
Subosic, Ivan, 240
Suez crisis (1956), 345–52, 356, 474
Sulzberger, Cyrus, 488
Summers, John, 91
Sunday Dispatch, 95, 98, 104–5, 107, 115, 120,
     327–8, 370
Sunday Express, 311, 370
Sunday Graphic, 88–9, 328–9
Sunday Telegraph, 91, 161, 395, 481, 486, 488
Sunday Times, 443, 448, 449, 470, 478, 481
Sunday Times, Johannesburg, 384
Sussex Square (No. 2), 26, 34
Sutherland, Graham, 322
Sutro, John, 342–3, 399–400
Sykes, Christopher, 250–1, 258, 342–3

Talbert, Ansel E., 303, 305, 306
Tatler, 312
Taylor, A.J.P., 419, 478, 490
Temple, Shirley, 139
Thadden, Adolf von, 481
Thatcher, Margaret (*later* Baroness), 378
Thomas, Hugh Lloyd, 149
Thomson, George, 355
Thomson, Roy (*later* Lord Thomson of Fleet), 482, 484
Thornton-Kemsley, Colin, 163
Time magazine, 371
Times, The, 80, 106, 108, 113, 130, 161, 274–5, 320, 321, 351, 354, 426, 436, 445, 460, 469, 478, 485 5
Titanic disaster, 9
Titmuss, Richard, 419
Tito, Marshal (Josip Broz): British Military Mission, 205, 232, 233; Drvar HQ, 236–7, 241, 243–5, 247, 249; attitude to King Peter, 238; RSC-Waugh mission, 250–2; Churchill meeting, 255, 260; Hebrang case, 261–4; Trieste discussions, 268; Moscow relations 282; visits Britain (1953), 312; RSC's death, 497
Tonypandy riots, 4, 383, 423
Topic magazine, 399
Toronto Globe, 312
Toynbee, Arnold, 415
Tree, Ronald, 335, 462, 483
Trethowan, Ian, 340
Trevor-Roper, Hugh, 436, 444
Tribune, 320, 419
Truman, Harry S., 289–90
Truth, 321, 322
Tshombe, Moïse, 421
Tudor Pembleton, Dr J., 475, 477
Twigg, Barbara, 400, 417, 490–1
Tynan, Kenneth, 491–2

Urquhart, Francis Fortesque 'Sligger', 64
Usborne, Peter, 425–6

Vansittart, Robert Gilbert, 123
Versailles Peace Conference, 25
Verwoerd, Hendrik Freusch, 383–4

Wall Street Crash, 63, 79
Wall Street Journal, 378
Ward, Dame Irene, 339
Warrender, Victor, 154
Warspite, HMS, 46
Washington, George, 294, 429
Watson, Graham, 395
Watts, John, 102, 105, 106

Waugh, Auberon, 274, 315
Waugh, Evelyn: *Decline and Fall*, 63, 386; *Vile Bodies*, 63; at Oxford, 63, 68, 399; advice to RSC, 176; joins Commando unit, 183, 184–5; Egypt posting, 186, 188; *Put Out More Flags*, 195–6; on Churchill marriage, 202; Croatian mission, 250–5, 256–9; Tito joke, 251–2, 312; meets RSC in Rome, 265; VJ-Day celebrations, 274; post-war life, 280; Nuremberg trials, 283–4; RSC's second marriage, 287–8; criticisms of *Fifteen Famous English Homes*, 314–16; reconciliation with RSC, 448–50; on RSC's title, 464; death, 468
Waugh, Laura, 280, 314, 315
Wavell, General Archibald, 188, 192
Wavertree constituency, 104–14, 121, 181
Wellington, Arthur Wellesley, 1st Duke of, 456
West Toxteth constituency, 121–2, 181
Western Morning News, 292, 295, 298
Westminster, Hugh Richard Arthur Grosvenor, 2nd Duke of, 48, 106, 108, 111
Westminster, Loelia, Duchess of, 400
Whicker, Alan, 307
White, Sir Thomas, 107, 120–1, 184
White-Thomas, C.R., 45
White's Club, 176, 183, 186, 250, 278, 287–8, 321, 336, 337, 350, 392, 448
Wigg, George, 351
Wilder, Mrs Billy, 409
Wilhelm II, Kaiser, 100
Willingdon, Freeman Freeman-Thomas, 1st Marquess, 110, 112
Wilson, Harold, 447, 453–4, 466, 468, 492
Wilson, Field Marshal Sir Henry, 30
Wilson, General Sir Henry Maitland ('Jumbo'), 238, 245–6, 247, 248, 251, 255
Wilson, Mary, 452–3
Wimborne, Ivor Churchill Guest, 1st Viscount, 87
Winant, John, 199, 265
Windsor, Duke and Duchess of, 147–9, 151, 170–1, 463
Wintour, Charles, 464
Wodehouse, P.G., 61
Wolff, Michael, 396–7, 413, 465, 493, 495, 498
Wolfson, Sir Isaac, 480–2, 487
Wood, Alan, 159
World Press News & Advertiser's Review, 411
World Telegram, 279, 280
World War, First, 12–13, 14–17
World War, Second, 169–265
Wyndham, John (*later* 1st Baron Egremont), 368

Yalta Conference, 264–5, 471–2
Yates, Ivan, 396